# CCNP: Building Cisco Multilaye Study Guide

## Building Cisco Multilayer Switched Networks Exam (BCMSN 642-811)

| OBJECTIVE | CHAPTER |
|---|---|
| **Technology** | |
| Describe the Enterprise Composite Model used for designing networks and explain how it addresses enterprise network needs for performance, scalability and availability. | 1 |
| Describe the physical, data-link and network layer technologies used in a switched network, and identify when to use each. | 1, 4 |
| Explain the role of switches in the various modules of the Enterprise Composite Model (Campus Infrastructure, Server Farm, Enterprise Edge, Network Management). | 1 |
| Explain the function of the Switching Database Manager [specifically Content Addressable Memory (CAM) and Ternary Content Addressable Memory (TCAM)] within a Catalyst switch. | 10 |
| Describe the features and operation of VLANs on a switched network. | 2, 3, 5 |
| Describe the features of the VLAN trunking protocols including 802.1Q, ISL (emphasis on 802.1Q) and dynamic trunking protocol. | 6 |
| Describe the features and operation of 802.1Q Tunneling (802.1QinQ) within a service provider network. | 3 |
| Describe the operation and purpose of managed VLAN services. | 3 |
| Describe how VTP versions 1 and 2 operate including domains, modes, advertisements, and pruning. | 3 |
| Explain the operation and purpose of the Spanning-Tree Protocol (STP) on a switched network. | 4, 5 |
| Identify the specific types of Cisco route switch processors, and provide implementation details. | 6, 10 |
| List and describe the operation of the key components required to implement interVLAN routing. | 6 |
| Explain the types of redundancy in a multilayer switched network including hardware and software redundancy. | 9 |
| Explain how IP multicast operates on a multilayer switched network, including PIM, CGMP and IGMP. | 8 |

| OBJECTIVE | CHAPTER |
|---|---|
| Describe the quality issues with voice traffic on a switched data network, including jitter and delay. | 9 |
| Describe the QoS solutions that address voice quality issues. | 9 |
| Describe the features and operation of network analysis modules on Catalyst switches to improve network traffic management. | 10 |
| Describe Transparent LAN Services and how they are implemented in a service provider network. | 9 |
| **Implementation and Operation** | |
| Convert CatOS to native IOS on Catalyst switches and manage native IOS images according to best practices. | 10 |
| Configure access ports for static and multi-VLAN membership. | 3, 6 |
| Configure and verify 802.1Q trunks. | 3, 6 |
| Configure and verify ISL trunks. | 3, 6 |
| Configure VTP domains in server, client and transparent modes. | 3 |
| Enable Spanning Tree on ports and VLANs. | 4, 5 |
| Configure Spanning Tree parameters including: port priority, VLAN priority, root bridge, BPDU guard, PortFast and UplinkFast. | 5 |
| Implement IP technology on a switched network with auxiliary VLANs. | 3 |
| Configure and verify router redundancy using HSRP, VRRP, GLBP, SRM, and SLB. | 9 |
| Configure QoS features on multilayer switched networks to provide optimal quality and bandwidth utilization for applications and data. | 9 |
| Configure Fast EtherChannel and Gigabit EtherChannel to increase bandwidth for interswitch connections. | 2, 5 |
| **Planning and Design** | |
| Compare end-to-end and local VLANs, determine when to use each. | 3 |
| Design a VLAN configuration with VTP to work for a given specific scenario. | 3 |
| Select multilayer switching architectures, given specific multilayer switching needs. | 7 |
| Describe the general design models when implementing IP telephony in a switched network environment. | 9 |
| Plan QoS implementation within a multilayer switched network. | 9 |

Exam objectives are subject to change at any time without prior notice and at Cisco's sole discretion. Please visit Cisco's website (www.cisco.com) for the most current exam objectives listing.

# CCNP:
# Building Cisco Multilayer Switched Networks
## Study Guide

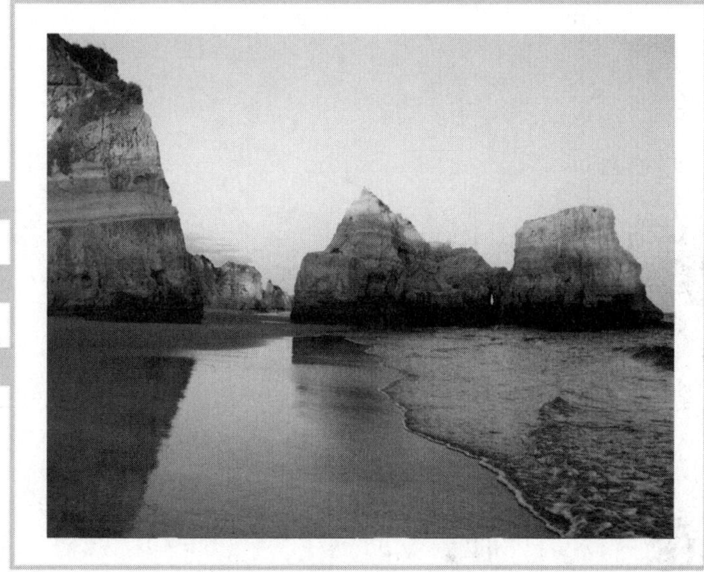

Jeff Lotan
CIS-122

# CCNP®:
# Building Cisco Multilayer Switched Networks
## Study Guide

Terry Jack

San Francisco • London

Associate Publisher: Neil Edde
Acquisitions Editor: Maureen Adams
Developmental Editor: Heather O'Connor
Production Editor: Mae Lum
Technical Editors: Patrick Bass, Arthur Pfund
Copyeditor: Suzanne Goraj
Compositor: Craig Woods, Happenstance Type-O-Rama
Graphic Illustrator: Jeffrey Wilson, Happenstance Type-O-Rama
CD Coordinator: Dan Mummert
CD Technician: Kevin Ly
Proofreaders: Emily Hsuan, Laurie O'Connell, Nancy Riddiough
Indexer: Ted Laux
Book Designers: Bill Gibson, Judy Fung
Cover Designer: Archer Design
Cover Photographer: Andrew Ward, Life File



Library of Congress Card Number: 2003109132

ISBN: 0-7821-4294-X



Manufactured in the United States of America

10 9 8 7 6 5 4 3 2

To Our Valued Readers:

Thank you for looking to Sybex for your CCNP certification exam prep needs. Sybex is proud to have helped thousands of Cisco certification candidates prepare for their exams over the years, and we are excited about the opportunity to continue to provide computer and networking professionals with the skills they'll need to succeed in the highly competitive IT industry.

We at Sybex are proud of the reputation we've established for providing certification candidates with the practical knowledge and skills needed to succeed in the highly competitive IT marketplace. It has always been Sybex's mission to teach individuals how to utilize technologies in the real world, not to simply feed them answers to test questions. Just as Cisco is committed to establishing measurable standards for certifying those professionals who work in the cutting-edge field of internetworking, Sybex is committed to providing those professionals with the means of acquiring the skills and knowledge they need to meet those standards.

The author and editors have worked hard to ensure that the Study Guide you hold in your hands is comprehensive, in-depth, and pedagogically sound. We're confident that this book will exceed the demanding standards of the certification marketplace and help you, the Cisco certification candidate, succeed in your endeavors.

As always, your feedback is important to us. Please send comments, questions, or suggestions to support@sybex.com. At Sybex we're continually striving to meet the needs of individuals preparing for IT certification exams.

Good luck in pursuit of your CCNP certification!

Neil Edde
Associate Publisher—Certification
Sybex, Inc.

## Software License Agreement: Terms and Conditions

The media and/or any online materials accompanying this book that are available now or in the future contain programs and/or text files (the "Software") to be used in connection with the book. SYBEX hereby grants to you a license to use the Software, subject to the terms that follow. Your purchase, acceptance, or use of the Software will constitute your acceptance of such terms.

The Software compilation is the property of SYBEX unless otherwise indicated and is protected by copyright to SYBEX or other copyright owner(s) as indicated in the media files (the "Owner(s)"). You are hereby granted a single-user license to use the Software for your personal, noncommercial use only. You may not reproduce, sell, distribute, publish, circulate, or commercially exploit the Software, or any portion thereof, without the written consent of SYBEX and the specific copyright owner(s) of any component software included on this media.

In the event that the Software or components include specific license requirements or end-user agreements, statements of condition, disclaimers, limitations or warranties ("End-User License"), those End-User Licenses supersede the terms and conditions herein as to that particular Software component. Your purchase, acceptance, or use of the Software will constitute your acceptance of such End-User Licenses.

By purchase, use or acceptance of the Software you further agree to comply with all export laws and regulations of the United States as such laws and regulations may exist from time to time.

### Software Support

Components of the supplemental Software and any offers associated with them may be supported by the specific Owner(s) of that material, but they are not supported by SYBEX. Information regarding any available support may be obtained from the Owner(s) using the information provided in the appropriate read.me files or listed elsewhere on the media.

Should the manufacturer(s) or other Owner(s) cease to offer support or decline to honor any offer, SYBEX bears no responsibility. This notice concerning support for the Software is provided for your information only. SYBEX is not the agent or principal of the Owner(s), and SYBEX is in no way responsible for providing any support for the Software, nor is it liable or responsible for any support provided, or not provided, by the Owner(s).

### Warranty

SYBEX warrants the enclosed media to be free of physical defects for a period of ninety (90) days after purchase. The Software is not available from SYBEX in any other form or media than that enclosed herein or posted to www.sybex.com. If you discover a defect in the media during this warranty period, you may obtain a replacement of identical format at no charge by sending the defective media, postage prepaid, with proof of purchase to:

SYBEX Inc.
Product Support Department
1151 Marina Village Parkway
Alameda, CA 94501
Web: http://www.sybex.com

After the 90-day period, you can obtain replacement media of identical format by sending us the defective disk, proof of purchase, and a check or money order for $10, payable to SYBEX.

### Disclaimer

SYBEX makes no warranty or representation, either expressed or implied, with respect to the Software or its contents, quality, performance, merchantability, or fitness for a particular purpose. In no event will SYBEX, its distributors, or dealers be liable to you or any other party for direct, indirect, special, incidental, consequential, or other damages arising out of the use of or inability to use the Software or its contents even if advised of the possibility of such damage. In the event that the Software includes an online update feature, SYBEX further disclaims any obligation to provide this feature for any specific duration other than the initial posting.

The exclusion of implied warranties is not permitted by some states. Therefore, the above exclusion may not apply to you. This warranty provides you with specific legal rights; there may be other rights that you may have that vary from state to state. The pricing of the book with the Software by SYBEX reflects the allocation of risk and limitations on liability contained in this agreement of Terms and Conditions.

### Shareware Distribution

This Software may contain various programs that are distributed as shareware. Copyright laws apply to both shareware and ordinary commercial software, and the copyright Owner(s) retains all rights. If you try a shareware program and continue using it, you are expected to register it. Individual programs differ on details of trial periods, registration, and payment. Please observe the requirements stated in appropriate files.

### Copy Protection

The Software in whole or in part may or may not be copy-protected or encrypted. However, in all cases, reselling or redistributing these files without authorization is expressly forbidden except as specifically provided for by the Owner(s) therein.

*To my ever-helpful, always-supportive, darling wife, Rose. For sharing the way through all my adventures to all my ambitions, once again, I thank you for proving that love conquers everything.*

# Acknowledgments

I want to thank everyone who was involved in creating my book. Without all the input from the people at Sybex, there would have been just my own thoughts and ideas, but certainly not a book. Thanks to Acquisitions Editor Maureen Adams; Technical Editors Patrick Bass and Arthur Pfund; Copy Editor Suzanne Goraj; Compositor Craig Woods of Happenstance Type-O-Rama; and Indexer Ted Laux.

I want to thank my pal Lloyd Wittebol, who supplied the test switches and regular advice. And Mae Lum, my Production Editor, and Heather O'Connor, my Developmental Editor. Without the tireless efforts and advice of these two ladies, this book would have been a poor shadow of itself. I look forward to working with you both again.

Finally, to my daughter Stephanie, who proofread, advised, cajoled, and encouraged me through the whole project, I offer my special thanks.

# Contents at a Glance

# Table of Contents

# Introduction

This book is intended to help you continue on your exciting new path toward obtaining your CCNP certification. Before reading this book, it is important to have at least read the *CCNA: Cisco Certified Network Associate Study Guide*, 4th Edition, by Todd Lammle (Sybex, 2004). You can take the CCNP tests in any order, but you should have passed the CCNA exam before pursuing your CCNP. Many questions in the Building Cisco Multilayer Switched Networks (BSMSN) exam are built on the CCNA material. However, we have done everything possible to make sure that you can pass the BSMSN exam by reading this book and practicing with Cisco routers—assuming that you are already a CCNA.

## Cisco Systems' Place in Networking

Cisco Systems has become an unrivaled worldwide leader in networking for the Internet. Its networking solutions can easily connect users who work from diverse devices on disparate networks. Cisco products make it simple for people to access and transfer information without regard to differences in time, place, or platform.

Cisco Systems' big picture is that it provides end-to-end networking solutions that customers can use to build an efficient, unified information infrastructure of their own or to connect to someone else's. This is an important piece in the Internet/networking-industry puzzle because a common architecture that delivers consistent network services to all users is now a functional imperative. Because Cisco Systems offers such a broad range of networking and Internet services and capabilities, users needing regular access to their local network or the Internet can do so unhindered, making Cisco's wares indispensable.

Cisco answers this need with a wide range of hardware products that are used to form information networks using any commands from the range of operating systems in use, including the Cisco Internetworking Operating System (IOS) and the CatOS software ranges. This software provides network services, paving the way for networked technical support and professional services to maintain and optimize all network operations.

Along with the Cisco IOS, one of the services Cisco created to help support the vast amount of hardware it has engineered is the Cisco Certified Internetworking Expert (CCIE) program, which was designed specifically to equip people to effectively manage the vast quantity of installed Cisco networks. The business plan is simple: If you want to sell more Cisco equipment and have more Cisco networks installed, ensure that the networks you installed run properly.

However, having a fabulous product line isn't all it takes to guarantee the huge success that Cisco enjoys—lots of companies with great products are now defunct. If you have complicated products designed to solve complicated problems, you need knowledgeable people who are fully capable of installing, managing, and troubleshooting them. That part isn't easy, so Cisco began the CCIE program to equip people to support these complicated networks. This program, known colloquially as the Doctorate of Networking, has also been very successful, primarily due to its extreme difficulty. Cisco continuously monitors the program, changing it as it sees fit, to make sure that it remains pertinent and accurately reflects the demands of today's internetworking business environments.

Building on the highly successful CCIE program, Cisco Career Certifications permit you to become certified at various levels of technical proficiency, spanning the disciplines of network design and support. So, whether you're beginning a career, changing careers, securing your present position, or seeking to refine and promote your position, this is the book for you!

## Cisco's Certifications

Cisco has created several certification tracks that will help you become a CCIE, as well as aid prospective employers in measuring skill levels. Before these new certifications, you took only one test and were then faced with the lab, which made it difficult to succeed. With these new certifications that add a better approach to preparing for that almighty lab, Cisco has opened doors that few were allowed through before. So, what are these new certifications, and how do they help you get your CCIE?

### Cisco Certified Network Associate (CCNA)

The CCNA certification is the first certification in the new line of Cisco certifications and is a prerequisite to all current Cisco certifications. With the new certification programs, Cisco has created a type of stepping-stone approach to CCIE certification. Now you can become a Cisco Certified Network Associate for the meager cost of the *CCNA: Cisco Certified Network Associate Study Guide*, 4th Edition, by Todd Lammle (Sybex, 2004), plus $125 for the test. And you don't have to stop there: you can choose to continue with your studies and select a specific track to follow. The Installation and Support track will help you prepare for the CCIE Routing and Switching certification, whereas the Communications and Services track will help you prepare for the CCIE Communication and Services certification. It is important to note that you do not have to attempt any of these tracks to reach the CCIE, but it is recommended that you do so.

### Cisco Certified Network Professional (CCNP)

The Cisco Certified Network Professional (CCNP) certification has opened up many opportunities for the individual wishing to become Cisco-certified but who is lacking the training, the expertise, or the bucks to pass the notorious and often failed two-day Cisco torture lab. The new Cisco certifications will truly provide exciting new opportunities for the CNE and MCSE who want to broaden rather than deepen their qualifications. So you're thinking, "Great, what do I do after I pass the CCNA exam?" Well, if you want to become a CCIE in Routing and Switching (the most popular certification), understand that there's more than one path to the CCIE certification. The first way is to continue studying and become a Cisco Certified Network Professional (CCNP). That means taking four more tests in addition to obtaining the CCNA certification.

We'll discuss requirements for the CCIE exams later in this introduction.

The CCNP program will prepare you to understand and comprehensively tackle the internetworking issues of today and beyond—not limited to the Cisco world. You will undergo an immense metamorphosis, vastly increasing your knowledge and skills through the process of obtaining these certifications.

Remember that you don't need to be a CCNP or even a CCNA to take the CCIE lab, but to accomplish that, it's extremely helpful if you already have these certifications.

## What Are the CCNP Certification Skills?

Cisco demands a certain level of proficiency for its CCNP certification. In addition to those required for the CCNA, these skills include the following:

- Installing, configuring, operating, and troubleshooting complex routed LAN, routed WAN, and switched LAN networks, and Dial Access Services.
- Understanding more complex networks than those covered on the CCNA, such as IP, IGRP, IPX, Async Routing, extended access lists, IP RIP, route redistribution, IPX RIP, route summarization, OSPF, VLSM, BGP, Serial, IGRP, Frame Relay, ISDN, ISL, X.25, DDR, PSTN, PPP, VLANs, Ethernet, access lists, 802.1Q, FDDI, and transparent and translational bridging.

To meet the Cisco Certified Network Professional requirements, you must be able to perform the following:

- Install and/or configure a network to increase bandwidth, quicken network response times, and improve reliability and quality of service.
- Maximize performance through campus LANs, routed WANs, and remote access.
- Improve network security.
- Create a global intranet.
- Provide access security to campus switches and routers.
- Provide increased switching and routing bandwidth—end-to-end resiliency services.
- Provide custom queuing and routed priority services.

## How Do You Become a CCNP?

After becoming a CCNA, the four exams that you must take to get your CCNP are as follows:

**Exam 642-801: Building Scalable Cisco Internetworks (BSCI)** A while back, Cisco retired the Routing (640-603) exam and now uses this exam to build on the fundamentals of the CCNA exam. BSCI focuses on large multiprotocol internetworks and how to manage them. The BSCI exam is also a required exam for the CCIP and CCDP certifications, which will be discussed later in this introduction.

**Exam 642-811: Building Cisco Multilayer Switched Networks (BCMSN)** The Building Cisco Multilayer Switched Networks exam tests your knowledge of the 2950 and 4500 series of Catalyst switches. You will also be challenged on your knowledge of switching technology, implementation and operation, and planning and design. This book covers all the topics you'll need to pass the BCMSN exam.

**Exam 642-821: Building Cisco Remote Access Networks (BCRAN)** The Building Cisco Remote Access Networks (BCRAN) exam tests your knowledge of installing, configuring, monitoring, and troubleshooting Cisco ISDN and dial-up access products. You must understand PPP, ISDN, Frame Relay, and authentication.

**Exam 642-831: Cisco Internetwork Troubleshooting Support (CIT)** The Cisco Internetwork Troubleshooting Support (CIT) exam tests you on troubleshooting information. You must be able to document a network; troubleshoot Ethernet LANs and IP networks, as well as ISDN, PPP, and Frame Relay networks.

If you hate tests, you can take fewer of them by signing up for the CCNA exam and the CIT exam, and then take just one more long exam called the Foundation R/S exam (640-841). Doing this also gives you your CCNP—but beware, it's a really long test that fuses all the material listed previously into one exam. Good luck! However, by taking this exam, you get three tests for the price of two, which saves you $125 (if you pass). Some people think it's easier to take the Foundation R/S exam because you can leverage the areas that you would score higher in against the areas in which you wouldn't. There is also an option to do three tests: the Composite Exam (642-891), which fuses the BSCI and BCMSN exams; the BCRAN exam; and the CIT exam.

Remember that exam objectives and tests can change at any time without notice. Always check the Cisco website for the most up-to-date information (`www.cisco.com`).

Sybex has a solution for each one of the CCNP exams. Each study guide listed in the table below covers all of the exam objectives for their respective exams.

| Exam Name | Exam # | Sybex Products |
|---|---|---|
| Building Scalable Cisco Internetworks | 642-801 | *CCNP: Building Scalable Cisco Internetworks Study Guide* by Carl Timm and Wade Edwards |
| Switching | 642-811 | *CCNP: Building Cisco Multilayer Switched Networks Study Guide* by Terry Jack |
| Remote Access | 642-821 | *CCNP: Building Cisco Remote Access Networks Study Guide* by Robert Padjen |
| Support | 642-831 | *CCNP: Cisco Internetwork Troubleshooting Study Guide* by Arthur Pfund and Todd Lammle |

Also available is the *CCNP Study Guide Kit,* 3rd Edition, which covers all four exams.

## Cisco Certified Internetwork Professional (CCIP)

After passing the CCNA, the next step in the Communications and Services track would be the CCIP. The CCIP is another professional-level certification, of a similar standard to the CCNP.

The CCIP will give you the skills necessary to understand and tackle the complex internetworking world of the service provider. Core competencies include IP routing, IP QoS, BGP, and MPLS. The skills you need to obtain for the CCIP will prepare you to move forward toward the ever-elusive CCIE Communications and Services certification, but are also of great value in themselves, as CCIP-certified individuals are likely to find work as level 2 engineers or deployment engineers.

### What Are the CCIP Certification Skills?

Cisco demands a certain level of proficiency for its CCIP certification. In addition to those required for the CCNA, these skills include the following:

- Performing complex planning, operations, installations, implementations, and troubleshooting of internetworks
- Understanding and managing complex communications networks—last mile, edge, or core
- Understanding how BGP can be implemented to provide a policy base for inter- and intra-ISP routing with globally large routing tables
- Understanding how MPLS can be used to create VPNs across an IP internet, providing an alternative to customers' private leased lines
- Knowing how and why QoS is of such importance in modern IPS networks, and be able to configure the various options

### How Do You Become a CCIP?

After becoming a CCNA, you must take the four exams listed next:

**Exam 642-901: Building Scalable Cisco Internetworks (BSCI)** A while back, Cisco retired the Routing (640-603) exam and now uses this exam to build on the fundamentals of the CCNA exam. BSCI focuses on large multiprotocol internetworks and how to manage them.

**Exam 642-641: Quality of Services (QoS)** This exam tests your knowledge of quality of service for internetworks. Subjects tested include IP Multicasting, QoS Classification and Marking, Traffic Shaping, Congestion Avoidance, and Signaling Mechanisms.

**Exam 640-910: Implementing Cisco MPLS (MPLS)** This exam tests your knowledge of multiprotocol label switching and its implementation. The test includes basic MPLS, frame and cell mode MPLS, MPLS VPNS, and MPLS Traffic Engineering. The *CCIP: MPLS Study Guide* by James Reagan (Sybex, 2002) covers all the exam objectives.

**Exam 642-661: Border Gateway Protocol (BGP)** This exam tests your knowledge of Border Gateway Protocol (BGP). You are tested on the design, implementation, and management of a large BGP network, and the test covers all aspects of BGP.

## Cisco's Network Design and Installation Certifications

In addition to the Network Installation and Support track and the Communications and Services track, Cisco has created another certification track for network designers. The two certifications within this track are the Cisco Certified Design Associate (CCDA) and Cisco Certified Design Professional (CCDP) certifications. If you're reaching for the CCIE stars, we highly recommend the CCNP and CCDP certifications before attempting the CCIE R/S Qualification exam.

These certifications will give you the knowledge to design routed LAN, routed WAN, and switched LAN.

### Cisco Certified Design Associate (CCDA)

To become a CCDA, you must pass the DESGN (Designing for Cisco Internetwork Solutions) test (640-861). To pass this test, you must understand how to do the following:

- Design simple routed LAN, routed WAN, and switched LAN and ATM LANE networks.
- Use network-layer addressing.
- Filter with access lists.
- Use and propagate VLAN.
- Size networks.

### Cisco Certified Design Professional (CCDP)

If you're already a CCNP and want to get your CCDP, you can simply take the ARCH (Designing Cisco Network Architectures) test (642-871). If you're not yet a CCNP, however, you must take the CCDA, CCNA, BSCI, BCMSN, Remote Access, and CID exams.

CCDP certification skills include the following:

- Designing complex routed LAN, routed WAN, and switched LAN and ATM LANE networks
- Building on the base level of the CCDA technical knowledge

CCDPs must also demonstrate proficiency in the following:

- Network-layer addressing in a hierarchical environment
- Traffic management with access lists
- Hierarchical network design
- VLAN use and propagation
- Performance considerations: required hardware and software; switching engines; memory; cost; and minimization

## Cisco's Security Certifications

There are quite a few Cisco security certifications to obtain. All of the Cisco security certifications also require a valid CCNA.

### Cisco Certified Security Professional (CCSP)

You have to pass five exams to get your CCSP. The pivotal one of those is the SECUR exam. Once you pass the SECUR exam, you need to take only four more. Here they are—the exams you must pass to call the CCSP yours:

**Exam 642-501: Securing Cisco IOS Networks (SECUR)** This exam tests your understanding of such concepts as basic router security, AAA security for Cisco routers and networks, Cisco

IOS Firewall configuration and authentication, building basic and advanced IPSec VPNs, and managing Cisco enterprise VPN routers. You can get help in passing the SECUR exam with the *CCSP: Securing Cisco IOS Networks Study Guide* by Todd Lammle (Sybex, 2003).

**Exam 642-521: Cisco Secure PIX Firewall Advanced (CSPFA)** This exam challenges your knowledge of the fundamentals of Cisco PIX Firewalls, as well as translations and connections, object grouping, advanced protocol handling and authentication, authorization, and accounting, among other topics. You can tackle the CSPFA exam with the help of the *CCSP: Secure PIX and Secure VPN Study Guide* by Wade Edwards, Tom Lancaster, Bryant Tow, and Eric Quinn (Sybex, 2004).

**Exam 642-511: Cisco Secure Virtual Private Networks (CSVPN)** The CSVPN exam covers the basics of Cisco VPNs as well as configuring various Cisco VPNs for remote access, hardware client, backup server, and load balancing, and IPSec over UDP and IPSec over TCP. Again, using the *CCSP: Secure PIX and Secure VPN Study Guide*, you'll approach the CSVPN exam with confidence.

**Exam 642-531: Cisco Secure Intrusion Detection System (CSIDS)** The CSIDS exam will challenge your knowledge of intrusion detection technologies and solutions, and test your abilities to install and configure ISD components. You'll also be tested on managing large-scale deployments of Cisco IDS sensors using Cisco IDS management software. Prepare for the CSIDS exam using the *CCSP: Secure Intrusion Detection and SAFE Implementation Study Guide* by Justin Menga and Carl Timm (Sybex, 2004).

**Exam 642-541: Cisco SAFE Implementation (CSI)** This exam tests such topics as security and architecture fundamentals, SAFE Network design for small and medium corporate and campus situations, and SAFE remote-user network implementation. The *CCSP: Secure PIX and Secure VPN Study Guide* mentioned earlier covers all the relevant details.

### Cisco Firewall Specialist

Cisco Security certifications focus on the growing need for knowledgeable network professionals who can implement complete security solutions. Cisco Firewall Specialists focus on securing network access using Cisco IOS Software and Cisco PIX Firewall technologies.

The two exams that you must pass to achieve the Cisco Firewall Specialist certification are Securing Cisco IOS Networks (SECUR) and Cisco Secure PIX Firewall Advanced (CSPFA).

### Cisco IDS Specialist

Cisco IDS Specialists can both operate and monitor Cisco IOS Software and IDS technologies to detect and respond to intrusion activities.

The two exams that you must pass to achieve the Cisco IDS Specialist certification are Securing Cisco IOS Networks (SECUR) and Cisco Secure Intrusion Detection System (CSIDS).

### Cisco VPN Specialist

Cisco VPN Specialists can configure VPNs across shared public networks using Cisco IOS Software and Cisco VPN 3000 Series Concentrator technologies.

The exams that you must pass to achieve the Cisco VPN Specialist certification are Securing Cisco IOS Networks (SECUR) and Cisco Secure Virtual Networks (CSVPN).

### Cisco Certified Internetwork Expert (CCIE)

Cool! You've become a CCNP, and now your sights are fixed on getting your Cisco Certified Internetwork Expert (CCIE) certification. What do you do next? Cisco recommends a *minimum* of two years of on-the-job experience before taking the CCIE lab. After jumping those hurdles, you then have to pass the written CCIE Exam Qualifications before taking the actual lab.

There are actually four CCIE certifications, and you must pass a written exam for each one of them before attempting the hands-on lab:

**CCIE Communications and Services (Exams 350-020, 350-021, 350-022, 350-023)** The CCIE Communications and Services written exams cover IP and IP routing, optical, DSL, dial, cable, wireless, WAN switching, content networking, and voice.

**CCIE Routing and Switching (Exam 350-001)** The CCIE Routing and Switching exam covers IP and IP routing, non-IP desktop protocols such as IPX, and bridge-and switch-related technologies.

You can get help in passing the CCIE Routing and Switching exam with the *CCIE: Cisco Certified Internetwork Expert Study Guide*, 2nd Edition, by Rob Payne and Kevin Manweiler (Sybex, 2003).

**CCIE Security (Exam 350-018)** The CCIE Security exam covers IP and IP routing as well as specific security components.

**CCIE Voice (Exam 351-030)** The CCIE Voice exam covers those technologies and applications that make up a Cisco Enterprise VoIP solution.

## Where Do You Take the Exam?

You may take the exams at any of the Sylvan Prometric or Virtual University Enterprises (VUE) testing centers around the world. For the location of a testing center near you, call Sylvan at (800) 755-3926 or VUE at (877) 404-3926. Outside of the United States and Canada, contact your local Sylvan Prometric Registration Center or VUE testing site by visiting their websites (`www.prometric.com` and `www.vue.com`, respectively).

To register for a Cisco Certified Network Professional exam:

1. Determine the number of the exam you want to take. (The BCMSN exam number is 642-811.)
2. Register with the nearest Sylvan Prometric or VUE testing center. At this point, you are asked to pay in advance for the exam. At the time of this writing, the exams are $125 each and must be taken within one year of payment. You can schedule exams up to six weeks in advance or as soon as one working day prior to the day you wish to take it. If something comes up and you need to cancel or reschedule your exam appointment, contact the testing center at least 24 hours in advance. Same-day registration isn't available for the Cisco tests.
3. When you schedule the exam, you'll get instructions regarding all appointment and cancellation procedures, the ID requirements, and information about the testing-center location.

## Tips for Taking Your CCNP Exam

The CCNP BCMSN test contains about 63 questions to be taken in 90 minutes. At least one of the questions will be a simulation, where you will actually have to configure switches in a given scenario. However, understand that your test may vary.

Many questions on the exam have answer choices that at first glance look identical—especially the syntax questions! Remember to read through the choices carefully because "close" doesn't cut it. If you put commands in the wrong order or forget one measly character, you'll get the answer wrong. So, to practice, do the hands-on exercises at the end of this book's chapters over and over again until they feel natural to you.

Unlike Microsoft or Novell tests, the exam has answer choices that are really similar in syntax—although some syntax is dead wrong, it is usually just *subtly* wrong. Some other syntax choices may be right, but they're shown in the wrong order. Cisco does split hairs, and it is not at all averse to giving you classic trick questions. Here's an example:

`access-list 101 deny ip any eq 23` denies Telnet access to all systems.

This item looks correct because most people refer to the port number (23) and think, "Yes, that's the port used for Telnet." The catch is that you can't filter IP on port numbers (only TCP and UDP). Another indicator is the use of an extended access list number but no destination address or "any" for the destination.

Cisco does have some simulation questions on the BCMSN exam. Make sure you've got the hands-on skills to take this test. Check out the hands-on labs in this book and for further practice with routers and switches, check out the *CCNP Virtual Lab* by Todd Lammle and Bill Tedder (Sybex, 2003).

Also, never forget that the right answer is the Cisco answer. In many cases, more than one appropriate answer is presented, but the *correct* answer is the one that Cisco recommends.

Here are some general tips for exam success:

- Arrive early at the exam center, so you can relax and review your study materials.
- Read the questions *carefully*. Don't just jump to conclusions. Make sure that you're clear about *exactly* what each question asks.
- Don't leave any questions unanswered. They count against you.
- When answering multiple-choice questions that you're not sure about, use the process of elimination to get rid of the obviously incorrect answers first. Doing this greatly improves your odds if you need to make an educated guess.
- As of this writing, you can no longer move forward and backward through the Cisco exams, so double-check your answer before clicking Next because you can't change your mind. However, it is best to always check the Cisco website before taking any exam to get the most up-to-date information.

After you complete the exam, you'll get immediate, online notification of your pass or fail status, a printed Examination Score Report that indicates your pass or fail status, and your exam results by section. (The test administrator will give you the printed score report.) Test scores are automatically forwarded to Cisco within five working days after you take the test, so you don't need to send your score to them.

## What Does This Book Cover?

This book covers everything you need to pass the CCNP BCMSN exam. It teaches you how to configure and maintain Cisco switches in a network of interconnected LAN segments. But because many of the newer switches have features traditionally associated with routing, we will also cover inter-VLAN routing, layer 3 switching, and Quality of Service. Each chapter begins with a list of the CCNP BCMSN topics covered, so make sure to read them over before working through the chapter.

Chapter 1 describes the traditional campus network model and compares this to the new campus model. In addition, this chapter discusses the Cisco three-layer model, the Cisco switching product line, and how to build switch and core blocks, and has an introduction to the layer 2, 3, and 4 switching technologies.

Chapter 2 describes the various Ethernet media types and connection options, and then shows you how to log in and configure both a set-based and an IOS-based Cisco Catalyst switch.

Chapter 3 covers VLANs—what they are, how they work, and how to configure them in a Cisco internetwork. Trunking and the VLAN Trunk Protocol (VTP) are described and implemented.

Chapter 4 gives you an in-depth look at the Spanning Tree Protocol (STP), its operation, and how to configure STP in a switch.

Chapter 5 shows you how to use different Spanning Tree incidences with different VLANs, and includes a discussion of root bridge selection. It then moves on to show you how to configure STP timers and other parameters. Creating redundant links in STP environments is also covered.

Chapter 6 covers Inter-VLAN routing using internal route processors and external route processors, as well as how to configure both internal and external route processors to connect multiple VLANs.

Chapter 7 provides the fundamentals of Multi-Layer Switching on both internal and external route processors. In addition to covering IP routing with MLS, we show you how to configure the MLS engine. Also covered is the other, more modern version of layer 3 switching, Cisco Express Forwarding (CEF).

Chapter 8 covers the rationale behind multicasting, the background of multicast addresses, and how to translate from a layer 3 multicast address to a layer 2 multicast address. This chapter also covers IGMP and CGMP, and joining a multicast group. In addition, we cover configuring multicast in a Cisco internetwork.

Chapter 9 outlines the reasons for the move toward Quality of Service (QoS)–driven IP networks, and then explains the options available to engineers in modern switched networks. The chapter also covers the configuration and implementation of QoS features, including packet classification, queuing, and forwarding.

Chapter 10 explains the internal workings of the Catalyst's switch range, focusing on how MAC addresses are stored and recalled to enable forwarding decisions, and how memory is managed. Particular attention is paid to the use of Content Addressable Memory (CAM) and Ternary CAM (TCAM).

Appendix A includes all the commands used in this book along with explanations of each command and how they are used with both access layer and distribution layer switches.

Appendix B is a list of all multicast addresses as listed in RFC 1112. It also includes a list of all the currently assigned multicast addresses.

Appendix C contains a list of commands for the 2924 switch series. This switch has not been included in the book because it is not as high-profile a switch as the mainstream 2950, 3550, 4000, and 6000 switches. Nonetheless, Cisco may very well ask a couple of questions on the slightly unusual operating system commands used in the 2924, and so I have created a list of the most important ones along with some usage information for you.

Each chapter ends with review questions that are specifically designed to help you retain the knowledge presented. To really nail down your skills, read each question carefully, and take the time to work through the hands-on labs in some of the chapters.

## How to Use This Book

This book can provide a solid foundation for the serious effort of preparing for the CCNP BCMSN exam. To best benefit from this book, use the following study method:

1. Take the Assessment Test immediately following this Introduction. (The answers are at the end of the test.) Carefully read over the explanations for any answer that you get wrong, and note which chapters the material comes from. This information should help you plan your study strategy.
2. Study each chapter carefully, making sure that you fully understand the information and the test topics listed at the beginning of each chapter. Pay extra-close attention to any chapter where you missed questions in the Assessment Test.
3. Complete all hands-on exercises in the chapter, referring to the chapter so that you understand the reason for each step you take. If you do not have Cisco equipment available, make sure to study the examples carefully. Also, check `www.routersim.com` for a router simulator. Answer the review questions related to that chapter. (The answers appear at the end of the chapter, after the review questions.)
4. Note the questions that confuse you, and study those sections of the book again.
5. Before taking the exam, try your hand at the two bonus exams that are included on the CD that comes with this book. The questions in these exams appear only on the CD. This will give you a complete overview of what you can expect to see on the real thing.
6. Remember to use the products on the CD that is included with this book. The electronic flashcards and the exam-preparation software have all been specifically picked to help you study for and pass your exam.
7. Study on the road with the *CCNP: Building Cisco Multilayer Switched Networks Study Guide* eBook in PDF, and be sure to test yourself with the electronic flashcards.

The electronic flashcards can be used on your Windows computer, Pocket PC, or Palm device.

8. Make sure that you read the Key Terms list at the end of each chapter. Additionally, Appendix A includes all the commands used in the book, along with an explanation for each command.

To learn all the material covered in this book, you'll have to apply yourself regularly and with discipline. Try to set aside the same time every day to study, and select a comfortable and quiet place to do so. If you work hard, you will be surprised at how quickly you learn this material. All the best!

## What's on the CD?

We worked hard to provide some really great tools to help you with your certification process. All of the following tools should be loaded on your workstation when studying for the test.

### The All-New Sybex Test Engine

New from Sybex, this test-preparation software prepares you to successfully pass the BCMSN exam. In this test engine, you will find all the review and assessment test questions from the book, plus two bonus exams that appear exclusively on the CD. You can take the assessment test, test yourself by chapter, or take the two bonus exams. Your scores will show how well you did on each BCMSN exam objective.

### Electronic Flashcards for PC, Pocket PC, and Palm Devices

After you read the *CCNP: Building Cisco Multilayer Switched Networks Study Guide*, read the review questions at the end of each chapter and study the practice exams included in the book and on the CD. But wait, there's more! Test yourself with the flashcards included on the CD. If you can get through these difficult questions, and understand the answers, you'll know you are ready for the BCMSN exam.

The flashcards include 150 questions specifically written to hit you hard and make sure you are ready for the exam. Between the review questions, bonus exams, and flashcards, you'll be more than prepared for the exam.

### *CCNP: Building Cisco Multilayer Switched Networks Study Guide* in PDF

Sybex offers this Cisco certification book on the accompanying CD so that you can read the book on your PC or laptop. It is in Adobe Acrobat format. Acrobat Reader 5.1 with Search is included on the CD as well. This could be extremely helpful to readers who travel and don't want to carry a book, as well as to readers who are more comfortable reading from their computer.

## How to Contact the Author

You can reach Terry Jack by e-mailing him at `terry@globalnettraining.co.uk`.

# Assessment Test

1. Transparent bridging uses which protocol to stop network loops on layer 2 switched networks?
   A. IP routing
   B. STP
   C. VSTP
   D. UplinkFast Bridging
2. Choose the three components that make MLS implementation possible.
   A. MLS-CP
   B. MLSP
   C. MLS-SE
   D. MLS-RP
3. Why would you configure VTP version 2 on your network? (Choose all that apply.)
   A. You need to support Token Ring VLANs.
   B. You want to correct TLV errors.
   C. You want to forward VTP domain messages without the switches checking the version.
   D. You have all Cisco switches.
4. An interface has been configured to use PIM sparse-dense mode. Which of the following criteria force the interface to operate in dense mode? (Choose all that apply.)
   A. DVMRP neighbors that are directly connected
   B. Non-pruned PIM neighbors
   C. Join request received by a host
   D. Interface connected to a Catalyst 4000 series switch
5. Which of the following is the proper syntax for enabling IP multicast on a router?
   A. `multicast ip routing`
   B. `ip-multicast routing`
   C. `ip multicast-routing`
   D. `ip mroute cache`
6. Which of the following are true regarding the blocking state of an STP switch port? (Choose all that apply.)
   A. Blocking ports do not forward any frames.
   B. Blocking ports listen for BPDUs.
   C. Blocking ports forward all frames.
   D. Blocking ports do not listen for BPDUs.

7. Choose the correct definition of an XTAG.

   A. A value assigned to each packet to assign it to an MLS flow

   B. A value assigned by the router to each MLS-SE in the layer 2 network

   C. A value assigned by each MLS-SE for each MLS-RP in the layer 2 network

   D. A value assigned by the NFFC or PFC to identify each flow

8. What Cisco Catalyst switches provide distribution layer functions? (Choose all that apply.)

   A. 2950

   B. 3550

   C. 4000

   D. 6000

   E. 8500

9. What is the difference between a bridge and a layer 2 switch? (Choose all that apply.)

   A. Switches are software based.

   B. Bridges are hardware based.

   C. Switches are hardware based.

   D. Bridges are software based.

10. What would you type at a 2950 console prompt to see the transmit and receive statistics of VTP?

    A. `show vtp counters`

    B. `show vtp status`

    C. `show vtp domain`

    D. `show interface e0/9`

11. If you wanted to configure VLAN 6 on an internal route processor with an IP address of 10.1.1.1/24, which of the following commands would you use?

    A. `set vlan6 ip address 10.1.1.1 255.255.255.0`

    B. `configure terminal, vlan6 ip address 10.1.1.1 255.255.255.0`

    C. `configure terminal, interface vlan 6, ip address 10.1.1.1 255.255.255.0`

    D. `set interface vlan6, ip address 10.1.1.1 255.255.255.0`

12. Which of the following is the correct multicast MAC address if it is mapped from the multicast IP address 224.127.45.254?

    A. 01-00-5e-7f-2d-fe

    B. 01-00-5e-7e-2d-fe

    C. 00-00-e0-7f-2d-fe

    D. 01-00-e0-7f-2d-fe

13. Which of the following describes local VLAN services?
    - **A.** Users do not cross layer 3 devices, and the network services are in the same broadcast domain as the users. This type of traffic never crosses the backbone.
    - **B.** Users cross the backbone to log in to servers for file and print services.
    - **C.** Users would have to cross a layer 3 device to communicate with the network services, but they might not have to cross the backbone.
    - **D.** Layer 3 switches or routers are required in this scenario because the services must be close to the core and would probably be based in their own subnet.
14. What is the command used to set the enable password to `terry` on a 2950 switch?
    - **A.** `enable secret terry`
    - **B.** `set password terry`
    - **C.** `enable password terry`
    - **D.** `set password enable terry`
15. Which of the following protocols is used to determine the locations of data loops and the election of a root bridge?
    - **A.** STP
    - **B.** VSTP
    - **C.** BPDU
    - **D.** BackboneFast
16. What is the syntax for configuring a router to be an RP Mapping Agent?
    - **A.** `ip multicast mapping-agent` *`scope`*
    - **B.** `ip pim send-rp-discovery` *`scope`*
    - **C.** `ip rp-mapping-agent` *`scope`*
    - **D.** `ip auto-rp mapping-agent` *`scope`*
17. Which of the following is an IEEE standard for frame tagging?
    - **A.** ISL
    - **B.** 802.3z
    - **C.** 802.1Q
    - **D.** 802.3u
18. How do you set the enable mode password to `terry` on a 4000 series switch?
    - **A.** `set sco password terry`
    - **B.** `set user password terry`
    - **C.** `set password terry`
    - **D.** `set enablepass`
    - **E.** `set enable password terry`

19. Which of the following is true?
    A. The 3550 uses CEF for layer 3 switching.
    B. The 3550 requires an external route processor to achieve layer 3 switching.
    C. The 3550 does not perform layer 3 switching without enhanced software.
    D. The 3550 integrates with the 2600 router to achieve layer 3 switching.

20. Which version of IGMP is the Cisco proprietary version?
    A. IGMPv1
    B. IGMPv2
    C. CGMP
    D. None

21. If you wanted to set a default route on a 4000 series switch, which of the following commands would you use?
    A. `route add 0.0.0.0 0.0.0.0 172.16.1.1`
    B. `set route default 0.0.0.0 172.16.1.1`
    C. `set route default 172.16.1.1`
    D. `set route 0.0.0.0 0.0.0.0 172.16.1.1`

22. Which of the following is a type of access policy that you can apply at the core layer?
    A. Port security
    B. Access lists
    C. High reliability
    D. Physical security

23. Which of the following defines remote VLAN services?
    A. Users do not cross layer 3 devices, and the network services are in the same broadcast domain as the users. This type of traffic never crosses the backbone.
    B. Users cross layer 2 devices only to find the network file and print services needed to perform their job function.
    C. Users would have to cross a layer 3 device to communicate with the network services, but they might not have to cross the backbone.
    D. Layer 3 switches or routers are required in this scenario because the services must be close to the core and would probably be based in their own subnet.

24. If you want to clear the VTP prune eligibility from all VLANs except VLAN 2, what command would you type in on a set-based switch?
    A. `delete pruneeligible 3, 4, 5,` and so on
    B. `delete vtp pruneeligible 1, 3-1005`
    C. `clear vtp pruneeligible 3-1005`
    D. `clear vtp pruneeligible 1, 3-1005`

25. Which of the following are valid QoS mechanisms? (Choose all that apply.)
    A. Differentiated services
    B. First in, first out
    C. Integrated services
    D. Best efforts

26. When must you run IGMPv1?
    A. When using Auto-RP
    B. When running DVMRP tunnels
    C. When hosts use IGMPv1
    D. You never have to use IGMPv1.

27. If you wanted to have a 4000 switch supervisor module in a VLAN other than the default of VLAN 1, what should you type?
    A. `set interface slo 3`
    B. `set interface sc0 2`
    C. `set sco2 3`
    D. `set vlan management 2`

28. What does a switch do with a multicast frame received on an interface?
    A. Forwards the switch to the first available link
    B. Drops the frame
    C. Floods the network with the frame looking for the device
    D. Sends back a message to the originating station asking for a name resolution

29. Choose the effects of configuring PIM SM on an interface.
    A. Enabling IGMP
    B. Enabling CGMP
    C. Enabling IGMP and CGMP
    D. Enabling Auto-RP

30. Choose the three basic steps in establishing a shortcut cache (MLS cache) entry.
    A. Identification of the MLS-RP
    B. Identification of the MLS-SE
    C. Identification of a candidate packet
    D. Identification of an enable packet
    E. Identification of ISL trunking

31. What is the default VLAN on all switches?

 A. VLAN 64

 B. VLAN 1005

 C. VLAN 1

 D. VLAN 10

32. Which of the following is a type of policy that you can apply at the distribution layer? (Choose all that apply.)

 A. Port security

 B. Access lists

 C. Distribute lists

 D. Physical security

33. Which of the following is true regarding the Cisco 2950-24 switch?

 A. Runs the Standard Image software version of IOS

 B. Supports a large number of connections and also supports an internal route processor module

 C. Supports MLS

 D. Recommended for use at the distribution layer

34. How many bits are available for mapping a layer 3 IP address to a multicast MAC address?

 A. 16

 B. 32

 C. 23

 D. 24

35. What command will set spanning to the per-VLAN mode (PVST) on a 2950 switch?

 A. `spanning-tree mode pvst`

 B. `spanningtree mode pvst+`

 C. `spanning-tree pvst`

 D. `spanning-tree pvst mode`

36. What does the PVST protocol provide?

 A. One instance of spanning tree per network

 B. One instance of STP per VLAN

 C. Port Aggregation Protocol support

 D. Routing between VLANs

**37.** What is the purpose of the IEEE 802.1p protocol?

**A.** It is an extension to 802.1D (STP), providing PVST options.

**B.** It is an extension to 802.1Q, providing CoS options.

**C.** It is an extension to 802.1Q, providing faster STP convergence.

**D.** It is an extension to 802.3, providing QoS options.

**38.** Which of the following are examples of ways to directly connect to a switch? (Choose all that apply.)

**A.** Console port

**B.** VTY line

**C.** Auxiliary port

**D.** Telnet

**39.** Which of the following IP address ranges is the valid multicast address range?

**A.** 127.0.0.0–127.255.255.255

**B.** 223.0.0.1–237.255.255.255

**C.** 224.0.0.1–239.0.0.0

**D.** 224.0.0.0–239.255.255.255

**40.** Which of the following defines enterprise services?

**A.** Users do not cross layer 3 devices, and the network services are in the same broadcast domain as the users. This type of traffic never crosses the backbone.

**B.** No layer 3 switches or devices are used in this network.

**C.** The users would have to cross a layer 3 device to communicate with the network services, but they might not have to cross the backbone.

**D.** Layer 3 switches or routers are required in this scenario because the services must be close to the core and would probably be based in their own subnet.

**41.** What is the command to enable trunking on interface fa0/1 on a 2950 switch?

**A.** `Terry_2950(config-if)#`**switchport trunk**

**B.** `Terry_2950(config-if)#`**switchport trunk mode**

**C.** `Terry_2950(config-if)#`**switchport mode trunk**

**D.** `Terry_2950(config-if)#`**mode trunk switchport**

**42.** Which of the following is true regarding IGMPv2?

**A.** It can be used only on Ethernet LANs.

**B.** It is used to update multicast caches on workstations.

**C.** IGMP works only with Unix devices.

**D.** It enables clients to inform routers of their intent to leave.

**43.** What type of cable must you use to connect between two switch uplink ports?

**A.** Straight

**B.** Rolled

**C.** Crossover

**D.** Fiber

**44.** Which LAN switch methods have a fixed latency time? (Choose all that apply.)

**A.** Cut-through

**B.** Store-and-forward

**C.** FragmentCheck

**D.** FragmentFree

**45.** Which of the following are true regarding a 2950T-24 switch? (Choose all that apply.)

**A.** It is recommended for use primarily at the distribution layer.

**B.** It supports frame classification and marking to create QoS options.

**C.** It uses the Enhanced Image version of the IOS software.

**D.** It supports rudimentary layer 3 switching.

**46.** What is the relationship between frame CoS (Class of Service) and IP ToS (Type of Service)?

**A.** There is no relationship unless you configure it to be so.

**B.** They are the same thing.

**C.** Conceptually, the 3 bits aim to identify the same prioritization.

**D.** They are a direct map to each other.

**47.** How do you set the usermode password to `terry` on a 4000 switch?

**A.** `set sco password terry`

**B.** `set user password terry`

**C.** `set password`

**D.** `set enable password terry`

**48.** What are the three problems that are associated with layer 2 switching and are solved by STP?

**A.** Address learning

**B.** Routing

**C.** Forwarding and filtering frames

**D.** Forwarding and filtering packets

**E.** Loop avoidance

**F.** IP addressing

**49.** When will a switch update its VTP database?

**A.** Every 60 seconds.

**B.** When a switch receives an advertisement that has a higher revision number, the switch will overwrite the database in NVRAM with the new database being advertised.

**C.** When a switch broadcasts an advertisement that has a lower revision number, the switch will overwrite the database in NVRAM with the new database being advertised.

**D.** When a switch receives an advertisement that has the same revision number, the switch will overwrite the database in NVRAM with the new database being advertised.

**50.** What is the typical time that it takes a switch port to go from blocking to forwarding state?

**A.** 5 seconds

**B.** 50 seconds

**C.** 10 seconds

**D.** 100 seconds

**51.** Which topology scenario(s) support Multi-Layer Switching (MLS)? (Choose all that apply.)

**A.** Router on a stick

**B.** Multiple switches connected via ISL trunks with only one switch connected to a router

**C.** Multiple switches connected to a router

**D.** Multiple routers connected to one switch

**52.** Which of the following commands is used to view the configuration of an external route processor?

**A.** `show vlan-config`

**B.** `show config`

**C.** `show running-config`

**D.** `show port` *`slot/type`*

**53.** To configure a root bridge on a set-based switch, what command would be used?

**A.** `set spanning tree backup`

**B.** `set spantree secondary`

**C.** `set spantree root`

**D.** `spanning tree 2`

**54.** What are the two types of distribution trees?

**A.** RP trees

**B.** Multicast trees

**C.** Shared root trees

**D.** Source root trees

55. When setting the VLAN port priority, what are the available values that you can use?

A. 0–63

B. 1–64

C. 0–255

D. 1–1005

56. What are valid ways that an administrator can configure VLAN memberships? (Choose all that apply.)

A. DHCP server

B. Static

C. Dynamic

D. VTP database

57. What is the distance that you can run an MMF, 62.5-micron Gigabit Ethernet cable?

A. 400 meters

B. 25 meters

C. 260 meters

D. 3 kilometers

E. 10 kilometers

58. You have just been hired as a consultant for a small company that has users distributed across many floors in the same building. Servers for the company are all located on the first floor, and 30 users access them from various parts of the building. What switch would you install for the access layer connection?

A. 2900 series

B. 3550 series

C. 4000 series

D. 6000 series

59. Which of the following commands will display XTAG information on a switch?

A. `show mls entry`

B. `show mls statistics`

C. `show mls`

D. `show mls rp ip`

60. Which statement about the 4000 series switches is true?

A. They run CatOS, but can be upgraded to run IOS.

B. The supervisor can be upgraded to run IOS, but CatOS remains on the switch cards.

C. IOS is supported only for the layer 3 switching portion of the configurations.

D. They can be upgraded to IOS from CatOS, but there is no mechanism to revert to CatOS.

# Answers to Assessment Test

1. B. The Spanning Tree Protocol was designed to help stop network loops that can happen with transparent bridge networks running redundant links. See Chapter 5 for more information.

2. B, C, D. MLSP is the routing protocol for MLS, MLS-SE is the switching engine, and MLS-RP is the route processor. MLS-CP is an invalid answer. See Chapter 7 for more information.

3. A, B, C. If you have Token Ring, you would want to run VTP version 2. See Chapter 3 for more information.

4. A, B. Join requests cause the interface to operate in PIM sparse mode. If a Catalyst is connected, the interface must be configured to use CGMP. See Chapter 8 for more information.

5. C. The first two are not valid commands. `ip mroute cache` allows the interface to use fast switching or other types of interface switching for multicast traffic. Refer to Chapter 8 for more information.

6. A, B. When a port is in blocking state, no frames are forwarded. This is used to stop network loops. However, the blocked port will listen for BPDUs received on the port. For more information on STP, see Chapter 4.

7. C. XTAG values are locally significant values that are assigned by the Multi-Layer Switching Switch Engine (MLS-SE) to keep track of the Multi-Layer Switching Route Processors (MLS-RPs) in the network. See Chapter 7 for more information.

8. B, C, D. The 3550, 4000 series, and 6000 series were specifically designed to provide distribution layer functions. See Chapter 1 for more information on the distribution layer and the Cisco switches designed to run at the distribution layer.

9. C, D. Bridges are considered software based and switches are considered hardware based. See Chapter 4 for more information.

10. A. The command `show vtp counters` is used to see VTP updates being sent and received on your switch. For more information, see Chapter 3.

11. C. The command `interface vlan #` is used to create a VLAN interface. The IP address of the interface is then configured with the `ip address` command. See Chapter 6 for more information on internal and external route processors.

12. A. 23 bits allows us to use the 127 value in the second octet. The MAC prefix is always 01-00-5e. See Chapter 8 for more information.

13. A. Local VLAN services are network services that are located in the same VLAN as the user trying to access them. Packets will not pass through a layer 3 device. See Chapter 1 for more information.

14. C. The 2950 uses Cisco IOS software, so the commands are the same as for a router. See Chapter 2 for more information.

15. C. Bridge Protocol Data Units are sent out every two seconds by default and provide information to switches throughout the internetwork. This includes finding redundant links, electing the root bridge, monitoring the links in the spanning tree, and notifying other switches in the network about link failures. See Chapter 5 for more information.

16. B. The router uses PIM to distribute RP information to multicast routers. The other syntax options are not valid. See Chapter 8 for more information.

17. C. Cisco's proprietary version of frame tagging is ISL. However, if you do not have all Cisco switches, the IEEE 802.1Q version would be used. See Chapter 3 for more information.

18. D. The command `set enablepass` will set the password on a 4000 series switch. See Chapter 2 for more information on configuring the 4000 series switches.

19. A. The 3550 uses Cisco Express Forwarding (CEF) to maintain tables that allow layer 3 switching to be carried out. See Chapter 6 for more information on layer 3 switching.

20. D. CGMP is not a version of IGMP but was developed by Cisco Systems. See Chapter 8 for more information.

21. C. The command `set route default` and the command `set route 0.0.0.0` are the same command and can be used to set a default gateway on a 4000 series switch. See Chapter 6 for more information on configuring a 4000 series switch.

22. C. A high level of reliability, including redundancy, is encouraged at the core layer. See Chapter 1 for more information on policies.

23. C. To communicate with another VLAN, packets must cross a layer 3 device. See Chapter 1 for more information on local and remote VLAN services.

24. C. You cannot turn off `pruneeligible` for VLAN 1, which makes `clear vtp pruneeligible 3-1005` the only correct answer. See Chapter 3 for more information.

25. A, C, D. First in, first out is a queuing mechanism. All the others are genuine models for QoS implementation. See Chapter 9 for more information.

26. C. Use IGMPv1 when the clients subscribing are using IGMPv1. See Chapter 8 for more information.

27. B. The command `set interface sc0` *`vlan#`* changes the default VLAN for the supervisor module to the specified VLAN. See Chapter 2 for more information.

28. C. The switch will flood the network with the frame looking for the device. For more information on LAN switching, see Chapter 4.

29. A. Adding the PIM configuration to the interface enables only Internet Group Management Protocol (IGMP) in addition to PIM. Auto-RP and Cisco Group Management Protocol (CGMP) must be configured separately. See Chapter 8 for more information.

30. A, C, D. The Multi-Layer Switching Switch Engine (MLS-SE) needs to know three things to create an entry: the Multi-Layer Switching Route Processor (MLS-RP), a candidate packet, and an enable packet. See Chapter 7 for more information.

31. C. VLAN 1 is a default VLAN and used for management by default. See Chapter 5 for more information.

32. B, C. Access lists can be configured at the distribution layer for packet filtering purposes, and a distribute list controls how routing traffic is forwarded. See Chapter 1 for more information on policies at each layer.

33. A. The 2950-24 is an entry-level switch. Running the SI IOS image, it is suitable for use at the access layer only. See Chapter 1 for more information.

34. C. Due to the prefix length and the high order bit already in use in the multicast MAC address, only 23 bits are left for mapping. See Chapter 8 for more information.

35. A. The command to set spanning tree to the pvst mode on a 2950 switch is `spanning-tree mode pvst`. See Chapter 5 for more information.

36. B. The Cisco proprietary protocol Per-VLAN Spanning Tree (PVST) uses a separate instance of spanning tree for each and every VLAN. See Chapter 5 for more information.

37. B. 802.1p uses 3 bits in the 802.1Q field to set Class of Service. See Chapter 9 for more information.

38. A, C. Connecting to the console port or auxiliary port is out-of-band management because you are not accessing the equipment from within the network. Instead, you are connecting directly to the switch. See Chapter 2 for more information on basic switch setup.

39. D. The first answer is a Class B range of addresses. 223.0.0.1 does not have the proper mask. The third answer is within the valid range, but it is not all-inclusive. See Chapter 8 for more information.

40. D. Enterprise services are defined as services that are provided to all users on the internetwork. See Chapter 1 for more information.

41. C. The command to set an interface to trunk mode on an IOS-based switch is `switchport mode trunk`. See Chapter 3 for more information on trunking configurations.

42. D. Internet Group Management Protocol (IGMP) version 2 is used by IGMP routers to enable clients to send messages, telling the router that they no longer want to subscribe to the multicast stream. See Chapter 8 for more information regarding IGMP.

43. C. A crossover cable is used to connect switches to switches and hubs to hubs. See Chapter 2 for more information on the Catalyst 4000 configuration.

44. A, D. Cut-through and FragmentFree always read only a fixed amount of a frame. For more information on LAN switch types, see Chapter 4.

45. B, C. The 2950T-24 uses the EI image of IOS and supports both frame classification and marking, but like all 2950 series, it is primarily used at the access layer and does not support layer 3 switching. See Chapter 9 for more information.

46. C. Although CoS is configured at layer 2 and ToS at layer 3, both of them are mechanisms to identify different traffic priorities, and thus are conceptually the same in their meaning. See Chapter 9 for more information.

**47.** C. The command `set password` sets the usermode password on a 4000 series switch. See Chapter 2 for more information on configuring 4000 series switches.

**48.** A, C, E. Layer 2 features include address learning, forwarding and filtering of the network, and loop avoidance. See Chapter 4 for more information.

**49.** B. Only when a VTP update is received with a higher data VTP revision number will a switch update its VTP database. See Chapter 3 for more information.

**50.** B. Fifty seconds is the default time for changing from blocking to forwarding state. This is to allow enough time for all switches to update their STP database. See Chapter 4 for more information on STP.

**51.** A, B, D. The router on a stick is the typical and simplest topology for Multi-Layer Switching (MLS). Multiple switches connected to each other can use MLS if only one switch is connected to the router. Multiple routers can be connected to one switch as long as each router has only one link to the switch. See Chapter 7 for more information.

**52.** C. The command `show running-config` is used to view the current configuration. See Chapter 6 for more information on internal and external route processors.

**53.** C. The `set spantree root` command enables you to configure a root bridge. See Chapter 5 for more information.

**54.** C, D. Multicast trees don't exist. Some protocols that are based in shared root trees can create RPTs (or RP trees) that are parallel to the shortest path tree, but this is a flavor of shared root tree distribution. See Chapter 8 for more information.

**55.** A. A priority from 0 to 63 can be set for each VLAN. See Chapter 3 for more information.

**56.** B, C. Static VLANs are set port by port on each interface or port. Dynamic VLANs can be assigned to devices via a server. See Chapter 3 for more information.

**57.** C. The maximum distance a Multi-Mode Fiber, 62.5-micron Gigabit Ethernet link can run is 260 meters. See Chapter 2 for more information.

**58.** A. Because the question involves a small company and no growth was specified, a couple of 2950s would be the most cost-effective solution. See Chapter 1 for more information.

**59.** C. The `show mls rp ip` command is used on routers and doesn't provide XTAG information. Neither do any of the other switch commands. See Chapter 7 for more information.

**60.** A. The default OS for older 4000 switches is CatOS, but they can be upgraded to IOS. Newer switches may be purchased with IOS already running. See Chapter 10 for more information.

# The Campus Network

## THE CCNP EXAM TOPICS COVERED IN THIS CHAPTER INCLUDE THE FOLLOWING:

- ✓ **Identify the correct Cisco Systems product solution given a set of network switching requirements**
- ✓ **Describe the Enterprise Composite Model (Campus Infrastructure, Server Farm, Enterprise Edge, Network Management) used for designing networks**
- ✓ **Identify enterprise network needs for performance, scalability, and availability**
- ✓ **Understand the physical, data-link, and network layer technologies used in a multi-layer switched network**
- ✓ **Describe the Enterprise Composite Model components and explain how switches fit into these roles.**

The definition of a campus network has never been straightforward, but the common description is a group of LAN segments within a building or group of buildings that connect to form one network. Typically, one company owns the entire network, including the wiring between buildings. This local area network (LAN) typically uses Ethernet, Token Ring, Fiber Distributed Data Interface (FDDI), or Asynchronous Transfer Mode (ATM) technologies. The size of the campus network is not defined, as it may be inside a single large building or spread across something as large as a distributed university campus. In fact, with the advent of Metro Ethernet, it may even be dispersed across different towns.

An Enterprise network connects all shared services and data within an enterprise. Some enterprises are global, and some are very self-contained. An Enterprise network may consist of several campus networks as well as possible WAN cores—that really depends on the size of the enterprise.

The main challenge for network administrators is to make the campus network run efficiently and effectively. To do this, they must understand current campus networks as well as the new emerging campus networks. Therefore, in this chapter, you will learn about current and future requirements of campus internetworks (the connecting of several campuses). We'll explain the limitations of traditional campus networks as well as the benefits of the emerging campus designs. You will learn how to choose from among the new generation of Cisco switches to maximize the performance of your networks. Understanding how to design for the emerging campus networks is not only critical to your success on the Switching exam, it's also critical for implementing production networks.

As part of the instruction in network design, we'll discuss the specifics of technologies, including how to implement Ethernet and the differences between layer 2, layer 3, and layer 4 switching technologies. In particular, you will learn how to implement FastEthernet, Gigabit Ethernet, Fast EtherChannel, and Multi-Layer Switching (MLS) in the emerging campus designs. This will help you learn how to design, implement, and maintain an efficient and effective internetwork.

You will learn about the Cisco hierarchical model, which is covered in all the Cisco courses. In particular, you will learn which Catalyst switches can—and should—be implemented at each layer of the Cisco model. You will also learn how to design networks based on switch and core blocks. Finally, you will learn about SAFE, the Cisco secure blueprint for enterprise networks, including a description of the network in terms of modules and how they are constructed and interact.

This chapter provides you with a thorough overview of campus network design (past, present, and future) and teaches you how, as a network administrator, to choose the most appropriate technology for particular network needs. This will enable you to configure and design your network now, with the future in mind.

# Understanding Campus Internetworks

The history of networking is a history of ebbs and flows. From the initial networks, which were designed to provide access to simple central, shared resources on the mainframe computer, we moved to the distributed architecture of networks in the 1990s. This has been followed by a move toward server farms, which in many ways appear to be a return to the old centralized networking from the past.

Mainframes were not always discarded; some still carry out huge batch processing tasks in banks and insurance companies, but many just became storage areas for data and databases. The NetWare or NT server took over as a file/print server and soon started running most other programs and applications as well. Groups of servers running sympathetic applications were clustered together in domains, or other administrative groups, and new directory services emerged to allow easy discovery of domain services. Networks were developed to find the simplest, cheapest, and most reliable mechanisms to establish and maintain connectivity with the resources.

Over the last 20 years, we have witnessed the birth of the LAN and the growth of WANs (Wide Area Networks) and the Internet. More than anything else, the Internet is changing our lives daily, with ever-increasing numbers of online transactions taking place, education and entertainment services becoming available, and people just plain having fun communicating with each other in exciting new ways.

So how will networks evolve in the twenty-first century? Are we still going to see file and print servers at all branch locations, or will servers migrate to common locations? Are all workstations going to connect to the Internet with ISPs to separate the data, voice, and other multimedia applications? I wish I had a crystal ball.

# Looking Back at Traditional Campus Networks

In the 1990s, the traditional campus network started as one LAN and grew and grew until segmentation needed to take place just to keep the network up and running. In this era of rapid expansion, response time was secondary to just making sure the network was functioning. Besides, the majority of applications were store-and-forward, such as e-mail, and there was little need for advanced quality of service options.

By looking at the technology, you can see why keeping the network running was such a challenge. Typical campus networks ran on 10BaseT or 10Base2 (thinnet). As a result, the network was one large collision domain—not to mention even one large broadcast domain. Despite these limitations, Ethernet was used because it was scalable, effective, and somewhat inexpensive compared to other options. (IBM "owned" Token Ring, and getting it installed frequently meant getting in IBM to do it—sometimes expensive and often impractical.) ARCnet was used in some networks, but Ethernet and ARCnet are not compatible, and the networks became two separate entities. ARCnet soon became history. Token Ring became marginalized. Ethernet became king.

Because a campus network can easily span many buildings, bridges were used to connect the buildings; this broke up the collision domains, but the network was still one large broadcast domain. More and more users were attached to the hubs used in the network, and soon the performance of the network was considered extremely slow.

## Performance Problems and Solutions

Availability and performance are the major problems with traditional campus networks. Availability is affected by the number of users attempting to access the network at any one time, plus the reliability of the network itself. The performance problems in traditional campus networks include collisions, bandwidth, broadcasts, and multicasts.

### Collisions

A campus network typically started as one large collision domain, so all devices could see and also collide with each other. If a host had to broadcast, then all other devices had to listen, even though they themselves were trying to transmit. And if a device were to exhibit a jabber (malfunction by continually transmitting), it could bring down the entire network.

Because routers didn't really become cost effective until the late 1980s, bridges were used to break up collision domains. That created smaller collision domains, and was therefore an improvement, but the network was still one large broadcast domain and the same old broadcast problems still existed. Bridges also solved distance-limitation problems because they usually had repeater functions built into the electronics and/or they could break up the physical segment.

### Bandwidth

The *bandwidth* of a segment is measured by the amount of data that can be transmitted at any given time. Think of bandwidth as a water hose; the amount of water that can go through the hose depends on two elements:

- Pressure
- Distance

The pressure is the current, and the bandwidth is the size of the hose. If you have a hose that is only ¼-inch in diameter, you won't get much water through it regardless of the current or the size of the pump on the transmitting end.

Another issue is distance. The longer the hose, the more the water pressure drops. You can put a repeater in the middle of the hose and re-amplify the pressure of the line, which would help, but you need to understand that all lines (and hoses) have degradation of the signal, which means that the pressure drops off the further the signal goes down the line. For the remote end to understand digital signaling, the pressure must stay at a minimum value. If it drops below this minimum value, the remote end will not be able to receive the data. In other words, the far end of the hose would just drip water instead of flow. You can't water your crops with drips of water; you need a constant water flow.

The solution to bandwidth issues is maintaining your distance limitations and designing your network with proper segmentation of switches and routers. Congestion on a segment happens when too many devices are trying to use the same bandwidth. By properly segmenting the network, you can eliminate some of the bandwidth issues. You never will have enough bandwidth for your users; you'll just have to accept that fact. However, you can always make it better.

## Broadcasts and Multicasts

Remember that all protocols have broadcasts built in as a feature, but some protocols can really cause problems if not configured correctly. Some protocols that, by default, can cause problems if they are not correctly implemented are Internet Protocol (IP), Address Resolution Protocol (ARP), Network Basic Input Output System (NetBIOS), Internetwork Packet Exchange (IPX), Service Advertising Protocol (SAP), and Routing Information Protocol (RIP). However, remember that there are features built into the Cisco router Internetworking Operating System (IOS) that, if correctly designed and implemented, can alleviate these problems. Packet filtering, queuing, and choosing the correct routing protocols are some examples of how Cisco routers can eliminate some broadcast problems.

Multicast traffic can also cause problems if not configured correctly. Multicasts are broadcasts that are destined for a specific or defined group of users. If you have large multicast groups or a bandwidth-intensive application such as Cisco's IPTV application, multicast traffic can consume most of the network bandwidth and resources.

To solve broadcast issues, create network segmentation with bridges, routers, and switches. However, understand that you'll move the bottleneck to the routers, which break up the broadcast domains. Routers process each packet that is transmitted on the network, which can cause a bottleneck if an enormous amount of traffic is generated.

**Understanding Broadcast Effects**

Just in case anyone is still confused about broadcasts, consider this analogy. Suppose you worked in an office where there was a telephone system that included a broadcast capability. Every time the phone rang, everyone would have to answer it and listen to who the broadcast transmission was aimed at—"Hello, is that the Domain Name Server?" How long would it be before all these interruptions caused you to throw the phone out of the window? That's what broadcasts do to PCs. Each interruption causes single-tasking operating systems to stop what they are doing—writing to the hard drive, processing, and so on—and answer the phone.

Virtual LANs (VLANs) are a solution as well, but VLANs are just broadcast domains with artificial boundaries. A VLAN is a group of devices on different network segments defined as a broadcast domain by the network administrator. The benefit of VLANs is that physical location is no longer a factor for determining the port into which you would plug a device into the network. You can plug a device into any switch port, and the network administrator gives that port a VLAN assignment. Remember that routers or layer 3 switches must be used for different VLANs to communicate.

## The 80/20 Rule

The traditional campus network placed users and groups in the same physical location. If a new salesperson was hired, they had to sit in the same physical location as the other sales personnel and be connected to the same physical network segment in order to share network resources. Any deviation from this caused major headaches for the network administrators.

The rule that needed to be followed in this type of network was called the *80/20 rule* because 80 percent of the users' traffic was supposed to remain on the local network segment and only 20 percent or less was supposed to cross the routers or bridges to the other network segments. If more than 20 percent of the traffic crossed the network segmentation devices, performance issues arose. Figure 1.1 shows a traditional 80/20 network.

**FIGURE 1.1** A traditional 80/20 network

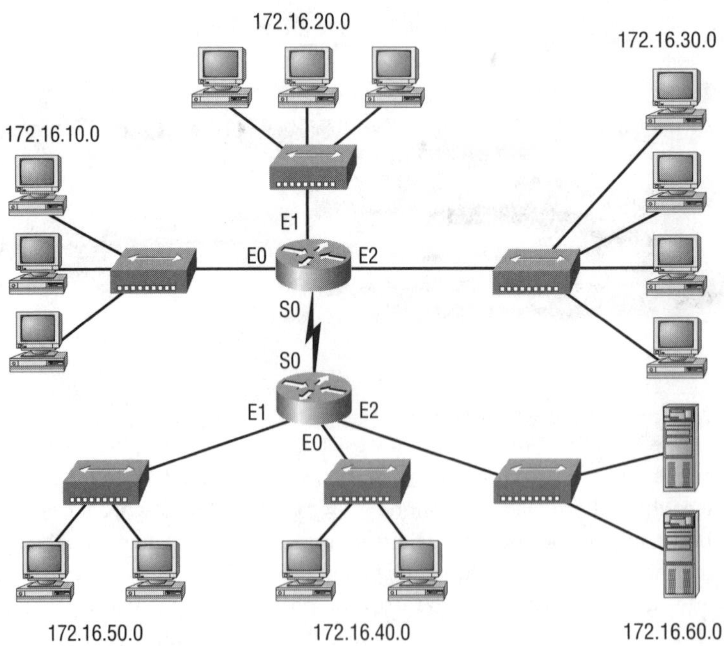

Because network administrators are responsible for network design and implementation, they improved network performance in the 80/20 network by making sure that all the network resources for the users were contained within the local network segment. The resources included network servers, printers, shared directories, software programs, and applications.

## The New 20/80 Rule

With new web-based applications and computing, any PC can be a subscriber or publisher at any time. Also, because businesses are pulling servers from remote locations and creating server farms (sounds like a mainframe, doesn't it?) to centralize network services for security, reduced cost, and administration, the old 80/20 rule is obsolete and could not possibly work in this environment. All traffic must now traverse the campus backbone, which means we now have a *20/80 rule* in effect. Twenty percent of what the user performs on the network is local, whereas up to 80 percent crosses the network segmentation points to get to network services. Figure 1.2 shows the new 20/80 network.

**FIGURE 1.2** A 20/80 network

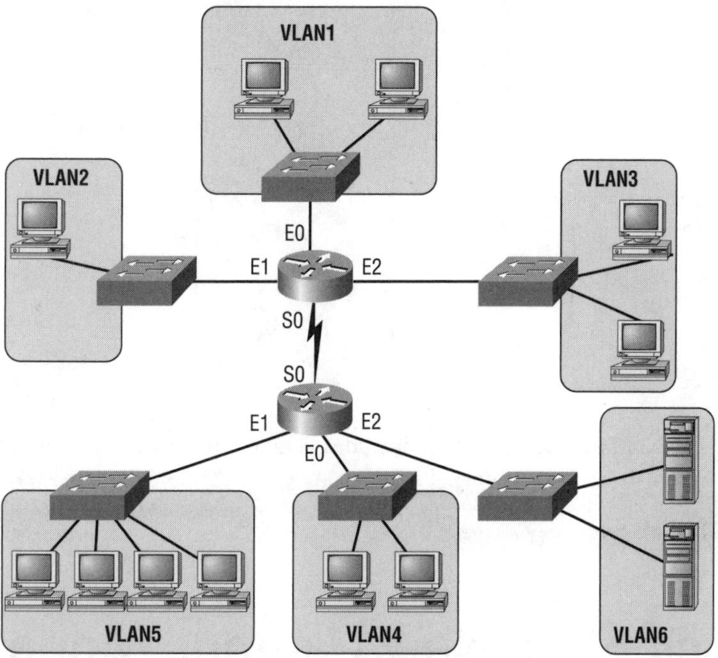


The problem with the 20/80 rule is not the network wiring and topology as much as it is the routers themselves. They must be able to handle an enormous number of packets quickly and efficiently at wire speed. This is probably where I should be talking about how great Cisco routers are and how our networks would be nothing without them. I'll get to that later in this chapter—trust me.

## Virtual LANs

With this new 20/80 rule, more and more users need to cross broadcast domains (VLANs), and this puts the burden on routing, or layer 3 switching. By using VLANs within the new campus model, you can control traffic patterns and control user access easier than in the traditional campus network. Virtual LANs break up broadcast domains by using either a router or a switch that can perform layer 3 functions. Figure 1.3 shows how VLANs are created and might look in an internetwork.

**FIGURE 1.3** VLANs break up broadcast domains in a switched internetwork.

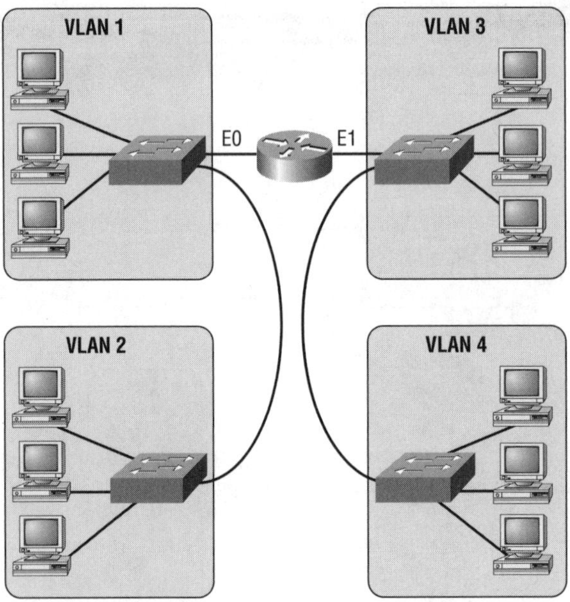


Chapter 3, "VLANs, Trunks, and VTP," includes detailed information about VLANs and how to configure them in an internetwork. It is imperative that you understand VLANs, because the traditional way of building the campus network is being redesigned and VLANs are a large factor in building the new campus model.

# Introducing the New Campus Model

The changes in customer network requirements—in combination with the problems with collision, bandwidth, and broadcasts—have necessitated a new network campus design. Higher user demands and complex applications force the network designers to think more about traffic patterns instead of solving a typical isolated department issue. We can no longer just think about creating subnets and putting different departments into each subnet. We need to create a network that makes everyone capable of reaching all network services easily. Server farms, where all enterprise servers are located in one physical location, really take a toll on the existing network infrastructure and make the way we used to design networks obsolete. We must pay attention to traffic patterns and how to solve bandwidth issues. This can be accomplished with higher-end routing and switching techniques.

Because of the new bandwidth-intensive applications, video and audio being delivered to the desktop, as well as more and more work being performed on the Internet, the new campus model must be able to provide the following:

**Fast convergence** When a network change takes place, the network must be able to adapt very quickly to the change and keep data moving swiftly.

**Deterministic paths** Users must be able to gain access to a certain area of the network without fail.

**Deterministic failover** The network design must have provisions that make sure the network stays up and running even if a link fails.

**Scalable size and throughput** As users and new devices are added to the network, the network infrastructure must be able to handle the new increase in traffic.

**Centralized applications** Enterprise applications accessed by all users must be available to support all users on the internetwork.

**The new 20/80 rule** Instead of 80 percent of the users' traffic staying on the local network, 80 percent of the traffic now crosses the backbone and only 20 percent stays on the local network.

**Multiprotocol support** Campus networks must support multiple protocols, both routed and routing protocols. Routed protocols are used to send user data through the internetwork (for example, IP or IPX). Routing protocols are used to send network updates between routers, which will in turn update their routing tables. Examples of routing protocols include RIP, Enhanced Interior Gateway Routing Protocol (EIGRP), and Open Shortest Path First (OSPF).

**Multicasting** Multicasting is sending a broadcast to a defined subnet or group of users. Users can be placed in multicast groups, for example, for videoconferencing.

**QoS** We need to be able to prioritize different traffic types.

## Network Services

The new campus model provides remote services quickly and easily to all users. The users have no idea where the resources are located in the internetwork, nor should they care. There are three types of network services, which are created and defined by the administrator and should appear to the users as local services:

- Local services
- Remote services
- Enterprise services

### Local Services

*Local services* are network services that are located on the same subnet or network as the users accessing them. Users do not cross layer 3 devices, and the network services are in the same broadcast domain as the users. This type of traffic never crosses the backbone.

### Remote Services

*Remote services* are close to users but not on the same network or subnet as the users. The users would have to cross a layer 3 device to communicate with the network services. However, they might not have to cross the backbone.

### Enterprise Services

*Enterprise services* are defined as services that are provided to all users on the internetwork. Layer 3 switches or routers are required in this scenario because an enterprise service must be close to the core and would probably be based in its own subnet. Examples of these services include Internet access, e-mail, and possibly videoconferencing. When servers that host enterprise services are placed close to the backbone, all users would be the same distance from the servers, but all user data would have to cross the backbone to get to the services.

# Using Switching Technologies

Switching technologies are crucial to the new network design. Because the prices on layer 2 switching have been dropping dramatically, it is easier to justify the cost of buying switches for your entire network. This doesn't mean that every business can afford switch ports for all users, but it does allow for a cost-effective upgrade solution when the time comes.

To understand switching technologies and how routers and switches work together, you must understand the Open Systems Interconnection (OSI) model. This section will give you a general overview of the OSI model and the devices that are specified at each layer.

You'll need a basic understanding of the OSI model to fully understand discussions in which it is included throughout the rest of this book. For more detailed information about the OSI model, please see *CCNA: Cisco Certified Network Associate Study Guide*, 4th edition, by Todd Lammle (Sybex, 2003).

## Open Systems Interconnection (OSI) Model

As you probably already know, the *Open Systems Interconnection (OSI) model* has seven layers, each of which specifies functions that enable data to be transmitted from host to host on an internetwork. Figure 1.4 shows the OSI model and the functions of each layer.

**FIGURE 1.4** The OSI model and the layer functions

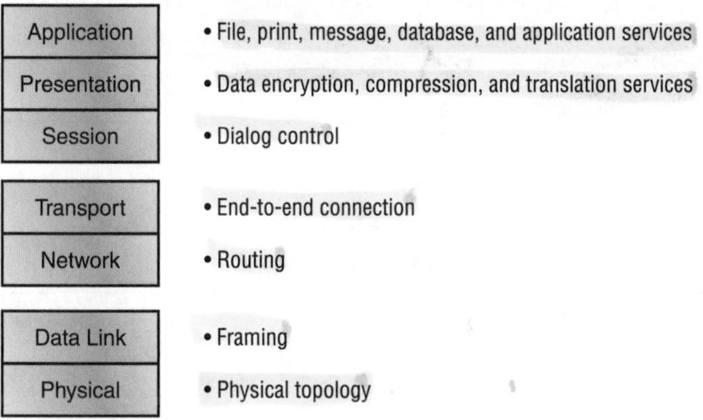


The OSI model is the cornerstone for application developers to write and create networked applications that run on an internetwork. What is important to network engineers and technicians is the encapsulation of data as it is transmitted on a network.

## Data Encapsulation

*Data encapsulation* is the process by which the information in a protocol is wrapped, or contained, in the data section of another protocol. In the OSI reference model, each layer encapsulates the layer immediately above it as the data flows down the protocol stack.

The logical communication that happens at each layer of the OSI reference model doesn't involve many physical connections, because the information each protocol needs to send is encapsulated in the layer of protocol information beneath it. This encapsulation produces a set of data called a packet (see Figure 1.5).

**FIGURE 1.5** Data encapsulation at each layer of the OSI reference model

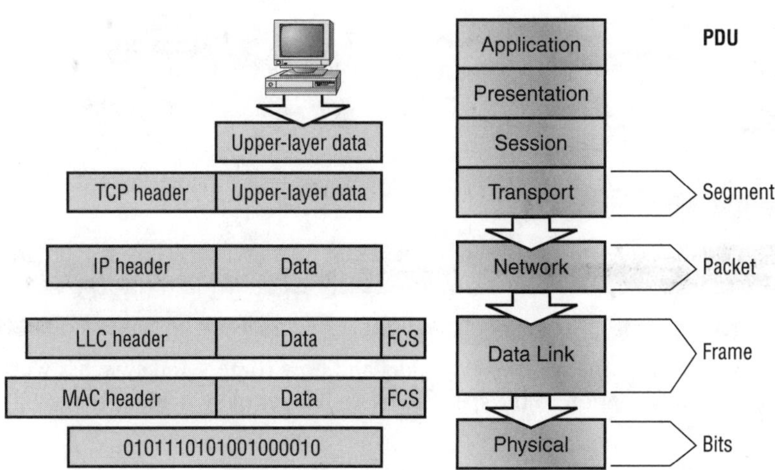

Looking at Figure 1.5, you can follow the data down through the OSI reference model as it's encapsulated at each layer. Cisco courses typically focus only on layers 2 through 4.

Each layer communicates only with its peer layer on the receiving host, and they exchange Protocol Data Units (PDUs). The PDUs are attached to the data at each layer as it traverses down the model and is read only by its peer on the receiving side. Each layer has a specific name for the PDU, as shown in Table 1.1.

**TABLE 1.1** OSI Encapsulation

| OSI Layer | Name of Protocol Data Units (PDUs) |
|---|---|
| Transport | Segments |
| Network | Packets |
| Data Link | Frames |
| Physical | Bits |

Starting at the Application layer, data is converted for transmission on the network, and then encapsulated in Presentation layer information. When the Presentation layer receives this information, it looks like generic data. The Presentation layer hands the data to the Session layer, which is responsible for synchronizing the session with the destination host.

The Session layer then passes this data to the Transport layer, which transports the data from the source host to the destination host in a reliable fashion. But before this happens, the Network layer adds routing information to the packet. It then passes the packet on to the Data Link layer for framing and for connection to the Physical layer. The Physical layer sends the data as 1s and 0s to the destination host. Finally, when the destination host receives the 1s and 0s, the data passes back up through the model, one layer at a time. The data is de-encapsulated at each of the OSI model's peer layers.

At a transmitting device, the data encapsulation method is as follows:

1. User information is converted to data for transmission on the network.
2. Data is converted to segments at the Transport layer, and any reliability parameters required are set up.
3. Segments are converted to packets or datagrams at the Network layer, and routing information is added to the PDU.
4. Packets or datagrams are converted to frames at the Data Link layer, and hardware addresses are used to communicate with local hosts on the network medium.
5. Frames are converted to bits, and 1s and 0s are encoded within the digital signal.

Now that you have a sense of the OSI model and how routers and switches work together, it is time to turn our attention to the specifics of each layer of switching technology.

## Layer 2 Switching

*Layer 2 switching* is hardware based, which means it uses the *Media Access Control (MAC)* address from the host's network interface cards (NICs) to filter the network. Switches use *application-specific integrated circuits (ASICs)* to build and maintain filter tables. It is okay to think of a layer 2 switch as a multiport bridge.

Layer 2 switching provides the following:

- Hardware-based bridging (MAC)
- Wire speed
- High speed
- Low latency
- Low cost

Layer 2 switching is so efficient because there is no modification to the data packet, only to the frame encapsulation of the packet, and only when the data packet is passing through dissimilar media (such as from Ethernet to FDDI).

Use layer 2 switching for workgroup connectivity and network segmentation (breaking up collision domains). This enables you to create a flatter network design and one with more network segments than traditional 10BaseT shared networks.

Layer 2 switching has helped develop new components in the network infrastructure:

**Server farms** Servers are no longer distributed to physical locations because virtual LANs can be used to create broadcast domains in a switched internetwork. This means that all servers can be placed in a central location, yet a certain server can still be part of a workgroup in a remote branch, for example.

**Intranets** These enable organization-wide client/server communications based on a web technology.

These new technologies are enabling more data to flow off local subnets and onto a routed network, where a router's performance can become the bottleneck.

### Limitations of Layer 2 Switching

Layer 2 switches have the same limitations as bridge networks. Remember that bridges are good if you design the network by the 80/20 rule: users spend 80 percent of their time on their local segment.

Bridged networks break up collision domains, but the network is still one large broadcast domain. Similarly, layer 2 switches (bridges) can not break up broadcast domains, which can cause performance issues and limits the size of your network. Broadcasts and multicasts, along with the slow convergence of spanning tree, can cause major problems as the network grows. Because of these problems, layer 2 switches can not completely replace routers in the internetwork.

## Routing

We want to explain how routing works and how routers work in an internetwork before discussing layer 3 switching next. Routers and layer 3 switches are similar in concept but not design. In this section, we'll discuss routers and what they provide in an internetwork today.

Routers break up collision domains as bridges do. In addition, routers also break up broadcast/multicast domains.

The benefits of routing include:

- Breakup of broadcast domains
- Multicast control
- Optimal path determination
- Traffic management
- Logical (layer 3) addressing
- Security

Routers provide optimal path determination because the router examines each and every packet that enters an interface and improves network segmentation by forwarding data packets to only a known destination network. Routers are not interested in hosts, only networks. If a router does not know about a remote network to which a packet is destined, it will just drop the packet and not forward it. Because of this packet examination, traffic management is obtained.

The Network layer of the OSI model defines a virtual—or logical—network address. Hosts and routers use these addresses to send information from host to host within an internetwork. Every network interface must have a logical address, typically an IP address.

Security can be obtained by a router reading the packet header information and reading filters defined by the network administrator (access lists).

## Layer 3 Switching

The only difference between a layer 3 switch and a router is the way the administrator creates the physical implementation. Also, traditional routers use microprocessors to make forwarding decisions, and the switch performs only hardware-based packet switching. However, some traditional routers can have other hardware functions as well in some of the higher-end models. Layer 3 switches can be placed anywhere in the network because they handle high-performance LAN traffic and can cost-effectively replace routers.

*Layer 3 switching* is all hardware-based packet forwarding, and all packet forwarding is handled by hardware ASICs. Layer 3 switches really are no different functionally from a traditional router and perform the same functions, which are listed here:

- Determine paths based on logical addressing
- Run layer 3 checksums (on header only)
- Use Time to Live (TTL)
- Process and respond to any option information

- Can update Simple Network Management Protocol (SNMP) managers with Management Information Base (MIB) information
- Provide security

The benefits of layer 3 switching include the following:

- Hardware-based packet forwarding
- High-performance packet switching
- High-speed scalability
- Low latency
- Lower per-port cost
- Flow accounting
- Security
- Quality of service (QoS)

## Layer 4 Switching

*Layer 4 switching* is considered a hardware-based layer 3 switching technology that can also consider the application used (for example, Telnet or FTP). Layer 4 switching provides additional routing above layer 3 by using the port numbers found in the Transport-layer header to make routing decisions. These port numbers are found in Request for Comments (RFC) 1700 and reference the upper-layer protocol, program, or application.

Layer 4 information has been used to help make routing decisions for quite a while. For example, extended access lists can filter packets based on layer 4 port numbers. Another example is accounting information gathered by NetFlow switching in Cisco's higher-end routers.

The largest benefit of layer 4 switching is that the network administrator can configure a layer 4 switch to prioritize data traffic by application, which means a QoS can be defined for each user. For example, a number of users can be defined as a Video group and be assigned more priority, or bandwidth, based on the need for videoconferencing.

However, because users can be part of many groups and run many applications, the layer 4 switches must be able to provide a huge filter table or response time would suffer. This filter table must be much larger than any layer 2 or 3 switch. A layer 2 switch might have a filter table only as large as the number of users connected to the network, maybe even smaller if some hubs are used within the switched fabric. However, a layer 4 switch might have five or six entries for each and every device connected to the network! If the layer 4 switch does not have a filter table that includes all the information, the switch will not be able to produce wire-speed results.

## Multi-Layer Switching (MLS)

*Multi-layer switching* combines layer 2, 3, and 4 switching technologies and provides high-speed scalability with low latency. It accomplishes this combination of high-speed scalability with low latency by using huge filter tables based on the criteria designed by the network administrator.

Multi-layer switching can move traffic at wire speed and also provide layer 3 routing, which can remove the bottleneck from the network routers. This technology is based on the concept of route once, switch many.

Multi-layer switching can make routing/switching decisions based on the following:

- MAC source/destination address in a Data Link frame
- IP source/destination address in the Network-layer header
- Protocol field in the Network-layer header
- Port source/destination numbers in the Transport-layer header

There is no performance difference between a layer 3 and a layer 4 switch because the routing/switching is all hardware based.

MLS will be discussed in more detail in Chapter 7, "Multi-Layer Switching."

It is important that you have an understanding of the different OSI layers and what they provide before continuing on to the Cisco three-layer hierarchical model.

# Understanding the Cisco Hierarchical Model

Most of us learned about hierarchy early in life. Anyone with older siblings learned what it was like to be at the bottom of the hierarchy! Regardless of where we were first exposed to hierarchy, most of us experience it in many aspects of our lives. *Hierarchy* helps us to understand where things belong, how things fit together, and what functions go where. It brings order and understandability to otherwise complex models. If you want a pay raise, hierarchy dictates that you ask your boss, not your subordinate. That is the person whose role it is to grant (or deny) your request.

Hierarchy has many of the same benefits in network design that it has in other areas. When used properly in network design, it makes networks more predictable. It helps us to define and expect at which levels of the hierarchy we should perform certain functions. You would ask your boss, not your subordinate, for a raise because of their respective positions in the business hierarchy. The hierarchy requires that you ask someone at a higher level than yours. Likewise, you can use tools such as access lists at certain levels in hierarchical networks and you must avoid them at others.

Let's face it, large networks can be extremely complicated, with multiple protocols, detailed configurations, and diverse technologies. Hierarchy helps us to summarize a complex collection of details into an understandable model. Then, as specific configurations are needed, the model dictates the appropriate manner for them to be applied.

The *Cisco hierarchical model* is used to help you design a scalable, reliable, cost-effective hierarchical internetwork. Cisco defines three layers of hierarchy, as shown in Figure 1.6, each with specific functionality.

**FIGURE 1.6** The Cisco hierarchical model

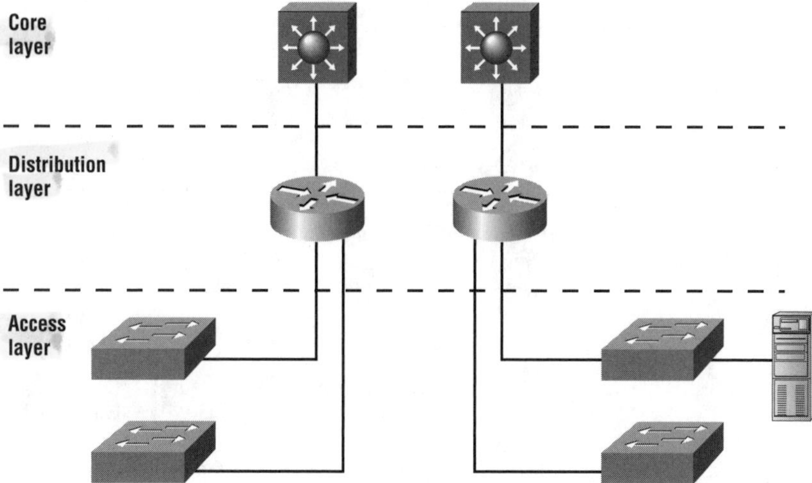


The three layers are as follows:

- Core
- Distribution
- Access

Each layer has specific responsibilities. Remember, however, that the three layers are logical and not necessarily physical. "Three layers" does not necessarily mean "three separate devices." Consider the OSI model, another logical hierarchy. The seven layers describe functions but not necessarily protocols, right? Sometimes a protocol maps to more than one layer of the OSI model, and sometimes multiple protocols communicate within a single layer. In the same way, when you build physical implementations of hierarchical networks, you might have many devices in a single layer, or you might have a single device performing functions at two layers. The definition of the layers is logical, not physical.

Before we examine these layers and their functions, consider a common hierarchical design, as shown in Figure 1.7. The phrase "keep local traffic local" has almost become a cliché in the networking world. However, the underlying concept has merit. Hierarchical design lends itself perfectly to fulfilling this concept. Now, let's take a closer look at each of the layers.

**FIGURE 1.7** A hierarchical network design

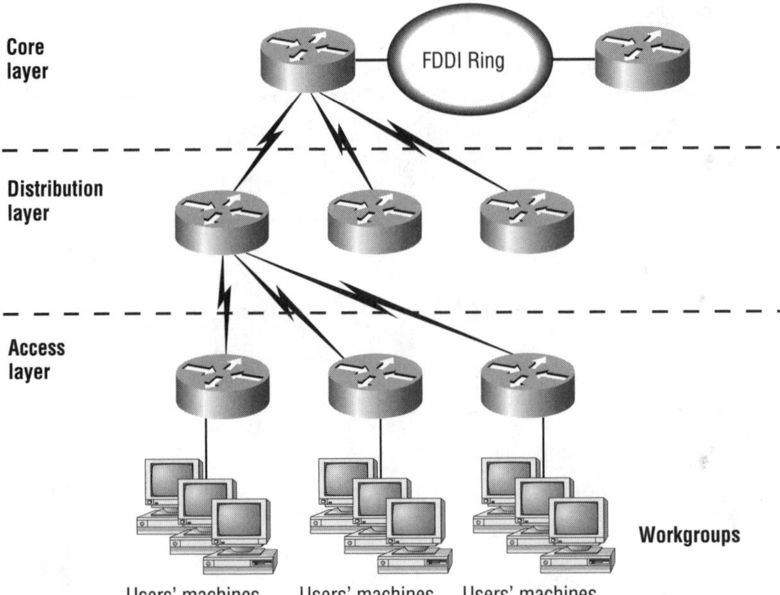


## Core Layer

The *core layer* is literally the core of the network. At the top of the hierarchy, the core layer is responsible for transporting large amounts of traffic both reliably and quickly. The only purpose of the core layer of the network is to switch traffic as quickly as possible. The traffic transported across the core is common to a majority of users. However, remember that user data is processed at the distribution layer, and the distribution layer forwards the requests to the core, if needed.

If there is a failure in the core, *every single* user can be affected. Therefore, fault tolerance at this layer is an issue. The core is likely to see large volumes of traffic, so speed and latency are driving concerns here. Given the function of the core, we can now look at some design specifics to consider. Let's start with some things you know you don't want to do:

- Don't do anything to slow down traffic. This includes using access lists, routing between VLANs, and packet filtering.
- Don't support workgroup access here.
- Avoid expanding the core when the internetwork grows (that is, adding routers). If performance becomes an issue in the core, give preference to upgrades over expansion.

There are a few things that you want to make sure to get done as you design the core:

- Design the core for high reliability. Consider Data Link technologies that facilitate both speed and redundancy, such as FDDI, FastEthernet (with redundant links), Gigabit Ethernet, or even ATM.
- Design with speed in mind. The core should have very little latency.
- Select routing protocols with lower convergence times. Fast and redundant Data Link connectivity is no help if your routing tables are shot!

## Distribution Layer

The *distribution layer* is sometimes referred to as the workgroup layer and is the communication point between the access layer and the core. The primary function of the distribution layer is to provide routing, filtering, and WAN access and to determine how packets can access the core, if needed. The distribution layer must determine the fastest way that user requests are serviced (for example, how a file request is forwarded to a server). After the distribution layer determines the best path, it forwards the request to the core layer. The core layer is then responsible for quickly transporting the request to the correct service.

The distribution layer is the place to implement policies for the network. Here, you can exercise considerable flexibility in defining network operation. Generally, the following should be done at the distribution layer:

- Implement tools such as access lists, packet filtering, and queuing.
- Implement security and network policies, including address translation and firewalls.
- Redistribute between routing protocols, including static routing.
- Route between VLANs and other workgroup support functions.
- Define broadcast and multicast domains.

Things to avoid at the distribution layer are limited to those functions that exclusively belong to one of the other layers.

## Access Layer

The *access layer* controls user and workgroup access to internetwork resources. The access layer is sometimes referred to as the desktop layer. The network resources that most users need are available locally. Any traffic for remote services is handled by the distribution layer. The following functions should be included at this layer:

- Continued (from distribution layer) access control and policies.
- Creation of separate collision domains (segmentation).
- Workgroup connectivity to the distribution layer.
- Technologies such as dial-on-demand routing (DDR) and Ethernet switching are frequently seen in the access layer. Static routing (instead of dynamic routing protocols) is seen here as well.

As already noted, having three separate levels does not have to imply having three separate routers. It could be fewer, or it could be more. Remember that this is a *layered* approach.

# Using Cisco Catalyst Products

Understanding the campus size and traffic is an important factor in network design. A large campus is defined as several or many colocated buildings, and a medium campus is one or more colocated buildings. Small campus networks have only one building.

By understanding your campus size, you can choose Cisco products that will fit your business needs and grow with your company. Cisco switches are produced to fit neatly within its three-layer model. This helps you decide which equipment to use for your network efficiently and quickly.

It should be noted that the Cisco range of switches is in a transitional phase between two operating systems. The Catalyst Operating System (CatOS) is the traditional method and is often referred to as using `set` commands because when configuring, the command often begins with the word "set." Switches in this line include the 4000 and the 6000/6500.

The switches based on the IOS are called Catalyst IOS (CatIOS) switches. The interface to configure these switches resembles that of the IOS router but isn't entirely the same. Anyone familiar with configuring a router, though, will be comfortable configuring one of these switches. The switches that use this include the 2950, the 3550, and the 8500 series.

With some switches—for instance, the 6000/6500 series—you have a choice between the two types of operating systems. When this occurs, the CatOS is the default OS.

Cisco Express Forwarding (CEF) allows for real layer 3 switches to forward traffic based on a complete layer 3 topology map. This map is shared with the ASICs at each port, enabling each port to know which port a packet should be forwarded to. Rather than forwarding based on MAC address, forwarding is done by layer 3 address. Only switches that have true layer 3 capabilities can do this type of switching. These devices include the 3550 series, the 4000 series, the 6000/6500 series with PFC2, and the 8500 series.

There are two general rules when it comes to Cisco switches: The lower model numbers usually cost less, and purchasing a device with more ports drives down the per-port cost. In addition, the model number may typically be split into two sections: For slot-based switches, the second number usually refers to the number of physical slots it has. The 6509 is a nine-slot device in the 6500 family of switches.

## Access Layer Switches

The access layer, as you already know, is where users gain access to the internetwork. The switches deployed at this layer must be able to handle connecting individual desktop devices to the internetwork. The switches here are usually characterized as having a large number of ports and being low cost. Most access switches don't have a lot of frills.

The Cisco solutions at the access layer include the following:

**2950** Provides switched 10/100 Mbps to the desktop. All ports are capable of full duplex, and options include Gigabit Ethernet interfaces. The standard Cisco IOS means that the switch supports functionality for basic data, video, and voice services. All Catalyst 2950 and 2955 switches also support the Cisco Cluster Management Suite (CMS) Software, which allows users to use a standard web browser to simultaneously configure and troubleshoot multiple Catalyst desktop switches.

**3550** Provides a range of stackable selections that can be used as access switches with the Standard Multilayer Software Image (SMI). Many options are available, including 24 and 48 ports, inline power for IP telephony, and a range of 10/100/1000Mbps ports.

If power for IP phones is required but a switch with inline power is not available, Cisco also has a product called the "Inline Power Patch Panel" that adds inline power to an existing Catalyst switch.

**4000** Provides a 10/100/1000Mbps advanced high-performance enterprise solution for up to 96 users and up to 36 Gigabit Ethernet ports for servers. Some models also support the delivery of inline power for IP telephones.

## Distribution Layer Switches

As discussed earlier, the primary function of the distribution layer is to provide routing, filtering, and WAN access and to determine how packets can access the core, if needed.

Distribution layer switches are the aggregation point for multiple access switches and must be capable of handling large amounts of traffic from these access layer devices. The distribution layer switches must also be able to participate in MLS and be able to handle a route processor.

The Cisco switches that provide these functions are as follows:

**3550 Series** This range includes a variety of stackable switches supporting a huge range of features. Full IOS operation complete with MLS is available, and this makes the switch suitable for both access layer and distribution layer switching.

**4000 Series** One of the most scalable switches, the 4000 can be used as a distribution switch if the supervisor IV engine supporting MLS is installed. The 4000 series support advanced QoS, security, and flexibility, achieved with a range of modules. Numerous chassis are available, providing advanced features such as non-blocking architecture and resilience through redundant supervisors. This range has been given a real boost by Cisco.

**6000** The Catalyst 6000 can provide up to 384 10/100Mbps Ethernet connections, 192 100FX FastEthernet connections, or 130 Gigabit Ethernet ports. (With the recent release of the 10/100/1000 card, the 6500 can now support up to 384 10/100/1000 Ethernet connections.) In addition to regular connections, IP telephone connections with inline power are also supported. The 6000 can be outfitted with a Multi-layer Switch Feature Card (MSFC) to provide router functionality as well as a Policy Feature Card (PFC) for layer 3 switching functionality.

### Core Layer Switches

The core layer must be efficient and do nothing to slow down packets as they traverse the backbone. The following switches are recommended for use in the core:

**6500** The Catalyst 6500 series switches are designed to address the need for gigabit port density, high availability, and multi-layer switching for the core layer backbone and server-aggregation environments. These switches use the Cisco IOS to utilize the high speeds of the ASICs, which allows the delivery of wire-speed traffic management services end to end.

**8500** The Cisco Catalyst 8500 is a core layer switch that provides high-performance switching. The Catalyst 8500 uses ASICs to provide multiple-layer protocol support including IP, IP multicast, bridging, ATM switching, and policy-enabled QoS.

All these switches provide wire-speed multicast forwarding, routing, and Protocol Independent Multicast (PIM) for scalable multicast routing. These switches are perfect for providing the high bandwidth and performance needed for a core router. The 6500 and 8500 switches can aggregate multiprotocol traffic from multiple remote wiring closets and workgroup switches.

## Applying the Building Blocks

Remember the saying, "Everything I need to know I learned in kindergarten"? Well, it appears to be true. Cisco has determined that following the hierarchical model they have created promotes a building-block approach to network design. If you did well with building blocks in your younger years, you can just apply that same technique to building large, multimillion-dollar networks. Kind of makes you glad it's someone else's money you're playing with, doesn't it?

In all seriousness, Cisco has determined some fundamental campus elements that help you build network building blocks:

**Switch blocks** Access layer switches connected to the distribution layer devices.

**Core blocks** Support of multiple switch blocks connected together with either 4000, 6500, or 8500 switches.

Within these fundamental elements, there are three contributing variables:

**Server blocks** Groups of network servers on a single subnet

**WAN blocks** Multiple connections to an ISP or multiple ISPs

**Mainframe blocks** Centralized services to which the enterprise network is responsible for providing complete access

By understanding how these work, you can build large, expensive networks with confidence (using someone else's money). After the network has been built, you need to allow the switches to talk to each other to allow for redundancy and to route around outages. We will cover these topics later in this section after the blocks are discussed.

## Switch Block

The *switch block* is a combination of layer 2 switches and layer 3 routers. The layer 2 switches connect users in the wiring closet into the access layer and provide 10Mbps or 100Mbps dedicated connections; 2950 Catalyst switches can be used in the switch block.

From here, the access layer switches connect into one or more distribution layer switches, which will be the central connection point for all switches coming from the wiring closets. The distribution layer device is either a switch with an external router or a multi-layer switch. The distribution layer switch then provides layer 3 routing functions, if needed.

The distribution layer router prevents broadcast storms that could happen on an access layer switch from propagating throughout the entire internetwork. The broadcast storm would be isolated to only the access layer switch in which the problem exists.

### Switch Block Size

To understand how large a switch block can be, you must understand the traffic types and the size and number of workgroups that will be using them. The number of switches that can collapse from the access layer to the distribution layer depends on the following:

- Traffic patterns
- Routers at the distribution layer
- Number of users connected to the access layer switches
- Distance VLANs must traverse the network
- Spanning tree domain size

If routers at the distribution layer become the bottleneck in the network (which means the CPU processing is too intensive), the switch block has grown too large. Also, if too many broadcasts or multicast traffic slow down the switches and routers, your switch blocks have grown too large.

Having a large number of users does not necessarily indicate that the switch block is too large; too much traffic going across the network does.

## Core Block

If you have two or more switch blocks, the Cisco rule of thumb states that you need a *core block*. No routing is performed at the core, only transferring of data. It is a pass-through for the switch block, the server block, and the Internet. Figure 1.8 shows one example of a core block.

The core is responsible for transferring data to and from the switch blocks as quickly as possible. You can build a fast core with a frame, packet, or cell (ATM) network technology. The Switching exam is based on an Ethernet core network.

**FIGURE 1.8** The core block

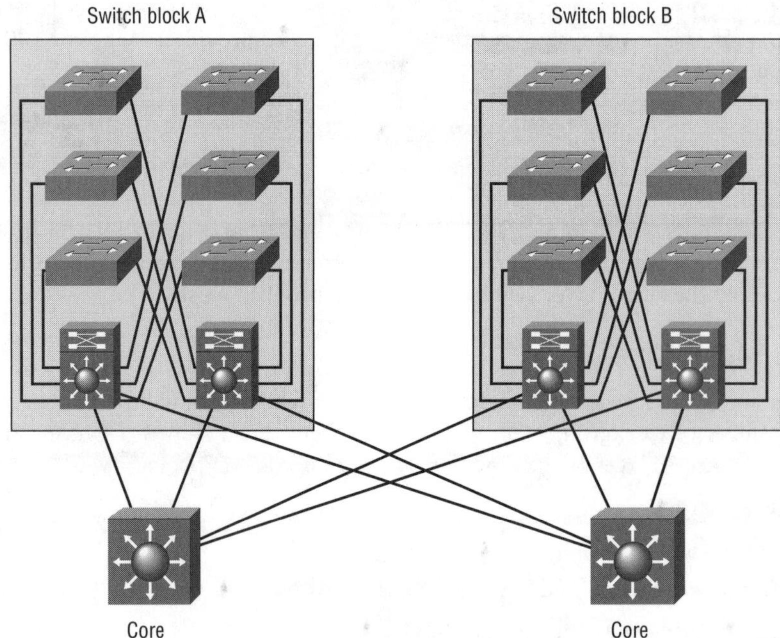


Typically, you would have only one subnet configured on the core network. However, for redundancy and load balancing, you could have two or more subnets configured.

Switches can trunk on a certain port or ports. This means that a port on a switch can be a member of more than one VLAN at the same time. However, the distribution layer will handle the routing and trunking for VLANs, and the core is only a pass-through after the routing has been performed. Because of this, core links do not carry multiple subnets per link; the distribution layer does.

A Cisco 6500 or 8500 switch is recommended at the core, and even though only one of those switches might be sufficient to handle the traffic, Cisco recommends two switches for redundancy and load balancing. You could consider a 4000 or 3550 Catalyst switch if you don't need the power of the 6500 or the 8500.

## Collapsed Core

A *collapsed core* is defined as one switch performing both core and distribution layer functions; however, the functions of the core and distribution layer are still distinct. The collapsed core is typically found in a small network.

Redundant links between the distribution layer and the access layer switches, and between each access layer switch, can support more than one VLAN. The distribution layer routing is the termination for all ports.

Figure 1.9 shows a collapsed core network design.

**FIGURE 1.9** Collapsed core

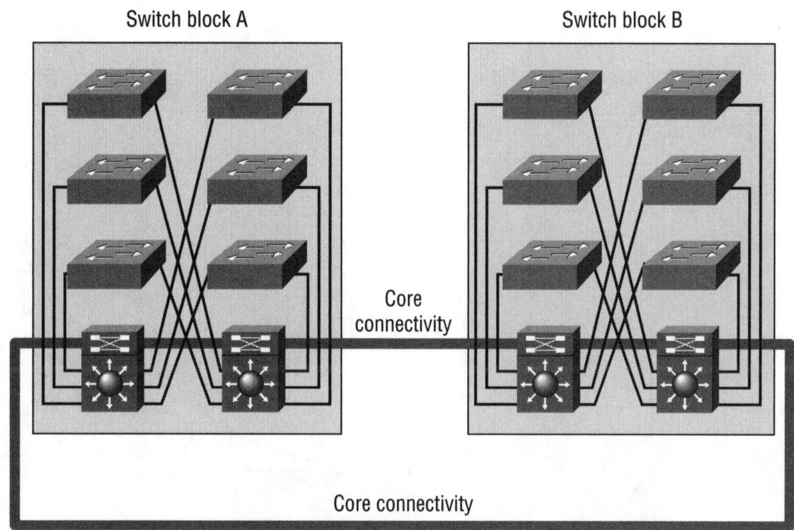


In a collapsed core network, Spanning Tree Protocol (STP) blocks the redundant links to prevent loops. Hot Standby Routing Protocol (HSRP) can provide redundancy in the distribution layer routing. It can keep core connectivity if the primary routing process fails.

## Dual Core

If you have more than two switch blocks and need redundant connections between the core and distribution layer, you need to create a dual core. Figure 1.10 shows an example dual-core configuration. Each connection would be a separate subnet.

In Figure 1.10, you can see that each switch block is redundantly connected to each of the two core blocks. The distribution layer routers already have links to each subnet in the routing tables, provided by the layer 3 routing protocols. If a failure on a core switch takes place, convergence time will not be an issue. HSRP can be used to provide quick cutover between the cores. (HSRP is covered in Chapter 9, "QoS and Redundancy.")

## Core Size

Routing protocols are the main factor in determining the size of your core. This is because routers, or any layer 3 device, isolate the core. Routers send updates to other routers, and as the network grows, so do these updates, so it takes longer to converge or to have all the routers update. Because at least one of the routers will connect to the Internet, it's possible that there will be more updates throughout the internetwork.

**FIGURE 1.10** Dual-core configuration

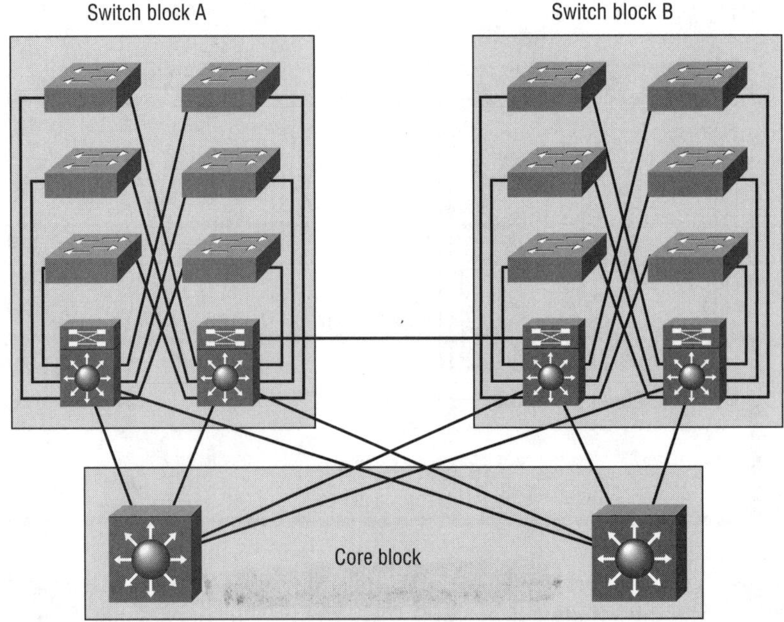


The routing protocol dictates the size of the distribution layer devices that can communicate with the core. Table 1.2 shows a few of the more popular routing protocols and the number of blocks each routing protocol supports. Remember that this includes all blocks, including server, mainframe, and WAN.

**TABLE 1.2** Blocks Supported by Routing Protocol

| Routing Protocol | Maximum Number of Peers | Number of Subnet Links to the Core | Maximum Number of Supported Blocks |
|---|---|---|---|
| OSPF | 50 | 2 | 25 |
| EIGRP | 50 | 2 | 25 |
| RIP | 30 | 2 | 15 |

## Scaling Layer 2 Backbones

Typically, layer 2 switches are in the remote closets and represent the access layer, the layer where users gain access to the internetwork. Ethernet switched networks scale well in this environment, where the layer 2 switches then connect into a larger, more robust layer 3 switch representing the distribution layer. The layer 3 device is then connected into a layer 2 device representing the core. Because routing is not necessarily recommended in a classic design model at the core, the model then looks like this:

| Access | Distribution | Core |
|---|---|---|
| Layer 2 switch | Layer 3 switch | Layer 2 switch |

## Spanning Tree Protocol (STP)

Chapter 4, "Layer 2 Switching and the Spanning Tree Protocol (STP)," and Chapter 5, "Using Spanning Tree with VLANs," detail the STP, but some discussion is necessary here. STP is used by layer 2 bridges to stop network loops in networks that have more than one physical link to the same network. There is a limit to the number of links in a layer 2 switched backbone that needs to be taken into account. As you increase the number of core switches, the problem becomes that the number of links to distribution links must increase also, for redundancy reasons. If the core is running the Spanning Tree Protocol, then it can compromise the high-performance connectivity between switch blocks. The best design on the core is to have two switches without STP running. You can do this only by having a core without links between the core switches. This is demonstrated in Figure 1.11.

**FIGURE 1.11** Layer 2 backbone scaling without STP

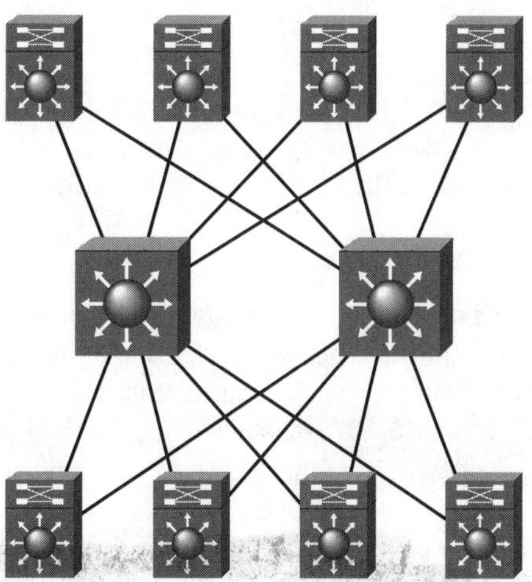

Figure 1.11 shows redundancy between the core and distribution layer without spanning tree loops. This is accomplished by not having the two core switches linked together. However, each distribution layer 3 switch has a connection to each core switch. This means that each layer 3 switch has two equal-cost paths to every other router in the campus network.

## Scaling Layer 3 Backbones

As discussed in the previous section, "Scaling Layer 2 Backbones," you'll typically find layer 2 switches connecting to layer 3 switches, which connect to the core with the layer 2 switches. However, it is possible that some networks might have layer 2/layer 3/layer 3 designs (layer 2 connecting to layer 3 connecting to layer 3). But this is not cheap, even if you're using someone else's money. There is always some type of network budget, and you need to have good reason to spend the type of money needed to build layer 3 switches into the core.

There are three reasons you would implement layer 3 switches into the core:

- Fast convergence
- Automatic load balancing
- Elimination of peering problems

### Fast Convergence

If you have only layer 2 devices at the core layer, the STP will be used to stop network loops if there is more than one connection between core devices. The STP has a convergence time of more than 50 seconds, and if the network is large, this can cause an enormous number of problems if it has just one link failure.

STP is not implemented in the core if you have layer 3 devices. Routing protocols, which can have a much faster convergence time than STP, are used to maintain the network.

### Automatic Load-Balancing

If you provide layer 3 devices in the core, the routing protocols can load-balance with multiple equal-cost links. This is not possible with layer 3 devices only at the distribution layer, because you would have to selectively choose the root for utilizing more than one path.

### Elimination of Peering Problems

Because routing is typically performed in the distribution layer devices, each distribution layer device must have "reachability" information about each of the other distribution layer devices. These layer 3 devices use routing protocols to maintain the state and reachability information about neighbor routers. This means that each distribution device becomes a peer with every other distribution layer device, and scalability becomes an issue because every device has to keep information for every other device.

If your layer 3 devices are located in the core, you can create a hierarchy, and the distribution layer devices will no longer be peers to each other's distribution device. This is typical in an environment in which there are more than 100 switch blocks.

# SAFE

SAFE is Cisco's Secure Blueprint for Enterprise Networks, the stated aim of which is to provide information on the best practice for designing and implementing secure networks. Recently, the issue of security in networking has been receiving a huge amount of attention. As part of this attention, Cisco has been at the forefront of developing this process, which is based upon the products of Cisco and its partners.

The SAFE methodology involves creating a layered approach to security, such that a failure at one layer does not compromise the whole network. Instead, it operates like a military "defense in depth."

Defense in depth is a concept that explains how it is expected that an enemy will be able to penetrate your defensive perimeter, but that it will take time and effort. Multiple lines of defense slow down an attacker and give you more time to discover and stop them. Additionally, each line of defense can have its own procedures, in the hope that the attacker may not be skilled in all countermeasures.

One of the main features of this new set of principles is that it defines a slightly different modular concept from the original core, distribution, and access layers. That is not to say that these original layers are no longer used in design; rather, the SAFE approach is to use an alternative. In practice, designers see both methods as useful and may appropriate features from each. The basis for the new modular design concept is shown in Figure 1.12.

**FIGURE 1.12** Enterprise Composite Module

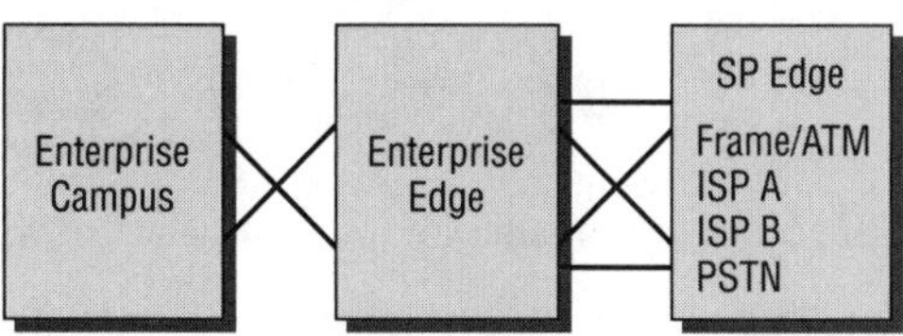


This high-level diagram shows only three blocks. Each block represents a different functional area, providing a modular understanding of the security issues. From our perspective, we need to focus in a little more on the detail, and this is expanded in the main SAFE block diagram, shown in Figure 1.13.

Figure 1.13 shows a much clearer breakout of the actual modules inside SAFE that need to be managed and secured. Each module has its own threats and protection issues. It is not expected that every network would be built using all modules, but rather that this provides a framework for understanding the security issues involved and isolating them.

From the perspective of the Cisco CCNP training program, we need to focus in again, this time looking in a little more detail at the Campus Module, as shown in Figure 1.14.

**FIGURE 1.13** Enterprise SAFE block diagram

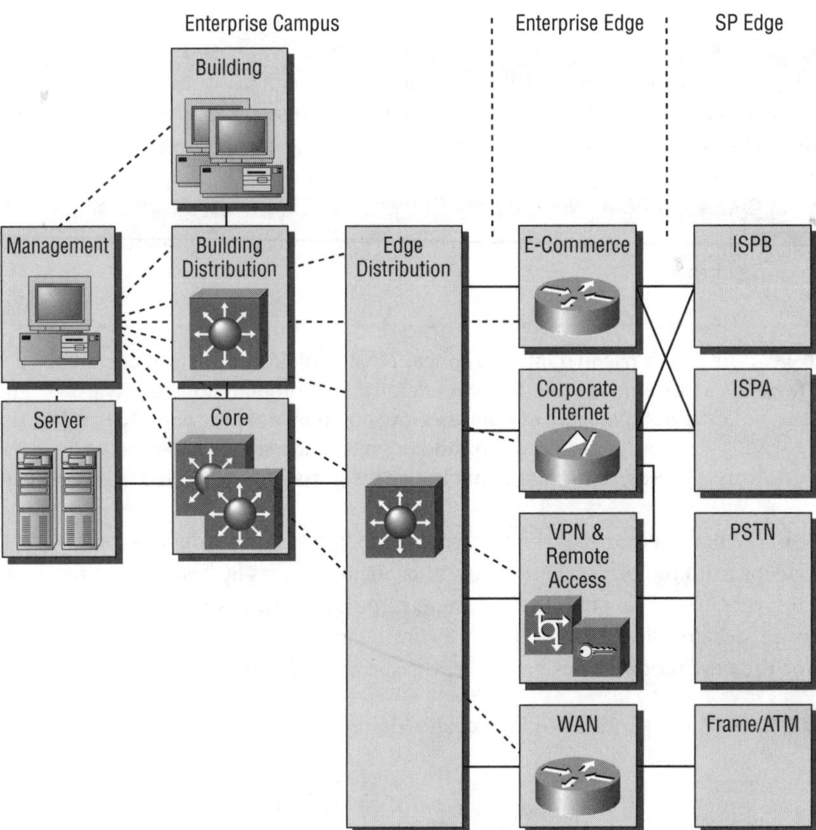


Note that the Campus Module contains a number of smaller modules, each of which is associated with a specific function.

**Management Module** Designed to facilitate all management within the campus network as defined by the SAFE architecture. The Management Module must be separated from the managed devices and areas by a firewall, by separate VLANs, and by separate IP addresses and subnet allocation.

**Building Module** SAFE defines the Building Module as the part of the network that contains end-user workstations and devices plus the layer 2 access points. Included in this are the Building Distribution Module and Building Access Module.

**Building Distribution Module** This module provides standard distribution-layer services to the building switches, including routing, access control, and, more recently, QoS (quality of service) support.

**Building Access Module** The Building Access Module defines the devices at the access layer, including Layer 2 switches, user workstations and, more recently, IP telephones.

**Core Module** This module follows the principles of the core part of the standard Cisco three-layer module, focusing on transporting large amounts of traffic both reliably and quickly.

**Server Module** The main goal of the Server Module is to provide access to the application services by end users and devices.

**FIGURE 1.14** Enterprise Campus Module detailed diagram

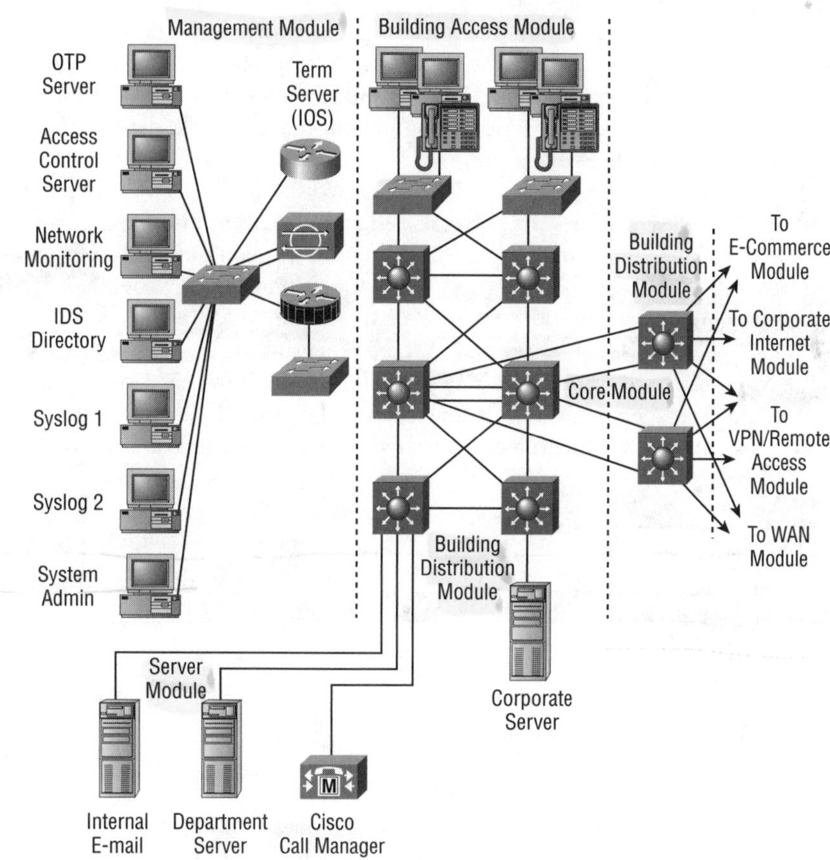

# Summary

Cisco Systems manufactures a large, varied, and ever-changing range of equipment. Over the years, the acquisition of a number of companies producing switches has meant that the range has not always appeared entirely consistent, but as time marches on, some of the differences in the underlying basics of the equipment are beginning to disappear. The most obvious differences in switch models now comes down to two factors: Are the switches modular (4000, 6500) or fixed footprint (2950, 3550), and do they support just layer 2 (2950) or can you buy a layer 3 capability (4000, 6500, 3550)?

Of course, the next question that arises is "Which switch should I choose?" Naturally there are issues of cost and size (in terms of ports and so on), but that may not be sufficient to help you design a complex network. So Cisco has pioneered some design guidelines that will help you put a specific Cisco box into a "location" in your internetwork, dependent upon the technologies required at that network point.

In order to understand all of this, there are two specific areas that we had to focus on. This first was how Cisco defines the network design model, in terms of redundancy, QoS, throughput, security, and so on, and how the Cisco models explain that to us. Cisco uses a three-layer model in which the access layer is used to provide redundant access to end users, the distribution layer manages policy, and the core layer provides fast access to the network backbone. Cisco also has a second model, related to its Secure Blueprint for Enterprise Networks (SAFE) guidelines, called the Enterprise Composite Module, which allows easy identification of modules such as the Management, Campus, Enterprise Edge, and SP Edge modules.

The second area we focused on was what technologies are available. Switches have traditionally been layer 2 devices, operating by forwarding data using MAC address tables. This is fast, but not very scalable, which means that routers, operating at layer 3, have been used. Modern devices can commonly combine the switching and routing processes, resulting in layer 3 switching. Layer 4 switching is an extension of that process, using the port fields inside TCP and UDP to assist with forwarding decisions. The total effect is commonly referred to as Multi-Layer Switching—MLS.

# Exam Essentials

**Understand the concept behind the three-layer model.** In order to provide some framework to the design process, Cisco has designed the three-layer model, with the built-in principles that functionality can be assigned to a specific layer. This allows easier equipment selection and configuration, as long as you remember which layer does what! The access layer is used to provide access for most users into the rest of the network. The distribution layer is used for routing, filtering, and for some access tasks. Finally, the core layer is used to link switch blocks, and nothing that slows traffic down should be run here.

**Understand the reasoning behind each of the switch block types.** A switch block is a collection of switching devices that provide access and distribution layer functions. Each of the block models has specific needs, and the Cisco range of equipment is designed to carry out the appropriate tasks. The result is that different switches perform optimally at different layers. Servers may benefit from duplex connectivity and larger bandwidth than clients, due to the aggregated traffic, and because SAFE planning demands that the network be protected in depth, blocks must be clearly defined.

**Understand the different product lines and the individual products that Cisco has available for switching tasks.** Some Cisco devices are standard layer 2 switches, and use just the MAC address for forwarding. This is simple, cheap, and pretty fast. But the limits of scalability mean that such devices can not be used throughout the network, so Cisco also manufactures switches that provide real layer 3 services. Understanding the needs of different layers assists with the selection of the correct switch and the planning of the appropriate configuration, which might be simple layer 2 switching, or possibly MLS.

# Key Terms

Before you take the exam, be sure you're familiar with the following terms:

20/80 rule

80/20 rule

access layer

application-specific integrated circuits (ASICs)

bandwidth

Cisco hierarchical model

collapsed core

core block

core layer

data encapsulation

distribution layer

enterprise services

hierarchy

layer 2 switching

layer 3 switching

layer 4 switching

layered

local services

Media Access Control (MAC)

multi-layer switching

Open Systems Interconnection (OSI) model

remote services

switch block

# Written Labs

In this section, you will complete the following written labs:

- Lab 1.1: Switching Definitions
- Lab 1.2: Cisco's Three-Layer Model
- Lab 1.3: Switching Theory

## Lab 1.1: Switching Definitions

In the following table, the first column contains definitions of different types of switching. Fill in the second column with the number or numbers of the correct switching technology.

1. Layer 2 switching
2. Layer 3 switching
3. Layer 4 switching
4. Multi-layer switching

| Definition | Switching Type |
|---|---|
| Based on "route once, switch many" | |
| Enables prioritization based on specific applications | |
| Creates security by using source or destination addresses and port numbers | |
| Can use NetFlow switching | |
| Enables you to create flatter networks | |
| Builds a filtering table based on application port numbers | |
| Communicates with peer layers in a different system with packets | |
| Reads the TCP and UDP port fields for filtering and forwarding information | |
| Uses access lists to control traffic | |
| Uses hardware-based routing | |
| Uses hardware-based bridging | |
| Uses an ASIC to handle frame forwarding | |
| Provides both layer 2 and layer 3 functions | |

## Lab 1.2: Cisco's Three-Layer Model

Options 1, 2, and 3 are the layers in the Cisco three-layer model. Match the functions to the correct layer.

1. Access layer
2. Distribution layer
3. Core layer

| Function | Layer |
|---|---|
| Routes traffic between VLANs | |
| Uses collision domains | |
| Uses broadcast domains | |
| Uses access lists | |
| Provides end users with access to the network | |
| Communicates between the switch blocks and to the enterprise servers | |
| Switches traffic as quickly as possible | |

## Lab 1.3: Switching Theory

Write the answers to the following questions:

1. Which device is used to break up broadcast domains?
2. Which device is used to break up collision domains?
3. What are the units of data at the lowest four layers of the OSI model, in top-to-bottom order?
4. Which Cisco layer is used to pass traffic as quickly as possible?
5. What is the Protocol Data Unit (PDU) used at the Transport layer?
6. What is the PDU used at the Network layer?
7. Which Cisco layer is used to break up collision domains?
8. Which OSI layer creates frames by encapsulating packets with a header and trailer?
9. What devices provide multicast control and packet-based security?
10. What breaks up broadcast domains in a layer 2 switched network?

# Review Questions

1. You work for a large company that needs to connect four buildings with a high-speed, high-bandwidth backbone. They are all on the same city block, and fiber already connects the buildings. There are multiple departments in each building and all run multiple protocols. The company already owns Cisco Catalyst 6000 series switches, which you can use for the distribution layer. What switch should you use for the core layer?

   A. 2950

   B. 4000

   C. 6500

   D. 8500

2. You need to install a large switched network for a company that has already defined its business requirements to be gigabit-speed data transfer, high availability, and ISL routing to the server farms for all 300 users. What switch would you install for the distribution layer?

   A. 2950 with gigabit uplinks

   B. 4000 series

   C. 3550 series

   D. 6000 series with a 16-port gigabit module

   E. 8500 series with gigabit uplinks

3. You just have been hired as a consultant for a small company that has users distributed across many floors in the same building. Servers for the company are all located on the first floor, and 30 users access them from various parts of the building. What switch would you install for the access layer connection?

   A. 2950

   B. 3550 series

   C. 6000

   D. 8000

4. You have just been promoted to network manager (congratulations!) for a large company. You need to connect four switch blocks; each contains 1500 users. You want to control broadcast domains at the switch blocks and use ISL to trunk between them. What switch would you purchase for the distribution layer?

   A. 2950 with gigabit links

   B. 3550 series

   C. 4000 with gigabit VLAN

   D. Catalyst 6000 with 16-port gigabit module

5. Which layer must be efficient and do nothing to slow down packets as they traverse the backbone?
   A. Access
   B. Distribute
   C. Distribution
   D. Backbone
   E. Core

6. Which of the following switches are recommended for use in the core? (Choose all that apply.)
   A. 3550 series
   B. 4000 series
   C. 6500
   D. 8500

7. Which of the following is the main factor in determining the size of your core?
   A. Routing protocols
   B. Routed protocols
   C. IP broadcasts
   D. ARPs
   E. ICMP redirects
   F. Number of distribution layer switches

8. The number of switches that can collapse from the access layer to the distribution layer depends on what? (Choose all that apply.)
   A. Traffic patterns
   B. Routers at the distribution layer
   C. Number of users connecting to the core layer
   D. Number of users connected to the access layer switches
   E. Number of distribution layer switches
   F. Distance VLANs must traverse the network
   G. Spanning tree domain size

9. Which of the following is generally performed at the distribution layer? (Choose all that apply.)
   A. Breaking up of collision domains
   B. No packet filtering
   C. Access lists, packet filtering, and queuing
   D. Routing between VLANs

10. Which of the following is also generally performed at the distribution layer? (Choose all that apply.)

    A. Broadcast and multicast domain definition

    B. Security and network policies

    C. Redistribution between routing protocols

    D. User access to the network

11. Which of the following is true regarding the access layer? (Choose all that apply.)

    A. This is where users gain access to the internetwork.

    B. The switches deployed at this layer must be able to handle connecting individual desktop devices to the internetwork.

    C. It is the aggregation point for multiple access switches.

    D. It can participate in MLS and handle a router processor.

12. Which of the following series of switches are suggested for use at the access layer? (Choose all that apply.)

    A. 2950

    B. 3550 series

    C. 4000 series

    D. 6000

    E. 8000

13. Which of the following Cisco switches provides a 10/100/1000Mbps advanced high-performance enterprise solution for up to 96 users and up to 36 Gigabit Ethernet ports for servers?

    A. 2950

    B. 3550 series

    C. 4000 series

    D. 6000

    E. 8000

14. Which of the following switches runs IOS by default? (Choose all that apply.)

    A. 2950

    B. 3550 series

    C. 4000 series

    D. 6000

15. Which of the following switches provides switched 10Mbps to the desktop or to 10BaseT hubs in small-to-medium campus networks?

    A. 2950

    B. 3550 series

    C. 4000 series

    D. 6000

16. Which layer of switching makes no modification of the data packet?

    A. Layer 2

    B. Layer 3

    C. Layer 4

    D. MLS

17. Layer 2 switching is ________________. (Choose all that apply.)

    A. Software based

    B. Hardware based

    C. Wire speed

    D. Asymmetrical

    E. Filtered using ASICs

18. Which Cisco switch can provide up to 384 10/100Mbps Ethernet connections, 192 100FX FastEthernet connections, or 130 Gigabit Ethernet ports?

    A. 2950

    B. 3550 series

    C. 4000 series

    D. 6000

19. Which of the following describes Cisco Catalyst 3550 series switches?

    A. They provide an enterprise solution for up to 96 users and up to 36 Gigabit Ethernet ports for servers.

    B. They run IOS in a mid-range switch with internal routing capability.

    C. They only use an external router processor such as a 4000 or 7000 series router.

    D. The 3550 series is the Catalyst low-end model.

20. Which of the following is true regarding the distribution layer switches? (Choose all that apply.)

    A. The distribution layer is the aggregation point for multiple access switches.

    B. This is where users gain access to the internetwork.

    C. The switches deployed at this layer must be able to handle connecting individual desktop devices to the internetwork.

    D. The distribution layer can participate in MLS and handle a router processor.

# Answers to Written Labs

## Answers to Lab 1.1

| Definition | Numbered Answer |
|---|---|
| Based on "route once, switch many" | 4 |
| Enables prioritization based on specific applications | 3 |
| Creates security by using source or destination addresses and port numbers | 3 |
| Can use NetFlow switching | 2, 3 |
| Enables you to create flatter networks | 1 |
| Builds a filtering table based on application port numbers | 3 |
| Communicates with peer layers in a different system with packets | 2 |
| Reads the TCP and UDP port fields for filtering and forwarding information | 3 |
| Uses access lists to control traffic | 2, 3 |
| Uses hardware-based routing | 2 |
| Uses hardware-based bridging | 1 |
| Uses an ASIC to handle frame forwarding | 1, 2 |
| Provides both layer 2 and layer 3 functions | 4 |

## Answers to Lab 1.2

| Function | Layer |
|---|---|
| Routes traffic between VLANs | 2 |
| Uses collision domains | 1 |
| Uses broadcast domains | 2 |
| Uses access lists | 2 |
| Provides end users with access to the network | 1 |
| Communicates between the switch blocks and to the enterprise servers | 3 |
| Switches traffic as quickly as possible | 3 |

## Answers to Lab 1.3

1. A layer 3 device, usually a router. Layer 2 devices do not break up broadcast domains.
2. A layer 2 device, typically a switch. Although routers break up both collision domains and broadcast domains, layer 2 switches are primarily used to break up collision domains.
3. Segment, packet, frame, bits. It is important to understand the question. This question asked for the units of data, which shows how data is encapsulated as user data goes from the Application layer down to the Physical layer.
4. The core layer should have no packet manipulation, if possible.
5. Segments are the name for the PDU used at the Transport layer.
6. A packet or datagram is the PDU used at the Network layer.
7. Access layer. Remember, the distribution layer is used to break up broadcast domains, and the access layer is used to break up collision domains.
8. Data Link. Data is encapsulated with header and trailer information at the Data Link layer.
9. Routers or layer 3 devices are the only devices that control broadcasts and multicasts, as well as providing packet filtering.
10. Virtual LANs. These are configured on the layer 2 switches, and layer 3 devices provide a means for moving traffic between the VLANs.

# Answers to Review Questions

1. D. A Cisco 6500 or 8500 switch is recommended at the core, and even though only one of those switches might be sufficient to handle the traffic, Cisco recommends two switches for redundancy and load balancing. You could consider a 4000 or a 3550 Catalyst switch if you don't need the power of the 6500 or the 8500. Because the customer is using 6500 at the distribution layer, you should use 8500s as the core switches. D is the best answer.
2. C. The Catalyst 6000 can provide up to 384 10/100Mbps Ethernet connections, 192 100FX FastEthernet connections, or 130 Gigabit Ethernet ports. Because there are 300 users, the 6000 series would be a good fit. The 8500 is a recommended core switch, and the question asks for an access layer/distribution layer solution.
3. A. A 3550 series switch might be overkill for the needs of the company. Because the question involves a small company and no growth was specified, a couple of 2950s would be the most cost-effective solution.
4. B. In this instance, the 3550 series have a number of switches capable of supporting the required layer 3 services.
5. E. The core layer should be designed to connect distribution layer devices. No packet manipulation should occur at this layer.
6. C, D. The core layer needs very fast switches to move data as quickly as possible between distribution layer devices.
7. A. Routing protocols are protocols that are used to update routers with network information. Routed protocols are used to send user data through an internetwork.
8. A, B, D, F, G. Traffic patterns, the number of routers, the number of users connected into access layer switches, distance, and spanning tree size are all factors that contribute to the number of switches that can collapse from the access layer to the distribution layer.
9. C, D. The distribution layer performs routing, which breaks up broadcast domains. Routers can be configured with access lists, packet filters, and queuing.
10. A, B, C. The distribution layer performs routing, which breaks up broadcast domains by default. Security can be performed as well as network policies implemented. Routing protocols can be redistributed with most Cisco routers.
11. A, B. The access layer breaks up collision domains and connects the access layer to the internetwork by connecting to the distribution layer.
12. A, B, C. Any switches from the 2950 series to the 4000 series can work at the access layer.
13. C. The Cisco 4000 series was created for high performance, up to 36 gigabit ports, and 96-user connectivity.
14. A, B. Both the 2950 and the 3550 runs IOS. The 4000 and 6000 can be upgraded from the default CatOS.

15. A. The 2950 is the current entry model that provides 10Mbps switched networking with up to 24 ports.

16. A. The Data Link layer (layer 2) encapsulates the packet but does not make any changes to it.

17. B, C, E. Layer 2 switching is considered hardware based because it uses an ASIC chip to make filtering decisions. It is also considered wire speed because no modification to the data packet takes place.

18. D. The Cisco Catalyst 6000 series provides up to 384 10/100Mbps Ethernet ports for user connectivity. It can also provide 192 100Mbps FastEthernet fiber uplinks or 130 Gigabit Ethernet ports.

19. B. The 3550 series Catalyst switches are the new kid on the block. With a range of different interface options from 10Mbps to gigabit speeds, they run IOS and perform full MLS internally.

20. A, D. The distribution layer connects the access layer devices, performs routing, and can provide multi-layer switching.

# Connecting the Switch Block

## THE CCNP EXAM TOPICS COVERED IN THIS CHAPTER INCLUDE THE FOLLOWING:

- ✓ **Describe LAN segmentation with VLANs**
- ✓ **Provide physical connectivity between two devices within a switch block**
- ✓ **Provide connectivity from an end user station to an access layer device**
- ✓ **Configure a switch for initial operation**
- ✓ **Apply IOS command set to diagnose and troubleshoot a switched network**
- ✓ **Configure Fast EtherChannel and Gigabit EtherChannel on interswitch links**

We have come a long way since the beginning of networking. We have lived through several mini-revolutions, and now we find ourselves at a time when Ethernet is king. Gaining ground over all rivals until most of them are left only in memory, this simple protocol has grown to support data transfer at 10, 100, 1000 and (almost) 10,000 Mbits/second. What a happy life being a network manager, knowing that your favorite protocol has expansion capability for the future.

This inherent growth capability, combined with the creation of a sound hierarchical network that follows the Cisco three-layer model, means that you too can be a LAN top gun.

This chapter will help you understand the different *contention media* available. Contention is the media access process used by Ethernet. This book covers only contention media because it is the most widely used; for the pragmatic reasons of cost, simplicity, and ease of implementation, Ethernet (or its variations) runs on most of the networks in the world.

But the development of faster Ethernets has changed many of the original concepts along the way. Full-duplex connectivity has removed the need for the contention algorithm, because each transmitting station has access to its own pair of wires. Some Gigabit Ethernet implementations may demand a larger minimum frame size, and switched Ethernet removes the need for the collision algorithm by using micro-segmentation to create mini collision domains. So, first we'll review the basics of Ethernet networking and then move on to how to use the various flavors of Ethernet networking in your access, distribution, and core networks.

After you have learned about the different Ethernet cable media types, you'll learn how to log in and configure both a set-based switch and an IOS-based switch. The set-based switch we will focus on is the modular 4000 series, and the IOS switches are the new 2950 and the excellent 3550, which supports several bells and whistles. Those old hands among you will notice the retirement of the 1900 series switches, which ran both a version of the IOS and a menu interface. You will also see that the 5000 series has gone as well. So long, old friend.

The chapter ends with a hands-on lab in which you'll connect the switches together and configure them.

# Understanding Cable Media

To know when and how to use the different kinds of cable media, you need to understand what users *do* on the corporate network. The way to find this information is to ask questions. After that, you can use monitoring equipment to really see what is going on inside the network cabling. Before you deploy an application on a corporate network, carefully consider bandwidth requirements as well as latency issues. More and more users need to compete for bandwidth on the network because of bandwidth-consuming applications. Although layer 2 switches break up collision domains and certainly help a congested network if correctly designed and installed, you must also understand the different cable media types available and where to use each type for maximum efficiency. That's where this chapter comes in.

## The Background of IEEE Ethernet

In 1980, the Digital Equipment Corporation, Intel, and Xerox (DIX) consortium created the original Ethernet. Predictably, Ethernet_II followed and was released in 1984. The standards-setting organization, the Institute of Electrical and Electronics Engineers (IEEE), termed this the 802.*x* project. The 802.*x* project was initially divided into three groups:

- The High Level Interface (HILI) group became the 802.1 committee, and was responsible for high-level internetworking protocols and management.
- The Logical Link Control (LLC) group became the 802.2 committee, and focused on end-to-end link connectivity and the interface between the higher layers and the medium-access-dependent layers.
- The Data Link and Medium Access Control (DLMAC) group became responsible for the medium-access protocols. The DLMAC ended up splitting into three committees:
  - 802.3 for Ethernet
  - 802.4 for Token Bus
  - 802.5 for Token Ring

DEC, Intel, and Xerox pushed Ethernet, while Burroughs, Concord Data Systems, Honeywell, Western Digital—and, later, General Motors and Boeing—pushed 802.4. IBM took on 802.5.

The IEEE then created the 802.3 subcommittee, which came up with an Ethernet standard that happens to be almost identical to the earlier Ethernet_II version of the protocol. The two differ only in their descriptions of the Data Link layer. Ethernet_II has a Type field, whereas 802.3 has a Length field. Even so, they're both common in their Physical layer specifications, MAC addressing, and understanding of the LLC layer's responsibilities.

See *CCNA: Cisco Certified Network Associate Study Guide,* 4th edition, by Todd Lammle (Sybex, 2003) for a detailed explanation of Ethernet frame types.

Ethernet_II and 802.3 both define a bus-topology LAN at 10Mbps, and the cabling defined in these standards is identical:

**10Base2/Thinnet** Segments up to 185 meters using RG58 coax at 50 ohms.

**10Base5/Thicknet** Segments up to 500 meters using RG8 or RG11 at 50 ohms.

**10BaseT/UTP** All hosts connect by using unshielded twisted-pair (UTP) cable with a central device (a hub or switch). Category 3 UTP is specified to support up to 10Mbps, category 5 to 100Mbps, category 6 to 155Mbps, and category 7 to 1Gbps.

## LAN Segmentation Using Switches

Ethernet is the most popular type of network in the world and will continue to be so. It is important to understand how hubs and switches work within an Ethernet internetwork.

By using *switched Ethernet* in layer 2 of your network, you no longer have to share bandwidth with the different departments in the corporation. With hubs, all devices have to share the same bandwidth (collision domain), which can cause havoc in today's networks. This makes a switched Ethernet LAN much more scalable than one based on shared Ethernet.

Hubs are layer 1 devices. The best way to think of them is as multi-port repeaters, repeating everything that comes their way, including runt frames, giant frames, and frames failing the frame check sequence at the end.

Even though layer 2 switches break the network into smaller collision domains, the network is still one large broadcast domain. Nowadays, switched Ethernet has largely replaced shared hubs in the networking world because each connection from a host to the switch is in its own collision domain. This is often referred to as *micro-segmentation* (as opposed to *segmentation*, where a legacy bridge may have created only two LAN segments). Remember that, with shared hubs, the network was one large collision domain and one large broadcast domain, whereas layer 2 switches break up collision domains on each port, but all ports are still considered, by default, to be in one large broadcast domain. Only virtual LANs, covered in Chapter 3, "VLANs, Trunks, and VTP," break up broadcast domains in a layer 2 switched network.

Switched Ethernet is a good way to dynamically allocate dedicated 10Mbps, 100Mbps, and 1000Mbps connections to each user. By also running full-duplex Ethernet, you can theoretically double the throughput on each link. In the next sections, we'll discuss how Ethernet is used in your internetwork, the differences between the Ethernet types, and half- and full-duplex.

# Using Ethernet Media in Your Internetwork

In this section, you'll learn the difference between the Ethernet media types and how to use them in your internetworks. We'll cover the following Ethernet types:

- 10BaseT
- FastEthernet
- Gigabit Ethernet

## 10BaseT

*10BaseT* stands for 10 million bits per second (Mbps), baseband technology, twisted-pair. This Ethernet technology has the highest install base of any network in the world. It runs the Carrier Sense Multiple Access/Collision Detection (CSMA/CD) protocol and, if correctly installed, is an efficient network. However, if it gets too large and the network is not segmented correctly, problems occur. It is important to understand collision and broadcast domains and how to correctly design the network with switches and routers.

### Using 10BaseT at the Access Layer

10BaseT Ethernet is typically used only at the access layer, and even then, FastEthernet (100BaseT) is quickly replacing it as the prices for 100BaseT continue to drop. It would be poor design to place 10BaseT at the distribution or core layers. You need transits that are much faster than 10BaseT at these layers.

### Distance

The distance that 10BaseT can run and be within specification is 100 meters (330 feet). The 100 meters includes the following:

- Five meters from the switch to the patch panel
- Ninety meters from the patch panel to the office punch-down block
- Five meters from the punch-down block to the desktop connection

This doesn't mean that you can't run more than 100 meters on a cable run; it just is not guaranteed to work.

## FastEthernet

*FastEthernet* is 10 times faster than 10Mbps Ethernet. The great thing about FastEthernet is that, like 10BaseT, it is still based on the CSMA/CD signaling. This means that you can run 10BaseT and 100BaseT on the same network without any problems. What a nice upgrade path this type of network can give you. You can put all your clients on 10BaseT and upgrade only the servers to 100BaseT if you need to. However, you can't even buy a PC that doesn't have a 10/100 Ethernet card in it anymore, so you really don't need to worry about compatibility and speed issues from the user's perspective.

### Using FastEthernet at All Three Layers

FastEthernet works great at all layers of the hierarchical model. It can be used to give high performance to PCs and other hosts at the access layer, provide connectivity from the access layer to the distribution layer switches, and connect the distribution layer switches to the core network. Connecting a server block to the core layer would need, at a minimum, FastEthernet or maybe even Gigabit Ethernet.

## IEEE Specifications for FastEthernet

There are two different specifications for FastEthernet, but the IEEE 802.3u is the most popular. The 802.3u specification is 100Mbps over category 3 or 5, twisted-pair (typically just category 5 or 5-plus is used for FastEthernet). The second Ethernet specification, called 802.12, used a different signaling technique, called Demand Priority Access Method (DPAM), which was more efficient than the CSMA/CD access method. The IEEE passed both methods in June 1995, but because 802.3 Ethernet had such a strong name in the industry, 802.12—also called 100VG-AnyLAN—has virtually disappeared from the market. As with the Macintosh and NetWare operating systems, it doesn't mean anything if you have a better product; it matters only how you market it.

The IEEE 802.3u committee's goals can be summarized as follows:

- Provide seamless integration with the installed base
- Provide 100BaseT at only two times (or less) the cost of 10BaseT
- Increase aggregate bandwidth
- Provide multiple-vendor standardization and operability
- Provide time-bounded delivery

Precisely speaking, 802.12 is usually referred to as 100VG-AnyLAN. 100 is for 100Mbps, VG is for voice-grade cable, and AnyLAN is because it was supposed to be able to use either Ethernet or token-ring frame formats. The main selling point—the use of all four pairs of voice-grade cable—was also its main drawback. This feature is useful if all you have is VG, but it's overshadowed completely by 100BaseT if you have category 5 cable or better. Developed at the time that category 5 was becoming popular, wide-scale implementations of new cabling systems just completely sidelined 802.12.

## Media Independent Interface (MII)

FastEthernet requires a different interface than 10BaseT Ethernet. 10Mbps Ethernet used the Attachment Unit Interface (AUI) to connect Ethernet segments. This provided a decoupling of the MAC layer from the different requirements of the various Physical layer topologies, which allowed the MAC to remain constant but meant the Physical layer could support any existing and new technologies. However, the AUI interface could not support 100Mbps Ethernet because of the high frequencies involved. 100BaseT needed a new interface, and the Media Independent Interface (MII) provides it.

100BaseT actually created a new subinterface between the Physical layer and the Data Link layer, called the Reconciliation Sublayer (RS). The RS maps the 1s and 0s to the MII interface. The MII uses a nibble, which is defined as 4 bits. AUI used only 1 bit at a time. Data transfers across the MII at one nibble per clock cycle, which is 25MHz. 10Mbps uses a 2.5MHz clock.

## Full-Duplex Ethernet and FastEthernet

Full-duplex Ethernet can both transmit and receive simultaneously and uses point-to-point connections. It is typically referred to as "collision free" because it doesn't share bandwidth with any other devices. Frames sent by two nodes can not collide because there are physically separate transmit and receive circuits between the nodes.

Both 10Mbps and 100Mbps Ethernet use four of the eight pins available in standard category 5 UTP cable. Pin 1 on one side and pin 3 on the other are linked, as are pins 2 and 6. When the connection is configured for half-duplex, the data can flow in only one direction at a time, while with full-duplex, data can come and go without collisions because the receive and send channels are separate.

Full-duplex is available when connected to a switch but not to a hub. Full-duplex is also available on 10Mbps, 100Mbps, and Gigabit Ethernet. Because it eliminates collisions, a full-duplex connection will disable the collision detection function on the port.

### Using Full-Duplex Ethernet in the Distribution Layer

Full-duplex Ethernet provides equal bandwidth in both directions. But because users typically work with client/server applications using read/write asymmetrical traffic, arguably the best performance increase gained by full-duplex connectivity would be in the distribution layer, not necessarily in the access layer. Nonetheless, the ease with which it can be implemented and the increase in throughput—no matter how incremental—means that many networks run full-duplex throughout the network.

Full-duplex with flow control was created to avoid packets being dropped if the buffers on an interface fill up before all packets can be processed. However, some vendors might not interoperate, and the buffering might have to be handled by upper-layer protocols instead.

## Auto-Negotiation

*Auto-negotiation* is a process that enables clients and switches to agree on a link capability. This is used to determine the link speed as well as the duplex being used. The auto-negotiation process uses priorities to set the link configuration. Obviously, if both a client and switch port can use 100Mbps, full-duplex connectivity, that would be the highest-priority ranking, whereas half-duplex, 10Mbps Ethernet would be the lowest ranking.

Auto-negotiation uses Fast Link Pulse (FLP), which is an extension to the Normal Link Pulse (NLP) standard used to verify link integrity. NLP is part of the original 10BaseT standard. Commonly, these auto-negotiation protocols do not work that well and you would be better off to configure the switch and NICs to run in a dedicated mode instead of letting the clients and switches auto-negotiate. Later in this chapter, we'll show you how to configure your switches with both the speed and duplex options.

Auto-negotiation is one of the most common causes of frame check sequence (FCS) and alignment errors. If two devices are connected, and one is set to full-duplex and the other to half-duplex, one is sending and receiving on the same two wires while the other is using two wires to send and two to receive. Statically configuring the duplex on the ports eliminates this problem.

Intermittent connectivity issues can often be traced to auto-negotiation problems. If a single user occasionally has long connectivity outages, statically setting speed and duplex on both ends often helps.

## Distance

FastEthernet does have some drawbacks. It uses the same signaling techniques as 10Mbps Ethernet, so it has the same distance constraints. In addition, 10Mbps Ethernet can use up to four repeaters, whereas FastEthernet can use only one or two, depending on the type of repeater. Table 2.1 shows a comparison of FastEthernet technologies.

Of course, the issue of the number of Ethernet repeaters in use is really only of concern when using a hub-based half-duplex system. Once we move to a switched Ethernet environment, the collision domains are considerably reduced in size and we don't need repeaters, and the use of full-duplex Ethernet removes the need to detect collisions entirely, changing the CSMA/CD operation to just CSMA.

**TABLE 2.1** Comparison of FastEthernet Technologies

| Technology | Wiring Category | Distance |
|---|---|---|
| 100BaseTX | Category 5 UTP wiring; categories 6 and 7 are now available. Category 6 is sometimes referred to as cat 5 plus. Two-pair wiring. | 100 meters |
| 100BaseT4 | Four-pair wiring, using UTP category 3, 4, or 5. | 100 meters |
| 100BaseFX | Multi-Mode Fiber (MMF) with 62.5-micron fiber-optic core with a 125-micron outer cladding (62.5/125). | 400 meters |

# Gigabit Ethernet

In the corporate market, *Gigabit Ethernet* is the new hot thing. What is so great about Gigabit is that it can use the same network that your 10Mbps and 100Mbps Ethernet now use. You certainly do have to worry about distance constraints, but what a difference it can make in just a server farm alone!

Just think how nice it would be to have all your servers connected to Ethernet switches with Gigabit Ethernet and all your users using 100BaseT-switched connections. Of course, all your switches would connect with Gigabit links as well. Add xDSL and cable to connect to the Internet and you have more bandwidth than you ever could have imagined just a few years ago. Will it be enough bandwidth a few years from now? Probably not. If you have the bandwidth, users will find a way to use it.

Parkinson's Law states that data expands to fill the space available for storage, but experience shows that it can be equally applied to bandwidth.

## Using Gigabit Ethernet in the Enterprise

Cisco's Enterprise model shows a number of different blocks, as defined in Chapter 1, "The Campus Network." Gigabit Ethernet has value in a number of these different blocks.

The Server Module is a natural choice, because the high demand placed on the network bandwidth by some modern applications would certainly be able to utilize gigabit availability.

The Building Distribution Module carries large amounts of inter-VLAN traffic, and as the 20:80 rule kicks in even more, this additional traffic would benefit from gigabit-speed data transfer.

The Core Module is responsible for connecting all other modules, and it is certain that gigabit throughput would suit the three general principles of core data requirements: speed, speed and more speed!

The Management Module, Building Module, and Edge Distribution Module are less likely at the moment to need gigabit speeds. Most management machines have less data to transfer than applications, most users would be more than satisfied with 100Mbps full-duplex, and the slower WAN speeds at the edge of the network does not need serving by gigabit transfer. Nonetheless, there is rarely such a thing as an average network, and you would be well advised to consider carefully where you might get the best from this exciting technology.

## Protocol Architecture

Gigabit Ethernet became an IEEE 802.3 standard in the summer of 1998. The standard was called 802.3z. Gigabit is a combination of Ethernet 802.3 and FiberChannel and uses Ethernet framing the same way 10BaseT and FastEthernet do. This means that not only is it fast, but it can run on the same network as older Ethernet technology, which provides a nice migration plan. The goal of the IEEE 802.3z was to maintain compatibility with the 10Mbps and 100Mbps existing Ethernet network. They needed to provide a seamless operation to forward frames between segments running at different speeds. The committee kept the minimum and maximum frame lengths the same. However, they needed to change the CSMA/CD for half-duplex operation from its 512-bit times to help the distance that Gigabit Ethernet could run.

Will Gigabit ever run to the desktop? Maybe. Probably. People said that FastEthernet would never run to the desktop when it came out, but it's now common. If Gigabit is run to the desktop, however, it's hard to imagine what we'll need to run the backbone with. 10000BaseT to the rescue! Yes, 10 Gigabit Ethernet is out!

In fact, there is now a 10 Gigabit Ethernet Alliance—a group of vendors and other interested parties who together have created the technology behind IEEE 802.3ae, the 10 Gigabit Ethernet standard.

## Comparing 10BaseT, FastEthernet, and Gigabit Ethernet

There are some major differences between FastEthernet and Gigabit Ethernet. FastEthernet uses the Media Independent Interface, and Gigabit uses the Gigabit Media Independent Interface (GMII). 10BaseT used the Attachment Unit Interface. A new interface was designed to help FastEthernet scale to 100Mbps, and this interface was redesigned for Gigabit Ethernet. The GMII uses an 8-bit data path instead of the 4-bit path that FastEthernet MII uses. The clocking must operate at 125MHz to achieve the 1Gbps data rate.

## Time Slots

Because Ethernet networks are sensitive to the round-trip-delay constraint of CSMA/CD, time slots are extremely important. Remember that in 10BaseT and 100BaseT, the time slots were 512-bit times. However, this is not feasible for Gigabit because the time slot would be only 20 meters in length. To make Gigabit usable on a network, the time slots were extended to 512 bytes (4096-bit times!). However, the operation of full-duplex Ethernet was not changed at all. Table 2.2 compares the new Gigabit Ethernet technologies.

**TABLE 2.2** Comparison of Gigabit Ethernet Technologies

| Technology | Wiring Category | Cable Distance |
|---|---|---|
| 1000BaseCX | Copper-shielded twisted-pair | 25 meters |
| 1000BaseT | Copper category 5, four-pair wiring, UTP | 100 meters |
| 1000BaseSX | MMF using 62.5 and 50-micron core, uses a 780-nanometer laser | 260 meters |
| 1000BaseLX | Single-mode fiber that uses a 9-micron core, 1300-nanometer laser | From 3 kilometers up to 10 kilometers |
| 1000BaseZX | 9-micron single-mode fiber or disposition-shifted fiber | Up to 100 kilometers |

**Real World Scenario**

**Jumbo Frames**

If Gigabit Ethernet is used from source to destination, you might consider using Jumbo frames. These are Ethernet frames that are 9000 bytes long. Jumbo frames don't work well if Gigabit is not used from end to end because fragmentation will take place, causing a small amount of latency. Although Jumbo frames aren't likely to be used to the desktop, they can speed up the process of data transfer between servers. An e-commerce web server that makes a lot of calls to a database and gets large amounts of data at once would be a good candidate.

# Connecting and Logging In to a Switch

The new range of Cisco switches—the 2950 and 3550—run a version of IOS. This makes configuring the switch very similar to configuring a router. The 4000 series is still set based, which means you use the command `set` to configure the router. Throughout the rest of this book, we'll show you commands for these switches.

As a general guideline, you would be expected to use the 2950 as an access-layer switch (because of its cheap per-port cost) and then utilize the more powerful 3550 at the distribution layer. Although these are only rough guidelines, the 3550 does support an internal routing option, which gives it the additional features essential in a modern distribution switch, and the 2950 has a number of different port types and densities, which provide relatively cheap connections for desktop PCs.

There are two types of operating systems that run on Cisco switches:

**IOS based** You can configure the Catalyst 2950 and 3550 switches from a command-line interface (CLI) that is almost identical to the one used on Cisco routers. The only differences are some of the commands, which are switch-specific.

**Set based** Uses older, set-based CLI configuration commands. The current Cisco switches that use the set-based commands are the 4000 and the 6000 series.

## Cabling the Switch Block Devices

You can physically connect to a Cisco Catalyst switch by connecting either to the console port or an Ethernet port, just as you would with a router.

### Connecting to the Console Port

The 2950, 3550, and 4000 series switches all have a console port on the back, which is an RJ-45 port. The console cables for these switches are rolled cables. (Older 5000 series switches have a console connector that uses only an RS-232-type connector, which comes with the switch when purchased).

After you connect to the console port, you need to start a terminal emulation program, such as HyperTerminal in Windows. The settings are as follows:

- 9600bps
- 8 data bits
- No parity
- 1 stop bit
- No flow control

Do not connect an Ethernet cable, ISDN, or live telephone line into the console port. The voltage levels are higher and the result may well be a burned-out console port.

## Connecting to an Ethernet Port

The Catalyst 2950 and 3550 series switches have a number of different arrangements of ports. They are not modular in the sense that the 4000 series switches are. All ports are at least 10/100, and some also support 1000 Mb/sec. Connecting hosts to any of these ports requires a straight-through cable, but to connect the ports to another switch as an uplink, you must use a crossover cable.

The Catalyst 4000 switches can run either 10Mbps or 100Mbps on any port, depending on the type of cards you buy. Gigabit cards are also available. The supervisor cards always take the first slot and have two FastEthernet or Gigabit Ethernet ports for uplinks using either copper or fiber. All devices connected into either the 2950/3550 or 4000 series switches must be within 100 meters (330 feet) of the switch port.

When connecting devices such as workstations, servers, printers, and routers to the switch, you must use a straight-through cable. Use a crossover cable to connect between switches.

When a device is connected to a port, the port status LED light (also called the port link LED or link state LED) on the switching module panel comes on and stays on. If the light does not come on, the other end might be off or there might be a cable problem. Also, if a light comes on and off, a speed matching or duplex problem may exist. I'll show you how to check that in the next section.

## 4000 Switch Startup

The 4000 series switch loads the software image from flash, and then asks you to enter a password, even if there isn't one set. Press Enter and you will see a `Console>` prompt. At this point, you can enter Enable mode and configure the switch by using `set` commands:

```
BOOTROM Version 5.1(2), Dated Apr 26 1999 10:41:04
BOOT date: 08/02/02 BOOT time: 08:49:03
```

```
Uncompressing NMP image.  This will take a minute...
Downloading epld sram device please wait ...
Programming successful for Altera 10K10 SRAM EPLD
Updating epld flash version from 0000 to 0600

Cisco Systems Console

Enter password: [Press return here]
2001 Mar 22 22:22:56 %SYS-5-MOD_OK:Module 1 is online
2001 Mar 22 22:23:06 %SYS-5-MOD_OK:Module 2 is online

Console>
```

## 2950 Switch Startup

When you connect to the 2950 console, the IOS is booted. As the switch boots, it will show diagnostics on the screen. It displays the version of code, information about the flash storage, various part and serial numbers, and so on. If there is no saved configuration file, you are presented with an option to enter the basic configuration using a process called *setup*.

```
System serial number: FOC0650W11A
         --- System Configuration Dialog ---
Would you like to enter the initial configuration dialog? [yes/no]:
```

If you enter **yes**, then the following menu is displayed:

```
Would you like to enter the initial configuration dialog? [yes/no]: yes

At any point you may enter a question mark '?' for help.
Use ctrl-c to abort configuration dialog at any prompt.
Default settings are in square brackets '[]'.


Basic management setup configures only enough connectivity
for management of the system, extended setup will ask you
to configure each interface on the system

Would you like to enter basic management setup? [yes/no]:
```

The menu is self-explanatory, but quite limited. You can set the switch name, enter passwords, set up vlan1 and assign IP addresses to interfaces. The rest of the configurations are defaults, and to be honest, it is rare for anyone to use this method of configuration.

You can exit the setup mode at any time using the Ctrl+C key entry, and you can enter the setup mode from the privileged mode by entering the command `setup`.

The alternative is to answer *no* to the option to enter setup, and then you are presented with the user-mode switch prompt (the initial name of the switch is, unsurprisingly, *switch*).

```
Switch>
```

No passwords are set, and entering the command word `enable` will take you to the privileged prompt.

```
Switch#
```

## Cisco IOS- and Set-Based Commands

In this section, you'll learn how to configure the basics on both types of switches. Specifically, you'll learn how to do the following:

- Set the passwords.
- Set the hostname.
- Configure the IP address and subnet mask.
- Identify the interfaces.
- Set a description on the interfaces.
- Configure the port speed and duplex.
- Verify the configuration.
- Erase the switch configuration.

### Setting the Passwords

The first thing you should do is configure the passwords. You don't want unauthorized users connecting to the switch. You can set both the user-mode and privileged-mode passwords, just as you can with a router. However, you use different commands.

As with any Cisco router, the login (user-mode) password can be used to verify authorization of the switch, including Telnet and the console port. The enable password is used to allow access to the switch so the configuration can be viewed or changed.

### 4000 Series Set-Based Switch

To configure the two passwords on a 4000 series switch, use the command `set password` for the user-mode password and the command `set enablepass` for the enable password:

```
2001 Mar 21 06:31:54 %SYS-5-MOD_OK:Module 1 is online
2001 Mar 21 06:31:54 %SYS-5-MOD_OK:Module 2 is online

Console> en

Enter password:
Console> (enable) set password ?
Usage: set password
Console> (enable) set password [Press enter]
Enter old password:
Enter new password:
Retype new password:
Password changed.
```

When you see the `Enter old password` prompt, you can leave it blank and press Enter if you don't have a password set. The output for the `Enter new password` prompt doesn't show on the console screen. If you want to clear the user-mode (login) password, type in the old password and then just press Enter when you're asked for a new password.

To set the enable password, use the command `set enablepass` and then press Enter:

```
Console> (enable) set enablepass
Enter old password:
Enter new password:
Retype new password:
Password changed.
Console> (enable)
```

You can type **`exit`** at this point to log out of the switch completely, which will enable you to test your new passwords.

### 2950 and 3550 Switches

The commands for setting the passwords are the same as for a router. Those of you used to configuring the password levels on a 1900 switch will find that they are optional on an IOS-based device. The enable secret password supersedes the enable password and automatically encrypts the displayed password by default.

```
Switch>enable
Switch#conf t
Enter configuration commands, one per line.  End with CNTL/Z.
Switch(config)#enable ?
```

```
  last-resort  Define enable action if no TACACS servers respond
  password     Assign the privileged level password
  secret       Assign the privileged level secret
  use-tacacs   Use TACACS to check enable passwords
```

As you can see from the script, the password can be set locally or can be assigned using a protocol called TACACS.

```
Switch(config)#enable secret ?
  0      Specifies an UNENCRYPTED password will follow
  5      Specifies an ENCRYPTED secret will follow
  LINE   The UNENCRYPTED (cleartext) 'enable' secret
  level  Set exec level password
```

Entering the password with no additional options causes the password to be encrypted automatically, thus preventing it from being read by unauthorized viewers. You can see that `san-fran` has become `$1$dytq$1j716VJbtocypNs1DgW2X.`

```
Switch(config)#enable secret san-fran
Switch(config)#^Z
Switch#show running-config

Building configuration...

Current configuration : 1404 bytes
!
version 12.1
no service pad
service timestamps debug uptime
service timestamps log uptime
no service password-encryption
!
hostname Switch
!
enable secret 5 $1$dytq$1j716VJbtocypNs1DgW2X.
!
```

Because the enable secret password takes precedence over the standard enable password, it is common practice for many users to set only the enable secret. More complex security is commonly obtained using TACACS.

The remote access telnet (vty) password prevents unauthorized access by other network users. By default, this is disabled, and the `show running-config` command will display no vty numbers. The passwords are set using the line mode, after which they will appear.

```
Switch#conf t
Enter configuration commands, one per line.  End with CNTL/Z.
Switch(config)#line vty 0 4
Switch(config-line)#login
% Login disabled on line 1, until 'password' is set
% Login disabled on line 2, until 'password' is set
% Login disabled on line 3, until 'password' is set
% Login disabled on line 4, until 'password' is set
% Login disabled on line 5, until 'password' is set
Switch(config-line)#password telnet
Switch(config-line)#^Z
Switch#
```

Now the running configuration displays both the lines configured for access and the password.

```
Switch#show running-config
Building configuration...

Current configuration : 1448 bytes

output omitted

line con 0
line vty 0 4
 password telnet
 login
line vty 5 15
 login
!
end
```

## Setting the Hostname

The hostname on a switch, as well as on a router, is only locally significant. A good rule of thumb is to name the switch after the location it is serving.

In this case, this means that it doesn't have any function whatsoever on the network or for name resolution. However, it is helpful to set a hostname on a switch so you can identify the switch when connecting to it.

Management applications, such as Cisco Works, and processes, such as the Cisco Discovery Protocol (CDP), will use the hostname of a device to differentiate it from other devices. Not changing the hostname can lead to some confusion and cause more work to find out just which "Switch" is having problems.

### 2950 and 3550 Switches

The switch command to set the hostname is exactly as it is with any router. The 2950 and 3550 begin life with a device name of "Switch." Setting the hostname is simple.

```
switch#
switch#conf t
Enter configuration commands, one per line.  End with CNTL/Z.
switch(config)#hostname Terry_2950
Terry_2950(config)#^Z
Terry_2950#
```

## Setting the IP Information

You do not have to set any IP configuration on the switch to make it work. You can just plug in devices and they should start working, as they do on a hub. IP address information is set so that you can either manage the switch via Telnet or other management software or configure the switch with different VLANs and other network functions.

### 4000 Series Set-Based Switch

To set the IP address information on a 4000 series switch, configure the supervisor engine that is plugged into slot 1 of every switch. This is called the in-band logical interface. Use the command set interface sc0:

```
Terry_4000> (enable) set interface sc0 172.16.10.17 255.255.255.0
Interface sc0 IP address and netmask set.
```

By default, the switch is configured for VLAN 1, which can be seen by using the `show interface` command. Notice also that the broadcast address for the subnet shows up and that you can change it by entering it with the `set interface` sc0 command (but we can think of only one reason that you would want to change it—to mess with the people in your MIS department):

```
Terry_4000> (enable) show interface
sl0: flags=51<UP,POINTOPOINT,RUNNING>
slip 0.0.0.0 dest 0.0.0.0
sc0: flags=63<UP,BROADCAST,RUNNING>
vlan 1 inet 172.16.10.17 netmask 255.255.255.0 broadcast 172.16.10.255
Terry_4000> (enable)
```

The command set `interface sl0` *`ip_address mask`* would be used for modem access to the switch. This enables addressing on the Serial Line Internet Protocol (SLIP) process. Before accessing the switch via a modem, the modem process must be enabled on the switch by using the `set system modem enable` command. The modem operates at a speed of 9600bps by default

**Real World Scenario**

**Remote Management**

Many organizations have a large number of switches that need to be managed, and administrators often need access directly to the console port for remote management. A setup that allows remote access direct to the console port is desirable because some problems will prevent telnet or management access, which means you have to physically be there. Not something you want to do at 3 A.M.!

Rather than installing several modems and telephone lines, consider an access server. A 3600 with asynchronous modules, for example, can have over 100 such connections for up to 16 devices at a time and also allow for security features such as a RADIUS or TACACS+ authentication server or an IOS firewall configuration.

### 2950 and 3550 Switches

Cisco recommends that you use VLAN 1 for management of the switch device and then create other VLANs for users. By default, all interfaces are in VLAN 1, supporting the plug-and-play operation of switches. To set the IP configuration, you should use the command `ip address` in interface mode, as shown next:

```
Terry_2950#conf t
Enter configuration commands, one per line.  End with CNTL/Z.
Terry_2950 (config)#int vlan 1
Terry_2950 (config-if)#ip address 172.16.1.1 255.255.255.0
Terry_2950(config-if)#no shut
Terry_2950 (config-if)#^Z
Terry_2950#
```

Don't worry just yet what a VLAN is; we will be covering that in Chapter 4, "Layer 2 Switching and the Spanning Tree Protocol (STP)." For the moment, just concentrate on getting the switch up and running, using as many defaults as possible.

Remember that as far as IP is concerned, the switch is simply another host. This means that the default gateway should also be set, and the command is `ip default-gateway`, which is a global-mode command:

```
Terry_2950(config)#ip default-gateway 172.16.1.254
Terry_2950(config)#^Z
Terry_2950#

Terry_2950#sho run
Building configuration...

[output cut]

interface Vlan1
 ip address 172.16.1.1 255.255.255.0
 no ip route-cache
!
ip default-gateway 172.16.1.254
ip http server
!
Terry_2950#
```

## Identifying Switch Interfaces

It is important to understand how to access switch ports. The 4000 series uses the *slot/port* command. The IOS-based switches use the `type` *slot/port* command.

### 4000 Series Set-Based Switch

You can use the `show` command to view port statistics on a 4000 switch. Notice that, by default, the duplex and speed of the port are both set to `auto`. Also, typically the ports on a 4000 and 6000 series switch can be enabled, but it might be necessary to configure the ports so that they can be enabled with the `set port enable` command. You can turn off any port with the `set port disable` command:

```
Terry_4000> (enable) show port ?
Usage: show port
       show port <mod_num>
       show port <mod_num/port_num>
Terry_4000> (enable) show port 2/1
Port  Name     Status   Vlan  Level  Duplex Speed  Type
----- -------------- ----------- ------- ------------
 2/1           connect   2    normal  auto  auto 10/100BaseTX
```

```
Terry_4000> (enable) set port disable 2/1
Port 2/1 disabled.
Terry_4000> (enable) show port 2/1
Port  Name     Status     Vlan     Level  Duplex Speed  Type
----- ---------------- -------- ------- ------ ------------
 2/1           disabled    1       normal  auto  auto 10/100BaseTX

Terry_4000> (enable) set port enable 2/1
Port 2/1 enabled.
Terry_4000> (enable) show port 2/1
Port  Name   Status     Vlan      Level  Duplex  Speed Type
---- ------ --------- ---------- ----- ------- ------------
 2/1         connect     1        normal  auto    auto 10/100BaseTX
```

The command show config displays the complete current configuration of the set-based switch.

### 2950 and 3550 Switches

These switches take the *type slot/port* command with either the `interface` command or the `show` command. The `interface` command enables you to set interface-specific configurations. As the range of 2950 and 3550 switches increases, it may be that several slots are available. The following example demonstrates a 2950:

```
Terry_2950#config t
Enter configuration commands, one per line.  End with CNTL/Z
Terry_2950(config)#interface fastEthernet ?
   <0-2>  FastEthernet interface number
Terry_2950(config)#interface fastEthernet 0/?
   <1-24>  FastEthernet interface number
Terry_2950(config)#interface fastEthernet 0/1
Terry_2950(config-if)#?
Interface configuration commands:
  arp                  Set arp type (arpa, probe, snap) or timeout
  bandwidth            Set bandwidth informational parameter
  carrier-delay        Specify delay for interface transitions
  cdp                  CDP interface subcommands

[output cut]

  spanning-tree        Spanning Tree Subsystem
```

```
speed               Configure speed operation.
storm-control       storm configuration
switchport          Set switching mode characteristics
timeout             Define timeout values for this interface
```

To configure the FastEthernet ports, the command is `interface fastethernet 0/#`.

You can switch between interfaces by using the `interface fa 0/#` command. Notice that we demonstrate the following commands with spaces or without—it makes no difference.

```
Terry_2950(config-if)#interface fa 0/2
Terry_2950(config-if)#interface fa0/3
Terry_2950(config-if)#exit
```

You can view the ports with the `show interface` command:

```
Terry_2950#show interface fa0/1
FastEthernet0/1 is down, line protocol is down
  Hardware is Fast Ethernet, address is 000b.be53.2c01 (bia 000b.be53.2c01)
  MTU 1500 bytes, BW 10000 Kbit, DLY 1000 usec,
     reliability 255/255, txload 1/255, rxload 1/255
  Encapsulation ARPA, loopback not set
  Keepalive set (10 sec)
  Auto-duplex, Auto-speed
  input flow-control is off, output flow-control is off

[output cut]
```

## Configuring Interface Descriptions

You can set a description on an interface, which will enable you to administratively set a name for each interface. As with the hostname, the descriptions are only locally significant.

### 4000 Series Set-Based Switch

To set a description for the 4000 switch, use the `set port name` *`slot/port`* command. Spaces are allowed. You can set a name up to 21 characters long:

```
Terry_4000> (enable) set port name 2/1 Sales Printer
Port 2/1 name set.
Terry_4000> (enable) show port 2/1
```

```
Port  Name          Status   Vlan Level  Duplex Speed  Type
----- ------------- -------- ---- ----- ------- ------ -----
2/1   Sales Printer notconnect 2  normal  auto  auto 10/100BaseTX
```

### 2950 and 3550 Switches

For the 2950 and 3550 series switches, use the `description` command. You can not use spaces with the `description` command, but you can use underscores if you need to:

```
Terry_2950#config t
Enter configuration commands, one per line.  End with CNTL/Z.
Terry_2950(config)#interface fa0/1
Terry_2950(config-if)#description Finance_VLAN
Terry_2950(config-if)#interface fa0/2
Terry_2950(config-if)#description trunk_to_Building_4
Terry_2950(config-if)#
```

You can view the descriptions with either the `show interface` command or the `show running-config` command:

```
Terry_2950#sho run
Building configuration...

Current configuration : 1387 bytes
!
version 12.1
no service pad
service timestamps debug uptime
service timestamps log uptime
no service password-encryption
!
hostname Terry_2950
!
ip subnet-zero
!
spanning-tree extend system-id
!
interface FastEthernet0/1
 description Finance_VLAN
 no ip address
!
interface FastEthernet0/1
 description trunk_to_Building_4
 no ip address
[output cut]
```

## Configuring the Port Speed and Duplex

By default, all 10/100 ports on the 2950, 3550, and 4000 are set to auto-detect the speed and duplex of the port.

### 4000 Series Set-Based Switch

Because the ports on a 10/100 card are auto-detect, you don't necessarily have to set the speed and duplex. However, there are situations where the auto-detect does not work correctly, and by setting the speed and duplex, you can stabilize the link:

```
Terry_4000> (enable) set port speed 2/1 ?
Usage: set port speed <mod_num/port_num>  <4|10|16|100|auto>
Terry_4000> (enable) set port speed 2/1 100
Port(s) 2/1 speed set to 100Mbps.
```

If you set the port speed to auto, both the speed and duplex are set to auto-negotiate the link. You can't set the duplex without first setting the speed:

```
Terry_4000> (enable) set port duplex 2/1 ?
Usage: set port duplex <mod_num/port_num> <full|half>
Terry_4000> (enable) set port duplex 2/1 full
Port(s) 2/1 set to full-duplex.
Terry_4000> (enable) ^C
```

Notice that the command Ctrl+C was used in the preceding code. This is a break sequence used on both types of switches.

You can view the duplex and speed with the show port command:

```
Terry_4000> (enable) show port 2/1
Port  Name          Status     Vlan  Level  Duplex Speed Type
----- ------------- ---------- ----- ------ ------- ----- -----
 2/1  Sales Printer notconnect 2     normal  full   100 10/100BaseTX
```

### 2950 and 3550 Switches

You can configure multiple options on any port. Speed can be set to 10, 100, or auto, and duplex can be set to half, full, or auto. You can not configure duplex to full if the speed is on auto. Here is an example from a 2950:

```
Terry_2950(config)#int fa0/1
Terry_2950(config-if)#speed ?
  10     Force 10 Mbps operation
  100    Force 100 Mbps operation
  auto   Enable AUTO speed configuration

Terry_2950(config-if)#speed 100
```

```
Terry_2950(config-if)#duplex ?
  auto  Enable AUTO duplex configuration
  full  Force full duplex operation
  half  Force half-duplex operation

Terry_2950(config-if)#duplex full
Terry_2950(config-if)#^Z
Terry_2950#

Terry_2950#sho int fa0/1
FastEthernet0/1 is down, line protocol is down
  Hardware is Fast Ethernet, address is 000b.be53.2c01 (bia 000b.be53.2c01)
  Description: Finance_VLAN
  MTU 1500 bytes, BW 10000 Kbit, DLY 1000 usec,
     reliability 255/255, txload 1/255, rxload 1/255
  Encapsulation ARPA, loopback not set
  Keepalive set (10 sec)
  Full-duplex, 100Mb/s
```

## Verifying Connectivity

It is important to test the switch IP configuration. You can use the "big three" tests of ping, trace, and telnet on all IOS-based switches and the 4000 and 6000 as well.

### 4000 Series Set-Based Switch

Use the IP utilities Ping, Telnet, and Traceroute to test the switch in the network:

```
Terry_4000> (enable) ping 172.16.10.10
172.16.10.10 is alive
Terry_4000> (enable) telnet ?
Usage: telnet <host> [port]
       (host is IP alias or IP address in dot notation: a.b.c.d)
Terry_4000> (enable) traceroute
Usage: traceroute [-n] [-w wait] [-i initial_ttl] [-m max_ttl] [-p dest_port]
   [-q nqueries] [-t tos] host
   [data_size]
(wait = 1..300, initial_ttl = 1..255, max_ttl = 1..255
dest_port = 1..65535, nqueries = 1..1000, tos = 0..255
data_size = 0..1420, host is IP alias or IP address in
dot notation: a.b.c.d)
```

You can use the keystrokes Ctrl+Shift+6, then X, as an escape sequence.

### 2950 and 3550 Switches

You can use the Ping and Trace programs, and you can telnet into and out of any of the switches, as long as a password has been set up.

```
Terry_2950#ping 172.16.10.10
Sending 5, 100-byte ICMP Echos to 172.16.10.10, time out is 2 seconds:
!!!!!
Success rate is 100 percent (5/5), round-trip min/avg/max 0/2/10/ ms
```

You can omit the word `telnet` and just enter the hostname or IP address of the target host, if you wish.

```
Terry_2950#conf t
Terry_2950(config)#ip host jack 172.16.10.10
Terry_2950(config)#^Z
Terry_2950#ping jack
Sending 5, 100-byte ICMP Echos to 172.16.10.10, time out is 2 seconds:
!!!!!
Success rate is 100 percent (5/5), round-trip min/avg/max 0/2/10/ms
```

### Physical Troubleshooting

If the ping test doesn't work, make sure IP addressing and gateways are set up correctly. If they are, and no other part of the network is having problems, there is a good chance that the problem has to do with the Physical layer.

When testing Physical layer connectivity, it is important to focus the tests on the cabling and on the interfaces. In those instances when it is possible, test the port on the switch by plugging in a laptop directly. Plugging the patch cord into a different port can test the cable inside the wall. Finally, test the NIC by plugging the PC into a different cable run and port.

## Saving and Erasing the Switch Configuration

The IOS-based switches hold their configuration in the running-config file. Using the command `copy running-config startup-config` copies this file to nonvolatile RAM (NVRAM), where it is saved as the startup-config file. The 4000 series switches automatically copy their configuration to NVRAM. You can delete the configurations if you want to start over.

It is also common to back up the configuration files on a TFTP server—despite your best efforts, things will go wrong at some time in any network. First, make sure that the TFTP server is available, using the `ping` command. Ensure that access to the server directory is authorized, and then enter the command **`copy running-config`** (or **`copy startup-config`**) **`tftp`**. A small menu follows, prompting you for the server IP address and filename to be stored.

## 2950 and 3550 Switches

The command `show running-config` (abbreviated here to `show run`), displays the configuration file the switch is currently implementing.

```
Terry_2950#show run
Building configuration...

Current configuration : 1411 bytes
!
version 12.1
no service pad
service timestamps debug uptime
service timestamps log uptime
no service password-encryption
!
hostname Terry_2950
!
[output cut]
```

The command `show startup-config` (abbreviated here to `show star`), displays the configuration file the switch has saved in NVRAM. It follows that this is the file that will be implemented when the switch is next started. Note that the two displays are slightly different.

```
Terry_2950#show star
Using 1411 out of 32768 bytes
!
version 12.1
no service pad
service timestamps debug uptime
service timestamps log uptime
no service password-encryption
!
hostname Terry_2950
!
[output cut]
```

To delete the startup configuration file, use the command `erase startup-config`. This will require a reboot of the switch to arrive at an empty configuration file. You can not erase the running config.

```
Terry_2950#erase ?
  flash:          Filesystem to be erased
  nvram:          Filesystem to be erased
  startup-config  Erase contents of configuration memory
```

### 4000 Series Set-Based Switch

To delete the configurations stored in NVRAM on the 4000 series switch, use the `clear config all` command. The `erase all` command deletes the contents of flash without warning. Be careful! Here is the code:

```
Terry_4000> (enable) clear config ?
Usage: clear config all
       clear config <mod_num>
       clear config rmon
       clear config extendedrmon
Terry_4000> (enable) clear config all
This command will clear all configuration in NVRAM.
This command will cause ifIndex to be reassigned on the next system startup.
Do you want to continue (y/n) [n]? y


System configuration cleared.
```

To delete the contents of flash, use the `erase all` command:

```
Terry_4000> (enable) erase all
FLASH on Catalyst:
Type            Address             Location
Intel 28F016    20000000            NMP (P3) 8MB SIM

Erasing flash sector...
Terry_4000> (enable)
Terry_4000> (enable) show flash
File      Version         Sector   Size    Built
--------- -------------- -------- ------- -------
```

Notice that when you type **`erase all`** and press Enter, the switch just starts erasing the flash and you can't break out of it. By using a `show flash` command, you can see that the contents of flash are now empty. You might not want to try this on your production switches. You can use the `copy tftp flash` command to reload the software.

# Summary

You can use several different types of Ethernet in an internetwork, and it's very important that you remember the distance each type of Ethernet media can run. For instance, the distance that 10BaseT can run is 100 meters, or 330 feet. The 100 meters includes five meters from the switch to the patch panel, 90 meters from the patch panel to the office punch-down block, and five meters from the punch-down block to the desktop connection.

For FastEthernet, there are various specifications for each type. For 100BaseTX, category 5 UTP wiring, categories 5e, 6, and 7 are now available. Category 5e is sometimes referred to as cat 5 plus. 100BaseTX requires two-pair wiring and a distance of 100 meters. 100BaseT4 requires four-pair wiring, using UTP category 3, 4, or 5. The distance for 100BaseT4 is 100 meters. 100BaseFX requires Multi-Mode Fiber with 62.5-micron fiber-optic core and a 125-micron outer cladding (62.5/125). The distance for the 100BaseFX is 400 meters.

For Gigabit Ethernet, the specifications for each type also vary. For instance, the 1000BaseCX requires a copper-shielded twisted-pair and a distance of 25 meters. The 1000BaseT requires copper category 5, four-pair wiring, UTP, and 100 meters distance. The 1000BaseSX requires MMF using 62.5 and 50-micron core, uses a 780-nanometer laser, and requires a distance of up to 260 meters.  1000BaseLX uses single-mode fiber with a 9-micron core and uses a 1300-nanometer laser. The distance for a 1000BaseLX is anywhere from 3 kilometers to 10 kilometers. Finally, the 1000BaseZX uses single-mode fiber with a 9-micron core or disposition-shifted fiber. The distance for a1000BaseZX is up to 100 kilometers.

You need to understand how to connect to and how to configure both a set-based switch and an IOS-based switch. It is not enough to just be able to copy down these commands and move on to the next section. The defaults, which are set on all Cisco switches, are there for the benefit of the plug-and-play kiddies—as a CCNP, you are expected to go far beyond that! You need to understand why these configurations are needed, so that you can make knowledge-based judgments on when to use the command options to move away from the default.

You can set hostnames and descriptions to identify your switch and the interfaces, enabling you to administer the network more efficiently. And you can control access to the switch in several ways, using console, telnet, and enable passwords to protect against unauthorized users. You should also be able to configure an IP address and default gateway on each switch so that you can make remote connections, which allows you to manage your switch without having to stand next to it. Finally, you should be able to verify the configuration by performing connectivity tests around the network using the standard IP tools of ping, trace, and telnet.

# Exam Essentials

**Understand how the set-based and IOS-based command lines are different.** Set-based commands belong to a legacy operating system purchased by Cisco when they bought the original switching company, so they bear no resemblance to the Cisco IOS at all. The only three commands in use—`set`, `clear`, and `show`—are used for all purposes. Interface/port configurations, passwords, and all VLAN and trunking options are changed from the defaults using `set` commands. Configurations are removed using `clear` commands, and `show` commands are used to display configurations, interfaces, memory, and so on.

Newer switches, such as the 3550 and 2950, use the familiar Cisco router IOS command set. Password, hostname, and other administrative commands are the same as for the router, and the only real difference is that because this is a switch, the command options may be reduced, omitting router specifics such as routing, on the 2950 switches. The 3550 switches, which support native routing, and the 4000 and 6500 series running the native IOS upgrade, actually support routing as well, and so have a full set of IOS commands.

**Understand physical network connectivity.** Some cables are suitable for some tasks but not for others, and the characteristics of each cable help determine which tasks they should be used for. For instance, Ethernet cables can be straight through, as used with PCs to switch connections, or crossover, as used for switch-to-switch links. You need to know the characteristics and limitations of each type of cable.

**Understand logical network connectivity.** There are several issues to confront with connectivity at layers 1 and 2. We know that hubs operate at layer 1 and switches at layer 2, which immediately identifies some major differences. For instance, a switch allows for full-duplex connectivity, but a hub does not. Also, turning on auto-detection for speed forces duplex into auto-detect mode.

# Key Terms

Before you take the exam, be sure you're familiar with the following terms:

10BaseT

auto-negotiation

contention media

FastEthernet

Gigabit Ethernet

switched Ethernet

# Written Lab

Write the answers to the following questions:

1. 100BaseFX is a point-to-point Ethernet topology that can run up to ___ meters.
2. 1000BaseSX uses a 780-meter laser that can run a distance of ___ meters.
3. 100BaseT can run a total distance of ___ meters.
4. What command saves the running configuration of an IOS-based switch to a TFTP server?
5. What command enables you to erase the configuration file on a 4000 series switch?
6. What command (other than `show run`) shows you the IP address of a 2950 switch?
7. How do you set the IP address on a 4000 series switch to `172.16.10.17 255.255.255.0`?
8. What command sets the enable password on an IOS-based switch?
9. What three IP commands are used to test the network connectivity of a device?
10. What type of Ethernet topology is suggested at the core layer?

# Review Questions

1. Which of the following is true about full-duplex Ethernet?
   A. Full-duplex Ethernet can both transmit and receive simultaneously and use point-to-multipoint connections.
   B. Full-duplex Ethernet can both transmit and receive simultaneously and use point-to-point connections.
   C. Full-duplex Ethernet can transmit and receive simultaneously and uses point-to-multipoint connections.
   D. Full-duplex Ethernet can not transmit and receive simultaneously and uses point-to-point connections.
2. Which of the following is *not* true regarding the 2950 switch? (Choose all that apply.)
   A. You can ping *from* a 2950 switch if configured.
   B. You can ping *to* a 2950 switch if configured.
   C. You can telnet *to* a 2950 switch if configured.
   D. You can not telnet *from* a 2950 switch if configured.
   E. You can trace *to* a 2950 switch if configured.
   F. You can not trace *from* a 2950 switch if configured.
3. What interface command sets interface fa0/10 on a 2950 switch to run full-duplex Ethernet?
   A. `full duplex on`
   B. `duplex on`
   C. `duplex full`
   D. `full-duplex`
   E. `set duplex on full`
4. Which command password protects a 2950 switch against unauthorized telnet access?
   A. `line vty 0 4, login, enable secret`
   B. `line vty 0 4, login, telnet enable`
   C. `line con 0, password cisco`
   D. `line vty 0 4, login, password cisco`
5. If port 2 on card 3 on a 4000 series switch were disabled, what command would enable this interface?
   A. `set enable port 3/2`
   B. `set port enable 3/2`
   C. `set port enable 2/3`
   D. `set enable port 2/3`

6. If you wanted to verify the duplex on a 2950 switch, port 16, what command should you use?
   A. `show port 16`
   B. `show interface 16`
   C. `show interface e0/16`
   D. `show interface fe0/16`
   E. `show interface fa0/16`
   F. `show interface f16`

7. Which of the following is not true of a 2950 switch?
   A. A port can be set to speed 10, full duplex.
   B. A port can be set to speed 100, full duplex.
   C. A port can be set to auto, full duplex.
   D. A port can be set to speed 10, auto.

8. What command (or commands) could you use to set a description of the Sales printer on card 2, interface 3 for a 4000 switch? (Choose all that apply.)
   A. `set port name 2/3 Sales Printer`
   B. `set port name 2/3 Sales_Printer`
   C. `description Sales Printer`
   D. `description Sales_printer`

9. If you wanted to set the hostname on a 3550 series switch to *`Terry_3550>`*, what command would you use?
   A. `host name Terry_3550`
   B. `hostname Terry_3550`
   C. `set prompt Terry_3550`
   D. `set system name Terry_3550>`

10. What is the distance that you can run an MMF, 62.5-micron Gigabit Ethernet cable?
   A. 400 meters
   B. 25 meters
   C. 260 meters
   D. 3 kilometers
   E. 10 kilometers

11. What is the distance that a single-mode, 9-micron Gigabit using a 1300-nanometer laser can run?
   A. 400 meters
   B. 25 meters
   C. 260 meters
   D. Up to 10 kilometers

12. What is the distance you can run an MMF with 62.5-micron fiber-optic core with a 125-micron outer cladding (62.5/125) using FastEthernet?
    A. 25 meters
    B. 400 meters
    C. 260 meters
    D. 3 kilometers
13. What is the distance you can run, and stay in spec, from a patch panel to a switch using 10BaseT?
    A. 5 meters
    B. 25 meters
    C. 90 meters
    D. 100 meters
    E. 330 feet
14. If you wanted interface fa0/22 on a 2950 switch to run only 100Mbps, what command would you use?
    A. `set port speed 100 0/22`
    B. `int fa 0/22, speed default`
    C. `set port 0/22, speed 100`
    D. `int fa 0/22, speed 100`
15. Which of the following is true regarding a port status light on a switch?
    A. It is used to see whether a loop has occurred on the network.
    B. It is used to identify RTS signaling.
    C. When a device is connected to a port, the port status LED light comes on and stays on.
    D. When a device is connected to a port, the port status LED light comes on and then goes off.
16. If you want to delete the startup configuration on a 2950 switch, what command do you use?
    A. `erase startup-config`
    B. `delete startup-config`
    C. `delete nvram`
    D. `delete startup`
17. If you want to delete the configuration on a 4000 series switch, what command do you use?
    A. `clear config all`
    B. `clear nvram`
    C. `delete nvram`
    D. `erase startup`

**18.** What command would you use to identify interface FastEthernet 0/3 on a 2950 switch to be Finance Server?

**A.** `interface fa0/3, description Finance Server`

**B.** `interface fa0/3, name Finance Server`

**C.** `set port name fa0/3 Finance server`

**D.** `set port name fa0/3 Finance_Server`

**19.** What is the IEEE specification for FastEthernet?

**A.** 802.3

**B.** 802.2

**C.** 802.3u

**D.** 802.3z

**20.** What is the IEEE specification for Gigabit Ethernet?

**A.** 802.3

**B.** 802.2

**C.** 802.3u

**D.** 802.3z

# Hands-On Lab

This lab will provide step-by-step instructions for configuring both access layer and distribution layer switches. You'll use a 2950 switch for the access layer and a 4000 series switch for the distribution layer. Figure 2.1 provides the network diagram that will be configured in this lab.

**FIGURE 2.1** Access layer to distribution layer configuration

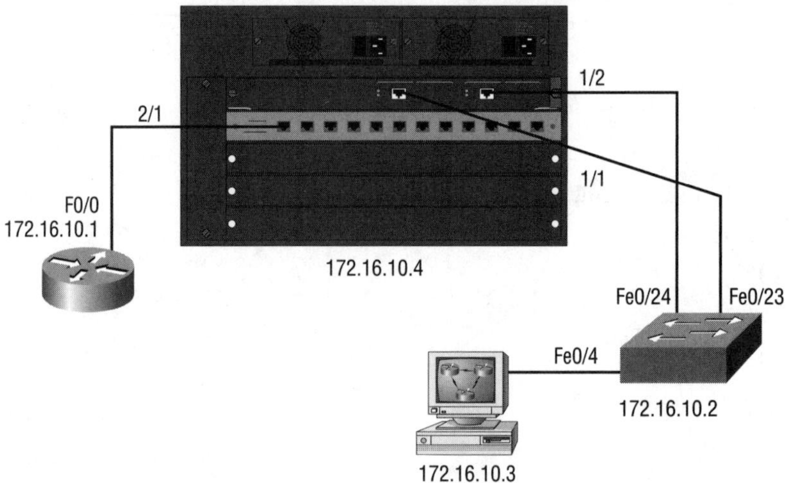


1. Configure the access layer switch by going to the console and pressing Enter.
2. Assign the console password:

   ```
   enable
   configure terminal
   line con 0
   login
   password cisco
   ```

3. Assign the enable password:

   ```
   enable password sanfran
   ```

4. Assign the enable secret, which will override the enable password:

   ```
   enable secret terry
   ```

5. Set the hostname of the switch:

   ```
   hostname 2950
   ```

6. Set the IP address of the switch:

   ```
   ip address 172.16.10.2 255.255.255.0
   ```

7. Set the default gateway for the switch:

```
ip default-gateway 172.16.10.1
```

8. Set interface 4 to run in full-duplex mode:

```
interface fastEthernet 0/4
duplex full
```

9. Set the description of the interface to Management PC:

```
interface fastEthernet 0/4
description Management PC
Control-Z
```

10. Type the command to view the current configuration:

```
show running-config
```

11. Verify the IP configuration of the switch:

```
show ip int
```

12. Verify the configuration of interface FastEthernet 0/4:

```
show interface fastEthernet 0/4
```

13. Configure the interface to full-duplex and add a description of Link to 4000:

```
configure terminal (if needed)
interface fa0/23
duplex full
description Link To 4000
```

14. Configure interface fa0/24 to connect to the FastEthernet port 1/2 of the 4000 switch. Set the description and duplex as well:

```
interface fa0/24
duplex full
description Another Link to 4000
```

15. Move your console cable to the 4000 series distribution switch. Set the hostname to be 4000:

```
enable
set system name 4000>
```

16. Set the user-mode and enable passwords:

```
set password cisco
set enablepass sanfran
```

17. Set the IP address of the 4000 switch:

```
set interface sc0 172.16.10.4 255.255.255.0
```

18. Configure the port speed and duplex of the connection to the access-layer switch:

    ```
    set port duplex 1/1 full
    set port speed 1/1 100
    ```

19. Set the description of port 1/1 to Link to Access Layer:

    ```
    set port name 1/1 Link to Access Layer
    ```

20. Set port 1/2 as the second connection to the access layer switch:

    ```
    set port duplex 1/2 full
    set port speed 1/2 100
    set port name 1/2 Link to Core Switch
    ```

21. Type the command to view port 1/1:

    ```
    show port 1/1
    ```

22. Type the command to view the configuration of the 4000 switch:

    ```
    show config
    ```

23. Test the connections by pinging all devices.

# Answers to Written Lab

1. 400
2. 260
3. 100
4. `copy running-config tftp`
5. `clear config all`
6. `show interface`
7. `set interface sc0 172.16.10.17 255.255.255.0`
8. `enable secret` *`password`*
9. `ping`, `telnet`, and `traceroute`
10. FastEthernet or Gigabit Ethernet

# Answers to Review Questions

1. B. Full-duplex Ethernet uses a point-to-point connection between the transmitter of the transmitting station and the receiver of the receiving station.

2. D, F. You can ping, trace, and telnet to and from all IOS-based switches. For telnet access, the password must be set.

3. C. The privileged command `duplex full` sets the duplex of a 2950 interface.

4. D. Telnet access is protected at the vty interface.

5. B. The 4000 series of switches uses the `set` commands. To set a parameter on a certain interface, use the `set port` command. To enable a port that has been disabled, use the command `set port enable` *`slot/port`*.

6. E. The 2950 switch command-line interface uses the `show interface` *`slot/port`* command, the same as any router that has modular interface cards. As all ports are 10/100, the FastEthernet description is used.

7. C. The speed must be set to 10 or 100 before the duplex configuration can be altered.

8. A, B. The `set port` command is used to change port parameters, and `set port name` *`slot/port`* `description` is used to identify the port to an administrator. The first answer is the best one.

9. B. Use the command `hostname` *`name`* to set the hostname on a 3550 series switch.

10. C. The maximum distance a Multi-Mode Fiber, 62.5-micron Gigabit Ethernet link can run is 260 meters.

11. D. Cisco supports up to 10 kilometers for a 1300-nanometer laser run using 9-micron Gigabit Ethernet.

12. B. FastEthernet point-to-point fiber runs can go a maximum distance of 400 meters.

13. A. Although many people break this rule, the specifications state that the patch panel-to-switch distance can be only 5 meters.

14. D. The `interface command speed 100` sets the parameters for individual ports. The `set port speed` *`port/slot speed`* command sets the port speed on a 10/100 port.

15. C. If a device is correctly connected to a port and the device is powered on, the port light-emitting diode (LED) will come on and stay on.

16. A. The command `erase startup-config` deletes the configuration file stored in NVRAM on all IOS-based switches.

17. A. The command that enables you to delete the configuration on a 4000 series switch is `clear config all`.

18. A. The interface needs to be identified by the keyword *description*.

19. C. The IEEE committee for FastEthernet is 802.3u.

20. D. The IEEE specification for Gigabit Ethernet is 802.3z.

# VLANs, Trunks, and VTP

## THE CCNP EXAM TOPICS COVERED IN THIS CHAPTER INCLUDE THE FOLLOWING:

- ✓ Describe LAN segmentation with VLANs
- ✓ Ensure broadcast domain integrity by establishing VLANs
- ✓ Configure access ports for static membership of single and multiple VLANs
- ✓ Describe the different Trunking Protocols
- ✓ Configure ports as 802.1Q trunks and verify their operation
- ✓ Configure ports as ISL trunks and verify their operation
- ✓ Understand the operation of VTPv1 and VTPv2, including the functions of domains, modes, advertisements, and pruning
- ✓ Configure switches in VTP domains in server, client, and transparent modes
- ✓ Understand local VLANs and end-to-end VLANs, and determine which to use
- ✓ Design VLAN configurations with VTP for operation in a specific scenario
- ✓ Understand managed VLAN services
- ✓ Know the features and functionality of 802.1Q Tunneling (802.1QinQ) in service provider networks
- ✓ Configure auxiliary VLANs with IP technology

You likely already know that a LAN is a group of stations that use broadcast frames to share common services. Most legacy protocols use broadcasts to carry out simple administrative functions, such as finding a server, advertising their services, and even acquiring naming and addressing information. These days, we can go much further using a virtual local area network (VLAN).

A VLAN is a logical grouping of network users and resources connected to administratively defined ports on a layer 2 switch. By creating these administrative groupings, you are able to create smaller broadcast domains within a switch by assigning different ports in the switch to different subnetworks. A VLAN is treated as its own subnet or broadcast domain. This means that when frames are broadcast, they are switched between ports only within the same VLAN.

By using VLANs, you're no longer confined to creating workgroups based on physical locations. VLANs can be organized by location, function, department, or even the application or protocol used, regardless of where the resources or users are located. VLANs can be created locally on a single switch, or can be extended across many switches in a LAN, using special trunk protocols to carry the additional VLAN header information. This technique is called *frame tagging*, and uses special identification methods that either encapsulate a frame or insert a new field in a frame, to identify it as belonging to a particular VLAN as it traverses a switched internetwork fabric.

One of the real problems facing network administrators managing large switched networks is that of consistency. With VLAN numbers and names requiring unique configuration, it is easy to lose control of the process, resulting in conflicting information about the same VLAN.

VTP—the VLAN Trunking Protocol—was developed to deal precisely with this problem. By creating a process where one switch can act as a server, updating other switches in the same domain, consistency of VLAN description can easily be achieved.

# Understanding the Design Benefits of Virtual LANs

Remember that layer 2 switches break up collision domains and that only routers can break up broadcast domains. However, virtual LANs can be used to break up broadcast domains in layer 2 switched networks. Routers are still needed in a layer 2 virtual LAN switched internetwork to enable the different VLANs to communicate with each other.

There are many benefits to creating VLANs in your internetwork. Remember that in a layer 2 switched network, the network is a *flat network*, as shown in Figure 3.1. Every broadcast packet transmitted is seen by every device on the network, regardless of whether the device needs to receive the data.

In a flat network, all users can see all devices. You can not stop devices from broadcasting or users from trying to respond to broadcasts. Your only security consists of passwords on the servers and other devices.

By creating VLANs, you can solve many of the problems associated with layer 2 switching.

**FIGURE 3.1** A flat network structure

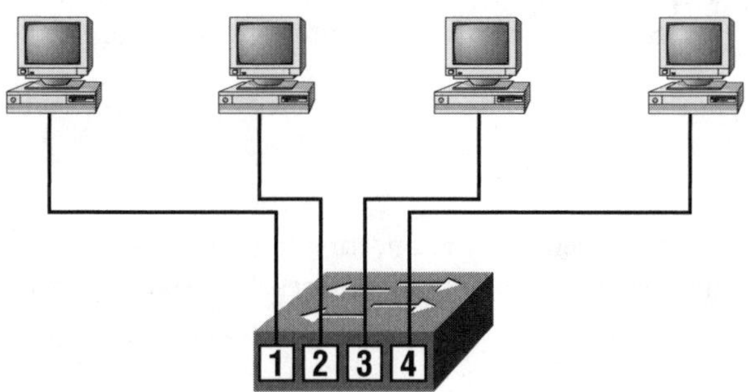


- Each segment has its own collision domain.
- All segments are in the same broadcast domain.

## Broadcast Control

Broadcasts occur in every protocol, but how often they occur depends on the protocol, the application(s) running on the internetwork, and how these services are used. VLANs can define smaller broadcast domains, which means that it is possible to stop application broadcasts to segments that do not use the application.

Although some older applications have been rewritten to reduce their bandwidth needs, there is a new generation of applications that are bandwidth greedy, consuming all they can find. These are multimedia applications that use broadcasts and multicasts extensively. Faulty equipment, inadequate segmentation, and poorly designed firewalls can also add to the problems of broadcast-intensive applications.

For the moment, you should consider multicast traffic to be the same as broadcast traffic. The switch has no default knowledge of multicast groups, and forwards it out of every port. We deal with this issue in detail in Chapter 7, "Multi-Layer Switching."

These bandwidth-gobbling applications have added a new factor to network design because broadcasts can propagate through the switched network. Routers, by default, send broadcasts only within the originating network, but layer 2 switches forward broadcasts to all segments. This is called a *flat network* because it is one broadcast domain.

As an administrator, you must make sure the network is properly segmented to keep problems on one segment from propagating through the internetwork. The most effective way of doing this is through switching and routing. Because switches have become more cost-effective, a lot of companies are replacing the hub-and-router network with a pure switched network and VLANs. The largest benefit gained from switches with defined VLANs is that all devices in a VLAN are members of the same broadcast domain and receive all broadcasts. The broadcasts, by default, are filtered from all ports that are on a switch and are not members of the same VLAN.

Every time a VLAN is created, a new broadcast domain is created. VLANs are used to stop broadcasts from propagating through the entire internetwork. Some sort of internal route processor, or an external router must be used in conjunction with switches to provide connections between networks (VLANs).

## Security

In a flat internetwork, security is implemented by connecting hubs and switches together with routers. Security is then maintained at the router, but this causes three serious security problems:

- Anyone connecting to the physical network has access to the network resources on that physical LAN.
- A user can plug a network analyzer into the hub and see all the traffic in that network.
- Users can join a workgroup just by plugging their workstation into the existing hub.

By using VLANs and creating multiple broadcast groups, administrators now have control over each port and user. Users can no longer just plug their workstation into any switch port and have access to network resources. The administrator controls each port and whatever resources it is allowed to use.

Because groups can be created according to the network resources a user requires, switches can be configured to inform a network management station of any unauthorized access to network resources. If inter-VLAN communication needs to take place, restrictions on a router can also be implemented. Restrictions can also be placed on hardware addresses, protocols, and applications.

## Flexibility and Scalability

VLANs also add more flexibility to your network by allowing only the users you want in the broadcast domain regardless of their physical location. Layer 2 switches read frames only for filtering; they do not look at the Network-layer protocol. This can cause a switch to forward all broadcasts. However, by creating VLANs, you are essentially creating separate broadcast domains. Broadcasts sent out from a node in one VLAN will not be forwarded to ports configured in a different VLAN. By assigning switch ports or users to VLAN groups on a switch—or a group of connected switches (called a *switch-fabric*)—you have the flexibility to add only the users you want in the broadcast domain regardless of their physical location. This can stop broadcast storms caused by a faulty network interface card (NIC) or stop an application from propagating throughout the entire internetwork.

When a VLAN gets too big, you can create more VLANs to keep the broadcasts from consuming too much bandwidth. The fewer users in a VLAN, the fewer are affected by broadcasts.

## The Collapsed Backbone and the VLAN

To understand how a VLAN looks to a switch, it's helpful to begin by first looking at a traditional collapsed backbone. Figure 3.2 shows a collapsed backbone created by connecting physical LANs to a router.

Each network is attached to the router, and each network has its own logical network number. Each node attached to a particular physical network must match that network number to be able to communicate on the internetwork. Now let's look at what a switch accomplishes. Figure 3.3 shows how switches remove the physical boundary.

Switches create greater flexibility and scalability than routers can by themselves because switches define the network VLANs and VLAN port assignments. You can group users into communities of interest, which are known as VLAN organizations.

Because of switches, we don't need routers anymore, right? Wrong. In Figure 3.3, notice that there are four VLANs, or broadcast domains. The nodes within each VLAN can communicate with each other but not with any other VLAN or node in another VLAN. When configured in a VLAN, the nodes think they are actually in a collapsed backbone, as in Figure 3.2. What do these hosts in Figure 3.2 need to do in order to communicate to a node or host on a different network? They need to go through the router, or other layer 3 device, just as they do when they are configured for VLAN communication, as shown in Figure 3.3. Communication between VLANs, just as in physical networks, must go through a layer 3 device.

**FIGURE 3.2** Switches remove the physical boundary.

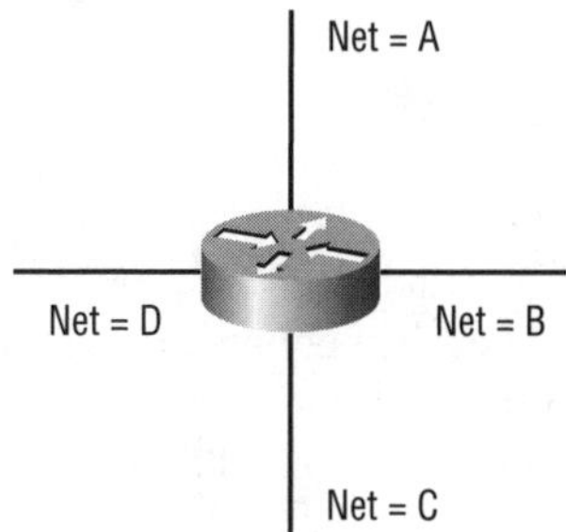

If the creation of VLANs using the existing addressing scheme does not produce the segmentation that you need, you may have to bite the bullet and renumber your network. But it's not all bad news. Creating a new IP addressing scheme from the ground up may seem like a huge task, but it is greatly simplified by using an automatic addressing process such as Dynamic Host Configuration Protocol (DHCP).

**FIGURE 3.3** Physical LANs connected to a router

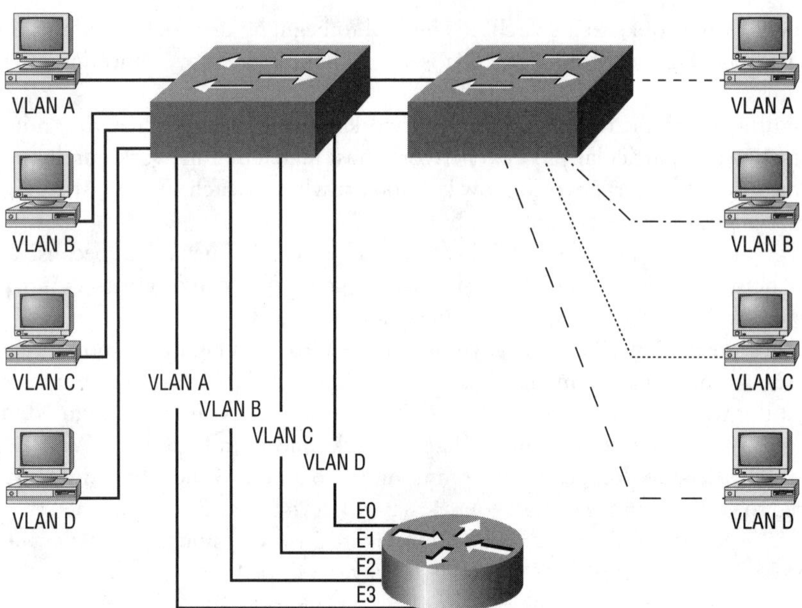


# Scaling the Switch Block

First introduced in Chapter 1, "The Campus Network," switch blocks represent a switch or group of switches providing access to users. These switches then connect to distribution-layer switches, which in turn handle routing issues and VLAN distribution.

To understand how many VLANs can be configured in a switch block, you must understand the following factors:

- Traffic patterns
- Applications used
- Network management
- Group commonality
- IP addressing scheme

Cisco recommends a one-to-one ratio between VLANs and subnets. For example, if you have 2000 users in a building, then you must understand how they are broken up by subnets to create your VLANs. If you had 1000 users in a subnet—which is ridiculous—you would create only 2 VLANs. If you had only 100 users in a subnet, you would create about 20 VLANs or more.

It is actually better to create your broadcast domain groups (VLANs) and then create a subnet mask that fits the need. That is not always possible, and you usually have to create VLANs around an already-configured network.

VLANs should not extend past the distribution switch on to the core.

## Defining VLAN Boundaries

When building the switch block, you need to understand two basic methods for defining the VLAN boundaries:

- End-to-end VLANs
- Local VLANs

### End-to-End VLANs

An *end-to-end VLAN* spans the switch-fabric from end to end; all switches with ports configured in end-to-end VLANs understand about any and all VLANs that may be configured on the network. End-to-end VLANs are configured to allow membership based on function, project, department, and so on.

The best feature of end-to-end VLANs is that users can be placed in a VLAN regardless of their physical location. The administrator defines the port the user is connected to as a VLAN member. If the user moves, the administrator defines their new port as a member of their existing VLAN. In accordance with the 80/20 rule, the goal of an administrator in defining end-to-end VLANs is to maintain 80 percent of the network traffic as local, or within the VLAN. Only 20 percent or less should extend outside the VLAN.

### Local VLANs

Unlike an end-to-end VLAN, a *local VLAN* is configured by physical location and not by function, project, department, and so on. Local VLANs are used in corporations that have centralized server and mainframe blocks because end-to-end VLANs are difficult to maintain in this situation. In other words, when the 80/20 rule becomes the 20/80 rule, end-to-end VLANs are more difficult to maintain, so you will want to use a local VLAN.

In contrast to end-to-end VLANs, local VLANs are configured by geographic location; these locations can be a building or just a closet in a building, depending on switch size. Geographically configured VLANs are designed around the fact that the business or corporation is using centralized resources, such as a server farm. The users will spend most of their time utilizing these centralized resources and 20 percent or less on the local VLAN. From what you have read in this book so far, you must be thinking that 80 percent of the traffic is crossing a layer 3 device. That doesn't sound efficient, does it?

Because many modern applications are not very tolerant of delay (a bit like users), you must design a geographic VLAN with a fast layer 3 device (or devices) for interconnecting your VLANs and for general site-to-site connectivity. Fortunately, layer 3 devices themselves are becoming faster. The benefit of this design is that it will give the users a predetermined, consistent method of getting to resources. But you can not create this design with a lower-end layer 3 model. In the past, these network types were only possible in large corporations with plenty of spending power, but as technology develops, the price is going down.

## Assigning VLAN Memberships

After your VLANs are created, you need to assign switch ports to them. There are two types of VLAN port configurations: static and dynamic. A static VLAN requires less work initially but is more difficult for an administrator to maintain. A dynamic VLAN, on the other hand, takes more work up front but is easier to maintain.

### Static VLANs

In a *static VLAN*, the administrator creates a VLAN and then assigns switch ports to it. The association does not change until the administrator changes the port assignment. This is the typical way of creating VLANs and it is the most secure. This type of VLAN configuration is easy to set up and monitor, working well in a network where the movement of users within the network is maintained by basically just locking the network closet doors. Using network management software to configure the ports can be helpful but is not mandatory.

### Dynamic VLANs

If the administrator wants to do a little more work up front and add all devices' hardware addresses to a database, hosts in an internetwork can be assigned VLAN assignments dynamically. By using intelligent management software, you can enable hardware (MAC) addresses, protocols, or even applications to create dynamic VLANs. A *dynamic VLAN* will tell the switch port which VLAN it belongs to, based on the MAC address of the device that connects to the port.

For example, suppose MAC addresses have been entered into a centralized VLAN management application. If a node is then attached to an unassigned switch port, the VLAN management database can look up the hardware address and assign and configure the switch port to the correct VLAN. This can make management and configuration easier for the administrator. If a user moves, the switch automatically assigns them to the correct VLAN. However, more administration is needed initially to set up the database than to set up static VLANs, and additional administration is required for upkeep of the database.

Cisco administrators can use the VLAN Management Policy Server (VMPS) service to set up a database of MAC addresses that can be used for dynamic addressing of VLANs. VMPS is a MAC-address-to-VLAN mapping database.

## Configuring Static VLANs

For the Switching exam, Cisco is primarily interested in static VLAN configuration. We'll show you how to configure VLANs on a Catalyst 4000 switch and a range of Catalyst IOS-based switches.

It is important to understand the difference between the Catalyst 4000 series VLAN configuration and the IOS-based VLAN configuration.

### Catalyst 4000 Series

To configure VLANs on a Catalyst 4000 switch, use the `set vlan vlan# name vlan_name` command. Then, after your VLANs are configured, assign the ports to each VLAN:

```
Terry_4000> (enable) set vlan 2 name Sales
Vlan 2 configuration successful
```

After the VLAN is configured, use the `set vlan vlan# slot/ports` com

```
Terry_4000> (enable) set vlan 2 2/1-2
VLAN  Mod/Ports
---- -----------------------
2     1/1-2
      2/1-2

Please configure additional information for VLAN 2.
Terry_4000> (enable)
```

The additional information the switch wants you to configure is the VLAN Trunk Protocol (VTP) information. (VTP and trunking are covered in more detail at the end of this chapter, where we will continue with the 4000 switch VLAN configuration.) The 4000 series switch enables you to configure as many ports as you wish to a VLAN at one time.

### Catalyst 2950 and 3550 Series - STATIC VLAN

To configure VLANs on an IOS-based switch, first you need to enter the *VLAN database*. This mode is entered by typing the command **vlan database**. This command changes the prompt, as can be seen from the example shown next. Once in this new privileged mode, use the `vlan` *`vlan#`* `name` *`vlan_name`*. Note that you do not enter the standard configuration mode to enter this configuration.

```
Terry_2950#vlan database
Terry_2950(vlan)#vlan ?
  <1-1005>  ISL VLAN index

Terry_2950(vlan)#vlan 2 ?
  are        Maximum number of All Route Explorer hops for this VLAN
  backupcrf  Backup CRF mode of the VLAN
  bridge     Bridging characteristics of the VLAN
  media      Media type of the VLAN
  mtu        VLAN Maximum Transmission Unit
  name       Ascii name of the VLAN
  parent     ID number of the Parent VLAN of FDDI or Token Ring type VLANs
  ring       Ring number of FDDI or Token Ring type VLANs
  said       IEEE 802.10 SAID
  state      Operational state of the VLAN
  ste        Maximum number of Spanning Tree Explorer hops for this VLAN
  stp        Spanning tree characteristics of the VLAN
  tb-vlan1   ID number of the first translational VLAN for this VLAN (or zero
             if none)
```

```
  tb-vlan2   ID number of the second translational VLAN for this VLAN (or zero
             if none)
  <cr>

Terry_2950(vlan)#vlan 2 name ?
  WORD  The ascii name for the VLAN

Terry_2950(vlan)#vlan 2 name marketing
VLAN 2 added:
    Name: marketing
Terry_2950(vlan)#vlan 3 name production
VLAN 3 added:
    Name: production
Terry_2950(vlan)#exit
APPLY completed.
Exiting....
```

Remember that a created VLAN is unused until it is mapped to a switch port or ports, and that all ports are always in VLAN 1 unless set otherwise.

After you create the VLANs that you want, you use the `show vlan` command to see the configured VLANs. However, notice that, by default, all ports on the switch are in VLAN 1. To change that, you need to go to each interface and tell it what VLAN to be a part of:

```
Terry_2950#show vlan

VLAN Name                             Status    Ports
---- -------------------------------- --------- -------------------------------
1    default                          active    Fa0/1, Fa0/2, Fa0/3, Fa0/4
                                                Fa0/5, Fa0/6, Fa0/7, Fa0/8
                                                Fa0/9, Fa0/10, Fa0/11, Fa0/12
                                                Fa0/13, Fa0/14, Fa0/15, Fa0/16
                                                Fa0/17, Fa0/18, Fa0/19, Fa0/20
                                                Fa0/21, Fa0/22, Fa0/23, Fa0/24
2    marketing                        active
3    production                       active
1002 fddi-default                     active
1003 token-ring-default               active
1004 fddinet-default                  active
1005 trnet-default                    active
```

```
VLAN Type  SAID       MTU   Parent RingNo BridgeNo Stp  BrdgMode Trans1 Trans2
---- ----- ---------- ----- ------ ------ -------- ---- -------- ------ ------
1    enet  100001     1500  -      -      -        -    -        0      0
2    enet  100002     1500  -      -      -        -    -        0      0
3    enet  100003     1500  -      -      -        -    -        0      0
1002 fddi  101002     1500  -      -      -        -    -        0      0
1003 tr    101003     1500  -      -      -        -    -        0      0

VLAN Type  SAID       MTU   Parent RingNo BridgeNo Stp  BrdgMode Trans1 Trans2
---- ----- ---------- ----- ------ ------ -------- ---- -------- ------ ------
1004 fdnet 101004     1500  -      -      -        ieee -        0      0
1005 trnet 101005     1500  -      -      -        ibm  -        0      0

Remote SPAN VLANs
------------------------------------------------------------------------------


Primary Secondary Type              Ports
------- --------- ----------------- ------------------------------------------
```

Configuring the interfaces on the 2950 and 3550 is very different. After the VLANs have been created, the interface needs to be made a member of the appropriate VLAN. The command `switchport mode access` is used to tell the port that it will be a member of a single VLAN. It is told what VLAN it is a member of with the command `switchport access vlan` *`vlan#`*.

```
Terry_2950(config-if)#switchport ?
  access          Set access mode characteristics of the interface
  host            Set port host
  mode            Set trunking mode of the interface
  nonegotiate     Device will not engage in negotiation protocol on this
                  interface
  port-security   Security related command
  priority        Set appliance 802.1p priority
  protected       Configure an interface to be a protected port
  trunk           Set trunking characteristics of the interface
  voice           Voice appliance attributes

Terry_2950(config-if)#switchport access ?
  vlan  Set VLAN when interface is in access mode

Terry_2950(config-if)#switchport mode access
Terry_2950(config-if)#^Z
Terry_2950#co
conf t
```

```
Enter configuration commands, one per line.  End with CNTL/Z.
Terry_2950(config)#int fa 0/2
Terry_2950(config-if)#switchport ?
  access         Set access mode characteristics of the interface
  host           Set port host
  mode           Set trunking mode of the interface
  nonegotiate    Device will not engage in negotiation protocol on this
                 interface
  port-security  Security related command
  priority       Set appliance 802.1p priority
  protected      Configure an interface to be a protected port
  trunk          Set trunking characteristics of the interface
  voice          Voice appliance attributes

Terry_2950(config-if)#switchport mode ?
  access   Set trunking mode to ACCESS unconditionally
  dynamic  Set trunking mode to dynamically negotiate access or trunk mode
  trunk    Set trunking mode to TRUNK unconditionally

Terry_2950(config-if)#switchport mode access
Terry_2950(config-if)#switchport access ?
  vlan  Set VLAN when interface is in access mode

Terry_2950(config-if)#switchport access vlan 2
Terry_2950(config-if)#^Z
```

Now you need to confirm that the configuration has been accepted and the port to VLAN relationship established. You can use the `show vlan` command we used earlier, but the VLANs will also be shown in the running configuration:

```
Terry_2950#show run
00:49:36: %SYS-5-CONFIG_I: Configured from console by consolesho run
Building configuration...

Current configuration : 1512 bytes
version 12.1

[output cut]

interface FastEthernet0/2
 switchport access vlan 2
 switchport mode access
 no ip address
```

Now, type **show vlan** to see the ports assigned to each VLAN:

```
Terry_2950#show vlan

VLAN Name                             Status    Ports
---- -------------------------------- --------- -------------------------------
1    default                          active    Fa0/1, Fa0/3, Fa0/4, Fa0/5
                                                Fa0/6, Fa0/7, Fa0/8, Fa0/9
                                                Fa0/10, Fa0/11, Fa0/12, Fa0/13
                                                Fa0/14, Fa0/15, Fa0/16, Fa0/17
                                                Fa0/18, Fa0/19, Fa0/20, Fa0/21
                                                Fa0/22, Fa0/23, Fa0/24
2    marketing                        active    Fa0/2
3    production                       active
1002 fddi-default                     active
1003 token-ring-default               active
1004 fddinet-default                  active
1005 trnet-default                    active

[output truncated]

Terry_2950#
```

# Identifying VLANs

VLANs can span multiple connected switches, which (as we stated earlier) Cisco calls a switch-fabric. Switches within the switch-fabric must keep track of frames as they are received on the switch ports, and they must keep track of the VLAN they belong to as the frames traverse the switch-fabric. Switches use frame tagging to perform this function. Switches can then direct frames to the appropriate port.

There are two types of links in a switched environment:

**Access link** An *access link* is a link that is part of only one VLAN, which is referred to as the native VLAN of the port. Any device attached to an access link is unaware of a VLAN membership. This device just assumes it is part of a broadcast domain, with no understanding of the physical network. Switches remove any VLAN information from the frame before it is sent to an access-link device. Access-link devices can not communicate with devices outside of their VLAN unless the packet is routed through a router.

**Trunk link** Trunks can carry multiple VLANs. Originally named after the trunks of the telephone system, which carry multiple telephone conversations, a *trunk link* is used to connect switches to other switches, to routers, or even to servers. Trunk links are supported on FastEthernet or Gigabit Ethernet only. To identify the VLAN that a frame belongs to, Cisco switches support two identification techniques: Inter-Switch Link (ISL) and 802.1Q. Trunk links are used to transport VLANs between devices and can be configured to transport all VLANs or just a few VLANs. Trunk links still have a native VLAN, and that VLAN is used if the trunk link fails.

## Frame Tagging

The switch in an internetwork needs a way to keep track of users and frames as they travel the switch-fabric and VLANs. Frame identification, called *frame tagging*, uniquely assigns a user-defined ID to each frame. This is sometimes referred to as a VLAN ID or color.

Frame tagging is used to identify the VLAN that the packet belongs to. The tag is placed on the frame as it enters the first switch it runs into. As long as the frame does not exit out a non-trunk port, the frame keeps the identifying tag. This enables each switch to see what VLAN the frame belongs to, and each switch that the frame reaches must identify the VLAN ID and then determine what to do with the frame based on the filter table. If the frame reaches a switch that has another trunk link, the frame can be forwarded out the trunk link port. After the frame reaches an exit to an access link, the switch removes the VLAN identifier. The end device receives the frames without having to understand the VLAN identification.

If you are using NetFlow switching hardware on your Cisco switches, this enables devices on different VLANs to communicate after taking just the first packet through the router. This means that communication can occur from port to port on a switch, instead of from port to router to port, when traversing VLANs.

## VLAN Identification Methods

To keep track of frames traversing a switch-fabric, VLAN identification is used to identify which frames belong to which VLAN. There are multiple trunking methods:

**Inter-Switch Link (ISL)** Proprietary to Cisco switches, ISL is used for FastEthernet and Gigabit Ethernet links only. It can be used on switch ports and router interfaces as well as server interface cards to trunk a server. Server trunking is good if you are creating functional VLANs and don't want to break the 80/20 rule. The server that is trunked is part of all VLANs (broadcast domains) simultaneously. The users do not have to cross a layer 3 device to access a company-shared server.

**IEEE 802.1Q** Created by the IEEE as a standard method of frame tagging. It actually inserts a field into the frame to identify the VLAN.

**LAN Emulation (LANE)** Used to communicate with multiple VLANs over ATM.

**802.10 (FDDI)** Used to send VLAN information over FDDI. Uses a SAID field in the frame header to identify the VLAN. This is proprietary to Cisco devices.

The Cisco Switching exam covers only the ISL and 802.1Q methods of VLAN identification.

It is possible for a packet to move from one type of network, such as FDDI, to another, such as Ethernet. Ethernet, FDDI, Token Ring, and ATM have standards enabling the switch to translate one type into a different type. The configuration on the switch requires specifically stating that VLAN 53 is the same thing as ATM ELAN 953, for example. The code for this is derived from translational bridging.

## Inter-Switch Link Protocol (ISL)

Inter-Switch Link Protocol (ISL) is a way of explicitly tagging VLAN information onto an Ethernet frame. This tagging information enables VLANs to be multiplexed over a trunk link through an external encapsulation method. By running ISL, you can interconnect multiple switches and still maintain VLAN information as traffic travels between switches on trunk links.

Cisco created the ISL protocol, and therefore ISL is proprietary to Cisco devices only. If you need a nonproprietary VLAN protocol, use the 802.1Q, which is covered next in this chapter.

ISL is an external tagging process, which means that the original frame is not altered but instead is encapsulated with a new 26-byte ISL header and a 4-byte frame check sequence (FCS) field at the end of the frame. Because the frame is encapsulated with information, only ISL-aware devices can read the frame. Token Ring devices can also be connected with the appropriate ports, if VTP version 2 is being used. The size of the frame can be up to 1548 bytes long for Ethernet and 17,878 bytes for Token Ring.

On multi-VLAN (trunk) ports, each frame is tagged as it enters the switch. ISL network interface cards (NICs) enable servers to send and receive frames tagged with multiple VLANs, so the frames can traverse multiple VLANs without going though a router, which reduces latency. This technology can also be used with probes and certain network analyzers. In addition, it enables users to attach to servers quickly and efficiently without going through a router every time they need to communicate with a resource. Administrators can use the ISL technology to simultaneously include file servers in multiple VLANs, for example.

It is important to understand that ISL VLAN information is added to a frame as soon as that frame enters the switch. The ISL encapsulation is removed from the frame if the frame is forwarded out an access link.

Preventing communication from one VLAN to another might be desirable, but the network design might still require that some devices have access to all VLANs. In addition to configuring a filter on a router, you can install a network card that is ISL or 802.1Q capable. This enables an e-mail server or database server to be directly connected to all VLANs without a router being involved.

## Standard for Virtual Bridged Local Area Networks (IEEE 802.1Q)

Unlike ISL, which uses an external tagging process and encapsulates a frame with a new ISL encapsulation, 802.1Q uses an internal tagging process by modifying the existing internal Ethernet frame. To access both links and trunk links, the frame looks as if it is just a standard Ethernet frame because it is not encapsulated with VLAN information. The VLAN information is added to a field within the frame itself.

Like ISL, the purpose of 802.1Q is to carry the traffic of more than one subnet down a single cable. 802.1Q tags the frame in a standard VLAN format, which allows for the VLAN implementations of multiple vendors. The standard tag allows for an open architecture and standard services for VLANs and a standard for protocols in the provision of these services. Because adding VLAN information to a frame affects the frame length, two committees were created to deal with this issue: 802.3ac and 802.1Q.

The VLAN frame format defined in both the 802.1Q and 802.3ac is a 4-byte field that is inserted between the original Ethernet frame Source address field and the Type or Length field. The CRC of the frame must be recomputed whenever the VLAN information is inserted or removed from the frame. The Ethernet frame size can now be up to 1522 bytes if a tag is inserted.

The VLAN Tag Protocol Identifier (TPID) is globally assigned and uses an EtherType field value of 0x81-00. The Tag Control Information (TCI) is a 16-bit value and has three fields contained within:

**User Priority** A 3-bit field used to assign up to eight layers of priority. The highest priority is 0, and the lowest is 7 (specified in 802.1Q).

**Canonical Format Indicator (CFI)** A 1-bit field that is always a 0 if running an 802.3 frame. This field was originally designed to be used for Token Ring VLANs, but it was never implemented except for some proprietary Token Ring LANs.

**VLAN ID (VID)** The actual VLAN number that the frame is assigned upon entering the switch (12 bits). The reserved VLAN IDs are as follows:

**0x0-00** Null, or no VLAN ID, which is used when only priority information is sent

**0x0-01** Default VLAN value of all switches

**0x-F-FF** Reserved

Because Ethernet frames can not exceed 1518 bytes, and ISL and 802.1Q frames can exceed 1518 bytes, the switch might record the frame as a baby giant frame.

# Trunking

Trunk links are point-to-point, 100Mbps or 1000Mbps links between two switches, between a switch and a router, or between a switch and a server. Trunk links carry the traffic of multiple VLANs, from 1 to 1005 at a time. You can not run trunk links on 10Mbps links.

Cisco switches use the Dynamic Trunking Protocol (DTP) to manage trunk negation in the Catalyst switch engine software release 4.2 or later, using either ISL or 802.1Q. DTP is a point-to-point protocol and was created to send trunk information across 802.1Q trunks. Dynamic ISL (DISL) was used to support trunk negation on ISL links only before DTP was released in software release 4.1; and before DISL, auto-negotiation of trunk links was not allowed.

A *trunk* is a port that supports multiple VLANs, but before it became a trunk, it was the member of a single VLAN. The VLAN it is a member of when it becomes a trunk is called a native VLAN. If the port were to lose the trunking ability, it would revert to membership in its native VLAN.

## Configuring Trunk Ports

This section shows you how to configure trunk links on the 4000 series and the 2950/3550 series IOS-based switches.

### 4000 Switch

To configure a trunk on a 4000 series switch, use the `set trunk` command, and on the IOS-based switch, use the `trunk on` command:

```
Terry_4000> (enable) set trunk 2/12 ?
Usage: set trunk <mod_num/port_num>
[on|off|desirable|auto|nonegotiate] [vlans] [trunk_type]
(vlans = 1..1005 An example of vlans is 2-10,1005)
       (trunk_type = isl,dot1q,dot10,lane,negotiate)

Terry_4000> (enable) set trunk 2/12 on isl
Port(s) 2/12 trunk mode set to on.
Port(s) 2/12 trunk type set to isl.
Terry_4000> (enable) 2003 Mar 21 06:31:54
%DTP-5-TRUNKPORTON:Port 2/12 has become isl trunk
```

Port 2/12 has become a trunk port that uses ISL encapsulation. Notice that we did not specify the VLANs to trunk. By default, all VLANs would be trunked. Take a look at a configuration in which we specified the VLANs to use:

```
Terry_4000> (enable) set trunk 2/12 on 1-5 isl
Adding vlans 1-5 to allowed list.
Please use the 'clear trunk' command to remove
vlans from allowed list.
Port(s) 2/12 allowed vlans modified to 1-1005.
Port(s) 2/12 trunk mode set to on.
Port(s) 2/12 trunk type set to isl.
```

Notice that, even though we told the switch to use VLANs 1–5, it added 1–1005 by default. To remove VLANs from a trunk port, use the `clear vlan` command. We'll do that in a minute.

We need to explain the different options for turning up a trunk port:

**on** The switch port is a permanent trunk port regardless of the other end. If you use the `on` state, you must specify the frame tagging method because it will not negotiate with the other end.

**off** The port becomes a permanent non-trunk link.

**desirable** The port you want to trunk becomes a trunk port only if the neighbor port is a trunk port set to `on`, `desirable`, or `auto`.

**auto** The port wants to become a trunk port but becomes a trunk only if the neighbor port asked the port to be a trunk. This is the default for all ports. However, because `auto` switch ports will never ask (they only respond to trunk requests), two ports will never become a trunk if they are both set to `auto`.

**nonegotiate** Makes a port a permanent trunk port, but because the port does not use DTP frames for communication, there is no negotiation. If you're having DTP problems with a switch port connected to a non-switch device, then use the `nonegotiate` command when using the `set trunk` command. This enables the port to be trunked, but you won't be sent any DTP frames.

Be careful when using the `nonegotiate` option. It is not unusual to set up switches initially with `auto` or `desirable` trunks and then lock them down with `on`, after the switch-fabric has settled down. If two trunk ports are configured with `auto` or `desirable`, they need to receive the negotiate packets to tell that there is another trunk-capable device on the other side. If two trunk ports are both set to `desirable` but `nonegotiate`, no trunk will come up.

## 2950 and 3550 Series

The 2950 switches support the same options but with different commands, as shown next. The 2950 series supports only IEEE 802.1Q VLANs, whereas the 3550 support ISL as well.

```
Terry_2950(config-if)#switchport trunk ?
  allowed  Set allowed VLAN characteristics when interface is in trunking mode
  native   Set trunking native characteristics when interface is in trunking
           mode
  pruning  Set pruning VLAN characteristics when interface is in trunking mode

Terry_2950(config-if)#switchport mode ?
  access   Set trunking mode to ACCESS unconditionally
  dynamic  Set trunking mode to dynamically negotiate access or trunk mode
  trunk    Set trunking mode to TRUNK unconditionally
```

```
Terry_2950(config-if)#switchport mode dynamic ?
  auto       Set trunking mode dynamic negotiation parameter to AUTO
  desirable  Set trunking mode dynamic negotiation parameter to DESIRABLE

Terry_2950(config-if)#switchport mode dynamic auto
Terry_2950(config-if)#^Z
Terry_2950#
```

## Clearing VLANs from Trunk Links

As demonstrated in the preceding sections, all VLANs are configured on a trunk link unless cleared by an administrator. If you do not want a trunk link to carry VLAN information because you want to stop broadcasts on a certain VLAN from traversing the trunk link, or because you want to stop topology change information from being sent across a link where a VLAN is not supported, use the `clear trunk` command.

This section shows you how to clear VLANs from trunk links on both the 4000 and IOS-based series of switches.

### 4000 Series

The command to clear a VLAN from a trunk link is `clear trunk` *`slot/port vlans`*. Here is an example:

```
Terry_4000> (enable) clear trunk 2/12 5-1005
Removing Vlan(s) 5-1005 from allowed list.
Port 1/2 allowed vlans modified to 1-4
```

### 2950 and 3550 Series Switches

The command `switchport trunk allowed vlan remove` *`vlan-list`* is used to limit which VLANs can use a particular trunk:

```
Terry_2950(config)# interface fa 0/10
Terry_2950(config-if)# switchport trunk allowed vlan remove 2-10,12,15
```

Use a hyphen to show a contiguous range of VLANs that are to be excluded and use a comma to separate VLANs that are not contiguous. Do not leave spaces. From the configuration, you can see that the specified VLANs have been removed from the supported list.

```
Terry_2950#show run
Building configuration...
version 12.1

[output cut]
```

```
interface FastEthernet0/10
 switchport trunk allowed vlan 1,11,13,14,16-1005
 switchport mode trunk
 no ip address
```

## Verifying Trunk Links

On the 4000 series, you can verify your trunk ports, using the `show trunk` command. If you have more than one port trunking and want to see statistics on only one trunk port, you can use the `show trunk` *`port_number`* command:

```
Terry_4000> (enable) show trunk 2/12
Port      Mode         Encapsulation  Status        Native vlan
--------  -----------  -------------  ------------  -----------
 2/12     on           isl            trunking      1

Port      Vlans allowed on trunk
--------  ---------------------------------------------------------
 2/12     1-4

Port      Vlans allowed and active in management domain
--------  ---------------------------------------------------------
 2/12     1

Port      Vlans in spanning tree forwarding state and not pruned
--------  ---------------------------------------------------------
 2/12     1
Terry_4000> (enable)
```

The 2950/3550 series of Catalyst switches continue to do it differently than the 4000. To view the trunk status of a port on one of these switches, the command `show interface` *`interface_id`* `switchport` needs to be used:

```
Terry_2950#show interface fa0/10 switchport
Name: Fa0/10
Switchport: Enabled
Administrative Mode: trunk
Operational Mode: down
Administrative Trunking Encapsulation: dot1q
Negotiation of Trunking: On
```

```
Access Mode VLAN: 1 (default)
Trunking Native Mode VLAN: 1 (default)
Administrative private-vlan host-association: none
Administrative private-vlan mapping: none
Operational private-vlan: none
Trunking VLANs Enabled: 1,11,13,14,16-1005
Pruning VLANs Enabled: 2-1001

Protected: false

Voice VLAN: none (Inactive)
Appliance trust: none
Terry_2950#
```

A VLAN that is enabled on the switch is one that the switch has learned exists in the switch-fabric of the LAN. Somewhere out there, a device needs that particular VLAN, or it might be configured for future use. An active VLAN is a VLAN in which one or more ports on this switch are members.

# Using VLAN Trunk Protocol (VTP)

VLAN Trunk Protocol (VTP) was created by Cisco to manage all the configured VLANs across a switched internetwork and to maintain consistency throughout the network. VTP enables an administrator to add, delete, and rename VLANs. These changes are then propagated to all switches.

VTP provides the following benefits to a switched network:

- Consistent configuration of global VLANs across all switches in the network
- Enabling VLANs to be trunked over mixed networks—for example, Ethernet to ATM LANE or FDDI
- Accurate tracking and monitoring of VLANs
- Dynamic reporting when VLANs are added to all switches
- Plug-and-play VLAN adding to the switched network

To enable VTP to manage your VLANs across the network, you must first create a VTP server. All servers that need to share VLAN information must use the same domain name, and a switch can be in only one domain at a time. This means that a switch can share VTP domain information only with switches configured in the same VTP domain.

A VTP domain can be used if you have more than one switch connected in a network. If all switches in your network are in only one VLAN, then VTP doesn't need to be used. VTP information is sent between switches via a trunk port between the switches.

Switches advertise VTP management domain information, such as the name, as well as a configuration revision number and all known VLANs with any specific parameters.

You can configure switches to receive and forward VTP information through trunk ports but not process information updates nor update their VTP database. This is called VTP transparent mode.

You can set up a VTP domain with security by adding passwords, but remember that every switch must be set up with the same password, which might be difficult. However, if you are having problems with users adding switches to your VTP domain, then a password can be used.

Switches detect the additional VLANs within a VTP advertisement and then prepare to receive information on their trunk ports with the newly defined VLAN in tow. The information would be VLAN ID, 802.10 SAID fields, or LANE information. Updates are sent out as revision numbers that are notification +1. Anytime a switch sees a higher revision number, it knows the information it receives is more current and will overwrite the current database with the new one.

Do you remember the `clear config all` command we talked about in Chapter 2, "Connecting the Switch Block"? Well, guess what? It really doesn't "clear all" after all. It seems that VTP has its own NVRAM, which means that VTP information as well as the revision number would still be present if you perform a `clear config all`. You can clear the revision number by power-cycling the switch.

**Real World Scenario**

**The Threat of High Revision Numbers**

Many organizations have discovered the need for physical security when a device with only VLAN 1 but a high configuration revision number is added to the network. If a switch is a part of a test lab and then needs to be placed into production, it is best to clear everything and then power-cycle it. There have been instances of wiped switches erasing the VLAN setup of large organizations because the new device had a higher configuration revision number but had only VLAN 1. If a port belongs to a VLAN and that VLAN is removed, the port shuts down until the VLAN exists again. Adding the VLANs back and propagating them is a snap. The hassle and stress occur with discovering the problem. Using a VTP password is encouraged to prevent people from accidentally causing problems.

## VTP Modes of Operation

There are three modes of operation within a VTP domain: server, client, and transparent. Figure 3.4 shows the three *VTP modes*.

**FIGURE 3.4** VTP modes

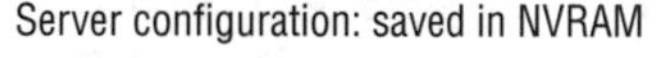


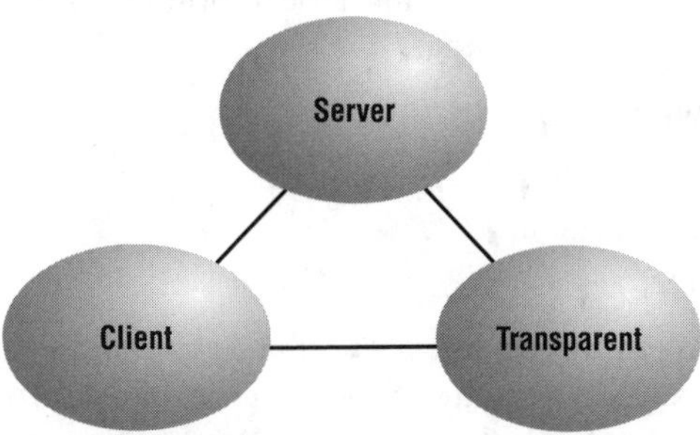


Client configuration: not saved in NVRAM

Transparent configuration: saved in NVRAM

## Server

VTP server mode is the default for all Catalyst switches. You need at least one server in your VTP domain to propagate VLAN information throughout the domain. The following must be completed within server mode:

- Create, add, or delete VLANs on a VTP domain.
- Change VTP information. Any change made to a switch in server mode is advertised to the entire VTP domain.

Global VLANs must be configured on a server. The server adds the VLANs to the switch configuration, so every time the switch boots up, the VLAN knowledge is propagated.

## Client

VTP clients receive information from VTP servers and send and receive updates, but they can not make any changes to the VTP configuration as long as they are clients. No ports on a client switch can be added to a new VLAN before the VTP server notifies the client switch about the new VLAN. If you want a switch to become a server, first make it a client so that it receives all the correct VLAN information and then change it to a server. No global VTP information is kept if the switch loses power.

## Transparent

VTP transparent switches do not participate in the VTP domain, but they still receive and forward VTP advertisements through the configured trunk links. However, for a transparent switch to advertise the VLAN information out the configured trunk links, VTP version 2 must be used. If not, the switch does not forward anything. VTP transparent switches can add and delete VLANs because they keep their own database and do not share it with other switches. Transparent switches are considered locally significant.

## VTP Advertisements

After the different types of VTP switches are defined, the switches can start advertising VTP information between them. VTP switches advertise information they know about only on their trunk ports. They advertise the following:

- Management domain name
- Configuration revision number
- VLANs the switch knows about
- Parameters for each VLAN

The switches use multicast MAC addresses so all neighbor devices receive the frames. A VTP server creates new VLANs, and that information is propagated through the VTP domain.

Figure 3.5 shows the three VTP advertisements: client, summary, and subset.

**FIGURE 3.5** VTP advertisement content

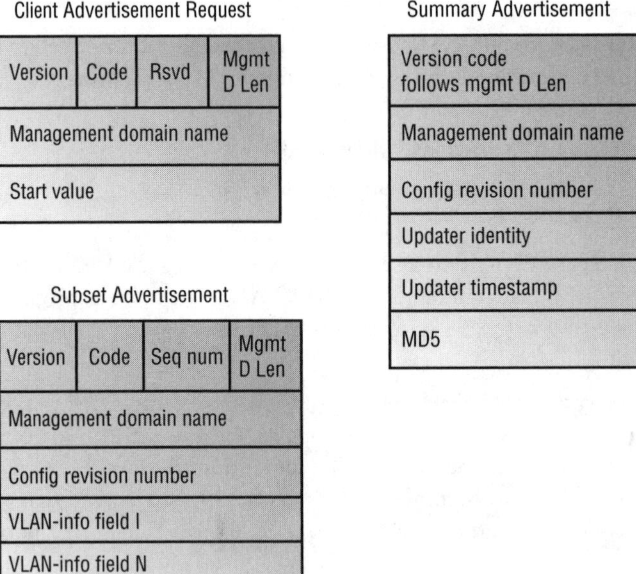


The three types of messages are as follows:

**Client requests** Clients can send requests for VLAN information to a server. Servers respond with both summary and subset advertisements.

**Summary** These advertisements are sent out every 300 seconds on VLAN 1 and every time a change occurs.

**Subset** These advertisements are VLAN specific and contain details about each VLAN.

The summary advertisements can contain the following information:

**Management domain name** The switch that receives this advertisement must have the name that is in this field or the update is ignored.

**Configuration revision number** Receiving switches use this to identify whether the update is newer than the one they have in their database.

**Updater identity** The name of the switch from which the update is sent.

**Updater timestamp** Might or might not be used.

**MD5Digest** The key sent with the update when a password is assigned to the domain. If the key doesn't match, the update is ignored.

## Subset Advertisements

The subset advertisements contain specific information about a VLAN. After an administrator adds, deletes, or renames a VLAN, the switches are notified that they are about to receive a VLAN update on their trunk links via the VLAN-info field 1. Figure 3.6 shows the VTP subset advertisement inside this field.

**FIGURE 3.6** Subset advertisement

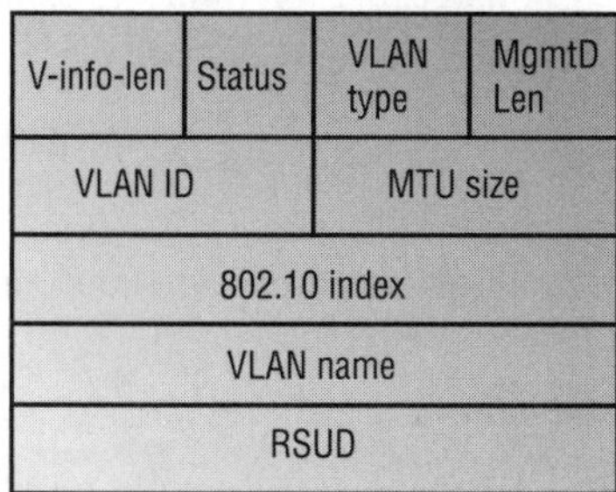


The following list includes some of the information that is advertised and distributed in the VLAN-info field 1:

**VLAN ID** Either ISL or 802.1Q

**802.10** SAID field that identifies the VLAN ID in FDDI

**VTP** VTP domain name and revision number

**MTU** Maximum transmission size for each VLAN

## Configuration Revision Number

The revision number is the most important piece in the VTP advertisement. Figure 3.7 shows an example of how a revision number is used in an advertisement.

**FIGURE 3.7** VTP revision number

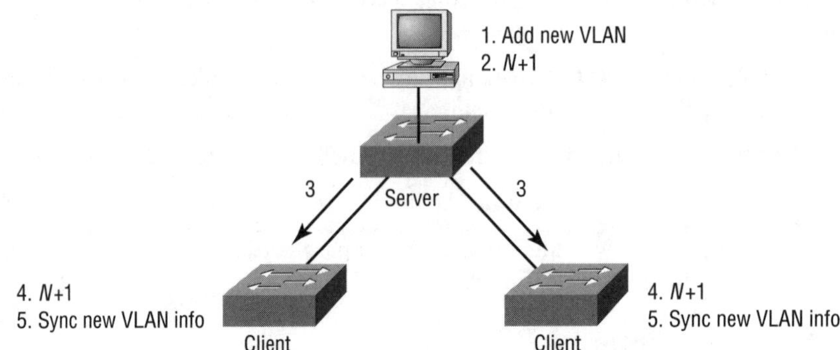


Figure 3.7 shows a configuration revision number as N. As a database is modified, the VTP server increments the revision number by 1. The VTP server then advertises the database with the new configuration revision number.

When a switch receives an advertisement that has a higher revision number, then the switch overwrites the database in NVRAM with the new database being advertised.

# Configuring VTP

There are several options that you need to be aware of before attempting to configure the VTP domain:

1. Consider the version number of the VTP you will run.
2. Decide if the switch is going to be a member of an already existing domain or if you are creating a new one. To add it to an existing domain, find the domain name and password, if used.
3. Choose the VTP mode for each switch in the internetwork.

After everything is configured, the new setup should be verified to ensure that the connections work properly.

## Configuring the VTP Version

There are two versions of VTP that are configurable on Cisco switches. Version 1 is the default VTP version on all switches and is typically used. No VTP version configuration is needed if you will be running version 1. Version 1 and version 2 are not compatible, so it is an all-or-nothing configuration for your switches. However, if all your switches are VTP version 2 compatible, changing one switch changes all of them. Be careful if you are not sure whether all your switches are version 2 compatible.

You would configure version 2 for the following reasons:

**Token Ring VLAN support** To run Token Ring, you must run version 2 of the VTP protocol. This means that all switches must be capable of running version 2.

**TLV support** Unrecognized type-length-value (TLV) support. If a VTP advertisement is received and has an unrecognized type-length-value, the version 2 VTP switches will still propagate the changes through their trunk links.

**Transparent mode** Switches can run in transparent mode, which means that they only forward messages and advertisements, not add them to their own database. In version 1, the switch checks the domain name and version before forwarding, but in version 2, the switches forward VTP messages without checking the version.

**Consistency checks** Consistency checks are run when an administrator enters new information in the switches, either with the CLI or other management software. If information is received by an advertisement or read from NVRAM, a consistency check is not run. A switch checks the digest on a VTP message, and if it is correct, no consistency check is made.

To configure VTP version 2 on a 4000 series, use the `set vtp v2 enable` command:

```
Terry_4000> (enable) set vtp v2 enable
This command will enable the version 2 function
in the entire management domain.
All devices in the management domain should
be version2-capable before enabling.
Do you want to continue (y/n) [n]? y
VTP domain  modified
Terry_4000> (enable)
```

The IOS-based switches once again demand that you access the VLAN database in order to configure VTP. Both versions are supported, as shown next:

```
Terry_2950#vlan database
Terry_2950(vlan)#?
VLAN database editing buffer manipulation commands:
  abort  Exit mode without applying the changes
  apply  Apply current changes and bump revision number
  exit   Apply changes, bump revision number, and exit mode
  no     Negate a command or set its defaults
  reset  Abandon current changes and reread current database
  show   Show database information
  vlan   Add, delete, or modify values associated with a single VLAN
  vtp    Perform VTP administrative functions.
```

```
Terry_2950(vlan)#vtp ?
  client       Set the device to client mode.
  domain       Set the name of the VTP administrative domain.
  password     Set the password for the VTP administrative domain.
  pruning      Set the administrative domain to permit pruning.
  server       Set the device to server mode.
  transparent  Set the device to transparent mode.
  v2-mode      Set the administrative domain to V2 mode.
```

## Configuring the Domain

After you decide which version to run, set the VTP domain name and password on the first switch. The VTP name can be up to 32 characters long. On both the 4000 and the IOS-based switches, you can set the VTP domain password. The password is a minimum of 8 characters and a maximum of 64 on the 4000, and although truncated to 64 characters on the IOS-based switches, it has no minimum value.

```
Terry_4000> (enable) set vtp domain ?
Usage: set vtp [domain <name>] [mode <mode>]
[passwd <passwd>]
[pruning <enable|disable>]
[v2 <enable|disable>
       (mode = client|server|transparent
        Use passwd '0' to clear vtp password)
Usage: set vtp pruneeligible <vlans>
       (vlans = 2..1000
        An example of vlans is 2-10,1000)
Terry_4000> (enable) set vtp domain Globalnet
VTP domain Globalnet modified
Terry_4000> (enable)

Terry_2950(vlan)#vtp password ?
  WORD  The ascii password for the VTP administrative domain.

Terry_2950(vlan)#vtp password globalnet
Setting device VLAN database password to globalnet.
Terry_2950(vlan)#
```

## Configuring the VTP Mode

Create your first switch as a server, and then create the connected switches as clients, or whatever you decided to configure them as. You don't have to do this as a separate command as we did; you can configure the VTP information in one line, including passwords, modes, and versions:

```
Terry_4000> (enable) set vtp domain
Usage: set vtp [domain <name>] [mode <mode>]
[passwd <passwd>]pruning <enable|disable>]
[v2 <enable|disable>
(mode = client|server|transparent
        Use passwd '0' to clear vtp password)
Usage: set vtp pruneeligible <vlans>
       (vlans = 2..1000
        An example of vlans is 2-10,1000)
Terry_4000> (enable) set vtp domain Globalnet mode server
VTP domain Globalnet modified
```

On the 2950 and 3550 switches, the commands are as follows:

```
Terry_2950#conf t
Enter configuration commands, one per line.  End with CNTL/Z.
Terry_2950(config)#vtp ?
  domain     Set the name of the VTP administrative domain.
  file       Configure IFS filesystem file where VTP configuration is stored.
  interface  Configure interface as the preferred source for the VTP IP updater
             address.
  mode       Configure VTP device mode.
  password   Set the password for the VTP administrative domain.
  pruning    Set the adminstrative domain to permit pruning.
  version    Set the adminstrative domain to VTP version.

Terry_2950(config)#vtp mode ?
  client       Set the device to client mode.
  server       Set the device to server mode.
  transparent  Set the device to transparent mode.
```

## Verify the VTP Configuration

You can verify the VTP domain information by using the commands `show vtp domain` and `show vtp statistics`.

The show vtp domain command shows you the domain name, mode, and pruning information:

```
Terry_4000> (enable) show vtp domain
Domain Name                  Domain Index VTP Version Local Mode  Password
--------------------- ------------ ----------- ----------------------
Globalnet        1             2           server
Vlan-count Max-vlan-storage Config Revision Notifications
---------- ---------------- --------------- -------------------------
5          1023             1               disabled

Last Updater    V2 Mode  Pruning  PruneEligible on Vlans
--------------- -------- -------- -----------------------------------
172.16.10.14    disabled disabled 2-1000
Terry_4000> (enable)
```

### 4000 Series

The show vtp statistics command shows a summary of VTP advertisement messages sent and received. It also shows configuration errors if detected:

```
Terry_4000> (enable) show vtp statistics
VTP statistics:
summary advts received         0
subset  advts received         0
request advts received         0
summary advts transmitted      5
subset  advts transmitted      2
request advts transmitted      0
No of config revision errors   0
No of config digest errors     0
VTP pruning statistics:
Trunk     Join Transmitted  Join Received  Summary advts received from
                                           non-pruning-capable device
--------  ----------------  -------------  ---------------------------
 2/12     0                 0              0
Terry_4000> (enable)
```

### 2950 and 3550 Series Switches

On the IOS-based switches, you have to use the show vtp counters command to achieve the same result:

```
Terry_2950#show vtp counters
VTP statistics:
```

```
Summary advertisements received     : 0
Subset advertisements received      : 0
Request advertisements received     : 0
Summary advertisements transmitted : 0
Subset advertisements transmitted  : 0
Request advertisements transmitted : 0
Number of config revision errors   : 0
Number of config digest errors     : 0
Number of V1 summary errors        : 0

VTP pruning statistics:

Trunk            Join Transmitted Join Received    Summary advts received from
                                                   non-pruning-capable device
---------------- ---------------- ---------------- --------------------
```

## Adding to a VTP Domain

You need to be careful when adding a new switch into an existing domain. If a switch is inserted into the domain and has incorrect VLAN information, the result could be a VTP database propagated throughout the internetwork with false information.

Before inserting a switch, make sure that you follow these three steps:

1. Perform a `clear config all` to remove any existing VLAN configuration on a set-based switch. On the IOS-based switches, you must ensure that the new switch has no VTP configuration. If it has, you should erase the startup-config (after saving it to a TFTP server or as a text file).
2. Power-cycle the switch to clear the VTP NVRAM.
3. Configure the switch to perform the mode of VTP that it will participate in. Cisco's rule of thumb is that you create several VTP servers in the domain, with all the other switches set to client mode.

## VTP Pruning

To preserve bandwidth, you can configure the VTP to reduce the number of broadcasts, multicasts, and other unicast packets. This is called *VTP pruning*. VTP restricts broadcasts to only trunk links that must have the information. If a trunk link does not need the broadcasts, the information is not sent. VTP pruning is disabled by default on all switches.

Figure 3.8 shows that if a switch does not have any ports configured for VLAN 5 and a broadcast is sent throughout VLAN 5, the broadcast would not traverse the trunk link going to the switch without any VLAN 5 members.

Enabling pruning on a VTP server enables pruning for the entire domain, and by default, VLANs 2 through 1005 are eligible for pruning. VLAN 1 can never prune.

**FIGURE 3.8** VTP pruning

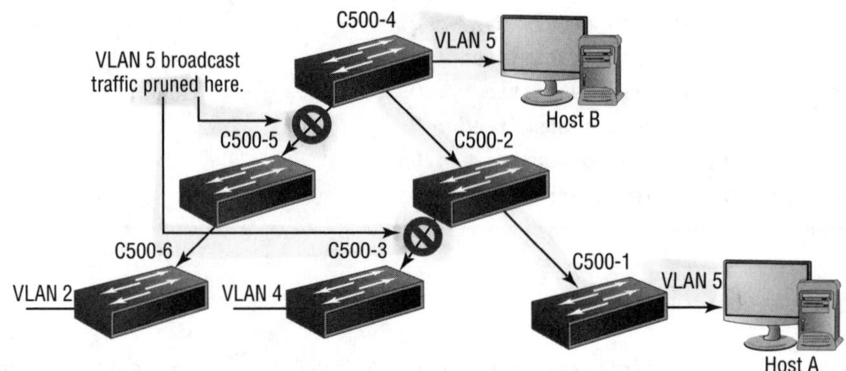


Use the following command to set VLANs to be eligible for pruning:

```
Terry_4000> (enable) set vtp pruneeligible ?
Usage: set vtp [domain <name>] [mode <mode>]
[passwd <passwd>] [pruning <enable|disable>]
[v2 <enable|disable> (mode = client|server|transparent
        Use passwd '0' to clear vtp password)
Usage: set vtp pruneeligible <vlans>
       (vlans = 2..1000
        An example of vlans is 2-10,1000)
Terry_4000> (enable) set vtp pruneeligible 2
Vlans 2-1000 eligible for pruning on this device.
VTP domain Globalnet modified.
```

Notice once again that when you enable a VLAN for pruning, by default, it configures all the VLANs. Use the following command to clear the unwanted VLANs:

```
Terry_4000> (enable) clear vtp pruneeligible 3-1005
Vlans 1,3-1005 will not be pruned on this device.
VTP domain Globalnet modified.
Terry_4000> (enable)
```

To verify the pruned state of a trunk port, use the `show trunk` command.

To set pruning on the 2950 and 3550, head into VLAN database mode. The command `vtp pruning` enables the pruning process while the command `switchport trunk pruning vlan remove` *`vlan-id`* removes VLANs from the list of pruning-eligible VLANs:

```
Terry_2950#vlan database
```

```
Terry_2950(vlan)#vtp ?
  client       Set the device to client mode.
  domain       Set the name of the VTP administrative domain.
  password     Set the password for the VTP administrative domain.
  pruning      Set the administrative domain to permit pruning.
  server       Set the device to server mode.
  transparent  Set the device to transparent mode.
  v2-mode      Set the administrative domain to V2 mode.

Terry_2950(vlan)#vtp pruning ?
  v2-mode  Set the administrative domain to V2 mode.
  <cr>

Terry_2950(vlan)#vtp pruning
Pruning switched ON
Terry_2950(vlan)#
Terry_2950#

Terry_2950#configure terminal
Terry_2950 (config)#interface fa 0/10
Terry_2950 (config-if)#switchport trunk pruning vlan remove 2-5,10
```

# Auxiliary VLANs

IP telephony involves the use of an IP-based network to replace the legacy telephony services provided by PBX (private branch exchange) systems. This involves the use of an IP telephone, a call manager, and gateway services for the access to the main telephone network. The call manager will probably be located in a network server, and many of the gateway functions will be provided inside the networking equipment. Cisco's 6500 series switches support many gateway functions.

IP packets traveling to and from the PC and to and from the phone share the same physical link to the same port of the switch. If the switch is already configured on a subnet-per-VLAN basis, this can cause problems if insufficient IP addresses are available.

One way of meeting the demands of mixed services, such as voice and data, is to allocate a VLAN specifically for the purpose of carrying voice traffic. These special VLANs are known as *auxiliary VLANs*. One advantage of auxiliary VLANs is that they can be used to ensure that data traveling across the shared link does not reduce the quality of service demanded by the IP phones. Another is that they allow the creation of a new VLAN with a new range of IP addresses just for the phones.

The IEEE 802.1p protocol is used to define quality of service at the MAC layer. Priorities are appended to the frame and these are regenerated at each layer 2 forwarding interface, based upon priorities established in the switches. This is covered in greater detail later in this book, but I just wanted to point out how QoS can be achieved with auxiliary VLANs.

# 802.1Q Tunneling

Modern networks are increasingly more complex, with new requirements being developed as new applications and ways of working appear. Sometimes there is a need for ISP customers to have their VLANs extended across the service provider network. The technique that supports this is called 802.1Q in Q, or more simply, 802.1Q tunneling. This is supported in the Catalyst 3550 series.

As you have read in this chapter, the 802.1Q protocol provides for a tag to be inserted inside the standard Ethernet frame carrying VLAN information. When 802.1Q tunneling is implemented, this happens twice. The first time, it is implemented by the customer, and the second time by the service provider.

At the tunnel boundary, the second tag, called the *metro tag*, is added, containing a VLAN ID unique to that customer. The frames are switched across the service provider network, and at the egress point, the metro tag is stripped and the exposed customer-specific 802.1Q frame is forwarded to the customer.

There are some restrictions to this technology, both in terms of the configuration options and the protocol operation. For example, these metro frames must be switched, not routed, and only layer 2 QoS is supported. Nonetheless, as more service providers offer switched networks across metropolitan areas, this is likely to become increasingly common.

# Summary

Broadcast domains exist as layer 2 switched networks, but can be broken up by creating virtual LANs. When you create VLANs, you are able to create smaller broadcast domains within a switch by assigning different ports in the switch to different subnetworks.

VLANs can be configured on both set-based and IOS-based switches, and it is still important to understand how to configure VLANs on both types as well as how to set the configuration of VLANs on individual interfaces.

Trunking enables you to send information about multiple VLANs down one link, in contrast to an access link that can send information about only one VLAN. Trunking is configured between switches, often between the access and distribution layer switches, but could be between any switches depending upon your particular topology. Trunking could be configured between a switch and a router, or a switch and a host, where special demands exist, such as the remote device needing to know about multiple VLANs.

VLAN Trunk Protocol (VTP) is used to maintain consistency of VLAN information across a domain. This doesn't really have much to do with trunking except that VTP information is only sent down trunk links. VTP is used to update all switches in the internetwork with VLAN information.

# Exam Essentials

**Understand what a trunk is.** A trunk is a link between a switch and another device that allows the traffic from multiple VLANs to cross it. Special trunk protocols are used to carry the additional information needed, which can not be incorporated into the standard Ethernet frame. Two protocols—the Cisco proprietary ISL and the standards-based IEEE 802.1Q—have been developed for this purpose. When a packet crosses a trunk, it retains any ISL or dot1q information detailing what VLAN the packet belongs to.

**Understand the difference between ISL and 802.1Q.** ISL is a Cisco proprietary VLAN format, whereas 802.1Q is a standard. Network cards are made to support both types, which enables PCs and servers to receive and send VLAN-specific traffic. The big difference between the two is that ISL encapsulates the original packet in a new 30-byte frame, whereas 802.1Q just inserts a 4-byte additional field into the existing Ethernet frame.

**Know the configuration differences between the different switches.** The 4000 series uses the standard `set` commands, whereas the 2950 and 3550 series use IOS commands. The IOS-based switches configure VLAN and VTP configurations in VLAN database configuration mode, but assign interfaces to VLANs in interface configuration mode. The 4000 makes no such distinctions.

**Understand when a VLAN should be used.** VLANs are used to separate broadcast traffic into different groupings. If a switch has ports 1–10 in VLAN 1 and ports 11–20 in VLAN 2, a packet arriving from a device connected to port 5 can't talk to a device connected to port 15 without some sort of routing engine participating. Know that VLANs can be used for security as well as to break up existing large broadcast domains.

**Understand what VTP is and how it is used.** VTP carries VLAN information between switches, which can be configured to be servers, clients, or transparent. VTP information is contained within a domain, and ensures that VLAN naming and numbering is consistent within a domain, as well as reducing configuration overhead.

# Key Terms

Before you take the exam, be sure you're familiar with the following terms:

access link

dynamic VLAN

end-to-end VLAN

flat network

frame tagging

local VLAN

static VLAN

switch-fabric

trunk link

VLAN database

VTP modes

VTP pruning

# Written Lab

Write the answers to the following questions:

1. What commands create VLAN 35 on a 4000 series switch named Sales using ports 5 through 9 on card 3?
2. What command sets the VTP domain name to Acme and the switch to a VTP client on a set-based switch?
3. What command would you use on a 2950 switch to see the configured VLANs?
4. What type of frame tagging places a VLAN identifier into the frame header?
5. What type of frame tagging encapsulates the frame with VLAN information?
6. What protocol handles the negotiation of trunk links?
7. How do you configure trunking on a set-based switch, port 1/1, using ISL tagging?
8. What command would you use to clear VLANs 10 through 14 from the trunk link 1/1 on a 4000 switch?
9. What command displays the VTP domain on an IOS-based switch?
10. If the VTP domain is already configured, how would you set a VTP password on an IOS-based switch to "cisco"?

# Review Questions

1. Which of the following is a true statement regarding VLANs?
   - **A.** You must have at least two VLANs defined in every Cisco switched network.
   - **B.** All VLANs are configured at the access layer and extend to the distribution layer.
   - **C.** VLANs should extend past the distribution switch on to the core.
   - **D.** VLANs should not extend past the distribution switch on to the core.
2. If you want to configure ports 3/1–12 to be part of VLAN 3, which command is valid on a set-based switch?
   - **A.** `console> (enable) set vlan 3 2/1, 2/2, 2/3, etc.`
   - **B.** `console> (config) vlan 3 set port  3/1-12`
   - **C.** `console> (enable) set vlan 3 3/1-12`
   - **D.** `console>  set vlan 3 3/1-12`
   - **E.** `console> vlan membership 3 3/1-12`
3. What are the two ways that an administrator can configure VLAN memberships? (Choose all that apply.)
   - **A.** DHCP server
   - **B.** Static
   - **C.** Dynamic
   - **D.** VTP database
4. How are local VLANs configured?
   - **A.** By geographic location
   - **B.** By function
   - **C.** By application
   - **D.** Doesn't matter
5. If you want to verify the VTP-configured information on an IOS-based switch, which of the following commands would you use?
   - **A.** `sh vtp status`
   - **B.** `sh domain`
   - **C.** `set vtp domain output`
   - **D.** `sho vtp info`

6. What size frames are possible with ISL and 802.1Q frames? (Choose all that apply.)
   - **A.** 1548 bytes
   - **B.** 1522 bytes
   - **C.** 4202 bytes
   - **D.** 8190 bytes

7. Which of the following is true regarding the Canonical Format Indicator (CFI)? (Choose all that apply.)
   - **A.** It is a 1-bit field that is always a 0 if running an 802.3 frame.
   - **B.** The CFI field was originally designed to be used for Token Ring VLANs, but it was never implemented except for some proprietary Token Ring LANs.
   - **C.** It is not used on any switch but the 4000 series.
   - **D.** It is used with FDDI trunk ports only.

8. Regarding 802.1Q, what is the TPID EtherType field always set to?
   - **A.** 17
   - **B.** 6
   - **C.** 0x81-00
   - **D.** 0x2102

9. How are dynamic VLANs configured?
   - **A.** Statically
   - **B.** By an administrator
   - **C.** By using a DHCP server
   - **D.** By using VLAN Management Policy Server

10. If you want to completely clear all configurations on an IOS-based switch, what two commands must you type in?
    - **A.** `clear config, reload`
    - **B.** `delete nvram, restart`
    - **C.** `delete vtp, delete nvram`
    - **D.** `erase start, reload`

11. What do VTP switches advertise on their trunk ports? (Choose all that apply.)
    - **A.** Management domain name
    - **B.** Configuration revision number
    - **C.** VLAN identifiers configured on Cisco routers
    - **D.** VLANs the switch knows about
    - **E.** Parameters for each VLAN
    - **F.** CDP information

12. Which of the following is true regarding VTP?
    A. VTP pruning is enabled by default on all switches.
    B. VTP pruning is disabled by default on all switches.
    C. You can run VTP pruning only on 4000 or higher switches.
    D. VTP pruning is configured on all switches by default if it is configured on just one switch.

13. Which of the following Cisco standards encapsulates a frame and even adds a new FCS field?
    A. ISL
    B. 802.1Q
    C. 802.3z
    D. 802.3u

14. What does setting the VTP mode to transparent accomplish?
    A. Transparent mode will only forward messages and advertisements, not add them to their own database.
    B. Transparent mode will forward messages and advertisements and add them to their own database.
    C. Transparent mode will not forward messages and advertisements.
    D. Transparent mode makes a switch dynamically secure.

15. Which of the following IEEE standards actually inserts a field into a frame to identify VLANs on a trunk link?
    A. ISL
    B. 802.3z
    C. 802.1Q
    D. 802.3u

16. How long a VTP domain name can there be on a 4000 series switch?
    A. The VTP name can be up to 23 characters.
    B. The VTP name can be up to 32 characters.
    C. The VTP name can be up to 48 characters.
    D. The VTP name can be up to 80 characters.

17. If you want to view the trunk status on port 24 of an IOS-based switch, which command would you use?
    A. `show switchport fa0/24`
    B. `show trunk interface fa0/24`
    C. `show trunk switchport fa0/24`
    D. `show trunk fa/24`
    E. `show interface fa0/24 switchport`

18. VTP provides which of the following benefits to a switched network? (Choose all that apply.)
    **A.** Multiple broadcast domains in VLAN 1
    **B.** Management of all switches and routers in an internetwork
    **C.** Consistent configuration of VLANs across all switches in the network
    **D.** Allowing VLANs to be trunked over mixed networks—for example, Ethernet to ATM LANE or FDDI
    **E.** Tracking and monitoring of VLANs accurately
    **F.** Dynamic reporting of added VLANs to all switches
    **G.** Plug-and-play VLAN adding
    **H.** Plug-and-play configuration

19. Which of the following is true regarding VTP?
    **A.** Changing the VTP version on one switch changes all switches in a domain.
    **B.** If you change the VTP version on one switch, you must change the version on all switches.
    **C.** VTP is on by default with a domain name of Cisco on all Cisco switches.
    **D.** All switches are VTP clients by default.

20. Which of the following is true regarding trunk links?
    **A.** They are configured by default on all switch ports.
    **B.** They work only with a type of Ethernet network and not with Token Ring, FDDI, or ATM.
    **C.** You can set trunk links on any 10Mbps, 100Mbps, and 1000Mbps ports.
    **D.** You must clear the unwanted VLANs by hand.

# Hands-On Lab

In this lab, you will continue to configure the network used in the hands-on lab in Chapter 2. This lab configures the network with VTP domain information and trunking. Figure 3.9 is a review of the lab we are configuring.

**FIGURE 3.9** Switched internetwork for hands-on lab

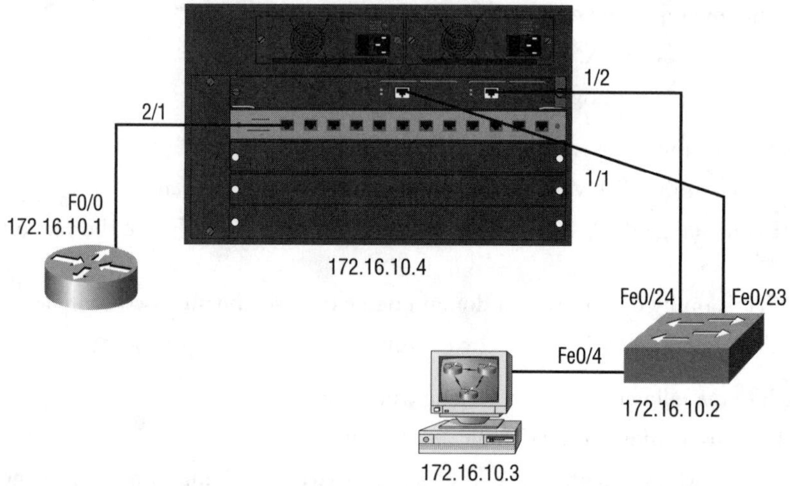


1. Start with the 4000 series switch and configure the VTP domain as globalnet:

   **set vtp domain globalnet**

2. The default VTP mode is server, which is what you want the 4000 series switch to be. The 2950 switch will be a VTP client. Create three VLANs on the 4000 series switch:

   - VLAN 1 is the default; it will be used for management.
   - VLAN 2 will be the Sales VLAN and will use IP network 172.16.20.0. Port 2 on card 2 will be used.
   - VLAN 3 will be the Mrkt VLAN and will use IP network 172.16.30.0. Ports 3 and 4 on card 2 will be used.
   - VLAN 4 will be the Accnt VLAN and will use IP network 172.16.40.0. Ports 5 and 6 on card 2 will be used.

   Here is the configuration:

   ```
   set vlan 2 name Sales
   set vlan 3 name Mrkt
   set vlan 4 name Accnt
   ```

```
set vlan 2 2/2
set vlan 3 2/3-4
set vlan 4 2/5-6
```

3. Type in the commands to verify the VLAN configuration and VTP configuration:

```
show vtp
show vlan
```

4. Because you want VLAN information to be propagated to the 2950 switch, a trunk link needs to be configured between both switches. Set the trunk link on port 1/1 and port 1/2 of the 4000 switch. These are your connections to the access layer switch (2950A). Remember that the 2950 switch can use only dot1q trunking, so the 4000 needs to be configured with the same:

```
set trunk 1/1 on dot1q
set trunk 1/2 on dot1q
```

5. Type the command to view the trunk link:

```
show trunk 1/1
show trunk 1/2
```

6. Connect to the 2950 switch and set the VTP domain name:

```
vlan database
vtp domain globalnet
```

7. Set the VTP mode to client:

```
vtp client
```

8. Before any VLAN information will be propagated through the internetwork, you need to make both interfaces f0/23 and f0/24 into trunk links:

```
Configure terminal
Interface f0/23
Switchport mode trunk
Interface f0/24
Switchport mode trunk
```

9. Verify that the trunk link is working:

```
show int fa0/23 tr
show int fa0/24 tr
```

10. Ping the 4000 series switch:

```
ping 172.16.10.4
```

11. Now verify that you have received VLAN information from the 4000 series switch:

```
show vlan
```

You should see all configured VLANs.

12. After you have the trunk link working and have received the VLAN information, you can assign VLANs to individual ports on the 2950. Assign ports 1 and 2 to VLAN 2, assign ports 3 and 4 to VLAN 3, and assign ports 5 and 6 to VLAN 4:

```
Configure terminal
Interface fa0/1
switchport access vlan 2
Interface fa0/2
switchport access vlan 2
Interface Fa0/3
switchport access vlan 3
Interface fa0/4
switchport access vlan 3
Interface fa0/5
switchport access vlan 4
Interface fa0/6
switchport access vlan 4
```

13. Verify the configuration:

```
show vlan
```

# Answers to Written Lab

1. `set vlan 35 name Sales, set vlan 35 3/5-9`
2. `set vtp domain Acme mode client`
3. `show vlan`
4. 802.1Q
5. ISL
6. Dynamic Trunk Protocol (DTP)
7. `set trunk 1/1 on isl`
8. `clear trunk 1/1 10-14`
9. `show vtp status`
10. `vtp password cisco`, in `vlan database` mode

# Answers to Review Questions

1. D. VLANs should not pass through the distribution layer. The distribution layer devices should route between VLANs.

2. C. The set-based switches can configure multiple ports to be part of a VLAN at the same time. The command is `set vlan` *`vlan# slot/ports`*.

3. B, C. Static VLANs are set port by port on each interface or port. Dynamic VLANs can be assigned to devices via a server.

4. A. Local VLANs are created by location—for example, an access closet.

5. A. The command `show vtp status` provides the switch's VTP mode and the domain name.

6. A, B. ISL encapsulates frames with another frame encapsulation type. This means that a data frame can extend past the regular frame size of 1518 bytes up to 1548 bytes, whereas 802.1Q frames can be up to 1522 bytes.

7. A, B. The CFI field is not used often, and only in proprietary Token Ring LANs. It will always be a 0 unless a programmer specifically programs it to be different.

8. C. The EtherType file is always a 0x81-00 when 802.1Q frame tagging is used.

9. D. A VLAN Management Policy Server (VMPS) must be configured with the hardware addresses of all devices on your internetwork. Then the server is allowed to hand out VLAN assignments configured by the administrator into the VMPS database.

10. D. Just as with routers, the command `erase startup-config` clears out the nvram files, and the `reload` command forces the switch to cycle and implement the startup-config, which is now empty.

11. A, B, D, E. VLAN Trunk Protocol is used to update switches within a domain with information about configured VLANs. This includes the management domain name and configuration revision number so that receiving switches know if new VLAN information (including configured parameters) has been added to the VTP database and all the VLANs the switch knows about.

12. B. VTP pruning stops VLAN information from traversing a trunk link if it would be discarded on the remote end because no VLANs are configured on the switch.

13. A. Inter-Switch Link (ISL) encapsulates a new header and trailer to an existing data frame.

14. A. VTP transparent switches do not update their VTP database with VLAN information received on trunk links. However, they will forward these updates.

15. C. 802.1Q does not encapsulate a data frame as ISL does. Instead, it puts a new field into the existing frame to identify the VLAN that the packet belongs to.

16. B. VTP domain names can be up to 32 characters and must be the same on all switches with which you want to share VLAN information.

17. E. The IOS-based switches use the `show interface` *`interface_number`* `switchport` to display trunk status.

**18.** B, C, D, E, F, G, H. VTP does not have anything to do with breaking up or configuring broadcast domains. All answers except A are correct.

**19.** A. If you change the VTP version on one switch, all other switches are changed automatically if they support the new version.

**20.** D. Trunk links, by default, are assigned to forward all VLANs. You must delete these by hand if you don't want all VLANs to be sent down a trunk link.

# Layer 2 Switching and the Spanning Tree Protocol (STP)

## THE CCNP EXAM TOPICS COVERED IN THIS CHAPTER INCLUDE THE FOLLOWING:

- ✓ **Understand the physical, data-link, and network layer technologies used in a multi-layer switched network**
- ✓ **Describe Spanning Tree (STP), and explain the operation of common and per-VLAN STP implementations**
- ✓ **Configure Spanning Tree in both Common Spanning Tree (CST) and per-VLAN modes**

In this chapter, we'll explore the three distinct functions of layer 2 switching: address filtering, forward/filter decision-making, and loop avoidance. We will probe the issue of loop avoidance in depth and discuss how the Spanning Tree Protocol (STP) works to stop network loops from occurring on your layer 2 network.

This chapter continues the discussion of layer 2 switching started in Chapter 1, "The Campus Network." We will consider the different modes of switching that may be employed, move on to see how network loops occur in a layer 2 network, and then provide an introduction to STP, including the different components of STP and how to configure STP on layer 2 switched networks. It is necessary for networking professionals to have a clear understanding of the STP, so by the end of this chapter, you will know how to use STP to stop network loops, broadcast storms, and multiple frame copies. In Chapter 5, "Using Spanning Tree with VLANs," we'll continue discussing STP and provide the more complex and advanced configurations used with it.

It is typical these days to create a network with redundant links; this provides consistent network availability when a network outage occurs on one link. STP provides the necessary loop-avoidance function, but there are several additional features that can be utilized. For example, it is possible to load-balance over the redundant links as well, and VLANs have a special part to play, so we will continue the discussion in Chapter 5.

# Layer 2 LAN Switching

You can think of layer 2 switches as bridges with more ports. Remember from Chapter 1 that layer 2 switching is hardware based, which means that it uses the Media Access Control (MAC) address from the hosts' network interface cards (NICs) to filter the network. You should also remember how switches use application-specific integrated circuits (ASICs) to build and maintain filter tables.

However, there are some differences between bridges and switches that you should be aware of. This section outlines those differences and then discusses the three functions of layer 2 switching.

## Comparing Bridges to Switches

The following list describes the differences between bridges and switches. Table 4.1 provides an overview of that comparison.

- Bridges are considered software based. Switches are hardware based because they use ASICs chips to help make filtering decisions.

- Bridges can have only one spanning-tree instance per bridge. Switches can have many. (Spanning tree is covered later in this chapter.)
- Bridges can have up to only 16 ports. A switch can have hundreds.

You probably won't go out and buy a bridge, but it's important to understand how bridges are designed and maintained because layer 2 switches function in a similar fashion.

**TABLE 4.1** Comparison of Bridges and Switches

| | Bridges | Switches |
|---|---|---|
| Filtering | Software based | Hardware based |
| Spanning tree numbers | One spanning tree instance | Many spanning tree instances |
| Ports | 16 ports maximum | Hundreds of ports available |

# Three Switch Functions at Layer 2

There are three distinct functions of layer 2 switching:

**Address learning** Layer 2 switches and bridges remember the source hardware address of each frame received on an interface and enter it into a MAC database.

**The forwarding and filtering decision** When a frame is received on an interface, the switch looks at the destination hardware address and looks up the exit interface in the MAC database.

**Loop avoidance** If multiple connections between switches are created for redundancy, network loops can occur. STP is used to stop network loops and allow redundancy.

These functions of the layer 2 switch—address learning, forward and filtering decisions, and loop avoidance—are discussed in detail next.

## Address Learning

The layer 2 switch is responsible for *address learning*. When a switch is powered on, the MAC filtering table is empty. When a device transmits and a frame is received on an interface, the switch takes the source address and places it in the MAC filter table. It remembers what interface the device is located on. The switch has no choice but to flood the network with this frame because it has no idea where the destination device is located.

If a device answers and sends a frame back, then the switch takes the source address from that frame, places the MAC address in the database, and associates this address with the interface on which the frame was received. Because the switch now has two MAC addresses in the filtering table, the devices can now make a point-to-point connection and the frames are forwarded only between the two devices. This is what makes layer 2 switches better than hubs. In a hub network, all frames are forwarded out all ports every time.

Figure 4.1 shows the procedures for building a MAC database.

**FIGURE 4.1** How switches learn hosts' locations

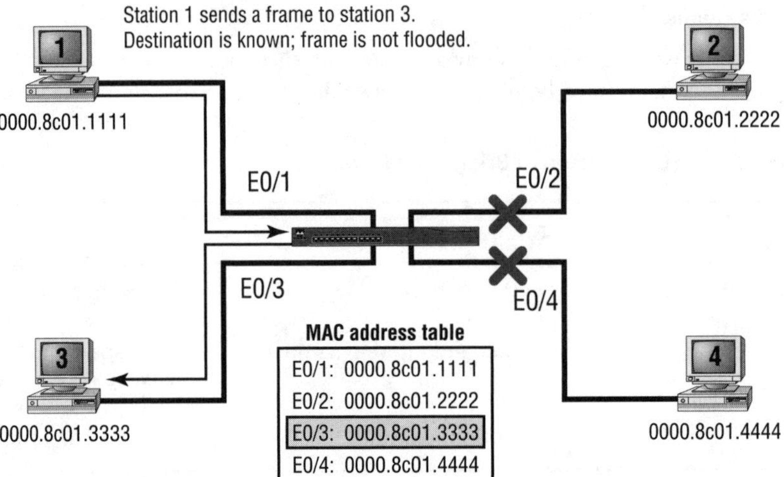


In the figure, four hosts are attached to a switch. The switch has nothing in the MAC address table when it is powered on. The figure shows the switch's MAC filter table after each device has communicated with the switch. The following steps show how the table is populated:

1. Station 1 sends a frame to station 3. Station 1 has a MAC address of 0000.8c01.1111. Station 3 has a MAC address of 0000.8c01.3333.
2. The switch receives the frame on Ethernet interface 0/1, examines the source and destination MAC addresses, and places the source address in the MAC address table.
3. Because the destination address is not in the MAC database, the frame is forwarded out of all interfaces.
4. Station 3 receives the frame and responds to station 1. The switch receives this frame on interface E0/3 and places the source hardware address in the MAC database.
5. Station 1 and station 3 can now make a point-to-point connection, and only the two devices will receive the frames. Stations 2 and 4 do not see the frames.

If the two devices do not communicate with the switch again within a certain time limit, the switch flushes the entries from the database to keep the database as current as possible.

## Forwarding/Filtering Decision

The layer 2 switch also uses the MAC filter table to both forward and filter frames received on the switch. This is called the *forwarding and filtering decision.* When a frame arrives at a switch interface, the destination hardware address is compared to the forward/filter MAC database. If the destination hardware address is known and listed in the database, the frame is sent out only on the correct exit interface. The switch does not transmit the frame out of any interface except for the destination interface, thus preserving bandwidth on the other network segments. This is called frame filtering.

If the destination hardware address is not listed in the MAC database, the frame is flooded out all active interfaces except the interface on which the frame was received. If a device answers, the MAC database is updated with the device location (interface).

In modern switches, the switching or bridging table is known as the CAM or TCM table. I will cover these in detail in Chapter 10, "Catalyst Switch Technologies." For the moment, please accept that these are just tables, optimized for pretty fast lookup.

### Broadcast and Multicast Frames

Remember, the layer 2 switches forward all broadcasts by default. The forwarding/filtering decision is a bit different because broadcast packets are designed to go to every device that is listening and multicasts are for every device listening for a particular type of packet. Whereas the MAC address of a given device is normally determined by the MAC address that is burned into the network card, broadcasts and multicasts need some way of targeting multiple devices.

A broadcast targets every device on the subnet by setting all the bits in the destination MAC address to 1. Thus, the 48-bit destination MAC address, which uses hexadecimal notation, looks like FFFF.FFFF.FFFF. Every device is trained to look for frames destined to its MAC address and frames destined to every MAC address. An example of a packet that needs to be addressed to every device that can hear is an ARP request.

A multicast is a slightly different animal in that it wants to go to every device that is participating in a certain process. If five routers are using the EIGRP routing protocol and one sends out an update, it sends the update to the multicast IP address 224.0.0.10. Each router is listening for any packet with that IP address as its destination, but devices don't look at the IP address when the frame is received—they look at the MAC address. There is a special format that MAC addresses follow when the packet is part of a multicast process. This process is covered in detail in Chapter 8, "Multicast Technologies."

When a switch receives these types of frames, the frames are then quickly flooded out of all active ports of the switch by default. To have broadcasts and multicasts forwarded out of only a limited number of administratively assigned ports, you create virtual LANs, which were discussed in Chapter 3, "VLANs, Trunks, and VTP."

## Loop Avoidance

Finally, the layer 2 switch is responsible for *loop avoidance*. It's a good idea to use redundant links between switches. They help stop complete network failures if one link fails. Even though redundant links are extremely helpful, they cause more problems than they solve. In this section, we'll discuss some of the most serious problems:

- Broadcast storms
- Multiple frame copies
- Multiple loops

### Broadcast Storms

If no loop avoidance schemes are put in place, the switches will flood broadcasts endlessly throughout the internetwork. This is sometimes referred to as a broadcast storm. Figure 4.2 shows how a broadcast might be propagated throughout the network.

### Multiple Frame Copies

Another problem is that a device can receive multiple copies of the same frame because the frame can arrive from different segments at the same time. Figure 4.3 shows how multiple frames can arrive from multiple segments simultaneously.

**FIGURE 4.2** Broadcast storms

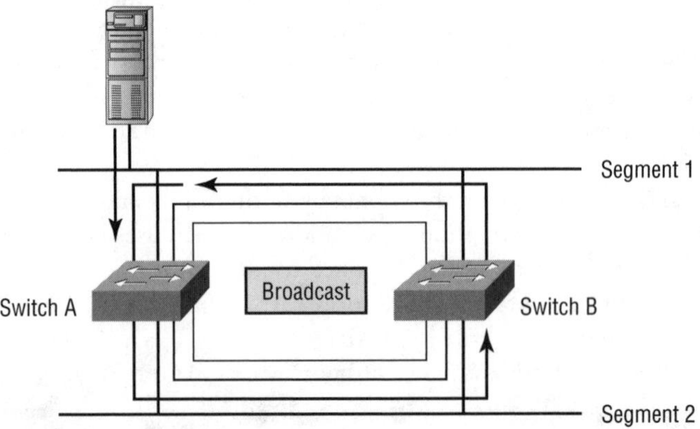


**FIGURE 4.3** Multiple frame copies

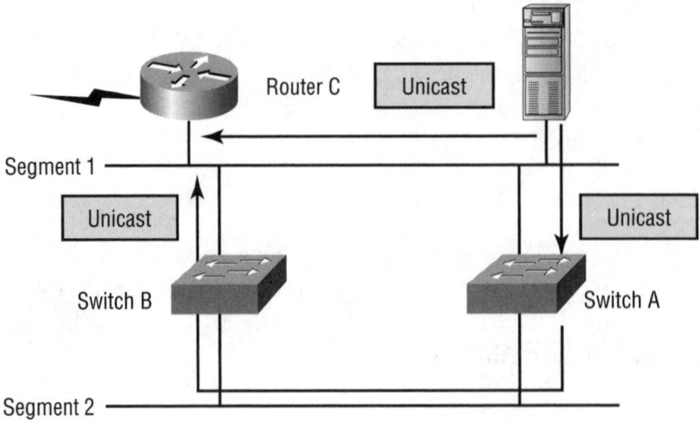

The MAC address filter table will be confused about where a device is located because the switch can receive the frame from more than one link. It is possible that the switch can't forward a frame because it is constantly updating the MAC filter table with source hardware address locations. This is called thrashing the MAC table.

### Multiple Loops

One of the biggest problems is multiple loops generating throughout an internetwork. This means that loops can occur within other loops. If a broadcast storm were to then occur, the network would not be able to perform packet switching.

To solve these three problems, the Spanning Tree Protocol was developed.

## Spanning Tree Operation

In layer 3 devices, which are typically routers, the routing protocols are responsible for making sure routing loops do not occur in the network. What is used to make sure network loops do not occur in layer 2 switched networks? That is the job of the *Spanning Tree Protocol (STP)*.

Digital Equipment Corporation (DEC), which was purchased by Compaq before the merger with Hewlett-Packard, was the original creator of STP. Actually, Radia Perlman is credited with the main development of STP and should get the credit. The IEEE created its version of STP, called 802.1D, using the DEC version as the basis. By default, all Cisco switches run the IEEE 802.1D version of STP, which is not compatible with the DEC version.

The big difference between the two types of STP from an administrative point of view is the range of values that can be set for the priority. A bridge using DEC STP can be set as high as 255, and a switch using IEEE STP can be set as high as 65535. If the two could be used together, a bridge set as a very low priority on DEC would stand a good chance of becoming the root in an IEEE STP network.

The big picture is that STP stops network loops from occurring on your layer 2 network (bridges or switches). STP is constantly monitoring the network to find all links and to make sure loops do not occur by shutting down redundant links.

The Spanning Tree Protocol executes an algorithm called the spanning-tree algorithm. This algorithm chooses a reference point in the network and calculates the redundant paths to that reference point. After it finds all the links in the network, the spanning-tree algorithm chooses one path on which to forward frames and shuts down the other redundant links to stop any network loops from occurring in the network. It does this by electing a root bridge that will decide on the network topology.

There can be only one *root bridge* in any given network. The root bridge ports are called designated ports, and designated ports operate in what is called forwarding state. Forwarding state ports send and receive traffic.

If you have other switches in your network, as shown in Figure 4.4, they are called non-root bridges. However, the port that has the lowest cost to the root bridge is called a root port and sends and receives traffic. The cost is determined by the bandwidth of a link.

**FIGURE 4.4** Spanning tree operations

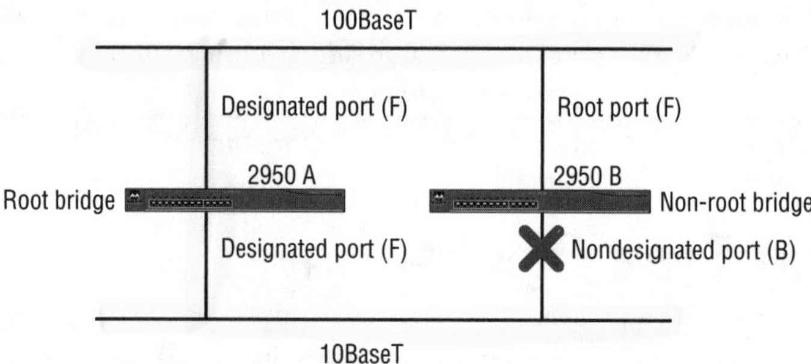


Ports that forward traffic away from the root bridge are called the *designated ports*. Because the root can forward traffic only away from itself, all its ports are designated ports. The other port or ports on the bridge are considered *nondesignated ports* and will not send or receive traffic. This is called blocking mode.

This section will cover exactly how a group of switches determines the best path throughout the network and how you can modify the results. This section will cover port selection and link cost values as well as the different spanning tree states a particular port might be in.

## Selecting the Best Path

Using spanning tree, a group of switches determines the best path from any point A to any point B. To do this, all the switches need to communicate and each switch needs to know what the network looks like. In order to know what links should be dynamically disabled, a root bridge must be selected and each switch needs to determine the type of each port.

### Selecting the Root Bridge

Switches or bridges running STP exchange information with what are called *Bridge Protocol Data Units (BPDUs)*. BPDUs are used to send configuration messages by using multicast frames. The bridge ID of each device is sent to other devices using BPDUs.

The *bridge ID* is used to determine the root bridge in the network and to determine the root port. The bridge ID is 8 bytes long and includes the priority and the MAC address of the device. The priority on all devices running the IEEE STP version is 32768 by default. The lower the bridge ID, the more likely a device is to become the root bridge.

To determine the root bridge, the switches in the network compare the bridge IDs they receive via the BPDUs. Whichever switch has the lowest bridge ID becomes the root bridge. If two switches or bridges have the same priority value, then the MAC address is used to determine which has the lowest ID.

For example, if two switches, A and B, both use the default priority of 32768, the MAC address will be used. If switch A's MAC address is 0000.0c00.1111 and switch B's MAC address is 0000.0c00.2222, switch A would become the root bridge.

Because each switch comes with a burned-in MAC address, if the switches use the default priority, then the one with the lowest MAC address becomes the root bridge. This means that this device will have a large number of packets passing through it. If you have a 6509 and have spent lots of money on the fabric upgrades to a 256Gb backplane, the last thing you want is for an old switch in a closet to become the root bridge. For this reason, it is strongly recommended that you lower the number on the priority for core switches. Chapter 5 gives more information on dealing with designs.

The following network analyzer output shows a BPDU broadcasted on a network. BPDUs are sent out every two seconds by default. That might seem like a lot of overhead, but remember that this is only a layer 2 frame, with no layer 3 information in the packet:

```
Flags:         0x80  802.3
Status:        0x00
Packet Length:64
Timestamp:     19:33:18.726314 02/28/2003
802.3 Header
  Destination:  01:80:c2:00:00:00
  Source:       00:b0:64:75:6b:c3
  LLC Length:   38
802.2 Logical Link Control (LLC) Header
  Dest. SAP:    0x42  802.1 Bridge Spanning Tree
  Source SAP:   0x42  802.1 Bridge Spanning Tree
  Command:      0x03  Unnumbered Information
802.1 - Bridge Spanning Tree
  Protocol Identifier:  0
  Protocol Version ID:  0
  Message Type:         0  Configuration Message
  Flags:                %00000000
  Root Priority/ID:     0x8000  /  00:b0:64:75:6b:c0
  Cost Of Path To Root: 0x00000000  (0)
  Bridge Priority/ID:   0x8000  / 00:b0:64:75:6b:c0
  Port Priority/ID:     0x80  /  0x03
  Message Age:                        0/256 seconds     (exactly 0seconds)
  Maximum Age:                        5120/256 seconds   (exactly 20seconds)
  Hello Time:                         512/256 seconds      (exactly 2seconds)
```

```
  Forward Delay:                          3840/256 seconds    (exactly 15seconds)
Extra bytes (Padding):
  ........              00 00 00 00 00 00 00 00
Frame Check Sequence:  0x2e006400
```

Notice the cost of path to root. It is zero because this switch is actually the root bridge. We'll discuss path costs in more detail in the upcoming section, "Selecting the Designated Port."

The preceding network analyzer output also shows the BPDU timers, which are used to prevent bridging loops because the timers determine how long it will take the spanning tree to converge after a failure.

BPDUs are susceptible to propagation delays, which happen because of packet length, switch processing, bandwidth, and utilization problems. This can create an unstable network because temporary loops might occur in the network when BPDUs are not received on time to the remote switches in the network. The STP uses timers to force ports to wait for the correct topology information.

As you can see in the output, the hello time is exactly 2 seconds, the maximum age is exactly 20 seconds, and the forward delay is exactly 15 seconds.

When a switch first boots up, the only MAC address it knows is its own, so it advertises itself as the root. As it collects BPDUs, it will acknowledge another device as the root, if necessary. When a switch receives a BPDU advertising a device as root, with a better bridge ID than the current root is using, the switch caches this information and waits. It will wait the duration of the MaxAge timer before using the new root, allowing other switches in the network to also receive the BPDU. This reduces the possibility of loops.

## Selecting the Root Port

After the root bridge selection process is complete, all switches must relate to the root bridge. Each switch listens to BPDUs on all active ports, and if more than one BPDU is received, the switch knows it has a redundant link to the root bridge. The switch has to determine which port will become the root port and which port will be put into blocking state.

To determine the port that will be used to communicate with the root bridge, the path cost is determined. The path cost is an accumulated total cost based on the bandwidth of the links. Table 4.2 shows the typical costs associated with the different Ethernet networks.

**TABLE 4.2** STP Link Cost

| Speed | New IEEE Cost | Original IEEE Cost |
|---|---|---|
| 10Gbps | 2 | 1 |
| 1Gbps | 4 | 1 |
| 100Mbps | 19 | 10 |
| 10Mbps | 100 | 100 |

The IEEE 802.1D specification was revised to handle the new higher-speed links, hence the different costs shown in Table 4.2.

Included in the BPDUs that a switch sends out is the cost of getting a frame to the root bridge. A neighboring device receives this information and adds the cost of the link the BPDU arrived on, and that becomes the cost for the neighboring device. For example, switch A sends out a BPDU to switch B saying that A can reach the root with a path cost of 38. The BPDU travels across a gigabit link between switch A and B. B receives the BPDU giving the cost of 38 and adds the cost of the link the BPDU arrived on, which is 4. Switch B knows that it can reach the root by sending frames through switch A with a total path cost of 42.

After the cost is determined for all links to the root bridge, the switch decides which port has the lowest cost. The lowest-cost port is put into forwarding mode, and the other ports are placed in blocking mode. If there are equal-cost paths, the port with the lowest port ID is put into the forwarding state. In the previous example, if switch B had two paths to the root, both with a cost of 42, the switch needs some other way of figuring out which single path will be used. If switch A is accessed via gigabit port 0/3 and switch C is accessed via gigabit port 0/7, switch B will send frames via switch A because it is attached to the lower numerical port number.

## Selecting the Designated Port

A designated port is one that is active and forwarding traffic, but doesn't lead to the root. Often, a designated port on one switch connects to the root port on another switch, but it doesn't have to. Because the root bridge doesn't have any ports that lead to itself and because its ports are never dynamically turned off, all its ports are labeled as designated ports.

The selection of a designated port is fairly easy. If there are two switches that have equal-cost paths to get to the root and are connected to each other, there must be some way of resolving the topological loop that exists. The switches simply examine the bridge IDs, and whichever device has the lower bridge ID is the one that will be responsible for forwarding traffic from that segment. Figure 4.4, shown earlier, illustrates this point.

## Spanning Tree Port States

The ports on a bridge or switch running the STP will go through four transitional states:

**Blocking** Won't forward frames; listens to BPDUs. All ports are in blocking state by default when the switch is powered on.

**Listening** Listens to BPDUs to make sure no loops occur on the network before passing data frames.

**Learning** Learns MAC addresses and builds a filter table, but does not forward frames.

**Forwarding** Bridge port is able to send and receive data. A port is never placed in forwarding state unless there are no redundant links or the port determines that it has the best path to the root bridge.

An administrator can put a port in disabled state, or if a failure with the port occurs, the switch puts it into disabled state.

Typically, switch ports are in either blocking or forwarding state. A forwarding port is a port that has been determined to have the lowest cost to the root bridge. However, if the network has a topology change because of a failed link, or the administrator adds a new switch to the network, the ports on a switch will be in listening and learning states.

Blocking ports are used to prevent network loops. After a switch determines the best path to the root bridge, all other ports may be placed in the blocking state. Blocked ports will still receive BPDUs.

If a switch determines that a blocked port should now be the designated port, it will go to listening state. It checks all BPDUs heard to make sure that it won't create a loop after the port goes to forwarding state.

Figure 4.5 shows the default STP timers and their operation within STP.

**FIGURE 4.5** STP default timers

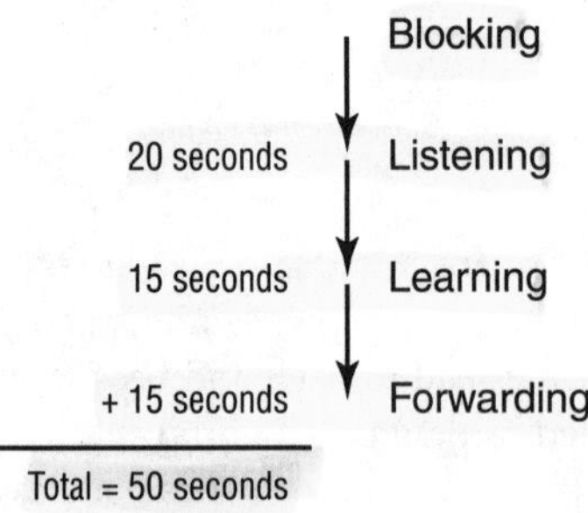


Notice the time from blocking to forwarding. Blocking to listening is 20 seconds. Listening to learning is another 15 seconds. Learning to forwarding is 15 seconds, for a total of 50 seconds. However, the switch could go to disabled if the port is administratively shut down or the port has a failure.

## Convergence

Convergence occurs when bridges and switches have transitioned to either the forwarding or blocking state. No data is forwarded during this time. Convergence is important in making sure that all devices have the same database.

The problem with convergence is the time it takes for all devices to update. Before data can start to be forwarded, all devices must be updated. The time it usually takes to go from blocking to forwarding state is 50 seconds. Changing the default STP timers is not recommended, but the timers can be adjusted if they need to be. The time it takes to transition a port from the listening state to the learning state or from the learning state to the forwarding state is called the forward delay.

**Real World Scenario**

**Sizing the Network**

Each device uses the timers configured on the root bridge. If the timers need to be changed, Cisco recommends that they not be changed directly. Instead, first experiment with the `spantree diameter` option. It will set the timers based on the size of the switched network. The larger the network, the more time is allowed for propagation, which increases the timers. The default diameter is seven switches across. Setting the diameter smaller than your actual network size increases the chance of broadcast storms.

## Spanning Tree Example

In Figure 4.6, the three switches all have the same priority of 32768. However, notice the MAC address of each switch. By looking at the priority and MAC addresses of each switch, you should be able to determine the root bridge.

Because 2950A has the lowest MAC address and all three switches use the default priority, 2950A will be the root bridge.

To determine the root ports on switches 2950B and 2950C, you need to look at the cost of the link connecting the switches. Because the connection from both switches to the root switch is from port 0 using a 100Mbps link, that has the best cost and both switches' root port will then be port 0.

Use the bridge ID to determine the designated ports on the switches. The root bridge always has all ports as designated. However, because both 2950B and 2950C have the same cost to the root bridge and because switch 2950B has the lowest bridge ID, the designated port will be on switch 2950B. Because 2950B has been determined to have the designated port, switch 2950C will put port 1 in blocking state to stop any network loop from occurring.

**FIGURE 4.6** Spanning tree example

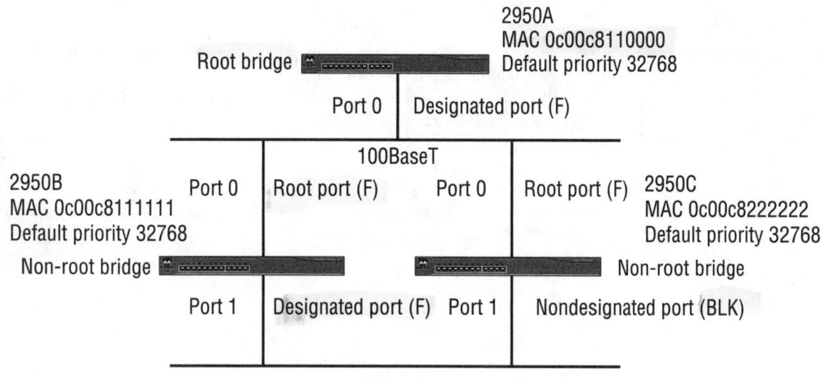

The STP algorithm is often referred to after the name of its creator, Edsger W. Dijkstra, as in Dijkstra's Algorithm. It's not as descriptive as the STP algorithm, but I still like to use it.

# LAN Switch Types

One last thing we need to cover before we can move on—the actual forwarding techniques used by switches. LAN switching forwards (or filters) frames based on their hardware destination—the MAC address. There are three methods by which frames can be forwarded or filtered. Each method has its advantages and disadvantages, and by understanding the different LAN switch methods available, you can make smart switching decisions.

Here are the three switching modes:

**Store-and-forward** With the *store-and-forward* mode, the complete data frame is received on the switch's buffer, a cyclic redundancy check (CRC) is run, and then the destination address is looked up in the MAC filter table.

**Cut-through** With the *cut-through* mode, the switch waits for only the destination hardware address to be received and then looks up the destination address in the MAC filter table.

**FragmentFree** *FragmentFree* is the default mode for the Catalyst 1900 switch; it is sometimes referred to as modified cut-through. The switch checks the first 64 bytes of a frame for fragmentation (because of possible collisions) before forwarding the frame.

Figure 4.7 shows the different points where the switching mode takes place in the frame. The different switching modes are discussed in detail next.

**FIGURE 4.7** Different switching modes within a frame

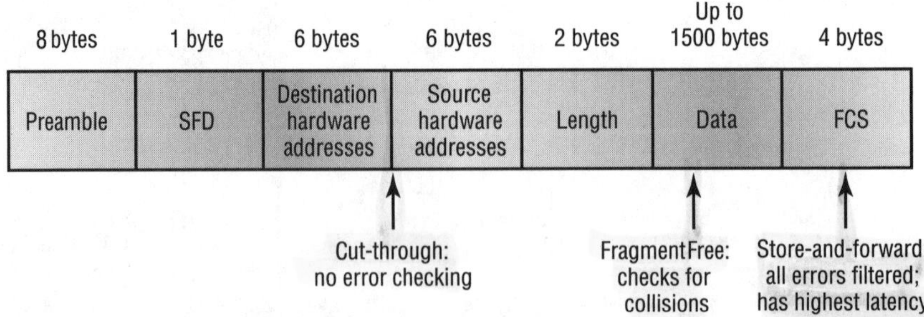

### Store-and-Forward

With the store-and-forward switching method, the LAN switch copies the entire frame onto its onboard buffers and computes the CRC. Because it copies the entire frame, latency through the switch varies with frame length.

The frame is discarded if it contains a CRC error, if it's too short (fewer than 64 bytes including the CRC), or if it's too long (more than 1518 bytes including the CRC). If the frame doesn't contain any errors, the LAN switch looks up the destination hardware address in its forwarding or switching table and determines the outgoing interface. It then forwards the frame to its destination.

This is the mode used by modern Catalyst switches, and it further allows for quality of service to be applied to the frame by reading additional data. QoS is covered in detail in Chapter 8.

### Cut-Through (Real Time)

With the cut-through switching method, the LAN switch copies only the destination address (the first six bytes following the preamble) onto its onboard buffers. It then looks up the hardware destination address in the MAC switching table, determines the outgoing interface, and forwards the frame toward its destination. A cut-through switch provides reduced latency because it begins to forward the frame as soon as it reads the destination address and determines the outgoing interface.

Some switches can be configured to perform cut-through switching on a per-port basis until a user-defined error threshold is reached. At that point, they automatically change over to store-and-forward mode so they will stop forwarding the errors. When the error rate on the port falls below the threshold, the port automatically changes back to cut-through mode.

### FragmentFree (Modified Cut-Through)

FragmentFree is a modified form of cut-through switching. In FragmentFree mode, the switch waits for the collision window (64 bytes) to pass before forwarding. If a packet has an error, it almost always occurs within the first 64 bytes. FragmentFree mode provides better error checking than the cut-through mode, with practically no increase in latency.

## Configuring Spanning Tree

The configuration of spanning tree is pretty simple unless you want to change your timers or add multiple spanning tree instances; then it can get complex. The timers and more advanced configurations are covered in Chapter 5.

STP is enabled on all Cisco switches by default. However, you might want to change your spanning tree configuration to have many spanning tree instances. This means that each VLAN can be its own spanning tree. This is known as Per-VLAN spanning tree.

To enable or disable spanning tree on a set-based switch, use the `set spantree` *`parameter`* command. This is performed on a VLAN-by-VLAN basis rather than a port-by-port configuration:

```
Terry_4000> (enable) set spantree disable 1-1005
Spantrees 1-1005 disabled.

Terry_4000> (enable) set spantree enable 1-1005
Spantrees 1-1005 enabled.
```

The preceding configuration shows the disabling of spanning tree on an individual VLAN basis. To enable spanning tree on an individual VLAN basis, use `set spantree enable` *`VLAN(s)`*. Cisco recommends that you do not disable spanning tree on a switch, particularly on uplinks where a loop can occur.

**Real World Scenario**

### Detecting Loops

On switches that have a CPU usage indicator, this is sometimes also called "the spanning tree loop indicator." It's relatively rare to see the CPU usage indicator get much past 20 percent utilization for more than a few seconds at a time. If network connectivity has been lost and you suspect a spanning tree loop is the culprit, take a look at the CPU usage indicator. If utilization reaches 70 percent or higher, when the switch never sees that level of usage during normal operation, that's a good indicator of a spanning tree loop.

Spanning Tree is enabled by default on modern switches, but you can enable or disable the protocol as needed. To enable or disable spanning tree on an IOS-based switch, use the `spanning-tree vlan` *`vlan_number`* command or the `no spanning-tree vlan` *`vlan_number`* command. Use the `show spanning-tree` command to view the spanning tree status. The following configuration shows how to enable and disable spanning tree on a 2950 switch:

```
Terry_2950#conf t
Terry_2950(config)#no spanning-tree vlan 1
Terry_2950(config)#^Z

Terry_2950#show spanning-tree

No spanning tree instances exist.
```

```
Terry_2950#conf t
Terry_2950(config)#spanning-tree vlan 1
Terry_2950(config)#^Z

Terry_2950#show spanning-tree

VLAN0001
  Spanning tree enabled protocol ieee
  Root ID    Priority    0
             Address     00b0.6414.1180
             Cost        100
             Port        1 (FastEthernet0/1)
             Hello Time   2 sec  Max Age 20 sec  Forward Delay 15 sec

  Bridge ID  Priority    32769  (priority 32768 sys-id-ext 1)
             Address     000b.be53.2c00
             Hello Time   2 sec  Max Age 20 sec  Forward Delay 15 sec
             Aging Time 300

Interface        Port ID                       Designated                 Port ID
Name             Prio.Nbr      Cost Sts       Cost Bridge ID             Prio.Nbr
---------------- -------- --------- --- --------- -------------------- --------
Fa0/1            128.1          100 LIS         0      0 00b0.6414.1180 128.1
Fa0/24           128.24         100 LIS       100 32769 000b.be53.2c00 128.24

Terry_2950#
```

Notice that the commands include mandatory references to the VLANs. You will remember that all ports are in VLAN 1 by default. In the next chapter we will be considering the use of different spanning trees for each VLAN, and these commands will make a little more sense then. In the meantime, just trust me and accept that the Cisco ISO demands that you enter a VLAN number at this time.

To see the spanning tree configuration and whether it is active on a Catalyst 4000 set-based switch, use the `show spantree` command as shown here:

```
Terry_4000> (enable) show spantree
VLAN 1
Spanning tree enabled
Spanning tree type          ieee

Designated Root             00-e0-34-88-fc-00
Designated Root Priority    32768
```

```
Designated Root Cost        0
Designated Root Port        1/0
Root Max Age   20 sec    Hello Time 2  sec   Forward Delay 15 sec

Bridge ID MAC ADDR          00-e0-34-88-fc-00
Bridge ID Priority          32768
Bridge Max Age 20 sec    Hello Time 2  sec   Forward Delay 15 sec

Port   Vlan  Port-State    Cost  Priority Fast-Start Group-Method
----- ---- ------------- ----- -------- ---------- -----
 1/1   1     forwarding      19       32     disabled
 1/2   1     not-connected   19       32     disabled
 2/1   1     not-connected  100       32     disabled
 2/2   1     not-connected  100       32     disabled
 2/3   1     not-connected  100       32     disabled
 2/4   1     not-connected  100       32     disabled
 2/5   1     not-connected  100       32     disabled
<Output truncated>
```

By default, the `show spantree` command provides information about VLAN 1. You can gather spanning tree information about other VLANs by using the `show spantree` *`vlan#`* command.

The `show spantree` command provides you the following information:

**Designated root** The MAC address of the root bridge.

**Designated root priority** The priority of the root bridge. All bridges have a default of 32768.

**Designated root cost** The cost of the shortest path to the root bridge.

**Designated root port** The port that is chosen as the lowest cost to the root bridge.

**Root timers** The timers received from the root bridge.

**Bridge ID MAC address** This bridge's ID. This plus the bridge priority make up the bridge ID.

**Bridge ID priority** The priority set; the preceding bridge output is using the default of 32768.

**Bridge timers** The timers used by this bridge.

**Ports in the spanning tree** Not all available ports are displayed in the preceding output. However, this field does show all ports participating in this spanning tree. It also shows whether they are forwarding.

Although the command abbreviation `show span` works on all the switches, you will get much different output if you use it on the 4000 series. This is because a SPAN (Switch Port ANalyzer) is the port used to connect to a sniffer. On the 4000, abbreviate `spantree` to no less than `spant` to avoid this.

# Summary

At layer 2 of the OSI model, we have very little to work with when it comes to forwarding data—essentially just the MAC address. And yet in layer 2 switching, functions including address learning, forwarding vs. filtering decision making, and loop avoidance can be taken. Obviously there are some clever things going on.

Forwarding and filtering is, of course, managed using the bridging (switching) table, constructed by reading source MAC addresses as frames are passed through the switch. This is very similar to legacy bridging, apart from the fact that multi-port switches support microsegmentation, and have several ways of forwarding frames, including store-and-forward, cut-through, and FragmentFree switching.

Additional links can be implemented to provide redundancy in a network; however, these redundant links can introduce problems such as broadcast storms, multiple frame copies, and multiple loops. The Spanning Tree Protocol can be used to break network loops by forcing some switches to place some of their ports into a blocking mode. This is effected by having one bridge assume a sort of control—the root—and other switches calculating the shortest distance to the root, thus allowing the loop to be seen and broken.

# Exam Essentials

**Understand that the Spanning Tree Protocol controls the switched network topology.** Redundancy is essential in modern networks, and without STP, switches would often have multiple paths to get to a given destination. Frame duplication due to the multiple paths, plus nonstop broadcast forwarding, would lead to broadcast storms and general instability.

**Understand the importance of the root bridge.** The root bridge is the center of the spanning tree universe; all STP calculations are based on which device is the root. You need to know how the root is selected and how to influence the process. Switches calculate which is the shortest path to the root and disable ports that promote redundancy.

**Know the different types of ports.** The root port is the port on a switch that has the least-cost path to the root bridge. A designated port is a port that is active but does not lead to the root. All the ports on the root bridge are active and are designated ports. You need to know how switches decide what state their ports will be in.

**Understand the method of breaking ties.** Whenever there is a tie, there is always a method of breaking it. Remember that a lower number is usually better. The bridge ID is a combination of the configured priority and the MAC address, so if two switches have the same priority value, the lowest MAC address will break the tie. If two ports on a single switch can reach the root with paths of the same cost, then the lowest-numbered one is used.

# Key Terms

Before you take the exam, be sure you're familiar with the following terms:

address learning

bridge ID

Bridge Protocol Data Units (BPDUs)

cut-through

designated ports

forwarding and filtering decision

FragmentFree

loop avoidance

nondesignated ports

root bridge

Spanning Tree Protocol (STP)

store-and-forward

# Written Lab

Write the answers to the following questions:

1. What command shows you whether a port is in forwarding mode?
2. What command would you use to disable spanning tree for VLAN 5 on a set-based switch?
3. What command(s) enables spanning tree for VLAN 6 on an IOS-based switch?
4. What is a switch's priority by default?
5. What is used to determine a bridge ID?
6. What is the default hello time of a BPDU?
7. What is the amount of time it takes for a switch port to go from blocking state to forwarding state?
8. What are the four states of a bridge port?
9. What are the two parameters used to determine which port forwards data and which ports block on a switch with redundant links?
10. True/False: A bridge must forward all broadcasts out all ports except for the port that initially received the broadcast.

# Review Questions

1. Which LAN switch method runs a CRC on every frame?
   A. Cut-through
   B. Store-and-forward
   C. FragmentCheck
   D. FragmentFree
2. Which LAN switch type checks only the hardware address before forwarding a frame?
   A. Cut-through
   B. Store-and-forward
   C. FragmentCheck
   D. FragmentFree
3. What is true regarding the STP blocked state of a port? (Choose all that apply.)
   A. No frames are transmitted or received on the blocked port.
   B. BPDUs are sent and received on the blocked port.
   C. BPDUs are still received on the blocked port.
   D. Frames are sent or received on the blocked port.
4. Layer 2 switching provides which of the following? (Choose all that apply.)
   A. Hardware-based bridging (MAC)
   B. Wire speed
   C. High latency
   D. High cost
5. What is used to determine the root bridge in a network? (Choose all that apply.)
   A. Priority
   B. Cost of the links attached to the switch
   C. MAC address
   D. IP address
6. What is used to determine the designated port on a bridge?
   A. Priority
   B. Cost of the links attached to the switch
   C. MAC address
   D. IP address

7. What are the four port states of an STP switch?
   - A. Learning
   - B. Learned
   - C. Listened
   - D. Heard
   - E. Listening
   - F. Forwarding
   - G. Forwarded
   - H. Blocking
   - I. Gathering

8. What are the three distinct functions of layer 2 switching?
   - A. Address learning
   - B. Routing
   - C. Forwarding and filtering
   - D. Creating network loops
   - E. Loop avoidance
   - F. IP addressing

9. Which of the following is true regarding BPDUs?
   - A. BPDUs are used to send configuration messages by using IP packets.
   - B. BPDUs are used to send configuration messages by using multicast frames.
   - C. BPDUs are used to set the cost of STP links.
   - D. BPDUs are used to set the bridge ID of a switch.

10. If a switch determines that a blocked port should now be the designated port, what state will the port go into?
    - A. Unblocked
    - B. Forwarding
    - C. Listening
    - D. Listened
    - E. Learning
    - F. Learned

11. What is the difference between a bridge and a layer 2 switch? (Choose all that apply.)
    - A. There can be only one spanning tree instance per bridge.
    - B. There can be many different spanning tree instances per switch.
    - C. There can be many spanning tree instances per bridge.
    - D. There can be only one spanning tree instance per switch.
12. What is the difference between a bridge and a layer 2 switch? (Choose all that apply.)
    - A. Switches are software based.
    - B. Bridges are hardware based.
    - C. Switches are hardware based.
    - D. Bridges are software based.
13. What does a switch do when a frame is received on an interface and the destination hardware address is unknown or not in the filter table?
    - A. Forwards the switch to the first available link
    - B. Drops the frame
    - C. Floods the network with the frame looking for the device
    - D. Sends back a message to the originating station asking for a name resolution
14. Which LAN switch type waits for the collision window to pass before looking up the destination hardware address in the MAC filter table and forwarding the frame?
    - A. Cut-through
    - B. Store-and-forward
    - C. FragmentCheck
    - D. FragmentFree
15. What is switching mode on a 4000 series switch?
    - A. Cut-through
    - B. Store-and-forward
    - C. FragmentCheck
    - D. FragmentFree
16. How is the bridge ID of a switch communicated to neighbor switches?
    - A. IP routing
    - B. STP
    - C. During the four STP states of a switch
    - D. Bridge Protocol Data Units
    - E. Broadcasts during convergence times

**17.** How is the root port on a switch determined?

**A.** The switch determines the highest cost of a link to the root bridge.

**B.** The switch determines the lowest cost of a link to the root bridge.

**C.** By sending and receiving BPDUs between switches. The fastest BPDU transfer rate on an interface becomes the root port.

**D.** The root bridge broadcasts the bridge ID, and the receiving bridge determines what interface this broadcast was received on and makes this interface the root port.

**18.** How many root bridges are allowed in a network?

**A.** 10

**B.** 1

**C.** 1 for each switch

**D.** 20

**19.** What could happen on a network if no loop avoidance schemes are put in place? (Choose all that apply.)

**A.** Faster convergence times.

**B.** Broadcast storms.

**C.** Multiple frame copies.

**D.** IP routing will cause flapping on a serial link.

**20.** What is the default priority of STP on a switch?

**A.** 32768

**B.** 3276

**C.** 100

**D.** 10

**E.** 1

# Answers to Written Lab

1. `show spantree`. This command displays the spanning tree information of a VLAN and all the ports' participation in STP.
2. `set spantree disable 5`. The `set spantree` command is used to enable or disable spanning tree for a VLAN.
3. `Terry_2950(config)#spanning-tree vlan 6`. This command is used to turn on spanning tree for a VLAN. You can disable STP for an interface with the interface command `spanning-tree vlan` *`vlan_number`* command.
4. 32768. This is the default priority on all switches and bridges.
5. Bridge priority and then MAC address. If the priorities of the switches are set the same, the MAC address would be used to determine the root bridge.
6. 2 seconds. Every 2 seconds, BPDUs are sent out all forwarding ports.
7. 50 seconds. From blocking to listening is 20 seconds, from listening to learning is 15 seconds, and from learning to forwarding is another 15 seconds.
8. Blocking, listening, learning, forwarding. Each state is used to stop network loops from occurring on redundant links.
9. The path cost and port ID are used to determine the designated port and nondesignated ports.
10. True. Bridges forward all frames that are received and are broadcasts or are not in the filter table.

# Answers to Review Questions

1. B. Store-and-forward LAN switching checks every frame for CRC errors. It has the highest latency of any LAN switch type.

2. A. The cut-through method does no error checking and has the lowest latency of the three LAN switch types. Cut-through checks only the hardware destination address before forwarding the frame.

3. A, C. BPDUs are still received on a blocked port, but no forwarding of frames and BPDUs is allowed.

4. A, B. Layer 2 switching uses ASICs to provide frame filtering and is considered hardware based. Layer 2 switching also provides wire-speed frame transfers, with low latency.

5. A, C. Layer 2 devices running the STP use the priority and MAC address to determine the root bridge in a network.

6. B. To determine the designated ports, switches use the cost of the links attached to the switch.

7. A, E, F, H. The four states are blocking, listening, learning, and forwarding. Disabled is a fifth state.

8. A, C, E. Layer 2 features include address learning, forwarding and filtering of the network, and loop avoidance.

9. B. Bridge Protocol Data Units are used to send configuration messages to neighbor switches. This includes the bridge IDs.

10. C. A blocked port always listens for BPDUs to make sure that a loop will not occur when the port is put into forwarding state.

11. A, B. Unlike a bridge, a switch can have many different spanning tree instances. Bridges can have only one.

12. C, D. Bridges are considered software based, and switches are considered hardware based.

13. C. Switches forward all frames that have an unknown destination address. If a device answers the frame, the switch will update the MAC address table to reflect the location of the device.

14. D. FragmentFree looks at the first 64 bytes of a frame to make sure a collision has not occurred. It is sometimes referred to as modified cut-through.

15. B. The 4000 series uses the store-and-forward method for frame switching.

16. D. The bridge ID is sent via a multicast frame inside a BPDU update.

17. B. Root ports are determined by using the lowest cost of a link to the root bridge.

18. B. Only one root bridge can be used in any network.

19. B, C. Broadcast storms and multiple frame copies are typically found in a network that has multiple links to remote locations without some type of loop avoidance scheme.

20. A. The default priorities on all switches are 32768.

# Using Spanning Tree with VLANs

## THE CCNP EXAM TOPICS COVERED IN THIS CHAPTER INCLUDE THE FOLLOWING:

- ✓ Describe LAN segmentation with VLANs
- ✓ Describe Spanning Tree (STP), and explain the operation of common and per-VLAN STP implementations.
- ✓ Configure Spanning Tree in both Common Spanning Tree (CST) and per-VLAN modes.
- ✓ Configure Spanning Tree parameters including: port priority, VLAN priority and root bridge selection.
- ✓ Enable advanced Spanning Tree features such as BPDU guard, PortFast and UplinkFast and BackboneFast.
- ✓ Configure Fast EtherChannel and Gigabit EtherChannel on inter-switch links.

Redundancy is the ability to provide an immediate backup solution to a fault in the network that might otherwise cause a network or component service outage. When you're building a redundant network—which is a network with redundant power, hardware, links, and other network-critical components—network loops can occur. The Spanning Tree Protocol (STP) was created to overcome the problems associated with transparent bridging at layer 2.

Unfortunately, STP is a far from optimal protocol. We can hardly blame the designers for this—all they had to work with was a forwarding system designed to transmit broadcasts out of every port, and the option of adding a little intelligence with Bridge Protocol Data Units (BPDUs). So legacy STP leaves us with suboptimal forwarding paths, unused spare links, and the possibility (probability, even) of very slow convergence after a network failure.

This chapter extends our coverage of STP by focusing on providing link redundancy by using STP and the IEEE 802.1D algorithm used to support STP on a per-VLAN basis. The Spanning Tree Protocol uses timers to make the network stable. You'll also learn how to manage the different STP timers to maximize the efficiency of your network, and how to implement specific additions to STP to decrease convergence times.

# Creating VLAN Standards

The history of using STP with VLANs is interesting, because it acts as a macro for how many standards have been developed. In the past, Cisco and the IEEE have differed in their approaches to the use of these two protocols together.

As we discovered in Chapter 4, "Layer 2 Switching and the Spanning Tree Protocol (STP)," STP has some well-defined problems. First, convergence can be slow because of the forwarding delays. This is unacceptable in modern networks where users and applications expect immediate recovery from equipment failures. Additionally, it is likely that a general Spanning Tree topology applied to all VLANs will result in suboptimal paths for some users. The result has been a spate of developments, some proprietary and some standards-based, to overcome these problems.

Per-VLAN Spanning Tree (PVST) is a Cisco proprietary implementation of STP. PVST uses Inter-Switch Link (ISL) routing and runs a separate instance of STP for each and every VLAN.

The IEEE uses Common Spanning Tree (CST), which is defined with IEEE 802.1Q. The IEEE 802.1Q defines one spanning tree instance for all VLANs. A new mechanism, recently standardized as 802.1s, allows multiple spanning tree instances but in a more complex fashion; it runs multiple instances of STP on a one-to-one basis with VLANs. There is one more implementation of STP, and that is called PVST+. Because it ends with a plus sign, it must be better, right? Well, maybe. What it does is allow CST information to be passed into PVST. Cisco thinks it would be easier if you simply had all Cisco switches; then you wouldn't even have to think about this issue.

This chapter covers the current protocols supported by Cisco, and compares the options. The following list includes a brief explanation of each STP implementation:

**Per-VLAN Spanning Tree (PVST)** Default for Cisco switches; runs a separate instance of spanning tree for each VLAN. Makes smaller STP implementations for easier convergence.

**Common Spanning Tree (CST)** The 802.1Q standard; runs one large STP on the entire network regardless of the number of VLANs. Problems with convergence can occur in large networks.

**Per-VLAN Spanning Tree+ (PVST+)** Allows Cisco switches to communicate with CST switches.

**Multiple Spanning Tree (MSP)** The 802.1s standard, supported by Cisco on IOS-based switches since versions of 12.1. Allows multiple instances of STP and group VLAN mapping.

In the rest of this section, we'll go into more detail about each type of STP implementation and its use with VLANs.

## Per-VLAN Spanning Tree (PVST)

The STP protocol does not scale well with large switched networks. In large switched networks, delays can occur in receiving BPDUs. These delays can cause instability in the STP database. Delays in larger switched networks can also cause convergence time problems, which means that the network will not be forwarding frames.

To solve late BPDUs and convergence problems, Cisco created a separate instance of *Per-VLAN Spanning Tree (PVST)*. It makes smaller STP implementations, which are easier for the switches to manage. Also, with PVST, each VLAN has a unique Spanning Tree Protocol topology for its root, port cost, path cost, and priority.

By running PVST, you still provide a loop-free network, but it is based within each VLAN. Each switch has a spanning tree process running for each VLAN. If a switch has five VLANs that it knows about, then it will have five instances of spanning tree running. The benefits of having a PVST are as follows:

- It reduces the STP recalculation time when the switched network is converging.
- The spanning tree topology is smaller because all links will not support all VLANs.
- It makes the switched network easier to scale.
- Recovery is faster than with a large network that has one STP instance.
- It allows administrative control of forwarding paths on a subnet basis.
- It allows for load balancing over redundant links when VLAN priorities are established for those links.

However, there are some disadvantages of using a spanning-tree-per-instance implementation:

- The utilization on the switch is a factor because it needs to manage all the STP instances.
- You must take into consideration that the trunk links have to support all the VLAN STP information as well.
- It requires ISL.
- PVST is a Cisco proprietary protocol.

## Common Spanning Tree (CST)

The IEEE 802.1Q is referred to as the *Common Spanning Tree (CST)*. It is also called the Mono-Spanning Tree because it uses only one spanning tree instance regardless of the size of the switched layer 2 network.

The CST runs on all VLANs by default, and all switches are involved in the election process to find the root bridge. The switches then form an association with that root bridge. Typically, using CST does not allow for optimization of the root bridge placement.

There are some advantages to CST. With one STP instance, there are fewer BPDUs consuming bandwidth. Because there is only one instance of STP in the network, there is less STP processing performed by the switches.

However, the disadvantages typically outweigh the advantages in a larger network. With a single root bridge, the path that has been calculated as the best cost to the root bridge might not be the most efficient for some users to send their data. Another disadvantage of CST is that the STP topology increases in size to make sure all ports in the network are found. This can cause delays in the update and convergence times if the network topology is too large.

## Per-VLAN Spanning Tree+ (PVST+)

*Per-VLAN Spanning Tree+ (PVST+)* is an extension of the PVST standard. Starting with the Catalyst software 4.1 or later, PVST+ is supported on Cisco Catalyst switches. This enables Cisco switches to support the IEEE 802.1Q standard. Basically, the PVST+ extension of the PVST protocol provides support for links across an IEEE 802.1Q CST region.

PVST+ also supports the Cisco default PVST and adds checking mechanisms to make sure there are no configuration problems on trunked ports and VLAN IDs across switches. PVST+ is plug-and-play compatible with PVST with no configuration necessary. To provide support for the IEEE 802.1Q standard, Cisco's existing PVST has been modified with additional features, enabling it to support a link across the IEEE 802.1Q Common Spanning Tree region.

PVST+ includes the following features:

- Provides notification of inconsistencies related to port trunking or VLAN identification across the switches.
- Adds mechanisms to ensure that there is no unknown configuration.
- Tunnels PVST BPDUs through the 802.1Q VLAN region as multicast data.
- Provides compatibility with IEEE 802.1Q's CST and Cisco's PVST protocols.

- Interoperates with 802.1Q-compliant switches using CST through 802.1Q trunking. A CST BPDU is transmitted or received with an IEEE standard bridge group MAC address.
- Blocks ports that receive inconsistent BPDUs in order to prevent forwarding loops.
- Notifies users via Syslog messages about all inconsistencies.

## Multiple Spanning Tree (MST)

Multiple Spanning Tree (MST) builds upon the proprietary PVST+ standard. With MST a number of spanning tree instances can be created, but they are not mapped one-to-one to VLANs. The reason for this is that in most networks, even those supporting hundreds of VLANs, there are a small number of optimal topologies. As each instance of STP demands its own root and all the associated BPDU activity, the processing overhead can be unnecessarily high if we allow each VLAN to have its own spanning tree. Better to create the STP instances and then map VLANs to those instances.

MST features include switches that are grouped together in MST "regions"—interconnected bridges that have the same MST configuration. Each switch in an MST region maintains three attributes: a configuration name, a revision number, and a table associating each of the VLANs supported per MST instance (up to the 4096 maximum). These attributes are common across a domain and must be shared by all switches. Different attributes signify a different domain, which changes the switch-to-switch relationship. Finally, different instances of STP have several VLANs mapped to them, creating the opportunity for VLANs to operate with optimal topology, but reducing the overhead associated with PVST.

MST was approved by the IEEE as 802.11g in June 2003, so a standards-based implementation of this protocol is likely to figure extensively in the future.

Readers wishing to know more about 802.1s than is covered in the CCNP program should visit `www.cisco.com/warp/public/473/147.html`.

# Scaling the Spanning Tree Protocol

The STP prevents loops in layer 2 switched networks and is basically plug-and-play. However, it might be advantageous to change some of the default timers and settings to create a more stable environment.

In this section, we'll discuss how to scale the STP protocol on a large, switched internetwork. It is important to understand how to provide proper placement of the root bridge to create an optimal topology. If the root bridge is automatically chosen through an election, which is the default, the actual path that the frames can take might not be the most efficient. As the administrator, you can then change the root placement to create a more optimal path. However, it's possible that your changes could cause more damage instead—so you want to think through your network design before making any changes.

To change the root placement, you need to do the following:

- Determine the root device.
- Configure the device.
- Set the port cost.
- Set the port priorities.
- Change the STP timers.

## Determining the Root

Determining the root device is the most important decision that you make when configuring the STP protocol on your network. If you place the root in the wrong place in your network, it will be difficult to scale the network, and, really, that is what you are trying to do: create a scalable layer 2 switched internetwork.

However, by placing the root switch as close as possible to the center of your network, more optimal and deterministic paths can be easily chosen. You can choose the root bridge and secondary and backup bridges as well. Secondary bridges are very important for network stability in case the root bridge fails. Choosing the root is typically the best thing to do, but if that root goes down for maintenance, spanning tree will select a new root—and because all other switches have the same priority, it might be a switch you wouldn't usually want to be the root bridge.

Because the root bridge should be close to the center of the network, the device will typically be a switch that a lot of traffic passes through, such as a distribution layer switch, a core layer switch, or one that does routing or multi-layer switching. An access layer switch would not usually be chosen.

After the root bridge has been chosen and configured, all the connected switches must determine the best path to the root bridge. The STP uses several different costs in determining the best path to the root bridge:

- Port cost
- Path cost
- Port priority

When a BPDU is sent out a switch port, the BPDU is assigned a port cost. The path cost, which is the sum of all the port costs, is then determined. The STP first looks at the path cost to figure out the forwarding and blocking ports. If the path costs are equal on two or more links to the root bridge, the port ID is used to determine the root port. The port with the lowest port ID is determined to be the forwarding port. You can change the port used by changing the port priority, but Cisco doesn't recommend this. However, we'll show you how to do it later in this section (so you can have some fun on a rainy Saturday).

## Configuring the Root

After you choose the best switch to become your root bridge, you can use the Cisco command-line interface (CLI) to configure the STP parameters in a switched network.

The command to configure the STP is `set spantree`. The following switch output (from our Catalyst 4000) shows the different command parameters you can use when configuring the STP. We are interested in the `set spantree root` and `set spantree root secondary` commands at this point:

```
Terry_4000(enable) set spantree ?
Set spantree commands:
----------------------------------------------------------------------------
set spantree disable         Disable spanning tree
set spantree enable          Enable spanning tree
set spantree fwddelay        Set spantree forward delay
set spantree hello           Set spantree hello interval
set spantree help            Show this message
set spantree maxage          Set spantree max aging time
set spantree portcost        Set spantree port cost
set spantree portfast        Set spantree port fast start
set spantree portpri         Set spantree port priority
set spantree portvlancost    Set spantree port cost per vlan
set spantree portvlanpri     Set spantree port vlan priority
set spantree priority        Set spantree priority
set spantree root            Set switch as primary or secondary root
set spantree uplinkfast      Enable or disable uplinkfast groups
set spantree backbonefast    Enable or disable fast convergence
Terry_4000 (enable)
```

The `set spantree root` command sets the primary root bridge for a specific VLAN, or even for all your VLANs. The `set spantree root secondary` command enables you to configure a backup root bridge.

In the following switch output, notice the options that are available with the `set spantree root` command:

```
Terry_4000> (enable) set spantree root ?
Usage: set spantree root [secondary] <vlans> [dia <network_diameter>]
                         [hello <hello_time>]
       (vlans = 1..1005, network_diameter = 2..7, hello_time = 1..10)
```

Table 5.1 shows the parameters available with the `set spantree` command and their definitions.

**TABLE 5.1** `set spantree root` Parameters

| Parameter | Definition |
|---|---|
| `root` | Designation to change the switch to the root switch. The `set spantree root` command changes the bridge priority from 32768 to 8192. |
| `secondary` | Designation to change the switch to a secondary root switch if the primary fails. This automatically changes the bridge priority from a default of 32768 to 16384. |
| `vlan_list` | Optional command that changes the STP parameters on a specified VLAN. If no VLAN is specified, then it changes only VLAN 1 by default. You can change the parameters for VLANs 1–1005. |
| `dia` *`network diameter`* | Another optional command that specifies the maximum number of bridges between any two points where end stations attach. You can set these parameters from 2 to 7. Figure the network diameter by starting at the root bridge and counting the number of bridges in the VLAN. The root bridge is 1, so if you have only one more switch, set the network diameter to 2. This changes the timers in the VLAN to reflect the new diameter. |
| `hello` *`hello time`* | Optional command that specifies in seconds the duration between configuration messages from the root switch. You can set this anywhere from 1 to 10 seconds (2 is the default). |

The following switch output is an example of using the `set spantree root` command:

```
Terry_4000> (enable) set spantree root 1-4 dia 2
VLANs 1-2 bridge priority set to 8192.
VLANs 1-2 bridge max aging time set to 10.
VLANs 1-2 bridge hello time set to 2.
VLANs 1-2 bridge forward delay set to 7.
Switch is now the root switch for active VLANs 1-4.
Terry_4000> (enable)
```

The `set spantree root` command tells the switch to change the bridge priority to 8192, which automatically changes the switch to the root bridge. The `1-4` represents the VLANs for which the STP will change the parameters, and the `dia 2` is the network diameter. To figure the network diameter, we simply counted the number of switches from the root, including the root bridge, which in our example equals 2.

Notice the output after the command. The bridge priority was changed to 8192, the maximum age time was changed to 10, hello time is still 2 seconds, and the forward delay was set to 7 seconds. If the network diameter is set, the STP sets the timers to what it would consider efficient for that size network.

**Real World Scenario**

**When a Root Isn't the Root**

Using the `set spantree root` command is great when the organization is very centralized. But in a decentralized environment, you might use this command only to find that a coworker set the priority of a different switch to a lower value by using the `set spantree priority` command. This will result in the switch you configured being no more than the backup root bridge. When setting a particular switch to become the root, always make sure that the switch you configured knows it's the root and that other switches know it as well. I find it useful to check one last time as I finish, just to make sure everything is well.

You can verify your STP configuration with the `show spantree` command. If you type the command **`show spantree`** with no parameters, it will show you the spanning tree configuration for all VLANs. You can type **`show spantree`** ***`vlan`*** to see the parameters for just a particular VLAN. The following switch output shows the spanning tree information for VLAN 1:

```
Terry_4000> (enable) show spantree 1
VLAN 1
Spanning tree enabled
Spanning tree type            ieee

Designated Root               00-e0-34-88-fc-00
Designated Root Priority      8192
Designated Root Cost          0
Designated Root Port          1/0
Root Max Age   10 sec    Hello Time 2  sec   Forward Delay 7  sec

Bridge ID MAC ADDR            00-e0-34-88-fc-00
Bridge ID Priority            8192
Bridge Max Age 10 sec    Hello Time 2  sec   Forward Delay 7  sec

Port      Vlan  Port-State     Cost  Priority  Fast-Start
--------- ----  -------------  ----- --------  ----------
 1/1      1     forwarding      19     32      disabled
```

```
 1/2      1    forwarding        19     32     disabled
 2/1      1    not-connected     100    32     disabled
 2/2      1    not-connected     100    32     disabled
 2/3      1    not-connected     100    32     disabled
 2/4      1    not-connected     100    32     disabled
 2/5      1    not-connected     100    32     disabled
<output truncated>
```

Notice that the bridge IP priority is set to 8192; the designated root and bridge ID MAC address are the same because this is the root bridge. The port states are both 19, which is the default for 100Mbps. Because both ports are in forwarding state, the 2950 switch must have one of its FastEthernet ports in blocking mode. Let's take a look by using the `show spanning-tree` command on the 2950:

```
Terry_2950# show spanning-tree

VLAN0001
  Spanning tree enabled protocol ieee
  Root ID     Priority    8192
              Address     00e0.3488.fc00
              Cost        5
              Port        1 (FastEthernet0/1)
              Hello Time   2 sec  Max Age 10 sec  Forward Delay 7 sec

  Bridge ID   Priority    32769  (priority 32768 sys-id-ext 1)
              Address     000b.be53.2c00
              Hello Time   2 sec  Max Age 10 sec  Forward Delay 7 sec
              Aging Time 300

Interface          Port ID                      Designated            Port ID
Name               Prio.Nbr     Cost Sts        Cost Bridge ID        Prio.Nbr
----------------   --------  ---------------  -------------------- --------
Fa0/1              128.1       100 FWD          0      1 00b0.6414.1180 128.1
Fa0/24             128.24      100 BLK          0      1 00b0.6414.1180 128.12
```

Notice that port fa0/24 is in blocking mode and port fa0/1 is in forwarding mode. If we want port fa0/24 to be in forwarding mode and fa0/21 in blocking mode, we can set the port costs to help the switch determine the best path to use. Note that we are not saying you should do this; we just wanted to show you how.

## Setting the Port Cost

The parameters in this next set are used to enable the network administrator to influence the path that spanning tree chooses when setting the port priority, port cost, and path cost.

Cisco does not recommend changing these settings unless it's absolutely necessary. However, the best way to get a good understanding of how the STP works is by changing the defaults. We do not recommend trying any of this on a production network unless you have permission from the network manager, who understands that you can bring the network down by doing so.

By changing the port cost, you can change the port ID, which means it can be a more desirable port to STP. Remember that STP uses the port ID only if there is more than one path to the root bridge and they are of equal cost. Path cost is the sum of the costs between a switch and the root bridge. The STP calculates the path cost based on the media speed of the links between the switch and the port cost of each port forwarding the frames. In the hands-on lab at the end of this chapter, both links are 100Mbps, so the port ID is important and will be used.

To change the path used between a switch and the root bridge, first calculate the current path cost. Then change the port cost of the port you want to use, making sure that you keep in mind the alternate paths if the primary path fails before making any changes to your switch. Remember that ports with a lower port cost are more likely to be chosen; this doesn't mean they always will be chosen.

To change the port cost of a port on a 4000 series switch, use the `set spantree portcost` command:

```
Terry_4000> (enable) set spantree portcost ?
Usage: set spantree portcost <mod_num/port_num> <cost>
       set spantree portcost <trcrf> <cost>
       (cost = 1..65535)
```

The parameters to set the cost of a port are the module and port number and the cost you want to configure. The following example shows how to set the port cost on port 1/1 from the default of 19 to 10:

```
Terry_4000> (enable) set spantree portcost 1/1 10
Spantree port 1/1 path cost set to 10.
```

You would verify the change with the `show spantree` command. However, because both ports are in forwarding mode, the preceding command will not change the switch's STP parameters. Notice in the following switch output that both ports are forwarding, but the costs of the ports are different:

```
Port      Vlan Port-State    Cost  Priority Fast-Start
--------- ---- ------------- ----- -------- ----------
 1/1      1    forwarding     10      32    disabled
 1/2      1    forwarding     19      32    disabled
```

Remember that a root switch will be forwarding on all active ports, so the port IDs are irrelevant to the switch. However, the 2950 must then choose a port to perform blocking on the interface with the lowest cost.

To change the port cost on an IOS-based switch, use the `spanning-tree cost` interface command. The cost value can be any number from 1 to 200000000; however, you can not make it less than the path cost of both links. What we need to do is to raise the port priority of the port we don't want STP to use for forwarding. Notice that we changed the cost of port fa0/24 to 20. This should make the fa0/24 port a more desirable path:

```
Terry_2950#conf t
Enter configuration commands, one per line.  End with CNTL/Z.
Terry_2950(config)#interface fa0/24
Terry_2950(config-if)#spanning-tree ?
  bpdufilter     Don't send or receive BPDUs on this interface
  bpduguard      Don't accept BPDUs on this interface
  cost           Change an interface's spanning tree port path cost
  guard          Change an interface's spanning tree guard mode
  link-type      Specify a link type for spanning tree protocol use
  port-priority  Change an interface's spanning tree port priority
  portfast       Enable an interface to move directly to forwarding on link up
  stack-port     Enable stack port
  vlan           VLAN Switch Spanning Tree

Terry_2950(config-if)#spanning-tree cost ?
  <1-200000000>  port path cost

Terry_2950(config-if)#spanning-tree cost 20
Terry_2950(config-if)#^Z
```

To verify the port priorities, use the `show spanning-tree` command:

```
Terry_2950#show spanning-tree

VLAN0001
  Spanning tree enabled protocol ieee

[Output cut]

Interface        Port ID                       Designated           Port ID
Name             Prio.Nbr    Cost Sts          Cost Bridge ID       Prio.Nbr
---------------- -------- --------------- -------------------- --------
Fa0/1            128.1          5 FWD          0      1 00b0.6414.1180 128.1
Fa0/24           128.24        20 BLK          0      1 00b0.6414.1180 128.12
```

In the preceding switch output, notice that port fa0/1 is forwarding and port fa0/24 is now blocking. In the output, the port path cost is 5 for port fa0/1 and 20 for port fa0/24. This is a pretty simple and straightforward configuration and worked fine, but the network suffered downtime due to convergence, so caution should be used when changing the port costs in a real production network. Also, you need to plan your final topology, because you can cause havoc in a network if the configuration is not thought out carefully. The port costs are propagated in the BPDUs, so a small change on one switch can affect how spanning tree chooses the various ports on a switch a few cable segments away.

You can get a good idea of the delays associated with Spanning Tree convergence if you try this out for yourself. Immediately after making the changes to the port cost, enter the **show spanning-tree** command on the 2950 switch. If you keep repeating the command, you will see the switch going through the blocking, listening, and learning modes on the way to forwarding. You can time the process with your watch.

## Setting the Port Priority

Another option you can use to help the switch determine the path selection that STP uses in your network is to set the port priorities. Remember, this only influences STP; it doesn't demand that STP do anything. However, between setting the port cost and priority, STP should always make your path selection.

The port priority and port cost configurations work similarly. The port with the lowest port priority will forward frames for all VLANs. The command to set a port priority is `set spantree portpri`:

```
Terry_4000> (enable) set spantree portpri ?
Usage: set spantree portpri <mod_num/port_num> <priority>
       set spantree portpri <trcrf> <trcrf_priority>
       (priority = 0..63, trcrf_priority = 0..7)
Terry_4000> (enable)
```

The possible port priority range is from 0 to 63, and the default is 32. If all ports have the same priority, then the port with the lowest port number will forward frames. For example, 2/1 is lower than 2/2. In the following example, the 4000 switch priority for port 1/1 is set to 20:

```
Terry_4000> (enable) set spantree portpri 1/1 20
Bridge port 1/1 port priority set to 20.
Terry_4000> (enable)
```

After you change your port priority, you can verify the configuration with the `show spantree 1/1` command:

```
Terry_4000> (enable) show spantree 1/1
Port      Vlan  Port-State     Cost   Priority  Fast-Start
--------- ----  -------------  -----  --------  ----------
 1/1      1     forwarding        10        20   disabled
 1/1      2     forwarding        10        20   disabled
 1/1      3     forwarding        10        20   disabled
 1/1      4     forwarding        10        20   disabled
 1/1      1003  not-connected     10        20   disabled
 1/1      1005  not-connected     10         4   disabled
Terry_4000> (enable)
```

Notice that, because port 1/1 is a trunked port, all VLAN priorities were changed on that port. Also notice in the following output that the priority is 20 for 1/1, but the default of 32 is set for 1/2:

```
Terry_4000> (enable)show spantree
[output cut]
Port      Vlan  Port-State     Cost   Priority  Fast-Start
--------- ----  -------------  -----  --------  ----------
 1/1        1   forwarding      10       20     disabled
 1/2        1   forwarding      19       32     disabled
```

You can go one step further and set the port priority on a per-VLAN basis. The port with the lowest priority will forward frames for the VLAN for which you've set the priority. Again, if all the ports have the same priority, the lowest port number wins and begins forwarding frames.

There is an advantage to setting the port priority per VLAN. If you have a network with parallel paths, STP stops at least one link from forwarding frames so a network loop will not occur. All traffic would then have to travel over only the one link. However, by changing the port priority for a specific group of VLANs, you can distribute the VLANs across the two links. This isn't quite as good as load sharing, but at least you get to use both links as opposed to having one sit idle.

To change the priority of STP for a certain VLAN or group of VLANs, use the `set spantree portvlanpri` command:

```
Terry_4000> (enable) set spantree portvlanpri ?
Usage: set spantree portvlanpri <mod_num/port_num>   <priority> [vlans]
(priority = 0..63)
Terry_4000> (enable)
```

The priority can be set for each VLAN from 0 to 63. In the following example, we'll set port 1/1 to forward only VLANs 1 and 2, and port 1/2 to forward VLANs 3 and 4. Figure 5.1 shows the physical topology involved.

**FIGURE 5.1** Prioritizing traffic by VLAN

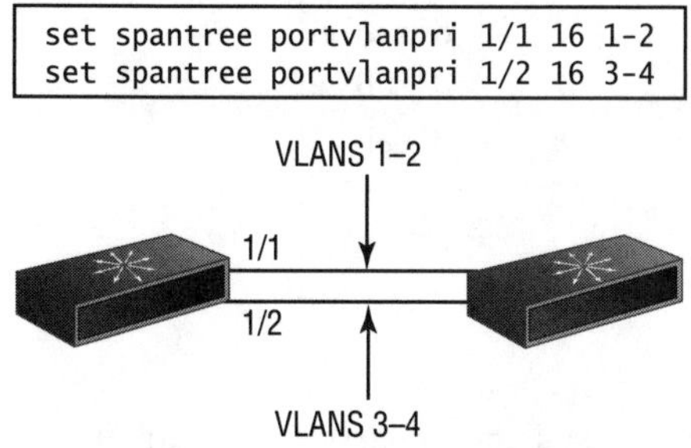


```
Terry_4000> (enable) set spantree portvlanpri 1/1 16 1-2
Port 1/1 vlans 1-2 using portpri 16.
Port 1/1 vlans 3-1004 using portpri 20.
Port 1/1 vlans 1005 using portpri 4.

Terry_4000> (enable) set spantree portvlanpri 1/2 16 3-4
Port 1/2 vlans 1-2,5-1004 using portpri 32.
Port 1/2 vlans 3-4 using portpri 16.
Port 1/2 vlans 1005 using portpri 4.
Terry_4000> (enable)
```

The preceding switch output displays the VLAN priority information. We set both VLAN port priorities to 16. Notice that for VLANs 1–4, the priority is 16. However, on port 1/1, all the other VLANs are listed as having a port priority of 20 because that is what we set the port priority to earlier in this chapter. On port 1/2, the switch thinks all the other ports have a port priority of 32, except for VLAN 1005, which becomes a default priority of 4.

You can view the changes by using the `show spantree` *`slot/port`* command, as shown here:

```
Terry_4000> (enable) show spantree 1/1
Port      Vlan Port-State    Cost  Priority Fast-Start
--------- ---- ------------- ----- -------- ----------
 1/1      1    forwarding      10       16  disabled
 1/1      2    forwarding      10       16  disabled
 1/1      3    forwarding      10       20  disabled
 1/1      4    forwarding      10       20  disabled
 1/1      1003 not-connected   10       20  disabled
 1/1      1005 not-connected   10        4  disabled

Terry_4000> (enable) show spantree 1/2
```

```
Port      Vlan Port-State    Cost  Priority Fast-Start
--------- ---- ------------- ----- -------- ----------
 1/2      1    forwarding      19      32   disabled
 1/2      2    forwarding      19      32   disabled
 1/2      3    forwarding      19      16   disabled
 1/2      4    forwarding      19      16   disabled
 1/2      1003 not-connected   19      32   disabled
 1/2      1005 not-connected   19       4   disabled
Terry_4000> (enable)
```

Setting the VLAN priority on the IOS-based switches is carried out using the interface command `spanning-tree vlan` *`vlan_number`* `port-priority` *`priority`*. Looking at the default configuration, we can see that the port priority is set to 128.

```
Terry_2950#show spanning-tree

VLAN0001
  Spanning tree enabled protocol ieee

[Output cut]

Interface        Port ID                     Designated           Port ID
Name             Prio.Nbr    Cost Sts        Cost Bridge ID       Prio.Nbr
---------------- -------- --------------- -------------------- --------
Fa0/1            128.1      100 BLK         0      1 00b0.6414.1180 128.1
Fa0/24           128.24      20 FWD         0      1 00b0.6414.1180 128.12
```

If we want to change the VLAN port priority on the 2950 switch to make the port more desirable, then we can reduce the priority as follows:

```
Terry_2950#conf t
Terry_2950(config)#interface fa0/1
Terry_2950(config-if)#spanning-tree vlan 1 port-priority 20
Terry_2950(config-if)#^Z
Terry_2950#sho span

VLAN0001
  Spanning tree enabled protocol ieee
  Root ID    Priority    1
             Address     00b0.6414.1180
             Cost        20
             Port        24 (FastEthernet0/24)
             Hello Time   2 sec  Max Age 20 sec  Forward Delay 15 sec
```

```
  Bridge ID  Priority    32769  (priority 32768 sys-id-ext 1)
             Address     000b.be53.2c00
             Hello Time   2 sec  Max Age 20 sec  Forward Delay 15 sec
             Aging Time 300

Interface        Port ID                     Designated               Port ID
Name             Prio.Nbr    Cost Sts        Cost Bridge ID           Prio.Nbr
---------------- -------- ------------- --------- -------------------- --------
Fa0/1             20.1        20 BLK        0        1 00b0.6414.1180 128.1
Fa0/24           128.24       20 FWD        0        1 00b0.6414.1180 128.12
```

By changing either the port priority or the port cost, you can persuade the switch to use your chosen paths. However, there are some miscellaneous other STP variables that you can change. We'll discuss those next.

## Changing the STP Timers

The timers are important in an STP network to stop network loops from occurring. The different timers are used to give the network time to update the correct topology information to all the switches and also to determine the whereabouts of all the redundant links.

The problem with the STP timers is that, if a link goes down, it can take up to 50 seconds for the backup link to take over forwarding frames. This is a convergence problem that can be addressed when instability is occurring in the network. The following timers can be changed:

**fwddelay** This interval indicates how long it takes for a port to move from listening to learning state and then from learning to forwarding state. The default is 15 seconds, but it can be changed to anywhere from 4 to 30 seconds. If you set this too low, the switch won't be allowed ample time to make sure no loops will occur before setting a port in forwarding mode. The following switch output shows how to set the `fwddelay` to 10 seconds:

```
Terry_4000> (enable) set spantree fwddelay ?
Usage: set spantree fwddelay <delay> [vlans]
       (delay = 4..30 seconds, vlan = 1..1005)
Terry_4000> (enable) set spantree fwddelay 10
Spantree 1 forward delay set to 10 seconds.
```

**hello** This is the time interval for sending BPDUs from the root switch. It is set to 2 seconds by default; you would think it couldn't be set any lower, but it can be increased or decreased. You can set it to 1 second to actually double the amount of BPDUs sent out that must be lost before triggering an unwanted convergence in the network. However, it doubles the CPU load and processing load as well. The following switch output shows how to change the BPDU timers to 1 second:

```
Terry_4000> (enable) set spantree hello ?
Usage: set spantree hello <interval> [vlans]
```

```
        (interval = 1..10, vlan = 1..1005)
Terry_4000> (enable) set spantree hello 1
Spantree 1 hello time set to 1 seconds.
```

**maxage** The max age is the amount of time that a switch will hold BPDU information. If a new BPDU is not received before the max age expires, then the BPDU is discarded and is considered invalid. The default is 20 seconds; it can be set to as low as 6 seconds. However, network instability will happen if too many BPDUs are discarded because this timer is set too low. The following output shows how to change the max age of a BPDU to 30 seconds:

```
Terry_4000> (enable) set spantree maxage ?
Usage: set spantree maxage <agingtime> [vlans]
        (agingtime = 6..40, vlan = 1..1005)
Terry_4000> (enable) set spantree maxage 30
Spantree 1 max aging time set to 30 seconds.
Terry_4000> (enable)
```

Rather than directly modifying the timers, it is usually better to modify the size of the network. Table 5.1 referred to a "diameter" value that can be set when selecting the spanning tree root. The diameter used is the width of the network from one side to the other. Three switches daisy-chained together would have a diameter of 3, whereas three configured in a triangle would have a diameter of 2.

The diameter automatically sets the timers to a value appropriate to the size of your network. Setting the timers yourself to low values in a large network risks topological loops because the delay might not be long enough to account for BPDU propagation delay. The best thing to do is to use the diameter option when setting the root and then modify the timers from there, if necessary.

We have been discussing redundant links and STP, but most of the discussion has been about how to make STP run efficiently, and that is by making the non-root port a blocking port. We discussed load balancing only when we showed you how to set the port priority on a per-VLAN basis. However, that really wasn't load balancing to the degree that is possible with a Cisco switched network. In the next section, we'll cover the most efficient ways of using redundant links in a large, switched internetwork.

To set similar parameters on the IOS-based switches, use the global command `spanning-tree vlan` *`vlan_number options`* as follows:

```
Terry_2950(config)#spanning-tree ?
  backbonefast   Enable BackboneFast Feature
  etherchannel   Spanning tree etherchannel specific configuration
  extend         Spanning Tree 802.1t extensions
  loopguard      Spanning tree loopguard options
  mode           Spanning tree operating mode
  pathcost       Spanning tree pathcost options
  pathcost       Spanning tree pathcost options
```

```
  uplinkfast    Enable UplinkFast Feature
  vlan          VLAN Switch Spanning Tree

Terry_2950(config)#spanning-tree vlan 1 ?
  forward-time  Set the forward delay for the spanning tree
  hello-time    Set the hello interval for the spanning tree
  max-age       Set the max age interval for the spanning tree
  priority      Set the bridge priority for the spanning tree
  root          Configure switch as root
  <cr>

Terry_2950(config)#spanning-tree vlan 1 forward-time ?
  <4-30>  number of seconds for the forward delay timer

Terry_2950(config)#spanning-tree vlan 1 hello-time ?
  <1-10>  number of seconds between generation of config BPDUs

Terry_2950(config)#spanning-tree vlan 1 max-age ?
  <6-40>  maximum number of seconds the information in a BPDU is valid
```

# Using Redundant Links with STP

*Fast EtherChannel* and *Gigabit EtherChannel* allow high-speed redundant links in a spanning tree environment by allowing dual parallel links to be treated as though they were one link. Cisco Fast EtherChannel technology uses the standards-based 802.3 Full-Duplex Fast Ethernet to provide a reliable high-speed solution for the campus network backbone. Fast EtherChannel can scale bandwidth within the campus, providing full-duplex bandwidth at wire speeds of 200Mbps to 800Mbps. It provides high bandwidth, load sharing, and redundancy of links in a switched internetwork.

Broadcast traffic, as well as unicast and multicast traffic, is distributed equally across the links in the channel. Fast EtherChannel also provides redundancy in the event of a link failure. If a link is lost in a Fast EtherChannel network, traffic is rerouted to one of the other links in just a few milliseconds, making the convergence transparent to the user.

Gigabit EtherChannel works in the same fashion that Fast EtherChannel does, except that it's faster. Each device has a limit to the number of ports that can participate but it's in the range of 2 to 8, giving a potential channel size of 16Gbps.

This section will introduce you to the several ways of configuring redundant links. In the part about EtherChannel, you'll learn about the communication protocol that switches use and how load balancing takes place. You will then learn how the switch can violate the usual rules that spanning tree lives by, to create a network that responds faster when there is a problem.

**Modifications to EtherChannel**

EtherChannel has undergone some changes in the last four years on Cisco switches. It used to be that you had to group the ports together in order to use them in a channel. Ports 1–4 had to be used together, 5–8 had to be used together, and so on. If you were using only two, then they had to be the first two ports in the group of four. Of course, they all had to be on the same blade as well. The first thing an administrator would do when troubleshooting was to make sure the correct ports were being used.

The restrictions aren't quite as difficult now, though. A CatOS version 5.3 or higher system enables you to use whatever ports you want to, as long as they are configured the same.

Different devices will also forward frames across the channel in different ways, and some can be set up to apply rules based on layer 3 or layer 4 headers. The secret to setting up an effective EtherChannel topology is to understand the limitations of your equipment and software.

## Parallel Fast EtherChannel Links

Fast EtherChannel uses load distribution to share the links in a bundle. A bundle is a group of FastEthernet or Gigabit Ethernet links managed by the Fast EtherChannel process. Should one link in the bundle fail, the Ethernet Bundle Controller (EBC) informs the Enhanced Address Recognition Logic (EARL) ASIC of the failure, and the EARL in turn ages out all addresses learned on that link. The EBC and the EARL use hardware to recalculate the source and destination address pair on a different link.

The convergence time is sometimes referred to as the failover time, which is the time it takes for the new address to be relearned—about 10 microseconds. Windowing flow control techniques can make this process a touch longer, but that depends on the particular application in use. The key is not having the application time out, and the failover time is fast enough to stop the time-out from happening.

### EtherChannel Guidelines

EtherChannel does not work under certain circumstances. This is to ensure that no network loops will occur if the bundle comes up. There are certain guidelines to follow when configuring EtherChannel technology:

- All ports must be in the same VLAN or they must all be trunk ports that belong to the same native VLAN.
- All ports must be configured as the same trunk mode if trunking is used.
- When trunking is used, all ports must be configured with the same VLAN range. If it is not the same, packets will be dropped and the ports will not form a channel when set to the auto or desirable mode.

- All ports must be configured with the same speed and duplex settings.
- If broadcast limits are configured on the ports, configure the limits for all the ports or packets might be dropped.
- The ports can not be configured in a channel as dynamic VLAN ports.
- Port security must be disabled on channeled ports.
- All ports must be enabled in the channel before the channel can come up. If you disable a port, a link failure occurs.

## Configuring EtherChannel

To create an EtherChannel bundle, use the `set port channel` command. You must first make sure that all the conditions for EtherChannel have been met.

Notice the switch output when we try to configure the ports on our 4000 switch as a bundle to the 2950 switch:

```
Terry_4000> (enable) set port channel 1/1-2 on
Mismatch in trunk mode.
Mismatch in port duplex.
Mismatch in STP port priority.
Failed to set port(s) 1/1-2 channel mode to on.
Terry_4000> (enable)
```

There is a mismatch in trunking, duplex, and STP port priority. All the ports must be configured the same for EtherChannel to work.

To view the configuration of a port, use the `show port capabilities` *`slot/port`* command:

```
Terry_4000> (enable) show port capabilities 1/1
Model                    WS-X5509
Port                     1/1
Type                     100BaseTX
Speed                    100
Duplex                   half,full
Trunk encap type         ISL
Trunk mode               on,off,desirable,auto,nonegotiate
Channel                  1/1-2
Broadcast suppression    percentage(0-100)
Flow control             no
Security                 yes
Membership               static,dynamic
Fast start               yes
Rewrite                  no
Terry_4000> (enable)
```

The preceding output shows the card model number and the configuration of the port. The easiest way for us to make sure all the ports we want to channel are configured the same is to just clear the configuration. We're not suggesting that you just clear your config whenever any problems come up, but the configuration we created in this chapter is pretty extensive, and it's easier to simply clear it out of the switch to perform the next function:

```
Terry_4000> (enable) clear config all
This command will clear all configuration in NVRAM.
This command will cause ifIndex to be reassigned on the next system startup.
Do you want to continue (y/n) [n]? y
........
.................
System configuration cleared.
Console> (enable)
```

Remember that you need to reset the switch after erasing the configuration to clear the configuration. We need to reconfigure the switch with an IP address and trunking on ports 1/1 and 1/2. We're also going to delete the configuration on the 2950, so then we will have both switches back to our STP default:

```
Terry_2950#erase startup-config
Erasing the nvram filesystem will remove all files! Continue? [confirm]
```

Now that we have both the switches back to their default configurations, we'll just configure the hostnames and IP addresses and turn on trunking on ports 1/1 and 1/2 of the 4000 and ports fa0/1 and fa0/24 of the 2950:

```
#configure terminal
(config)#hostname Terry_2950
Terry_2950(config)#int vlan 1
Terry_2950(config-if)#ip address 172.16.10.2 255.255.255.0
Terry_2950(config-if)#ip default-gateway 172.16.10.1
Terry_2950(config)#int fa 0/1
Terry_2950(config-if)#switchport ?
  access         Set access mode characteristics of the interface
  host           Set port host
  mode           Set trunking mode of the interface
  nonegotiate    Device will not engage in negotiation protocol on this
                 interface
  port-security  Security related command
  priority       Set appliance 802.1p priority
  protected      Configure an interface to be a protected port
  trunk          Set trunking characteristics of the interface
  voice          Voice appliance attributes
```

```
Terry_2950(config-if)#switchport mode trunk
Terry_2950(config-if)#int fa 0/24
Terry_2950(config-if)#switchport mode trunk
Terry_2950(config-if)#^Z
```

```
Console> (enable) set prompt Terry_4000>
Terry_4000> (enable) set interface sc0 172.16.10.4 255.255.255.0
Interface sc0 IP address and netmask set.
Terry_4000> (enable) set trunk 1/1 on
Port(s) 1/1 trunk mode set to on.
Terry_4000> (enable) set trunk 1/2 on
Port(s) 1/2 trunk mode set to on.
Terry_4000> (enable)
```

To verify that the ports are trunking, use the `show trunk` command:

```
Terry_4000> (enable) show trunk
Port     Mode        Encapsulation  Status      Native vlan
-------- ----------- ------------- ---------- -----------
  1/1    on          isl            trunking    1
  1/2    on          isl            trunking    1
```

Let's try to configure EtherChannel between the switches again:

```
Terry_4000> (enable) set port channel 1/1-2 on
Port(s) 1/1-2 channel mode set to on.
Terry_4000> (enable) 2003 Jul 25 23:08:20 %PAGP-5
PORTFROMSTP:Port 1/1 left bridge  port 1/1
2003 Jul 25 23:08:20 %PAGP-5-PORTFROMSTP:Port 1/2 left   bridge port 1/2
2003 Jul 25 23:08:20 %PAGP-5-PORTTOSTP:Port 1/1 joined   bridge port 1/1-2
2003 Jul 25 23:08:21 %PAGP-5-PORTTOSTP:Port 1/2 joined   bridge port 1/1-2
```

To verify the EtherChannel bundle, use the `show port channel` command:

```
Terry_4000> (enable) show port channel
Port  Status     Channel   Channel     Neighbor  Neighbor
                 mode      status      device    port
----- ---------- --------- ----------- --------- -------
 1/1  errdisable on        channel
 1/2  errdisable on        channel
----- ---------- --------- ----------- --------- -------
Terry_4000> (enable)
```

You can see that the status is error disabled and that no neighbors are found. This is because we still need to configure Fast EtherChannel on the 2950 switch. If this were a remote switch, you would lose contact with the switch and have to go to the site and console into the switch to configure EtherChannel. You should configure the remote site first; then you will lose contact with it until you configure the local switch bundle.

To configure the EtherChannel bundle on a 2950 switch, use the interface command `channel-group` *`group_number`* `mode` *`mode_type`*:

```
Terry_2950(config)#int fa 0/1
Terry_2950(config-if)#channel-group ?
  <1-6>  Channel group number

Terry_2950(config-if)#channel-group 1 ?
  mode  Etherchannel Mode of the interface

Terry_2950(config-if)#channel-group 1 mode ?
  auto       Enable PAgP only if a PAgP device is detected
  desirable  Enable PAgP unconditionally
  on         Enable Etherchannel only

Terry_2950(config-if)#channel-group 1 mode on
Terry_2950(config-if)#int fa 0/24
Terry_2950(config-if)#channel-group 1 mode on
Terry_2950(config-if)#exit
```

To view the channel status on the IOS-based switch, use the `show etherchannel` *`options`* command.

```
Terry_2950#show etherchannel ?
  <1-6>         Channel group number
  brief         Brief information
  detail        Detail information
  load-balance  Load-balance/frame-distribution scheme among ports in
                port-channel
  port          Port information
  port-channel  Port-channel information
  summary       One-line summary per channel-group

Terry_2950#show etherchannel det
                Channel-group listing:
                -----------------------
```

```
Group: 1
----------
Group state = L2
Ports: 3   Maxports = 8
Port-channels: 1 Max Port-channels = 1
                Ports in the group:
                -------------------
Port: Fa0/1
------------

Port state    = Up Mstr In-Bndl
Channel group = 1           Mode = On/FEC     Gcchange = 0
Port-channel  = Po1         GC   = 0x00010001    Pseudo port-channel = Po1
Port index    = 0           Load = 0x00

Age of the port in the current state: 00d:00h:10m:25s

Port: Fa0/24
------------

Port state    = Up Mstr In-Bndl
Channel group = 1           Mode = On/FEC     Gcchange = 0
Port-channel  = Po1         GC   = 0x00010001    Pseudo port-channel = Po1
Port index    = 0           Load = 0x00

Age of the port in the current state: 00d:00h:05m:45s
                Port-channels in the group:
                ----------------------

Port-channel: Po1
------------

Age of the Port-channel   = 00d:00h:10m:26s
Logical slot/port   = 1/0          Number of ports = 2
GC                  = 0x00010001     HotStandBy port = null
Port state          = Port-channel Ag-Inuse

Ports in the Port-channel:

Index   Load   Port    EC state
------+------+------+------------
```

```
00      Fa0/1    on
00      Fa0/24   on

Time since last port bundled:    00d:00h:05m:45s    Fa0/24
```

To verify the EtherChannel on the 4000 series switch, use the `show port channel` command:

```
Terry_4000> (enable) show port channel
Port  Status     Channel   Channel     Neighbor                  Neighbor
                 mode      status      device                    port
----- ---------- --------- ----------- ------------------------- ----------
 1/1  connected  on        channel     cisco 2950  Terry_2950      A
 1/2  connected  on        channel     cisco 2950  Terry_2950      B
----- ---------- --------- ----------- ------------------------- ----------
Terry_4000> (enable)
```

The preceding switch output shows the port numbers, status, mode, channel status, neighbor device, and neighbor port ID. Our EtherChannel is working!

## Port Aggregation Protocol (PAgP)

The *Port Aggregation Protocol (PAgP)* is used to add more features to the EtherChannel technology. This protocol is used to learn the capabilities of the neighbors' EtherChannel ports. By doing this, it allows the switches to connect via Fast EtherChannel automatically. PAgP has four options when configuring the channel: `on`, `off`, `desirable`, and `auto`. The first two, `on` and `off`, are self-explanatory. A `desirable` link wants to become a channel, whereas a link set to `auto` doesn't want to but will if it has to. A channel will form if one of the following combinations are used: `on-on`, `on-desirable`, `on-auto`, `desirable-desirable`, `desirable-auto`.

The PAgP protocol groups the ports that have the same neighbor device ID and neighbor group capability into a channel. This channel is then added to the Spanning Tree Protocol as a single bridge port.

For PAgP to work, all the ports must be configured with static, not dynamic, VLANs, and all the ports must also be in the same VLAN or be configured as trunk ports. All ports must be the same speed and duplex as well. In other words, all the ports must be configured the same or PAgP will not work.

If an EtherChannel bundle is already working and you make a change on a port, all ports in that bundle are changed to match the port. If you change the speed or duplex of one port, all ports will then run that speed or duplex.

## Load Balancing and Redundancy

Each switch operates a channel in a different fashion, but there are two main issues that all the switches must face. The first is how they forward traffic across the bundle of physical links, and the second is what happens if a link fails. This section will cover the basics. Cisco provides a guide at `www.cisco.com/warp/public/473/4.html`, detailing how each of the switches deal with these two topics.

### Load Balancing

A channel is nothing more than a bundle of circuits that pretend to act like a single cable. Although this is convenient for increasing bandwidth without causing problems with spanning tree, it leaves us wondering which link gets used when a frame wants to cross the channel. The following list shows how each switch approach this task.

**The 4000** Will send frames across the channel in a fashion that depends on the source and destination MAC addresses. An X-OR process is run on the last bit in the MAC addresses. The output will be one of 0.0, 0.1, 1.0, or 1.1. All frames where the source and destination MAC addresses end in 1 will use the same circuit. All frames where the last bit in the source is 0 and the last bit in the destination is 1 will use a different circuit. There is no load balancing between the circuits.

**The 2950 and 3550** Will also send frames across the channel in a fashion that depends on the source and destination MAC addresses, but with the following caveats. If source-MAC address forwarding is used, frames are sent to hosts across the ports the source MAC address is associated with. If destination-MAC address forwarding is implemented, frames are forwarded according to the destination host's MAC address/port association. In either case, there is symmetry in the frame transfer, with frames following predictable paths according to entries in the bridging tables. Source-based forwarding is enabled by default.

**Layer 3+ switches** A switch that can recognize layer 3 or higher information can be configured to forward frames based on higher-layer header information. For example, the 6000 series can be configured with hardware that enables it to choose what circuit to use based on source, destination, or both. For addressing, it can use MAC addressing, IP addressing, or port values.

### Redundancy

Because of the dynamic, load-balancing nature of 2950 and 3550 switches, redundancy and the management of traffic after a port failure are almost transparent. Frames previously carried over the port that fails are transferred to the port with the least traffic load at the moment of failure.

The 4000 works in a similar fashion, in that frames previously carried over the failed link are switched to the remaining segments within the EtherChannel.

## PortFast

By default, the Spanning Tree Protocol (STP) runs on all ports on a switch. Because most of the ports connect to workstations, printers, servers, routers, and so on, it's basically a waste of resources for these point-to-point ports to be running the Spanning Tree Protocol. When a device—let's say, a workstation—powers up, it takes up to 50 seconds before the switch forwards data on the port because the STP is making sure no loops are going to occur when the port is in forwarding mode. Not only is this a waste of time (because a loop does not occur with point-to-point links), but some protocols or applications could time out.

*PortFast* is used to make a point-to-point port almost immediately enter into forwarding state by decreasing the time of the listening and learning states. This is very helpful for switch ports that have workstations or servers attached, because these devices will connect immediately instead of waiting for the STP to converge. If you connect a hub to a port configured with PortFast and then accidentally connect another port into the switch from the hub, you will have a network loop, and STP will not stop it. It is important to make sure that PortFast is used only on point-to-point links connected only to workstations or servers.

## Configuring PortFast

To configure PortFast on a switch, use the `set spantree portfast` command. The following switch output shows how to configure ports 2/1–12 with PortFast:

```
Terry_4000> (enable) set spantree portfast ?
Usage: set spantree portfast <mod_num/port_num>   <enable|disable>
       set spantree portfast <trcrf> <enable|disable>

Terry_4000> (enable) set spantree portfast 2/1-12 enable
Warning: Spantree port fast start should only be enabled on ports connected
to a single host. Connecting hubs, concentrators, switches, bridges, etc. to a
fast start port can cause temporary spanning tree loops. Use with caution.
Spantree ports 2/1-12 fast start enabled.
Terry_4000> (enable)
```

Notice the nice warning received on the switch console when PortFast was turned on. Also notice that we were able to turn on all 12 ports of our 10/100 card.

To configure PortFast on an IOS-based switch, use the `spanning-tree portfast` interface command:

```
Terry_2950(config)#int fa 0/12
Terry_2950(config-if)#switchport mode access

Terry_2950(config-if)#spanning-tree ?
  bpdufilter     Don't send or receive BPDUs on this interface
  bpduguard      Don't accept BPDUs on this interface
  cost           Change an interface's spanning tree port path cost
  guard          Change an interface's spanning tree guard mode
  link-type      Specify a link type for spanning tree protocol use
  port-priority  Change an interface's spanning tree port priority
  portfast       Enable an interface to move directly to forwarding on link up
  stack-port     Enable stack port
  vlan           VLAN Switch Spanning Tree
```

```
Terry_2950(config-if)#spanning-tree port

Terry_2950(config-if)#spanning-tree portfast ?
  disable  Disable portfast for this interface
  trunk    Enable portfast on the interface even in trunk mode
  <cr>

Terry_2950(config-if)#spanning-tree portfast
%Warning: portfast should only be enabled on ports connected to a single host.
Connecting hubs, concentrators, switches, bridges, etc. to this interface
when portfast is enabled, can cause temporary bridging loops.

Use with CAUTION

%Portfast has been configured on FastEthernet0/12 but will only have effect
when the interface is in a non-trunking mode.
Terry_2950(config-if)
```

This parameter must be configured on each port you want to run PortFast. Note the words of caution associated with this command.

**PortFast and BPDUs**

Some switches support an addition to PortFast called BPDUGuard. When you enable PortFast on a port, there is no guarantee that someone won't add a switch at their desk. Then, for redundancy, they also connect that switch to the LAN drop at their neighbor's desk. Congratulations, you now have a spanning tree loop!

BPDUGuard is a feature that can be set on many switches that enable PortFast. It monitors for BPDUs on that port. If a BPDU arrives, the switch shuts down the port, placing it in the `errdisable` state, and generates a status message.

## UplinkFast

*UplinkFast* is used to minimize network downtime by ensuring that network loops do not occur when the network topology changes. STP convergence time is very time-consuming, so network loops can occur when the convergence is taking place. Additionally, some hosts will not be available for communication during the convergence time because STP has disabled ports on a switch during convergence. The key to both problems is decreased convergence time, which UplinkFast was developed to provide.

UplinkFast enables a blocked port on a switch to begin forwarding frames immediately when a link failure is detected on the root port. For the switch to change a port from blocking to forwarding mode, UplinkFast must have direct knowledge of the link failure: otherwise a loop might occur.

To utilize UplinkFast, several criteria must be met. First, UplinkFast must obviously be enabled on the switch. The switch must have at least one blocked port, and the failure must be on the root port. If the failure is not on a root port, UplinkFast ignores it and normal STP functions will occur.

When a link fault occurs on the primary root link, UplinkFast transitions the blocked port to a forwarding state. UplinkFast changes the port without passing through the listening and learning phases, which enables the switch to skip the normal convergence time and start forwarding in about 3 to 4 seconds instead of the usual 50 seconds.

UplinkFast was designed to work with access-layer switches, not core switches, because the switch running UplinkFast must not be the root bridge.

## Configuring UplinkFast

When configuring UplinkFast, remember that all VLANs on the switch are affected and that you can not configure UplinkFast on individual VLANs.

To configure UplinkFast on a set-based switch, use the `set spantree uplinkfast` command:

```
Terry_4000> (enable) set spantree uplinkfast ?
Usage: set spantree uplinkfast <enable> [rate <station_   update_rate>]
[all-protocols <off|on>]
       set spantree uplinkfast <disable>
```

The options are really just `enable` or `disable`. The station update rate value is the number of multicast packets transmitted per 100 milliseconds (by default, it is set to 15 packets per millisecond). It is not recommended that you change this value.

The switch provides an output describing what the command changed on the switch, as shown here:

```
Terry_4000> (enable) set spantree uplinkfast enable
VLANs 1-1005 bridge priority set to 49152.
The port cost and portvlancost of all ports set to above 3000.
Station update rate set to 15 packets/100ms.
uplinkfast all-protocols field set to off.
uplinkfast enabled for bridge.
Terry_4000> (enable)
```

The VLAN priorities are automatically changed to 49152, and the port costs are set to above 3000. These are changed to make it unlikely that the switch will become the root switch.

You can verify the UplinkFast configuration with the `show spantree uplinkfast` command:

```
Terry_4000> (enable) show spantree uplinkfast
```

```
Station update rate set to 15 packets/100ms.
uplinkfast all-protocols field set to off.

VLAN           port list
-----------------------------------------------
1              1/1(fwd)
2              1/1(fwd)
3              1/1(fwd)
4              1/1(fwd)
Terry_4000> (enable)
```

Notice that all four VLANs are changed and that we were not asked which VLANs to run UplinkFast on.

To configure UplinkFast on an IOS-based switch, use the command `spanning-tree uplinkfast` in global configuration mode:

```
Terry_2950(config)#spanning-tree ?
  backbonefast  Enable BackboneFast Feature
  etherchannel  Spanning tree etherchannel specific configuration
  extend        Spanning Tree 802.1t extensions
  loopguard     Spanning tree loopguard options
  mode          Spanning tree operating mode
  pathcost      Spanning tree pathcost options
  portfast      Spanning tree portfast options
  uplinkfast    Enable UplinkFast Feature
  vlan          VLAN Switch Spanning Tree

Terry_2950(config)#spanning-tree uplinkfast ?
  max-update-rate  Rate at which station address updates are sent
  <cr>

Terry_2950(config)#spanning-tree uplinkfast
Terry_2950(config)#
```

To verify that UplinkFast is configured and running, use the command `show spanning-tree uplinkfast`:

```
Terry_2950#show spanning-tree uplinkfast
UplinkFast is enabled

Station update rate set to 150 packets/sec.
```

```
UplinkFast statistics
-----------------------
Number of transitions via uplinkFast (all VLANs)            : 0
Number of proxy multicast addresses transmitted (all VLANs) : 0

Name                 Interface List
-------------------- ------------------------------------
VLAN0001
VLAN0002
VLAN0003

Terry_2950
```

The default frame generation rate is 150pps, which is displayed with the `show uplinkfast` command. The next command used to help STP maintain a consistent network is BackboneFast.

## BackboneFast

Sometimes a switch might receive a BPDU from another switch that identifies the second switch as the root bridge when a root bridge already exists. This shouldn't happen, except when a new switch comes on line and the BPDU is considered "inferior."

BPDUs are considered inferior when a switch has lost its link to the root bridge. The switch transmits the BPDUs with the information that it is now the root bridge as well as the designated bridge. The receiving switch ignores the inferior BPDU for the max age time, to prevent spanning tree loops.

After receiving inferior BPDUs, the receiving switch tries to determine whether there is an alternate path to the root bridge. If the port that the inferior BPDUs are received on is already in blocking mode, then the root port and other blocked ports on the switch become alternate paths to the root bridge. However, if the inferior BPDUs are received on a root port, then all presently blocking ports become the alternate paths to the root bridge. Also, if the inferior BPDUs are received on a root port and there are no other blocking ports on the switch, the receiving switch assumes that the link to the root bridge is down and the max age time expires, which turns the switch into the root switch.

If the switch finds an alternate path to the root bridge, it uses this new alternate path. This new path, and any other alternate paths, will be used to send a Root Link Query BPDU. By turning on *BackboneFast*, the Root Link Query BPDUs are sent out as soon as an inferior BPDU is received. This can enable faster convergence in the event of a backbone link failure. To ensure proper operation, BackboneFast should be enabled on all switches, including the root, if it is enabled at all.

### Configuring and Verifying BackboneFast

Configuring BackboneFast is pretty easy, but it sounds difficult, which is the cool part about this command. You turn it on with the `set spantree backbonefast` command. Here is an example of this command being enabled:

```
Terry_4000> (enable) set spantree backbonefast
Usage: set spantree backbonefast <enable|disable>

Terry_4000> (enable) set spantree backbonefast enable
Backbonefast enabled for all VLANs
```

Notice in the preceding switch output that BackboneFast is enabled for all VLANs, and it must be enabled on all switches in your network to function. To verify that it is running on a switch, use the `show spantree backbonefast` command:

```
Terry_4000> (enable) show spantree backbonefast
Backbonefast is enabled.
Terry_4000> (enable)
```

The preceding command shows that BackboneFast is enabled. That's all there is to it. It is a little different with the IOS-based switches:

```
Terry_2950(config)#spanning-tree ?
  backbonefast   Enable BackboneFast Feature
  etherchannel   Spanning tree etherchannel specific configuration
  extend         Spanning Tree 802.1t extensions
  loopguard      Spanning tree loopguard options
  mode           Spanning tree operating mode
  pathcost       Spanning tree pathcost options
  portfast       Spanning tree portfast options
  uplinkfast     Enable UplinkFast Feature
  vlan           VLAN Switch Spanning Tree

Terry_2950(config)#spanning-tree backbonefast ?
  <cr>
```

## Rapid Spanning Tree

In the beginning, all bridges were inherently slow and it was accepted by users and applications developers alike that convergence would be slow. Cisco engineers have worked to develop solutions that overcame the basic flaws in STP that became obvious only when switching matured and took over from legacy bridging. All of the previous enhancements to the STP, such as PortFast, UplinkFast, and BackboneFast, have been proprietary.

*Rapid Spanning Tree Protocol (RSTP)*, which has been standardized as 802.1w, can be regarded as a replacement for the proprietary extensions. Recalling the two core concepts of the 802.1D STP from Chapter 4, let us compare the old with the new.

First, 802.1D specifies that there are five different states that a port can be in. Each state is accompanied by a port mode, so a blocking port, for example, can not be a root or designated port.

RSTP assumes that three of these states can be regarded as essentially the same from the perspective of other switches. Listening, blocking, and disabled modes are all characterized by the facts that they do not forward frames and they do not learn MAC addresses, so RSTP places them all into a new mode, discarding. Learning and forwarding ports remain more or less the same. The effect of this change is to decouple the port states from the port roles.

The second big difference is the timing operation. In 802.1D STP, bridges would only send out a BPDU when they received one on their root port. These legacy bridges essentially act as forwarding agents for BPDUs that are generated by the root. In contrast, 802.1w-enabled switches send out BPDUs every hello time, containing current information.

The combination of these two changes forces spanning tree to operate in a much faster mode, with convergence being achieved in just a few seconds (typically about three times the 2-second update timer), largely because if a switch fails to receive BPDUs on an interface for 6 seconds, it presumes that the port at the other end of the link is down.

This rapid transition to the forwarding state, caused by switches no longer having to wait for the timer mechanism, is similar in concept to the proprietary PortFast mechanism, and only operates on edge ports and point-to-point links. Other enhancements in RSTP, such as the synchronization of root port information and the explicit forwarding authorization granted by switches to other switches, have parallels with the UplinkFast and BackboneFast extensions.

It is likely that, as time passes, greater emphasis will be placed by Cisco on the standardized mechanisms of 802.1w rather than the proprietary extensions to 802.1D.

Those wishing to learn more about RSTP than is covered in the CCNP program should visit `www.cisco.com/warp/public/473/146.html`.

# Summary

The Spanning Tree Protocol was originally designed to work on bridged networks, which in turn were designed to segment LANs to allow for additional growth—remember that collision domains have some upper limits, largely based upon the back-off algorithm inside Ethernet, which gradually nibbles away at the available bandwidth. These networks carried slow applications data, often FTP or e-mail, and although redundancy was planned to cover for bridge failures, slow convergence was readily accepted.

Modern-day switches have replaced bridges, and the design criteria have shifted dramatically. Now we have expectations of almost instant recovery from network failures because the applications themselves place those demands on the network. With so many applications having an interactive or multimedia component, and with business relying so heavily on the LAN infrastructure, slow legacy STP no longer meets our needs and expectations.

You should now be familiar with all of the bells and whistles that bring STP into the 21st century. Whether they be proprietary implementations of PortFast, UplinkFast, or BackboneFast, or their soon-to-happen replacement by standards-based alternatives such as 802.1s and 802.1w, we need their help to get STP to work the way we want. Related to this, you have several configuration options for changing the STP timers to speed up convergence in a legacy network.

These days it's possible to configure separate spanning trees on different VLANs, giving us the multiple benefits of planning optimal topologies while also creating faster converging and smaller (hence more efficient) spanning trees. Finally, it is often advantageous to increase bandwidth at certain places in the network using port aggregation protocols such as EtherChannel. These "channelizing" protocols provide an inexpensive and simple mechanism for increasing bandwidth on point-to-point links using existing interfaces.

# Exam Essentials

**Know the types of spanning tree available.** STP comes in a variety of different flavors, and you need to be sure which one to configure. It's not necessarily a case of which one is best, because not every switch supports every option, but you do need to understand the different types of spanning tree and know what their limitations and benefits are. ISL is Cisco proprietary and allows for one spanning tree instance per VLAN (PVST), whereas the standards-based 802.1Q supports only Common Spanning Tree, unless you also implement 802.1s and the MST option.

**Know what can be configured to reduce the delay a port must go through with a topology change.** A perennial STP problem is slow convergence. The Cisco proprietary options of PortFast, BackboneFast, and UplinkFast are capable of speeding up the process, and you need to understand what they are doing and under what circumstances you can use them. At the time this book went to press, these are the main players, but the recent standardization of 802.1w—RSTP—means that they may be used less in the future.

**Understand how an EtherChannel works.** An EtherChannel is formed from bonding together between two and eight ports connecting the same two switches. A single command on each switch logically binds the circuits together, but only if each circuit is configured in an identical fashion.

# Key Terms

Before you take the exam, be sure you're familiar with the following terms:

BackboneFast

Common Spanning Tree (CST)

Fast EtherChannel

Gigabit EtherChannel

Per-VLAN Spanning Tree (PVST)

Per-VLAN Spanning Tree+ (PVST+)

Port Aggregation Protocol (PAgP)

PortFast

Rapid Spanning Tree (RSTP)

UplinkFast

# Written Lab

Write the answers to the following questions:

1. Write the command to set a switch to become the root bridge for VLANs 50–1000 with four switches in the internetwork on a 4000 series switch.
2. What command shows you the port cost and priority for VLAN 1 on an IOS-based switch?
3. Write the command to set the port cost on a 4000 switch port 2/1 from the default of 19 to 10.
4. Write the command to set the priority for port fa0/1 to 20 on a 3550 switch. What mode is the command entered in?
5. After you change your port priority, you can verify the configuration with which command?
6. Write the command to set port 1/1 priority on a set-based switch to 16 for VLANs 1 and 2 only.
7. Write the commands to turn on PortFast on ports 2/1–12 on an IOS-based switch.
8. Write the command to set UplinkFast on a set-based switch to on.
9. Write the command to create an EtherChannel bundle on a set-based switch using ports 1/1–2.
10. Write the command to change the `fwddelay` to 10 seconds on a set-based switch.

# Review Questions

1. The Spanning Tree Protocol was created to overcome the problems of what type of bridging?
   - **A.** Source route bridging
   - **B.** Shorter path bridging
   - **C.** Transparent bridging
   - **D.** UplinkFast bridging

2. Bridge Protocol Data Units (BPDUs) are responsible for providing information for which four services in a spanning tree?
   - **A.** Determining the locations of data loops
   - **B.** Electing a root bridge
   - **C.** Monitoring the spanning tree
   - **D.** Deciding the manufacturer's MAC address on a physical interface
   - **E.** Notifying other switches of network changes

3. On what VLAN are Bridge Protocol Data Units (BPDUs) sent by default?
   - **A.** VLAN 64
   - **B.** VLAN 1005
   - **C.** VLAN 1
   - **D.** VLAN 10

4. Which of the following provides a separate instance of Spanning Tree Protocol for every VLAN?
   - **A.** Common Spanning Tree (CST)
   - **B.** Spanning Tree Algorithm (STA)
   - **C.** Port Aggregation Protocol (PAgP)
   - **D.** Per-VLAN Spanning Tree (PVST)

5. To configure a backup root bridge on a set-based switch, what command would be used?
   - **A.** `set spanning tree backup`
   - **B.** `set spantree secondary`
   - **C.** `set spantree root secondary`
   - **D.** `spanning tree 2`

6. How many Spanning Tree Protocol instances are supported on the 2950 switch?
   A. 1005
   B. 10
   C. 512
   D. 64

7. Which of the following would change the VLAN port priority on an IOS-based switch to a value of 16?
   A. `spanning-tree vlan` *`vlan_number`* `priority 16`
   B. `spanning-tree priority 16`
   C. `config spantree priority 16`
   D. `spanning-tree priority 16 vlan` *`vlan_number`*

8. When setting the VLAN port priority, what are the available values you can use?
   A. 0–63
   B. 1–64
   C. 0–255
   D. 1–1005

9. When you're using EtherChannel on your switches and a link failure occurs, what controlling device notifies the EARL of the failure?
   A. SAMBA
   B. CPU
   C. EBC
   D. SAINT

10. From which of the following can PAgP form a bundle?
   A. Only statically assigned VLAN ports
   B. Dynamically assigned VLAN ports
   C. Dynamically and statically assigned VLAN ports
   D. Ports using different duplex types

11. What does the STP use to choose a forwarding port if the port costs are equal on a switch?
   A. Port ID
   B. MAC address
   C. Bridge name
   D. Hello timer

12. What is used to make a point-to-point port enter almost immediately into forwarding state by decreasing the time of the listening and learning states?

    A. PortUp

    B. PortFast

    C. Priority

    D. BackboneFast

13. What protocol sends Root Link Query BPDUs upon receiving an inferior BPDU?

    A. PortUp

    B. PortFast

    C. Priority

    D. BackboneFast

14. Which of the following commands is used to create a bundle on a 4000 series switch?

    A. `port set channel`

    B. `set port channel`

    C. `etherchannel on`

    D. `set bundle slot/port`

15. Which of the following global configuration commands is used to turn on BackboneFast on an IOS-based switch?

    A. `port channel backbonefast`

    B. `spanning-tree backbonefast`

    C. `spantree backbonefast`

    D. `enable spanning-tree backbone-fast`

16. Which of the following is true regarding PVST+? (Choose all that apply.)

    A. It is a Cisco proprietary protocol.

    B. It adds checking mechanisms to make sure there are no configuration problems on trunked ports and VLAN IDs across switches.

    C. It is set on a port-by-port basis.

    D. It enables Cisco switches to support the IEEE 802.1Q standard.

17. What is the IEEE implementation of the STP?

    A. CST

    B. PVST

    C. PVST+

    D. 802.1u

18. How many spanning tree instances are defined with the PVST protocol running on a switch with six VLANs configured?
    - A. 1005
    - B. 1
    - C. 6
    - D. 64

19. How many spanning tree instances are defined with the CST protocol running on a switch with six VLANs configured?
    - A. 1005
    - B. 1
    - C. 6
    - D. 64

20. Which three of the following can STP use to determine the best path to the root bridge?
    - A. STP protocol
    - B. Port cost
    - C. Path cost
    - D. Bridge priority
    - E. Port priority

# Hands-On Lab

In this lab, you'll test PortFast and UplinkFast on the network; then you'll configure the 4000 series switch as an STP root and add EtherChannel between the 4000 and 2950 switches. Figure 5.2 shows the network configuration used in this lab. Make sure the configurations of your switches are deleted and the default STP configuration is on both switches.

**FIGURE 5.2** Network diagram for the hands-on lab

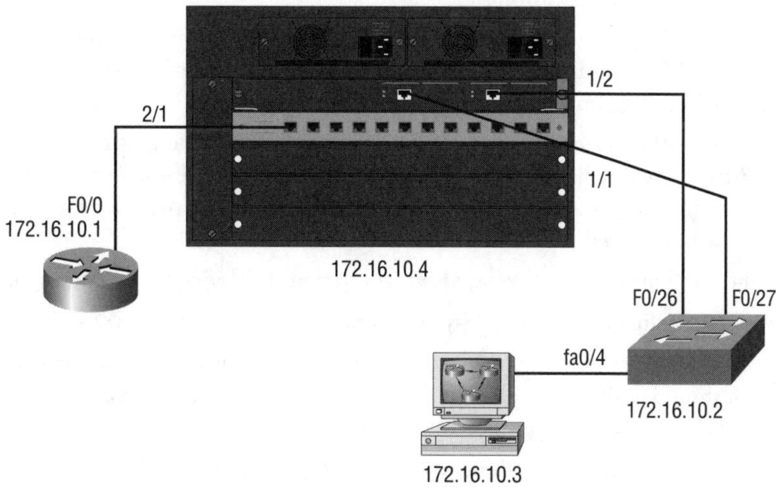


Configure both the 4000 series switch and the 2950 switch with the hands-on labs from Chapter 2, "Connecting the Switch Block," and Chapter 3, "VLANs, Trunks, and VTP." Each switch should have the hostname, interface descriptions, passwords, VTP domain information, and VLANs configured and trunk links on. Test by pinging from the workstation to the 2950 and 4000 switch.

1. Remember that PortFast is disabled on all ports of a switch by default. By turning on PortFast, you can start forwarding up to 50 seconds sooner when bringing up a device. To test this, connect your workstation into interface fa0/4 of the 2950 switch and then from the DOS prompt of your workstation, ping the 4000 series switch.

   ```
   Ping -t 172.16.10.4
   ```

2. The `-t` will keep the ping running. Go to the 2950 switch and perform a `shutdown` and `no shutdown` on interface fa0/4. Then notice how long it takes before the pings resume. This could be up to 50 seconds (although, if you have a small network, it might resume faster).
3. Leave the pings running. Go to int fa0/4 and type **`spanning-tree portfast`**, which turns on PortFast for that port.
4. Go to the 2950 switch and perform a `shutdown`, then a `no shutdown` on fa0/4. The pings will time out but should resume after only a few seconds.

5. Leave the Ping program running. Type **show spanning-tree vlan 1** and notice which port is forwarding and which port is blocking.
6. Leave the Ping program running. Perform a shutdown on the forwarding interface. Notice that the pings have timed out, but they should resume after a few seconds.
7. Type **show spanning-tree vlan 1** and notice which port is forwarding.
8. Perform a no shutdown on the port that you originally shut down. Notice that the pings have timed out again, but the pings should resume after a few moments.
9. Turn on UplinkFast on your 2950 forwarding port by typing **spanning-tree uplink-fast** from global configuration mode.
10. Perform steps 5 through 8 again and notice that the ping's time-out and resume cycle was shorter. UplinkFast demonstrated an almost immediate transition to the second trunk link when the forwarding link was shut down.
11. Configure the 4000 series switch as the STP root switch by typing **set spantree root 1-4 dia 2** from the enable mode of the switch. The diameter of the network is determined by counting the switches connected to the root, including the root, which in this case is 2. The VLANs configured are 1–4.
12. Verify the configuration by typing **show spantree 1**. Notice the root designation.
13. Make sure your links are trunked by typing **show trunk** on the 4000 series switch.
14. Go to the 2950 and verify the forwarding port. Change the cost of the forwarding port to 20, which should make the blocked port the forwarding port. Type **spanning-tree cost 20** in interface configuration mode on the forwarding port.
15. Verify the configuration with the show spanning-tree command and notice that the blocked port is now forwarding and the forwarding port has been changed to blocked. Also notice the port costs.
16. Set the port priority on the forwarding port as well, to make sure that STP always uses this port to forward, by typing **spanning-tree port-priority 64** from interface configuration, which is half of the 128 default interface priority.
17. Verify the configuration with the show spantree command.
18. Create an EtherChannel bundle between your two switches, but before you do, make sure your port configurations are exactly the same. Change the 2950 switch back to the default configuration. Type **spanning-tree cost 10** and **spanning-tree port-priority 128** from interface configuration mode. Also, set the duplex of the links to full-duplex on both the 2950 and 4000. Set the 4000 to be 100Mbps as well.
19. From the 2950 interface configuration mode, type **duplex full** on both ports.
20. From the 4000 series switch, type **set port speed 100** and **set port duplex full** for ports 1/1 and 1/2.
21. Set the EtherChannel bundle to on for the 2950 switch by typing the interface command **channel-group *group_number* mode *mode_type***.
22. From the 4000 series switch, turn on EtherChannel by typing **set port channel 1/1-2 on**.
23. Verify the EtherChannel bundle by typing **show port channel**.

# Answers to Written Lab

1. `set spantree root 50-1000 dia 4`
2. `show spanning-tree vlan 1`
3. `set spantree portcost 2/1 10`
4. `spanning-tree port-priority 20`, entered in interface mode
5. `show spanning-tree`
6. `set spantree portvlanpri 1/1 16 1-2`
7. `spanning-tree portfast` entered in interface configuration mode *for each desired interface*
8. `set spantree uplinkfast enable`
9. `set port channel 1/1-2 on`
10. `set spantree fwddelay 10`

# Answers to Review Questions

1. C. The Spanning Tree Protocol was designed to help stop network loops that can happen with transparent bridge networks running redundant links.

2. A, B, C, E. The Bridge Protocol Data Units are sent out every 2 seconds by default and provide information to switches throughout the internetwork. This includes finding redundant links, electing the root bridge, monitoring the links in the spanning tree, and notifying other switches in the network about link failures.

3. C. VLAN 1 is a default VLAN and used for management by default.

4. D. The Cisco proprietary protocol Per-VLAN Spanning Tree (PVST) uses a separate instance of spanning tree for each and every VLAN.

5. C. The `set spantree root secondary` command enables you to configure a backup root bridge.

6. D. The 2950 switch can support up to 1005 VLANs but only up to 64 STP instances.

7. A. On an IOS-based switch, use the `spanning-tree vlan` *`vlan_number`* `priority 16` from interface configuration to change the port priority.

8. A. A priority from 0 to 63 can be set for each VLAN.

9. C. Should one link in the bundle fail, the Ethernet Bundle Controller (EBC) informs the Enhanced Address Recognition Logic (EARL) ASIC of the failure, and the EARL in turn ages out all addresses learned on that link.

10. A. PAgP bundled ports must all be configured the same, including the duplex and speed. Also, dynamic VLANs will not work, so VLANs must be assigned statically or must all be trunked ports.

11. A. The switch uses the port ID to find the best forwarding port if the link costs are equal.

12. B. PortFast is used to put a blocked port into forwarding state immediately upon a bootup of a point-to-point device such as a workstation or server.

13. D. When BackboneFast is turned on, the Root Link Query BPDUs are sent out as soon as an inferior BPDU is received. This can enable faster convergence in the event of a backbone link failure.

14. B. The command `set port channel` *`slot/port`* `[on/off]` is used to create an EtherChannel bundle.

15. B. To enable BackboneFast on an IOS-based switch, use the `spanning-tree backbonefast` command, which turns the protocol on for every VLAN.

16. A, B, D. PVST is proprietary to Cisco, and PVST+ is an extension of PVST. PVST+ enables non-PVST information to be accepted and received into PVST, adds configuration checking, and enables Cisco switches to support 802.1Q.

17. A. The IEEE uses what is called Common Spanning Tree (CST), which is defined with IEEE 802.1Q. The IEEE 802.1Q defines one spanning tree instance for all VLANs.

18. C. The PVST protocol defines one instance of STP per VLAN.

19. B. The CST protocol defines one instance of STP per network regardless of the number of VLANs configured.

20. B, C, E. The port cost, path cost, and port priority are used to determine the best path to the root bridge.

# Inter-VLAN Routing

## THE CCNP EXAM TOPICS COVERED IN THIS CHAPTER INCLUDE THE FOLLOWING:

- ✓ Understand VLAN trunking protocols including 802.1Q, ISL, and the dynamic trunking protocol
- ✓ Describe inter-VLAN routing and name the components
- ✓ Configure access ports for static membership of single and multiple VLANs
- ✓ Configure ports as 802.1Q trunks and verify their operation
- ✓ Configure ports as ISL trunks and verify their operation
- ✓ Identify the Cisco Route Switch processors and explain how they are implemented

First, let's have a quick review. Routers break up broadcast domains and layer 2 switches are used to break up collision domains. If you connect all your switches together, they will be in one broadcast domain. You can break up broadcast domains in layer 2 switched networks by creating virtual LANs (VLANs). However, the hosts within a VLAN can communicate only within the same VLAN by default.

Obviously you can not bridge together VLANs because that would allow the forwarding of broadcasts across the VLAN boundary, and would just create a larger single VLAN. For devices in one VLAN to communicate with devices in a different VLAN, they must be routed through a layer 3 device. This is called *inter-VLAN routing.* You can perform inter-VLAN routing with internal route processors in a layer 2 switch or with an external router called an *external route processor*.

In this chapter, we cover both internal route processors and external route processors and how to configure them for inter-VLAN configuration.

The term *route processor* is used commonly when discussing the device used for inter-VLAN communications, but we should be clear. This is really just a router, either running externally or as firmware or software in a switch. Modern implementations of route processors run IOS and support routing protocols in common with routers.

# Routing Between VLANs

The main reason for the creation of a VLAN is to keep traffic within local workgroups. We have already mentioned in this book that you can not communicate between VLANs without a router (layer 3 device), so understanding the configuration of VLANs and understanding routing need to go hand in hand in order to understand the full process of inter-VLAN communications.

Route processors provide the communication that hosts need between VLANs. However, if you are using local VLANs (see Chapter 3, "VLANs, Trunks, and VTP" for a thorough explanation), a good rule of thumb is to design your networks so at least 80 percent of the users' traffic does not cross over into another VLAN. Therefore, you should design the network so that the users have access to local servers and other needed resources to prevent excessive packets from crossing the route processor.

## Real World Scenario

### ISL Network Cards

It is worth repeating that many network card vendors nowadays make NICs that can understand ISL and 802.1Q encapsulated packets. When attempting to keep a large percentage of traffic from straying from the local VLAN, these cards can be very useful. Fitting a server with an ISL or 802.1Q-aware NIC means that the server can be a member of multiple VLANs and connect to a switch via a trunk link.

Example scenarios include installing one of these NICs in an e-mail server or a database server. Anything that a large number of people, across several VLANs, need to access is a candidate for this type of connection. It often makes more fiscal sense to upgrade a server NIC than to upgrade an entire router.

Cisco recommends that VLANs should be configured one for one with IP subnet designs. This means that you need to create a subnet design for your network taking into account the needs of the various VLANs. If you are using VLSM, this is pretty straightforward, but if for some reason you are constrained to a single subnet mask, you may need to select the mask first and then design your VLANs around the subnet design. For example, if you have engineering, marketing, sales, and support departments, you will typically—not always, but typically—create a subnet for each department, making sure you have room for growth. You would then create a VLAN for each department. In Chapter 3, we discussed the differences between local and end-to-end VLANs. Regardless of the type of VLAN you configure, each of these types would be associated with a subnet.

The route processor managing the inter-VLAN routing would have multiple interfaces (real or virtual) and each would have an IP address in the subnet associated with the interface VLAN. Each device within a VLAN would have a default gateway of the IP address of the inter-VLAN device connected to its VLAN. The inter-VLAN device would then route any packets with a destination not on the local network.

Before configuring routing between your VLANs, you need to understand the type of data sharing that is needed. By understanding the user and business needs, you can design the network with load balancing and/or redundant links if needed.

When configuring routing, you can choose from three options:

- Multiple links
- A single trunk link
- An internal or external route processor

VLSM (Variable Length Subnet Masking) is a technique designed to create flexible subnets and get the most from your available IP address space. It is covered in detail in the *CCNP: Building Scalable Cisco Internetworks Study Guide*, by Carl Timm and Wade Edwards (Sybex, 2003).

## Multiple Links

You can configure your VLANs to inter-communicate by connecting a separate router interface into separate switch ports that are configured for each VLAN. Each workstation in the VLAN would have its default gateway configured for the physical router interface's own VLAN/subnet. Figure 6.1 shows how this might look in an internetwork.

**FIGURE 6.1** Routers with multiple links

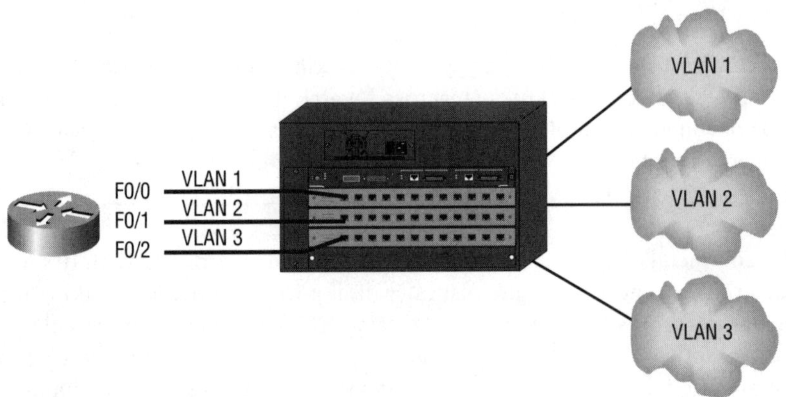


This is a perfectly workable solution for small networks, but it does not scale well when you have more than a few VLANs. It depends on the type of router you have. For every VLAN, you need to have a router interface (typically FastEthernet or Gigabit Ethernet), so a larger, more expensive router can have more interfaces without being saturated—but sooner rather than later, you will run out of physical interfaces.

The more VLANs you have, the more router interfaces you have to purchase with the router. Also, you should have a fast router such as a high-end (at least a 4700 or 7200 series) router that can route quickly so the router does not become a bottleneck. Cost then becomes the issue with multiple links, and the possible requirement for multiple or redundant route-processors doubles the cost.

**Real World Scenario**

### Using Legacy Equipment

Using multiple links is not a desirable thing to do in most cases, but there are times when it might be the only solution. The alternate solutions—using a trunk, for example—require Fast Ethernet at the least. Trunks do not run over 10Mbits/second Ethernet. So if you have some routers with only slower Ethernet interfaces, such as the 2500 series, then you would be able to effect inter-VLAN routing with one of those—albeit quite slowly.

## A Single Trunk Link

Another possible solution to routing between VLANs is creating a trunk link on a switch and then using a frame-tagging protocol such as ISL or 802.1Q (which are used to identify VLAN/frame relationships as they traverse FastEthernet and Gigabit Ethernet links) on the router. Cisco calls this solution "router on a stick."

Figure 6.2 shows how the internetwork might look with a single trunk link for all VLANs.

**FIGURE 6.2** Single trunk link for all VLANs

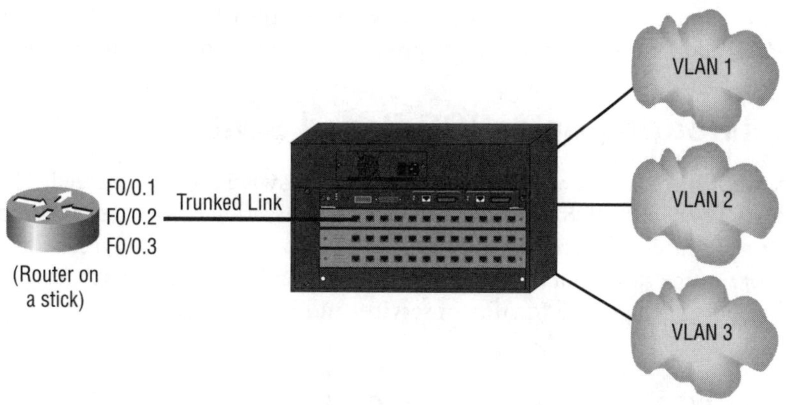


This solution uses only one router interface on the router, but it also puts all the traffic on one interface. You really have to have a fast router to do this. Also, to even perform this function, you need, at minimum, a FastEthernet interface on a 2600 series router. ISL does not work on 10BaseT interfaces, nor would you want to run this on 10BaseT because it is processor- and bandwidth-intensive.

## An Internal Route Processor

An *internal route processor* is a router on a card that fits inside the switch. This enables a switch to route packets without having the packets leave the box that the switch resides in. You need to add an internal route processor to a layer 2 device—for example, a 4000 Catalyst switch—to be able to provide forwarding of layer 3 packets without an external router.

Adding an internal route processor makes a layer 2 switch into a multi-layer switch and can integrate layer 2 and layer 3 (and possibly layer 4) functionality in a single box. The 4000 series uses a *Layer 3 Switching Module (L3SM)*, and the 6000 series uses the *Multi-layer Switch Module (MSM)* and the *Multi-layer Switch Feature card (MSFC)* to perform this function. The MSM and MSFC (and older RSMs and RSFCs) are configured in exactly the same way on older switches.

The 4000 series router module (WS-X4232-L3) consists of a 4GB routing switch fabric with 4GB interfaces. Two of these gigabit connections appear on the front panel, making externally accessible gigabit router ports, while the two remaining ports are connected internally to the switch backplane. (There are also 32 10/100M ports, which are standard layer 2 ports and not linked into the routing fabric.)

Most of the time, ports 3 and 4 are configured as part of the same channel and subinterfaces are added as needed using either ISL or 802.1q encapsulation. The configuration of gigabit ports 3 and 4 on the router module must be consistent with the configuration of port slot/1 and slot/2 on the switch.

The traffic flow between the module and the switch can be seen using the global commands `show interface port-channel` or `show interface gigabit`.

The L3SM is plugged directly into the switch, and runs the Cisco IOS in order to perform inter-VLAN communication. The 4000 series switch sees the RSM as a single trunked port with a single MAC address. In other words, it appears as a router on a stick to the switch.

## Internal Routing on an IOS-Based Switch

More recently, an entirely new method for inter-VLAN switching has emerged. The migration of Cisco switches over to IOS has meant that a new generation of switches is equipped with native routing capabilities. Not only are these faster than those switches with additional daughter boards or routing cards, but they support a variety of enhanced features that we will examine later in the book, such as QoS (quality of service) and layer 3 switching.

# Using ISL and 802.1Q Routing

The best solution to inter-VLAN routing might be to provide a Gigabit Ethernet router interface for each VLAN. Obviously this can be cost prohibitive, as well as stretching the physical limitations of router options. What if you have 200 VLANs? Can you really afford a router with 200 Gigabit Ethernet ports? That would be an interesting configuration.

Well, there are some other options open to you, because you can use just one interface for all your VLANs. Using either the Cisco proprietary Inter-Switch Link (ISL) or the standards-based 802.1Q protocol, you can configure routing between VLANs with only one FastEthernet or one Gigabit Ethernet interface. To run either ISL or 802.1Q, you need to have two VLAN-capable FastEthernet or Gigabit Ethernet devices, such as a Cisco 4000 or 6500 switch and a 7000 (or larger) series router. (We will be using a 2600 router in the hands-on lab, but that is a little low-powered for larger networks.)

Remember from Chapter 3 that both ISL and 802.1Q are trunking protocols, ways of explicitly tagging VLAN information onto an Ethernet frame? This tagging information enables VLANs to be multiplexed over a trunk link through an external encapsulation method. By running a trunking protocol on the switch and router interfaces, you can interconnect both devices and maintain VLAN information end to end.

You can configure inter-VLAN routing with either an external router or an internal route processor that can be placed in a slot of a modular Catalyst switch, such as the 4000 and 6500 series (as well as the old 5000 series). In this section, we take a look at both options.

## Configuring ISL/802.1Q with an External Router

An external layer 3 device can be used to provide routing between VLANs. You can use almost any router to perform the function of external routing between VLANs, but if trunking is being used, the selected router must support the VLAN tagging method used, whether it's ISL or 802.1Q; then the FastEthernet or Gigabit Ethernet interface would be your choice.

If you have a few small VLANs that perform 80 percent or more of their network function on the local VLAN, then you can probably get away with a 10Mbps Ethernet connection into each VLAN. Just remember that 10Mb interfaces do not support trunking, so the configuration would be one VLAN per interface. You should get FastEthernet if you can.

The external router interface needs to be configured with a trunking protocol encapsulation, such as ISL or 802.1Q, thus allowing different VLANs to be assigned to different subinterfaces. These subinterfaces give you an extremely flexible solution for providing routing between VLANs. To perform ISL routing on a single interface, the interface must be at least a FastEthernet interface that supports ISL routing. The Cisco 1750 is the least expensive router that can perform this function.

To configure ISL/802.1Q routing on a single interface, you must first configure the subinterfaces. These are configured by using the *`int.subinterface_number`* global command. Here is an example on a 2600 router with a FastEthernet interface:

```
Terry_2620#configure terminal
Enter configuration commands, one per line.  End with CNTL/Z.
Terry_2620(config)#interface fa0/0.?
  <0-4294967295>  FastEthernet interface number

Terry_2620(config)#interface fa0/0.1
Terry_2620(config-subif)#
```

Notice the number of subinterfaces available (4.2 billion). You can choose any number that feels good because the subinterfaces are only locally significant to the router. However, we usually like to choose the VLAN number for ease of administration. Notice that the prompt on the router is now telling you that you are configuring a subinterface (`config-subif`).

After you configure the subinterface number you want, you then need to define the type of encapsulation you are going to use. Here is an example of the different types of trunking protocols you can use:

```
Terry_2620(config-subif)#encapsulation ?
  dot1Q   IEEE 802.1Q Virtual LAN
  isl     Inter Switch Link - Virtual LAN encapsulation
  sde     IEEE 802.10 Virtual LAN - Secure Data Exchange
  tr-isl  Token Ring Inter Switch Link - Virtual LAN encapsulation
```

You're not done yet. You need to tell the subinterface which VLAN it is a member of, and you provide this information on the same line as the encapsulation command. Here is an example:

```
Terry_2620(config-subif)#encapsulation isl ?
  <1-1000>  Virtual LAN Identifier.
```

Notice that you can configure the subinterface to be a part of any VLAN up to 1000. The `dot1Q` encapsulation is for the IEEE standard 802.1Q trunking, and `isl` is for ISL encapsulation.

After you choose the interface and encapsulation type and VLAN number, configure the IP address that this subinterface is a member of. The complete configuration looks like this:

```
Terry_2620#configure terminal
Enter configuration commands, one per line.  End with CNTL/Z.
Terry_2620(config)#interface fa0/0.1
Terry_2620(config-subif)#encapsulation isl 1
Terry_2620(config-subif)#ip address 172.16.10.1 255.255.255.0
```

The preceding configuration is for subinterface fa0/0.1 to VLAN 1. You would create a subinterface for each VLAN. You can verify your configuration with the `show running-config` command:

```
!
interface FastEthernet0/0.1
 encapsulation isl 1
 ip address 172.16.10.1 255.255.255.0
```

If you had elected the 802.1Q encapsulation, the complete router configuration would look like this:

```
Terry_2620#configure terminal
Enter configuration commands, one per line.  End with CNTL/Z.
Terry_2620(config)#interface fa0/0.1
Terry_2620(config-subif)#encapsulation dot1Q 1
Terry_2620(config-subif)#ip address 172.16.10.1 255.255.255.0
```

Once again, you can verify your configuration with the `show running-config` command:

```
!
interface FastEthernet0/0.1
 encapsulation dot1Q 1
 ip address 172.16.10.1 255.255.255.0
!
```

## Configuring ISL/802.1Q on an Internal Route Processor

Up until recently, the situation was that if you did not have an external router or if you had many VLANs, you should use a L3SM to provide the layer 3 routing for your 4000/6500 series switch.

The introduction of the Supervisor III and IV engines for the Catalyst 4000 and above changes all this. These new Supervisor engines run IOS, and this means that they can route natively without the need for additional hardware. Obviously, Cisco might recommend an upgrade if you are planning much inter-VLAN routing, which is probably a good idea. The faster switching available with these native IOS devices will certainly improve packet forwarding.

First, however, we will look at the configuration of the older design switches, which have a native switching fabric supplemented by some sort of routing module. We will look at a 4000 series switch that has a Layer 3 Services Module in slot 3. Let's first confirm the hardware configuration of the switch:

```
Terry_4000> (enable) show module
Mod Slot Ports Module-Type               Model               Sub Status
--- ---- ----- ------------------------- ------------------- --- --------
1   1    0     Switching Supervisor      WS-X4012            no  ok
2   2    34    10/100/1000 Ethernet      WS-X4232            no  ok
3   3          Router Switch Card        WS-X4232-L3         no  ok

Mod Module-Name         Serial-Num
--- ------------------- --------------------
1                       JAE044001T8
2                       JAE04271V1N
3                       JAE0427155N

Mod MAC-Address(es)                        Hw     Fw         Sw
--- -------------------------------------- ------ ---------- -----------------
1   00-03-e3-7a-6b-00 to 00-03-e3-7a-6e-ff 2.1    5.4(1)     4.5(2)
2   00-02-b9-61-89-e0 to 00-02-b9-61-8a-0f 2.3
3   00-03-4a-a0-d3-ab to 00-02-4b-a0-d0-cf 1.0    12.0(7)W5( 12.0(7)
```

Now that we have confirmed that the switch sees the router module in port 3, we need to access the L3SM using the `session` command:

```
Terry_4000> (enable) session 3
Trying Router...
Connected to Router.
Escape character is \Q^]'.
Router>
```

You are now connected to the internal route processor and you should continue to configure the device as you would any other router. Notice in the following router output that we set the hostname and routing protocol as well:

```
Router>
Router>enable
Router#
Router#configure terminal
Enter configuration commands, one per line.  End with CNTL/Z.
Router(config)#hostname Terry_L3SM
Terry_L3SM(config)#router eigrp 10
Terry_L3SM (config-router)#network 172.16.0.0
```

As we mentioned, the route processor looks like any Cisco router, because it is running IOS. Remember that it's just as important to configure the routing protocols on this device as it is to configure them on any other router. The route processor is able to handle most of the routing protocols that a traditional router can. Be careful of large routing tables, though.

## Configuring VLANs on an Internal Route Processor

First, it would be common practice to set up the internal gigabit interfaces to act as Gigabit-EtherChannel trunks. This needs to be done at both the L3SM and switch parts of the internal link. On the L3SM, the configuration looks like this:

```
Terry_L3SM#configure terminal
Terry_L3SM(config)#interface GigabitEthernet3
Terry_L3SM(config-if)#channel-group 1
Terry_L3SM(config)#interface GigabitEthernet4
Terry_L3SM(config-if)#channel-group 1
```

And on the Catalyst it looks like this:

```
Terry_4000> (enable)set port channel 3/1-2 mode on
Terry_4000> (enable)set trunk 3/1  nonegotiate dotlq 1-1005
Terry_4000> (enable)set trunk 3/2  nonegotiate dotlq 1-1005
```

Next, instead of creating subinterfaces as you would with an external router, you need to configure each VLAN with the `interface vlan #` command. This establishes a direct virtual connection between the switch backplane and the routing module, and what you are actually doing is associating each VLAN with a virtual interface. Here is an example of how to configure the processor to route between three VLANs:

```
Terry_L3SM#configure terminal
Terry_L3SM(config)#interface vlan 1
Terry_L3SM(config-if)#ip address 172.16.1.1 255.255.255.0
```

```
Terry_L3SM(config-if)#interface vlan 2
Terry_L3SM(config-if)#ip address 172.16.2.1 255.255.255.0
Terry_L3SM(config-if)#interface vlan 3
Terry_L3SM(config-if)#ip address 172.16.3.1 255.255.255.0
Terry_L3SM(config-if)#no shutdown
```

The interesting part of the configuration is the necessary `no shutdown` command for each VLAN interface. Notice in the preceding configuration that we performed a `no shutdown` only on interface VLAN 3. Take a look at the output of interface VLAN 2:

```
Terry_L3SM#show interface vlan 2
Vlan2 is administratively down, line protocol is down
```

It is important to think of each VLAN interface as a separate interface that needs an `IP address` and a `no shutdown` performed, just as with any other router interface.

You can then verify your configuration with the `show running-config` command:

```
Terry_L3SM#show running-config
Current configuration:
!
version 12.0
service timestamps debug uptime
service timestamps log uptime
no service password-encryption
!
hostname Terry_L3SM
!
interface Vlan1
 ip address 172.16.1.1 255.255.255.0
!
interface Vlan2
 ip address 172.16.2.1 255.255.255.0
!
interface Vlan3
 ip address 172.16.3.1 255.255.255.0
!
router eigrp 10
 network 172.16.0.0
```

To view the routing table on the internal processor, use the `show ip route` command:

```
Terry_L3SM#show ip route
Codes: C - connected, S - static, I - IGRP, R - RIP,   M – [output cut]
Gateway of last resort is not set
```

```
     172.16.0.0/24 is subnetted, 3 subnets
C       172.16.3.0 is directly connected, Vlan3
C       172.16.2.0 is directly connected, Vlan2
C       172.16.1.0 is directly connected, Vlan1

Terry_L3SM#
```

## Assigning MAC Addresses to VLAN Interfaces

The RSM uses only one global MAC address for all VLAN interfaces on the device. If you want to assign a specific MAC address to a VLAN interface, use the `mac-address` command. You might want to configure this option to enhance the operation of the RSM interface. Here is an example:

```
Terry_L3SM#configure terminal
Terry_L3SM(config)#interface vlan 2
Terry_L3SM(config-if)#mac-address 4004.0144.0011
Terry_L3SM(config-if)#exit
Terry_L3SM(config)#exit
Terry_L3SM#show running-config
[output cut]
interface Vlan2
 mac-address 4004.0144.0011
 ip address 172.16.2.1 255.255.255.0
```

## Defining a Default Gateway

One thing to keep in mind before configuring ISL on your switches is that the switches must be configured correctly with an IP address, subnet mask, and default gateway. Understand that this has nothing to do with routing, because the switches work only at layer 2. However, the switches need to communicate with IP through the network. Remember that this will not affect data that is passing through the switch. You can think of layer 2 switches as being just like any host on the network. To be able to send packets off the local network, you need to have a default gateway configured.

To configure a default gateway on a 4000 series switch, use the `set ip route` command:

```
Terry_4000> (enable) set ip route 0.0.0.0 172.16.1.1
Route added.
```

You can also use the command `set ip route default 172.16.1.1`, which configures the route the same as the `set ip route 0.0.0.0 172.16.1.1` command does.

The IOS switch `default-gateway` command was covered in Chapter 2, "Connecting the Switch Block."

## Configuring Internal Routing on an IOS-Based Switch

At this stage of learning, it is a simple matter to configure internal routing. The configuration on the modular L3SM is just about identical to that on the modern IOS-based layer 3 switches. This example shows a 3550 configured as a VTP server, and with two VLANs configured. In addition, two interfaces are placed into the created VLANs. No routing protocols are needed unless the requirement exists to route outside the connected VLAN table.

```
Terry_3550# configure terminal
Terry_3550(config)#vtp domain globalnet
Terry_3550(config)#vtp mode server
Terry_3550(config)#vlan 2
Terry_3550(config-vlan)#name PRODUCTION
Terry_3550(config-vlan)#ip address 172.16.2.1 255.255.255.0
Terry_3550(config-vlan)#exit
Terry_3550(config)#vlan 3
Terry_3550(config-vlan)#name SALES
Terry_3550(config-vlan)#ip address 172.16.3.1 255.255.255.0
Terry_3550(config-vlan)#exit
Terry_3550(config)#vlan 1
Terry_3550(config-vlan)#ip address 172.16.1.1 255.255.255.0
Terry_3550(config-vlan)#exit

Terry_3550(config)#interface FastEthernet0/1
Terry_3550(config-if)#description PRODUCTION MANAGER
Terry_3550(config-if)#switchport access vlan 2
Terry_3550(config-if)#switchport mode access

Terry_3550(config)#interface FastEthernet0/2
Terry_3550(config-if)#description SALES MANAGER
Terry_3550(config-if)#switchport access vlan 3
Terry_3550(config-if)#switchport mode access
```

This gives rise to the following running configuration, viewed with the IOS standard `show running-config` statement:

```
Terry_3550#show run
```

```
!
[output cut]
!
interface FastEthernet0/1
 description PRODUCTION MANAGER
 switchport access vlan 2
 switchport mode access
 no ip address
!
interface FastEthernet0/2
 description SALES MANAGER
 switchport access vlan 3
 switchport mode access
 no ip address
!
[output cut]
!
interface Vlan1
 ip address 172.16.1.1 255.255.255.0
!
interface Vlan2
 ip address 172.16.2.1 255.255.255.0
!
interface Vlan3
 ip address 172.16.3.1 255.255.255.0
!
[output truncated]
!
Terry_3550#
```

The only other thing we need to do is make sure that the routing table is properly populated. By default, IP routing is not enabled on a layer 3 switch, so we need to configure that with the global command `ip routing`. After this is done, you can view the routing table in the normal way.

```
Terry_3550#
Terry_3550#conf t
Terry_3550(config)#ip routing
Terry_3550(config)#exit
Terry_3550#

Terry_3550#show ip route
```

```
Codes: C - connected, S - static, I - IGRP, R - RIP, M - mobile, B - BGP
       D - EIGRP, EX - EIGRP external, O - OSPF, IA - OSPF inter area
       N1 - OSPF NSSA external type 1, N2 - OSPF NSSA external type 2
       E1 - OSPF external type 1, E2 - OSPF external type 2, E - EGP
       i - IS-IS, L1 - IS-IS level-1, L2 - IS-IS level-2, ia - IS-IS inter area
       * - candidate default, U - per-user static route, o - ODR
       P - periodic downloaded static route

Gateway of last resort is not set

     172.16.0.0/24 is subnetted, 2 subnets
C       172.16.1.0 is directly connected, Vlan1
C       172.16.2.0 is directly connected, Vlan2
C       172.16.3.0 is directly connected, Vlan3
Terry_3550#
```

Notice that the complete range of routing protocols is available for use. This immensely powerful piece of equipment can be used for full multi-layer switching and routing as needed. So far we have not needed to configure a routing protocol, as all of our subnets are directly attached, but as the internetwork grows we shall undoubtedly need to configure dynamic routing.

# Summary

VLANs are designed to keep broadcasts within artificial limits, and this makes them a useful design tool. But nobody can expect that all of the data in one VLAN will remain there. Users will need to communicate with services and hosts on other VLANs, and that means going through a router.

Question: What do you get when you bridge two VLANs together?

Answer: A bigger VLAN!

So, to get from one VLAN to another, data needs to be forwarded across a router! Routers are needed to enable hosts on different networks to communicate, and also for inter-VLAN communication. The router in question can be either an external router or an internal route processor. Both are suitable and can do the task, but the advantages of internal processors are clear—cost, simplicity, and speed of link to the router fabric are all factors.

You can use both internal routers and external routers to configure an ISL/802.1Q. You can also use them for inter-VLAN configuration. Further, both ISL and 802.1Q are able to differentiate between VLANs at the router interface.

# Exam Essentials

**Know the difference between an internal and an external route processor.** An external route processor is a standard router that is routing between VLANs. An external router can accept packets across a trunk terminating at a single Ethernet interface or it can have several connections, one per VLAN. The second method is required if there are only 10Mb Ethernet interfaces available, because you can not configure trunks on standard Ethernet.

An internal route processor is a special card inside the switch that routes between VLANs. Once connected internally to the route processor, you can configure it in a similar fashion to the external processor/router, as it will run IOS. Modern layer 3 switches with an intelligent matrix run IOS and can be configured in the same way.

**Know how to configure VLANs on each of the routers.** On an internal route processor, the router has VLAN interfaces as opposed to the Ethernet or serial interfaces found on an external router. The interfaces are accessed in the same fashion, but on an internal router, each VLAN interface gets an IP address and the `no shut` command must be issued to activate the interface.

On an external router, you must select the appropriate FastEthernet or Gigabit Ethernet interface and create subinterfaces, preferably labeling them the same as the VLAN that will reside there. Configure each subinterface with the appropriate encapsulation and IP address and then issue the `no shut` command on the physical interface.

**Know how to configure routing on the router and on the switch.** Both internal and external route processors can be configured to route packets from one network to another based on routing protocol information. To configure a dynamic routing protocol, you must enter global configuration mode and use the `router` command followed by routing-protocol-specific information. No routing protocol may be needed if all VLANs in your network have an interface on the route processor and there are no external links.

To configure routing on a switch, you must configure a default gateway on the switch. Use the command `set ip route` to accomplish this, pointing to an IP address that can forward packets to other networks, something like a router interface.

# Key Terms

Before you take the exam, be sure you're familiar with the following terms:

| | |
|---|---|
| external route processor | L3SM |
| internal route processor | Multi-layer Switch Feature card (MSFC) |
| inter-VLAN routing | Multi-layer Switch Module (MSM) |

# Written Lab

Write the answers to the following questions:

1. Write the commands to configure ISL routing for VLAN 1 with an IP address of 172.16.10.1 with a 24-bit mask, on FastEthernet interface 0/0.
2. Write the command to view the different types of cards in a 4000 series switch.
3. Write the command to connect to an RSM module in slot 3.
4. Write the commands to configure two VLANs on an IOS-based switch. VLAN 1 has an IP address of 172.16.1.1 and VLAN 2 has an IP address of 172.16.2.1. Both addresses use a 24-bit mask.
5. Write the command to set a hardware address on the VLAN 2 interface of 4004.0144.0011.
6. What type of link is needed to run ISL routing on a FastEthernet interface?
7. What is the IEEE alternative to ISL?
8. True/False: You can assign a MAC address to a VLAN ISL interface.
9. How many VLANs can you create with subinterfaces on a FastEthernet interface?
10. What command would you use to see the configuration on a Catalyst 3550 switch?

# Review Questions

1. What command is used to connect to an RSM from a set-based switch CLI?

   A. `connect`

   B. `telnet`

   C. `session`

   D. `module`

2. What command shows you the hardware address of each card in a 4000 series switch?

   A. `sh cards`

   B. `show session`

   C. `show version`

   D. `show module`

3. What command is used to set a virtual hardware address on a VLAN interface?

   A. `mac-address` *`mac_address`*

   B. `config mac` *`slot/port mac-address`*

   C. `set vlan mac-address` *`mac-address`*

   D. `set mac` *`mac-address`*

4. What are the two types of frame-tagging encapsulation methods used with FastEthernet and Gigabit Ethernet trunk links?

   A. `dot1Q`

   B. `sde`

   C. ISL

   D. `tr-isl`

5. What are the two options you can consider when you need to have inter-VLAN communication and you have only an external router?

   A. One router interface for every switch in the internetwork

   B. One router interface for every single VLAN

   C. Two router interfaces for every switch in the internetwork

   D. One router interface into one switch port running a trunking protocol

6. What is the correct configuration for a subinterface on a modular router?

   A. `int 10.f0/0`

   B. `int fa0/0.3980`

   C. `faste 0/0 subinterface 3`

   D. `set int f0/0.1`

7. Which of the following is true regarding layer 2 switches?

   A. They break up collision domains by default.

   B. They break up broadcast domains by default.

   C. They provide inter-VLAN routing by default.

   D. An external route processor can be attached to the backplane of the switch to provide inter-VLAN routing.

8. What is an advantage of running an integral layer 3 switch as opposed to one with an additional plug-in module?

   A. Integral layer 3 switches run an enhanced version of IOS.

   B. Integral switches are more scalable.

   C. Integral switches are more resilient.

   D. There are no obvious advantages at the moment; different switches suit different tasks.

9. Which of the following is true regarding the configuration of the internal route processors?

   A. The 6000 series internal processors use the `set` commands.

   B. The 4000 series internal processors use a menu-driven interface.

   C. The 8500 series of switches does not support internal route processors.

   D. Internal route processors all use IOS commands.

10. Which two commands can be used to set a default route on a 4000 series switch to 172.16.1.1?

    A. `route add 0.0.0.0 0.0.0.0 172.16.1.1`

    B. `set ip route default 0.0.0.0 172.16.1.1`

    C. `set ip route default 172.16.1.1`

    D. `set ip route 0.0.0.0 172.16.1.1`

11. Which of the following is used to configure VLAN 1 on an internal route processor with an IP address of 208.211.78.200/28?

    A. `set vlan1 ip address 208.21.78.200 255.255.255.240`

    B. `config t, vlan1 ip address 208.21.78.200 255.255.255.240`

    C. `int vlan 1, ip address 208.211.78.200 255.255.255.240`

    D. `set int vlan1, ip address 208.211.78.200 255.255.255.224`

12. Which of the following is true?
   A. You are required to assign a password to an RSM interface CLI.
   B. You must perform a `no shutdown` command for every subinterface on an external route processor.
   C. You must perform a `no shutdown` command for every VLAN on an internal route processor.
   D. You can use a 2500 series router for ISL routing.

13. What routing protocols must be configured on an internal router to route between directly connected VLANs?
   A. RIP, as long as the same subnet is used throughout.
   B. None—directly connected subnets automatically appear in the routing table.
   C. Routing protocols are enabled by default.
   D. EIGRP or IGRP with ISL, RIP or OSPF with 802.1Q.

14. If you wanted to view the IP routing table on a 3550 switch, which command would you use?
   A. `sh vlan route`
   B. `show ip route`
   C. `sho ip vlan`
   D. `show route vlan`

15. To view the routing table on the internal route processor, use the ________ command.
   A. `show routing protocol`
   B. `show vlan`
   C. `show config`
   D. `show ip route`

16. If you assigned a virtual hardware address to VLAN 2 on an internal route processor, how do you view this configuration? (Choose all that apply.)
   A. `show virtual address`
   B. `show vlan 2`
   C. `show interface vlan 2`
   D. `show run`

17. Which command displays the BIA address of a VLAN on an internal route processor?
   A. `show virtual address`
   B. `show vlan 2`
   C. `show interface vlan 2`
   D. `show run`

18. What type of link must be used on a switch port if you are running ISL on an external router interface?

    A. Access

    B. Trunk

    C. Virtual

    D. Ethernet

19. Which of the following sets VLAN 3 to run ISL on an external route processor with one FastEthernet interface?

    A. `(config)#encap isl vlan3`

    B. `(config)#encap vlan3 isl`

    C. `(config-if)#encap isl 3`

    D. `(config-if)encap 3 isl`

20. Which of the following is true regarding inter-VLAN routing using an external router?

    A. Only ISL can be used with gigabit Ethernet.

    B. ISL or 802.1Q can be used only with gigabit Ethernet.

    C. Only 802.1Q can be used with gigabit Ethernet.

    D. ISL or 802.1Q can be used with gigabit and Fast Ethernet.

# Hands-On Labs

In these hands-on labs, you will configure a 4000 series switch, two 2950 switches, and one 2621 router to provide ISL routing between VLANs.

You will complete the following labs:

- Lab 6.1: External Inter-VLAN Routing
- Lab 6.2: Internal Inter-VLAN Routing

In both of the labs, refer to Figure 6.3 for configuring inter-VLAN communication.

**FIGURE 6.3** Configuring inter-VLAN communication for the hands-on labs

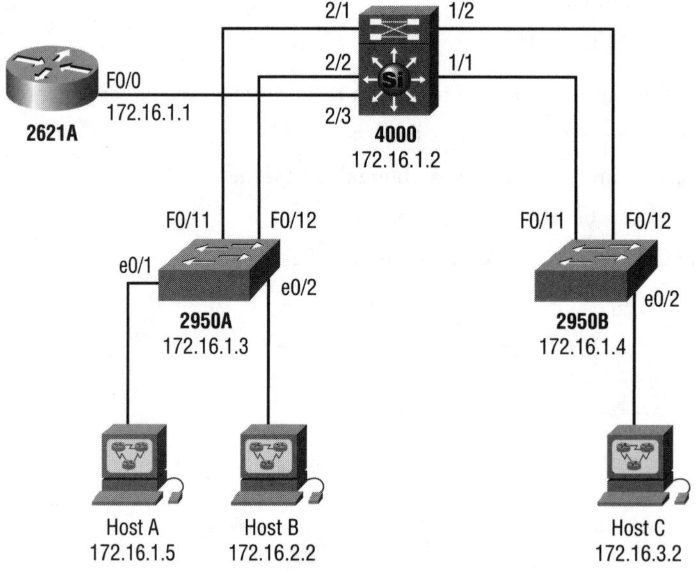


## Lab 6.1: External Inter-VLAN Routing

In this lab, you'll configure the 2621 with ISL routing. First you'll configure the two 2950 switches, then the 4000 switch, and then the 2621 router.

### Configuring the 2950A Switch

Start by configuring the basic features of the switch, including the hostname, passwords, and IP configuration. After that, you will configure the VTP parameters and set the trunks. This is straightforward, and is largely a repeat of previous configurations that you have undertaken.

1. Plug into the 2950A console port.
2. Enter privileged mode by typing **enable**.
3. Enter configuration mode and set the hostname:

```
#config t
(config)#hostname 2950A
```

4. Set the user mode and privileged mode passwords:

```
2950A(config)#enable password level 1 terry
2950A(config)#enable secret jack
```

5. Set the IP address of the switch by using the IP address assigned in Figure 6.3. Set the default gateway address by using interface f0/0 of the 2621 as the gateway:

```
2950A(config)#ip address 172.16.1.3 255.255.255.0
2950A(config)#ip default-gateway 172.16.1.1
```

6. Verify the IP configuration on the switch by typing **show ip**.
7. Set the VTP domain to **globalnet** and then make the switch a VTP client so that when you set the VLANs on the 4000 switch, the 2950A switch will automatically be updated with VLAN information:

```
2950A(config)#vtp domain globalnet
2950A(config)#vtp client
```

8. Set the FastEthernet interfaces to **trunk on** so that all VLAN information will be sent down both links from the 4000 series switch:

```
2950A(config)#int fa0/11
2950A(config-if)#trunk on
2950A(config-if)#int fa0/12
2950A(config-if)#trunk on
```

9. Configure the FastEthernet connection to the 4000 series switch to be full-duplex:

```
2950A(config)#int fa0/11
2950A(config-if)#duplex full
2950A(config-if)#int fa0/12
2950A(config-if)#duplex full
```

## Configuring the 2950B Switch

The configuration of the second switch is very similar to the first, and involves the basic switch naming and addressing, plus setting up VTP and the trunks.

1. Plug into the 2950B switch console.
2. Enter privileged mode by typing **enable**.

3. Enter configuration mode and set the hostname:

```
#config t
(config)#hostname 2950B
```

4. Set the user mode and privileged mode passwords:

```
2950B(config)#enable password level 1 terry
2950B(config)#enable secret jack
```

5. Set the IP address of the switch by using the IP address assigned in Figure 6.3. Set the default gateway address by using interface f0/0 of the 2621 as the gateway:

```
2950B(config)#ip address 172.16.1.4 255.255.255.0
2950B(config)#ip default-gateway 172.16.1.1
```

6. Verify the IP configuration on the switch by typing **show ip**.
7. Set the VTP domain to **globalnet** and then make the switch a VTP client so that when you set the VLANs on the 4000 switch, the 2950B switch will automatically be updated with VLAN information:

```
2950B(config)#vtp domain globalnet
2950B(config)#vtp client
```

8. Set the FastEthernet interfaces to **trunk on** so that all VLAN information will be sent down both links from the 4000 series switch:

```
2950B(config)#int fa0/11
2950B(config-if)#trunk on
2950B(config-if)#int fa0/12
2950B(config-if)#trunk on
```

9. Configure the FastEthernet connection to the 4000 series switch to be full-duplex:

```
2950B(config)#int fa0/11
2950B(config-if)#duplex full
2950B(config-if)#int fa0/12
2950B(config-if)#duplex full
```

10. Set the ports to configure an EtherChannel bundle when the 4000 series is configured. This can be run only on the Supervisor card or a specific EtherChannel card. EtherChannel will be run only on the 2950B connection to the 4000 switch.

```
2950B(config-if)#port-channel mode on
```

## Configuring the 4000 Series Switch

Now move on to the larger switch. This switch is running CatOS, and you have to remember to change back to the relevant command set. Configure the basic switch parameters, and set up VTP and the trunks.

1. Connect your console cable to the 4000 series switch and press Enter. Press Enter at the password prompt; then, again at the password prompt, type **enable** and press Enter.
2. Set the hostname of the switch:

```
#(enable)set system name Cat4000>
```

3. Set the user mode and privileged mode passwords:

```
Cat4000>(enable)set password [press enter]
Enter old password: [press enter]
Enter new password: [this doesn't show]
Retype new password: [this doesn't show]
Password changed.
Cat4000> (enable)set enablepass
Enter old password:[press enter]
Enter new password: [this doesn't show]
Retype new password: [this doesn't show]
Password changed.
Cat4000> (enable)
```

4. Set the IP address and default gateway of the switch:

```
Cat4000>(enable)set int sc0 172.16.1.2 255.255.255.0
Cat4000>(enable)set ip route default 172.16.1.1
```

5. Verify this configuration by typing **show int**.
6. Set the VTP domain name to **globalnet** and the mode to server:

```
Cat4000>(enable)set vtp domain globalnet mode server
```

7. Set all ports connected to the 2950 switches as 100Mbps and full-duplex. The two ports on the Supervisor engine are labeled 1/1 and 1/2 and run in only 100Mbps, so only the duplex can be set on those ports.

```
Cat4000> (enable) set port duplex 1/1 full
Port(s) 1/1 set to full-duplex.
Cat4000> (enable) set port duplex 1/2 full
Port(s) 1/2 set to full-duplex.
Cat4000> (enable) set port speed 2/1 100
Port(s) 2/1 speed set to 100Mbps.
Cat4000> (enable) set port speed 2/2 100
Port(s) 2/2 speed set to 100Mbps.
Cat4000> (enable) set port duplex 2/1 full
Port(s) 2/1 set to full-duplex.
Cat4000> (enable) set port duplex 2/2 full
Port(s) 2/2 set to full-duplex.
Cat4000> (enable)
```

8. It is possible that the ports on the 4000 have been disabled because of mismatched port configurations between the 2950 and 4000. Type the command **show port *slot/port*** to see the status. If it is disabled, use the **set port enable *slot/port*** command.

```
Cat4000> (enable) set port enable 1/1
Port 1/1 enabled.
```

9. Configure trunking on all ports connected to the 2950A and 2950B switches:

```
Cat4000> (enable) set trunk 2/1 on isl
Port(s) 2/1 trunk mode set to on.
Port(s) 2/1 trunk type set to isl.
Cat4000> (enable) set trunk 2/2 on isl
Port(s) 2/2 trunk mode set to on.
Port(s) 2/2 trunk type set to isl.
Cat4000> (enable) set trunk 1/1 on isl
Port(s) 1/1 trunk mode set to on.
Port(s) 1/1 trunk type set to isl.
Cat4000> (enable) set trunk 1/2 on isl
Port(s) 1/2 trunk mode set to on.
Port(s) 1/2 trunk type set to isl.
```

10. Verify that the trunk ports are working by typing **show trunk**:

```
Cat4000>(enable)show trunk
Port      Mode        Encapsulation  Status     Native vlan
--------  ----------- -------------  ---------  --------
 1/1      on          isl            trunking      1
 1/2      on          isl            trunking      1
 2/1      on          isl            trunking      1
 2/2      on          isl            trunking      1
 5/1      on          isl            trunking      1

[output cut]
```

11. Configure EtherChannel on both ports connected to the 2950B switch:

```
Cat4000> (enable) set port channel 1/1-2 on
Port(s) 1/1-2 channel mode set to on.
```

12. Verify that the EtherChannel is working by typing **show port channel**:

```
Cat4000> (enable) show port channel
Port  Status     Channel   Channel     Neighbor        Neighbor
                 mode      status      device            port
----- ---------- --------- ----------- --------------  -----
 1/1  connected  on        channel   cisco 2950   2950B  A
```

```
 1/2  connected  on        channel   cisco 2950  2950A  B
----- ---------- --------- ----------- --------------- -----
Cat4000> (enable)
```

13. At this point, the three switches should be up and working, and you should be able to ping all devices in the 172.16.1.0 network:

```
Cat4000> (enable) ping 172.16.1.3
172.16.1.3 is alive
Cat4000> (enable) ping 172.16.1.4
172.16.1.4 is alive
```

## Configuring VLANs

Because the 4000 series switch is a VTP server and the two 2950 switches are VTP clients, you can configure VLANs on just the 4000 series switch, and the 4000 switch will automatically update the VLAN information on the 2950 switches.

1. On the 4000 series switch console, create two new VLANs:

   VLAN 2: **Sales**

   VLAN 3: **Admin**

```
Cat4000> (enable) set vlan 2 name Sales
Vlan 2 configuration successful
Cat4000> (enable) set vlan 3 name Admin
Vlan 3 configuration successful
Cat4000>(enable)
```

2. Type the command **show vlan** to view the configured VLANs on the switch:

```
Cat4000>(enable)show vlan
VLAN Name                 Status    IfIndex Mod/Ports, Vlans
---- --------------    --------- ------- -------------------
1    default              active    5       2/3-12
2    Sales                active    10
3    Admin                active    11
1002 fddi-default         active    6
1003 token-ring-default   active    9
1004 fddinet-default      active    7
1005 trnet-default        active    8       1003
[output cut]
```

3. Verify that VTP is up and running correctly by telneting into 2950A and 2950B and typing **show vlan**. The same VLANs should appear if VTP is working properly. If not, verify that you spelled the VTP domain the same on all switches.

4. Configure Host A to be in VLAN 1, Host B to be in VLAN 2, and Host C to be in VLAN 3:

```
2950A#config t
Enter configuration commands, one per line.  End with CNTL/Z.
2950A(config)#int e0/1
2950A(config-if)#vlan-membership static 1
2950A(config-if)#int e0/2
2950A(config-if)#vlan-membership static 2

2950B#config t
Enter configuration commands, one per line.  End with CNTL/Z.
2950B(config)#int e0/2
2950B(config-if)#vlan-membership static 3
```

5. Type the **show vlan** command on the 2950B switch and verify that e0/2 is a member of VLAN 3. Type the same command on 2950A and verify that e0/1 is a member of VLAN 1 and that e0/2 is a member of VLAN 2.

```
2950B#show vlan
VLAN Name             Status     Ports
---------------------------------------------------
1    default          Enabled    1, 3-12, AUI, A, B
2    Sales            Enabled
3    Admin            Enabled    2
[output cut]
2950A#show vlan
VLAN Name             Status     Ports
---------------------------------------------------
1    default          Enabled    1, 3-12, AUI, A, B
2    Sales            Enabled    2
3    Admin            Enabled
[output cut]
```

6. Configure each host with the following IP addresses:

   Host A: 172.16.1.5/24 default gateway 172.16.1.1

   Host B: 172.16.2.2/24 default gateway 172.16.2.1

   Host C: 172.16.3.2/24 default gateway 172.16.3.1

7. Try pinging from host to host. This should fail. However, you should be able to ping from Host A to all switches in the network, and all switches should be able to ping to Host A because they are all in the same VLAN. To enable hosts in different VLANs to communicate, you need to configure inter-VLAN routing.

## Configuring the 2621 Router

The 2621 router will provide the inter-VLAN routing and enable the hosts to communicate with each other.

1. Go to the privileged mode of the router and enter global configuration mode:

```
Router>enable
Router#configure terminal
Router(config)#
```

2. Set the hostname and passwords on the 2621 router:

```
Router(config)#hostname 2621A
2621A(config)#enable secret jack
2621A(config)#line console 0
2621A(config-line)password console
2621A(Config-line)login
2621A(config)#line vty 0 4
2621A(config-line)password telnet
2621A(Config-line)login
```

3. Configure the FastEthernet interface to run ISL routing for all three VLANs:

```
2621A(config-line)#exit
2621A(config)#interface f0/0.1
2621A(config-subif)#encapsulation isl 1
2621A(config-subif)#ip address 172.16.1.1 255.255.255.0
2621A(config-subif)#interface f0/0.2
2621A(config-subif)#encapsulation isl 2
2621A(config-subif)#ip address 172.16.2.1 255.255.255.0
2621A(config-subif)#interface f0/0.3
2621A(config-subif)#encapsulation isl 3
2621A(config-subif)#ip address 172.16.3.1 255.255.255.0
2621A(config-subif)#interface f0/0
2621A(config-if)#no shutdown
2621A(config-if)#
```

4. Before this will work, you need to set the port on the 4000 to trunk mode. Go to the 4000 switch and configure the port:

```
Cat4000> (enable) set trunk 2/3 on
Port(s) 2/3 trunk mode set to on.
Cat4000> (enable)
```

5. Test the configuration by pinging to all devices from the router:

```
2621A#ping 172.16.3.2
Type escape sequence to abort.
Sending 5, 100-byte ICMP Echos to 172.16.3.2, timeout  is 2 seconds:
.!!!!
Success rate is 80 percent (4/5), round-trip min/avg/   max = 1/1/4 ms
2621A#ping 172.16.1.3
Type escape sequence to abort.
Sending 5, 100-byte ICMP Echos to 172.16.1.3, timeout  is 2 seconds:
.!!!!
Success rate is 80 percent (4/5), round-trip min/avg/  max = 4/5/8 ms
2621A#ping 172.16.2.2
Type escape sequence to abort.
Sending 5, 100-byte ICMP Echos to 172.16.2.2, timeout  is 2 seconds:
.!!!!
Success rate is 80 percent (4/5), round-trip min/avg/  max = 4/5/8 ms
2621A#ping 172.16.1.5
Type escape sequence to abort.
Sending 5, 100-byte ICMP Echos to 172.16.2.2, timeout  is 2 seconds:
.!!!!
Success rate is 80 percent (4/5), round-trip min/avg/  max = 4/5/8 ms
2621A#ping 172.16.1.4
Type escape sequence to abort.
Sending 5, 100-byte ICMP Echos to 172.16.2.2, timeout  is 2 seconds:
.!!!!
Success rate is 80 percent (4/5), round-trip min/avg/  max = 4/5/8 ms
2621A#
```

6. Verify that all hosts can communicate by pinging from host to host.

The reason for less than 100 percent success rate is that the IP hosts have not communicated before and the first ping timed out waiting for the ARP protocol to resolve the hardware addresses of each device. If you like, you can type **show arp** before and after the ping and see the comparison between a populated and an empty arp cache.

## Lab 6.2: Internal Inter-VLAN Routing

In this second lab, you'll configure the L3SM in the 4000 switch for inter-VLAN routing using ISL. The 2950s will be configured first, then the 4000. The 2621 router is not needed in this lab.

1. Unplug the 2621 router from the 4000 series switch. The hosts should no longer be able to ping each other.
2. Configure the L3SM on the 4000 series switch to provide inter-VLAN routing.
3. Start by connecting to the L3SM through the 4000 console:

```
Cat4000> (enable) session 3
Trying Router-3...
Connected to Router-3.
Escape character is '^]'.
Router>
```

Remember to use the show module command to identify the correct slot for your switching module

4. Configure three VLAN interfaces, one for each VLAN configured in the switched internetwork:

```
Router>enable
Router#configure terminal
Enter configuration commands, one per line.  End with CNTL/Z.
Router(config)#hostname 4000L3SM
4000L3M(config)#interface vlan 1
4000L3SM(config-if)#ip address 172.16.1.1 255.255.255.0
4000L3SM(config-if)#no shutdown
4000L3SM(config-if)#interface vlan 2
4000L3SM(config-if)#ip address 172.16.2.1 255.255.255.0
4000L3SM(config-if)#no shutdown
4000L3SM(config-if)#interface vlan 3
4000L3SM(config-if)#ip address 172.16.3.1 255.255.255.0
4000L3SM(config-if)#no shutdown
```

5. Verify that the L3SM is working by pinging between hosts.

# Answers to Written Lab

1. Router#**configure terminal**

   ```
   Enter configuration commands, one per line.  End with CNTL/Z.
   Router(config)#interface fa 0/0.1
   Router(config-subif)#encapsulation isl 1
   Router(config-subif)#ip address 172.16.10.1  255.255.255.0
   ```

2. show module
3. session 3
4. Terry_L3SM#**configure terminal**

   ```
   Terry_L3SM(config)#interface vlan 1
   Terry_L3SM(config-if)#ip address 172.16.1.1 255.255.255.0
   Terry_L3SM(config-if)#no shutdown
   Terry_L3SM(config-if)#interface vlan 2
   Terry_L3SM(config-if)#ip address 172.16.2.1 255.255.255.0
   Terry_L3SM(config-if)#no shutdown
   ```

5. Terry_L3SM#**configure terminal**

   ```
   Terry_L3SM(config)#interface vlan 2
   Terry_L3SM(config-if)#mac-address 4004.0144.0011
   ```

6. A trunk link
7. 802.1Q
8. True
9. 1000
10. show running-config

# Answers to Review Questions

1. C. The `session` command is used to create a session from the switch CLI to the RSM CLI.

2. D. The `show module` command displays the type of cards in each slot, the hardware address, and the serial number of each card.

3. A. The command `mac-address` *`mac_address`* is used under the `interface vlan #` command to set a virtual MAC address to a VLAN interface.

4. A, C. The frame-tagging encapsulation methods are `dot1Q` and ISL. `dot1Q` is the IEEE standard for frame tagging between disparate systems. ISL is a Cisco proprietary FastEthernet and Gigabit Ethernet frame-tagging method.

5. B, D. If you have an external router, you certainly can have a router interface for every single VLAN. However, you can also have one FastEthernet or Gigabit Ethernet interface connected into a switch running a trunking protocol that will provide inter-VLAN routing.

6. B. You can create subinterfaces on a FastEthernet or Gigabit Ethernet modular interface by using the *`type slot/port.subinterface_number`* command.

7. A. Layer 2 switches break up only collision domains by default. A layer 3 device is needed for inter-VLAN routing. An external route processor can not attach to the backplane of a switch, only into a switch port.

8. D. At the moment, there are a variety of switches available, and the modular nature of some larger switches such as the 6500 makes them ideal as core switches. But the 2950 is a wonderful and powerful access layer switch. So currently, there is no clear distinction—just pick one at the scale and price that suits your needs.

9. D. All internal route processors use IOS-based commands.

10. C, D. The command `set ip route default` and the command `set ip route 0.0.0.0` are the same command and can be used to set a default gateway on a 4000 series switch.

11. C. The command `interface vlan #` is used to create a VLAN interface. The IP address of the interface is then configured with the `ip address` command.

12. C. An external route processor configured with subinterfaces does not need a shutdown performed on each subinterface, only the main interface. However, an internal route processor must have a `no shutdown` command performed under every VLAN interface.

13. B. Directly connected subnets appear in the routing table as directly connected—so no routing protocol is needed unless you need to get to non–directly connected subnets.

14. B. The commands are the same as they are for any Cisco IOS router, and `show ip route` is used to view the current routing table entries.

15. D. To view the routing table on the internal processor, use the `show ip route` command, just as you would with any IOS-based router.

**16.** C, D. The commands `show interface vlan #` and `show running-config` display the virtual hardware address of an interface, if set.

**17.** C. The command `show interface vlan` *`vlan#`* shows both the virtual MAC address, if set, and the burned-in address (BIA) of the VLAN interface.

**18.** B. A switch port must be configured with a trunking protocol to run ISL inter-VLAN communication to a single router interface.

**19.** C. The subinterface command `encapsulation` *`type vlan`* is used to set the VLAN ID and encapsulation method on a subinterface.

**20.** D. ISL and 802.1Q may be configured on both Fast and Gigabit Ethernet links, but not on 10BaseT.

# Multilayer Switching (MLS)

## THE CCNP EXAM TOPICS COVERED IN THIS CHAPTER INCLUDE THE FOLLOWING:

- ✓ Identify the components necessary to effect multilayer switching
- ✓ Apply flow masks to influence the type of MLS cache
- ✓ Describe layers 2, 3, 4 and multilayer switching
- ✓ Verify existing flow entries in the MLS cache
- ✓ Describe how MLS functions on a switch
- ✓ Configure a switch to participate in multilayer switching
- ✓ Determine appropriate multilayer switching architectures for specific needs

The expression *Multilayer Switching (MLS)* can be very confusing. If you ask 10 different vendors what it means, you will probably get 11 different answers! After all, you already know that switching is a layer 2 function, where frames are forwarded using just the MAC address and a dynamic table. You may also recall that routing, a layer 3 function where packets are forwarded using IP addresses, sometimes also uses some layer 4 information.

Some people will argue that there is really no such thing as layer 3 switching, and that this is all vendor-speak, just smoke and mirrors to confuse poor buyers into selecting a product. This is rather harsh, but it is true that defining layer 3 switching can be problematical.

So let's get down to business. Why do you need layer 3 switching when you have layer 3 routing? The answer to both of these questions is simple: enhanced performance. Why do you implement any features on any piece of Cisco equipment? To improve performance and to take advantage of the robust feature set provided by Cisco. Routers, by their nature, need to analyze packets in great detail before forwarding them. This takes time, and anything that we can do to reduce the time is of benefit, especially in the modern world of QoS-hungry applications.

MLS can be implemented using more than one technology, because it really is just a vendor description for how routing can be speeded up. Cisco has two separate techniques. One involves the use of a route processor (either external or internal) that communicates specific information to a Cisco switch. The other technique is called Cisco Express Forwarding (CEF), and this requires that the switch have a routing function such as the 3550 series or the 4000 series running native IOS. In this chapter, you'll learn about both.

# Understanding the Fundamentals of MLS

The first of the Cisco MLS implementations involves the use of a *router on a stick*. Figure 7.1 depicts the router-on-a-stick architecture. As you can see from the diagram, there are multiple hosts using two separate VLAN assignments. One segment is running on VLAN 10 and the other is running on VLAN 50. Both VLANs are connected to the same switch. The switch is then connected to a router. Here we show an external router, but an RSM provides the same functionality, just internally.

By now, you understand that for Host A on VLAN 10 to communicate to Host D on VLAN 50, packets must be routed through Router A. Because of the VLAN assignments, the switch must send the packet to the router on interface FE0/0.10. The router knows that the route to the network assigned to VLAN 50 is through interface FE0/0.50. The packet is then sent back to the switch and forwarded to Host D.

**FIGURE 7.1** Router-on-a-stick diagram

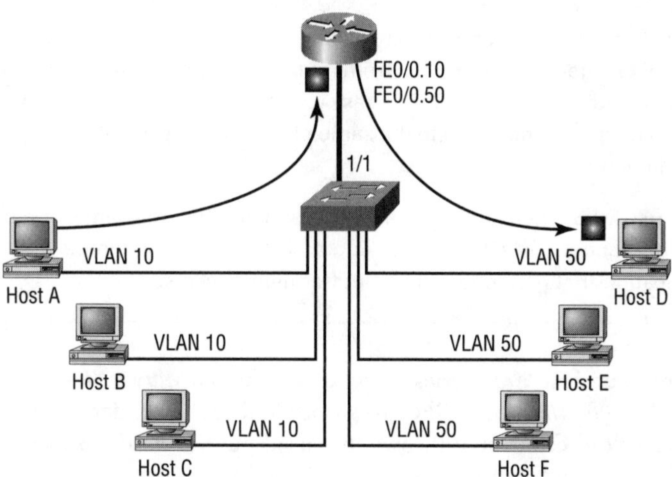


Now back to our original question. Why use layer 3 switching? You can see in Figure 7.1 that it is very inefficient to have to use a router to move a packet from Host A to Host D when they are connected to the same switch. MLS is used to bypass the router on subsequent packets of the same flow. A *flow* is a table entry for a specific conversation, created by using source and destination header information for layers 3 and 4. The switch caches the routing information for that particular flow to make changes to future packets. Several fields within a packet make it unique:

- Source and destination IP addresses
- Source and destination MAC addresses
- Type of Service (ToS)
- Protocol type (for example, HTTP, FTP, ICMP, and so on)

These are just some of the characteristics of a packet that can be used to establish a flow. A switch can be configured to support simple flows, such as IP address to IP address, or the switch can support complex flows dealing with port and protocol information.

To summarize, we use MLS to enable the switch to forward the first packet in the flow to the router and then learn what should be done with the rest of the packets in the flow so the router doesn't need to route them. In Figure 7.1, the switch makes the necessary VLAN and destination MAC address changes in the subsequent packets.

## MLS Requirements

Some Cisco Catalyst switches require additional hardware to make use of the packet header information. While the 3550 series and the 4000 series with the Supervisor IV card have

**Large Packet Streams**

MLS tends to work better when the packet stream is fairly large. If a user is browsing the corporate intranet, they might be getting information from multiple servers located in various areas. If that same user is downloading a file via FTP, it is easy to see that the hundreds of fragments are all coming from the same place and going to the same place. Only the initial fragment needs to be routed; the rest of them are layer 3 switched.

For the best results, use MLS when large files are accessed or when the same type of information is accessed on a frequent basis. Users checking their e-mail every minute would be an example of an application that generates small but frequent packets.

on-board processing, Catalyst 6000 series switches use the *Multilayer Switch Feature Card (MSFC)* and the *Policy Feature Card (PFC)* to gather and cache header information. (You may remember that the old Catalyst 5000 switches used the *NetFlow Feature Card (NFFC)* to gather this information and cache it.) A detailed process, which will be discussed later in this chapter, enables switches to establish flows.

MLS requires three components to function in any network (we have already briefly discussed two of them):

- *Multilayer Switching Route Processor (MLS-RP)* is a directly attached router. This can be an MLS-capable external router or an RSM installed in the switch.
- *Multilayer Switching Switch Engine (MLS-SE)* is an MLS-capable switch (a 6000 with an MSFC and PFC).
- *Multilayer Switching Protocol (MLSP)* is a protocol that runs on the router and enables it to communicate to the MLS-SE regarding topology or security changes.

Now that you have a basic understanding of what MLS does and what is required for MLS to function in a network, let's get into the nitty-gritty of how it works. Throughout the rest of the chapter, you will see the preceding abbreviations many times.

## MLS Procedures

We discussed the three required components of MLS. It is important to understand how they work together to enable layer 3 switching. Let's look at a sample network topology that supports MLS.

Figure 7.2 shows a simple architecture of a router and a switch with two connected hosts on the switch. Again, the hosts have different VLAN assignments, requiring the router's intervention to route packets. Notice that the figure depicts the main interface with two subinterfaces, FE0/0.2 and FE0/0.3. As it stands, the current topology requires that all packets sent from the client on VLAN 3 to the client on VLAN 2 be routed by the external router. If there are a large number of packets, this creates a lot of unnecessary work.

**FIGURE 7.2** MLS example topology

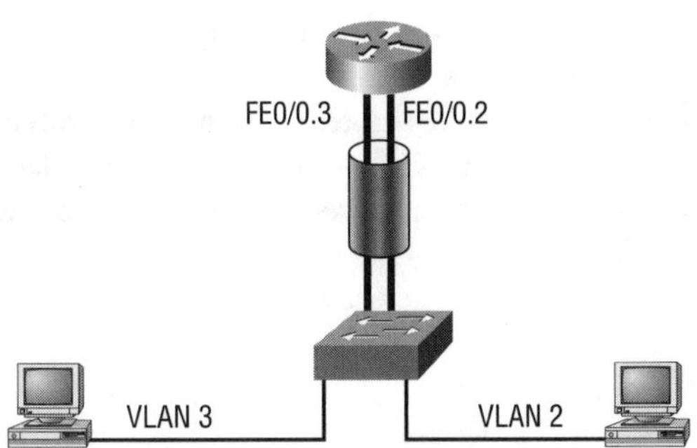


MLS follows a four-step process to establish the layer 3 switching functionality. These four steps can then be broken down into more detailed processes, which will be discussed shortly. If these descriptions leave you a bit confused, the detailed explanation should clear things up. The four steps required to enable MLS are as follows:

**MLSP discovery** The MLS-RP uses MLSP to send hello packets out all interfaces to discover any MLS-SE devices and establish the MLS-RP/MLS-SE neighbor relationships.

**Identification of candidate packets** The NFFC or PFC watches incoming packets and as it forwards the packets to the router, it creates partial cache entries for them, thus identifying the packets as potential candidates for a flow. A candidate packet is one that has yet to return from the router.

**Identification of enable packets** The NFFC or PFC watches packets coming from the MLS-RP and tries to match them with candidate packet entries. If matches are made, the packets are tagged as enable packets and a shortcut forwarding entry is made in the CAM table. This shortcut tells the switch how to duplicate the effect of routing. Everything that the router did to the packet, the switch is now able to do.

**Layer 3 switching of subsequent flow packets** Incoming packets are compared against CAM table entries. If the packets match the flow criteria, the switch will take the shortcut information and make any necessary changes, and the packet is directly forwarded to the appropriate exit port for the flow.

As we said, the preceding list is an overview of the steps that must take place before packets can be switched at layer 3. We'll discuss each step in detail next.

## MLSP Discovery

Switches need routers to perform the initial route table lookup and the packet rewrite. This dependency requires that MLS adjacencies are established between the switch and the router. This is accomplished by using MLSP.

Initially, the router, or MLS-RP, sends hello packets containing all the MAC addresses and VLANs configured for use on the router. These messages are sent every 15 seconds to a layer 2 multicast address of 01-00-0C-DD-DD-DD. This is the address for the CGMP process on a Cisco switch. CGMP is covered in detail in Chapter 8, "Understanding and Configuring Multicast Operation," and Chapter 9, "Quality of Service (QoS)." The intended recipients of these hello packets are the MLS-SE devices on the network.

When an MLS-SE receives the information, it makes an entry in the CAM table of all the MLS-RP devices in the layer 2 network. Layer 2 is mentioned because MLS-SE devices are not concerned with devices that are not directly connected to layer 2 devices, such as switches. Figure 7.3 depicts the MLSP discovery process.

**FIGURE 7.3** MLSP discovery

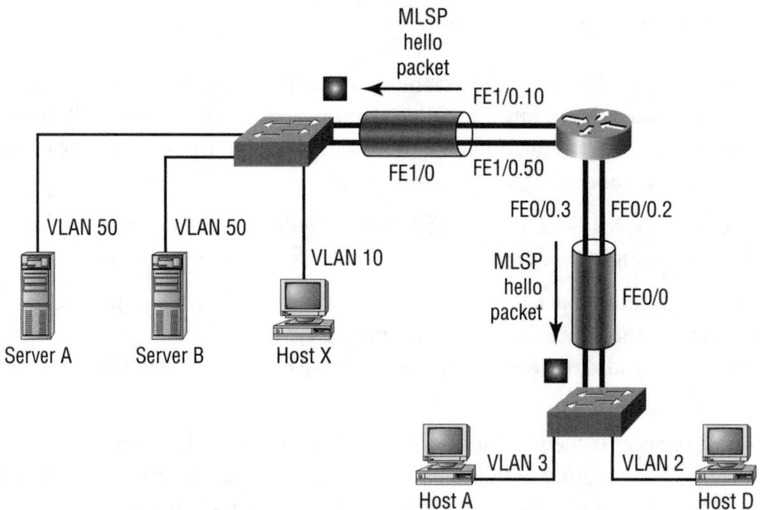


Part of the information that is stored in the CAM table after an MLSP hello packet is received is an ID called an XTAG. The following is a description of the significance and purpose of the XTAG.

## XTAGs

An *XTAG* is a unique identifier that MLS switches use to keep track of the MLS routers in the network. All the MAC addresses and VLANs in use on the MLS-RP are associated with the XTAG value in the CAM table.

The following output is from a Catalyst 6509 with an MSFC and PFC. The `show mls` command was issued to provide the output:

```
Terry_6509> (enable) show mls
Total packets switched = 4294967295
Total Active MLS entries = 85
IP Multilayer switching aging time = 256 seconds
IP Multilayer switching fast aging time = 0 seconds,  packet
```

```
threshold = 0
IP Current flow mask is Destination flow
Active IP MLS entries = 85
Netflow Data Export version: 7
Netflow Data Export disabled
Netflow Data Export port/host is not configured.
Total packets exported = 0

IP MSFC ID      Module XTAG MAC               Vlans
--------------- ------ ---- ----------------- ----------
172.16.100.5    15     1    00-d0-bc-e3-70-b1 2,3

IPX Multilayer switching aging time = 256 seconds
IPX flow mask is Destination flow
IPX max hop is 0
Active IPX MLS entries = 0

IPX MSFC ID     Module XTAG MAC               Vlans
--------------- ------ ---- ----------------- ----------
172.16.100.5    15     1    -                 -

Terry_6509> (enable)
```

You can clearly see that the MSFC has been assigned the XTAG value of 1. The MSFC is a daughter card residing on the Supervisor card, which is why it uses module 15. The MSFC receives the assignment because the MSFC was configured as the MLS-RP. In this example, only one MAC address is associated with XTAG 1. However, two VLANs are associated with it.

### MLS Cache

After MLS-SEs have established CAM entries for MLS-RPs, the switch is ready to start scanning packets and creating cache entries. This was described previously as the identification of candidate and enable packets.

The cache entries are made in order to maintain flow data. Flow data enables the MLS-SE to rewrite the packets with the new source and destination MAC address and then forward the packets. All of this is done without sending the packets to the router for a route lookup and to be rewritten.

Cache entries happen in two steps:

- Candidate packet entries
- Enable packet entries

After these entries have been made in the MLS-SE, subsequent packets are matched against existing flow entries and dealt with accordingly.

## Identifying Candidate Packets

The process of identifying *candidate packets* is quite simple. As has already been established, the MLS-SE has MAC address entries for any and all interfaces that come from the MLS-RP. Using this information, the MLS-SE starts watching for incoming frames destined for any MLS-RP-related MAC addresses.

An incoming frame will match one of the following three criteria:

- Not destined for an MLS-RP MAC address
- Destined for an MLS-RP MAC address, and a cache entry already exists for this flow
- Destined for an MLS-RP MAC address, but no cache entry exists for this flow

Different actions will be taken by the MLS-SE, depending on which criteria match.

### Destination Other Than the MLS-RP

If the incoming frame is not destined for a MAC address associated with the MLS-RP, no cache entry is made. No cache entry is made because MLS is used to avoid additional route lookups. If the frame is destined for another MAC address in the CAM table, the frame is layer 2 switched.

Figure 7.4 depicts the occurrence of a candidate packet.

### Cache Entry Exists

When frames destined for an MLS-RP MAC address enter the switch, the switch checks whether a cache entry has been made that matches the attributes of the current packet.

**FIGURE 7.4** Candidate packet

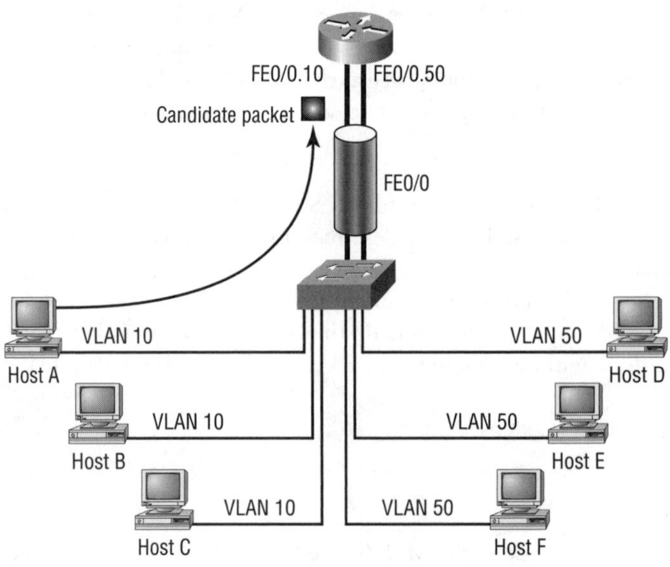

As was previously mentioned briefly, each frame has distinguishing characteristics or attributes that enable the MLS-SE to categorize a packet into a flow. For instance, all packets from a particular IP address and destined for a different IP address can be placed by a switch into a flow. A flow entry can use IP addresses as well as, optionally, layer 4 information. The MLS-SE uses these cache attributes to match header information in future incoming packets. If an incoming packet has the same attributes as an established flow cache entry, the packet is layer 3– or shortcut-switched.

### No Cache Entry

When an incoming frame destined for the MLS-RP is compared against the cache and no existing flow entry is found, a new cache entry is made. At this point, the packet is tagged as a candidate packet.

After the cache entry is made, the packet is forwarded to the router (MLS-RP) for normal processing. Here the router performs the route lookup, rewrites the layer 2 header, and sends the packet out the next-hop interface, whichever it might be.

The state of the MLS cache is only partial at this stage. A complete flow cache has not been established because the MLS-SE has only seen a packet come in and be forwarded to the router. It still needs to see the packet come back from the router before the flow is complete.

## Identifying Enable Packets

*Enable packets* are the missing piece of the flow cache puzzle. Just as the MLS switch watches all incoming frames destined for the MLS router's MAC addresses, it also watches all the packets coming from the MLS router.

It watches these packets, hoping for a match with the candidate packet cache entry. If it can make the match, the packet is tagged as an enable packet and the remaining elements of the flow cache are completed in the CAM table. Figure 7.5 depicts the occurrence of an enable packet.

The match is made by using the following criteria:

- The source MAC address is from an MLS-RP.
- The destination IP matches the destination IP of a candidate packet.
- The source MAC address is associated with the same XTAG value as the candidate packet's destination MAC address.

If all three of these criteria are met, the MLS-SE completes the shortcut cache entry.

### Frame Modification

It is important to understand that this shortcut switching occurs at layer 3. The layer 2 frames that are a part of the conversation but come after the first frame are rewritten by the switch. Normally, a router (layer 3 device) would rewrite the frame with the necessary information. A rewrite consists of changing the VLAN assignment, the source and destination MAC addresses, and the checksums. The MLS-SE can also modify the TTL, TOS, and encapsulation.

Because these packets are no longer sent to the router, the MLS-SE must perform the rewrite function. When the switch changes the source and destination MAC addresses, the MLS-SE uses the MAC address of the MLS-RP for the source, and it changes the destination MAC to the MAC of the directly connected host. Through this procedure, the frame appears to the destination host as if it had come through the router. Figure 7.6 depicts the differences between the incoming frame and the exiting frame.

**FIGURE 7.5** Enable packet

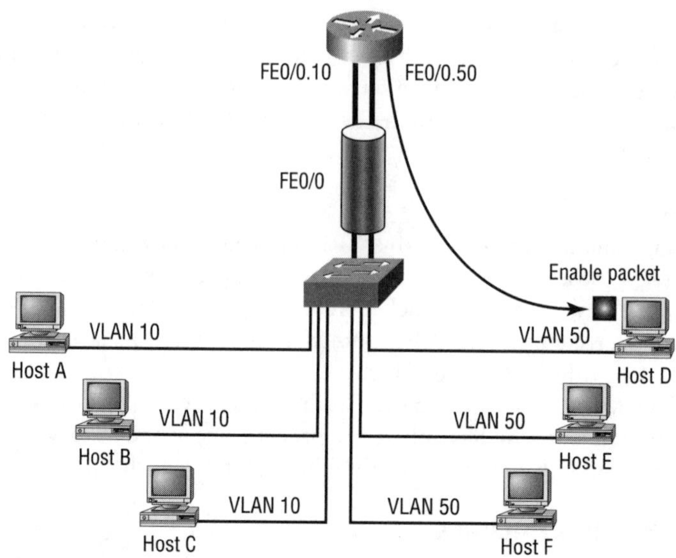


### Subsequent Packets

After the candidate and enable packets have been identified and a shortcut, or flow cache, has been established, subsequent packets are forwarded by the switch to the destination without the use of the router. Because the MLS-SE has the capability to rewrite the frames, it can make the necessary modifications and forward the frame directly to the destination host.

The MLS-SE caches the necessary information, such as the source and destination IP addresses, the source and destination MAC addresses, and the MLS-RP-related MAC addresses. Using this information, the MLS-SE is then capable of identifying packets belonging to a specific flow, rewriting the frame, and forwarding the packets to the proper destination.

## Disabling MLS

There is a right way and a wrong way to disable MLS on a router or switch. Both methods are discussed here.

### The Right Way

The correct way to disable MLS depends on the equipment that you are using. Disabling MLS on a router can be paralleled with disabling MLS on an MSFC for a 6500 series switch. The command is even the same: `no mls rp ip` issued from the interface on either the router or the MSFC. To disable it completely, you can issue the same command from global configuration mode. The consequences of this action vary depending on the system on which it is issued. When the command is issued on the router, the router alone disables MLS. When it's issued on an MSFC, MLS is disabled on the MSFC and the switch itself.

MLS is enabled by default for IP traffic and disabled for IPX. To disable MLS on a 6000 series, MLS should be disabled by issuing the `no ip mls` command on the MSFC.

**FIGURE 7.6** Frame modification

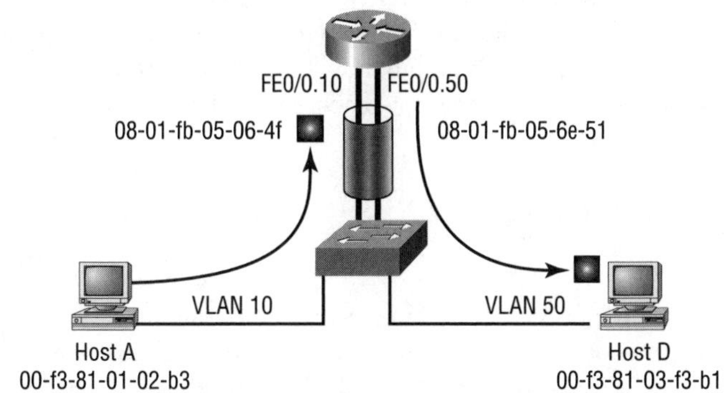


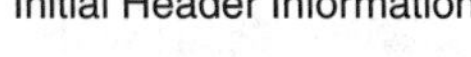


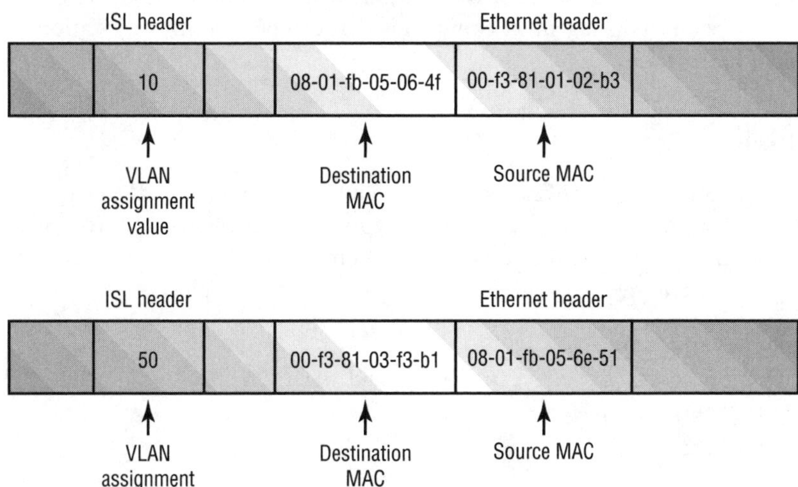


## The Wrong Way

There are several ways to inadvertently disable MLS on switches. Some are temporary, and others are permanent. Here is a list of MSFC/router commands that can disable MLS:

- `no ip routing`
- `ip security`

- `ip tcp compression-connections`
- `ip tcp header-compression`
- `clear ip route`

By disabling IP routing on the MSFC or router, you automatically disable MLS. The `ip security` command disables MLS on the interface to which the command is applied. The same results occur with the `ip tcp` compression commands. Finally, the `clear ip route` command simply clears the MLS cache entries, and the flow caches must be reestablished.

# Configuring MLS-RP

To fully enable MLS, you must properly configure all participating devices. This section will cover the different configurations and settings that must be executed on the MLS-RP. Remember, the MLS-RP can be an external router or an MSFC on a 6000 series switch.

We will discuss optional configuration settings. These options depend on the existing layer 2 network and configuration. All the remaining subsections, except for "Verifying the MLS Configuration," apply only to external routers. We will start with the most basic and essential commands and then move on to management commands that can be used for verification and troubleshooting if necessary.

## Enabling MLS

Although MLS is enabled on an MSFC, other routers may or may not need MLS enabled before it can be used. To enable MLS on a route processor, type the command **`mls rp ip`** while in global configuration mode. Much like the `ip routing` command, enabling MLS on a router just begins the process; you still need to configure more. Here is an example:

```
Terry_2620#configure terminal
Enter configuration commands, one per line.  End with CNTL/Z.
Terry_2620(config)#mls rp ip
Terry_2620(config)#^Z
Terry_2620#

!
ip subnet-zero
mls rp ip
!
```

Enabling MLS on the router is just the tip of the iceberg as far as required configuration tasks are concerned. We'll continue with the domain information that is needed.

## VTP Domain Assignments

If a router interface is connected to a switch that is a VTP server or client, assigning the VLAN Trunk Protocol (VTP) domain is also a necessary step for MLS to work properly. It is very important to note that this step should be executed before any further MLS interface-specific commands are entered.

Failing to assign the VTP domain before configuring interfaces will place interfaces into a "null domain" rather than the proper one. Fixing this requires disabling MLS on the interfaces, and then fixing the domain and adding the interfaces back in.

### Verifying the VTP Domain

First you should verify which VTP domain the interface belongs to. This is done with the `show vtp domain` command from the switch. You can also obtain this information by looking at the switch configuration. Here are the two examples:

```
Terry_6509> show vtp domain
Domain Name   Domain Index VTP Version Local Mode  Password
-----------   ------------ ----------- ----------  --------
test          1            2           server      -

Vlan-count Max-vlan-storage Config Revision Notifications
---------- ---------------- --------------- -------------
7          1023             2               disabled

Last Updater   V2 Mode  Pruning  PruneEligible on Vlans
-------------- -------- -------- -------------------------
172.16.10.1    disabled disabled 2-1000
Terry_6509>

Terry_6509> (enable) show running-config
.....
.........
.........
.........
.........
..
-- omitted text --
!
```

```
#vtp
set vtp domain test
set vtp mode server
```

## VTP Interface Configuration

After you have the VTP domain name, you are ready to assign the router interface to that VTP domain. This is done with the execution of the command `mls rp vtp-domain` *`domain_name`* on the specified interface.

Here is an example:

```
Terry_2620#configure terminal
Enter configuration commands, one per line.  End with CNTL/Z.
Terry_2620(config)#interface fastethernet 4/0
Terry_2620(config-if)#mls rp vtp-domain test
Terry_2620(config-if)#^Z
Terry_2620#

!
interface FastEthernet4/0
 ip address 172.16.10.1 255.255.255.0
 no ip directed-broadcast
 no ip route-cache
 no ip mroute-cache
 mls rp vtp-domain test
!
```

# VLAN Assignments

The command to establish a VLAN is used only if an external router's interface is not using ISL or 802.1Q encapsulation. (RSMs and MSFCs use logical VLAN interfaces.) An example is a router that has two physical interfaces connected to the same switch, each to a different VLAN. This scenario doesn't require that the router be aware of VLAN assignments and would typically be found on routers that have only 10Mb interfaces.

If you wish to enable MLS on interfaces that don't use VLANs, you can issue the `mls rp vlan-id` *`vlan_id_number`* command to assign a VLAN to the interface. Here is an example:

```
Terry_2620#configure terminal
Enter configuration commands, one per line.  End with CNTL/Z.
Terry_2620(config)#interface fastethernet 4/0
Terry_2620(config-if)#mls rp vlan-id 10
Terry_2620(config-if)#^Z
```

```
Terry_2620#

!
interface FastEthernet4/0
 ip address 172.16.10.1 255.255.255.0
 no ip directed-broadcast
 no ip route-cache
 no ip mroute-cache
 mls rp vtp-domain test
 mls rp vlan-id 10
!
```

## Interface Configurations

After VTP and VLAN assignments have been made, you can finally enable MLS on the interface. This is done with the same command that was used to globally enable MLS, `mls rp ip`. Here is an example:

```
Terry_2620#configure terminal
Enter configuration commands, one per line.  End with CNTL/Z.
Terry_2620(config)#interface fastethernet 4/0
Terry_2620(config-if)#mls rp ip
Terry_2620(config-if)#^Z
Terry_2620#

!
interface FastEthernet4/0
 ip address 172.16.10.1 255.255.255.0
 no ip directed-broadcast
 no ip route-cache
 no ip mroute-cache
 mls rp vtp-domain test
 mls rp vlan-id 10
 mls rp ip
!
```

## MSA Management Interface

As you may remember, MLS has three components. The third component is MLSP, the communication protocol itself. Well, in order for MLS to function between a switch and a router, MLSP must be able to communicate between both devices.

This requirement makes this next configuration step essential for MLS functionality. At least one interface on the router that is connected to the same switch must be enabled as the management interface. This indicates which interface is going to participate in MLSP exchanges.

Another requirement is that there be at least one management interface per VLAN on the switch. To specify a router interface as a management interface, issue the `mls rp management-interface` command on the specified interface. Here is an example of the syntax for the command:

```
Terry_2620#configure terminal
Enter configuration commands, one per line.  End with CNTL/Z.
Terry_2620(config)#interface fastethernet 4/0
Terry_2620(config-if)#mls rp management-interface
Terry_2620(config-if)#^Z
Terry_2620#
```

## Verifying the MLS Configuration

After all the pieces have been configured, you can issue the `show mls rp` command to view the MLS status and information on the router. There are two options in correlation with the main command. All three commands are shown here:

`show mls rp` Provides global MLS information.

`show mls rp interface` *`interface`* Provides interface-specific MLS information.

`show mls rp vtp-domain` *`domain_name`* Provides MLS information for the VTP domain.

Here is an example of the global command:

```
Terry_2620#show mls rp
multilayer switching is globally enabled
mls id is 0010.a6a9.3400
mls ip address 172.16.21.4
mls flow mask is destination-ip
number of domains configured for mls 1

vlan domain name: test
   current flow mask: destination-ip
   current sequence number: 3041454903
   current/maximum retry count: 0/10
   current domain state: no-change
   current/next global purge: false/false
   current/next purge count: 0/0
   domain uptime: 00:34:35
   keepalive timer expires in 4 seconds
```

```
   retry timer not running
   change timer not running
   fcp subblock count = 1

   1 management interface(s) currently defined:
      vlan 10 on FastEthernet4/0

   1 mac-vlan(s) configured for multi-layer switching:

      mac 0010.a6a9.3470
         vlan id(s)
         10

   router currently aware of following 1 switch(es):
      switch id 00-e0-4e-2d-43-ef

Terry_2620#
```

Here is an example of the interface option:

```
Terry_2620#show mls rp interface fastethernet 4/0
mls active on FastEthernet4/0, domain test
interface FastEthernet4/0 is a management interface
Terry_2620#
```

These are the `show` commands, and as with any IOS, there are debugging opportunities. Table 7.1 provides a summary of the debug commands available for MLS troubleshooting.

**TABLE 7.1** MLS Debug Command Summary

| Command | Description |
|---|---|
| `all` | Performs all MLS debugging |
| `error` | Displays information about MLS errors |
| `events` | Displays information from MLS events |
| `ip` | Displays IP MLS events |
| `locator` | Displays MLS locator information |
| `packets` | Displays information for all MLS packets |
| `verbose packets` | Displays information on all MLS verbose packets |

## Access Control Lists (ACLs)

It's not unusual to want to use an access control list to filter traffic from one VLAN to another, especially if one VLAN needs higher security than the others do. The problem is that you usually want all the packets to be examined by the access control list, and the switch is forwarding only the first one.

Until IOS release 12.0(2), inbound access control lists were not supported. If a router interface had an inbound access control list applied, MLS was disabled. With versions after 12.0(2), inbound access control lists are supported, but the support is not enabled by default. Use the command `mls rp ip input-acl` from global configuration mode to enable the router to use MLS with inbound access control lists.

Outbound access control lists are a little more problematic. Although they have always been supported, applying the access control list to an interface will clear the MLS cache information for connections passing through that interface. Another packet needs to be forwarded to the router to start the MLS process again. Also, outbound lists utilizing the following functions will disable MLS on the interface to which they are applied:

- TOS
- Established
- Log
- Precedence
- Reflexive

This is because these features require the router to examine every packet. Because these features tend to be more security related than a simple access control list often is, using these features disables MLS on the interface in question.

# Configuring the MLS Switch Engine

Switch configuration of MLS is very simple. MLS is on by default for the 6000. The only time when it is necessary to perform configuration tasks on the MLS-SE is when you want to change specific MLS attributes or when the device requires configuration. Here are some examples:

- Using an external router
- Establishing flows
- Changing the MLS cache aging timers
- Enabling NetFlow Data Export (NDE)

Each of these topics are addressed in this section.

## Enabling MLS on the MLS-SE

As mentioned, the only time you need to actually enable MLS on the switch is when it has been disabled or on a system on which MLS is off by default.

To enable MLS on the MLS-SE, issue the command `set mls enable`. Here is an example:

```
Terry_6506> (enable) set mls enable
Multilayer switching is enabled
Terry_6506> (enable)
```

If the MLS route processor being used is an external router, the switch needs to be told to send MLSP packets to the appropriate IP address. Use the command `set mls include` *`rp_ip_address`* to tell the switch which IP address that is. The command `show mls include` displays the list of IP addresses of external route processors.

## Configuring Flow Masks

A flow is the cache entry on the switch that is used for layer 3 switching. The switch learns the appropriate information from the MLS router and the switch caches the information for subsequent packets in the stream. Typically, flow information is received from a router based on what type of access control list is configured on the outbound interface.

There are three ways of configuring flow masks:

**Destination-IP** This is the default mask and is the least specific. A flow is created for each destination IP address, and all packets—no matter the source—get layer-3 switched if they match the destination. This mask is used if no outbound access control list is used.

**Source-Destination-IP** The switch engine will have a flow entry for each source/destination pair of addresses. No matter what applications are used between the two addresses, all traffic that matches the source and destination IP addresses will be switched according to this flow. This mask is used if there is a standard access control list used on the outbound interface.

**IP-Flow** This mask builds flows that have a specific source and destination port in addition to specific source and destination IP addresses. Two different processes—for example, HTTP and Telnet—from one client to a single server will create two different masks because the port numbers are different. This mask is used if the outbound access control list is extended.

If no outbound access control list is configured on the router but either IP-Flow or Source-Destination-IP is desired, it is possible to configure the switch to build flows in a more specific fashion. The command `set mls flow [destination|destination-source|full]` can be used to tell the MLS switch what information to cache with candidate packets.

## Using Cache Entries

MLS entry or shortcut cache exists on the PFC for 6000 series switches. The purpose of the cache is consistent across all platforms: The cache is a layer 3 switching table. It maintains the flow information that facilitates MLS.

Here is a sample of a layer 3 cache table:

```
Terry_6509> (enable) show mls entry
```

```
Dest-IP  Source-IP Prot DstPrt SrcPrt Dest-Mac Vlan EDst  ESrc DPort SPort
Stat-Pkts  Stat-Bytes  Uptime   Age
--------------- --------------- ----- ------ ------ ----------------- ---- ----
---- ------ ------ ---------- ----------- -------- --------
MSFC 10.10.100.5 (Module 15):
172.16.10.1 -               -    -     -       00-30-96-2d-24-20   188  ARPA
ARPA 2/7     2/6     870          157785       00:05:29 00:00:27
172.16.55.115    -               -    -     -       00-30-96-2d-24-20  188
ARPA ARPA 2/7    2/6    2407        642886      00:00:39  00:00:00
172.16.96.101   -                -    -     -       00-d0-bc-f3-69-44  4     ARPA
ARPA 2/2     2/7     2710       2200670      00:12:23  00:00:00
172.16.8.35    -                 -    -     -       00-d0-bc-f3-66-9c  180  ARPA
ARPA 3/7     3/3     76634      24951932     00:24:31  00:00:00
172.16.8.17    -                 -    -     -       00-30-96-2d-24-20  188  ARPA
ARPA 2/7     2/6     81752      26599352     00:18:32  00:00:00
172.16.8.102   -                 -    -     -       00-30-96-2d-24-20  188  ARPA
ARPA 2/7     2/6     313        148298       00:00:24  00:00:22
```

This command has many options, but the most basic ones involve viewing cache information based on the source and destination IP addresses. The syntax of the command is `show mls entry [rp|destination|source]` *`ip_address`*. Also, be aware that the display has room for many pieces of information, but you won't see them unless the flow is based on that information. For example, when using the preceding Destination-IP flow, the source IP address isn't displayed. You will always be able to see the destination IP address as well as the destination MAC address.

Cache entries are kept while the flow is active. After the flow no longer receives traffic, the cache entry gets aged out and removed from the layer 3 cache on the NFFC or PFC. This attribute can be modified and adjusted. You'll learn how to do that next.

A candidate entry is cached for five seconds to allow for an enable packet to arrive from the router. If the enable packet doesn't arrive in that time, the switch assumes that the best path is not through itself and removes the entry.

## Modifying the Cache Aging Time

A layer 3 cache entry remains in cache for 256 seconds after the last packet for the flow has passed through the switch. This is the default value. The value can be changed to different values depending on your needs as a network administrator.

The syntax is `set mls agingtime` *`agingtime`*, where *`agingtime`* is a value of seconds. The value is a multiple of 8. The valid range is from 8 to 2032. If the value specified is not a multiple of 8, the nearest multiple is used. Here is an example:

```
Terry_6506> (enable) set mls agingtime 125
Multilayer switching aging time set to 128
Terry_6506> (enable)
```

## Modifying Fast Aging Time

When the layer 3 cache grows greater than 32KB in size, the possibility increases that the PFC or NFFC will not be able to perform all layer 3 switching, causing some packets to be forwarded to the router. To aid in maintaining a layer 3 cache smaller than 32KB, you can enable and adjust fast aging times.

Because some flows can be very short—a DNS query, for example—you can enable packet thresholds that can be used in correlation with the fast aging time to quickly age out these entries. Both of these attributes are thresholds. When you set the fast aging time, you specify the amount of time for which *n* number of packets (defined by the packet threshold) must have used the cache entry.

When a flow is initialized, the switch must see a number of packets equal to or greater than the packet threshold set within the time specified by the fast aging time. If this criterion isn't met, the cache entry is aged out immediately.

Valid values for the fast aging time are 32, 64, 96, and 128. Valid values for the packet threshold are 0, 1, 3, 7, 15, 31, and 63. Let's try an example so you can understand how this works.

Say you configured a fast aging time of 64 seconds and set the packet threshold to 31 packets by using the `set mls agingtime fast 64 31` command on the switch. This is telling the MLS-SE that a layer 3 cache entry has 64 seconds in which 31 packets or more must utilize the entry. If this doesn't happen, the cache entry is removed.

The actual syntax for the command is `set mls agingtime fast` *`fastagingtime pkt_threshold`*. An example configuration follows:

```
Terry_6506> (enable) set mls agingtime fast 64 31
Multilayer switching fast aging time set to 64 seconds for
   entries with no more than 31 packets switched.
Terry_6506> (enable)
```

## Verifying the Configuration

MLS-SE configuration settings can be seen by using the `show mls ip` command. The command provides information regarding the aging time, the fast aging time, and the packet threshold values. In addition, it gives summary statistics for the type of flow mask and MLS entries. Finally, it provides details about the MLS-RP, including XTAG, MAC, and VLAN values. Here is an example:

```
Terry_6509> show mls ip
IP Multilayer switching aging time = 256 seconds
IP Multilayer switching fast aging time = 64 seconds,  packet threshold = 31
IP Current flow mask is Destination flow
Active IP MLS entries = 87
Netflow Data Export version: 7
Netflow Data Export disabled
```

```
Netflow Data Export port/host is not configured.
Total packets exported = 0

IP MSFC ID       Module XTAG MAC               Vlans
--------------- ------ ---- ----------------- ------------
172.16.10.1     15     1    00-d0-bc-f4-81-c0 10,100
Terry_6509>
```

## Displaying the MLS Cache Entries

There are several methods of viewing MLS cache entries. The base command is `show mls entry`. However, many options are available to customize the output of this basic command.

If you are on a switch and issue the help command for `show mls entry`, this is what you get:

```
Terry_6509> (enable) show mls entry ?
Usage: show mls entry [mod] [long|short]
       show mls entry ip [mod] [destination <ip_addr_spec>]
       [source <ip_addr_spec>] [protocol <protocol>]
       [src-port <src_port>] [dst-port <dst_port>]
       [short|long]
   show mls entry ipx [mod] [destination <ipx_addr_spec>]        [short|long]
    (mod = 15 or 16
ip_addr_spec = ip_addr|ip_addr/netmask|ip_addr/maskbit (maskbit: 0..32)
     protocol = 1..255|ip|ipinip|icmp|igmp|tcp|udp
     src_port, dst_port = 1..65535|dns|ftp|smtp|telnet|x|www
     ipx_addr_spec = dest_net.dest_node|dest_net/mask)
Terry_6509> (enable)
```

As you can see, there are quite a few options. This command, with the options shown, enables the administrator to view very general information or very specific information. To get an idea of what can be generated from this command, let's review the options.

You can show MLS entries based on the module. The `long` and `short` options modify the output in different ways. `Long` displays the information all on one line, and `short` displays the information by using carriage returns. It is impossible to give an example due to the formatting limitations in this book.

More specific information can be obtained by specifying an IP address or port information. By specifying options, you can refine your output. Instead of getting pages and pages of cache entries, you get entries that match your criteria.

## Removing MLS Cache Entries

If you do not want to wait for aging times to expire, or if you want to clear the cache immediately, you can issue the `clear mls entry` command. This command also has options that enable the network administrator to clear specific cache entries instead of the entire table.

The syntax of the command is as follows:

```
clear mls entry destination ip_addr_spec source ip_addr_spec flow
   protocol src_port dst_port [all]
```

The use of the `all` optional keyword causes all MLS cache entries to be removed. If you use specific IP addresses, ports, or protocols, specific cache entries can be removed.

# Using Acceptable MLS Topologies

Few topologies support MLS. Due to the nature of MLS, only certain system topologies allow candidate and enable packets to transit the router and switch properly. If both candidate and enable packets cannot be identified, no complete flow cache entry can be made. Acceptable topologies include the following:

**Router on a stick** This includes one router (internal RSM/MSFC or external) and one switch. The router has a single connection to the network, which is the stick (see Figure 7.7).

**Multiple switches, one router** This is acceptable if only one switch connects to the router and the switches are connected via an ISL trunk (see Figure 7.8).

The second of the Cisco MLS implementations involves a process called Cisco Express Forwarding (CEF), which we will discuss in the next section.

**FIGURE 7.7** Router on a stick

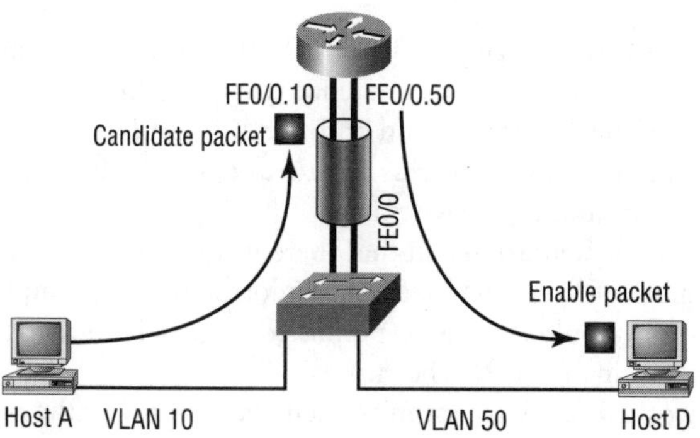

**FIGURE 7.8** Multiple switches, one router

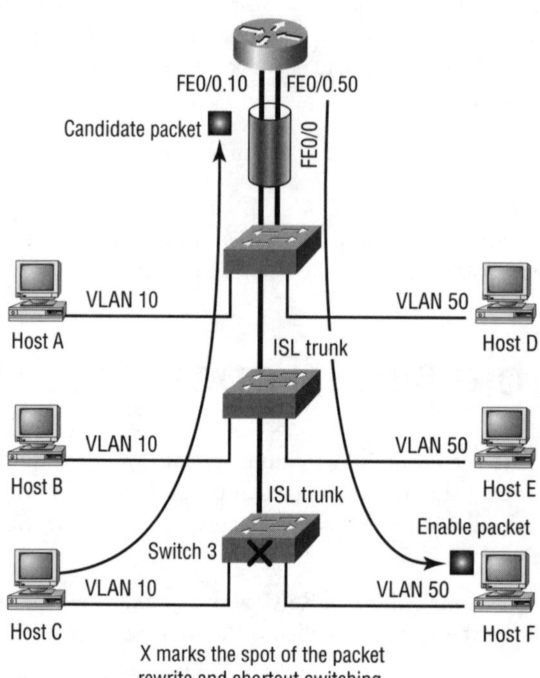


# Cisco Express Forwarding (CEF)

Two of the newer additions to the Cisco range (the 3550 and 4000 series) are sometimes described as Multilayer Switches, with the obvious inference that something beyond legacy routing is going on. With respect to the 3550 series and both the 4000 and 6500 series using the Supervisor IV engine, that something is *Cisco Express Forwarding (CEF)*. In fact, the 3550 is advertised as supporting CEF-based multilayer switching.

CEF differs from other MLS implementations, in that there is no caching in the traditional sense. Caching introduces a number of issues that need to be addressed. For example, how long should a cache stay valid? How big should a cache be permitted to grow? And how do we deal with routing topology changes that invalidate cache entries?

Well, Cisco has constantly worked to try to optimize cache behavior, but the problems remain. It seems that the only good way to do layer 3 data forwarding is to use a routing table. But that slows everything down again, right? Actually, no, not necessarily. You see, if you create a stripped-down version of the routing table, and a separate adjacency table (which is similar to a separate ARP cache), then you can get the best of both worlds. The table resides close to the interfaces (figuratively speaking), keeping data away from the busy route processor and its buses. And because the table is in communication with the main routing table, it is always as up-to-date as the main table.

## The Trouble with CEF and Layer 3 Switching

It may seem wrong to refer to CEF as layer 3 switching, but layer 3 switching is so poorly defined that it is easy to see how someone could become confused. Remember, though, that the CEF process has much in common with the way we have previously described layer 3 switching.

The routing decision is taken for the first packet at the route processor, and the frame address is rewritten to allow the packet to be properly forwarded. This is true in both CEF and layer 3 switching. It is also true to say that subsequent frames are forwarded (and the MAC address rewritten) according to cached information, and that they never get to the route processor.

I guess that, arguably, the story of layer 3 switching began a long time ago with the introduction of fast switching, and it has just progressed to caches further away from the route processor. Sometimes the cache is moved all the way to a separate box, namely the switch. But once modern switches incorporate IOS and the associated routing capability, the cache would naturally move back into the same housing.

The point here is that layer 3 switching really is vendor-speak, and in an ideal world we would not even have a chapter with this title—we would be calling it something like "How to Speed Up the Routing Process." The problem is that Cisco is under pressure from other vendors who call *their* offerings layer 3 switching, and so the myth continues to be propagated. And as long as Cisco exams are going to have questions on this topic, we have to use the same language. The term means little enough, but once you start building boxes with IOS that have the capability to perform both switching *and* routing, all this business of switch-router intercommunications disappears inside the proprietary architecture, and you can't see it anymore. So the early switches didn't do layer 3 switching at all, the (dying) range of CatOS-based switches do it in a complex fashion (as in the first part of this chapter), and the new IOS-based switches do it wonderfully, but it's a secret!

CEF, then, is not a first-generation attempt to speed up the forwarding process, but is the most recent mechanism to be tested. I think that it would assist us in placing CEF in the proper context if we looked at how we got here, so I propose to first consider the actual forwarding mechanisms that have traditionally been used by Cisco routers.

## Legacy Routing and Layer 3 Switching

Over the years, as Cisco routers have matured from the early days of the IGS and AGS platforms, faster processors have been employed to make the forwarding decisions more quickly. Nonetheless, it is not only the processor power that determines the latency of a switch. Right up there with processing delay is the time taken to forward packets around inside the router, hence the move toward ever faster router architectures.

Designers soon realized that even with faster buses, there were still some delays associated with internal packet forwarding that might benefit from other techniques, and this gave rise to the different switching modes employable in modern routers. Because the 3550 and Supervisor IV–equipped 4000 are really routers as well as switches, these processes suddenly became relevant to those engineers studying switches.

In order to really see the progression here from legacy routing to layer 3 switching, let's look at some of the history, specifically that of process switching (which you could easily call legacy routing), fast switching, and optimum switching (both cache-based methods for speeding up the forwarding process). Finally, we'll look properly at CEF.

## Process Switching

When packets are process switched, the complete packet is forwarded across the internal architecture to the route processor. This is the "heart" of the router, and is a busy place to be! Often accessed via two buses—the Cbus and the systems bus—it involves a long trip through the router and out to the forwarding interface for the whole packet. At the route processor, the forwarding interface and the MAC header rewrite information is applied. Delay is considerable, but there are some advantages: if the routing table holds multiple paths of equal cost to the destination, then load balancing can be carried out on a per-packet basis.

The routing process is shown in Figure 7.9. This diagram illustrates the linear nature of process switching, where a packet travels right through the "heart" of the router, resulting in slow forwarding.

**FIGURE 7.9** Process switching flow

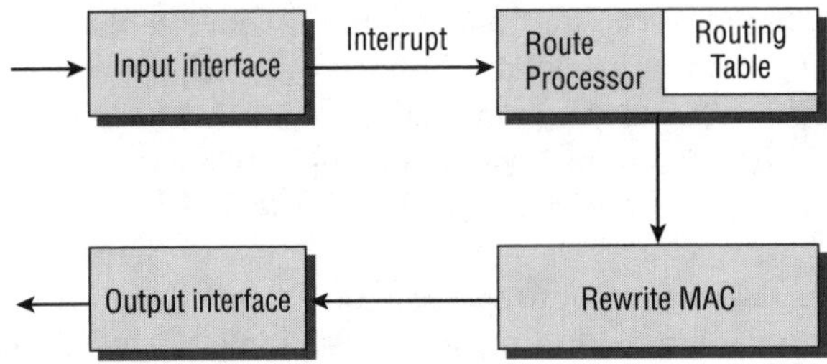


## Fast Switching

Like process switching, fast switching has been available on all Cisco platforms for many years, including the ubiquitous 2500 series. Fast switching involves the use of a cache on the route processor where forwarding information is maintained. The first packet in a conversation is passed to the route processor, matched against routes, and process switched. The fast switching cache is updated, and subsequent packets have only the header matched in the cache. The result is that the rest of the conversation is forwarded without being passed to the route processor.

Forwarding information is stored in the form of a binary tree, which allows bit-by-bit decision making to be carried out regarding the next hop. This binary tree may require up to 32 levels of comparison to fully match a route, but the decision is often reached much more quickly, and is considered to be a very efficient lookup mechanism.

Entries in the fast cache are created at the beginning of a conversation, and therefore suffer the perennial problems of caches—how do updates to other information, such as the ARP cache, affect the cached information? And the answer is that they don't, leaving the possibility that changes in the ARP cache may leave the fast cache with out-of-date and incorrect information. In that case, the cache must be recreated. The second problem with fast switching is that the cache can construct only a single route to a destination, so any load sharing must be on a conversation-by-conversation basis (sometimes caller per-destination load sharing) with a cache entry for each conversation.

Nonetheless, fast switching is perhaps ten times faster than process switching and is widely used.

The fast switching tree is shown in Figure 7.10. Each bit in the destination address is compared with the table, and because each possibility is either a one or a zero, a single match is gained with every pass.

**FIGURE 7.10** Fast switching tree

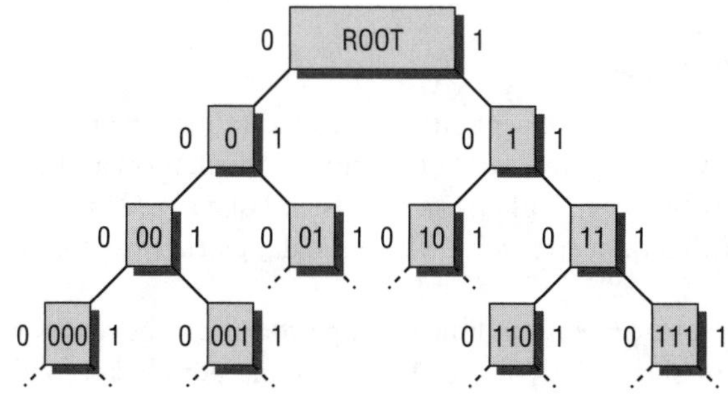


## Optimum Switching

Optimum switching also relies on a caching mechanism, but there are important differences from fast switching. The first difference is in the operation of the tree. Instead of a binary tree, with each level being a single comparison (one or zero in the binary string), optimum switching employs a 256-way multi-way tree (mtree). Each level allows selection of a single octet in the destination address, resulting in a maximum of four lookup probes to find any target.

Optimum switching is very fast, but still suffers from the same problems of cache invalidation and therefore needs to be aged out regularly, interrupting the optimum flow while caches are rebuilt from requests to the route processor again.

The optimum switching tree is shown in Figure 7.11. Each octet in the 32-bit dotted-decimal address is matched individually, resulting in a far faster lookup process.

**FIGURE 7.11** Optimum switching tree

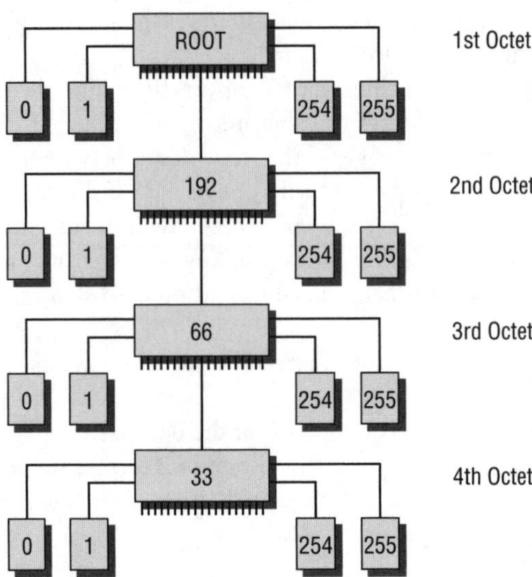


## The CEF Forwarding Process

At last we come to CEF. CEF maintains two separate but related tables, the forwarding table and the adjacency table. The forwarding table contains routing information and the adjacency table contains layer 2 next-hop addressing. CEF uses a trie instead of a tree. No, that's not a misprint. A *trie* is a pointer used with a data structure, where the data structure does not actually contain the data.

The separation in the data structure means that the lookup process can be recursive, allowing different routes to be selected for successive packets, thus enabling per-packet load sharing. Also, if information in a cache changes, because the lookup is performed individually each time, the most up-to-date information is always used.

The CEF forwarding process is shown in Figure 7.12. This simple diagram illustrates that the lookup is much swifter because the 256-way data structure is the most efficient of all lookup methods, and is directly associated with the adjacency table.

**FIGURE 7.12** CEF forwarding process

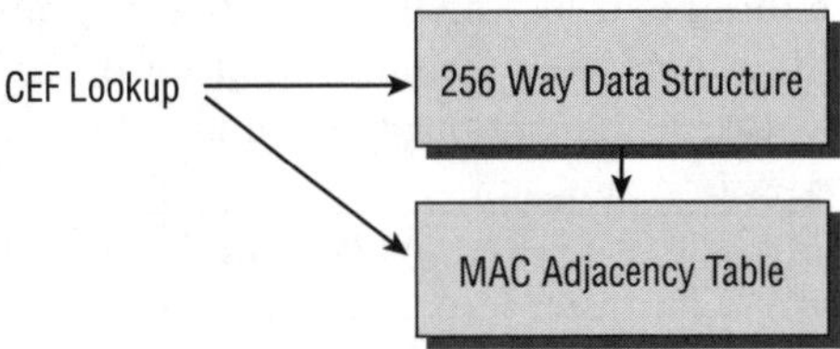

The result of CEF forwarding is a much higher throughput. True, a lot of this increased speed is due to proprietary architecture inside the switch or router, including the increased use of ASICs and specialized buses and memory arrangements. But it is also true that packets no longer need to be forwarded across internal buses to the busy route processor, which is where most of the router latency is introduced. And there are other benefits to CEF, such as the ability to support packet-by-packet load sharing, which cannot be achieved using cached entries as in fast or optimum switching.

## Configuring CEF

To configure CEF on a 3550 switch, you first have to enable IP routing. Remember that because this is a multilayer switch, only the layer 2 switching processes are enabled by default, to maintain the plug-and-play nature of all switches. Use the global command `ip routing` to enable ip routing, and use the global command `ip cef` to enable cef.

```
Terry_3550#
Terry_3550#conf t
Enter configuration commands, one per line.  End with CNTL/Z.
Terry_3550(config)#ip routing
Terry_3550(config)#ip cef ?
  accounting           Enable CEF accounting
  load-sharing         Load sharing
  table                Set CEF forwarding table characteristics
  traffic-statistics   Enable collection of traffic statistics
  <cr>
```

Next, you have to convert the layer 2 interface to layer 3. To do this, use the interface command `no switchport`. Enable IP on the interface using the standard command, and then enable CEF on the interface using the `ip route-cache cef` interface command.

```
Terry_3550#
Terry_3550#
Terry_3550#conf t
Enter configuration commands, one per line.  End with CNTL/Z.
Terry_3550(config)#int fa 0/1
Terry_3550(config-if)#no switchport
Terry_3550(config-if)#ip address 192.168.1.1 255.255.255.0
Terry_3550(config-if)#no shut
Terry_3550(config-if)#ip route-cache cef
Terry_3550(config-if)#^Z
```

Finally, you can confirm that CEF is running on the interface by using the `show ip interface` command:

```
Terry_3550#show ip int fa 0/1
```

```
FastEthernet0/1 is down, line protocol is down
  Internet address is 192.168.1.1/24
  Broadcast address is 255.255.255.255

[output cut]

  IP fast switching is enabled
  IP fast switching on the same interface is disabled
  IP Flow switching is disabled
  IP CEF switching is enabled
  IP CEF Fast switching turbo vector
  IP multicast fast switching is enabled

[output cut]

Terry_3550#
```

Any entries in the CEF table will be displayed in the following format, using the `show ip cef` command:

```
Terry_3550#sho ip cef fastEthernet 0/1
Prefix              Next Hop            Interface
Terry_3550#
```

# Summary

The helpful thing about VLANs is that you can place users into the broadcast domain that suits them. This is great if your network works like the old 80:20 rule, because that's where most of their data will remain—inside their own VLAN. But that may not be the case, and you may need to transfer a lot of packets between VLANs.

In itself, transferring packets between VLANs is not a problem. Routers are very capable when moving data between subnets. The problem is that routers are traditionally a lot slower than switches, because they have to interrogate more of the packet, which naturally takes more time. Hence the development of MLS.

Given that there are different definitions of MLS, it is no surprise that MLS behaves differently on different platforms, employing different components. The 6500, for example, runs "classic" MLS, in that the first packet is routed, subsequent packets are frame-switched, and the whole process can be cleanly seen because the routing and switching functions are not terribly well integrated, even with the use of an internal route processor. This requires you to understand the flow process intimately and to be able to configure MLS on both routers and switches.

More modern switches, on the other hand, running an IOS that fully integrates the switching and routing processes, carry out the same process (route once, switch many), but do so internally, and therefore make a much better job of it. In fact, most of the process is automatic, transparent, and hard to examine.

Integrated switch-routers can forward data at incredible speeds due to the fast architecture employed. Is the routing (layer 3 switching) process much slower? Well, hardly, when you consider that the boxes all operate in a store-and-forward mode. Lots of time (comparatively speaking) is available during standard packet arrival latency for fast processes such as CEF to make up their minds how to forward packets or frames.

# Exam Essentials

**Know the components of MLS.** Multilayer Switching is made of three components. The first is the MLS-SE, the switch. The second is the MLS-RP, the router that makes the changes to the initial packet. The third is MLSP, the communication protocol that is used between the router and any switches.

**Understand what a flow is and how a switch uses them.** A flow is nothing more than a conversation, a stream of packets between two devices. A switch caches information about the conversation and information about how the packets are supposed to be manipulated. When a packet arrives that matches a packet stream that the switch has already seen, the switch makes the necessary changes.

**Know what information a switch can use to identify flows.** A switch can use various pieces of information to identify flows, but only three broad configurations are allowed. The first tells the switch to identify flows based only on the destination IP address. The second says to use both source and destination IP addresses. The third uses the protocol as well as the source and destination IP addresses and ports.

**Understand how access control lists on the router affect MLS.** Outbound access control lists have always been supported and are the primary way of telling the switch what information to use to identify the flow. Inbound access control lists are supported with additional configuration. Reflexive lists and IP security on the interface disable the MLS process for that interface.

# Key Terms

Before you take the exam, be sure you're familiar with the following terms:

| | |
|---|---|
| candidate packets | Multilayer Switching Route Processor (MLS-RP) |
| Cisco Express Forwarding (CEF) | Multilayer Switching Switch Engine (MLS-SE) |
| enable packets | NetFlow Feature Card (NFFC) |
| flow | Policy Feature Card (PFC) |
| Multilayer Switch Feature Card (MSFC) | router on a stick |
| Multilayer Switching (MLS) | trie |
| Multilayer Switching Protocol (MLSP) | XTAG |

# Written Lab

Write the answers to the following questions:

1. Write the command that enables MLS globally on an external router.
2. Write the command that assigns the VTP domain to the external router's interface. Use *cisco* as the VTP domain name.
3. Write the command that assigns VLAN 5 to the interface.
4. Write the command that configures an external router interface to allow MLSP packets across it.
5. Write the command that shows you MLS information on a switch.
6. Write the command that shows you the XTAG information on a switch.
7. Write the command that displays all the layer 3 cache entries.
8. Write the command that displays a layer 3 cache entry based on the destination IP address of 172.16.10.100.
9. Write the command to clear all MLS cache entries.
10. Write the command that sets the fast aging time to 64 and the packet threshold to 63.

# Review Questions

1. Which of the following is one of the three components of MLS?
   A. MFSC
   B. PCF
   C. MLS-P
   D. MLSP

2. Which of the following is one of the three components of MLS?
   A. MLS
   B. MLS-SW
   C. MLS-ES
   D. MLS-SE

3. Which of the following is one of the three components of MLS?
   A. RP
   B. RSP
   C. MLS-RP
   D. MLS-MSFC

4. Which of the following describes the router-on-a-stick topology? (Choose all that apply.)
   A. A router connected to a switch with coax
   B. A single external router connected to a single switch
   C. A single internal router (MSFC) installed in a switch
   D. A switch with an MSFC connected to an external router

5. Which of the following elements are *not* used to create a flow or shortcut cache entry? (Choose all that apply.)
   A. ToS
   B. Protocol
   C. CRC
   D. Payload
   E. Source MAC
   F. Destination MAC
   G. Destination IP

6. Which answer best describes the MLSP discovery process?

   A. The MLS-SE sends hello packets to the multicast address 01-00-0C-DD-DD-DD. MLS-RPs then respond to these hello packets.

   B. The MLS-RP sends hello packets to the multicast address 01-00-0C-DD-DD-DD. MLS-SEs then respond to these hello packets.

   C. The MLS-RP sends hello packets to the multicast address 01-00-0C-DD-DD-DD. MLS-SEs then record the hello packet information.

   D. The MLS-SE sends hello packets to the multicast address 01-00-0C-DD-DD-DD. MLS-RPs then record the hello packet information.

7. What is the XTAG used for, and what is its significance?

   A. XTAG is a numerical value assigned by the MLS-SE to identify an MLS-RP. It must be unique throughout the VTP domain.

   B. XTAG is a numerical value assigned by the MLS-SE to identify an MLS-RP. It is locally significant.

   C. The XTAG is the MLS-RP router ID and is used to uniquely identify the MLS-RP to the MLS-SE. It is a unique value throughout the layer 2 network.

   D. The XTAG is the MLS-SE ID and is used to identify each MLS-SE in the layer 2 network. Therefore, it must be unique across all switches.

8. What must you do on a 3550 switch before enabling CEF?

   A. `Enable IP routing.`

   B. `Disable layer 2 switching.`

   C. `Nothing, the box is ready to run CEF.`

   D. `Nothing, CEF is enabled by default.`

9. What are the two prerequisites before a complete shortcut entry can be entered into cache?

   A. Identification of the MLS-SE

   B. Identification of the candidate packet

   C. Identification of the MLS topology

   D. Identification of the enable packet

10. Which of the following criteria qualify a packet as a candidate packet?

    A. Any incoming packet that is destined for a MAC address associated with the MLS-RP

    B. Incoming packets sourcing from 224.0.0.1 and destined for the MAC address of the MLS-SE

    C. Incoming packets sourcing a MAC address associated with the MLS-RP

    D. Outbound packets destined for a remote host

11. Which of the following criteria qualify a packet as an enable packet? (Choose all that apply.)
    A. The packet is sourced from an MLS-RP MAC address.
    B. The XTAG value matches the candidate packet XTAG value.
    C. The destination MAC address is the same as the corresponding candidate packet's source MAC address.
    D. The destination IP address matches the destination IP of the corresponding candidate packet.
12. Which component or device performs the frame rewrite?
    A. PFC
    B. MLSRP
    C. MSFC
    D. DCAM
13. Which of the following fields can be rewritten by the MLS-SE? (Choose all that apply.)
    A. ISL header
    B. DEST MAC
    C. Source MAC
    D. Destination IP address
14. Which of the following fields can be rewritten by the MLS-SE? (Choose all that apply.)
    A. Source IP address
    B. ToS
    C. CRC
    D. Payload
15. At what MLS cache size does the probability of involving the router increase dramatically?
    A. 8KB
    B. 64KB
    C. 32KB
    D. 128KB
    E. 256KB
16. What command can inadvertently disable MLS on a router or interface? (Choose all that apply.)
    A. `no ip routing`
    B. `ip security`
    C. `ip access-group access-list-number [in|out]`
    D. `no tcp-small-servers`

17. What command can inadvertently disable MLS on a router or an MLS-configured interface?

    A. `clear ip route`

    B. `ip tcp header-compression`

    C. `route-map`

    D. `ip router rip`

18. Which of the following caches does CEF consider when forwarding a packet? (Choose all that apply.)

    A. The CEF table

    B. The adjacency table

    C. The forwarding table

    D. The optimum route cache

19. Which of the following commands enables MLS on an external router?

    A. `set mls ip enable`

    B. `set mls enable`

    C. `mls rp ip`

    D. `mls ip`

20. When must you configure the VTP domain on an interface of an external router?

    A. Always

    B. When it uses ISL encapsulation

    C. When it doesn't use ISL or 802.1Q encapsulation

    D. When it is connected to a VTP server or client

# Hands-On Lab

Refer to Figure 7.13 for the topology of this lab. This lab uses the simplest architecture: router on a stick using a Catalyst 6500 and an external router (7200 series).

**FIGURE 7.13** Lab topology

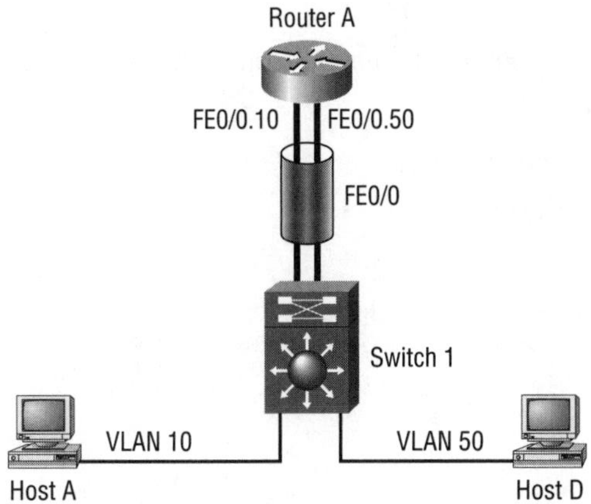


1. Assume that Router A does not have MLS enabled. You can assume that the subinterfaces are running ISL and have VLAN assignments. Switch 1 is a VTP server for the Sybex domain. Configure MLS to work on Router A:

```
RouterA#configure terminal
Enter configuration commands, one per line.  End with CNTL/Z.
RouterA(config)#mls rp ip
RouterA(config)#interface fastethernet 4/0
RouterA(config-subif)#mls rp vtp-domain sybex
RouterA(config-subif)#interface fastethernet4/0.50
RouterA(config-subif)#mls rp management-interface
RouterA(config-subif)#mls rp ip
RouterA(config-subif)#interface fastethernet4/0.10
RouterA(config-subif)#mls rp ip
RouterA(config-subif)#^Z
RouterA#
```

2. The aging timers need to be adjusted to be shorter than the default of 256 seconds. Make the new value 128. In addition to changing the aging timers, add a command that will help keep the layer 3 cache size under 32KB. To do this, use values of aging timer = 64 and packet threshold = 31:

```
Switch1> (enable) set mls agingtime 128
Multilayer switching aging time set to 128
Switch1> (enable) set mls agingtime fast 64 31
Multilayer switching fast aging time set to 64 seconds  for entries with no
more than 31 packets switched.
Switch1> (enable)
```

3. Verify MLS status on the switch and router. Provide samples of the MLS entries and XTAG values.

   Results will vary on this answer; here are the commands that should be issued:

   - `show mls` (executed on the switch)
   - `show mls rp` (executed on the router)
   - `show mls entry` (executed on the router)

# Answers to Written Lab

1. `mls rp ip`
2. `mls rp vtp-domain cisco`
3. `mls rp vlan-id 5`
4. `mls rp management-interface`
5. `show mls`
6. `show mls`
7. `show mls entry`
8. `show mls entry ip destination 172.16.10.100`
9. `clear mls entry destination all`
10. `set mls agingtime fast 64 63`

# Answers to Review Questions

1. D. MLSP is the proper acronym for Multilayer Switching Protocol. MFSC should be MSFC; PCF should be PFC.

2. D. Multilayer Switching Switch Engine is the name of the component. The proper acronym is provided in the last answer.

3. C. MLS-RP represents the broad spectrum of route processors. RP, RSP, and MSFC are all types of route processors.

4. B, C. The topology name comes from the original look of an external router connected to a switch. With the implementation of MSFC, the same functional topology is achieved in the same chassis. The media connection type does not define the topology.

5. C, D. CRC can vary from packet to packet and is used for error checking. The payload is also unique for each packet. Flows are established by using packet similarities.

6. C. The key to this question is twofold. The MLS-RP is the only device that sends hello packets. Because the packets are sent to a multicast address, the MLS-RP doesn't require a response from the switch. The MLS-RP doesn't need to establish an actual connection with the switch.

7. B. XTAGs are used by the MLS-SE to identify each MLS-RP connected to the layer 2 network. Each switch can utilize the same XTAG values; they are used only locally.

8. A. The 3550 is a multilayer switch, but only layer 2 switching is enabled by default. You must specifically enable IP routing.

9. B, D. Both packets must be identified to complete the shortcut entry.

10. A. Incoming packets must be destined for a MAC address that is associated with the MLS-RP via the XTAG value. If the packet is not destined for this address, the packet is not tagged as a candidate packet.

11. A, B, D. Enable packets have more criteria to match than do candidate packets. Because the destination MAC address is different for every hop, there is no way that a packet could match using the destination MAC address and still use MLS.

12. A. MSFCs are layer 3 devices that are used in Catalyst switches. Pattern matching and frame rewrites are done by the PFC.

13. A, B, C. Although the rewrite engine can modify some fields in the IP header, it does not change the IP addresses.

14. B, C. The MLS-SE has to rewrite the CRC because it changes the values for the source MAC and destination MAC addresses. It calculates a new CRC for the new frame.

15. C. After the MLS cache size exceeds 32KB, chances are that the MLS-SE will not be able to shortcut-switch all flows, and packets will be sent to the router.

16. A, B. Other commands also can inadvertently disable MLS, but access control lists no longer do. They can cause the cache to be cleared, but since IOS 12.0(2), inbound as well as outbound access control lists are supported and do not disable MLS.

17. B. Using header compression disables MLS on the configured interface. `clear ip route` is not a correct answer because it temporarily clears the cache but it doesn't disable MLS.

18. B, C. CEF looks at the route forwarding table and then the adjacency table.

19. C. The command `set mls enable` is used to enable MLS on a 6500 series switch, and the command `mls rp ip` is used to enable MLS on an external router.

20. D. Internal routers such as MSFCs don't require a VTP domain configuration because they are physically connected to a single switch. However, external routers that have connections to VTP servers or clients must configure the interface for the VTP domain.

# Understanding and Configuring Multicast Operation

## THE CCNP EXAM TOPICS COVERED IN THIS CHAPTER INCLUDE THE FOLLOWING:

✓ Describe the functionality of CGMP

✓ Describe how switches facilitate Multicast Traffic

✓ Translate Multicast Addresses into MAC addresses

✓ Enable CGMP on the distribution layer devices

✓ Describe how IP multicast operates on a multilayer switched network, including IGMP versions 1, 2, and 3 and CGMP

✓ Understand how IP multicast operates on a routed network, including PIM in both sparse and dense modes

Today's web and enterprise applications are directed to larger audiences on the network than ever before, causing increased bandwidth requirements. This increased demand on bandwidth can be accommodated with as little cost increase as possible by using multicast. For example, voice and video are being sourced for larger and larger audiences and one-on-one communications can overwhelm both servers and network resources. Unlike unicast and broadcast, however, multicast services can eliminate these problems.

This chapter will help you understand the differences in unicast, broadcast, and multicast communication methods and when each should be used. Unicast is an excellent method of point-to-point communication, whereas broadcast traffic is imperative for many systems and protocols to work on a network. Multicast comes in as a bridge between these two communication extremes by efficiently allowing point-to-multipoint data forwarding. It is essential that you understand how multicast addressing spans both layer 3 and layer 2 of the OSI model. You will also learn about the protocols and tools used to implement and control multicast traffic on your network. As with any service that runs on your network, you must understand the resources needed and the potential implications of enabling multicast forwarding.

You will also cover the steps and syntax for configuring IP multicast on Cisco routers and switches. You will see several new commands in this chapter. By the time you finish this chapter, and its review questions and lab, you will be thoroughly familiar with multicast and its implementation. Pay attention to small details that might usually seem unimportant. They are often the key to a successful implementation of an IP multicast network.

You will learn how to deploy an IP multicast network, and after you have a plan in place, you will move on to configuring equipment. Not only do the routers have to be IP multicast enabled, but you must enable a multicast protocol on every interface through which you want to be able to forward multicast traffic.

An IP multicast network can result in traffic flows that are very hard to predict. One way of preventing this problem is to try and force traffic along specific paths, and using specified routers as Rendezvous Points (RPs) to assist in this process is quite common, so you have to configure them as well. Then, to keep your multicast local to the enterprise network, you need to configure the Time to Live (TTL) thresholds on your external interfaces.

After the routers have been configured, you can concentrate on the hosts. Of course, we won't discuss host configuration in this chapter, but we will enable Cisco Group Management Protocol (CGMP) on the routers and switches, so that after the hosts are configured, the network will be available.

# Multicast Overview

Just as blue, yellow, and red are different and each has its own place within the spectrum of visible light, unicast, broadcast, and multicast are different in that each is used to achieve a specific purpose or fulfill requirements of a specific part of the communication spectrum. It is important to know where each falls within the spectrum as well as the potential applications for each.

RFC 1112 discusses multicast and goes into great detail about host extensions and multicast groups. In addition to address assignment for multicast applications and hosts, protocol methods and procedures are discussed. For example, it covers the methods by which hosts join and leave multicast groups, and it also covers group advertisements and multicast forwarding.

## Unicast

*Unicast* is used for direct host-to-host communication. When the layer 3 Protocol Data Unit (PDU, or packet) is formed, two layer 3 IP addresses are added to the IP header. These are the source and destination IP addresses. They specify a particular originating and receiving host. After the layer 3 PDU is formed, it is passed to layer 2 to create the layer 2 PDU, or frame. The frame consists of all the previous layers' headers in addition to the layer 2 header. With an Ethernet frame, for example, the two 48-bit source and destination MAC addresses are specified in the layer 2 header. Other protocols such as IEEE 802.5 (Token Ring) and FDDI also have headers that contain specific host source and destination addresses.

Unicast communication is used when two hosts need to exchange data with only each other and are not concerned with sharing the data with everyone. A MAC address must *uniquely* identify a host. No two MAC addresses, on a single network, can be the same. Therefore, unicast capitalizes on the unique MAC address of each host. With the specific address, any source host should be able to contact the destination host without confusion.

**FIGURE 8.1** Unicast communication

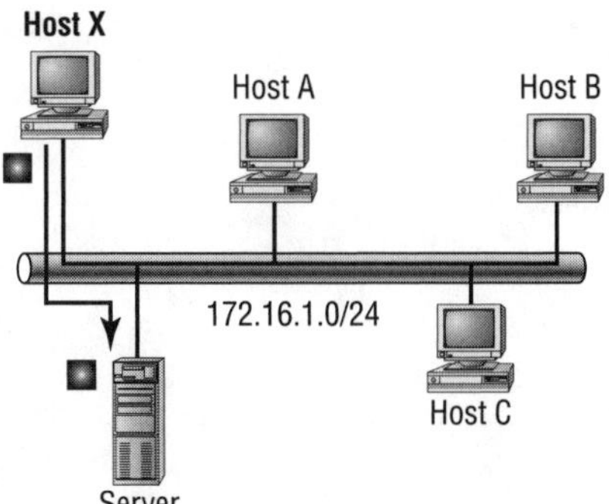

One of the caveats with unicast communication is that the source host must know or be able to learn what every destination MAC is for every station it wishes to communicate with. In order to figure out which MAC address the source should send frames to, it uses an ARP request, as explained in the following section. The normal operation is that the host has a default gateway assigned for use when the logical destination address does not reside on the same subnet as the source host. Figure 8.1 depicts how unicast traffic works on the same subnet.

Of course, unicast traffic may differ inside an internetwork interconnected by routers. In those circumstances, you will remember that the transmitting client needs to know the IP (and MAC) addresses of the default gateway.

The unicast process occurs between two hosts only. A single destination address is used to ensure that data is sent to only one host. This could be client-to-server, server-to-client, or peer-to-peer. It doesn't matter, so long as the frames are addressed to a unicast address. So when one host wants to send data to multiple hosts or all the hosts on the same network segment, things have to change. That is where multicast and broadcast communication comes in.

## Broadcast

Now that you have a good understanding of unicast, we can discuss the principle of broadcast communication on networks. Whereas unicast messages target a single host on a network (unicast communication can be compared to sending an e-mail to a friend; the mail is addressed to the friend, and it is sent from you), *broadcast* messages are meant to reach all hosts on a broadcast domain (such as when you shout out to everyone in the room, "Who wants an ice cream?"). Figure 8.2 depicts a broadcast message sent from Host X to all machines within the same broadcast domain.

**FIGURE 8.2** Broadcast message on a network

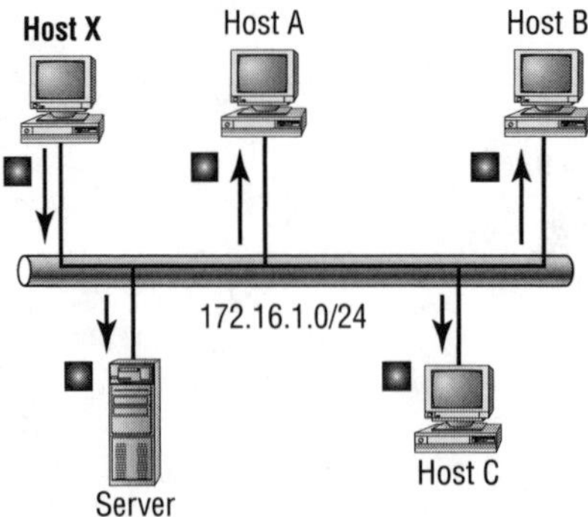


A good example of a broadcast message is an Address Resolution Protocol (ARP) request. When a host has a packet, it knows the logical address of the destination. To get the packet to the destination, the host needs to forward the packet to a default gateway if the destination resides on a different IP network. If the destination is on the local network, the source will forward the packet directly to the destination. Because the source doesn't have the MAC address it needs to forward the frame to, it sends out a broadcast, something that every device in the local broadcast domain will listen to. This broadcast says, in essence, "If you are the owner of IP address 192.168.2.3, please forward your MAC address to the source address of this frame. Each device will answer a request for its own IP address, but a correctly configured router can serve as a proxy as well, with the process of Proxy ARP.

This brings up another good point: Broadcasts can cause problems on networks. Because the broadcast frame is addressed to include every host, every host must process the frame. CPU interruption occurs so that the frame can be processed. This interruption affects other applications that are running on the host. When unicast frames are seen by a router, a quick check is made to identify whether the frame is intended for the host. If it isn't, the frame is discarded.

## Multicast

Multicast is a different beast entirely. At first glance, it appears to be a hybrid of unicast and broadcast communication, but that isn't quite accurate. Multicast does allow point-to-multipoint communication, which is similar to broadcasts, but it happens in a different manner. The crux of *multicast* is that it enables multiple recipients to receive messages without flooding the messages to all hosts on a broadcast domain.

Multicast works by sending messages or data to IP *multicast group* addresses. Routers then forward copies of the packet out every interface that has hosts *subscribed* to that group address. This is where multicast differs from broadcast messages. With multicast communication, copies of packets are sent only to subscribed hosts.

The difference between multicast and unicast is comparable to the difference between mailing lists and spam. You subscribe to a mailing list when you want to receive mail from a specific group regarding specific information—for example, a Cisco User Group mailing list. You expect to get messages only from other members of the group regarding topics related to the user group. In contrast, spam is unsolicited mail that arrives in your inbox. You aren't expecting it from the sender, nor are you likely to be interested in the content.

Multicast works in much the same way as a mailing list. You (as a user) or an application will subscribe to a specific IP multicast group to become a member. After you become a member of the group, IP multicast packets containing the group address in the destination field of the header arrive at your host and are processed. If the host isn't subscribed to the group, it will not process packets addressed to that group. Refer to Figure 8.3 for a reference on how multicast works.

Broadcast and multicast traffic can occur at different layers of the OSI model. Each is characterized by the fact that they are addressed to a wide group of hosts, and are not usually acknowledged. At the data link layer, broadcasts manage useful concepts such as ARP. At the network layer, they may be responsible for routing updates or server requests. At the application layer, they may be misused. E-mail broadcasts are often referred to as spam.

**FIGURE 8.3** Multicast communication

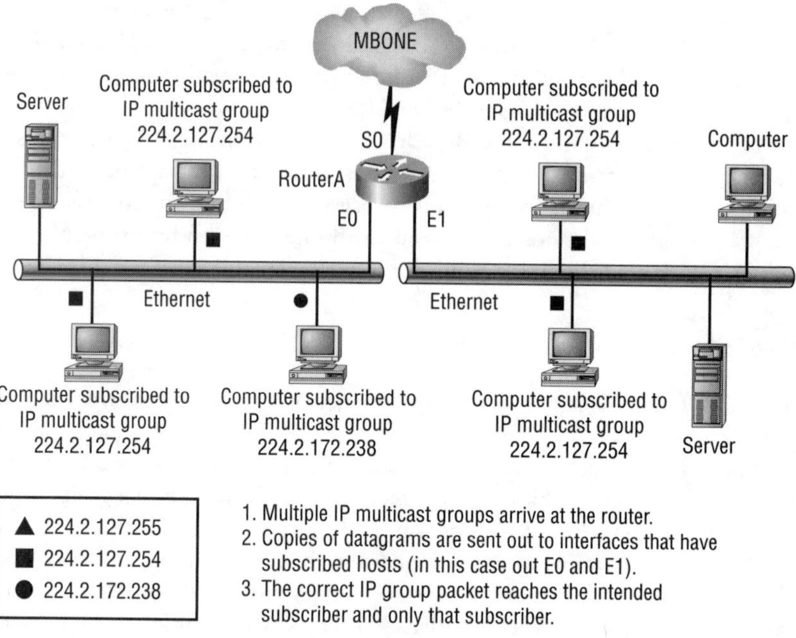


The key to multicast is the addressing structure. This is key because all communication is based on addressing. In unicast communication, there is a unique address for every host on a network. In broadcast communication, a global address that all hosts will respond to is used. Multicast uses addressing that only some hosts will respond to. The next section covers multicast addressing in detail.

# Using Multicast Addressing

Just as with mailing lists, there are several different groups that users or applications can subscribe to. The range of multicast addresses starts with 224.0.0.0 and goes through 239.255.255.255. As you can see, this range of addresses falls within IP Class D address space based on classful IP assignment. This is denoted by the first four bits in the first octet being set to 1110. Just as with regular IP addresses, there are some addresses that can be assigned and there are ranges of reserved addresses.

It is important to recognize that the reserved addresses are categorized. Table 8.1 depicts some of the reserved addresses and their corresponding categories. For a full listing of these assignments, you can go to `www.iana.org/assignments/multicast-addresses`.

**TABLE 8.1** IP Multicast Reserved Addresses

| Address | Purpose | Reserved Category |
|---|---|---|
| 224.0.0.0–224.0.0.18 | Use by network protocols | Local-link |
| 224.0.0.1 | All hosts | Local-link |
| 224.0.0.2 | All routers | Local-link |
| 224.0.0.19–224.0.0.255 | Unassigned | Local-link |
| 224.0.1.0–224.0.1.255 | Multicast applications | Misc. applications |
| 224.0.1.1 | NTP | Misc. applications |
| 224.0.1.8 | NIS+ | Misc. applications |
| 224.0.1.39 | Cisco-RP-Announce | Misc. applications |
| 224.0.1.40 | Cisco-RP-Discovery | Misc. applications |
| 224.0.1.80–224.0.1.255 | Unassigned | Misc. applications |
| 224.0.0.10 | EIGRP | Local-link |
| 239.0.0.0–239.255.255.255 | Private multicast domain | Administratively scoped |

Each address range is managed by the Internet Address Number Authority (IANA). Due to the limited number of multicast addresses, there are very strict requirements for new assignments within this address space. The 239.0.0.0–239.255.255.255 range is equivalent in purpose to the private networks defined by RFC 1918.

The difference between the IP multicast ranges of 224.0.0.0–224.0.0.255 and 224.0.1.0–224.0.1.255 is that addresses in the first range will not be forwarded by an IP router. Both ranges of addresses are used by applications and network protocols. The first group, classified as local-link, is meant to remain local to the subnet or broadcast domain on which the system resides. The second group is a global address that can be routed and forwarded across multiple IP routers.

## Mapping IP Multicast to Ethernet

Multicast addressing began on MAC addresses. Growth needs required that there be a way to use multicast across routers instead of limiting it to the physical segment where hosts were located. In regular unicast, MAC addresses are layer 2 addresses, and in order for the local host to reach remote hosts, layer 3 logical IP addresses are used to route data to the destination. After the packet reaches the remote subnet, the ARP is used to find the MAC address of the host. By using an existing ARP table, or via an ARP request, the MAC address that is associated to the layer 3 IP address is found and the packet is forwarded to the destination host.

IP multicast generates a MAC address based on the layer 3 IP multicast address. The MAC frame has a standard prefix of 24 bits. This prefix, 01-00-5e, is used for all Ethernet multicast addresses. This leaves another 24 bits for use in creating the multicast MAC address. When the MAC address is generated, the 25th bit (or high order bit) is set to 0 and then the last 23 bits of the IP address are mapped to the remaining 23 bits of the MAC address. Figure 8.4 depicts how this looks.

**FIGURE 8.4** IP multicast mapped to MAC multicast

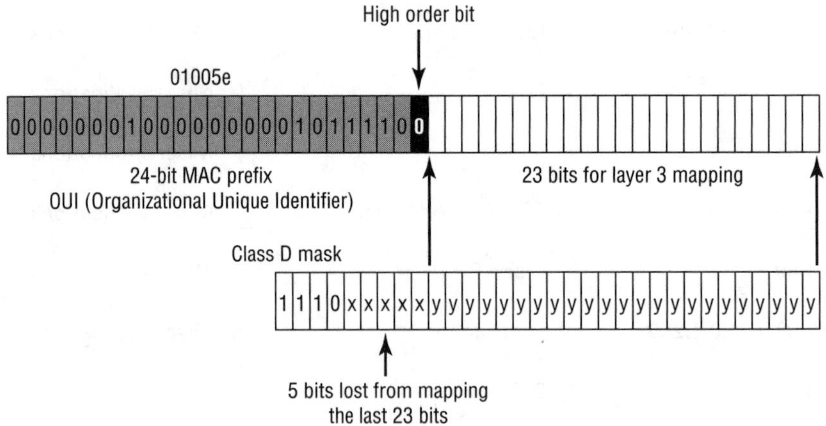

MAC addresses are made up of two sets of addresses, each with 24 bits. The first set is an address reserved for a particular manufacturer. The second set identifies a particular device by that manufacturer. This is why Cisco devices always seem to have one of a small number of "first halves." Multicast MAC addresses use 01-00-5E for the vendor code, with the device code based on the IP address.

Let's look at some examples of mapping layer 3 multicast addresses to layer 2 multicast addresses. A local IP multicast address is 224.0.0.1. Refer to Figure 8.5 to see how this is mapped. The conversion from binary to hexadecimal reveals the MAC multicast address. The prefix was 01-00-5e. The last 23 bits, including the high order bit, give you 00-00-01. Put them together and you get 01-00-5e-00-00-01 as the MAC address.

Now let's try one a little bit harder. Suppose, for example, you have the IP multicast address of 225.1.25.2 (follow along in Figure 8.6). Part of the 225 octet falls within the Class D mask. However, there is one bit that is not masked. By looking carefully at the location of the bit, you see that it is part of five lost bits and is not mapped to the layer 2 MAC multicast address.

**FIGURE 8.5** Example 1 for mapping IP multicast to MAC multicast addresses

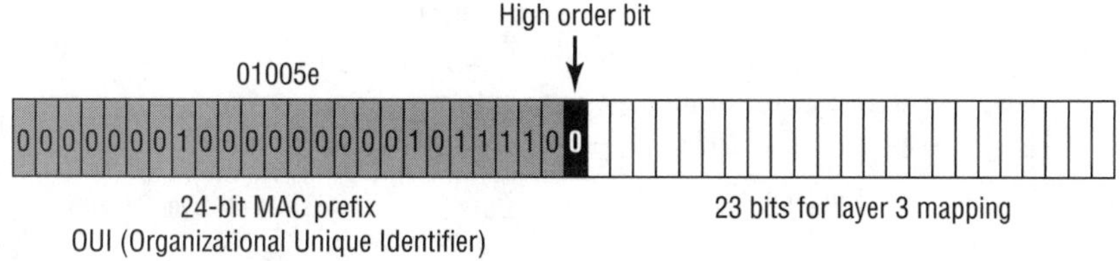


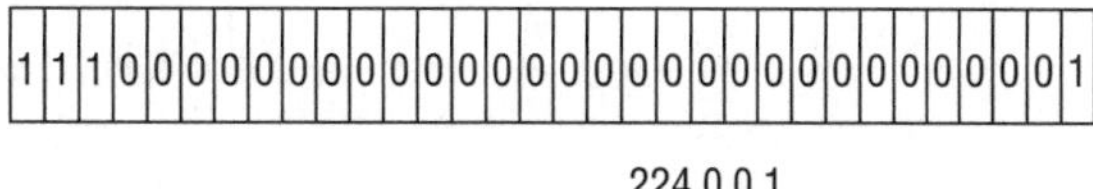


Final MAC
multicast address

01-00-5e-00-00-01

0 0 0 0 0 0 0 1 0 0 0 0 0 0 0 0 0 1 0 1 1 1 1 0 0 0 0 0 0 0 0 0 0 0 0 0 0 0 0 0 0 0 0 0 0 0 0 1

Convert the octets from decimal into binary so you can get a clear picture of what the last 23 bits are. Here you would see the following address (the last 23 bits are indicated in bold font): 11100001.**00000001.00011001.00000010**. Also, as you can see, Figure 8.6 depicts the last 23 bits that are mapped to the free spaces of the multicast MAC address. After the mapping has occurred in binary, convert the binary value to hex and you have the new MAC multicast address.

After you do the math and map the last 23 bits, the MAC address becomes 01-00-5e-01-19-02. The easiest way to map layer 3 to layer 2 manually is to do the math and make the binary conversion so you can see what the last 23 bits of the layer 3 IP address are. After you have that number, all you have to do is insert it into the MAC address and then calculate the remaining 3 hex octet values. The first three octets is always the same, 01-00-5e.

It is important that you spend time studying this procedure and the steps needed to convert a layer 3 IP multicast address to a layer 2 MAC multicast address.

There is one last method of determining the last 23 bits, but this method works only on some addresses. Keep in mind that the highest value you can get in the second octet is 127 and still have it be included in the 23 bits that will map to the MAC address. You know that the last two octets (3 and 4) will map no matter what. So you have 7 bits from the second octet, and 16 bits from the last two octets, for a total of 23 bits. After your value goes above 127 in the second octet, you have to break down the octet into binary so you can see the values of the first seven fields.

**FIGURE 8.6** Example 2 for mapping IP multicast to MAC multicast addresses

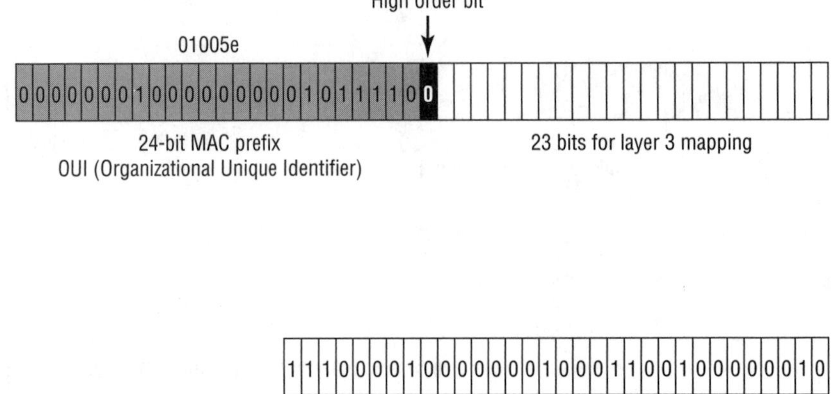

## Layer 3 to Layer 2 Overlap

By the time you've done a few of these conversions, you'll notice that there is a problem with this conversion scheme. By not using all available bits for a Class D address, you can not get an accurate map of layer 3 to layer 2 addresses. If you look at properties of a Class D address, you will see that the high order bit lies in the first octet and is in the 16's value position. This leaves 28 bits for host specification. However, by using only 23 bits of the layer 3 IP address, you leave five bits out of the mapping. This causes an overlap of $2^5$, or 32 layer-3 addresses for every one layer-2 address. With a ratio of 32:1, you can expect to see a significant amount of address ambiguity. It is safe to say that any IP addresses that have the same values in the last 23 bits will map to the same MAC multicast address.

For example, 224.0.1.1 and 225.128.1.1 map to the same MAC address. Figure 8.7 shows why this is true. You can see that the bits that differ between 224.0.1.1 and 225.128.1.1 are all within the lost five bits. The last 23 bits are equivalent.

The impact of this overlap can be significant. The overlap creates a window for multiple multicast groups' data to be forwarded to and processed by machines that didn't intentionally subscribe to the multiple groups. To give another example, a machine that subscribes to multicast group 224.2.127.254 would be given a MAC address of 01-00-5e-02-7f-fe. This host also processes packets that come from multicast group 225.2.127.254 because the layer 2 MAC address is identical.

**FIGURE 8.7** Multicast addressing overlap

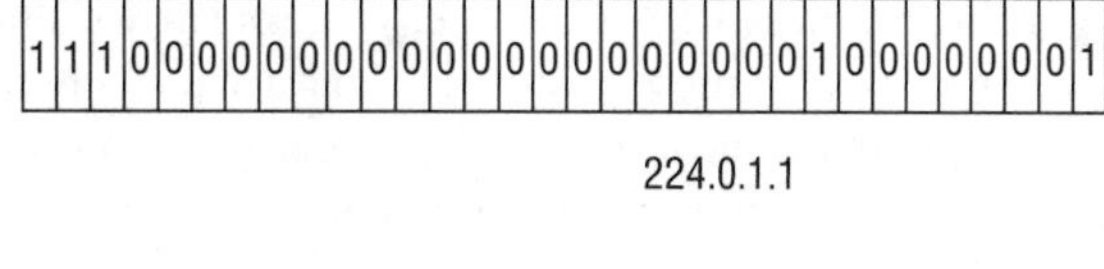


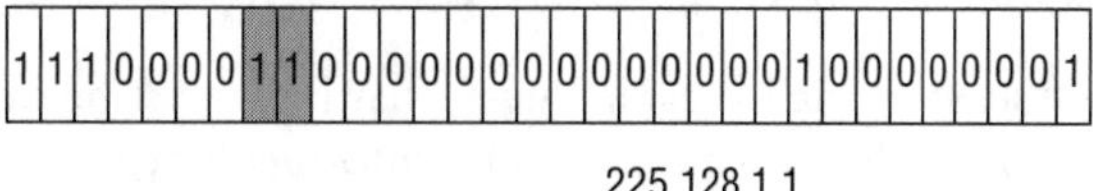


Final MAC
multicast address

01-00-5e-00-01-01

The problem this creates is that the end host must now process packets from both multicast groups even though it is interested only in data from 224.2.127.254. This causes unwanted overhead and processor interrupts on the host machine.

# Managing Multicast in an Internetwork

As a user on the network, you can understand that spam is not something that is managed by a systems administrator, whereas valid mailing lists require maintenance to keep a current list of valid subscribers. The same can be said of multicast. As we said earlier, one of the major differences between broadcast and multicast communication is that broadcast traffic goes to all hosts on a subnet, whereas multicast traffic goes only to the hosts that request it. The distinguishing factor that puts multicast traffic so far ahead of broadcast traffic in utility is the ability to specify which multiple hosts will receive the transmission.

This isn't done magically; routers and switches don't know who and where the recipients are just because it's multicast traffic. As with any application, protocols are needed to make things happen. Multicast works on the basis of host subscription to groups.

Several methods and protocols have been developed and implemented to facilitate multicast functionality within the internetwork:

- Subscribing groups
- Maintaining groups
- Joining groups
- Leaving groups

Each of these protocols and methods is used for specific tasks or to achieve specific results within the multicast environment. More importantly, each device in the network must know its role regarding multicasting; otherwise, you are left with nothing except a broadcast.

We will now look at these protocols and learn just where they fit in and what they are needed for. We begin with the most important, subscription and group maintenance, and then move on to enhancements for multicast deployment and distribution.

## Subscribing and Maintaining Groups

For multicast traffic to reach a host, that host must be running an application that sends a request to a multicast-enabled router informing the router that it wishes to receive data belonging to the specified multicast group. If this request were never to take place, the router wouldn't be aware that the host was waiting for data from the specified group.

As an overview: A multicast-enabled router receives all group advertisements and routes. It listens on all interfaces, waiting for a request from a host to forward multicast group traffic. After a host on an interface makes a request to become a member of a group, the interface activates the requested group on itself and only on itself. While the host is a member, multicast data is forwarded to that interface, and any host subscribed to the group receives the data.

That was a simple overview; now let's look at how this is accomplished in more detail. We start by discussing five major host subscription protocols:

- IGMPv1
- IGMPv2
- IGMPv3
- CGMP
- IGMP Snooping

The differences among them will become apparent as we get further into the discussion.

## Internet Group Management Protocol Version 1 (IGMPv1)

As the name indicates, *Internet Group Management Protocol version 1 (IGMPv1)* was the first version of the protocol. It was a result of RFC 1112. The purpose of this protocol is to enable hosts to subscribe to or join specified multicast groups. By subscribing to groups, the hosts are thereby enabled to receive multicast data forwarded from the router.

IGMP has several processes that it executes to manage multicast group subscription and maintenance. We will discuss them in greater detail so you can get an understanding of what happens.

Three processes are employed by version 1 of IGMP:

- Query
- Join
- Leave

These processes are the means by which multicast group membership is maintained. The first two processes are functional processes, whereas the Leave process is more of a time-out than a formal request. Each process is defined in detail next.

## Membership Query Process

One important process is the *IGMP Query process*, which is kindred to a keep-alive procedure. Because the router needs to keep tabs on which multicast groups need to remain active, or be made active or inactive, it sends a Membership Query out each interface. The query is directed to the reserved address of 224.0.0.1, to which all multicast hosts will answer.

After the request is received, the hosts report back with their group subscription information. After a specific group has been reported to the router, subsequent reports for the same group coming from different hosts are suppressed. This is done because only one host on a subnet/VLAN needs to request membership for the router to activate that group on the interface. Once active on the router interface, any host on that segment wanting to receive data for that specific group will receive it. Figure 8.8 depicts how this process works.

**FIGURE 8.8** IGMPv1 Query routine

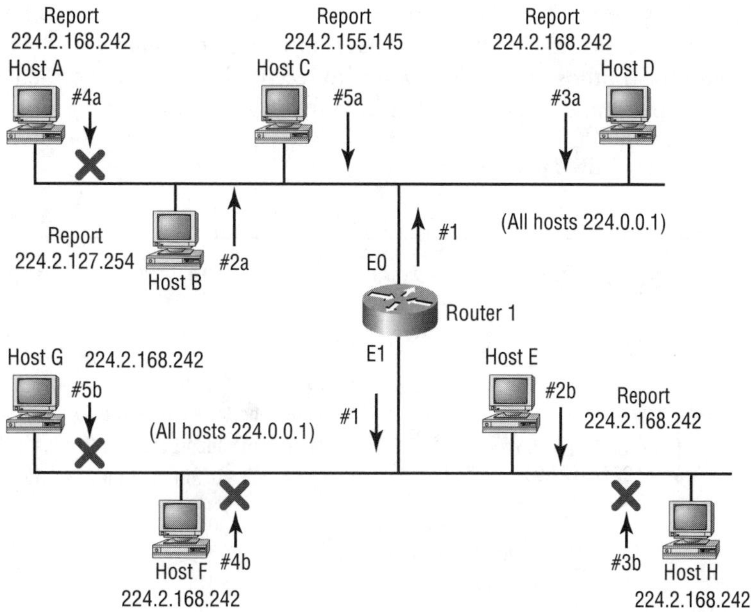


You can follow the numbers indicated in the figure. First, the query to 224.0.0.1 is sent, and subsequently, the hosts begin to report back. The first host to respond (#2a) is Host B, requesting data for the multicast group 224.2.127.254. Host D responds next (#3a) with a request for the group 224.2.168.242. The next host to reply is Host A (#4a). However, because the report from Host D was already multicast to the 224.2.168.242 group, Host A heard the report and suppressed its own report to the group.

The protocol is "smart" enough to understand that after one host has reported, more hosts don't need to report as well. This helps prevent unwanted and unnecessary bandwidth and processor utilization. To accomplish this, when a query is sent, each participating device sets a random countdown timer. The first device whose timer runs out will respond; the others will reset their timers.

Host C (#5a) responds with a different group number, 224.2.155.145. After all the hosts have responded to the query, Router 1 can maintain activity for these groups on interface E0.

Notice that this description applies to interface E0 on Router 1. Simultaneously, a multicast flood to 224.0.0.1 was sent out interface E1 as well. The first host to respond on this segment is Host E (#2b), and it is reporting membership to 224.2.168.242. Notice that this report was not suppressed, even though Host D had already multicast a report to this group, because it occurred on a different interface. The router queries the local All Hosts address 224.0.0.1, which is not forwarded by the router. That is why the same query is sent out all interfaces on the router. Now that Host E has multicast to the group for that segment, none of the other hosts on the E1 segment will report because they are all members of the 224.2.168.242 group.

## Join Process

The other processes are joining and leaving multicast groups. Both of these processes are quite simple and straightforward. You understand how interfaces are maintained in an active state through Membership Queries. The query process runs only every 60 seconds. If a host wants to join a multicast group outside the Membership Query interval, it can simply send an unsolicited report to the multicast router stating that it wants to receive data for the specified multicast group. Figure 8.9 depicts how this occurs. This is known as the *IGMP Join process*.

**FIGURE 8.9** Unsolicited join requests

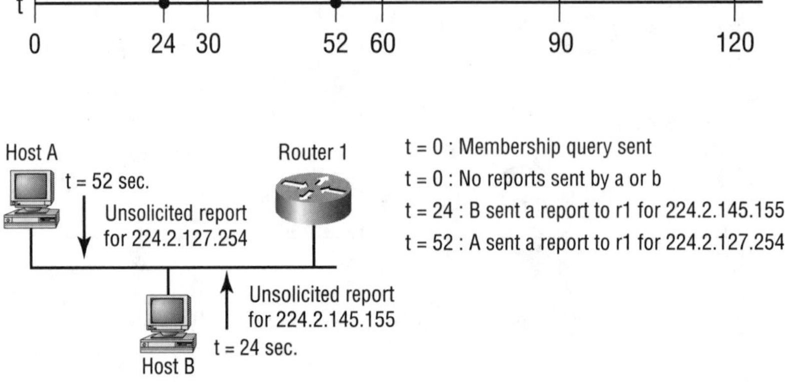


## Leave Process

Withdrawal from a group is not initiated by the host, as one would imagine. The router hosts a timer that is reset every time a response is received from a host on the subnet. The timer runs for three minutes, which is equivalent to three Membership Query cycles (a cycle lasts 60 seconds). If the timer expires and no response is received from the hosts on the interface, the router disables multicast forwarding on that interface. If the router was forwarding for a specific group and doesn't get responses for that group but continues to get responses for other groups, it stops forwarding only for the group that no longer has hosts listening.

## Internet Group Management Protocol Version 2 (IGMPv2)

As with any software revision, features are made better. Defined by RFC 2236, *Internet Group Management Protocol version 2 (IGMPv2)* provides the same functionality as version 1 did, but with a few enhancements:

- The Leave process in version 2 was included to avoid long time-outs that are experienced in version 1.
- There are two Query forms, General and Group-Specific.
- Network traffic is less bursty due to new timing mechanisms.

In this section, these enhancements are discussed.

It is important to be aware of issues when both versions of IGMP are present on the network. Version 2 provides backward compatibility with version 1, but the functionality of version 2 is lost when it's operating with version 1 devices. A version 2 host has to use version 1 frame formats when talking with a version 1 router. The same applies when a version 2 router tries to communicate with a version 1 host; it must use the version 1 format.

### General and Group-Specific Query Processes

One enhancement that was made to IGMPv2 processes was the creation of a new query type. The Membership Query, as it was called in IGMPv1, was renamed General Queries, and the new type is Group-Specific Query. The new query type is used to query a specific multicast group (kind of obvious from the name). The overall procedure is the same as it is in IGMPv1.

When multiple IGMPv1 routers existed on the same segment, a multicast routing protocol made the decision as to which of all the multicast routers would perform the Membership Queries. Now, the decision is made by using a feature added to IGMPv2. This feature is known as the Querier Election Process.

The frame for the query was changed to enable a maximum response time that allows the hosts on the segment more time to respond to the query. This reduces the bursty traffic on the network.

### IGMPv2 Leave Process

IGMPv2 implemented the capability for hosts to remove themselves from the multicast group immediately (in a matter of seconds) instead of the router having to wait up to three minutes. The process is known as the *IGMP Leave process*. The two new additions of the Leave and Group-Specific messages work together to enable a host to remove itself from the multicast group immediately without interrupting the state of the interface on the multicast router.

Figure 8.10 depicts how the IGMPv2 Leave process works. First, Host A sends a Leave message to the All multicast routers address (224.0.0.2), expressing the intent to withdraw from the multicast group. Because Router 1 doesn't know how many hosts on the segment belong to group 224.2.155.145, it must send a Group-Specific Query to see whether any hosts remain members of the group. If no responses are received, the router disables multicast forwarding out of the interface for the 224.2.155.145 group. If any hosts respond to the query, the router leaves the interface status quo. In the figure, you can see that Host B responds because it is still participating in the group 224.2.155.145. Hence, the interface is left active for that group.

**FIGURE 8.10** IGMPv2 Leave process

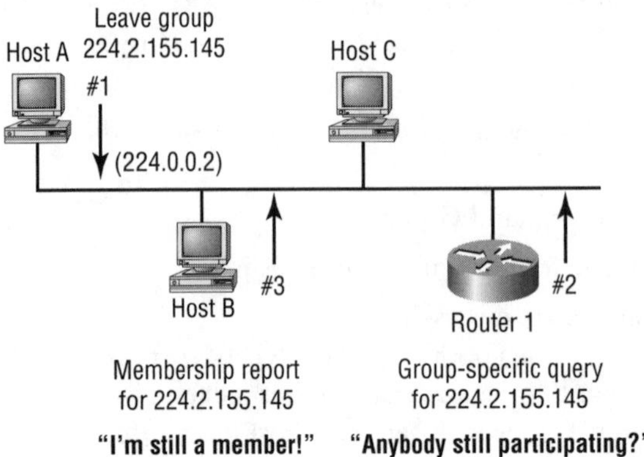


# Internet Group Management Protocol Version 3 (IGMPv3)

Multicasting is a rapidly evolving world of multicast traffic flows. No surprise, then, that version 2 of IGMP is not without its own flaws.

Known problems with IGMPv2 (which were not obvious in the past) include the possibility of two multicast applications being "live" at the same time with the same multicast address, the lack of knowledge about the multicast server source address causing routing tree instability, and the ease with which multicast groups can be subjected to Denial-of-Service attacks (or even simple spamming).

*Internet Group Management Protocol Version 3 (IGMPv3)* addresses these problems specifically by allowing hosts to specify the list of hosts from whom they want to receive traffic, blocking traffic from other hosts transmitting the same stream, and allowing hosts to block packets that come from sources sending unwanted traffic.

Only two types of message exists in IGMPv3: Membership Query and Membership Report.

## Membership Query

The Query message is used to determine if there are any extant members in a particular group. Two types of query exist: Group-Specific Queries and Group-and-Source-Specific Queries.

**Group-Specific Queries** If a host receives an IGMPv3 Group-Specific Query in its source-specific range, it must respond with a report.

**Group-and-Source-Specific Queries** An IGMPv3 router will query any source-specific channel that a host has requested to leave with a Group-and-Source-Specific Query. Hosts must respond to any Group-and-Source-Specific Query for which both the group and source match any channel to which they are subscribed.

### Membership Report

IGMPv3 receivers signal their membership to a multicast host group in one of two possible modes, Include and Exclude.

**Include** When operating in Include mode, the receiver announces its membership to a host group and provides a list of IP addresses (referred to as the *include* list) from which it wants to receive traffic.

**Exclude** When operating in Exclude mode, the receiver announces membership to a host group and provides a list of IP addresses (referred to as the *exclude* list) from which it does not want to receive traffic. Obviously, this indicates that the host will only receive traffic from other sources whose IP addresses are not listed in the exclude list.

To receive traffic from all sources, a host transmits an empty exclude list.

## Cisco Group Management Protocol (CGMP)

We have discussed IGMPv1, IGMPv2, and IGMPv3, which are open standard protocols for host membership of multicast groups. When running multicast at layer 2, things get a little complicated for the switch. It doesn't know which packets are membership report messages or which are actual multicast group data packets because all of them have the same MAC address. *Cisco Group Management Protocol (CGMP)* was implemented to fill this void. It runs on both routers and switches.

**Real World Scenario**

**Multicast Design**

If the router interface is connected to a hub or a switch that doesn't understand multicasting, when the router forwards the multicast, the stream acts like a broadcast. In other words, every device gets a copy. In IGMPv1, the router would keep forwarding the multicast stream out to the hub, which forwards it to every connected client. Multicast routers work well because they can forward a broadcast from one router to the next, something that doesn't happen with true broadcasts. The problem is that clients on a multicast segment get the stream whether they want it or not.

This type of scenario is fine when the CEO wants to give a speech to every desktop, but what about video that is only for a specific division, department, or business unit? If the packets need to go to five different locations, and after you get past the routers all you have are switches, everyone will receive the multicast stream. This doesn't reduce bandwidth utilization!

So far, corporate multicasting with IGMP, either version, works well at the router level. Too bad most clients aren't connected directly to router ports. Because IGMP is essentially nothing more than intelligent broadcast propagation, Cisco created something that would enable switches to participate as well, CGMP.

The key feature of CGMP is that it uses two MAC addresses:

**Group Destination Address (GDA)** The GDA is the multicast group address mapped to the MAC multicast address.

**Unicast Source Address (USA)** The USA is the unicast MAC address of the host. USA enables the host to send multicast membership reports to the multicast router—the multicast router can also be a Route Switch Module (RSM) or Multi-layer Switch Feature Card (MSFC)—and still tell the switch which port needs to receive the multicast data.

In addition to being able to make port assignments on the switch, CGMP also handles the interface assignment on the router. If a switch doesn't have any ports that need to receive multicast data, CGMP informs the router that it doesn't need to forward multicast group data out the router interface.

CGMP uses many of the same processes IGMP uses. The main difference is that CGMP is used between the router and switch. When switches are involved, the IGMP requests must be translated to CGMP and passed on to the switch. These processes include the following:

- CGMP Join process
- Switch host management
- CGMP Leave process

## CGMP Join

Hosts do not use CGMP; only the switches and routers that the host connects to use it. When a host sends an IGMP report (membership report) advertising membership of a multicast group, the message is forwarded to the router (that is, an actual multicast router, an RSM, or an MSFC) for processing. The router sees the request and processes it accordingly. The multicast group is set up, and the two MAC addresses are generated. The router then gives the switch the CGMP message. With the CGMP message, the switch can assign the multicast group to the port of the requesting host. You can see the entire process in Figure 8.11.

**FIGURE 8.11** CGMP Join process

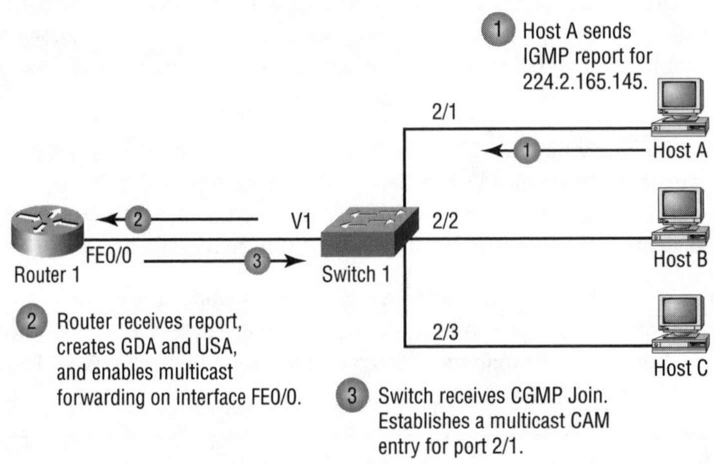

### Host Management

Host management is performed by the router. The router continues to receive IGMP messages from the host. Then the router converts the message into a CGMP message and forwards it to the switch. The switch then performs the port maintenance as directed by the router. This process is followed for the multiple types of messages that the host can generate. The router forwards three critical pieces of information to the switch in the CGMP message:

- Request type
- MAC address of the requesting host
- Multicast group the request is for

The CGMP Leave process is done in the same manner. The router receives the request and then informs the switch that the multicast group address needs to be removed from the Content Addressable Memory (CAM) table for the host's port.

## IGMP Snooping

While CGMP is a Cisco proprietary protocol to enable switches and routers to communicate regarding multicast traffic patterns, *IGMP Snooping* is referenced in IGMPv3 and does that same thing. Several vendors have created implementations of IGMP Snooping that don't quite play well with each other.

IGMP Snooping doesn't require any sort of translation into a different protocol at the switch. IGMP is used from the client to the router. The switch monitors, or sniffs, the IGMP packets as they pass through and records the MAC addresses and the port that requested to be a part of the process.

Because the switch becomes an integral part of the process of IGMP, the router forwards status messages to the switch and the switch forwards them out the appropriate ports. This is the process of Fast-Leave and is done on both CGMP and IGMP Snooping:

- Client A is listening to a multicast stream and decides to stop listening. The client sends an IGMP Leave message to the switch.
- The switch responds with an IGMP Query to find out whether other clients exist that still want that multicast stream.
- If a client exists out that port, the switch makes no changes.
- If there is no reply out that port but other ports are receiving the stream, the switch does nothing.
- If there is no reply to the Query and there are no other ports participating, the switch forwards the Leave message to the router.

**Real World Scenario**

**Multicast and Spanning Tree**

It might seem that CGMP and IGMP Snooping are the way to go. That is true—if you have a very stable network. Remember that STP is used to allow for redundancy but that it disables the redundant links until they are needed. If you have a switched network with redundant connections and a link drops, spanning tree takes over and figures out the next best topology. Unfortunately, the spanning tree process doesn't tell the multicasting process that this is happening. The switch will still forward the multicast message out the port that it was using. This can cause delays and dropped connections. Eventually it settles down, unless the topology changes are always going on.

# Routing Multicast Traffic

Up to this point, we have been discussing the host side of multicast. You have learned how hosts interact with switches and routers to join multicast groups and receive the traffic. It is now time to move on to discuss how multicast traffic travels across the Internet (or intranet) from a source on a remote network to a local router and host.

Unicast data uses routing protocols to accomplish the task of getting data to and from remote destinations. Multicast does the same, but it goes about it in a somewhat different manner. Unicast relies on routing tables. Multicast uses a sort of spanning tree system to distribute its data. This section describes the tree structures that can be implemented to enable multicast routing. In addition to trees, several different protocol methods can be used to achieve the desired implementation of multicast.

## Distribution Trees

Two types of trees exist in multicast:

**Source trees** *Source trees* use the architecture of the source of the multicast traffic as the root of the tree.

**Shared trees** *Shared trees* use an architecture in which multiple sources share a common rendezvous point.

Each of these methods is effective and enables sourced multicast data to reach an arbitrary number of recipients of the multicast group. Let's discuss each of them in detail.

### Source Tree

Source trees use special notation. This notation is used in what becomes a multicast route table. Unicast route tables use the destination address and next-hop information to establish a topology for forwarding information. Here is a sample from a unicast routing table:

```
B     210.70.150.0/24 [20/0] via 208.124.237.10, 3d08h
B     192.5.192.0/24 [20/0] via 208.124.237.10, 2w1d
B     193.219.28.0/24 [20/0] via 208.124.237.10, 1d03h
B     136.142.0.0/16 [20/0] via 208.124.237.10, 3d07h
B     202.213.23.0/24 [20/0] via 208.124.237.10, 1w2d
      202.246.53.0/24 is variably subnetted, 2 subnets, 2 masks
B        202.246.53.0/24 [20/0] via 208.124.237.10, 1w2d
B        202.246.53.60/32 [20/0] via 208.124.237.10, 1w2d
```

Multicast route tables are somewhat different. A sample of a multicast table follows. Notice that the notation is different. Instead of having the destination address listed and then the next hop to get to the destination, source tree uses the notation (S, G). This notation specifies the source host's IP address and the multicast group address for which it is sourcing information. Let's take the first one, for example. This is seen as (198.32.163.74, 224.2.243.55), which means that the source host is 198.32.163.74 and it is sourcing traffic for the multicast group 224.2.243.55:

```
(198.32.163.74, 224.2.243.55), 00:01:04/00:01:55, flags: PT
  Incoming interface: POS1/0/0, RPF nbr 208.124.237.10, Mbgp
  Outgoing interface list: Null
(198.32.163.74, 224.2.213.101), 00:02:06/00:00:53, flags: PT
  Incoming interface: POS1/0/0, RPF nbr 208.124.237.10, Mbgp
  Outgoing interface list: Null
(195.134.100.102, 224.2.127.254), 00:00:28/00:02:31, flags: CLM
  Incoming interface: POS1/0/0, RPF nbr 208.124.237.10, Mbgp
  Outgoing interface list:
    FastEthernet4/0/0, Forward/Sparse, 00:00:28/00:02:54
    FastEthernet4/1/0, Forward/Sparse, 00:00:28/00:02:31
(207.98.103.221, 224.2.127.254), 00:00:40/00:02:19, flags: CLM
  Incoming interface: POS1/0/0, RPF nbr 208.124.237.10, Mbgp
  Outgoing interface list:
    FastEthernet4/0/0, Forward/Sparse, 00:00:41/00:02:53
    FastEthernet4/1/0, Forward/Sparse, 00:00:41/00:02:19
(128.39.2.23, 224.2.127.254), 00:04:43/00:02:06, flags: CLMT
  Incoming interface: POS1/0/0, RPF nbr 208.124.237.10, Mbgp
  Outgoing interface list:
    FastEthernet4/0/0, Forward/Sparse, 00:04:43/00:02:43
```

```
    FastEthernet4/1/0, Forward/Sparse, 00:04:43/00:03:07
(129.237.25.152, 224.2.177.155), 00:17:58/00:03:29, flags: MT
  Incoming interface: POS1/0/0, RPF nbr 208.124.237.10, Mbgp
  Outgoing interface list:
    FastEthernet4/0/0, Forward/Sparse, 00:17:58/00:02:44
```

Figure 8.12 gives you a good picture of how source trees work.

Also notice in the drawing that the shortest path to the receivers was chosen. This is known as choosing the shortest path tree (SPT). You can see from the preceding output that there are three sources for the same group of 224.2.127.254. This indicates that there are three SPT groups shown here: (195.134.100.102, 224.2.127.254), (207.98.103.221, 224.2.127.254), and (128.39.2.23, 224.2.127.254). Each of these sources has its own shortest path tree to the receivers.

## Shared Tree

There are two types of shared tree distribution:

- Unidirectional
- Bidirectional

**FIGURE 8.12** Source tree forwarding

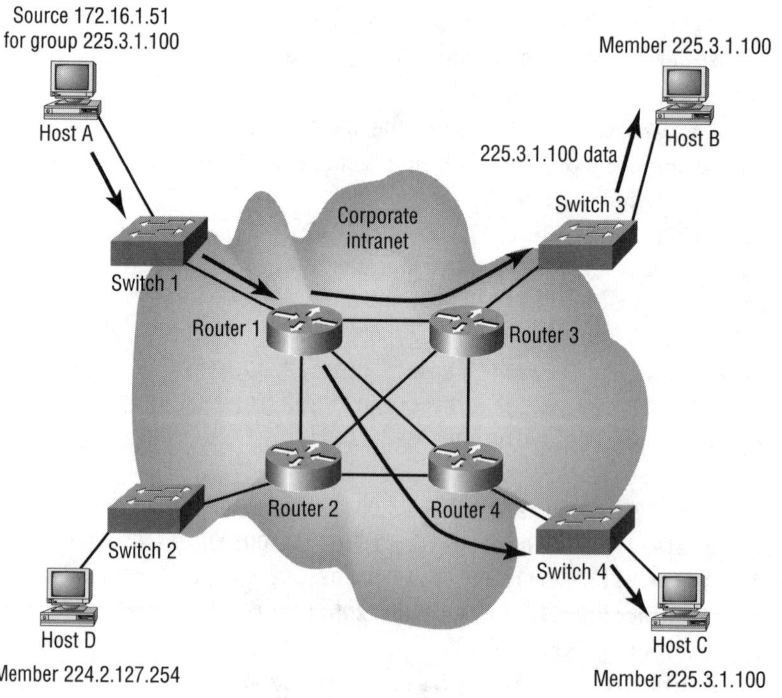

Both of them work a little differently from source tree distribution. Shared tree architecture lies in the possibility that there might be multiple sources for one multicast group. Instead of each individual source creating its own SPT and distributing the data apart from the other sources, a shared root is designated. Multiple sources for a multicast group forward their data to a shared root or rendezvous point (RP). The rendezvous point then follows SPT to forward the data to the members of the group. Figure 8.13 depicts how the shared tree distribution works.

### Unidirectional Shared Tree Distribution

*Unidirectional shared tree* distribution operates as shown in Figure 8.13. All recipients of a multicast group receive the data from a RP no matter where they are located in the network. This is very inefficient if subscribers are close to the source because they need to get the multicast stream from the RP.

### Bidirectional Shared Tree Distribution

*Bidirectional shared tree* distribution operates somewhat differently. If a receiver lives upstream from the RP, it can receive data directly from the upstream source. Figure 8.14 depicts how this works. As you can see, Host A is a source for group 224.2.127.254, and Host B is a receiver of that same group. In a bidirectional shared tree, data goes directly from Host A to Host B without having to come from the RP.

**FIGURE 8.13** Shared tree forwarding

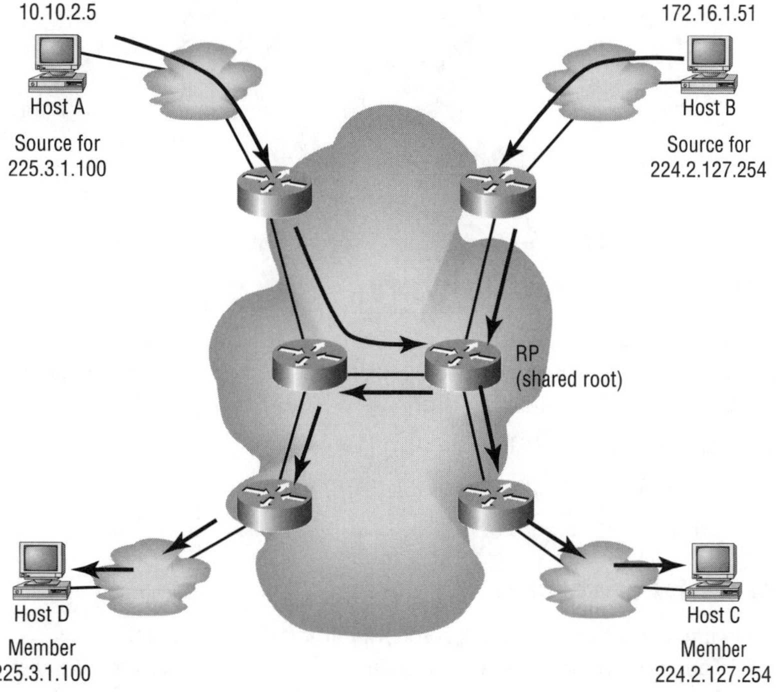

**FIGURE 8.14** Bidirectional shared tree

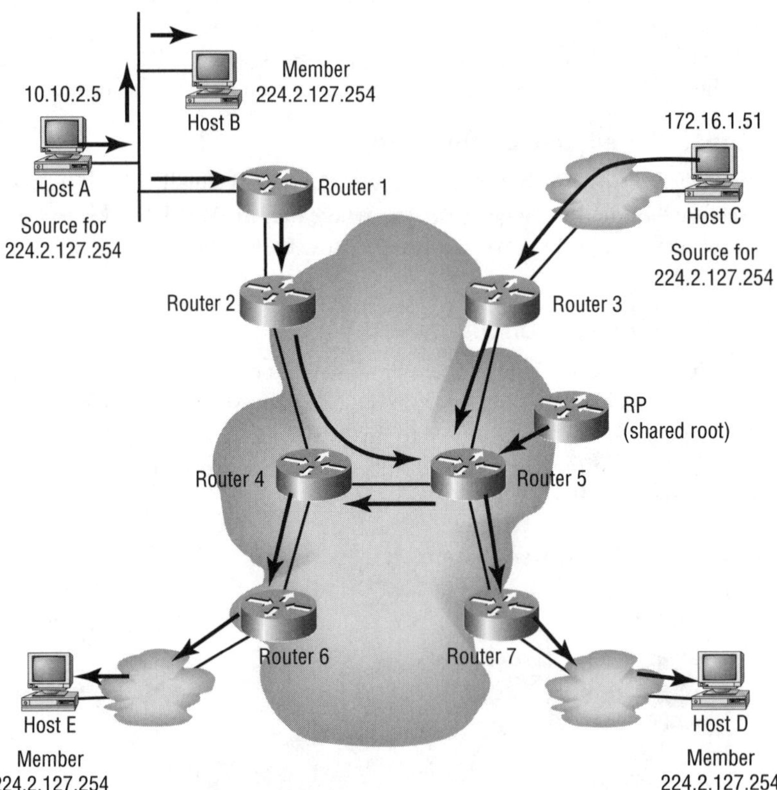


## Managing Multicast Delivery

The tree distributions explain how source information is managed; now we must discuss how the actual data delivery is managed. There are several methods of making sure that delivery is as efficient as possible. The following is discussed here:

- Reverse Path Forwarding (RPF)
- Time to Live (TTL) attributes
- Routing protocols

### Reverse Path Forwarding

RPF works in tandem with the routing protocols, but it is described briefly here. As you have seen in Figures 8.13 and 8.14, the traffic goes only to the multicast group receivers. We also indicated that bidirectional distribution eliminates the need to forward data upstream. You might ask, "How do you define upstream?" It is easy to clarify. By means of the routing protocols, routers are aware of which interface leads to the source(s) of the multicast group. That interface is considered *upstream*.

The Reverse Path Forwarding process is based on the upstream information. After receiving an incoming multicast packet, the router verifies that the packet came in on an interface that leads back to the source. The router forwards the packet if the verification is positive; otherwise, the packet is discarded. This check stops potential loops. To avoid increased overhead on the router's processor, a multicast forwarding cache is implemented for the RPF lookups.

## Time to Live (TTL)

You can also control the delivery of IP multicast packets through the TTL counter and TTL thresholds. The Time to Live counter is decremented by one every time the packet hops a router. After the TTL counter is set to zero, the packet is discarded.

Thresholds are used to achieve higher granularity and greater control within one's own network. Thresholds are applied to specified interfaces of multicast-enabled routers. The router compares the threshold value of the multicast packet to the value specified in the interface configuration. If the TTL value of the packet is greater than or equal to the TTL threshold configured for the interface, the packet is forwarded through that interface.

TTL thresholds enable network administrators to bound their network and limit the distribution of multicast packets beyond the boundaries. This is accomplished by setting high values for outbound external interfaces. The maximum value for the TTL threshold is 255. Refer to Figure 8.15 to see how network boundaries can be set to limit distribution of multicast traffic.

**FIGURE 8.15** TTL threshold utilization

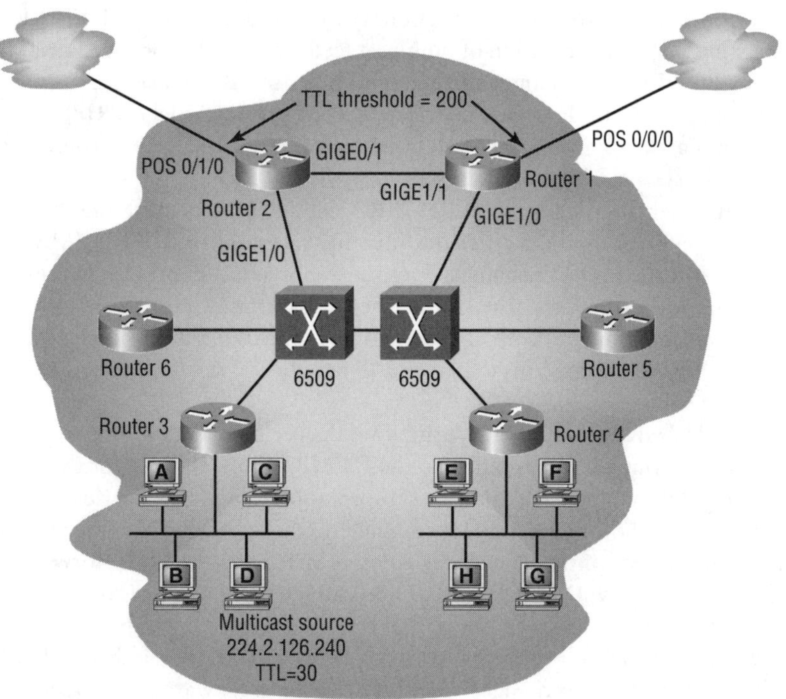

The multicast source initially sets the TTL value for the multicast packet and then forwards it on throughout the network. In this scenario, the TTL threshold values have been set to 200 on both of the exiting Packet over Sonet (POS) interfaces. The initial TTL value has been set to 30 by the application. There are three to four router hops to get out of the campus network. Router 3 will decrement by one, leaving a TTL value of 29; the Catalyst 6509's MSFC will decrement by one as well, leaving the value set to 28. After the packet reaches Router 2 or Router 1, the value will be 27 or 26, respectively. Both of these values are less than the TTL threshold of 200, which means that Router 1 and Router 2 will drop any outbound multicast packets.

## Routing Protocols

Unicast has several routing protocols that build route tables enabling layer 3 devices such as routers and some switches to forward unicast data to the next hop toward its final destination. We have also discussed some of the methods that multicast, in general, uses to distribute multicast data. Similar to unicast, multicast has a variety of routing protocols, including distance vector and link state protocols.

Protocols are used to enhance the efficiency by which multicast application data is distributed and to optimize the use of existing network resources. This section covers Distance Vector Multicast Routing Protocol (DVMRP), Multicast Open Shortest Path First (MOSPF), and Protocol Independent Multicast dense mode (PIM DM).

### Distance Vector Multicast Routing Protocol (DVMRP)

*Distance Vector Multicast Routing Protocol (DVMRP)* has achieved widespread use in the multicast world. A few years ago, you might have often heard the term "DVMRP tunnel" used when discussing the implementation of multicast feeds from an ISP or a feed from the Multicast Backbone (MBONE). As the name indicates, this protocol uses a distance-vector algorithm. It uses several of the features that other distance-vector protocols (such as RIP) implement. Some of these features are a 32 max hop-count, poison reverse, and 60-second route updates. It also allows for IP classless masking of addresses.

Just as with other routing protocols, DVMRP-enabled routers must establish adjacencies in order to share route information. After the adjacency is established, the DVMRP route table is created. Route information is exchanged via route reports. It is important to remember that the DVMRP route table is stored separately from the unicast routing table. The DVMRP route table is more like a unicast route table than the multicast route table that was shown earlier in this chapter. A DVMRP table contains the layer 3 IP network of the multicast source and the next hop toward the source.

Because the DVMRP table has this form, it works perfectly with source tree distribution, as discussed earlier. Using the information in the DVMRP table, the tree for the source can be established. In addition, the router uses this information to perform the Reverse Path Forwarding check to verify that the multicast data coming into the interface is coming in an interface that leads back to the source of the data. DVMRP uses SPT for its multicast forwarding.

Figure 8.16 shows how DVMRP works. You can see that not every router in the network is a DVMRP router. You should also notice that the adjacencies are established over tunnel interfaces. DVMRP information is tunneled through an IP network. On either end of the tunnel, information is learned and exchanged to build a multicast forwarding database or route table.

**FIGURE 8.16** DVMRP tunnels

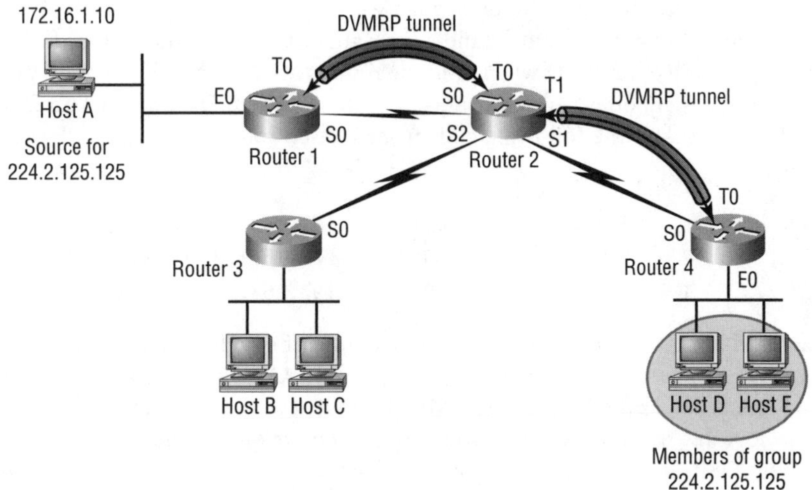


### Multicast Open Shortest Path First (MOSPF)

*Multicast Open Shortest Path First (MOSPF)* is a link state protocol. OSPFv2 includes some changes that allow multicast to be enabled on OSPF-enabled routers. This eliminates the need for tunnels such as those used for DVMRP.

To completely understand the full functionality of MOSPF, you must have a thorough understanding of OSPF itself. Here we cover only the basic functionality of MOSPF, so you should be fine with just a basic understanding of OSPF.

For more on OSPF, see *CCNP: Building Scalable Cisco Internetworks Study Guide,* by Carl Timm and Wade Edwards (Sybex, 2003).

MOSPF's basic functionality lies within a single OSPF area. Design gets more complicated as you route multicast traffic to other areas (inter-area routing) or to other autonomous systems (inter-AS routing). This additional complication requires more knowledge of OSPF routing. We briefly discuss how this is accomplished in MOSPF, but most of the details will be regarding MOSPF intra-area routing.

### Intra-Area MOSPF

OSPF route information is shared via different Link State Advertisement (LSA) types. LSAs are flooded throughout an area to give all OSPF-enabled routers a logical image of the network topology. When changes are made to the topology, new LSAs are flooded to propagate the change.

In addition to the unicast-routing LSA types, in OSPFv2 there is a special multicast LSA for flooding multicast group information throughout the area. This additional LSA type required some modification to the OSPF frame format.

Here is where you need to understand a little about OSPF. Multicast LSA flooding is done by the Designated Router (DR) when multiple routers are connected to a multi-access media, such as Ethernet. On point-to-point connections, there are no DR and Backup Designated Router (BDR). Look at the following code from a Cisco router running OSPF over point-to-point circuits:

```
Neighbor ID    Pri   State          Dead Time   Address         Interface
172.16.1.2      1    FULL/  -       00:00:31    172.16.1.2      Serial3/0
192.168.1.2     1    FULL/  -       00:00:39    192.168.1.2     Serial3/1
```

On a multi-access network, the DR must be multicast enabled—that is, running MOSPF. If any non-MOSPF routers are on the same network, their OSPF priority must be lowered so that none of them becomes the DR. If a non-MOSPF router were to become the DR, it would not be able to forward the multicast LSA to the other routers on the segment.

Inside the OSPF area, updates are sent describing which links have active multicast members on them so that the multicast data can be forwarded to those interfaces. MOSPF also uses (S, G) notation and calculates the SPT by using the Dijkstra algorithm. You must also understand that an SPT is created for each source in the network.

### Inter-Area and Inter-AS MOSPF

When discussing the difference between intra-area and inter-area MOSPF, you must remember that all areas connect through Area 0, the backbone. In large networks, having full multicast tables in addition to all the unicast tables flow across Area 0 would cause a great deal of overhead and possibly latency.

Unicast OSPF uses a Summary LSA to inform the routers in Area 0 about the networks and topology in an adjacent area. This task is performed by the area's Area Border Router (ABR). The ABR summarizes all the information about the area and then passes it on to the backbone (Area 0) routers in a summary LSA. The same is done for the multicast topology. The ABR summarizes which multicast groups are active and which groups have sources within the area. This information is then sent to the backbone routers.

In addition to summarizing multicast group information, the ABR is responsible for the actual forwarding of multicast group traffic into and out of the area. Each area has an ABR that performs these two functions within an OSPF network.

OSPF implements Autonomous System Border Routers to be the bridges between different autonomous systems. These routers perform much the same as an ABR but must be able to communicate with non-OSPF-speaking devices. Multicast group information and data is forwarded and received by the Multicast Autonomous System Border Router (MASBR). Because MOSPF runs natively within OSPF, there must be a method or protocol by which the multicast information can be taken from MOSPF and communicated to the external AS. Historically, DVRMP has provided this bridge.

## PIM DM

There are three types of *Protocol Independent Multicast (PIM)*: sparse mode, dense mode, and a combination of the two. Although *PIM dense mode (PIM DM)* maintains several functions, the ones that are discussed here are flooding, pruning, and grafting. We'll talk about sparse mode later in this chapter.

PIM is considered "protocol independent" because it actually uses the unicast route table for RPF and multicast forwarding. PIM DM understands classless subnet masking and uses it when the router is running an IP classless unicast protocol.

PIM DM routers establish neighbor relationships with other routers running PIM DM. It uses these neighbors to establish an SPT and forward multicast data throughout the network. The SPT created by PIM DM is based on source tree distribution.

PIM, either sparse mode or dense mode, is the method that Cisco recommends for multicast routing on their routers.

**Flooding** When a multicast source begins to transmit data, PIM runs the RPF, using the unicast route table to verify that the interface leads toward the source. It then forwards the data to all PIM neighbors. Those PIM neighbors then forward the data to their PIM neighbors. This happens throughout the network, whether there are group members on the router or not. Every multicast-enabled router participates; that is why it is considered *flooding* and is where the term "dense mode" comes from.

When multiple, equal-cost links exist, the router with the highest IP address is elected to be the incoming interface (used for RPF). Every router runs the RPF when it receives the multicast data.

Figure 8.17 depicts the initial multicast flooding in a PIM DM network. You can see that the data is forwarded to every PIM neighbor throughout the network. After a PIM neighbor does the RPF calculation, the router then forwards the data to interfaces that have active members of the group.

**Pruning** After the initial flooding through the PIM neighbors, pruning starts. *Pruning* is the act of trimming down the SPT. Because the data has been forwarded to every router, regardless of group membership, the routers must now prune back the distribution of the multicast data to routers that actually have active group members connected.

Figure 8.18 shows the pruning action that occurs for the PIM DM routers that don't have active group members. Router 5 does not have any active group members, so it sends a prune message to Router 3. Even though Router 4 has a network that does not have members, it does have an interface that does, so it will not send a prune message.

Four criteria merit a prune message being sent by a router:

- The incoming interface fails the RPF check.
- There are no directly connected active group members and no PIM neighbors. (This is considered a leaf router because it has no downstream PIM neighbors.)
- A point-to-point non-leaf router receives a prune request from a neighbor.
- A LAN non-leaf router receives a prune request from another router, and no other router on the segment overrides the prune request.

If any of these criteria are met, a prune request is sent to the PIM neighbor and the SPT is pruned back.

**FIGURE 8.17** PIM DM flooding

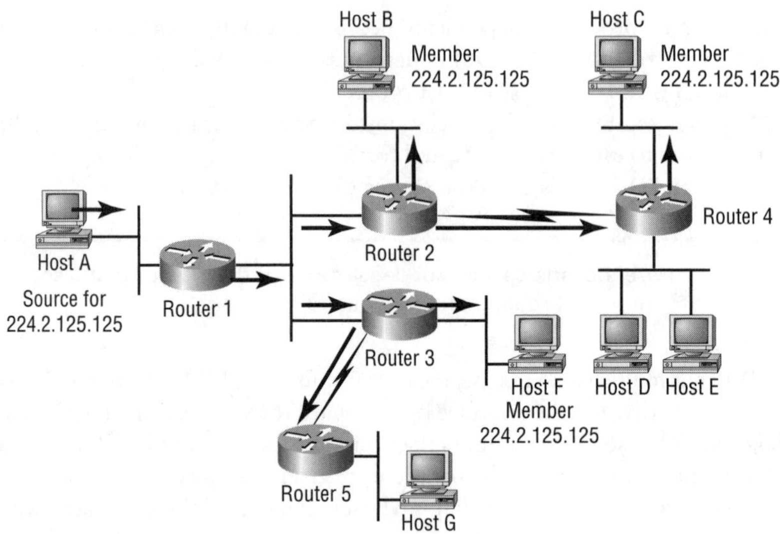


**FIGURE 8.18** PIM DM pruning

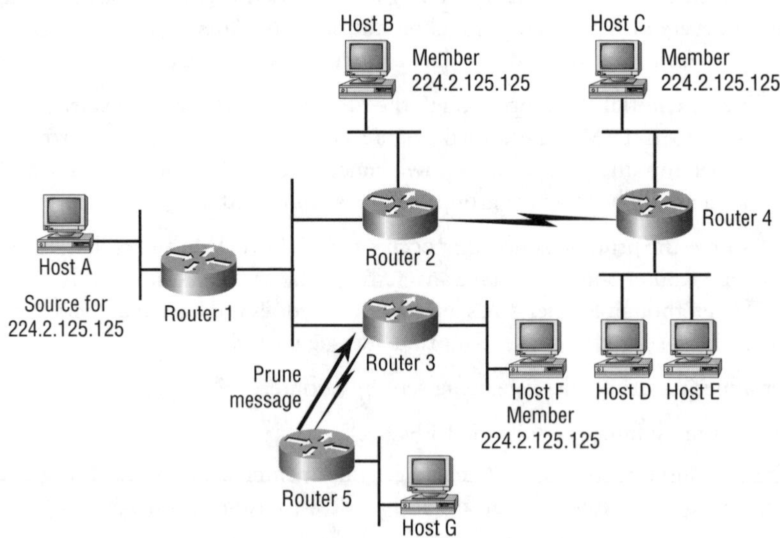

**Grafting** PIM DM is also ready to forward multicast data after a previously inactive interface becomes active. This is done through the process of *grafting*. When a host sends an IGMP group membership report to the router, the router then sends a Graft message to the nearest upstream PIM neighbor. After this message is acknowledged, multicast data begins to be forwarded to the router and on to the host. Figure 8.19 depicts the grafting process.

## Sparse Mode Routing Protocols

Sparse mode protocols use shared tree distribution as their forwarding methods. This is done to create a more efficient method of multicast distribution. Two sparse mode protocols are discussed in this section:

- Core-based trees (CBT)
- Protocol Independent Multicast sparse mode (PIM SM)

### Core-Based Trees

When we discussed shared trees, you learned that there were two types, unidirectional and bidirectional. CBT utilizes the bidirectional method for its multicast data distribution. Because CBT uses a shared tree system, it designates a core router that is used as the root of the tree, enabling data to flow up or down the tree.

**FIGURE 8.19** PIM DM grafting

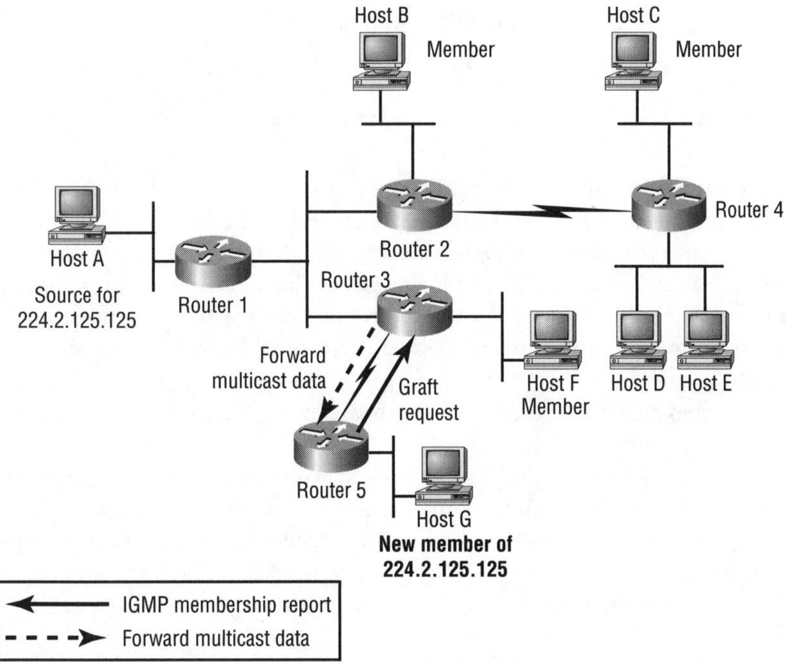

Data forwarding in a CBT multicast system is similar to the shared tree distribution we covered earlier. If a source to a multicast group sends multicast data to the CBT-enabled router, the router then forwards the data out all interfaces that are included in the tree, not just the interface that leads to the core router. In this manner, data flows up and down the tree. After the data gets to the core router, the core router then forwards the information to the other routers that are in the tree. Figure 8.20 depicts this process.

**FIGURE 8.20** CBT data distribution

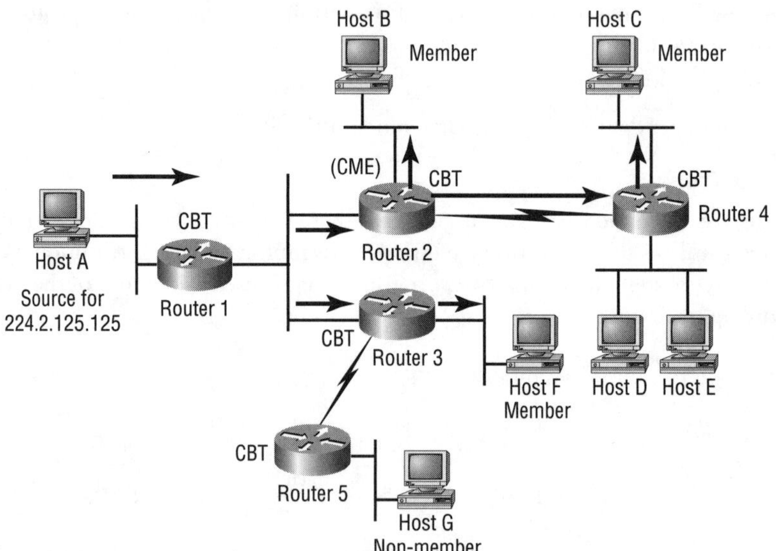


It is important to see the difference between this sparse mode method and the dense mode method. In sparse mode operation, routers are members of the tree only if they have active members directly connected. Notice in Figure 8.20 that Router 5 is not participating. Dense mode operates on the initial premise that all PIM neighbors have active members directly connected. The tree changes when the directly connected routers request to be pruned from the tree.

A CBT router might become part of the tree after a host sends an IGMP Membership Record to the directly connected router. The router then sends a join tree request to the *core* router. If the request reaches a CBT tree member first, that router will add the *leaf* router to the tree and begin forwarding multicast data.

Pruning the tree is done much the same way. When there are no more active members on a router's interfaces, the router sends a prune request to the upstream router. The answering router removes the interface from the forwarding cache if it is on a point-to-point circuit, or it waits for a timer to expire it if is on a shared access network. The timer gives enough time for other CBT routers on the segment to override the prune request.

### PIM SM

*PIM sparse mode (PIM SM)* also uses the architecture of shared tree distribution. There is an RP router that acts as the root of the shared tree. Unlike CBT, however, PIM SM uses the unidirectional shared tree distribution mechanism. Because PIM SM uses the unidirectional method, all multicast sources for any group must register with the RP of the shared tree. This enables the RP and other routers to establish the RPT, or RP tree (synonymous with SPT in source tree distribution).

Just as with CBT, PIM SM routers join the shared tree when they are notified via IGMP that a host requests membership of a multicast group. If the existing group entry (*, G) does not already exist in the router's table, it is created and the join tree request is sent to the next hop toward the RP. The next router receives the request. Depending on whether it has an existing entry for (*, G), two things can happen:

- If an entry for (*, G) exists, the router simply adds the interface to the shared tree and no further join requests are sent toward the RP.
- If an entry for (*, G) does not exist, the router creates an entry for the (*, G) group and adds the link to the forwarding cache. In addition to doing this, the router sends its own join request toward the RP.

This happens until the join request reaches a router that already has the (*, G) entry or a join request reaches the RP.

The next facet of PIM SM is the shared tree pruning. With PIM SM, pruning turns out to be just the opposite of the explicit Join mechanism used to construct the shared tree.

**FIGURE 8.21** PIM SM pruning

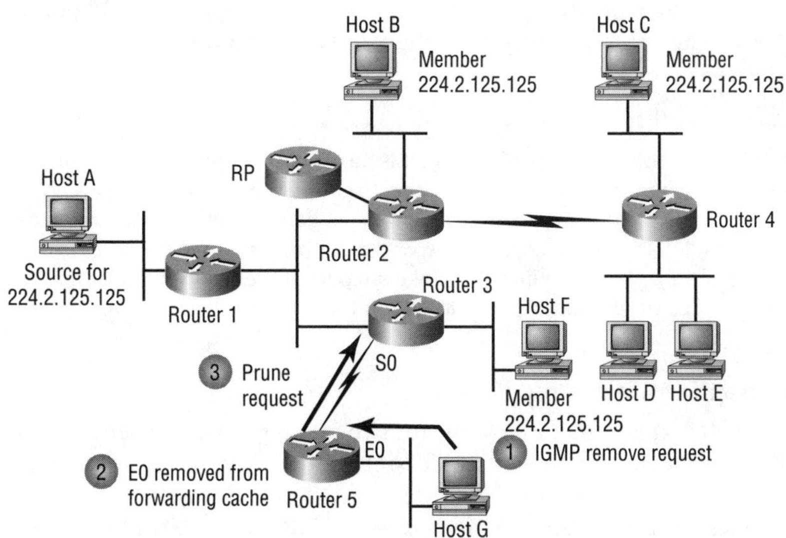

When a member leaves a group, it does so via IGMP. When it happens to be the last member on a segment, the router removes the interface from the forwarding cache entry and then sends a prune request toward the RP of the shared tree. If there is another router with active members connected to the router requesting the prune, it is removed from the outgoing interface list and no additional Prune messages are sent to the RP. See Figure 8.21 for a visual description.

Router 5 receives an IGMP message requesting the removal of Host G from the group. Because Host G was the last active member of the group, the (*, G) entry is set to null 0 and a prune request is sent by Router 5 to Router 3. When Router 3 receives the request, it removes the link for interface S0 from the forwarding table. Because Host F is a directly connected active member of the group, the entry for (*, G) is not null 0, so no prune request is sent to Router 2 (the RP for this example).

If Host F were not active, the entry for (*, G) would have been set to null 0 also and a prune request would have been sent to the RP.

### Multicast Source Discovery Protocol (MSDP)

In PIM sparse mode, the routers closest to the sources and receivers register with the RP, and so the RP knows about all the sources and receivers for any group. But it is possible that several RPs may need to be created, resulting in several PIM SM domains. Naturally, RPs don't know about multicast sources in other domains. *Multicast Source Discovery Protocol (MSDP)* was developed to address this issue.

ISPs offering multicast routes to their customers faced a dilemma. Naturally, they didn't want to have to rely on an RP maintained by another ISP, but they needed to access multicast traffic coming from the Internet. MSDP allows them to each run their own RP. RPs peer together using a TCP-based connection that allows them to share information about active sources inside their own domains.

ISPs have the option of which sources they will forward to other MSDP peers, or which sources they will accept, using filtering configurations. PIM SM is used to forward traffic between the RP domains.

ISPs have no problem with this peering relationship. ISP border routers already establish peering relationships with neighboring ISPs, running *Border Gateway Protocol (BGP)* version 4 to exchange routing information as part of the Internet architecture. ISPs with such peering relationships have regular meetings, and their inter-ISP links are part of their commercial raison d'etre. MSDP peering is simply an addition to the agenda.

### Source-Specific Multicasting (SSM)

Within any multicast group, it is possible for two sources to exist. Therefore, as multiple listeners join the group, they all receive multicast streams from both sources. This can be filtered out, but possibly not until the last router is reached, in which case considerable unnecessary traffic will have been transmitted. *Source-Specific Multicasting (SSM)* is an extension to the PIM protocol that removes that problem without having to resort to MSDP source discovery. SSM requires the network be running IGMPv3.

In SSM multicast networks, the router closest to the receiver receives a request from that receiver to join to a multicast source. The receiver application uses the Include option to specify the required source. Once the multicast router knows the specific source of the multicast stream, it no longer needs to communicate via the RP, but can instead forward data to the receiver directly, using a source-based share tree distribution system.

# Planning and Preparing for Using IP Multicast

You now know that multicast networks behave differently from unicast networks. It is important to keep this in mind when planning the deployment of an IP multicast network. You should take several factors into consideration, including bandwidth implications, use of multicast applications, application requirements, user requirements, the location of the recipients, required equipment, cost, and, most importantly, what multicast source(s) will be used.

All these factors require attention and planning for a successful deployment of IP multicast throughout the network. You must also think upside down when thinking about multicast routing. As discussed in the preceding chapter, distribution trees are built based on the position of the root (source) of the tree. Therefore, when planning the routing for the multicast network, you must know where your sources or RPs will be located.

By taking the time to plan and prepare for a multicast deployment, you will avoid headaches later. You must become familiar with the customer's requirements as well as the effects that multicast will have on the existing network.

There are many methods of implementing multicast on a network. Commonly, institutions will want to connect with the Multicast Backbone (MBONE) multicast sessions; therefore, they must implement multicast through a Distance Vector Multicast Routing Protocol (DVMRP) tunnel or with Multicast Border Gateway Protocol (MBGP). If the multicast source is within the network and meant to stay within the confines of the network, other design issues come into play. It is important that you understand what each multicast routing protocol brings to the table when it comes to operational functionality.

By better understanding the many protocols and possible implementations of multicast, you will be able to better plan and prepare for its deployment. With so many options, there is bound to be a solution for almost any requirement. Through understanding requirements, and through preparing and planning, you can successfully implement an IP multicast network.

## End-to-End IP Multicast

Part of deploying multicast is the determination of how much of the network should be multicast enabled. This is an important decision because it directly affects many aspects of multicast implementation. To strategically place the RPs, you must know where all the multicast leaf routers will be. Knowing the approximate number of potential multicast subscribers can have an effect on which protocols are run in the network to allow efficient multicast forwarding and routing.

The decision to use end-to-end deployment can be based on the applications that will be used or the intent of multicast implementation. If you are enabling multicast for a corporate application, you would need to enable multicast on every interface on every router throughout the enterprise. However, if you need to provide access to only the MBONE for the engineering department, or some other department within the organization, perhaps the most efficient method would not include end-to-end configuration and deployment.

It is important to keep in mind that the state of technology is dynamic. Today, you might receive a request from a single department for multicast access. Before jumping on the project and planning for just that department, consider that in the near future, it is likely that other departments will also request access. Applications that require end-to-end multicast capability might be purchased or integrated into the enterprise. It is far better to plan an end-to-end deployment and initially activate only the routers and interfaces that are needed than to plan your implementation on a limited initial activation. It is easier to "build it right the first time" than to try to come back and work around or rebuild a poor IP multicast deployment.

# Configuring IP Multicast Routing

When configuring multicast, keep in mind that many options and protocols can be configured. This is why it is so important that you have previously prepared and planned for the actual configuration. It isn't something that you can just sit down and throw together (not without a lot of problems, anyway).

Configuring routers for IP multicast is different from enabling CGMP on switches. You must also remember that switches do not understand Internet Group Management Protocol (IGMP) by default, and that you need to enable multicasting on switches and routers for hosts to be able to subscribe to a multicast group.

This section of the chapter covers the basics of configuring multicast on routers and switches. It also covers the configuration of rendezvous points. This is a very important task because without a rendezvous point, you will not be able to send or receive multicast packets across a network. We also cover the individual interface configurations on routers. CGMP processes are discussed in a little more detail than in the preceding chapter. Later, we will describe the multicast settings that can be made on a multicast-enabled router (and switches). "Enabling IP Multicast Routing" and "Enabling PIM on an Interface" describe required configuration, whereas the configuration described in the rest of this section is optional.

It is best to prepare a configuration task list before setting out to configure a group of routers. The configuration list should be specific to the device that will be configured. That fact makes it hard to present a set list of configuration tasks that would apply to all scenarios. However, two items definitely must be configured on a router in order for multicast to even begin working: enabling multicast routing and enabling PIM on the interfaces that will carry multicast traffic.

## Enabling IP Multicast Routing

As we have said, multicast routing must be enabled on the router. This step is very straightforward, but without it, multicast will not work. Let's look at a configuration of a router that does not have multicast enabled:

```
Current configuration:
!
version 12.0
service timestamps debug uptime
service timestamps log uptime
no service password-encryption
!
hostname Terry_3640
!
aaa new-model
aaa authentication login default tacacs+ line
aaa authentication login oldstyle line
aaa accounting exec default start-stop tacacs+
enable secret 5 $1$G7Dq$em.LpM4Huem9uqjZDHLe4.
!
!
!
ip subnet-zero
ip telnet source-interface FastEthernet3/0
[output truncated]
```

Notice that no multicast information is running on this machine. If we were to try to execute a multicast-related command, we wouldn't get any information returned. For example, look at what happens when the `show ip mroute` command is issued:

```
Terry_3640#sho ip mroute
IP Multicast Routing Table
Flags: D - Dense, S - Sparse, C - Connected, L - Local,
P - Pruned R - RP-bit set, F - Register flag,
 T - SPT-bit set,J - Join SPT, M - MSDP created entry,
X - Proxy Join Timer Running
       A - Advertised via MSDP
Timers: Uptime/Expires
Interface state: Interface, Next-Hop or VCD, State/Mode

Terry_3640#
```

The syntax for the command is `ip multicast-routing`, and an example of the execution follows:

```
Terry_3640#configure terminal
Enter configuration commands, one per line.  End with CNTL/Z.
Terry_3640(config)#ip multicast-routing
Terry_3640(config)#^Z
Terry_3640#
```

This enables the multicast on the router. Notice that it was executed while in global configuration mode. However, the router still can not exchange multicast information with any neighbors because none of the interfaces have been enabled. This step is next.

## Enabling PIM on an Interface

PIM is one of the required elements for multicast configuration. It enables IGMP on the router and enables it to receive and forward traffic on the specified interface. PIM must be enabled on every interface that is to participate in the multicast network.

PIM interface configuration has many options. Take a look at the available options in IOS 12.0(10)S1, shown in Table 8.2. Most of these options are for advanced multicast configuration that won't be addressed in detail here. The ones that are discussed are `dense-mode`, `sparse-mode`, and `sparse-dense-mode`.

**TABLE 8.2** IP PIM Configuration Options

| IP PIM Options | Description |
|---|---|
| `bsr-border` | Specifies border of PIM domain |
| `dense-mode` | Enables PIM dense-mode operation |
| `nbma-mode` | Specifies use of Non-Broadcast Multi-Access (NBMA) mode on interface |
| `neighbor-filter` | Specifies PIM peering filter |
| `query-interval` | Specifies PIM router query interval |
| `sparse-dense-mode` | Enables PIM sparse-dense-mode operation |
| `sparse-mode` | Enables PIM sparse-mode operation |
| `version` | Displays PIM version |

## IP PIM Dense Mode

PIM dense mode functions by using the source root shared tree. It also assumes that all PIM neighbors have active multicast members directly connected and, therefore, it initially forwards multicast group data out all PIM-enabled interfaces.

The syntax for this command is simple: `ip pim dense-mode`. An example of placing an interface in PIM dense mode follows:

```
Terry_3640#configure terminal
Enter configuration commands, one per line.  End with CNTL/Z.
Terry_3640(config)#interface FastEthernet3/0
Terry_3640(config-if)#ip pim dense-mode
Terry_3640(config-if)#^Z
Terry_3640#
```

This is what the interface configuration looks like now:

```
!
interface FastEthernet3/0
 ip address 172.16.21.4 255.255.255.0
 no ip directed-broadcast
 ip pim dense-mode
!
```

## IP PIM Sparse Mode

Sparse mode was developed to use shared root source tree distribution and relies on the knowledge of a RP. If a RP can not be found, the router is unable to forward multicast information, strictly because it does not know the source of the multicast traffic. If it can't determine where the traffic is supposed to be coming from, the Reverse Path Forwarding (RPF) check fails and no interfaces are added to the multicast forwarding table.

Configuration of PIM sparse mode is just as simple as it is for IP dense mode. The command for enabling IP PIM sparse mode is `ip pim sparse-mode`. Sparse mode PIM also activates IGMP on the interface, allowing the interface to listen for IGMP membership reports. Here is an example of enabling IP PIM sparse mode multicast on an interface:

```
Terry_3640#configure terminal
Enter configuration commands, one per line.  End with CNTL/Z.
Terry_3640(config)#interface FastEthernet3/0
Terry_3640(config-if)#ip pim sparse-mode
Terry_3640(config-if)#^Z
Terry_3640#
```

Here is a look at the interface configuration after the preceding execution:

```
!
interface FastEthernet3/0
 ip address 172.16.21.4 255.255.255.0
 no ip directed-broadcast
 ip pim sparse-mode
!
```

All forms of sparse mode also require a rendezvous point to be configured.

## IP PIM Sparse-Dense Mode

The name of this command gives an indication of the functionality it provides. Due to the increasing use of multicast and the variety of applications available today, it is best to configure an interface to be able to use both sparse mode and dense mode. With the previous commands, the interface was assigned the operating mode, and the interface could not change between modes depending on the need at the time.

PIM sparse-dense mode configuration now enables the interface to use whichever forwarding method is needed by the application or multicast group. The interface uses the multicast group notation to decide which mode it needs to operate in. If the interface sees something with the notation (S, G), it operates in dense mode. If the interface sees a notation similar to (*, G), the interface operates in sparse mode.

An added benefit of implementing sparse-dense mode on the interfaces is the elimination of the need to hard-configure the RP at every leaf router. The Auto-RP information is sent out across the network by using dense mode forwarding.

IP PIM sparse-dense mode is enabled by using `ip pim sparse-dense-mode` on the interface command line. Here is an example:

```
Terry_3640#configure terminal
Enter configuration commands, one per line.  End with CNTL/Z.
Terry_3640(config)#interface FastEthernet3/0
Terry_3640(config-if)#ip pim sparse-dense-mode
Terry_3640(config-if)#^Z
Terry_3640#
```

Again, here is what the interface looks like after the preceding lines have been entered:

```
!
interface FastEthernet3/0
 ip address 172.16.21.4 255.255.255.0
```

```
 no ip directed-broadcast
 ip pim sparse-dense-mode
!
```

In summary, when using the sparse-dense mode configuration on an interface, you need to understand that three criteria will activate the interface and place it into the multicast forwarding table. The first criterion applies to either sparse or dense mode; the others cause the interface to operate specifically for sparse or dense mode. Table 8.3 provides the details.

**TABLE 8.3** Interface Activation Criteria for Sparse-Dense Mode Interfaces

| Criteria | Mode of Operation |
|---|---|
| Directly connected group members or DVMRP neighbors | Sparse and dense |
| Non-pruned PIM neighbors | Dense |
| Join request received | Sparse |

# Configuring a Rendezvous Point

If you are using PIM-DM throughout the multicast network, configuring a rendezvous point is an optional task. There are two ways of configuring a rendezvous point for a router. Notice that we did not say "configuring a router *to be*" a rendezvous point. You can manually specify the IP address of the RP on a router, or you can enable Auto-RP. Both are described in this section.

## Manual RP Configuration

The syntax for the manual RP configuration command is simple: `ip pim rp-address` *`ip_address group_access_list_number`* *[override]*. The *`ip_address`* is the IP address of the router that is the RP. The *`access_list_number`* is for a standard IP access list (1–99) or an expanded range from 1300 to 1999. These lists are used to define which multicast groups can or can not use this RP. If no access list is specified, all multicast groups will use the configured RP. Finally, the `override` option can be used to override any RP information that might be learned via an Auto-RP update. The static RP takes precedence over any Auto-RP-learned RP. Here is a sample configuration for manual RP configuration:

```
Terry_3640#configure terminal
Enter configuration commands, one per line.  End with CNTL/Z.
Terry_3640(config)#ip pim rp-address 172.16.1.253 50 override
Terry_3640(config)#^Z
Terry_3640#
```

Here is a look at the router after the execution. Notice that the command is a global command. Following the global configuration, you will see `access-list 50`. The list allows only groups within the range of 224.0.0.0 to 224.255.255.255 to use 172.16.1.253 as the RP. Other groups need Auto-RP information or another statically configured RP in order to work properly:

```
!
no ip classless
ip route 0.0.0.0 0.0.0.0 172.16.22.2
ip pim rp-address 172.16.1.253 50 override
!
access-list 50 permit 224.0.0.0 0.255.255.255
access-list 50 deny   any
!
```

## Auto-RP Configuration

Because multiple RPs can exist in a multicast network, the *Auto-RP* function aids by distributing the RP information across a multicast network. Different multicast groups can use different RPs, so this feature keeps track of which groups are using which RP. It will also fine-tune the leaf router's RP by choosing the RP nearest to the leaf. If you don't like to use static routes in a unicast network, you probably don't want to statically configure multicast RPs either.

There are also two procedures that can be used to enable Auto-RP; which one you use depends on the state of your multicast network. If you are beginning a new deployment, it isn't necessary to create a default RP. If you are modifying an existing multicast network, you need to designate a default RP router in the network.

Here is a list of configuration tasks that must be completed to successfully implement Auto-RP in a multicast network:

- Designate a default RP (only when modifying an existing multicast network).
- Advertise each RP and the multicast groups associated with the RP.
- Enable an RP Mapping Agent.

As you can see, the list is short and simple. Now that you know what has to be done, let's discuss each step individually.

### Designating a Default RP

This step is somewhat tricky, not so much because the configuration is tricky, but because of the decision regarding when to execute the step. The only time you need to designate a default RP is when you are running sparse mode only on any of your interfaces in an existing multicast network. If you are using sparse-dense mode, as suggested, you do not need to execute this step.

This step is executed as described in the "Manual RP Configuration" section earlier in this chapter. The default RP becomes the statically mapped RP on all the leaf routers. The default RP should serve all global multicast groups. That is all that has to be done.

### Advertising RP Group Assignments

From each RP, a statement needs to be added that assigns and advertises multicast groups to that RP. The multicast groups are then advertised so the RP Mapping Agent can keep track of which RP hosts which multicast groups and resolve conflicts when necessary.

The syntax for the command is `ip pim send-rp-announce` *type number* `scope` *ttl* `group_list` *access_list_number*. The command is entered in global configuration mode. The first two options, *type* and *number*, are the interface type and number that indicate the RP IP address. *Scope* defines the boundary of the RP advertisement by using a high TTL value that will be effectively blocked by interfaces with the TTL threshold set. The *group_list* uses the specified access list to determine which multicast group ranges the RP is allowed to announce.

Here is an example of the command as well as a valid access list:

```
Terry_3640#configure terminal
Enter configuration commands, one per line.  End with CNTL/Z.
Terry_3640(config)#access-list 5 permit 224.0.0.0 0.0.255.255
Terry_3640(config)#ip pim send-rp-announce fastethernet4/0 scope 230 group-list 5
Terry_3640(config)#^Z
Terry_3640#

Terry_3640#write terminal
. . .
!
ip pim send-rp-announce FastEthernet4/0 scope 230  group-list 5
!
access-list 5 permit 224.0.0.0 0.0.255.255
!
. . .
```

### Configuring the RP Mapping Agent

This router is in charge of learning all the rendezvous point routers in the network along with the multicast group assignments that each RP advertises. The Mapping Agent then tells all the routers within the multicast network which RP should be used for their source.

This is done with the `ip pim send-rp-discovery scope` *ttl* command. As you can see, this command is similar to the command in the preceding section. The scope defines the TTL value for the discovery. After the TTL is reached, the discovery packets are dropped. Here is an example:

```
Terry_3640#configure terminal
Enter configuration commands, one per line.  End with CNTL/Z.
Terry_3640(config)#ip pim send-rp-discovery scope 23
Terry_3640(config)#^Z
Terry_3640
```

In this example, you can see that the TTL value was set to 23. This means that after 23 hops, the discovery has expired. This command actually assigns to the router the role of RP Mapping Agent.

This concludes the tasks for configuring a rendezvous point in a multicast network. Keep in mind that the RP Mapping Agent can be an RP, although it doesn't have to be. The Mapping Agent's role is to learn of all the deployed rendezvous points throughout the network and then advertise which groups are available via the closest RP for all multicast-enabled routers in the network.

## Configuring TTL

TTL threshold configuration is done to limit the boundary of scope of the IP multicast network. As you learned earlier in this chapter, limiting the scope of a multicast network is based on the TTL value in the multicast packet. Because this command is used to create a boundary, it must be executed on each border interface.

The default value for the TTL threshold is zero. The value can be changed with the `ip multicast ttl-threshold` ***`ttl`*** command. The syntax is straightforward, and the ***`ttl`*** value that is used is up to the discretion of the network administrator. The range of valid values for this option is between 0 and 255. However, the value should be high enough to stop multicast packets from exiting the interface. Here is an example:

```
Terry_3640#configure terminal
Enter configuration commands, one per line.  End with CNTL/Z.
Terry_3640(config)#interface FastEthernet0/0
Terry_3640(config-if)#ip multicast ttl-threshold 230
Terry_3640(config-if)#^Z
Terry_3640#
```

```
!
interface FastEthernet0/0
 ip address 172.16.5.1 255.255.255.0
 no ip directed-broadcast
 ip pim sparse-dense-mode
 ip multicast ttl-threshold 230
 no ip route-cache
 no ip mroute-cache
 full-duplex
!
```

## Joining a Multicast Group

After the main configuration is done on the router to enable multicast, PIM, rendezvous points, and RP Mapping Agents, the only other major task is enabling hosts to join multicast groups.

Within Cisco IOS, the network administrator has the opportunity to verify functionality and connectivity before users use the multicast system and applications. You can configure a router to join any number of IP multicast groups and thus verify functionality.

This is achieved through the `ip igmp join-group` *`group_address`* command. The *`group_address`* is the multicast address of the group you want the router to join. An example follows:

```
Terry_3640(config)#interface FastEthernet4/0
Terry_3640(config-if)#ip igmp join-group 224.2.127.254
Terry_3640(config-if)#^Z
Terry_3640#
```

This tells the router to become a member of the 224.2.127.254 multicast group. Joining a group facilitates troubleshooting multicast connectivity issues as well.

### Troubleshooting IP Multicast Connectivity

Multicast can be a difficult protocol to troubleshoot. However, a few basic tools (mostly `show` commands) can provide enough information for you to verify that connectivity is active or to determine whether other steps, such as debugging, are needed to troubleshoot the problem.

If you do need to debug a multicast-enabled interface, you must first disable the multicast fast switching on the interface. This is done so that the debug messages can be logged. The command to disable fast switching is `no ip mroute-cache`. The standard unicast fast (or other forms of) switching can be left enabled.

You are familiar with the troubleshooting tools for unicast connectivity, Ping and traceroute. Well, these tools are also available for troubleshooting multicast connectivity. There is one minor difference, though: multicast requires a special version of traceroute—called mtrace, or "multicast-traceroute."

**Ping** After a device on the network becomes a member of a group, it can be identified by its layer 3 multicast address as well as the layer 2 MAC address. Because the device has an active address on its interface, it can respond to ICMP request packets. Here is an example:

```
Terry_3640#ping
Protocol [ip]:
Target IP address: 224.2.143.55
Repeat count [1]: 5
Datagram size [100]:
Timeout in seconds [2]:
Extended commands [n]:
Sweep range of sizes [n]:
Type escape sequence to abort.
```

```
Sending 5, 100-byte ICMP Echos to 224.2.143.55, timeout is  2 seconds:
.!!!!
Terry_3640#
```

This tool can be used to verify connectivity among RPs or other multicast routers.

**mtrace** Cisco also provides a multicast traceroute tool. The multicast version of traceroute is somewhat different from the unicast version. The complete syntax for *mtrace* is `mtrace` *`source_ip destination_ip group`*. The *`source_ip`* is the unicast IP address for the source of the multicast group. The *`destination_ip`* is used when following the forwarding path established by the source or shared tree distribution toward a unicast destination. The *`group`* option is used to establish the tree for the specified group. If no destination or group options are specified, the mtrace will work from the incoming multicast interfaces back toward the multicast source. Here are a few samples of the command and its output:

```
Jack_3640#mtrace 198.32.163.74
Type escape sequence to abort.
Mtrace from 198.32.163.74 to 172.16.25.9 via RPF
From source (blaster.oregon-gigapop.net) to destination  (?)
Querying full reverse path...
 0  172.16.25.9
-1  172.16.25.9 PIM/MBGP  [198.32.163.0/24]
-2  172.16.25.10 PIM/MBGP  [198.32.163.0/24]
-3  ogig-den.oregon-gigapop.net (198.32.163.13) [AS 4600]
 PIM  [198.32.163.64/26]
-4  Ocar-Ogw.oregon-gigapop.net (198.32.163.26) [AS 4600]
 PIM  [198.32.163.64/26]
-5  blaster.oregon-gigapop.net (198.32.163.74)
Jack_3640#

Jack_3640#mtrace 198.32.163.74 224.2.243.55
Type escape sequence to abort.
Mtrace from 198.32.163.74 to 172.16.25.9 via group  224.2.243.55
From source (blaster.oregon-gigapop.net) to destination  (?)
Querying full reverse path...
 0  172.16.25.9
-1  172.16.25.9 PIM/MBGP Reached RP/Core [198.32.163.0/24]
-2  172.16.25.10 PIM/MBGP Reached RP/Core [198.32.163.0/24]
-3  ogig-den.oregon-gigapop.net (198.32.163.13) [AS 4600]
 PIM Reached RP/Core [198.32.163.64/26]
-4  Ocar-Ogw.oregon-gigapop.net (198.32.163.26) [AS 4600]
 PIM  [198.32.163.64/26]
Jack_3640#
```

As you can see, the outputs differ very little, but it is important to see how the paths are established. From the first sample output, no group or destination was specified, so the router strictly used RPF to calculate the path from the source to the router. In the other output, a group address was specified. This caused the router to specifically use the existing forwarding tree for group 224.2.243.55 to get back to the router.

These tools can be useful to determine connectivity as well as the effectiveness of the placement of RPs and multicast sources. There are other `show` commands that can aid you as well, but they are not related to the topic of this chapter.

## Changing the IGMP Version

Several settings can be tweaked in the router to enhance or change performance. The majority of them are beyond the scope of this chapter. However, in this section, we discuss one important feature: changing the IGMP version. It is important that you understand and know how to perform this change because of the compatibility issues between IGMP versions, as discussed earlier in this chapter in the section "Changing the IGMP Version."

To put it simply, the IGMP version that runs on the hosts must also run on the router. Cisco routers use IGMPv2 by default and do not auto-detect the IGMP version that the host is using. The command to change from IGMPv2 to IGMPv1, or vice versa, is `ip igmp version (2 | 1)`. Because the IGMP version needs to match only on the subnet, the command must be entered on the interface that connects to the subnet housing the IGMPv1 hosts. The other interfaces on the router can remain on IGMPv2.

## Enabling CGMP and IGMP Snooping

When hosts connect to a router via a Catalyst switch, either CGMP or IGMP Snooping can be used to enable the switch to learn appropriate information. Catalysts run both so they can manage multicast membership reports from the router accordingly and so they can manage multicast ports on the switch. The router is the device that listens for the IGMP membership report; it then tells the switch which port needs to be activated. CGMP or IGMP Snooping must be activated on both the router and the switch.

### CGMP Router Configuration

The router configuration syntax is simple. It must be applied to the interface connected to the Catalyst switch. The command is `ip cgmp` *`proxy`*. The *`proxy`* option is used for routers that are not CGMP capable. It enables them to use the proxy router for CGMP. Here is a sample configuration:

```
Terry_3640#configure terminal
Enter configuration commands, one per line.  End with CNTL/Z.
Terry_3640(config)#interface FastEthernet4/0
Terry_3640(config-if)#ip cgmp
Terry_3640(config-if)#^Z
Terry_3640#
```

Use the command `show running-config` to see whether CGMP is enabled or disabled on a particular router interface, as shown here:

```
!
interface FastEthernet4/0
 ip address 172.16.10.1 255.255.255.0
 no ip directed-broadcast
 ip pim sparse-dense-mode
 no ip route-cache
 ip igmp join-group 224.2.127.254
 ip cgmp
!
```

## Catalyst Switch Configuration

The Catalyst syntax is just as simple as the syntax for the router configuration, if not simpler. By default, CGMP is turned off on the switch. If you want multicast to work properly, you must enable CGMP or IGMP Snooping on the switch. Enabling CGMP is done by using the syntax `set cgmp enable`. Here is a sample:

```
Terry_4000> (enable) set cgmp enable
CGMP support for IP multicast enabled.
Terry_4000> (enable)
Terry_4000> (enable) show cgmp statistics
CGMP enabled

CGMP statistics for vlan 1:
valid rx pkts received          6
invalid rx pkts received        0
valid cgmp joins received       6
valid cgmp leaves received      0
valid igmp leaves received      0
valid igmp queries received     0
igmp gs queries transmitted     0
igmp leaves transmitted         0
failures to add GDA to EARL     0
topology notifications received 0
number of packets dropped       0
Terry_4000> (enable)
```

After CGMP is enabled, you can look at statistics by using the `show cgmp statistics` command. This is all that is needed to enable CGMP on the switch so that it can communicate with the router.

A CGMP-enabled switch can also be configured to detect IGMPv2 Leave messages generated by clients. To do this, simply use the command `set cgmp leave enable`. This command takes place globally on the switch.

The switch collects multicast group MAC addresses for each group address. To see what multicast groups your switch knows about, use the command `show multicast group cgmp`.

## IGMP Snooping

IGMP Snooping can be configured to enable the switch to learn multicast information by examining the frames as they pass through the switch. The switch doesn't depend wholly on information received from the multicast router.

To configure IGMP Snooping on the switch, use the command `set igmp enable`. You can not have CGMP and IGMP Snooping enabled on the same switch at the same time. To enable IGMP Snooping on the router, use the command `ip igmp snooping` while in global configuration mode.

Fast-Leave processing is a new feature that works only with IGMP Snooping and is one of the main reasons for its use. Fast-Leave processing enables a switch to receive an IGMP Leave message and immediately remove the interface from the table that lists which ports receive the multicast stream. Thus, if a client on port 2/5 generates a Leave message, the switch immediately removes port 2/5 from the list of ports receiving the multicast stream. To enable Fast-Leave processing on the switch, use the command `set igmp fastleave enable`.

Just as with CGMP, IGMP Snooping has a way of displaying the configuration and statistics. Using the command `show igmp statistics` will display the status of IGMP Snooping on the switch as well as the amount of traffic that has been processed.

**Real World Scenario**

### The Fast-Leave Trap

Fast Leave is a great tool in an organization that uses quite a bit of multicasting. There can be a problem though, when using it in a network where Spanning Tree changes frequently.

When a switch configured for Fast Leave receives a Leave message, the switch will remove the port at which the message arrived from the forwarding table for the particular stream. What happens if this occurs on a core switch, on the port going out to a closet switch or stack? The core switch will remove all entries associated with that port. If several clients were listening to the stream and one leaves, the core switch will remove them all.

Whenever possible, only enable Fast-Leave processing on switches that have clients terminating at individual ports. Turn this feature on at the closets but think twice before doing so at core and distribution layer switches.

It is early to be too definite about this, but it would seem that Cisco is moving away from CGMP towards IGMP Snooping as a preference. With pressure on all the giant companies moving them toward a standards-based intercommunications approach, this would make sense, as would the fact that IGMP Snooping supports the Fast-Leave process. Readers should note that IGMP Snooping is enabled by default on both the 2950 and 3550 switches.

# Summary

Multicast forwarding is relatively new. Until the growth of applications that required multicast delivery, it was used by service protocols such as "all OSPF routers". Now, many multimedia applications—such as video—and wide distribution applications—such as market data feeds—all require multicast delivery.

We have therefore given a lot of time to understanding the many facets of IP multicast. We started with an overview of multicast and compared it to unicast and broadcast communication, and then discussed how IP addresses were designated as multicast addresses. These layer 3 addresses must be converted to layer 2 MAC addresses using a standard mapping process.

Of course, theoretical knowledge needs to be backed up with an understanding of how to configure multicast on both Cisco routers and switches, because the routers carry the multicast traffic over the internetwork and the switches deliver it to the multicast hosts. The syntax of the commands is straightforward, but you need to ensure that the network is properly planned before starting the implementation. Care needs to be taken when considering the IGMP version to be used, for example.

When considering the multicast distribution, you need to select between PIM-DM, PIM-SM, and CBT. All three are independent protocols that use tree distribution to manage multicast data delivery in a network, but all affect the network operation in different ways, and require different configurations.

# Exam Essentials

**Know the difference between IGMP and IGMPv2 and IGMPv3.** IGMPv1 and IGMPv2 are very similar. The major difference is that IGMPv2 has a message that the client sends when it doesn't want to receive the multicast stream anymore. The result of this small difference is that they don't work well together, and it makes sense for you to have only one version running. IGMPv3 is better still, and supports extras such as SSM, but because it is very new, you have to make sure that all the hosts in your network support it.

The Catalyst switch can listen for client Leave messages with both CGMP and IGMP Snooping. A switch configured for CGMP can listen for IGMPv2 and v3 Leave messages by being configured with the command `set cgmp leave enable`. A switch configured for IGMP Snooping can be configured for IGMP Fast-Leave processing with the command `set igmp fastleave enable`.

**Know the difference between CGMP and IGMP Snooping.** Although both CGMP and IGMP Snooping allow a switch to get involved in a multicast stream, they are rather different. CGMP is a Cisco proprietary protocol communication based upon communication between a router and any attached switches. Routers receiving IGMP packets from other routers forward specific information to appropriate switches containing information on multicast memberships.

IGMP Snooping enables the switch to learn information from watching IGMP packets go through the switch. IGMP is an Internet standard. Snooping is being considered by the IETF as a standard and is currently in draft. Remember that snooping can't be enabled if CGMP is enabled, so you first need to make sure that CGMP is turned off. Next, enable IGMP Snooping with the `ip igmp snooping` command.

**Know the difference between the multicast routing protocols.** There are several options for routing multicast traffic. DVMRP is a distance-vector-based routing protocol, and MOSPF uses OSPF, but neither is the recommended method of doing multicast routing with Cisco equipment. Cisco recommends that PIM be used to route multicast streams because it learns from the preexisting routing protocol. This means that EIGRP can be used to route multicast information.

PIM has two broad modes, sparse and dense. In dense mode PIM, each router is automatically included in the multicast table and has to prune itself off if no clients need the stream. Sparse mode assumes no routers wish to participate. Routers are added as connected clients request access to the multicast streams, and a special router is used as the base for the entire tree. This router, a rendezvous point, needs to be referenced in each multicast router's configuration. Use the command `rp pim ip-address` *`ip_address`* to define the IP address of the rendezvous point.

**Know how to troubleshoot your multicast setup.** There are many `show` commands that can be done on the router and switch to show communication but you still need to test the transport. You can use the `ping` command to reach out and touch a particular multicast IP address. If you want to do a traceroute, use the command `mtrace`.

# Key Terms

Before you take the exam, be sure you're familiar with the following terms:

Auto-RP

bidirectional shared tree

Border Gateway Protocol (BGP)

broadcast

Cisco Group Management Protocol (CGMP)

core

Distance Vector Multicast Routing Protocol (DVMRP)

flooding

grafting

IGMP Join process

IGMP Leave process

IGMP Query process

IGMP Snooping

Internet Group Management Protocol version 1 (IGMPv1)

Internet Group Management Protocol version 2 (IGMPv2)

Internet Group Management Protocol Version 3 (IGMPv3)

leaf

`mtrace`

multicast

multicast group

Multicast Open Shortest Path First (MOSPF)

Multicast Source Discovery Protocol (MSDP)

PIM dense mode (PIM DM)

PIM sparse mode (PIM SM)

Protocol Independent Multicast (PIM)

pruning

rendezvous points (RPs)

shared trees

Source Specific Multicasting (SSM)

source trees

subscribed

unicast

unidirectional shared tree

uniquely

upstream

# Written Lab

Write the answers to the following questions:

1. Write the command that enables multicast routing on a router.
2. Write the commands that enable PIM SM on interface FastEthernet 4/0.
3. Write the configuration commands that enable PIM DM on interface FastEthernet 3/0.
4. Write the configuration for enabling PIM sparse-dense mode on interface FastEthernet 0/0.
5. Write the command that shows you the multicast route table.
6. Manually configure a router to be an RP by using the IP address of 172.16.25.3 and apply access list number 30.
7. Write the command to use when implementing Auto-RP so that the RP announces only specific multicast groups. Use access list number 10 and interface FastEthernet 4/0. Use a TTL value of 220.
8. Write the command that enables an RP Mapping Agent. Use a TTL value of 32.
9. Apply a command that sets a TTL threshold of 235 on interface FastEthernet 2/0.
10. Write the commands that enable CGMP on a router for interface FastEthernet 3/0, and then write the command that enables CGMP on a switch.

# Review Questions

1. Which of the following commands are necessary in order for multicast to work? (Choose all that apply.)

   A. `ip mroute cache`

   B. `ip pim [sparse-mode | dense-mode | sparse-dense-mode]`

   C. `ip cgmp`

   D. `ip multicast-routing`

2. Which of the following addresses are within the range of valid IP multi-cast addresses? (Choose all that apply.)

   A. 242.127.1.1

   B. 224.0.0.1

   C. 239.255.255.254

   D. 225.128.1.1

3. What three configuration tasks are necessary to enable multicast Auto-RP?

   A. Perform IP multicast routing.

   B. Assign the default RP (for existing multicast networks).

   C. Assign the RP Mapping Agent.

   D. Advertise RP/group associations.

4. What is the main difference between broadcast and multicast communication?

   A. Multicast data is distributed to subscribed hosts on specific groups.

   B. Broadcast data is distributed to subscribed hosts on specific groups.

   C. Multicast data uses unicast route tables to flood the network instead of using the network's broadcast address.

   D. There really is no difference.

5. What is the destination of the reserved IP multicast address 224.0.0.2?

   A. All DVMRP routers

   B. All routers

   C. All hosts

   D. All CGMP-enabled routers

6. How many layer 3 IP multicast addresses can be represented by the same layer 2 MAC address?
   A. 1
   B. 23
   C. 32
   D. 24
7. Which of the following multicast route notations indicates the operation of sparse mode?
   A. (*, G)
   B. (G, *)
   C. (S, G)
   D. (G, S)
8. What are the primary functions of RP Mapping Agents? (Choose all that apply.)
   A. Mapping unicast addresses of all RP routers in a multicast network
   B. Sourcing multicast traffic
   C. Resolving multicast group/RP conflicts
   D. Providing member topologies to the RP routers in the network
9. Which of the following is a method of limiting the scope of a multicast network?
   A. Passive interface applied to border interfaces
   B. Distribution lists within an IGP such as EIGRP or OSPF
   C. TTL threshold setting on border interfaces
   D. RPF settings within the RP routers
10. What is the layer 2 MAC address for the layer 3 IP address 224.2.127.254?
    A. 01-00-5E-02-7E-FF
    B. 01-00-5E-02-7F-FE
    C. 01-00-5E-00-7E-FF
    D. 01-00-5E-00-7F-FE
11. Which are tools that can be used to troubleshoot multicast connectivity? (Choose all that apply.)
    A. Ping
    B. `show ip mroute`
    C. traceroute
    D. mtrace

12. Which of the following protocols can hosts use to subscribe to a multicast group? (Choose all that apply.)
    A. IBMP
    B. IGMPv1
    C. IGMPv2
    D. CGMP
    E. DVMRP
    F. MOSPF
    G. PIM (DM/SM)
    H. CBT

13. From which direction is the mtrace established?
    A. From the default RP of the multicast network to the source
    B. From the source to the RP
    C. From the source to the router interface
    D. From the router interface to the source

14. What two address values does CGMP use compared to IGMP?
    A. CGMP uses the USA and GDA.
    B. CGMP uses the MAC address and IP address.
    C. CGMP uses the GSA and UDA.
    D. CGMP uses the MAC address and switch port.

15. What are the two types of distribution trees?
    A. RP trees
    B. Multicast trees
    C. Shared root trees
    D. Source root trees

16. What command is used to manually configure a router to be an RP?
    A. `ip multicast RP` *`ip_address`*
    B. `ip pim RP` *`ip_address`*
    C. `ip pim rp-address` *`ip_address`*
    D. `ip igmp rp-address` *`ip_address`*

17. Which of the following criteria activates an interface that is configured to use dense mode? (Choose all that apply.)

    A. Directly connected hosts

    B. Directly connected PIM routers

    C. Router configured as a border router

    D. When the interface receives a prune statement from a directly connected PIM router

18. What are two types of shared root tree distributions?

    A. Unidirectional

    B. Unicast

    C. Multidirectional

    D. Bidirectional

19. Which criteria activates an interface in sparse mode when the interface is configured to use sparse-dense mode? (Choose all that apply.)

    A. Directly connected DVMRP neighbor.

    B. Explicit join request.

    C. Any PIM-configured interface is made active.

    D. The interface has directly connected hosts.

20. How does PIM DM differ from PIM SM? (Choose all that apply.)

    A. PIM DM assumes that all PIM neighbors have active members directly connected and initially forwards multicast data out every interface.

    B. PIM SM requires an explicit join from a router before the router is added to the shared tree.

    C. PIM DM is based on a source root tree distribution mechanism.

    D. PIM SM is based on bidirectional shared root tree distribution.

# Hands-On Lab

Refer to Figure 8.22 as the diagram for this lab. The objective of this lab is to configure an IP multicast network from scratch. You will implement Auto-RP, PIM sparse-dense mode, and CGMP on all routers and switches. You will not have to configure host applications in this lab. Assume that Routers C and D have multicast sources attached to them. In order for the CGMP version of the lab to have the greatest value, the switches used will be 4000 series running CatOS.

**FIGURE 8.22** Configuring an IP multicast network

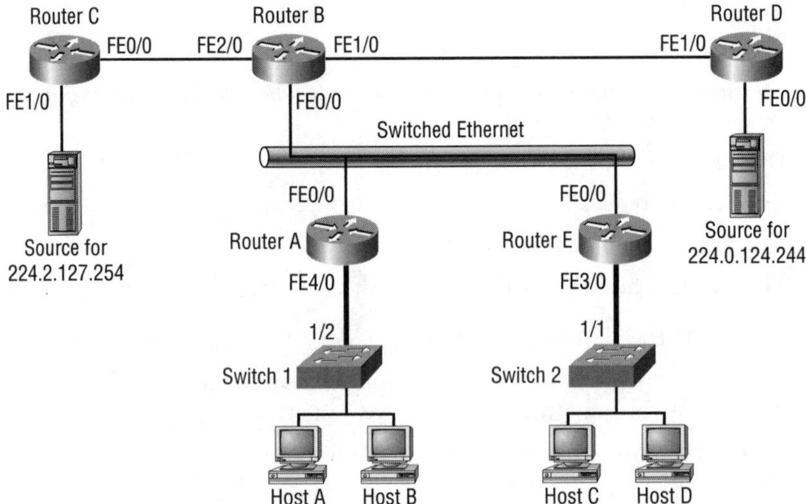


1. Because you are starting from scratch, the first step is to enable multicast on all routers:

```
RouterA#configure terminal
Enter configuration commands, one per line.  End with CNTL/Z.
RouterA(config)#ip multicast-routing
RouterA(config)#^Z
RouterA#

RouterB#configure terminal
Enter configuration commands, one per line.  End with CNTL/Z.
RouterB(config)#ip multicast-routing
RouterB(config)#^Z
RouterB#
```

```
RouterC#configure terminal
Enter configuration commands, one per line.  End with CNTL/Z.
RouterC(config)#ip multicast-routing
RouterC(config)#^Z
RouterC#

RouterD#configure terminal
Enter configuration commands, one per line.  End with CNTL/Z.
RouterD(config)#ip multicast-routing
RouterD(config)#^Z
RouterD#

RouterE#configure terminal
Enter configuration commands, one per line.  End with CNTL/Z.
RouterE(config)#ip multicast-routing
RouterE(config)#^Z
RouterE#
```

2. Now, enable PIM sparse-dense mode on all shown connected interfaces:

```
RouterA#configure terminal
Enter configuration commands, one per line.  End with CNTL/Z.
RouterA(config)#interface FastEthernet4/0
RouterA(config-if)#ip pim sparse-dense-mode
RouterA(config-if)#interface fastethernet0/0
RouterA(config-if)#ip pim sparse-dense-mode
RouterA(config-if)#^Z
RouterA#

RouterE#configure terminal
Enter configuration commands, one per line.  End with CNTL/Z.
RouterE(config)#interface fastethernet3/0
RouterE(config-if)#ip pim sparse-dense-mode
RouterE(config-if)#interface fastethernet0/0
RouterE(config-if)#ip pim sparse-dense-mode
RouterE(config-if)#^Z
RouterE#

RouterB#configure terminal
Enter configuration commands, one per line.  End with CNTL/Z.
RouterB(config)#interface fastethernet0/0
RouterB(config-if)#ip pim sparse-dense-mode
```

```
RouterB(config-if)#interface fastethernet1/0
RouterB(config-if)#ip pim sparse-dense-mode
RouterB(config-if)#interface fastethernet2/0
RouterB(config-if)#ip pim sparse-dense-mode
RouterB(config-if)#^Z
RouterB#

RouterC#configure terminal
Enter configuration commands, one per line.  End with CNTL/Z.
RouterC(config)#interface fastethernet0/0
RouterC(config-if)#ip pim sparse-dense-mode
RouterC(config-if)#interface fastethernet1/0
RouterC(config-if)#ip pim sparse-dense-mode
RouterC(config-if)#^Z
RouterC#

RouterD#configure terminal
Enter configuration commands, one per line.  End with CNTL/Z.
RouterD(config)#interface fastethernet0/0
RouterD(config-if)#ip pim sparse-dense-mode
RouterD(config-if)#interface fastethernet1/0
RouterD(config-if)#ip pim sparse-dense-mode
RouterD(config-if)#^Z
RouterD#
```

3. Enable CGMP on all router interfaces and switches (some may not be shown):

```
RouterA#configure terminal
Enter configuration commands, one per line.  End with CNTL/Z.
RouterA(config)#interface fastethernet0/0
RouterA(config-if)#ip cgmp
RouterA(config-if)#interface fastethernet4/0
RouterA(config-if)#ip cgmp
RouterA(config-if)#^Z
RouterA#

RouterE#configure terminal
Enter configuration commands, one per line.  End with CNTL/Z.
RouterE(config)#interface fastethernet0/0
RouterE(config-if)#ip cgmp
RouterE(config-if)#interface fastethernet3/0
RouterE(config-if)#ip cgmp
```

```
RouterE(config-if)#^Z
RouterE#

RouterB#configure terminal
Enter configuration commands, one per line.  End with CNTL/Z.
RouterB(config)#interface fastethernet0/0
RouterB(config-if)#ip cgmp
RouterB(config-if)#interface fastethernet1/0
RouterB(config-if)#ip cgmp
RouterB(config-if)#interface fastethernet2/0
RouterB(config-if)#ip cgmp
RouterB(config-if)#^Z
RouterB#

RouterC#configure terminal
Enter configuration commands, one per line.  End with CNTL/Z.
RouterC(config)#interface fastethernet0/0
RouterC(config-if)#ip cgmp
RouterC(config-if)#interface fastethernet1/0
RouterC(config-if)#ip cgmp
RouterC(config-if)#^Z
RouterC#

RouterD#configure terminal
Enter configuration commands, one per line.  End with CNTL/Z.
RouterD(config)#interface fastethernet0/0
RouterD(config-if)#ip cgmp
RouterD(config-if)#interface fastethernet1/0
RouterD(config-if)#ip cgmp
RouterD(config-if)#^Z
RouterD#

switch1> (enable) set cgmp enable
CGMP support for IP multicast enabled.
switch1> (enable)
switch2> (enable) set cgmp enable
CGMP support for IP multicast enabled.
```

4. Assign multicast group 224.2.127.254 to Router C via access list 5. This assignment allows only Router C to advertise that group. Assign a TTL value of 12. Then assign group 224.0.124.244 to Router D via access list 6:

```
RouterC#configure terminal
Enter configuration commands, one per line.  End with CNTL/Z.
RouterC(config)#access-list 5 permit 224.2.127.254  0.0.0.0
RouterC(config)#ip pim send-rp-announce fastethernet1/0  scope 12 group-list 5
RouterC(config)#^Z
RouterC#

RouterD#configure terminal
Enter configuration commands, one per line.  End with CNTL/Z.
RouterD(config)#access-list 6 permit 224.0.124.244  0.0.0.0
RouterD(config)#ip pim send-rp-announce fastethernet1/0  scope 12 group-list 6
RouterD(config)#^Z
RouterD#
```

5. Now configure Router B to be the RP Mapping Agent, using a scope of 12:

```
RouterB#configure terminal
Enter configuration commands, one per line.  End with CNTL/Z.
RouterB(config)#ip pim send-rp-discovery scope 12
RouterB(config)#^Z
RouterB#
```

# Answers to Written Lab

1. `ip multicast-routing`
2. `configure terminal, interface fastethernet4/0, ip pim sparse-mode`
3. `configure terminal, interface fastethernet3/0, ip pim dense-mode`
4. `configure terminal, interface fastethernet0/0, ip pim sparse-dense-mode`
5. `show ip mroute`
6. `ip pim rp-address 172.16.25.3 30`
7. `ip pim send-rp-announce fastethernet 4/0 scope 220 group-list 10`
8. `ip pim send-rp-discovery scope 32`
9. `configure terminal, interface fastethernet2/0, ip multicast ttl-threshold 235`
10. `configure terminal, interface fastethernet3/0, ip cgmpset cgmp enable`

# Answers to Review Questions

1. B, D. These two commands must be entered for multicast forwarding to work. The `ip mroute cache` command enhances performance but is not necessary. CGMP is necessary only when hosts are connected to a router via a Catalyst switch using CGMP.

2. B, C, D. The first response is outside of the valid range for IP multicast addresses. The other choices are valid host addresses within the range.

3. B, C, D. IP multicast routing is not part of the Auto-RP configuration.

4. A. Broadcast communications use the broadcast IP or MAC address to communicate information to all hosts. Multicast data is sent only to hosts subscribing to groups that are active on the network.

5. B. IANA reserved the address 224.0.0.2 to indicate all local multicast routers. This address is not forwarded by any routers in the network.

6. C. Due to the lost 5 bits in the mapping, 32 IP addresses may be represented by the same multicast MAC address ($2^5 = 32$).

7. A. (S, G) and (*, G) are the only valid notations. (*, G) indicates a shared root tree distribution. Sparse mode uses shared root trees.

8. A, C. RP Mapping Agents keep track of all RP routers in the network via their unicast addresses. They then provide the nearest RP for the multicast groups it sources to all leaf routers in the multicast network.

9. C. The correct way to limit the scope of the multicast network is to configure TTL thresholds for external or border interfaces. RPF is used strictly for reverse path lookup.

10. B. The MAC prefix is 01-00-5E. You know you don't have to worry about the lost bits because the second octet of the IP address is less than 127. Therefore, the value is 02. The last two octets are mapped with no problem.

11. A, B, D. Traceroute is used for unicast connectivity; mtrace, however, is used for multicast connectivity.

12. B, C. CGMP is Cisco's proprietary version of IGMP. IBMP is not a valid protocol. The other protocols are for routing purposes and group management within a network.

13. C. From the examples given in this chapter, you can see that the path is established from the source toward the multicast router interface.

14. A. The USA is the Unicast Source Address (the unique MAC address of the machine) and the GDA is the Group Destination Address (the newly mapped layer 2 multicast MAC address). By using these two values, the switch knows which port to make a CAM entry for.

15. C, D. Multicast trees don't exist. Some protocols that are based in shared root trees can create RPTs (or RP trees) that are parallel to the shortest path tree, but this is a flavor of shared root tree distribution.

16. C. The correct syntax is provided by the third answer. The other answers are not valid.

17. A, B. Hosts activate the interface through membership reports. PIM interfaces automatically receive multicast forwarding until a prune request is received.

18. A, D. We are discussing multicast in this chapter, so unicast is not a valid answer. Because there are only two directions on a tree, the correct answers are bidirectional and unidirectional.

19. A, B, D. A PIM-configured interface is considered active only when in dense mode.

20. A, B, C. The problem with the last answer is that PIM SM is based on unidirectional shared root tree distribution. The other answers are correct.

# Quality of Service (QoS)

## THE CCNP EXAM TOPICS COVERED IN THIS CHAPTER INCLUDE THE FOLLOWING:

- ✓ Describe the needs of isochronous voice traffic on a switched data network
- ✓ Understand QoS solutions to voice quality issues such as jitter and delay
- ✓ Configure QoS features on multilayer switched networks
- ✓ Describe the general design models for switched networks requiring integrated IP telephony
- ✓ Plan the implementation of QoS features in a multilayer switched network
- ✓ Configure router redundancy using HSRP and VRRP, and verify operation
- ✓ Explain how both hardware and software redundancy is achieved in a multilayer switched network
- ✓ Understand the general design models for switched networks requiring integrated IP telephony
- ✓ Understand transparent LAN services and explain their use in service provider networks
- ✓ Configure load balancing using GLBP and SLB, and verify operation
- ✓ Implement QoS features in a multilayer switched network

*Quality of service (QoS)* is a largely new concept to bring into the world of LANs. Traditional Ethernet networks have been constructed on base protocols that allow for best efforts delivery and little else. Legacy switched networks—if you will pardon the term—have been designed and built using the same principles. After all, Ethernet suffers from collisions, broadcasts are LAN-wide random events, and frame sizes are unpredictable. All of this pretty much guarantees that quality of service will also have some random aspects, doesn't it?

Well, maybe not. Over the last few years, considerable effort has been applied to the development of techniques designed to provide the Internet Protocol (IP) with some added bells and whistles. Many of these are associated with providing quality of service beyond the best efforts nature of IP, in order to make the Internet a better place for the transport of time-sensitive traffic, such as voice, video, and multimedia applications.

Once these developments started to bear fruit, much of the effort shifted away from IP toward the edges of the networks. The idea is that if we can somehow create QoS-based switched networks in the campus, then it might be possible to create end-to-end QoS provision from LAN to LAN across the Internet.

This chapter deals primarily with the QoS options currently available on Cisco switches. We will have to start, however, with some detail about the QoS options in IP, so we can see how they may also be employed in multi-layer switched networks and how the layer 3 and layer 2 QoS options map together at the campus edge.

In the last section, "Redundancy in Switched Networks," we will look at redundancy in several of its implementations, including router redundancy and server redundancy. Although these techniques may not normally be considered QoS protocol, they do nonetheless add to the general availability of network services. The chapter will end with a brief discussion of one of the more interesting technologies to emerge from the new-look Ethernet, transparent Ethernet.

# Understanding Application Needs

Understanding the needs of different applications is the key to developing an understanding of the many factors contributing to the selection of the most appropriate QoS options. Obviously, there are an enormous number of applications in use, but we can use some basic categories to define their needs and expectations in general terms.

One method is to define applications using some sort of classification, and then apply QoS based on specific classes. I have selected three applications to illustrate this principle—e-mail, World Wide Web traffic, and voice over Ethernet—each of which possesses different characteristics.

## E-mail

A number of different e-mail packages exist on the market today, and all have idiosyncrasies of some sort. Nonetheless, the basic method of operation (from the perspective of the bottom layers of the OSI model) is very similar in all cases.

E-mail uses a store-and-forward transfer mechanism, gaining its reliability from the TCP protocol. Data is formatted by the application and by TCP and IP into a reliable sequence of datagrams (packets) that are individually transmitted to the server or e-mail client. Little in the way of QoS needs to be applied to e-mail, largely because the users and the application both agree that this is not an instantaneous protocol.

Figure 9.1 shows e-mail packets traversing a network. As you can see, Figure 9.1 shows an e-mail message traveling from host Terry to host Stephanie. The message is fragmented into packets that are sent across the intervening internetwork, and then are reassembled at the destination by the application. Because e-mail is designed from the top down to be a store-and-forward (rather than real-time) application, greater emphasis was placed on guaranteed delivery than on delay, and so each packet will be of the maximum size permitted by the media.

**FIGURE 9.1** E-mail application fragments

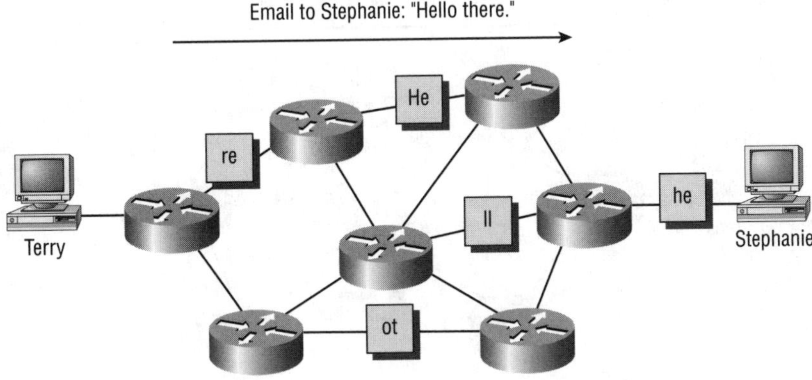


Obviously, if the delay in packet delivery was so large that users complained and the system became unusable, then something would have to be done, but this would generally be a low priority.

## WWW Traffic

All WWW traffic starts from somewhere. Assuming that you are connecting to the Web from a LAN, that's the first place where problems can affect the connection and the upload or download speed.

This is just a small part of the story, however. The weakest link in a chain always sets the strength for the whole chain, and the same is true of networks. So as far as transfer speed is concerned, we need to spend most of our time working on the narrowest bandwidth (generally the lowest speed). And that is unlikely to be the switched Ethernet LAN.

After all, your LAN is probably running 100BaseT, switched, possibly with duplex links to important machines. The connection to the Internet is probably through the company firewall (a packet-filtering engine introducing its own delay), and the Internet speed itself available to your PC is probably be a fraction of an E1 or T1 at best!

Obviously, if the service runs too slowly to be of use, and if you can identify the switched Ethernet LAN that you are connected to as the choke point, then you need to do something about it. But for the moment, let's leave the problems with WWW to the WAN guys.

What is important to us is that the size of each WWW packet may be different. Even though we tend to equate being connected to a website as having a single flow, that is rarely true. The construction of modern sites and the surfing behavior of Internet users means that TCP sessions are being opened and closed all the time, and the download of different format content ensures that the service is very patchy (see Figure 9.2).

**FIGURE 9.2** HTTP application fragments

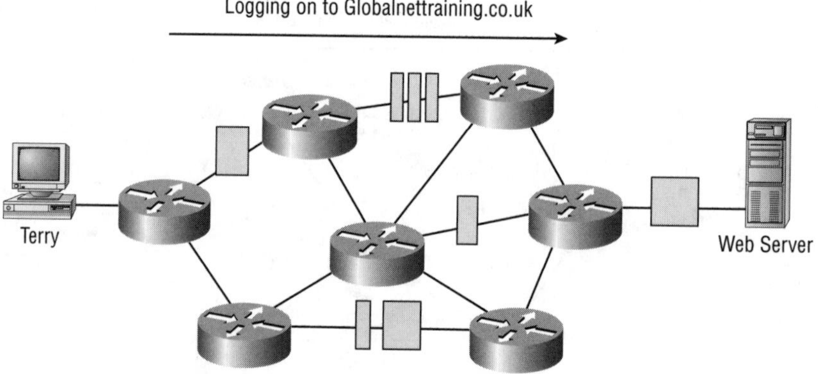


## Voice over Ethernet

Now, at last. Something that we can really get our teeth into! Voice traffic is very unusual, in that it presents an entirely different set of demands to an Ethernet LAN. We are all used to the usual pressures from applications, namely bandwidth and delay, but jitter is a new problem for us. In short, jitter is the variation in the delay experienced by successive packets in a flow.

Voice is a streaming protocol. As the analog signal is encoded and broken down into packets, each packet is transmitted across the network as a unique entity, and the whole is reassembled into a stream at the receiving end. Obviously, humans don't speak in packets, and we take pauses and breaks at random moments, uttering words when we need to. If the packets received at the end of the link are delayed too long, or if the delay is too variable for the decoder, then the voice stream cannot be properly reconstructed.

There is a name for this transmission type: *isochronous*. Derived from the Greek words for "equal" and "time," it describes processes that require timing to be coordinated. In other words, isochronous traffic requires that data flow continuously and at a steady rate in close timing with the ability of the display mechanism to receive and display the image data. Figure 9.3 demonstrates how jitter can affect the output of the playback buffers.

**FIGURE 9.3** Voice playback buffers

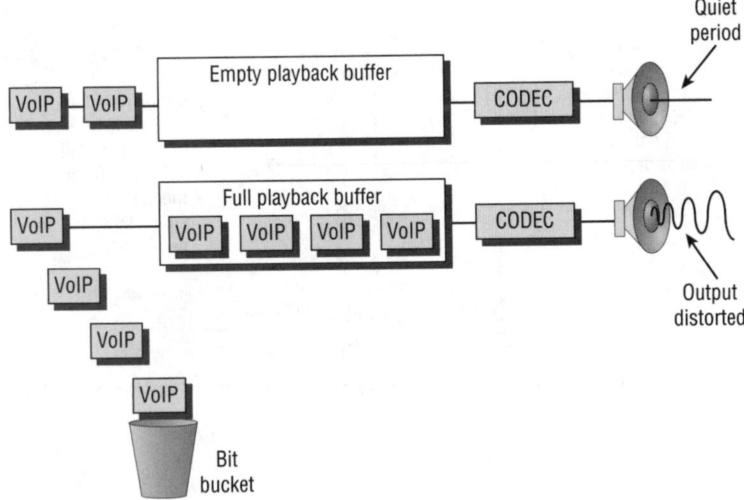


As you can see, the possibility exists for the playback buffer to be empty, full, or half-full. If the buffer is half-full, then a smoothly created output audio signal will result in good quality voice reception.

If the buffer is empty, then no audio signal output can be created; this is not a problem if the reason for the empty buffer is a genuine lack of transmitted data. But if the buffer is full, then there may be a problem. First, any new arriving packets will be dropped, and time is insufficient for them to be retransmitted, so they are lost forever. This, however, may not be the largest problem, because if the reason for the buffer alternating between full and empty is a variability in the arrival rate of voice-encapsulated data packets, then the output stream will be of poor quality.

Jitter is probably of greater significance than simple delay in voice networks, because (up to a certain limit) delay just means that the receiver has to wait a short time for the words. But jitter results in poor quality voice reception that may be unacceptable to the listener. Figure 9.4 illustrates a general design model for multimedia traffic, showing how voice will be integrated into the IP infrastructure. Obviously, we are focusing on the campus network, but you can see clearly that as IP datagrams carry voice into the IP cloud, inconsistencies start to appear in the delivery process.

**FIGURE 9.4** Voice design model

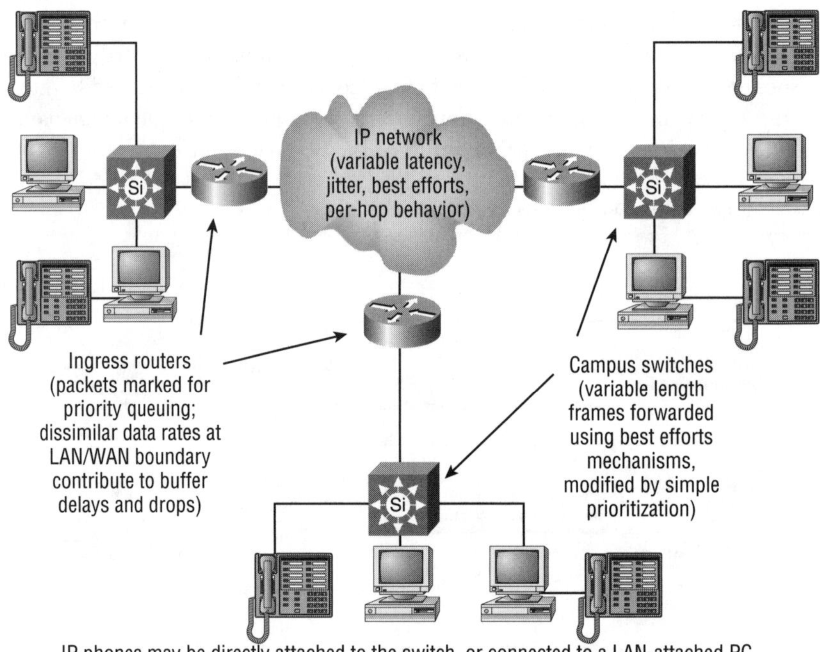


# Understanding the Fundamentals of QoS

In order to fully understand QoS, there are a few changes we need to apply to our common mindset regarding network traffic. We need to consider the mechanisms behind our existing traffic forwarding, usually comprising a combination of connectionless and connection-oriented delivery, per-hop router/switch forwarding, and FIFO (first in, first out) queuing. We need to review what we know about networks where no QoS features are added to the basic protocol activity. These networks are called best efforts networks.

## Best Efforts Networks

In a *best efforts network*, as illustrated in Figure 9.5, data is transmitted in the hope (an expectation) that it will be delivered. It's similar to the mail system. You write your letter, address it, and put it in the mailbox. And that's it. You hope (and expect) that it will be delivered, but it's out of your control. If something goes wrong with the system, your mail is undelivered. And you may not even know that it failed to get through!

 Best efforts packets

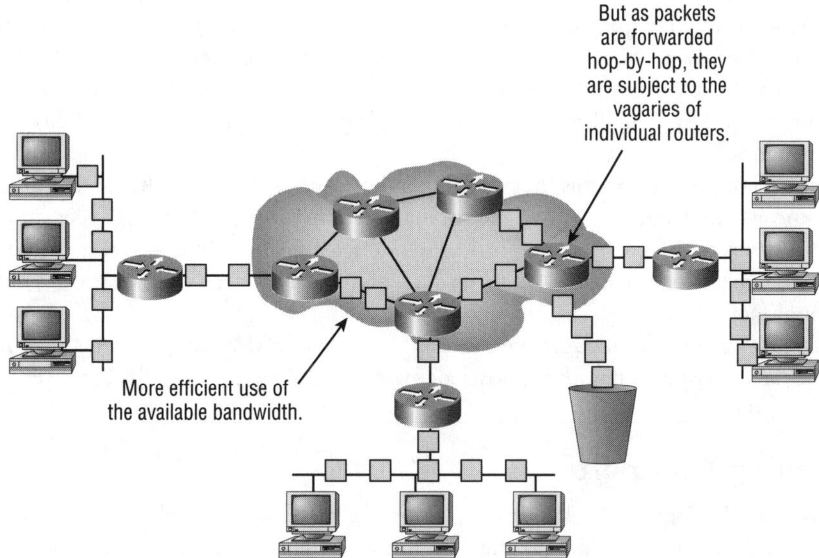
But as packets
are forwarded
hop-by-hop, they
are subject to the
vagaries of
individual routers.
More efficient use of
the available bandwidth.

Of course, if the mail system were truly unreliable, you would complain loudly, and eventually stop using it, so it can't be all that bad. But because there is no reliability built in, we refer to it as unreliable.

Under these circumstances, there are two choices open to us. We can either live with the unreliability, or try to do something about it.

## Connection-Oriented Transport

One thing we could do is ask for a receipt to be signed at the far end so that we know it got through. This would make our system more reliable, but obviously the service would not be free, because there is greater overhead and therefore greater cost. In IP networks, we use TCP (Transport Control Protocol) to handle that receipting process for us, and we call those receipts acknowledgments. And it isn't free, because we have to wait for a packet to be acknowledged before we can send the next one, and that slows down the data throughput.

So in order to work properly, both the sequence number and the acknowledgment numbers must be synchronized at the start of the data transfer. In fact, other additional parameters also need to be set at this time, and so TCP has a complex process to initiate the data transfer, called the *connection sequence*.

In a way, this puts us on the road to QoS-based networks, because we have at least guaranteed that our data will be delivered. Now we have to deal with all of the other issues surrounding how it will be delivered.

## Connectionless Transport

Sometimes the need for reliable data transfer is overridden by another, more pressing requirement. If the protocol in question uses broadcasts to deliver its data, then we cannot reasonably expect acknowledgments. It's bad enough that every station on the segment is disturbed by the original broadcast, without compounding the felony! Protocols such as RIP (the ubiquitous routing protocol) operate like this, resending their data at regular intervals to ensure that data gets through.

Another family of protocols that remain connectionless are the multicasts. Multicast traffic (as we know from Chapter 8, "Understanding and Configuring Multicast Operation") is delivered to stations that have joined a particular multicast group. Once again, it would be unreasonable to expect acknowledgments from such a potentially large receiver group, but there are additional factors.

Multicast streams often contain either time-sensitive or streaming information. In either case, the delays associated with acknowledgments would be unacceptable, interfering with the flow of the data.

## Streaming Transport

There is one other option. Multicast traffic may not be acknowledged, but that is no reason for us to abandon all efforts to deliver the data in the sequence in which it was transmitted.

Real Time Protocol (RTP) is one option to assist us here. RTP runs over UDP and provides both sequence information and a timestamp for each datagram. Although this in itself doesn't provide any service guarantees, it does mean that the receiver can make adjustments by changing the order of packet arrival to restore simple out-of-sequence deliveries, and packets arriving too late for insertion into the stream decoders can be ignored.

## Common Problems in Best Efforts Networks

Best efforts networks attempt to deliver packets, but are characterized by a variety of conditions that interfere in some way with forwarding data.

### Simple Delay

Simple delay causes packets to arrive later than might be expected. There are several contributing factors to simple delay:

**Laws of Physics Delay** *Laws of physics delay* is caused by the fact that data cannot be propagated through either copper or fiber instantaneously, or even at anything like the speed of light. In fact, about 60 percent of light speed in copper, and not much faster in fiber, is the norm. The good news is that this delay is standard.

Data traveling across copper for a distance of 100 meters takes about 0.5 microseconds to arrive. This might seem very small, almost insignificant. But for data traveling at 100Mbits/second, this is a delay of about 50 bits!

**Serialization Delay** *Serialization delay* is caused by store-and-forward devices such as switches and routers having to read the frame or packet into the buffers before any decision-making process can be implemented. This is obviously unpredictable, as varying frame/packet sizes will result in different delays.

**Processing Delay** *Processing delay* is caused by the router or switch having to make a forwarding decision. This is again variable and unpredictable, because it may depend upon the processing overhead on that device at the moment of search, the internal buffer architecture and load, internal bus load, and the searching algorithm in use. There may be some statistically measurable average, but that's no good for individual packets.

**Output Buffer Priorities** *Output buffer priorities* are the final stage of the delay. Should a buffer become full, then the mechanism for discarding may be simple tail-drop, or something more complex such as Random Early Discard. And if the queuing method is FIFO, then that favors larger frames/packets, whereas if we implement sophisticated queuing, we must always remember that putting one data stream at the front of the queue is bound to result in another stream being at the back.

## Jitter

Jitter is what happens when packets arrive either earlier or later than expected, outside established parameters for simple delay. The effect is to interfere with the smooth playback of certain types of streaming traffic (voice, video, and so on), because the playback buffers are unable to cope with the irregular arrival of successive packets. Jitter is caused by variations in delay, such as the following:

**Serialization Delay** Serialization delay can cause jitter, with subsequent packets being of different sizes. One technique that might be used to standardize this delay would be to make all frames the same size, irrespective of their data content. This is the method used by Frame Relay using the FRF.11 (for voice) recommendation, and by ATM. This solution is good for voice but bad for data, because of the overhead created by increasing the number of frames per packet.

**Queue Disposition** *Queue disposition* can affect delay, because while packets at the front of the queue may have constancy of delay, packets further back are behind an unknown number of frames/packets at the front, giving rise to variability. Cisco provides a number of different queuing options, allowing the most appropriate to be selected on a case-by-case basis.

**Per-Hop Routing** *Per-hop routing* behavior can affect delay variably, because subsequent packets may travel to the same destination via different paths due to routing changes.

## Packet Loss

Packet loss may seem to be the most important issue, but that is often not the case. If packet loss occurs in connection-oriented services, then the lost packet will be requested and retransmitted. This may be annoying if it slows down the data transfer too much, but connection-oriented applications are built to manage this problem.

In a connectionless network, once lost, the data is gone forever. If the loss exceeds certain parameters (different for each application), then the application will be deemed unusable and terminated either by the user (quality too poor) or by the application itself. In either case, the user and application are exposed to the poor quality with the resulting dissatisfaction regarding the network. Packet loss can occur in a number of places, with each location introducing loss in a different way:

**Line Loss** *Line loss* is usually caused by data corruption on unacknowledged links. Corrupted packets may fail a checksum and are discarded, but are not scheduled for retransmission. In a well-designed Ethernet network, this should be a rare occurrence.

**Buffer Overflows** *Buffer overflows* occur when network devices are too busy internally, or when the output network is congested. The key to managing buffer overflows lies in early detection of the problem and careful application throttling.

**Discard Eligible** *Discard eligible* packets are flagged to be deliberately dropped when congestion occurs on Frame Relay and ATM networks. There is no exactly comparable process with Ethernet LANs, but if we establish traffic classes in order to create priorities, then it follows that those frames in the lowest priority traffic streams run the risk of being dropped more frequently as network congestion occurs.

# QoS Options

Obviously, the ultimate Quality of Service would be if we were able to guarantee that every packet/frame on the network were delivered reliably, in the correct sequence, and with zero delay. Well, guess what—that's not going to happen! But a variety of techniques can be applied to try to get close enough to the end of the rainbow to allow the applications to manage the rest themselves.

The following parameters are considered essential for measuring and providing any QoS:

- Service availability
- Frame loss
- Frame order
- Frame duplication
- The transit delay experienced by frames
- Frame lifetime
- The undetected frame error rate
- Maximum service data unit size supported
- User priority
- Throughput

Two main mechanisms exist for dealing with end-to-end QoS, *Differentiated Services* and *Integrated Services*. Both are contenders for the ultimate solution, but we will focus on Differentiated Services because that's what Cisco uses with Ethernet.

The Integrated Services model involves setting up an end-to-end connection across an internetwork of RSVP-enabled routers using an new IP-based signaling protocol called Resource Reservation Setup Protocol (RSVP). RSVP routers request and reserve bandwidth across an internetwork and release it back to the internetwork after the connection is terminated.

## The Differentiated Services Model

The QoS implementation in Catalyst switches is based on the Differentiated Services (DiffServe) architecture. This reference model states that packets are marked (classified) at the entry point into the network, and that every subsequent router or switch, implementing hop-by-hop forwarding, uses the *classification* to try to match the forwarding process to the classification. This is achieved by each DiffServe router in the path having a locally configured queuing priority for forwarding marked packets. Non-DiffServe-enabled routers will simply forward packets based upon default queues. Figure 9.6 shows the DiffServe architecture, with routers in the end-to-end path either being in the domain or without. The entry point to the domain is called the ingress, and the exit point is called the egress.

**FIGURE 9.6** Differentiated Services model

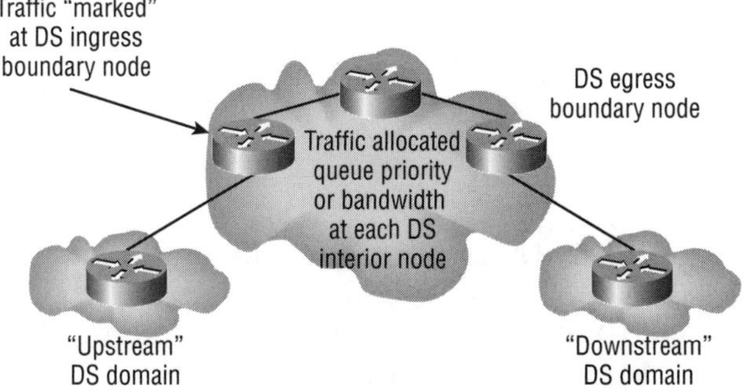


At layer 3, this classification and marking is established by setting bits in the IP Type of Service (TOS) field to differing values. At layer 2, however, this is a little more difficult, as there are no fields inside legacy Ethernet available for this purpose. Even so, there are some clever mechanisms that allow us to map layer 2 priorities to layer 3.

The basic QoS model underlying all efforts is closely related to the DiffServe architecture. Shown in Figure 9.7, it consists of a series of discrete stages. First, the packets are classified and tested to see if they conform to the configured classification. This stage is called *policing*.

Next, the packet is marked and forwarded to the DiffServe network, where the marking will be used to set priorities in queues and establish any other forwarding rules, before reaching the egress point. The last router or switch in the path forwards the data to the target client according to locally configured rules.

**FIGURE 9.7** Basic QoS model

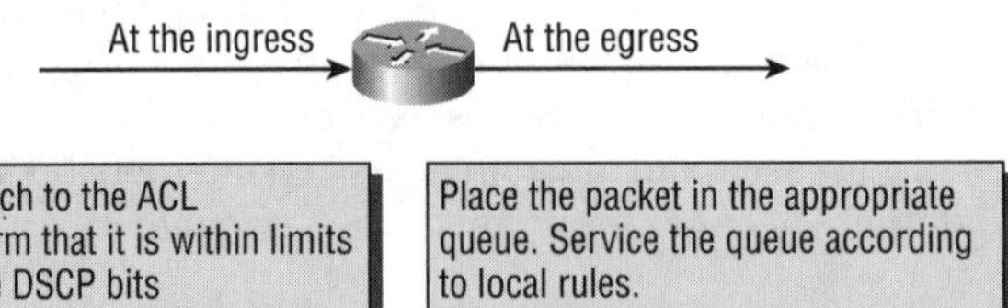
At the ingress
At the egress
Classify: match to the ACL
Police: confirm that it is within limits
Mark: set the DSCP bits
Place the packet in the appropriate queue. Service the queue according to local rules.

It is not a condition of basic IP that routers understand the TOS or DS fields. Non-DiffServe routers in a path will treat the IP datagram in the same way as all other datagrams, forwarding it in a best-efforts fashion. This is quite useful because it means that DiffServe is easy to implement in phases on a network.

DiffServe uses some specific bits in the IP header to mark the service class required. All DiffServe routers understand these settings and administrators are responsible for configuring router queues in such a way as to best meet the needs of the specific traffic class. The DiffServe field is part of the IP header, which is extended and changed slightly from the original TOS field.

The original IPv4 TOS field was defined years ago in RFC 791, when nobody had any idea how the Internet and its applications would pan out. This single octet has 3 bits of Precedence configurable as a group, providing seven levels of Precedence. In addition, a further 4, individually configurable, bits are available to request one of four types of service, with 1 bit unused (which must be zero):

- Minimize delay
- Maximize throughput
- Maximize reliability
- Minimize monetary

A replacement header field, called the DS field, is defined in RFC 2474, which is intended to supersede the existing definition. Six bits of the DS field are used as a Differentiated Services Code Point (DSCP) to select the PHB a packet experiences at each node. A 2-bit currently unused (CU) field is reserved. All 6 bits must be tested by DiffServe-compliant routers.

There is no backward compatibility with the TOS fields, but the implementation of one does not prevent implementation of the other. In either case, the actual forwarding mechanism applied by each router in the path is established by local configuration of queues and priorities, and is likely to be proprietary, so routers could forward along planned paths according to either TOS or DS bits.

In order to classify packets, we need to determine some traffic types to use as templates. Table 9.1 defines traffic types.

# IEEE 802.1p

The *IEEE 802.1p* standard defines important methods for traffic class expediting and dynamic multicast filtering, thus providing Quality of Service at the MAC level. This standard may be considered an extension to the 802.1Q standard discussed in Chapter 3, "VLANs, Trunks, and

VTP." Three bits are allocated inside the 802.1Q insert that were unspecified at the time, but have been allocated by 802.1p.

802.1p establishes eight levels of priority that are conceptually similar to the 3 bits specified by IP Precedence. Layer 2 switches can prioritize data in their output buffers according to these priority bits, and many layer 3 switches are capable of "mapping" the 802.1p Precedence to the TOS or DiffServe fields inside IP so as to achieve end-to-end QoS across integrated switched and routed internetworks.

**TABLE 9.1** Differentiated Services Traffic Types

| Traffic Type | Characteristics of Traffic Needs |
|---|---|
| Network Control | High requirement to get through to maintain and support the network infrastructure |
| Voice | Less than 10 milliseconds delay |
| Video | Less than 100 milliseconds delay |
| Controlled Load | Important applications |
| Excellent Effort | Best efforts for important users |
| Best Effort | Ordinary LAN priority |
| Background | Bulk transfers, games, and so on |

## Applying the QoS Model

The first stage in determining how the switches and routers in the network will prioritize traffic is the classification process. Essentially, the idea is to somehow mark traffic with an indication that it should be treated differently from packets with dissimilar marking.

The second stage is traffic policing. This is the process whereby a switch/router determines whether the frame/packet matches the preconfigured profiles. Packets that exceed specified limits are considered to be nonconforming. The policing process specifies the action to take for packets by either setting bandwidth limits for conforming traffic, or dropping or remarking nonconforming traffic.

The third stage is to actually mark the frame/packet. Data can be marked at layer 2 (in the 802.1p header) or at layer 3 (inside the IP header), depending upon the device. Switches that operate at layer 3 are able to mark at either layer, but switches operating purely at layer 2 are able to mark only the frame.

So if the switch is a layer 3 switch, we have the option of forwarding a packet with QoS. Then, using the general principles of traffic types, we need to "map" the traffic type to a TOS or DiffServe number. After the packet has been through the classification, policing, and marking processes, it is assigned to the appropriate queue before exiting the switch. If the switch has received the packet inside an 802.3 frame with 802.1p priority specified, this process may be automated. If not, then we must map it manually.

Finally, the packet must be forwarded out of a shared output buffer onto the media toward the next hop. This is usually accomplished by establishing a queuing process and placing traffic into different queues according the policies defined earlier.

## Prioritizing Traffic Classes

Traffic marking is normally carried out using mapping commands. There is a wide range of mapping commands in the Cisco IOS, including route-maps (for manipulating route parameters), crypto-maps (for establishing encryption parameters), and others. The ones we are most interested in are the policy-maps and the class-maps.

All IOS maps have some things in common. Maps begin with a `match` command, which unambiguously identifies some form of traffic, at the frame, packet, or even application layers. This would involve the additional use of an access list. Class-maps allow for the matching of an IP address, a protocol, or an incoming interface.

Once traffic has been matched, then the map (sometimes the same map, sometimes a "sister" map, as in the case of policy- and class-maps) is used to "set" an attribute. A wide variety of attributes can often be associated with matched traffic in this way, but the policy-map allows only for the setting of the DSCP code point. Figure 9.8 shows where the marking takes place in both the Data Link and Network PDUs.

**FIGURE 9.8** Frame and packet marking

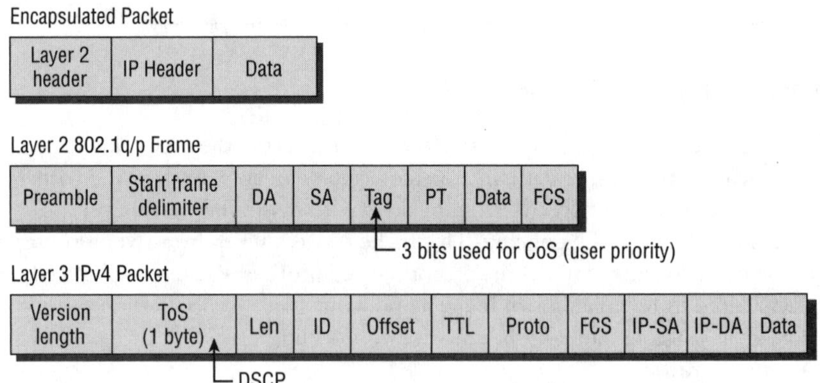


## Queuing Mechanisms

A number of different queuing mechanisms exist on Cisco layer 2 and layer 3 switches. The reason for this is that across the globe, different network managers require different prioritization for different networks running a wide variety of legacy, common, and emerging applications. No single queuing mechanism could support these diverse needs, so several mechanisms exist. It is up to the intelligent network administrator to apply the method available for their network that best suits their needs. Here is a short list of the most prevalent methods available across the spectrum of Cisco layer 2 and layer 3 switches:

**First In, First Out Queuing** *First in, first out* (FIFO) queuing transmits frames/packets according to the timed arrival of the first bits in the frame/packet at the input interface. This is often the default method.

**Weighed Fair Queuing** *Weighed Fair Queuing (WFQ)* places data into different queues according to the conversation index associated with each packet. The conversation index is a term applied to different applications, whose packets are then marked with a number inside the switch or router. The selection of the data type and queue is internal and proprietary, but results in low-volume interactive traffic (voice) being granted higher priority than high-volume non-interactive traffic (FTP).

**Custom Queuing** *Custom Queuing* allows administrators to create up to 16 queues, each with configurable sizes and forwarding thresholds. Data is placed in queues according to access lists, and queues are emptied on a round-robin basis.

**Priority Queuing** *Priority Queuing* allows the administrator to create a number of queues and configure the size of each. Data is placed into queues according to access lists, and queues are emptied on a strict priority basis. Packets in the highest priority queue are always transmitted first, and packets in lower priority queues are not transmitted until the queues higher up are emptied.

**Weighted Round Robin Queuing** *Weighted Round Robin Queuing* is a simplified version of custom queuing. A fixed number of queues are serviced in round-robin fashion, each being configurable only as to the size of the queue.

**Multistage Queuing** *Multistage Queuing* can be implemented on some platforms, and involves the creation of multiple queuing processes in a dependency fashion. For example, a mixture of priority and WFQ could be used.

Figure 9.9 shows how packets arriving at three interfaces at the same time need to be sorted into an output queue to be transmitted serially. Of course, it is in the output queue that we can influence packet delay by arranging how the queue works.

**FIGURE 9.9** Queuing overview

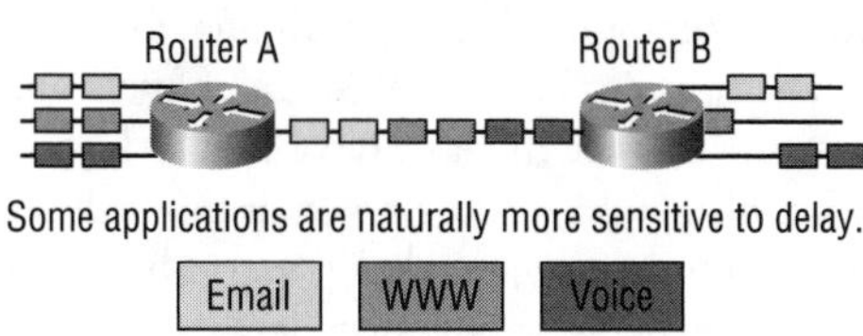
Router A
Router B
Some applications are naturally more sensitive to delay.
Email
WWW
Voice
It makes sense to give those a higher priority in the queues.

## Auto-QoS

Obviously, implementing QoS can be an administrative headache. Some configurations have the potential to affect application delivery across a wide spectrum of the network, and without practical skills and experience it's easy to make mistakes. To help administrators build QoS-based networks with the minimum of effort, Cisco has created something called auto-QoS.

*Auto-QoS* can be used to simplify the deployment of QoS features. Auto-QoS makes certain assumptions about the network design, allowing the switch to prioritize different traffic flows and use the output queues appropriately instead of just using the default QoS behavior of best-efforts service from a single queue. Auto-QoS uses the input packet label and traffic type to automatically classify traffic. The switch then uses this classification to place traffic in the appropriate output queue.

One of the main features of auto-QoS is the ability of the switch to identify ports that have IP telephones attached to them and allocate sufficient buffer space to afford the VoIP (Voice over IP) calls the correct QoS. This does not just apply to the ports with the IP phones connected, but also to uplinks that carry the VoIP calls to the next switch. This process is called *trust*.

Trust allows for ports that may carry VoIP traffic (but not actually have IP phones directly connected) to recognize that a packet marked as carrying such a service must be afforded the same QoS as if it were directly connected, and therefore proven to be VoIP. Trust is configured across a QoS domain. Packets are marked only at the ingress to the domain and trusted from there on, obviating the need to mark again at every switch or router.

Trust will be pretty important in the future, when all networks start to use QoS. Obviously, QoS is not going to be free, and ISPs will probably charge more for better QoS on the Internet. It follows that when an arriving packet demands a better QoS because of some bits set in an IP header, we should be certain that we are prepared to agree to those demands; otherwise the system would be open to abuse. Disreputable users would be able to manipulate the DSCP code bits to create higher priorities for web browsing, for example.

# Configuring QoS on Cisco Switches

The Cisco range of switches is currently undergoing one of the largest series of changes I have ever seen. As you may know, Cisco became one of the largest switch vendors in the world, partly by buying up some of the best competition. Companies such as Kalpana, Grand Junction, and Catalyst all provided input to the range. The result has been a mixture of operating systems and command-line interfaces that Cisco engineers and technicians have had to learn.

As Cisco standardizes the range, we are also experiencing an emerging need for something better than best-efforts data delivery on our computer networks. The combination of the newer operating systems, new switch architectures, and new application demands means that there is a lot more to learn. Because the process is ongoing, not every Cisco switch will support every QoS feature. And because the IOS now plays such a large part in all this, new versions of the IOS may offer enhancements over previous versions.

In this section, I will cover the main commands used in the three current operating system options, CatOS and the standard and enhanced IOS images. But you need to stay up-to-date on this, because a major new IOS revision will almost certainly cause some things to change.

## 2950 Series Switches

The 2950 switch transmits network traffic in the following fashion. Frames are classified by assigning priority-indexed Class of Service (CoS) values to them and giving preference to higher-priority traffic such as telephone calls.

Each transmit port has a default normal-priority transmit queue and may be configured with up to four additional high-priority transmit queues. Frames in the high-priority queue are forwarded before frames in the normal-priority queue. Frames are forwarded to queues dependent upon the defined priority-to-queue mapping. Queues can be emptied using strict Priority Queuing or Weighted Round Robin Queuing as desired.

If your 2950 switch is running the standard software image, there are some restrictions on what you can configure. In fact, you are limited to configuring the CoS priorities and the WRR settings. To do this, use the `wrr-queue cos-map` global command to establish the queues, and the `wrr-queue bandwidth` statement to set the queue thresholds if needed.

```
Terry_2950#conf t
Terry_2950(config)#wrr-queue ?
  bandwidth  Configure WRR bandwidth
  cos-map    Configure cos-map for a queue
Terry_2950(config)#wrr-queue cos-map ?
  <1-4>  enter cos-map queue id (1-4)
Terry_2950(config)#wrr-queue cos-map 1 ?
  <0-7>  cos values separated by spaces (up to 8 values total)
Terry_2950(config)#wrr-queue cos-map 1 0 1
Terry_2950(config)#wrr-queue cos-map 2 2 3
Terry_2950(config)#wrr-queue cos-map 3 4 5
Terry_2950(config)#wrr-queue cos-map 4 6 7
Terry_2950(config)#wrr-queue bandwidth 10 20 30 40
Terry_2950(config)#
Terry_2950#
```

If your switch has the enhanced image, you will be able to carry out classification and marking in addition to being able to perform DSCP mapping.

The example shown here will identify a particular traffic stream, identified by MAN address, and associate a DiffServe value with it. First, we need to establish the way that we will identify the traffic to be classified. Use the `class-maps` *name* global command to define the match criteria when classifying traffic.

```
Terry_2950(config)# class-map terry1
Terry_2950(config-cmap)# match access-group 701
Terry_2950(config-cmap)# exit
```

There are a selection of match options inside a class map:

```
Terry_2950(config-cmap)#match ?
  access-group      access group
  input-interface   Select an input interface to match
  mpls              Multi Protocol Label Switching values
  protocol          Protocol
  <cr>
```

In this example, we will use an access list in conjunction with the class map to clearly identify the traffic to be classified.

```
Terry_2950(config)#access-list 701 permit 0011.2345.6789 00aa.1234.5678
```

Finally, we need to determine what the classification will be. Use the global configuration command `policy-map name` to determine the classification criteria to be set for incoming traffic.

```
Terry_2950(config)#policy-map macpolicy1
Terry_2950(config-pmap)#class terry1
Terry_2950(config-pmap-c)#set ip dscp 56
Terry_2950(config-pmap-c)#exit
Terry_2950(config)#int fa0/1
Terry_2950(config-if)#service-policy input macpolicy1
```

For a full explanation of the differences between the standard and enhanced images available on the 2950 switch range, see Chapter 10, "Catalyst Switch Technologies."

## 3550 Series Switches

The 3550 supports an entirely greater range of QoS options because of the layer 3 capability of the hardware and the IOS. There is, in fact, a good case for referring to the 3550 as a multiport router with layer 2 capabilities rather than a switch with layer 3 capabilities.

Essentially, the combined layer 2 and layer 3 QoS functionality means that the switch can classify traffic using sophisticated access lists, mark at both layers, forward using either DSCP or 802.1p priority bits, and even translate from one to the other. This combined functionality involves accepting the default mapping that places DSCP traffic into Ethernet frames with a closely related CoS (or maps the IP datagram inside an incoming Ethernet with CoS set to the IP datagram itself as a DSCP). If the defaults are not suitable for your network, you can use an `mls qos-map` to establish your own translation values.

This large range of options means that we have to restrict ourselves a little, because the subject of QoS as applied by routers and other layer 3 devices is large enough to warrant a book all by itself. In fact, it is one of the core subjects of a new advanced Cisco certification, the CCIP (Cisco Certified Internetwork Professional). So, to stay on target, we will concentrate our efforts on those configurations that are likely to appear on the BCMSN exam.

### Configured QoS

To configure QoS on a 3550 switch, first enable QoS globally with the `mls qos` command.

The use of class-maps and policy-maps to define the match and classification criteria for incoming traffic is very similar to the way they are used inside the 2950.

Class-maps can be configured using an extension allowing the matching of either all or any of the criteria specified in the map. To manage this feature, use either the `class-map match-all` or the `class-map match-any` global commands. In addition, the class-map supports matching against a VLAN or a group of up to 30 VLANs. To select this match option, use the `match vlan vlan-list` c-map command.

The following example shows traffic arriving at interface gigabitethernet0/1, sourced from VLAN 66 or being already marked with an IP Precedence of 1, having the DSCP set to 63 at the ingress.

```
Terry_3550(config)#mls qos
Terry_3550(config)#access-list 101 permit ip any any precedence 1
Terry_3550(config)#class-map match any terry2
Terry_3550(config-cmap)#match access-group 101
Terry_3550(config-cmap)#match vlan 66
Terry_3550(config-cmap)#exit
Terry_3550(config)#policy-map ip_or_VLAN66
Terry_3550(config-pmap)#class terry2
Terry_3550(config-pmap-c)#set ip dscp 63
Terry_3550(config-pmap-c)#exit
Terry_3550(config-pmap)#exit
Terry_3550(config)#interface gigabitethernet0/1
Terry_3550(config-if)#service-policy input ip_or_VLAN66
```

If you are configuring QoS inside a trusted domain and you do not use auto-QoS, then you have to decide what to do about trust. If you wish to trust incoming CoS values, use the interface command `mls qos trust cos` to ensure that the CoS value in received traffic is trusted, and use the `mls qos trust device cisco-phone` command to specify that the Cisco IP phone is a trusted device and ensure that a non-trusted device does not misuse the CoS available. Remember to enable cdp.

```
Terry_3550(config)#int fa0/1
Terry_3550(config-if)#cdp enable
Terry_3550(config-if)#mls qos trust ?
  cos           Classify by packet COS
```

```
  device          trusted device class
  dscp            Classify by packet DSCP
  ip-precedence   Classify by packet IP precedence
  <cr>
Terry_3550(config-if)# mls qos trust cos
Terry_3550(config-if)# mls qos trust device cisco-phone
Terry_3550(config-if)#^c
```

Because trusted traffic will automatically gain access to the process whereby CoS is mapped to DSCP, there is an option to forward CoS values without changing the existing DSCP (and vice versa) through the switch. This is called pass-through, and can be configured for either option:

```
Terry_3550(config-if)# mls qos trust cos pass-through dscp
```

or

```
Terry_3550(config-if)# mls qos trust dscp pass-through cos
```

### Auto-QoS

The implementation of auto-QoS simplifies the configuration of switches inside a trusted domain. First, enable QoS in the usual way, with the `mls qos` command:

```
Terry_3550(config)#mls qos
```

Now you have a choice. If the interface has an IP phone directly connected, use the commands shown next:

```
Switch(config)#interface fastethernet0/1
Switch(config-if)#auto qos voip cisco-phone
```

And if the interface is not directly connected to an IP phone, but is a trusted device, then enter this alternative:

```
Switch(config)#interface gigabitethernet0/1
Switch(config-if)#auto qos voip trust
```

Note that up to release 12.1(14)EA1 of the IOS, auto-QoS configures only the switch for VoIP with Cisco IP phones.

## 4000 Series Switches

If your 4000 switch has been upgraded to run IOS, then the classification, marking, and forwarding of packets is the same as for the 3550. But when running the legacy CatOS operating system, the QoS options available for the 4000 series switches are relatively unsophisticated. This section describes the CatOS QoS options.

Each transmit port has three possible queues. There is one non-configurable queue and two queues where some configuration is possible. The drop thresholds can be configured, but tail drop occurs in all cases when the queue is full.

The switch has a default 802.1p CoS of 0 (zero), but this can be changed. In that case, all unmarked frames entering the switch are marked with the specified CoS value. Marked frames cannot be changed.

The default condition is for QoS to be disabled, so first you have to enable QoS on the switch. Take care that any configuration changes are carried out at an appropriate time, because some of them will reset ports, and possibly cause Spanning Tree instability if the network converges. You can turn on QoS using the `set qos enable` command.

The port type is defined by the number of transmit queues and the number of drop thresholds that are supported on the port. For example, the 2q1t port type supports two transmit queues each with a single configurable drop threshold.

Port types on the Catalyst 4000 are dependent upon the hardware. Use the `show port capabilities` command to find out what port type you are configuring.

To configure the CoS mapping and set the thresholds on a configurable port, use `the set qos map` *`port_type q# threshold#`* `cos` *`cos_list`*. The port type you will already know. You need to decide which threshold to apply to which queue, and the CoS values to map to the specified transmit queue. The following example shows the two queues on a 2q1t port being configured, one with CoS 2-4 and the other with CoS 5-7:

```
Terry_4000> (enable) set qos map 2q1t 1 1 cos 2-4
Terry_4000> (enable) set qos map 2q1t 2 1 cos 5-7
Qos tx priority queue and threshold mapped to cos successfully.
Terry_4000> (enable)
```

To view the QoS configuration, use the `show qos info config` command.

# Queuing Mechanisms

In addition to setting the QoS parameters, it is common for devices operating at layer 3 to have to receive and transmit packets, applying simple queuing mechanisms to the forwarding process. The most common of the configurable queuing mechanisms are Priority Queuing and Custom Queuing.

## Priority Queuing

*With Priority Queuing, d*ata is placed into one of four different queues, defined as high, medium, normal, and low. These queues are emptied on a strict priority basis. Packets in the highest priority queue are always transmitted first, and packets in lower priority queues are not transmitted until the queues with higher priorities are emptied.

Configuration options available to the administrator include how to define the traffic, what queue to place the traffic into, and how large each queue should be. To define the traffic for a particular priority queue, use the `priority-list` global command.

```
Terry_3550(config)#priority-list 1 ?
  default      Set priority queue for unspecified datagrams
  interface    Establish priorities for packets from a named interface
  protocol     priority queueing by protocol
  queue-limit  Set queue limits for priority queues

Terry_3550(config)#priority-list 1 protocol ?
  arp            IP ARP
  bridge         Bridging
  cdp            Cisco Discovery Protocol
  compressedtcp  Compressed TCP
  ip             IP

Terry_3550(config)#priority-list 1 protocol ip ?
  high
  medium
  normal
  low

Terry_3550(config)#priority-list 1 protocol ip high ?
  fragments  Prioritize fragmented IP packets
  gt         Prioritize packets greater than a specified size
  list       To specify an access list
  lt         Prioritize packets less than a specified size
  tcp        Prioritize TCP packets 'to' or 'from' the specified port
  udp        Prioritize UDP packets 'to' or 'from' the specified port
  <cr>

Terry_3550(config)#priority-list 1 prot ip high list ?
  <1-199>      IP access list
  <1300-2699>  IP expanded access list
Terry_3550(config)#^Z
Terry_3550#
```

To define the maximum queue size for a particular priority queue, use the `priority-list` *`priority-queue`* `queue-limit` global command:

```
Terry_3550(config)#priority-list 1 ?
  default      Set priority queue for unspecified datagrams
  interface    Establish priorities for packets from a named interface
  protocol     Priority queueing by protocol
  queue-limit  Set queue limits for priority queues
```

```
Terry_3550(config)#priority-list 1 queue-limit ?
  <0-32767>  High limit
Terry_3550(config)#priority-list 1 queue-limit 5000
Terry_3550(config)#^Z
Terry_3550#
```

Allocating the priority queue to a particular outgoing interface is achieved using the `priority-list` *`priority-queue`* interface command.

```
Terry_3550(config)#int fastEthernet 0/1
Terry_3550(config-if)#priority-group 1
Terry_3550(config)#^Z
Terry_3550#
```

It is common to make the queue sizes increasingly larger as the priority decreases. Naturally, packets in the lowest priority queue stand a statistically greater change of spending more time in the queue, and it makes sense to allow the packets somewhere to wait.

The following configuration uses access list 101 to place telnet traffic between any two hosts into the high-priority queue, uses access list 102 to place web traffic between any two hosts into the medium-priority queue, and places all other IP traffic into the normal-priority queue, while cdp traffic is placed into the low-priority queue. The list is applied to interface FastEthernet 0/24:

```
Terry_3550(config)#priority-list 1 prot ip high list 101
Terry_3550(config)#priority-list 1 prot ip medium list 102
Terry_3550(config)#priority-list 1 prot ip normal
Terry_3550(config)#priority-list 1 protocol cdp low
Terry_3550(config)#access-list 101 permit tcp any any eq telnet
Terry_3550(config)#access-list 102 permit tcp any any eq www
Terry_3550(config)#int fastEthernet 0/24
Terry_3550(config-if)#priority-group 1
Terry_3550(config)#^Z
Terry_3550#
```

## Custom Queuing

*With Custom Queuing, d*ata is placed into one of up to sixteen different queues, defined by queue number. These queues are emptied on a strict rotational basis. Once a queue's transmit threshold has been reached, the next queue is serviced, irrespective of whether the current queue still has packets in it.

Configuration options available to the administrator include how to define the traffic, what queue to place the traffic into, how large each queue should be, and how large each queue's service threshold should be.

To define the traffic for a particular custom queue, use the `queue-list` global command:

```
Terry_3550(config)#queue-list ?
  <1-16>  Queue list number

Terry_3550(config)#queue-list 1 ?
  default        Set custom queue for unspecified datagrams
  interface      Establish priorities for packets from a named interface
  lowest-custom  Set lowest number of queue to be treated as custom
  protocol       Priority queueing by protocol
  queue          Configure parameters for a particular queue
  stun           Establish priorities for stun packets

Terry_3550(config)#queue-l 1 interface ?
  Async                 Async interface
  BVI                   Bridge-Group Virtual Interface
  Dialer                Dialer interface
  FastEthernet          FastEthernet IEEE 802.3
  GigabitEthernet       GigabitEthernet IEEE 802.3z
  Group-Async           Async Group interface
  Lex                   Lex interface
  Loopback              Loopback interface
  Multilink             Multilink-group interface
  Null                  Null interface
  Port-channel          Ethernet Channel of interfaces
  Transparent           Transparent interface
  Tunnel                Tunnel interface
  Virtual-Template      Virtual Template interface
  Virtual-TokenRing     Virtual TokenRing
  Vlan                  Catalyst Vlans
  fcpa                  Fiber Channel

Terry_3550(config)#queue-l 1 interface fastEthernet 0/12 ?
  <0-16>  queue number

Terry_3550(config)#queue-l 1 interface fastEthernet 0/12 1
Terry_3550(config)#queue-l 1 interface fastEthernet 0/13 2
Terry_3550(config)#queue-l 1 interface fastEthernet 0/14 2
Terry_3550(config)#^Z
Terry_3550#
```

To define the maximum queue size for a particular custom queue, use the `queue-list queue-limit` *queue-number* `byte-count` global command:

```
Terry_3550(config)#queue-list 1 ?
  default        Set custom queue for unspecified datagrams
  interface      Establish priorities for packets from a named interface
  lowest-custom  Set lowest number of queue to be treated as custom
  protocol       Priority queueing by protocol
  queue          Configure parameters for a particular queue
  stun           Establish priorities for stun packets

Terry_3550(config)#queue-list 1 queue 1 ?
  byte-count  Specify size in bytes of a particular queue
  limit       Set queue entry limit of a particular queue

Terry_3550(config)#queue-list 1 queue 1 byte-count ?
  <1-16777215>  Size in bytes

Terry_3550(config)#queue-list 1 queue 1 byte-count 10000 ?
  limit  Set queue entry limit of a particular queue
  <cr>

Terry_3550(config)#queue-list 1 queue 1 byte-count 10000 limit ?
  <0-32767>  Number of queue entries
Terry_3550(config)#queue-list 1 queue 1 byte-count 10000 limit 10
Terry_3550(config)#^Z
Terry_3550#
```

Allocating the priority queue to a particular outgoing interface is achieved using the `custom-queue-list` *custom-queue* interface command:

```
Terry_3550(config)#int fastEthernet 0/1
Terry_3550(config-if)#custom-queue-list 1
Terry_3550(config)#^Z
Terry_3550#
```

The following configuration uses access list 101 to place telnet traffic between any two hosts into queue 1, uses access list 102 to place web traffic between any two hosts into queue 2, and places all other IP traffic into queue 3, while cdp traffic is placed into queue 4. Changing the queue sizes has the effect of "fairly" allocating queue space to traffic:

```
Terry_3550(config)#queue-list 1 protocol ip 1 list 101
Terry_3550(config)#queue-list 1 protocol ip 2 list 102
```

```
Terry_3550(config)#queue-list 1 protocol ip 3
Terry_3550(config)#queue-list 1 protocol cdp 4
Terry_3550(config)#access-list 101 permit tcp any any eq telnet
Terry_3550(config)#access-list 102 permit tcp any any eq www
Terry_3550(config)#queue-list 1 queue 1 byte-count 2000 limit 25
Terry_3550(config)#queue-list 1 queue 2 byte-count 5000 limit 20
Terry_3550(config)#queue-list 1 queue 3 byte-count 10000 limit 10
Terry_3550(config)#queue-list 1 queue 4 byte-count 1000 limit 5
Terry_3550(config)#^Z
Terry_3550#
```

The 16 queues are all configurable, but you only need to configure as many as you need or want to. A separate 17th queue is created by the router for use by systems traffic. This queue is not configurable.

# Redundancy in Switched Networks

Redundancy is the art of ensuring that even when a component or service fails, network availability remains. This is obviously difficult to achieve in areas of the network where a single point of failure exists. One of the most common single points of failure is the default gateway used by non-routing hosts.

Here is a reminder of the basic IP connection procedure. When an IP host needs to access a second IP host, it knows the three things: its own IP address and mask and the address of the target. Using its own mask, a host decoded the target IP address in what is colloquially known as a *test for adjacency*. If the target host is on the same network, the host ARPs the target IP address directly. If the test for adjacency fails—the target is on a different subnet—then the host must send the data to a router. The most common method used to identify the default gateway is a statically configured default gateway.

Under normal circumstances, if the default gateway is unavailable, the result would be that the host would not receive a reply to an ARP request, would not be able to create Ethernet frames addressed to the default gateway, and would be unable to send data outside the local subnet. Even if a second default gateway were configured on the host, there would be a delay while the host realized that the first default gateway was not going to reply.

There are other ways of allowing a host to find a router. Hosts could run passive RIP, which would allow them to listen to RIP routing updates from local routers and complete a proper routing table. This is common in some UNIX implementations, but is slow to converge and can use a lot of memory for the routing tables. The Internet Router Discovery Protocol (IRDP) and IPv6 with its ICMP router discovery hello packets may also be suitable. But most Microsoft Windows machines use the static default gateway configuration.

Cisco's Hot Standby Routing Protocol was designed to provide a solution to this perennial problem.

# Hot Standby Router Protocol

The principles behind the Hot Standby Routing Protocol are marvelously simple. Two or more routers are configured in such a way that they act as a sort of cluster, creating a single, virtual router. Hosts are configured to use the address of the virtual router as their default gateway, and the *Hot Standby Routing Protocol (HSRP)* manages the decision-making regarding which router acts as the real default gateway.

Figure 9.10 shows the general layout of an HSRP group, with two routers sharing a standby IP address, and hosts using that address as their default gateway.

**FIGURE 9.10** HSRP virtual router

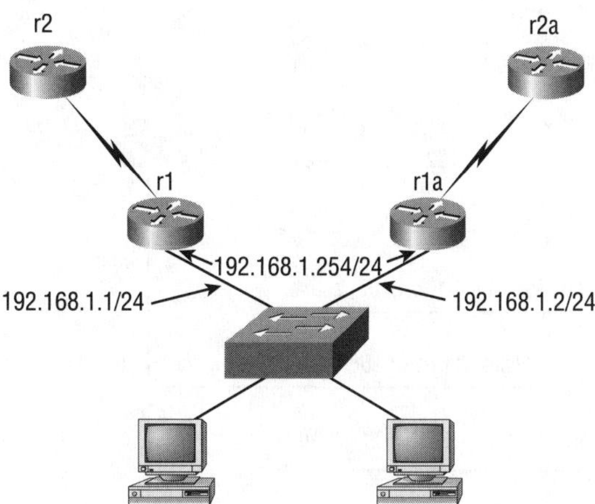


Each member of the virtual router cluster can also act as a standard router, as long as all clients wishing to use the (non-virtual) router as their default gateway have the correct configuration—in other words, the standard IP address of the router interface.

## HSRP Operation

Routers assume membership of an HSRP group after being configured with a standby IP address on an Ethernet interface in addition to the regular IP address. All routers in a group are configured with the same standby IP address, and an internal process in each router creates a standby MAC address of 0000.0c07.ac**, where the two stars represent the HSRP group number. (It follows that up to 256 HSRP groups could be configured.)

HSRP routers send hello packets, based on a 3-second default timer (configurable, of course), out of this interface, advertising the fact that they are now in a virtual router group. These hello packets contain the group ID of the HSRP group and the advertised priority of the router sending the hello.

Based on a priority system, one router assumes the role of the active router in the group. Other routers will adopt the standby condition. Active routers, on receipt of a packet that needs to be forwarded, will forward the packet. Standby routers will drop the packet, even though they also have a route.

This state remains static as long as the hello packets are continually received from the active router. Should these fail to arrive, then after the hold time has been exceeded, the next senior standby router assumes the active role and starts to forward packets. The default hold timer is 10 seconds, but is configurable.

Figure 9.11 shows the activity of the hello packets as they advertise their priorities on a specific standby group. The diagram shows router Terry sending hellos with a default priority of 100, and router Jack switched off. When router Jack is started, it sends out a hello with the configured priority of 105. Router Terry realizes that it is no longer the active router and now advertises that it is standby. Note that the hellos come from the "natural" Ethernet IP address.

**FIGURE 9.11** HSRP hello process

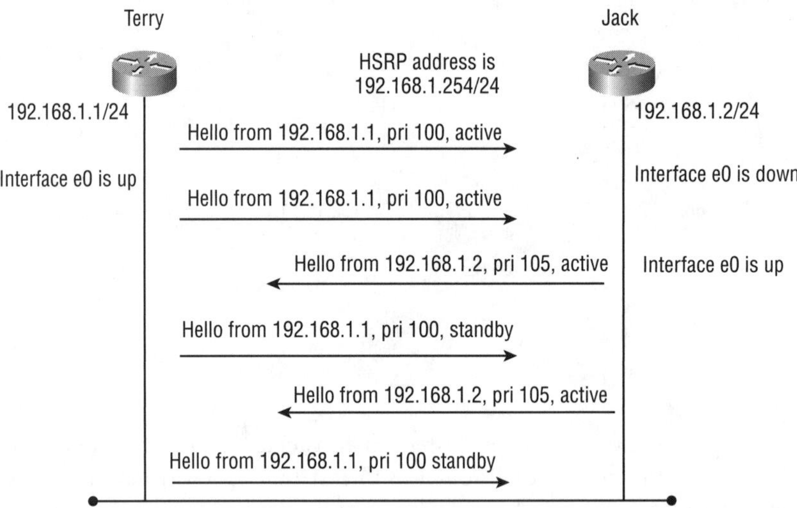


## Preemption

Preemption is the process whereby the router with the highest configured priority becomes the active router. In the case of HSRP, the highest priority is the highest number in the range 0–255 (one octet).

The result is that if an active router fails, and then comes back online, it is able to take over being the active router once again. Without the preempt process, the standby router that had become active would remain as the active router until a new election process was started.

### Interface Tracking

One additional advantage of the preemption process is that it allows the selection of the active router at arbitrary moments on a network without having to wait for formal elections. Thus if a standby router receives a hello from the active router and the active router is lower than its own configured priority, it will preempt and become active itself. By the same process, if an active router receives a hello from a router with a higher priority; it will cease to remain active.

This leads to a rather clever situation where a router can be configured to track another interface, with a view to reducing the standby priority on the standby interface should the other interface fail. There is a default reduction of 10, but this is configurable, allowing for complex scenarios to be created.

### Multiple HSRP Groups

Within a group of VLANs, there will be more than one default gateway specified. If the Cisco advice of a subnet per VLAN is followed, then there will be the same number of default gateways.

Redundancy is both expensive and necessary, but we need not create full redundancy by having each default gateway backed up by another physical device. We can use multiple HSRP groups to do this in a more cost-effective fashion. One router could be used to act as the standby router for several different groups.

Furthermore, it is possible to create two groups on a pair of routers, and make each router active in one group and standby in the other. In this way, each router would forward traffic for its own group while providing redundancy to the other, thus providing a kind of load sharing.

Given that this scenario can be expanded to a much larger implementation by creating up to 256 HSRP groups, it follows that some very complex configurations can be created to meet a variety of different needs.

## Configuring HSRP

To configure HSRP on a Cisco router, use the `standby ip` *`ip_address`* command in interface configuration mode.

```
Terry_1#conf t
Terry_1(config)#
Terry_1(config)#int e0
Terry_1(config-if)#standby ?
  <0-255>         group number
  authentication  Authentication string
  ip              Enable hot standby protocol for IP
  mac-address     Specify virtual MAC address for the virtual router
  mac-refresh     Refresh MAC cache on switch by periodically sending packet
                  from virtual mac address
  name            Name string
  preempt         Overthrow lower priority designated routers
  priority        Priority level
  timers          Hot standby timers
```

```
  track          Priority tracks this interface state
  use-bia        Hot standby uses interface's burned in address

Terry_1(config-if)#standby ip 172.16.1.254
Terry_1(config)#^Z
Terry_1#

Terry_1#show standby
Ethernet0 - Group 0
  Local state is Active, priority 100
  Hellotime 3 holdtime 10
  Next hello sent in 00:00:00.358
  Hot standby IP address is 172.16.1.254 configured
  Active router is local
  Standby router is unknown expired
  Standby virtual mac address is 0000.0c07.ac00
  2 state changes, last state change 00:03:34
Terry_1#
```

Note that if no HSRP group is specified, the default group of 0 is used, resulting in a standby MAC address of 0000.0c07.ac00 being used.

To configure preemption, use the `standby preempt` command in interface configuration mode:

```
Terry_1#conf t
Terry_1(config)#int e0
Terry_1(config-if)#standby preempt ?
  delay     Wait before preempting
  priority  Priority level
  <cr>

Terry_1(config-if)#standby preempt
Terry_1(config-if)#
Terry_1#
```

Note the options with this command. The `delay` option allows you to specify minimum delay timers prior to a router preempting. The `priority` option allows you to select which router is going to become the active router. The default is 100, and the highest priority wins.

To configure interface tracking, use the `standby track` command in interface configuration mode:

```
Terry_1#conf t
Terry_1(config)#int e0
Terry_1(config-if)#standby track ?
```

```
  Async               Async interface
  BRI                 ISDN Basic Rate Interface
  BVI                 Bridge-Group Virtual Interface
  Dialer              Dialer interface
  Ethernet            IEEE 802.3
  Lex                 Lex interface
  Loopback            Loopback interface
  Multilink           Multilink-group interface
  Serial              Serial
  Tunnel              Tunnel interface
  Virtual-Template    Virtual Template interface
  Virtual-TokenRing   Virtual TokenRing
  Vlan                Catalyst Vlans
Terry_1(config-if)#
Terry_1#
```

Shown next is the configuration for an active HSRP router, with a priority of 105, tracking interface serial 0, with authentication and modified timers:

```
Terry_1#show run
Building configuration...
!
output cut
!
hostname Terry_1
!
interface Ethernet0
 ip address 172.16.1.1 255.255.255.0
 no ip redirects
 standby timers 1 4 advertise 2
 standby priority 105 preempt
 standby authentication globalnet
 standby ip 172.16.1.254
 standby track Serial0
!
interface Serial0
 ip address 172.16.2.1 255.255.255.252
!
[output cut]
!
end
```

The dynamic information on the HSRP group and interface can be seen using the `show standby` command:

```
Terry_1#sho stand
Ethernet0 - Group 0
  Local state is Active, priority 105, may preempt
  Hellotime 1 holdtime 4 configured hellotime 1 secholdtime 4 sec
     advertise 2 secs
  Next hello sent in 00:00:00.004
  Hot standby IP address is 172.16.1.254 configured
  Active router is local
  Standby router is 172.16.1.2 expires in 00:00:03
  Standby virtual mac address is 0000.0c07.ac00
  2 state changes, last state change 00:40:59
  Tracking interface states for 1 interface, 0 up:
    up Serial0
Terry_1#
```

**Real World Scenario**

### HSRP in Action at the ISP Edge

Many Internet service providers (ISPs) use HSRP when providing dual-homed, resilient Internet connections. BGP is perfectly suitable for managing the flow of traffic to the client, and the ISP will certainly be running BGP in any case. But for the client end of the connection, where BGP may not be running and clients demand high-speed responses to link or topology failures, HSRP is a better bet.

An example would be where a customer is dual-homed to an ISP, with connections going from his site to different Points of Presence (POPs). It is possible to use a single router at the client site to connect both serial links to the client network, but that still leaves the router (in other words, the default gateway) as a single point of failure. Using more than one router makes the connection to the Internet more resilient, but would cause confusion among client PCs if multiple default gateway addresses were needed. HSRP allows the implementation of multiple routers with a common default gateway IP address and an automatic failover. The two HSRP routers would be configured with a common standby IP address as the default gateway, and prioritization used to select the active router and therefore the path taken out of the customer network. Symmetry (ensuring that return packets take the same path, whatever the active HSRP router) is achieved using BGP attribute manipulation. You can learn more about BGP in the *CCNP: Building Scalable Cisco Internetworks Study Guide* (Sybex, 2003).

## Server Load Balancing

The *Server Load Balancing (SLB)* protocol can be considered an extension to HSRP, which Cisco recommends should be already configured on the switches performing Server Load Balancing. The purpose of SLB is to share the load normally associated with multiple traffic streams terminating on a single server, across several servers.

A virtual server represents a cluster of real servers. Clients connect to the virtual address and—according to a load-balancing algorithm—to a selected real server. Obviously, clients and servers need to be on separate LANs or VLANs for SLB to work, because packets have to traverse the SLB switch.

Two different methods of load sharing may be used: weighted round robin (WRR) and weighted least connections (WLC). WRR specifies the next server to be connected to using a circular selection, modified by a weight that allows more clients to connect to particular servers prior to stepping to the next one. WLC connects to servers based on the number of existing active connections, weighting this with the server capacity, which can be specified.

It is also possible to use SLB to load-share between firewalls, in which case the real group of devices is called a firewalls farm.

### Configuring SLB

To configure SLB redundancy on a switch, use the `ip slb serverfarm` *`serverfarm_name`* global command. This will create a new prompt during which you can start to configure the SLB options. You then need to specify the virtual IP address to be used by clients wishing to connect to the servers under SLB control using the `real` *`ip-address`* `[port_number]` command, plus any other options that you want to select. You can configure more servers, but each server entry must be followed by the `inservice` command to enable the preceding server.

The second part of the configuration requires you to enter the global command `ip slb vserver` *`virtual_server-name`*, which changes the prompt again to the mode required to create the virtual IP address. Now you can enter the command `virtual ip-address [`*`network-mask`*`] {tcp | udp} [port-number | wsp | wsp-`*`wtp`*` | wsp-`*`wtls`*` | wsp-`*`wtp-wtls`*`] [service `*`service-name`*`]` to establish the virtual server IP address. Once again, you need to enter the `inservice` command to enable the specified IP address. Collectively, these commands will create a name for the server farm, associate it with the real IP addresses of the servers, and enable the process.

A basic configuration, providing a virtual IP address of 10.1.1.1 for a group called vserver_one, serving two e-mail servers with real IP addresses of 192.168.1.1 and 192.168.1.2, is shown next:

```
Terry_4840#configure terminal
Enter configuration commands, one per line.  End with CNTL/Z.
Terry_4840#(config)ip slb serverfarm email
Terry_4840#(config-slb-sfarm)real 192.168.1.1
Terry_4840#(config-slb-sfarm)inservice
Terry_4840#(config-slb-sfarm)real 192.168.1.2
Terry_4840#(config-slb-sfarm)inservice
Terry_4840#(config-slb-sfarm)exit
Terry_4840#(config)ip slb vserver vserver_one
Terry_4840#(config-slb-vserver)virtual 10.1.1.1 tcp 25
Terry_4840#(config-slb-vserver)serverfarm email
Terry_4840#(config-slb-vserver)inservice
Terry_4840#(config-slb-vserver)exit
Terry_4840#(config)^z
Terry_4840#
```

### SLB Stateful Backup

The most advanced configuration would be to implement SLB in a stateful backup mode. This involves configuring one virtual server group per VLAN, and using HSRP to determine which switch would act as the SLB active device. The configuration of more switches, each one acting as the default for a different VLAN (or VLANs), would mean that load sharing could be on a per-VLAN basis, with a range of complex possibilities for full redundancy.

## Virtual Router Redundancy Protocol

HSRP is a Cisco proprietary protocol, only usable on Cisco devices. Nonetheless, it is such a useful protocol that other vendors have wanted something similar in the open standards domain.

The *Virtual Router Redundancy Protocol (VRRP)* is an Internet standard, defined in RFC 2338. Specifically, VRRP specifies the protocol responsible for selecting one of a group of VRRP routers on a LAN to be the Master. Any of the virtual router IP addresses on the LAN may be used as the default router by hosts using a statically configured default gateway.

The Master VRRP router forwards packets sent to IP addresses associated with the VRRP group. As with HSRP, the election process has dynamic failover should the Master become unavailable.

There seems to be no obvious benefit to changing over to VRRP if you are already running HSRP in a satisfactory configuration. But if you intend to mix with some non-Cisco routers, or have a bee in your bonnet about proprietary protocols, then a change may be required.

## Gateway Load Balancing Protocol

As a grand generalization, the *Gateway Load Balancing Protocol (GLBP)* can be regarded as an alternative to both HSRP and VRRP, in that GLBP also provides a virtual default gateway as the target for hosts on an Ethernet. The main difference between the protocols is that both HSRP and VRRP select an active router, and the standby routers are not used at all.

GLBP uses the same principle for the virtual IP address as the default gateway, but uses more than one virtual MAC address to bind this to. This has the impact of allowing hosts to select different routers as the default gateway while still using the virtual IP address that guarantees redundancy.

GLBP is very similar to HSRP, apart from the fact that more than one MAC address will be used to map to the virtual IP address. It may be hard to see why you should choose to use GLBP, given the fact that HSRP has such a large following. In fact, the load-sharing capacity of GLBP, while very useful, can almost be achieved by HSRP if you have several VLANs to support, as each VLAN can be configured with its own default gateway mapped to a unique HSRP group.

Nonetheless, when using HSRP in a single VLAN environment, and with a single default gateway address, it is true that only one router will be forwarding in the group. GLBP will change that.

The design of the GLBP group is very simple in basic networks, but in large networks where you require multiple groups, time must be taken to consider how different groups can interact.

Remember to plan your entire configuration beforehand, because this protocol starts running as soon as it is enabled.

Many of the commands that you have seen in HSRP have a parallel inside GLBP, so don't expect any surprises in the next sections.

## Active Gateway Selection

The active gateway is selected using a similar mechanism to HSRP. GLBP routers are configured with a priority (the default is 100) and the one with the highest priority becomes the active router, called the *Active Virtual Gateway (AVG)* on GLBP. As with HSRP, non-AVG routers in the same group provide router redundancy.

Once a router is elected to AVG, the clever part begins. The AVG now allocates virtual MAC addresses to other members of the group. All routers in the group forward packets, but each router is individually responsible for forwarding packets addressed to their assigned virtual MAC address.

## Addressing

Up to four virtual MAC addresses are possible per GLBP group. The non-AVG routers are assigned MAC addresses in sequence by the AVG. A non-AVG router is referred to as an *active virtual forwarder (AVF)*.

AVF routers fall into two categories. Any one assigned a virtual MAC address by the AVG directly is known as a primary virtual forwarder. Group members arriving late do not know the real IP address of the AVG and use hellos to discover its identity. They are then allocated MAC addresses and are known as secondary virtual forwarders.

## Prioritization, Redundancy, and Failover

If the AVG fails, then an election takes place to determine which AVF will take over and be responsible for allocating MAC addresses. This election uses the same principle as the initial election, and the remaining routers select a new AVG based on the (configurable) priorities of the remaining routers. The highest priority wins. To configure the priority on an interface in GLBP mode, use the `glbp` *group* `priority` *level* interface command.

As with HSRP, the ability for a higher priority router to become the AVG, and even the delay before the election is forced, can be configured. To do either of these things, use the interface command `glbp` *group* `preempt [delay` *minimum seconds*`]`.

Additionally, interfaces can be tracked (as in HSRP), with the result that failed interfaces cause the priority of a router to be reduced by a configurable amount. This has the effect of forcing a new election for the position of AVG. To track interfaces and change the priority based on an interface failure, use the interface command `glbp` *group* `weighting track` *object-number* [*decrement value*].

## Load Balancing

Up to 1024 separate GLBP groups can be established, each with its own AVG. Different user groups (VLANs, for example) can be configured with different group AVGs as their default gateways, thus sharing out the traffic loading.

## Configuring GLBP

To configure GLBP on a Cisco router, use the `glbp` *group* `ip` [*ip-address* [*secondary*]] command in interface configuration mode.

```
Terry_1#conf t
Terry_1(config)#
Terry_1(config)#int fastethernet 0/0
Terry_1(config-if)#ip address 10.1.1.1
Terry_1(config-if)#glbp 99 ip 10.1.1.254
Terry_1(config-if)#glbp 99 priority 105
Terry_1(config-if)#glbp 99 preempt delay 10
Terry_1(config-if)#glbp 10 weighting track int S0 10
Terry_1(config)#^Z
Terry_1#
```

This configuration shows a router configured with a single GLBP group. The regular IP address is set to 10.1.1.1. The virtual address is 10.1.1.254 and the priority is set to 105, so in the absence of other routers having their default priority of 100 changed, this will be the AVG for group 10. In addition, interface serial 0 is being tracked, and if it fails, the priority drops to 95, allowing a router with a default 100 priority to take over as AVG. Also, if interface serial 0 comes up again, then this router will preempt and take back over the task of AVG.

To view the entered configuration, use the standard `show running-config` command:

```
interface fastethernet 0/0
 ip address 10.1.1.1 255.0.0.0
 glbp 99 ip 10.1.1.255
```

```
glbp 99 preempt delay minimum 10
glbp 99 priority 105
glbp 99 weighting track interface S0 10
```

## Transparent Ethernet

Ethernet has become a clear winner in the LAN environment, for all the reasons that we have considered in this book. Factors such as cost, simplicity of implementation, and scalability have been powerful reasons to select Ethernet. In this chapter, we have focused on how to provide reliable and QoS-driven Ethernet networks.

It's not too much of a step to consider that this very friendly protocol may have uses beyond the LAN—perhaps into the metropolitan area, and maybe, somehow, into the wide area. After all, with the end of shared media LANs and the advent of duplex connectivity, distance is not the same problem as it was. And with Ethernet data rates many times the data rates of traditional WAN services, replacing some MAN and WAN links with Ethernet seems very seductive.

Many Cisco Ethernet switches now have special "metro" interfaces; sometimes even a particular switch is manufactured specifically to provide the correct interfaces needed to drive the signals much further. Services such as these are available in the 3550, 4000, and 6500 series switches.

New technologies are under development, including the ability to encapsulate Ethernet into either SONET or SDH frames, thus allowing Ethernet to be transported over unlimited distances.

SONET (Synchronous Optical Networks), widely used in the USA, and SDH (Synchronous Digital Hierarchy), used throughout the rest of the world, are ultra-high-speed technologies used to transport data over fiber-optic cables.

In fact, several technologies exist that allow Ethernet to be transported inside another protocol over unlimited distances, including:

- Long-distance Ethernet-over-fiber (EOF) using Cisco Catalyst switches
- Ethernet over SONET or SDH
- Ethernet over DWDM
- Ethernet inside IP using MPLS
- Ethernet tunneled over native IP using Layer 2 Tunneling Protocol version 3 (L2TPv3)

The benefit to the end user of these services is in the way that the network is perceived. Because the wide or metropolitan connection now behaves like a LAN, users can connect using standard broadcast protocols to servers and services that are large distances away. VLANs can be extended into other offices, and mobile users may be able to connect directly to their regular VLAN even when in a remote company site. Because the network would like Ethernet end-to-end, the term *transparent Ethernet* has been coined.

This is still new to service providers, and not all ISPs provide all services—in fact, some don't provide transparent Ethernet at all. But transparent Ethernet is still in its early stages, and as the Internet becomes more stable and the QoS that we have covered in this chapter becomes more widespread, we are likely to see transparent Ethernet cropping up in the strangest of places.

The IEEE is in the process of considering standards for running Ethernet in the metropolitan area network. This is called Ethernet in the First Mile (EFM) and the appropriate standard is IEEE 802.3ah. Consideration is being given to different subscriber topologies using point-to-point connections over the existing copper infrastructure.

# Summary

Quality of Service is a broad descriptive term, and can be applied to a variety of different processes. Traditional network design is driven by throughput and reliability. Tomorrow's networks will be driven by the need to support multimedia, time-sensitive applications. Today's networks are somewhere in between.

When considering reliability, many factors need to be taken into account. All over the network, single points of failure abound, from the host PC right through to the Internet access router. We cannot hope to solve all of the problems in one go, and it may not be our responsibility to do so. But we can focus on the areas where we can have a large impact. HSRP is one of those areas, where a failure of the default gateway is such a critical factor that Cisco developed a proprietary protocol, HSRP, to manage the problem.

The second side to QoS is the approach taken to try to provide connection-oriented-like services over best efforts networks. This is a serious challenge, as both Ethernet (at the Data Link layer) and IP (at the Network layer) provide genuine best-efforts connectivity, and without the addition of extra content, we would make no progress.

The result has been a spate of new protocol extensions developed by various standards bodies, from the IEEE to the IETF. In IP, we have the Type of Service bits, and their new implementation, the Differentiated Services Code Points. In Ethernet, we have the Class of Service extensions to 802.1Q, specified in 802.1p. Naturally, the DSCP is supported properly only in layer 3 switches, but there is some automatic mapping between the layers in the higher-specification switches.

Cisco switches, at layer 2 and layer 3, support a variety of these new protocols, although they are somewhat limited as yet. This is partly because we in the networking community have yet to achieve consensus on what we want and how we will implement it. When we provide the lead, you can be sure the IOS will follow.

# Exam Essentials

**Understand what Quality of Service is.** QoS is a combination of processes and procedures for trying to enhance the service usually allocated to a frame or packet delivered by a best efforts network. This involves identifying the data, marking it, and then using that marking as a key for how the data will be managed inside queues across a network.

**Understand why some applications benefit from QoS.** Not every application benefits greatly from applying priorities to its data. Many legacy applications are built to run as store-and-forward flows, and are satisfied with the simple reliability that they get from TCP. E-mail, FTP, and so on do not have the same urgency as mission-critical data with a delay limit. In addition, some applications place considerable demands across the network because although the bandwidth needs may be small, they cannot manage jitter. Defined as the variation in *latency* between successive frames or packets, jitter spells the death knell for multimedia applications.

**Understand what QoS features Cisco switches can support.** Not every Cisco switch can support every QoS feature. This is true largely because QoS can be applied at either layer 2 or layer 3. Some Cisco switches are simple layer 2 devices, whereas others have so much layer 3 capability that they could easily be called routers. Obviously, layer 2 switches cannot support layer 3 QoS. Layer 2 QoS is limited to setting and responding to the TOS bits inside the 802.1p extension to 802.1Q. Layer 3 QoS uses either the TOS bits from legacy IPv4, or the newer DSCP implementation of the same field. Both can be mapped to the layer 2 TOS at a device supporting both layers.

**Understand how to configure QoS on Cisco switches.** There are still different versions of operating systems on Cisco switches. From the 4000 and 6500 running CatOS, to the same switches running IOS, to the 3550 running a full IOS and the 2950 running IOS in either the standard or enhanced image options, many differences occur. Using the basic information regarding layer 2 and layer 3 QoS, you need to be able to configure any of these switches for QoS. Remember that the BCMSN exam has simulations and is new, so there may be more in the future. Simulations carry several extra marks, so make sure you are familiar with all the commands in this book.

**Understand how redundancy is achieved using Cisco switches and routers.** Redundancy can be applied to many places in the network, but this course, focusing as it does upon the campus network, exposes the fact that most PCs use a default gateway to get off-LAN. This critical device can be a single point of failure. Cisco's HSRP and less commonly VRRP can be used to provide that redundancy. By creating a virtual router IP address and using that as the default gateway, we can configure more than one router to be prepared to forward data sent to the group, with options for prioritized selection and preempting of control. Both SLB and GLBP can be used to load share the cross-router traffic.

# Key Terms

Before you take the exam, be sure you're familiar with the following terms:

active virtual forwarder (AVF)
Active Virtual Gateway (AVG)
auto-QoS
best efforts network
buffer overflows
classification
Custom Queuing
Differentiated Services
discard eligible
first in, first out
Gateway Load Balancing Protocol (GLBP)
Hot Standby Router Protocol (HSRP)
IEEE 802.1p
Integrated Services
isochronous
latency
laws of physics delay
line loss
Multistage Queuing
output buffer priorities
per-hop routing
policing
Priority Queuing
processing delay
Quality of service (QoS)
queue disposition
serialization delay
Server Load Balancing (SLB)
transparent Ethernet
Virtual Router Redundancy Protocol (VRRP)
Weighed Fair Queuing (WFQ)
Weighted Round Robin Queuing

# Written Lab

Write the answers to the following questions:

1. What command enables QoS on a 3550 switch?
2. What is the command used to display QoS information on a 4000 switch running CatOS?
3. Write the command to set the bandwidth of the Weighted Round Robin Queues on a 2950 to 40, 30, 20, and 10, respectively.
4. What mode is used to enable QoS on an IOS-based switch?
5. What match options in a class-map are available on a 2950 switch running standard edition software?

6. What is the interface command to enable auto-QoS for a connected Cisco IP phone to be implemented?
7. Write the command to set the class of service to 0 for the only configurable threshold on queue 1 of a 2q1t port on a Catalyst 4000 running CatOS.
8. What command is used to display information about the QoS configuration, with respect to DSCP mapping, on a 3550 switch?
9. What is the command used to set the HSRP priority to 105?
10. What is the default hello timer for HSRP?

# Review Questions

1. Which of the following describes isochronous data transfer most accurately?
   A. Time sensitive
   B. Delay sensitive
   C. Reliable
   D. Connection oriented
2. Which of the following describes SLB most accurately?
   A. An alternative to HSRP
   B. A protocol allowing server load sharing
   C. A server redundancy protocol
   D. An alternative to switching
3. Which of the following best describes a best efforts network?
   A. Unreliable
   B. Guaranteed
   C. Connectionless
   D. Streaming
4. Which of the following best describes jitter?
   A. Packets arriving with variations in delay
   B. Packets arriving later than expected
   C. Packets arriving all at once
   D. Packets not arriving at all
5. Which of the following best describes TOS (Type of Service)?
   A. TOS is the classification of different IP streams.
   B. TOS is a field in the IP header that can be used to classify packets.
   C. TOS is applied by DiffServe routers to forward packets.
   D. TOS applies only to IPv6.
6. Which of the following best describes DiffServe?
   A. Packets marked and forwarded by each DiffServe router
   B. Packets forwarded by each DiffServe router using per-hop forwarding according to TOS
   C. Packets following a predetermined path through the DiffServe cloud
   D. Packets forwarded using DiffServe parameters

7. Which of the following might cause variable delay in packet forwarding? (Choose all that apply.)
   A. Congested switches
   B. First in, first out queuing
   C. Varying frame sizes in the switch output buffers
   D. Unstable network topology

8. Which protocol defines Type of Service at the Data Link layer?
   A. 802.1D
   B. 802.1Q
   C. DiffServe
   D. 802.1p

9. What queuing mechanisms are supported by the 2950 switches, running standard edition IOS software? (Choose all that apply.)
   A. Custom Queuing
   B. Low Latency Priority Queuing
   C. Weighted Round Robin Queuing
   D. Strict Priority Queuing
   E. First in, first out queuing

10. What is a policy-map used for?
   A. To set the different classes of service
   B. To determine which traffic is to be matched to specific criteria to be set for incoming traffic
   C. To determine the classification criteria to be set for incoming traffic
   D. To define the match criteria when classifying traffic

11. What is a class-map used for?
   A. To set the different classes of service
   B. To define the match criteria when classifying traffic
   C. To determine which traffic is to be matched to specific criteria to be set for incoming traffic
   D. To determine the classification criteria to be set for incoming traffic

12. Which of the following describes GLBP most accurately?
   A. An extension to HSRP
   B. An alternative to HSRP
   C. A replacement for HSRP
   D. A firewall load balancing protocol

13. If a `show port capabilities` command on a 4000 series router tells you that a port is type 2q1t, what does that mean?
    A. The port has two configurable queues, with one drop threshold.
    B. The port has one configurable queue with two drop thresholds.
    C. The port has the option of one or two configurable queues.
    D. The port has two queues but a single timer.

14. What queue types are supported on the 2950 switch?
    A. One normal priority and two configurable high priority
    B. One normal priority and four configurable high priority
    C. One normal priority and one configurable high priority
    D. One normal priority or our configurable high priority

15. Which of the following services could be described as supporting transparent Ethernet LANs? (Choose all that apply.)
    A. Ethernet over Fiber
    B. Ethernet over ADSL
    C. Ethernet over DWDM
    D. Ethernet over IP networks
    E. Ethernet over wireless

16. Which of the following best describes Weighted Round Robin Queuing?
    A. A queuing mechanism where each queue is the same length and is serviced in turn
    B. A queuing mechanism where each queue is of configurable length and is serviced in turn
    C. A queuing mechanism where each queue is of different length and is serviced in priority of size
    D. A queuing mechanism where each queue is of configurable length and is serviced using strict priority

17. What is the default QoS configuration on a 3550 switch?
    A. QoS is globally disabled, so no classification occurs.
    B. QoS is globally enabled, so a default classification is applied.
    C. QoS is globally disabled; packets arriving with the DSCP set will be discarded.
    D. QoS is globally disabled; packets arriving with the DSCP set will be forwarded, but error messages will be created.

18. How does auto-QoS discover whether a Cisco IP telephone is connected to a switch port?
    A. Cisco proprietary IP hellos
    B. Cisco Discovery Protocol (CDP)
    C. It does not discover; you have to manually configure the interface.
    D. Enhanced Cisco Discovery Protocol (ECDP)

**19.** Which of the following best describes the preempt function in HSRP?

**A.** Can take over when active fails

**B.** Works only in groups of two routers

**C.** Will not release to higher priority routers

**D.** Will take over from lower-priority active routers

**20.** Which of the following interface commands sets the standby IP address on an interface to 192.168.1.200?

**A.** `standby ip address 192.168.1.200`

**B.** `hsrp address 192.168.1.200`

**C.** `standby ip 192.168.1.200`

**D.** `ip address 192.168.1.200 standby`

# Hands-On Lab

In this lab, you will configure two HSRP groups, with one of the routers acting as the active gateway for one VLAN and vice versa. Refer to Figure 9.12 for the topology of this lab. This lab will use the two routers shown to configure HSRP in such a way as to provide load sharing to the Internet for attached hosts.

**FIGURE 9.12** Network diagram for the hands-on lab

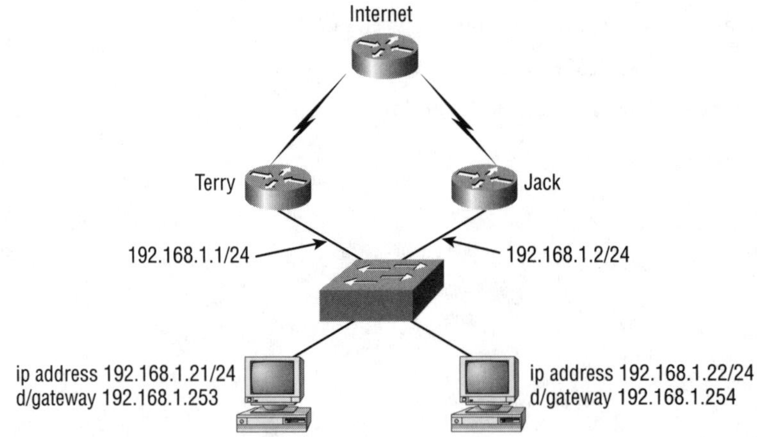


First, make sure the configurations of your routers and switches are fully deleted. Then configure the switch with the basic hostname and password details as covered in Chapter 2, "Connecting the Switch Block." Create and name one VLAN, and assign ports to the VLAN as shown in the diagram. These configuration commands were covered in Chapter 3. On the routers, set the hostname and passwords also, using standard IOS commands.

1. Now set the IP addresses on the two PCs to the values in the diagram, and remember to set the default gateways to the values shown as the correct standby group IP address of the HSRP router pair. Note that the two PCs, although belonging to the same subnet, use different default gateway addresses.
2. Configure the two HSRP routers with individual IP addresses on the Ethernet interfaces. Test that the Ethernet is working properly by pinging between routers. Here are the commands:

```
Terry#conf t
Terry(config)#int e0
Terry(config-if)#ip address 192.168.1.1 255.255.255.0

Jack#conf t
Jack(config)#int e0
Jack(config-if)#ip address 192.168.1.2 255.255.255.0
```

3. Configure the two HSRP routers with individual IP addresses on the serial interfaces. As you are using a null-modem cable, remember to configure a clock on the DCE end of the cable, and to start up the interfaces. Here are the commands:

```
Terry1#conf t
Terry1(config)#int s0
Terry1(config-if)#ip address 192.168.2.1 255.255.255.0
Terry1(config-if)#clock rate 64000
Terry1(config-if)#no shutdown
Terry1(config-if)#exit
Terry1(config)#router rip
Terry1(config-router)#network 192.168.1.0
Terry1(config-router)#network 192.168.2.0
Terry1(config)#^c

Jack#conf t
Jack(config)#int s0
Jack(config-if)#ip address 192.168.3.1 255.255.255.0
Jack(config-if)#clock rate 64000
Jack(config-if)#no shutdown
Jack(config-if)#exit
Jack(config)#router rip
Jack(config-router)#network 192.168.1.0
Jack(config-router)#network 192.168.3.0
Jack(config)#^c
```

4. Configure the Internet router to connect to the two HSRP routers over the serial links. Here are the commands:

```
Internet#conf t
Internet(config)#int s0
Internet(config-if)#ip address 192.168.2.2 255.255.255.0
Internet(config)#no shutdown
Internet(config)#int s1
Internet(config-if)# ip address 192.168.3.2 255.255.255.0
Internet(config-if)#no shutdown
Internet(config)#^c
```

5. In order to test the path that packets take through the network, we need to configure a target IP address. We will do this by configuring interface loopback 0 on the Internet router as follows:

```
Internet#conf t
Internet(config)# int lo0
Internet(config-if)#ip address 192.168.4.1 255.255.255.0
```

6. We now need to build a simple routing table, just to allow us to test the configuration. Use RIP v1, and remember to include the locally connected networks to each router in the configuration. For example:

```
Internet#conf t
Internet(config)#router rip
Internet(config-router)#network 192.168.2.0
Internet(config-router)#network 192.168.3.0
Internet(config-router)#network 192.168.4.0
Internet(config)#^c
```

7. Now we need to build the HSRP configuration proper. This configuration is carried out only on the two HSRP routers. The router called Terry will be the active router for group 1, and the router Jack will be the active router for group 2. Each router will act as the standby router for the other HSRP group.

```
Terry(config)#int e0
Terry(config-if)#standby 1 ip 192.168.1.253
Terry(config-if)#standby 1 priority 105
Terry(config-if)#standby 1 preempt
Terry(config-if)#standby 2 ip 192.168.1.254
Terry(config-if)#standby 2 preempt

Jack(config)#int e0
Jack(config-if)#standby 1 ip 192.168.1.253
Jack(config-if)#standby 1 preempt
Jack(config-if)#standby 2 ip 192.168.1.254
Jack(config-if)#standby 2 preempt
Jack(config-if)#standby 2 priority 105
```

8. We must test this configuration. If you have a traceroute application running on your PC, you can easily trace the route a packet takes. If not, then you must do the following:

   Open a command window on the PC, and start a continuous ping to the loopback address of the Internet router. Once the ping starts to be returned, open the console window on both routers and enter the command **debug ip packet detail**.

   This command will show which of the two routers is carrying the IP traffic from the ping. Testing using pings from both PCs should show that traffic from one travels via the router Terry and the other transmits via the router Jack.

9. The last part of the lab is to see what happens when a failure occurs. First, we need to carry out some additional configuration.

   We have already set the priority for the active router to 105 (remember that the default is 100). Now we need to make sure that when the serial link fails, the active router becomes standby. This involves tracking the serial interface, as shown in the following commands:

```
Terry(config)#int e0
Terry(config-if)#standby 1 track serial 0
Terry(config)#^c

Jack(config)#int e0
Jack(config-if)#standby 2 track serial 0
Jack(config)#^c
```

10. To test the tracking configuration, start a continuous ping as in step 8, and determine the path taken.

    Remove the serial cable carrying the ping traffic and see the interruption in the returned pings to the PC. After a few seconds, the pings should resume, demonstrating that the second router has become active.

    For a different view of the same event, enter the command **debug standby**, and restore the serial connection. You should see the hello packets change to include the higher value once the serial link becomes active, and the standby router will preempt. This should cause no loss to returned pings at all.

# Answers to Written Lab

1. `mls qos`
2. `show qos info config`
3. `wrr-queue bandwidth 40 30 20 10`
4. Global configuration mode
5. access-group, input-interface, mpls, protocol
6. `auto qos voip cisco-phone`
7. `set qos map 2q1t 2 1 cos 0`
8. `show mls qos map cos-dscp`
9. `standby priority 105`
10. 3 seconds

# Answers to Review Questions

1. A. The word *isochronous* comes from the Greek words iso (equal) and chrono (time). So isochronous traffic is time sensitive.

2. B. SLB stands for Server Load Balancing, and although some redundancy may be configured, it is designed to load-balance connections across more than one server.

3. A. Best efforts networks deliver datagrams as best they can. Without any additional features, such as acknowledgments and requests for retransmission, they are regularly termed unreliable.

4. A. Jitter is the term used to describe the effect caused by successive packets arriving with different delay times.

5. B. Inside IPv4, the limited provisions for prioritization are encoded in the 3 bits entitled Type of Service.

6. B. Differentiated Services (DiffServe) provides no integrated capabilities. Each DiffServe router must be configured to forward data using local priorities.

7. A, B, C, D. In a best efforts network, almost anything can cause delay to occur, and to occur variably.

8. D. Inside the 802.1Q standard for VLAN definition, 3 bits are allocated to the priority of the Ethernet frame. These 3 bits are fully defined inside 802.1p.

9. C, D, E. Custom Queuing and Low Latency Priority Queuing are usually associated with layer 3 functionality in the IOS.

10. C. Class-maps define the criteria for matching, and policy-maps define the classification for setting.

11. B. Class-maps define the criteria for matching , and policy-maps define the classification for setting.

12. B. Gateway Load Balancing Protocol operates in almost exactly the same way as HSRP, but with the added advantage of utilizing standby routers that HSRP does not utilize.

13. A. The queue type on a port is fixed in the hardware, and the `show port capabilities` command allows you to determine what you have.

14. B. Even so, the queues have some independence. You can just use the normal priority queue and FIFO, or you can enable QoS to get access to the other queues.

15. A, C, D. Although the technology for extending Ethernet is constantly under review, only Ethernet over Fiber, Ethernet over DWDM, and Ethernet over IP networks are correct.

16. B. Round robin queuing means servicing each queue in turn. Weighted means configuring the length of each queue to modify the fairness of the traffic distribution.

17. A. By default, QoS is disabled on all Cisco switches.

**18.** B. The proprietary Cisco Discovery Protocol multicasts machine properties based on a (configurable) timer. Cisco IP telephones therefore announce to Cisco switches that they are connected using a CDP hello.

**19.** D. Preemption allows HSRP routers to take over at any time if they have the highest configured priority in a group.

**20.** C. The interface command `standby ip` *`ip_address`* sets the standby IP address.

# Catalyst Switch Technologies

## THE CCNP EXAM TOPICS COVERED IN THIS CHAPTER INCLUDE THE FOLLOWING:

- ✓ **Identify the Cisco Route Switch processors and explain how they are implemented**
- ✓ **Understand the function of the Content Addressable Memory (CAM) and Ternary CAM (TCAM) within a Catalyst switch**
- ✓ **Describe how network analysis modules on Catalyst switches can be used to improve network traffic management**
- ✓ **Be able to convert CatOS to native IOS on Catalyst switches and manage native IOS images using best practice methods**
- ✓ **Describe the operation of both the Content Addressable Memory (CAM) and Ternary Content Addressable Memory (TCAM) as implemented in different Catalyst switches**

Cisco switches are at the forefront of modern technology, and comprise some of the most flexible devices on the market. But the changing nature of applications' demands upon switching is reflected in the variety in the range. Some of the older switches still use a bus technology on the backbone, whereas newer switches use a shared memory forwarding engine. The most modern employ a matrix fabric at the heart of the switch.

The reason for this is the continuing growth of multimedia applications. Voice and video place unique demands upon the network that can be satisfied only by a combination of high availability and configurable QoS. High availability means that the switches have to be non-blocking. In other words, we don't want them to get in the way!

In this chapter, you will learn what the different switch architectures are, and which type relates to which Cisco switch. I will explain how the switch memory functions, and how the bridging tables are stored and accessed. We will look at the different Cisco switches currently offered, and see how these technologies are implemented.

We end the chapter with a discussion of the techniques that can be used to manage and troubleshoot an integrated switch network.

# The Switching Process

All of the descriptions of the switching process contain the same words and phrases. We hear people using terms such as "wire speed" and "low latency," but these expressions don't tell us what is going on inside the switch, only how long it takes to happen! If you are anything like me, you want to know what goes on inside. But the inside of a switch is not like the inside of the family auto—taking it to bits doesn't always let you see the interesting stuff. Let me explain.

When frames arrive at an ingress interface, they must be buffered. Unless the switch is operating in cut-through or fragment-free mode, the frame check sequence needs to be calculated and tested against the arriving FCS. After the frame is confirmed as uncorrupted, it must be passed to a switching "fabric" of some sort, where it can go through the forwarding process to the egress interface.

This forwarding will be expedited by a table lookup process, which must be very quick if the frame is not to be delayed. Finally, there may be contention for the egress interface, and the frame will have to be held in a buffer until the output channel is clear. This complete process will involve a number of discrete steps taken by specific devices.

I am using the term *switching fabric* here for two reasons. First, you will hear the term used throughout the industry, often by people who are not quite sure what it means, but who will expect you to know. Second, because it is a broad descriptive term, without a single definition, and because I also intend to use it throughout this chapter. What I mean is the "heart" of the switch, where frames are redirected to an outgoing interface. It might be a crossbar, a bus, or shared memory. Read on and see what I mean.

## Switch Architecture and Components

Switches come in a variety of shapes and sizes, as you would expect; after all, as long as the standards are complied with when stated, how you make that happen can be entirely proprietary. And Cisco, which has a range of switches in the portfolio—some designed in-house and others the result of canny purchases—has more than one type of switch.

Modern switches differ from bridges because they support micro-segmentation, and because they do everything very quickly. So they have to be both scalable and efficient, which means that the architecture needs to be designed for the job. You can't make a world-class switch by purchasing chips from the corner shop and soldering them together.

So modern switches have a number of key components designed for specific purposes, and an architecture that describes how they are connected together.

### Non-Blocking Switches

The term non-blocking comes from the telecommunications industry, specifically that section concerned with telephone exchange design. It means that the *non-blocking switch* must have sufficient capacity in the switching fabric to be able to avoid delaying the frame forwarding. Figure 10.1 shows a non-blocking switch architecture, with eight Gigabit Ethernet interfaces and a 4Gb fabric. This would be the minimum fabric to be truly non-blocking.

**FIGURE 10.1** Non-blocking switch fabric

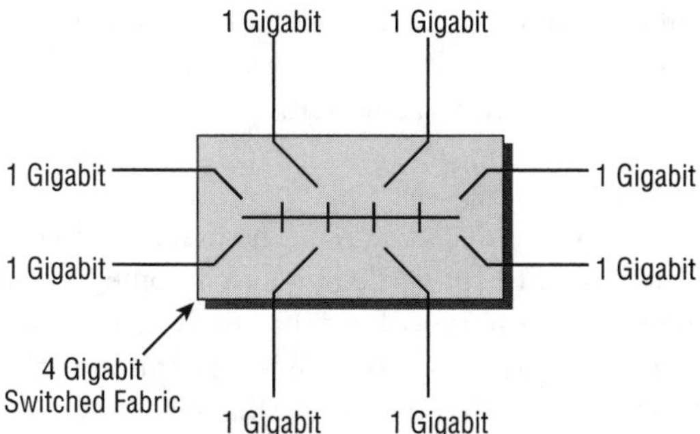

The comparison to telephone exchanges is worth following up, especially as we move toward VoIP. How often do you try to make a telephone call these days and get a tone that says "the exchange is busy"? Not very often, I'll bet. That is because modern telephone exchanges are non-blocking. But it wasn't always so. It has taken exchange and network designers some years to get to this advanced stage. And in the data communications industry, we are not there yet!

Now, it doesn't take too much effort to see that there are really only two ways to create this type of switch. You could use a *crossbar*, which has a cross-point for every possible interface pair in any given frame-forwarding action (crossbars are described fully in the next section), or you could have some sort of *shared memory* coupled to a multi-tasking operating system (also in the next section). Everything else will result at some time in a frame being queued because the fabric is busy. This has led to the rise of the term "essentially non-blocking."

Switches that are essentially non-blocking are so described because the manufacturers deem that the chances of frames being delayed in the fabric, or of any delays being significant, are almost non-existent. This gives the designers of such switches more leeway, and opens the door for fabrics comprising bus architectures.

The term "essentially non-blocking" is statistically sound when applied to telephone networks, as it sometimes is. That's because we can predict with some accuracy the distribution of telephone calls throughout the network across the day. This is less predictable with data, and some forwarding delays will occur. You have to keep an eye on your switch port statistics to ensure that it is not a problem on your network.

Non-blocking switches are sometimes referred to as *wire speed* switches, in an attempt to explain that, in the absence of any other delays, the switch can forward data at the same rate as which it is received.

## Switch Fabrics

There are three main switch fabrics in use today: bus, shared memory, and matrix. Each has its own advantages and disadvantages, and manufacturers select designs based upon the throughput demanded by the switch and the cost required to achieve it.

### Bus Switching Fabric

A *bus fabric* involves a single frame being forwarded at a time. The first issue that this raises is one of contention. Although the frames could be forwarded on a first-come first-served basis, this is unlikely to prove "fair" to all ports, and so most bus fabrics have a contention process involving a second bus just used for contention and access. The most common approach is for an ingress buffer to make a request for access to the forwarding bus when there is a queued frame. The resulting permission from some central logic allows the buffer to forward the frame to the forwarding bus.

Of course, this forwarding bus need not be a simple serial affair, where bits are transmitted one after the other. As the whole frame is already stored in a buffer prior to being forwarded, the bus could be parallel, allowing the frame to be forwarded much more quickly. For example, a 48-bit-wide bus clocked at only 25MHz would result in a possible throughput of 1.2Gbs/second.

Figure 10.2 shows four line cards connected to a shared bus switching fabric.

**FIGURE 10.2** Bus switching fabric

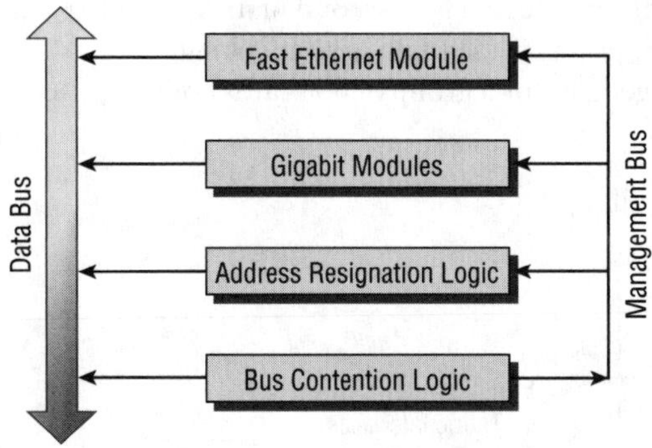


## Shared Memory Switching Fabric

Shared memory fabrics pass the arriving frame directly into a large memory block, where all of the checking for corruption is carried out. Corrupted frames are discarded from here.

The header of the frame is checked against the bridging table on the processor, which has direct access to the shared memory. The forwarding decision results in the frame being forwarded to the egress port, and scheduling or prioritization will be managed as the frame leaves the shared memory.

One advantage of shared memory fabrics is that the frame may only have to be queued once as it passes through the switch. Under light loads, very high throughput can be achieved from such architecture. In addition, the line cards don't need to have the same level of intelligence as with bus architectures, because there is no requirement for a contention mechanism to access the fabric.

Figure 10.3 shows four line cards connected to a shared memory fabric.

**FIGURE 10.3** Shared memory switching fabric

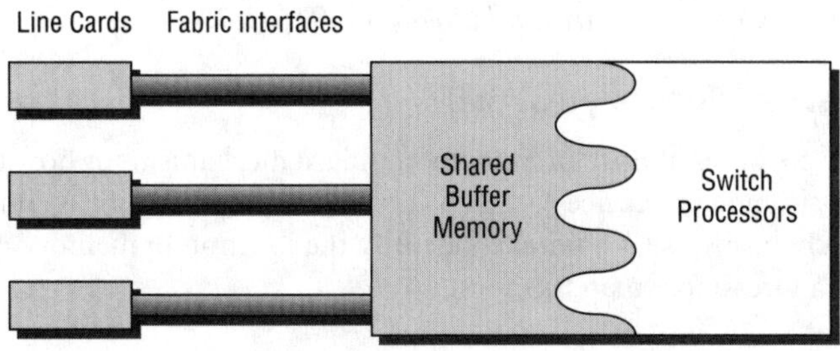

### Crossbar Switching Fabric

Crossbar switching uses a fabric composed of a *matrix*. In other words, the core of the switch is a series of cross-points, where every input interface has direct access to the matrix, resulting in a truly non-blocking architecture. This design is at the heart of many telephone switches.

What is common, however, is to reduce the size of the matrix by not giving every port its own path to the matrix, but instead giving every line card direct access. Of course, some prioritization and contention management is needed on the line cards, but the system is still extremely fast. Add to this the additional availability created by a second matrix (with line cards attached to each), and you might rightly refer to it as "essentially non-blocking."

Figure 10.4 shows the basic arrangement for a group of line cards connected to a single crossbar switch.

**FIGURE 10.4** Crossbar switching fabric

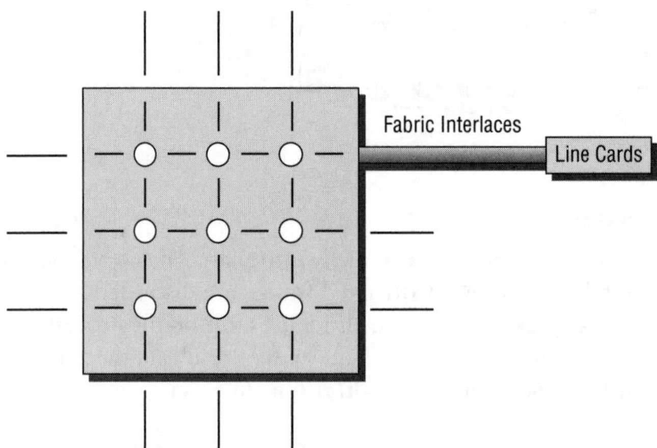


## Bridging Table Operation

Naturally, the bridging table is one of the most important parts of a switch. There is little point in being able to forward data at wire speed if it takes ages to make a decision as to where to forward it. The main mechanisms for table lookup in use today are the *Content Addressable Memory (CAM)* and the *Ternary Content Addressable Memory (TCAM)*.

### Content Addressable Memory (CAM)

CAM is not unique to Cisco, but is almost an industry standard mechanism for how the lookup process for data operates in modern devices. CAM is not the same as a traditional indexing method. These older mechanisms use a pointer to identify the location in memory of specific information (such as an address/port match).

With CAM, a precise relationship exists between the information in the data and its location in the data store. This means that all data with similar characteristics will be found close together in the store. CAM could therefore be defined as any kind of storage device that includes some comparison logic with each bit of data stored.

CAM is sometimes called *associative memory*.

### Ternary Content Addressable Memory (TCAM)

In normal CAM lookups, all of the information is important—in other words, there is nothing you wish to ignore. This is a function of the fact that binary has just the two bits, "ones" and "zeros." This is restricting, because time must be spent looking for a match for the whole data structure, 48 bits in a MAC address and 32 bits in an IP address.

Ternary mechanisms add a third option to the binary possibilities, that of "don't care," commonly shown as the letter *X*. This means that data can be searched for using a masking technique where we want to match 1s and 0s and ignores Xs.

For example, in a standard CAM, a lookup for the IP address 172.16.0.0 would require a match of 32 bits of 1s and 0s. But if we were trying to find a match on the network 172.16.0.0/16, then we really only need to match the first 16 bits. The result is a much faster lookup because we only have to search for the bits we want to match—extraneous bits would be flagged with a mask of Xs.

TCAMs are useful when there may be bits in a lookup that we can afford to ignore. Good examples are layer 2 and layer 3 forwarding tables and access control lists.

## Memory

One of the most important aspects of a switch is the memory. Switches are often presented with interfaces running at different speeds. In fact, the differences are commonly factors of 10 (10/100/1000 Ethernet). Combined with this possible bandwidth mismatch between interfaces, the fact that switches move frames from one interface to another at very high speed means that buffer space can fill up very quickly. The result is that the science of data buffering is quite advanced, and the simple serial shift-register memory of the past is no longer suitable.

The reason for using fixed-size buffers in the first place is not necessarily intuitive. You might think that better use would be made of shared memory by just placing arriving frames/packets into the next free space and making an entry in a table, rather like the way your hard drive manages files. But the problems that arise from this are in fact very similar to the hard drive file storage mechanism. In short, how do we use space that has been released after data has been forwarded from memory?

Obviously, the space made available after a packet has left the memory block is likely to be the wrong size to exactly fit the next occupant. If the next packet is too small, space will be wasted. If it is too large, it won't fit, and we would need to fragment it. After a while, throughput would slow down and more and more packets would have to be chopped up for storage and reassembled for transmission. On our hard drive, we'd have to defragment our disk regularly. In shared memory, we'd just end up with smaller and smaller memory spaces, with the resulting loss of throughput.

Fixed size buffers allow us to control the way that memory is allocated.

## Rings

In order for arriving packets to be placed into the shared memory buffers, it is common to use a buffer control structure called a ring. Shared memory devices usually have two rings, one to control the receive packet buffering and one to control transmit packet buffering.

Rings act effectively as a control plane (if you have a telecommunications background, think out-of-band signaling) that carries information about which frame may go where.

## Contiguous Buffers

*Contiguous buffers* are fixed-size buffers where different units of data (frame, packet, and so on) are placed in separate buffers. This has the advantage of creating easily addressed blocks where data can quickly be both stored and accessed efficiently. In general, contiguous buffers are easy to manage. But there is also a disadvantage in that considerable space can be wasted if, for example, a 64-byte frame has to be placed into a 1500-byte buffer.

On Cisco switches (and routers) that use this method, the contiguous buffers are created in a variety of fixed sizes at startup of the switch. The size of the contiguous buffers is designed to be suitable for a variety of frames/packets of common sizes to be properly stored with the minimum of wasted space.

The contiguous buffering allocation can be most wasteful on routers, where the need to create buffers to support the MTU of all interfaces may mean that some buffers as large as 18 kilobytes may be reserved (FDDI or high-speed token ring, for example). Under these circumstances, very few frames or packets may demand a buffer this large, but once created, the memory is not available for other purposes. And the maximum memory on switches and routers may be quite limited.

Figure 10.5 shows the disadvantages of the contiguous buffering system. Despite the different-sized buffers that have been created, there is always going to be waste.

**FIGURE 10.5** Contiguous buffering

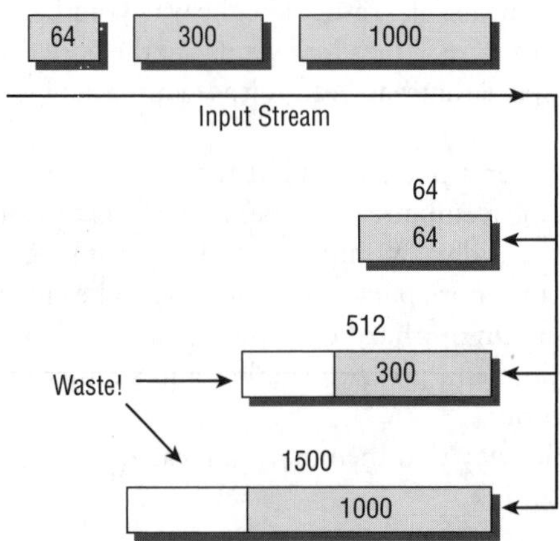

Shown next is the output of the `show buffers` command executed on a WS-C2950-24 switch. You can see the sizes of the system buffers, and the default number that are created at startup by this particular switch.

```
Terry_2950#show buffers
Buffer elements:
     500 in free list (500 max allowed)
     58 hits, 0 misses, 0 created

Public buffer pools:
Small buffers, 104 bytes (total 52, permanent 25, peak 52 @ 00:16:09):
     52 in free list (20 min, 60 max allowed)
     50 hits, 9 misses, 0 trims, 27 created
     0 failures (0 no memory)
Middle buffers, 600 bytes (total 30, permanent 15, peak 39 @ 00:16:09):
     30 in free list (10 min, 30 max allowed)
     24 hits, 8 misses, 9 trims, 24 created
     0 failures (0 no memory)
Big buffers, 1524 bytes (total 5, permanent 5):
     5 in free list (5 min, 10 max allowed)
     4 hits, 0 misses, 0 trims, 0 created
     0 failures (0 no memory)
VeryBig buffers, 4520 bytes (total 0, permanent 0):
     0 in free list (0 min, 10 max allowed)
     0 hits, 0 misses, 0 trims, 0 created
     0 failures (0 no memory)
Large buffers, 5024 bytes (total 0, permanent 0):
     0 in free list (0 min, 5 max allowed)
     0 hits, 0 misses, 0 trims, 0 created
     0 failures (0 no memory)
Huge buffers, 18024 bytes (total 0, permanent 0):
     0 in free list (0 min, 2 max allowed)
     0 hits, 0 misses, 0 trims, 0 created
     0 failures (0 no memory)

Interface buffer pools:
Calhoun Packet Receive Pool buffers, 1560 bytes (total 512, permanent 512):
     480 in free list (0 min, 512 max allowed)
     56 hits, 0 misses

Terry_2950#
```

You can change the buffer allocations by using the `buffers` *`buffer_size buffer_setting number`* command, but this is a skilled task with considerable ramifications. If too much memory is allocated to buffers, performance will suffer. If you think you need to alter the default buffer allocations, either liaise with the Cisco TAC or, at the very least, model the impact on a non-production switch.

### Particle Buffers

*Particle buffers* are a new mechanism designed to overcome the limitations of the contiguous buffering system. Instead of allocating a contiguous block, particle-based systems allocate small, discontiguous blocks of memory called particles, which are then linked together to form a logically contiguous packet buffer. These packet buffers are therefore spread across multiple physical particles in different locations.

The advantage of this method is that no buffers of specific sizes need to be allocated in advance; instead, buffers are created as needed, and of the optimum size (within the limits of the particle sizes, which are usually split into pools of 128 and/or 512 bytes).

Figure 10.6 shows how the use of particles may not completely eliminate waste, but sure cuts it down to a minimum!

**FIGURE 10.6** Particle buffers

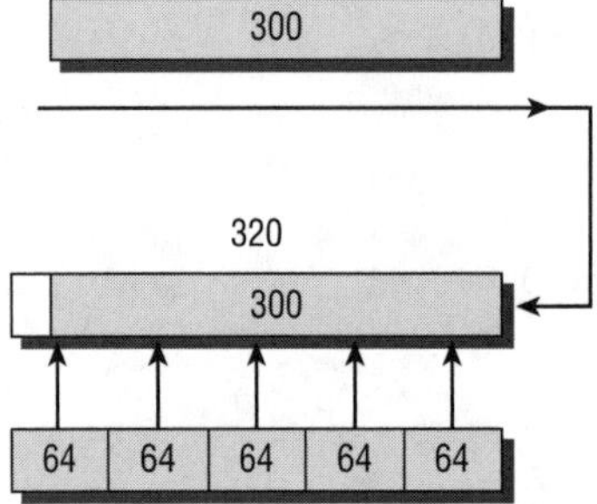


## Software

At the heart of the switch is the software. At the moment, a variety of different images appear in the range. This is partly because Cisco is in a transitional stage between the legacy operating systems of the older switches and the completion of the migration toward IOS-based switches. It is also partly because some switches do more than just layer 2 switching. The minute a switch operates at layer 3, it is, in effect, a router as well—which means a router-compliant IOS.

The two main issues that you must understand when considering software are

- On a 2950 switch, is the IOS *Standard Image (SI)* or *Enhanced Image (EI)*?
- On a 4000 or 6500 series switch, is the IOS a hybrid of CatOS and IOS, or is it true IOS?

## 2950 Series Software

Taking the first subject first, Cisco produces the IOS for the 2950 in two versions, Standard Image and Enhanced Image. The images are platform dependent, and when you buy a switch with SI installed, you cannot upgrade to EI.

### Standard Image IOS

The SI is installed on the 2950SX-24, 2950-12, and 2950-24. The SI supports basic IOS functionality, and includes functionality to support basic data, video, and voice services at the access layer. In addition to basic layer 2 switching services, the SI supports:

- IGMP snooping
- L2 CoS classification
- 255 multicast groups
- 8000 MAC addresses in up to 64 VLANs

### Enhanced Image IOS

The EI is installed on the 2950G-12, 2950G-24, 2950G-48, 2950G-24-DC, 2950T-24, and 2950C-24. The EI supports all features of the SI, plus several additions, including enhanced availability, security, and quality of service (QoS). In addition to the services provided by the SI, the EI supports:

- 8000 MAC addresses in up to 250 VLANs
- 802.1s Multiple Spanning Tree Protocol
- 802.1w Rapid Spanning Tree Protocol
- Gigabit EtherChannel
- Port-based Access Control Lists
- DSCP support for up to 13 values
- Rate limiting on Gigabit Ethernet

A full breakdown of the components of both the SI and EI images is available at Cisco's website: `www.cisco.com/en/US/products/hw/switches/ps628/prod_bulletin09186a00800b3089.html`.

## 4000 and 6500 Series Software

The 6500 and 4000 series routers are the ones most exposed to the changing face of Cisco operating systems. Coming from a history of native CatOS, they have moved to a hybrid CatOS/IOS operating system, on the path to becoming fully IOS supported. These changes have brought with them increased functionality and faster throughput.

### CatOS/IOS Hybrids

The native operating system on the two platforms has always been *CatOS*, with the familiar set, show, and clear commands used for almost all control aspects. The introduction of routing and layer 3 switching features on a separate module created the concept of two operating systems on a single switch.

By using an internal telnet connection, or a separate console port on the front of the introduced module, access is gained to the IOS-based routing engine. The Catalyst 4000 4232-L3 module and the Catalyst 6000 Multilayer Switch Feature Card 1 (MSFC 1) and 2 (MSFC 2) fall into this category.

### Native IOS

There are some limitations to running two operating systems, not including the most obvious one of having to understand and remember two different sets of commands. The CatOS was written before Cisco acquired the Catalyst company, and represents a different configuration philosophy. It is cumbersome, unfriendly, and very limited when compared with the Cisco *IOS*, which is mature and flexible.

It makes sense to be able to integrate the complete layer 2 and layer 3 functionality available in the combined switching engines, and this can only be leveraged through the use of an operating system that understands everything. Enter IOS, ready to run in native format on the integrated platform.

Upgrading the IOS is a well-defined process involving a series of steps:

- Confirm that your platform will support the new IOS.
- Confirm that you have the correct IOS from Cisco.
- Establish a TFTP server that your switch can access.
- Ensure that your switch has sufficient flash memory for the new image.
- Copy the new IOS into flash.
- Reload the switch with the new IOS running.

A reference document on the Cisco website contains detailed instructions for the step-by-step upgrade process on all platforms (including the old 5000 series switches). It can be found at `www.cisco.com/en/US/products/hw/switches/ps700/products_tech_note09186a00801347e2.shtml`.

## Switches: The Current Range

The current Cisco range of switches represents the most powerful yet. Many of them have layer 3 switching capabilities in addition to layer 2, which means that they can almost be configured as a multi-port router. Many also run a version of the IOS as standard. The only two still running the set-based CatOS have an upgrade path to allow them to run IOS. Despite figuring in the current exam, CatOS is doomed.

This next section looks at the four main switch families in turn, and links together the technologies we have discussed so far in this chapter with the real world of Cisco products.

## 2950 Series Switches

The 2950 series comprises a number of fixed configuration switches that can be operated in a stand-alone fashion or joined together in a stack. There are two distinctly different IOS-based software images (which are platform dependent and not interchangeable), allowing users to purchase the most suitable system for their environment.

The Standard Image (SI) software offers IOS-based basic data, video, and voice services. The Enhanced Image (EI) software provides additional features such as advanced quality of service (QoS), rate limiting, and security filtering for more exposed locations in the topology.

All Catalyst 2950 and 2955 models have the Cisco Cluster Management Suite (CMS) software embedded in the operating system. (CMS is discussed later in this chapter.)

The basic architecture of the 2950 switches is shown in Figure 10.7.

**FIGURE 10.7** 2950 switch architecture

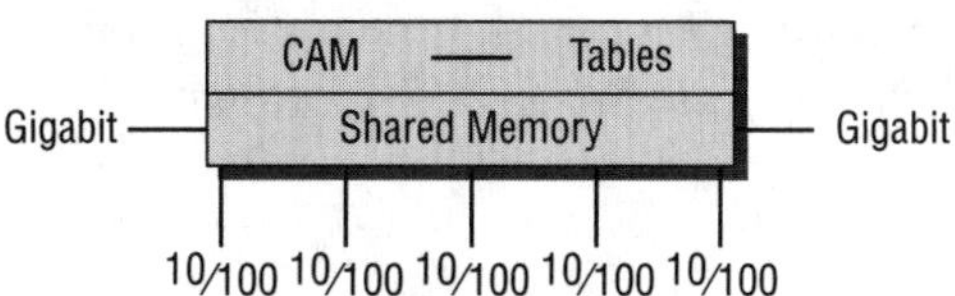


A wide range of switch configurations and port densities is available. You can determine the switch model and the version of the IOS by entering the `show version` command. Shown next is the output from the `show version` command executed on a WS-C2950-24 switch (the underlines are mine to highlight the image and switch model):

```
Terry_2950#show version
Cisco Internetwork Operating System Software
IOS (tm) C2950 Software (C2950-I6Q4L2-M), Version 12.1(11)EA1, RELEASE SOFTWARE
(fc1)
Copyright (c) 1986-2002 by cisco Systems, Inc.
Compiled Wed 28-Aug-02 10:25 by antonino
Image text-base: 0x80010000, data-base: 0x80528000
ROM: Bootstrap program is CALHOUN boot loader
Terry_2950 uptime is 19 minutes
System returned to ROM by power-on
System image file is "flash:/c2950-i6q4l2-mz.121-11.EA1.bin"
cisco WS-C2950-24 (RC32300) processor (revision G0) with 20402K bytes of memory.
```

```
Processor board ID FOC0650W11A
Last reset from system-reset
Running Standard Image
24 FastEthernet/IEEE 802.3 interface(s)
32K bytes of flash-simulated non-volatile configuration memory.
Base ethernet MAC Address: 00:0B:BE:53:2C:00
Motherboard assembly number: 73-5781-11
Power supply part number: 34-0965-01
Motherboard serial number: FOC06500D9W
Power supply serial number: PHI06460AS1
Model revision number: G0
Motherboard revision number: A0
Model number: WS-C2950-24
System serial number: FOC0650W11A
Configuration register is 0xF

Terry_2950#
```

The 2950 series switches operate only at layer 2, and all use a CAM for address lookup, and a shared memory switching fabric for forwarding frames. Shown next is the output from the `show mac-address-table` command executed on a WS-C2950-24 switch:

```
Terry_2950#show mac-address-table
          Mac Address Table
------------------------------------------

Vlan    Mac Address       Type        Ports
----    -----------       ----        -----
   1    00e0.b063.c196    DYNAMIC     Fa0/1
   1    00e0.b064.6ee5    DYNAMIC     Fa0/2
   2    0000.0c76.1f30    DYNAMIC     Fa0/3
   2    00e0.b063.c197    DYNAMIC     Fa0/4
Total Mac Addresses for this criterion: 4
Terry_2950#
```

The 2950 stores the VLAN information in a separate database file (`vlan.dat`) from the one used for the configuration files (`config.text`). Shown next is the output from the `show flash` command executed on a WS-C2950-24 switch:

```
Terry_2950#show flash

Directory of flash:/
```

```
  2  -rwx    2664051   Mar 01 1993 00:04:35  c2950-i6q412-mz.121-11.EA1.bin
  3  -rwx        269  Jan 01 1970 00:02:46  env_vars
  5  -rwx        676  Mar 01 1993 00:48:45  vlan.dat
  6  -rwx             Mar 03 1993 05:25:47  private-config.text
  7  drwx        704  Mar 01 1993 00:05:13  html
 19  -rwx        109  Mar 01 1993 00:05:14  info
 20  -rwx        109  Mar 01 1993 00:05:14  info.ver
 21  -rwx       1580  Mar 03 1993 05:25:47  config.text

7741440 bytes total (3778048 bytes free)
Terry_2950#
```

## 3550 Series Switches

The 3550 Series Intelligent Ethernet switch comprises a number of fixed configuration switches that can be operated in a stand-alone fashion or joined together in a stack. More powerful than the 2950 switches, they provide several enhancements to both security and Quality of Service (QoS), thanks in part to the additional layer 3 capability of the IOS.

All Catalyst 3550 models have the Cisco Cluster Management Suite (CMS) software embedded in the operating system. (CMS is discussed later in this chapter.)

The 3550 series switches operate using a distributed shared-memory switching fabric. The forwarding decisions, at layers 2, 3, and 4, as well as CEF, are taken by "satellite" ASICs located near the main shared memory. Figure 10.8 shows the relationship between the shared memory, the decision-making satellite ASICs, and the ring request mechanism.

**FIGURE 10.8** 3550 switch architecture

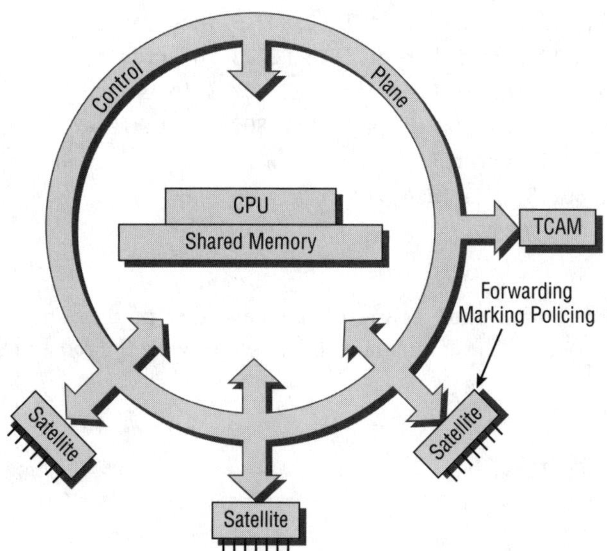

The 3550 switches operate at both layer 2 and layer 3, and use a CAM for address lookup at both layers for 10/100 Mbits/second interface traffic. All switches in the range use TCAM for faster switching because of the proliferation of Gigabit interfaces. You can tell which version of the switch you are connected to by using the `show version` command.

```
Terry_3550#show version
Cisco Internetwork Operating System Software
IOS (tm) C3550 Software (C3550-I5K2L2Q3-M),
   Version 12.1(13)EA1a, RELEASE SOFTWARE (fc1)
Copyright (c) 1986-2003 by cisco Systems, Inc.
Compiled Tue 25-Mar-03 23:56 by yenanh
Image text-base: 0x00003000, data-base: 0x008BA914

ROM: Bootstrap program is C3550 boot loader

Terry_3550 uptime is 4 days, 23 hours, 10 minutes
System returned to ROM by power-on
System image file is "flash:/c3550-i5k2l2q3-mz.121-13.EA1a.bin"

[output cut]

cisco WS-C3550-24-PWR (PowerPC) processor
   (revision B0) with 65526K/8192K bytes of memory.
Processor board ID CAT0709X07M
Last reset from warm-reset
Bridging software.
Running Layer2/3 Switching Image
Ethernet-controller 1 has 12 Fast Ethernet/IEEE 802.3 interfaces
Ethernet-controller 2 has 12 Fast Ethernet/IEEE 802.3 interfaces
Ethernet-controller 3 has 1 Gigabit Ethernet/IEEE 802.3 interface
Ethernet-controller 4 has 1 Gigabit Ethernet/IEEE 802.3 interface
24 FastEthernet/IEEE 802.3 interface(s)
2 Gigabit Ethernet/IEEE 802.3 interface(s)

Terry_3550#
```

Shown next is the output from the `show tcam` command executed on the same switch. Very few entries exist in this TCAM, but the command can be used to view the remaining TCAM capacity.

```
Terry_3550#show tcam ?
  inacl    Show Ingress ACL TCAM
```

```
  outacl  Show Egress ACL TCAM
  pbr     Show PBR TCAM
  qos     Show Ingress QoS TCAM

Terry_3550#show tcam qos ?
  <1-1>   TCAM ID

Terry_3550#show tcam qos 1 ?
  entries       Show entry information
  masks         Show mask information
  port-labels   Show port label information
  size          Show size
  statistics    Show statistics
  vlan-labels   Show vlan label information

Terry_3550#show tcam qos 1 statistics
QoS TCAM#1: Number of active labels: 0
QoS TCAM#1: Number of masks   allocated: 4,available:412
QoS TCAM#1: Number of entries allocated: 1,available:3327

Terry_3550#
```

## 4000 Series Switches

The Cisco Catalyst 4000 Series switches are modular in construction, and are based around the Catalyst 4003 and Catalyst 4006 chassis, both of which operate using a shared memory switching fabric. A range of line cards supporting different arrangements of port numbers and speeds is available and is compatible with both chassis. The Cisco Catalyst 4000/4500 Supervisor Engine IV is the current "heart" of the machine, comprising a fabric that Cisco defines as supporting, among other features:

- Integrated resiliency
- Cisco Express Forwarding (CEF)-based Layer 2/3/4 switching
- Advanced Quality of Service (QoS)
- Non-blocking switch fabric forwarding at 48Mbps

(Other Cisco documentation defines the 4000 series switching as "Layer 2 switching powered by a 24-Gbps, 18-Mbps engine and Layer 3 switching powered by a scalable, 8-Gbps, 6-Mbps engine," thus allowing you calculate the 48Mbps by yourself.)

Cisco also offer a Catalyst 4500 Series Supervisor Engine II-Plus engine, running Cisco IOS software.

The basic architecture of the 4000 series switches is shown in Figure 10.9.

**FIGURE 10.9** 4000 switch architecture

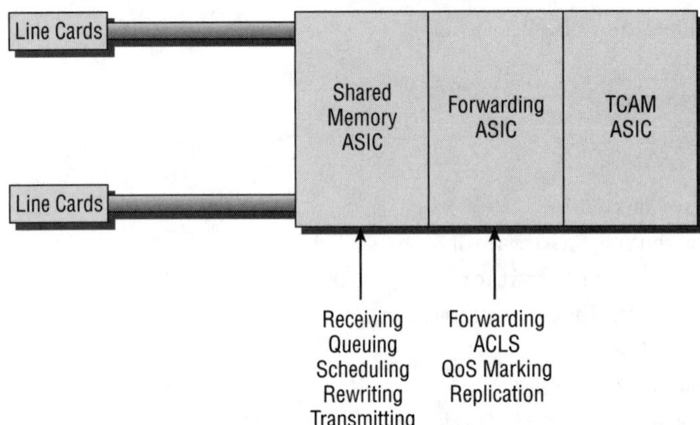


The model number of the 4000 series and details of the operating system are displayed using the `show version` command. The following shows the output when the command is executed on a WS-C4003 switch:

```
Terry_4003 (enable)show version
WS-C4003 Software, Version NmpSW: 4.5(2)
Copyright (c) 1995-1999 by Cisco Systems, Inc.
NMP S/W compiled on Jun 25 1999, 15:53:36
GSP S/W compiled on Jun 25 1999, 15:38:34

System Bootstrap Version: 5.4(1)

Hardware Version: 2.1  Model: WS-C4003  Serial #: JAE044001T8

Mod Port Model           Serial #         Versions
--- ---- ----------      ------------------------------
1   0    WS-X4012        JAE044001T8      Hw : 2.1
                                          Gsp: 4.5(2.0)
                                          Nmp: 4.5(2)
2   48   WS-X4148-RJ     JAE04271V1N      Hw : 2.3
3   34   WS-X4232-GB-RJ  JAE043203CK      Hw : 2.3

       DRAM                    FLASH                   NVRAM
Module Total   Used    Free    Total   Used    Free    Total Used  Free
------ ------- ------- ------- ------- ------- ------- ----- ----- -----
1      65536K  17723K  47813K  12288K  3764K   8524K   480K  126K  354K
```

```
Uptime is 183 days, 3 hours, 32 minutes
Terry_4003 (enable)
```

The bridging table in a 4000 series switch is held in the CAM. While this is considered fast enough for the 10/100 interfaces, the Gigabit Ethernet interfaces need more speed, and so a TCAM is used for both layer 2 and layer 3 lookup when the faster interfaces are installed.

Shown next is the output from the `show cam` command executed on a WS-C4003 switch. Note that it is possible to see either dynamic or static entries, and also to have them displayed by VLAN.

```
Terry_4003 (enable) show cam
Usage: show cam [count] <dynamic|static|permanent|system> [vlan]
       show cam <dynamic|static|permanent|system> <mod_num/port_num>
       show cam <mac_addr> [vlan]
       show cam agingtime

Terry_4003 (enable) show cam dynamic
* = Static Entry. + = Permanent Entry. # = System Entry.
   R = Router Entry. X = Port Security Entry

VLAN  Dest MAC/Route Des   Destination Ports or VCs / [Protocol Type]
----  ------------------   ------------------------------------------
1     00-00-00-1d-f0-b6    2/26 [ALL]
1     00-00-85-07-7d-ba    2/25 [ALL]
1     00-02-a5-03-69-e0    2/23 [ALL]
1     00-02-a5-09-ef-08    2/31 [ALL]
1     00-02-a5-09-ef-14    2/43 [ALL]
1     00-02-a5-0c-ab-01    2/36 [ALL]
1     00-02-a5-0c-f9-c7    2/46 [ALL]
1     00-02-a5-22-8f-b4    2/24 [ALL]
1     00-02-a5-31-ac-d8    2/32 [ALL]

[output cut]
```

## 6500 Series Switches

The 6500 series switches use a crossbar switching fabric. This is good, because as the heart of the Cisco high-end range, they are widely used as core switches, and need to ensure non-blocking throughput at very high speeds.

The 6500 series switches have 8 usable slots, with 2 fabric channels per slot and 8 Gigabits/sec per fabric channel, providing an advertised 256 Gigabits/second (full-duplex) switching fabric.

A TCAM lookup mechanism is applied to the architecture for the fastest possible address-matching decision, and the actual forwarding mechanism is assisted by a distributed forwarding mechanism using the Distributed Forwarding Card. (This is similar to the satellite ASICs in the 3550 series.)

In addition, the 6500 series gains a large increase in throughput speed by using a process called Demand-Base Switching. This involves updating an ASIC-based cache with information from the first layer 3 packet forwarded at routing table speeds, and then switching the rest of the packets along the same path. The use of ASICs to manage this table increases the throughput by a factor of thousands. This is in addition to standard fast CEF table. The basic architecture of the 6500 switches is shown in Figure 10.10.

**FIGURE 10.10** 6500 switch architecture

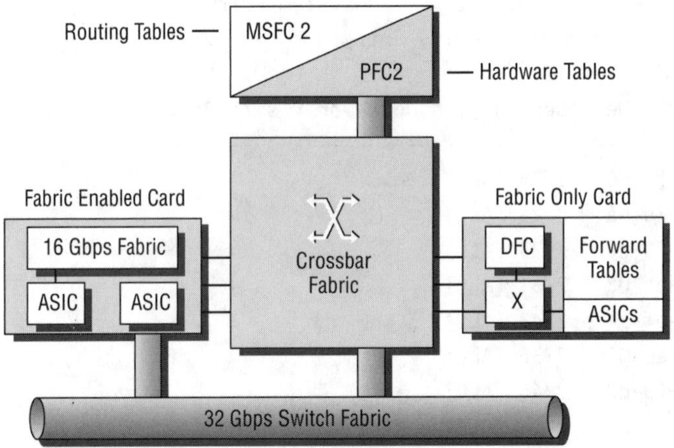


You can select the options you need in this modular architecture, taking into account both cost and requirements. For example, line cards can be installed with several configuration options, including:

- Classic line cards: bus connectivity only
- Fabric-enabled line cards: switch fabric and bus connectivity
- Fabric-only line cards: dual switch fabric, no bus connectivity
- Switch fabric: line cards that contain the actual 256 Gigabits fabric

For details of the full range of line cards available for the 6500 series, see the Cisco website for the most up-to-date details: `www.cisco.com/en/US/products/hw/switches/ps708/products_data_sheets_list.html`.

# Debugging, Management, and System Testing

Modern switches are usually part of a large, possibly integrated network topology. As such, two different management techniques need to be established. First, administrators need to be able to view the complete network, taking a holistic approach to managing the environment. The second technique relates to managing individual switches.

For the first problem, Cisco designed the Cisco Cluster Management Suite, and all modern switches are enabled with the correct processes to support this centralized management. For the second problem, we have the regular range of show commands, supplemented by a process called debugging. Read on, MacDuff.

## The Cisco Cluster Management Suite (CMS)

The Cisco Cluster Management Suite represents the smallest of the management options supplied by Cisco. Larger offerings fall into the CiscoWorks range of SNMP-based management programs.

CMS supports the management of up to 16 distributed switches. Access is via a standard browser interface, providing a web-based interface for managing the IOS commands on a Cisco switch. CMS is used as an alternative to connecting to the console or establishing a Telnet session to a switch and using the standard command-line interface (CLI).

The use of a standard browser plus the enhancements made possible by customization of the interface mean that this is a simple-to-use application. CMS provides a topology map to enable you to identify the switch that you wish to configure simply by looking at the diagram. Built-in applets include report creation and alarm monitoring. CMS supports all of the advanced features found on the CLI, including MLS forwarding options and QoS for voice and video.

## Debugging

Debugging may be new to you. It is available only on IOS-based switches, and there is no comparable feature in CatOS. Of course, debugging has been inside routers since time began, so those of you familiar with router IOS already know something about it. For those wanting to learn the complete story of debugging, I refer you to *CCNP: Cisco Internetwork Troubleshooting Study Guide*, 3rd ed., by Arthur Pfund and Todd Lammle (Sybex, 2004).

Debugging is the process whereby you can gather information about specific activities going on in the switch as they happen. Bearing in mind that debugging commands often have several extensions allowing greater granularity of capture, you must remember that the context-sensitive help provides the best guide to what debugging commands you can use.

Debugging is not free. Debugging takes place in the router processor at the heart of the switch, and uses system buffers to store debugging information. If you try to debug too much all at once, then you run the genuine risk of preventing the switch from functioning due to an overworked processor and overloaded memory. Debugging should therefore be used like a surgeon's scalpel, cutting finely into what you need to see. Don't use debugging like a club!

It is easy to forget precisely which debugging command you have entered, and therefore commands exist to disable all debugging activity. There are two choices; `no debug all` and `undebug all` work equally well.

```
Terry_2950#no debug all
All possible debugging has been turned off
Terry_2950#undebug all
All possible debugging has been turned off
Terry_2950#
```

**Real World Scenario**

**Debugging Danger!**

Not too long ago, I was consulting for a large ISP, and we were working as a team making lots of changes to customer networks in the wee small hours of the morning. At one stage, one of the guys needed to debug some activity on the customer router, and he was a little worried about the effect. Because we had no time to run tests on the debug, I suggested that he set a reload timer on the router in question so that it would reboot in five minutes if everything went wrong. Well, things started off fine, but when he typed the `undebug all` command, he got a little confused and typed `debug all` instead.

The target router lasted about 30 seconds before it terminated his Telnet session and overloaded the memory and processor. Fortunately, it reloaded about two minutes later, and all was well. He bought the beers. The moral of this story is don't ever use the `debug all` command outside the lab or classroom!

## System Testing

In addition to the sophisticated debugging option, a huge variety of `show` commands are available to allow you to take snapshot views of everything from the configuration to information about the frame flow on an interface. In the absence of a photographic memory, the context-sensitive help is the first step in determining which command you need. This can best be demonstrated by using the `show help` command below.

```
Terry_3550#show ?
  access-expression  List access expression
  access-lists       List access lists
  accounting         Accounting data for active sessions
  adjacency          Adjacent nodes
  aliases            Display alias commands
```

```
arp                 ARP table
auto                Show Automation Template
boot                show boot attributes
```

One command you may wish to familiarize yourself with is the `show processes` command. In addition to providing an (almost indecipherable) list of the processes running, it provides a very valuable snapshot of the processor overhead. (The underlines are mine.)

```
Terry_3550#show processes ?
  cpu      Show CPU use per process
  memory   Show memory use per process
  |        Output modifiers
  <cr>
Terry_3550#show processes cpu
CPU utilization for five seconds: 20%/20%; one minute: 16%; five minutes: 10%
 PID Runtime(ms)   Invoked      uSecs   5Sec   1Min   5Min TTY Process
   1           0         1          0  0.00%  0.00%  0.00%   0 Chunk Manager
   2           4    105887          0  0.00%  0.00%  0.00%   0 Load Meter
   3           0        72          0  0.00%  0.00%  0.00%   0 SpanTree Helper
   4           0         2          0  0.00%  0.00%  0.00%   0 IpSecMibTopN
   5      106752     53797       1984  0.00%  0.01%  0.00%   0 Check heaps
   6           4       477          8  0.00%  0.00%
[output cut]
```

One additional module that can be implemented with the 6500 series switches is the Network Analysis Module (NAM), which constitutes an integrated traffic monitoring solution, enabling network managers to gain "application-level visibility" into network traffic. The NAM supplies an embedded, web-based traffic analyzer, providing remote monitoring and troubleshooting through a browser. Main features include

- Integrated monitoring
- Real-time and historical data gathering
- Performance management
- Fault isolation
- QoS and VoIP monitoring
- Capacity planning

# Summary

The architecture of modern switches does not conform to a single model. Vendors, in competition with each other, devise their own mechanisms to create faster, more scalable switches to suit every niche in the modern network. Cisco is no exception; in fact, they are probably among the world's greatest innovators.

New technologies such as the Content Addressable Memory lookup system are used in the entry-level 2950 series switches, and CAM's big brother, the Ternary CAM, is used in the 3550, 4000, and 6500 series. This provides the speedy lookup required for fast decision-making. In turn, this decision-making is itself speeded up by the use of processors external to the memory tables. In the 3550, these are satellite ASICs, and in the 6500 they are provided by the Distributed Forwarding Card.

All of this is bound together by the selection of the most appropriate switching fabric. Whether it is the shared memory of the 2950 and the 4000, the distributed shared memory of the 3550, or the crossbar of the 6500, each switch has a fabric that matches its needs and position in the network. In addition, a range of software options is currently available, with the biggest decisions centering around whether to purchase SI or EI for the 2950, and whether to use hybrid IOS or native IOS on the 4000 and 6500.

Finally, switch management has never been more difficult. With the range of newer technologies such as voice and video demanding newer QoS options, we find ourselves with an almost bewildering array of configuration options. To manage this environment, we have the legacy range of `show` and `debug` commands, although `debug` will be new to many of you without a router background. But we also have the Cisco Cluster Management Suite, which allows us to manage up to 16 switches using a single front end.

# Exam Essentials

**Understand what switching architecture is.** Switches have come a long way in the last few years. From simple systems using shared buses and interrupt-drive access, we have arrived at the crossbar switch—a truly non-blocking architecture suitable for building the largest switches in the busiest environments. But the crossbar is expensive and other mechanisms exist that are suitable for lesser needs. These include the shared memory and distributed shared memory fabrics. And you need to understand how they work, and remember which Cisco switch uses which.

**Understand CAM and TCAM.** Storing addressing information in memory is quite easy. The difficult part is referencing it and accessing it quickly. A number of different techniques have emerged in the past to carry out this task, including simple pointing and hash referencing, but all have been slow. A modern, more intelligent process is called a Content Addressable Memory. In the CAM, the location of the data in the memory block is somehow related to the type of data that is stored, making for a much faster lookup.

Even so, the CAM is limited by the fact that there are only two binary numbers, and that means checking every bit. By adding a third bit (the "don't care" bit) in a mask, the resulting Ternary CAM can provide even faster lookups by ignoring unnecessary bits of information.

**Understand switch types.** Cisco switches come in a variety of shapes and sizes. As the range changes and becomes more modern, some new switches have appeared. Some of them, such as the fixed-configuration 3550 series, are almost multi-port routers, running native IOS. Others, such as the 4000 and 6500 series, are modular, running updated versions of the IOS. You need to know which switches have which features, and know how to upgrade the CatOS to IOS.

**Understand switch management.** Switches need to be managed, and in an increasingly complex network topology, that task also becomes more complex. Cisco has the Cluster Management Suite to help, and there are also a range of `show` and `debug` commands that you need to learn, practice, and remember.

# Key Terms

Before you take the exam, be sure you're familiar with the following terms:

bus fabric

CatOS

Content Addressable Memory (CAM)

contiguous buffers

crossbar

Enhanced Image (EI)

IOS

matrix

non-blocking switch

particle buffers

shared memory

Standard Image (SI)

switching fabric

Ternary Content Addressable Memory (TCAM)

wire speed

# Written Lab

Write the answers to the following questions:

1. What command shows the size of the image file running on a 3550?
2. What two commands disable all debugging on a Cisco switch?
3. How many VLANs are supported on the SI IOS image on a 2950 switch?
4. What command displays the CAM entries on a 2950 switch?
5. What command displays the CPU overhead on an IOS-based switch?
6. How many MAC addresses can be stored on a 2950 switch?
7. Which switch range supports the NAM?
8. What command displays the interface buffer sizes on an IOS-based switch?
9. What command displays the bridging table on a 4000 series switch?
10. What is the name of the file in flash that stores the configuration in a 2950 series switch?

# Review Questions

1. Which of the following is used to search the bridging tables in a 3550 switch?
   A. CAM
   B. DCAM
   C. TCAM
   D. Bridging database

2. Which switching fabric is used by the 2950 switch series?
   A. Dynamic
   B. Shared memory
   C. Crossbar
   D. Bus

3. What does the term non-blocking mean when referring to an Ethernet switch?
   A. The switch has dual power supplies.
   B. The switch has sufficient capacity to forward data without delay.
   C. The switch has enhanced management to allow frames to pass through undelayed.
   D. The switch has more than one bus.

4. What does the TCAM on a 3550 switch do?
   A. Searches for matches on "1s," "0s," and "don't cares"
   B. Searches for matches on binary "1s" and "0s"
   C. Searches for the longest prefix match
   D. Searches for the match with the most bits

5. What type of buffer creates buffers as needed?
   A. Particle buffering
   B. Virtual buffering
   C. Contiguous buffering
   D. Ring buffering

6. What command is used to display the system buffers in a 3550 switch?
   A. `show memory`
   B. `show system-buffers`
   C. `show buffers`
   D. `show buffers system`

7. What command is used to stop all debugging activity on an IOS-based switch?

   A. `stop debug all`

   B. `no debug all`

   C. `disable debug all`

   D. `undebug all`

8. What does CMS stand for?

   A. Cisco Management Suite

   B. Cluster Management Session

   C. Cluster Management Suite

   D. Cisco Management Session

9. What are the two chassis options available with the 4000 series switches?

   A. 4000 and 4003

   B. 4003 and 4006

   C. 4000 and 4006

   D. 4000 and 4500

10. In the 2950 switch range, where is the VLAN information held?

    A. In flash, in its own file called vlan.dat

    B. In ROM, in its own file called vlan.dat

    C. In flash, in the config.text file

    D. In the VTP server

11. What can a TCAM process be used for? (Choose the best answer.)

    A. Layer 2 lookups

    B. Layer 3 lookups

    C. Layer 2 and Layer 3 lookups

    D. Layer 2, Layer 3, and ACL lookups

12. If a switch is running "hybrid IOS," what do you understand it to be using?

    A. Software that is a combination of CatOS and IOS

    B. CatOS on the switch and IOS on the routing module

    C. Software that has commands from both operating systems running in tandem

    D. IOS on the switch and CatOS on the router

13. What does EI mean when referring to 2950 series IOS?
    A. Enterprise Image
    B. Extended Image
    C. Enhanced Image
    D. Excellent Image

14. Which of the following is supported inside the EI IOS on a 2950 switch? (Choose all that apply.)
    A. IGMP snooping
    B. DSCP for 13 values
    C. 255 VLANs
    D. 802.1w

15. Which command is used to show the non-configured entries in a CAM table on a 2950 series switch?
    A. `show cam dynamic`
    B. `show bridge dynamic`
    C. `show dynamic cam`
    D. `show cam`

16. What type of switching fabric exists inside a 2950G-24-DC switch?
    A. Distributed shared bus
    B. Crosspoint
    C. Shared memory
    D. Distributed shared memory

17. What is a particle buffer?
    A. A buffer made up from small particles of memory
    B. A small piece of a larger buffer
    C. A buffer designed to handle frame particles
    D. A group of contiguous buffer

18. What is a CAM?
    A. A special memory block where the location of the data is related to its type
    B. Another name for the bridging table
    C. A special table where data is grouped for easy access
    D. A special memory block where data is accessed using fast pointer lookups

19. Why are system buffers made in so many different sizes?

  A. Because different systems allow different frames to be received

  B. Because different interfaces support different MTUs

  C. Because the buffers can be used as particles to create larger buffers

  D. Because buffers have to be discarded once they are used

20. The Network Analysis Module on the 6500 series switches can be used to do what? (Choose all that apply.)

  A. Remotely gather traffic statistics.

  B. Remotely configure QoS options.

  C. Remotely change passwords.

  D. Remotely measure traffic parameters.

# Answers to Written Lab

1. `show flash`
2. `no debug all` and `undebug all`
3. 64
4. `show mac-address-table`
5. `show processes cpu`
6. 8000
7. The 6500 series
8. `show buffers`
9. `show cam (options)`
10. `config.text`

# Answers to Review Questions

1. C. The 3550 uses a TCAM for searching the forwarding tables.
2. B. The 2950 switch uses a shared memory switching fabric.
3. B. Non-blocking switches have sufficient built-in capacity to ensure that frames are forwarded without delay being introduced by waiting for fabric availability.
4. A. TCAM looks for matches of "1s" "0s" and "don't cares."
5. A. Particle buffering uses small blocks of memory, called particles, to create buffers as needed.
6. C. The command `show buffers` is used to display both the system and interface buffers in IOS.
7. B, D. The command `disable debug all` is used to stop all debugging activity on an IOS-based switch.
8. C. CMS is the Cluster Management Suite.
9. B. The two chassis options currently available are the 4003 and the 4006.
10. A. VLAN information is held in a separate database, and stored under the name `vlan.dat` in flash.
11. D. TCAM lookup can be performed on any structure where addresses contain masks, including Layer 2, Layer 3, and ACL lookups.
12. B. Switches are said to be running hybrid software when they have CatOS on the switch and IOS on the router.
13. C. EI is the abbreviation of Enhanced Image.
14. A, B, C, D. EI supports all of the possible options.
15. A. The command `show cam dynamic` shows the dynamically discovered MAC addresses.
16. D. The 3550 series switches all use a distributed shared-memory switching architecture.
17. A. A particle buffer is a logically contiguous buffer constructed from particles of memory.
18. A. With Content Addressable Memory (CAM), a precise relationship exists between the information in the data and its location in the data store.
19. B. Different interfaces on a router support different MTUs. Different buffer sizes are created at switch-on to support the different MTUs.
20. A, D. The NAM is a remote monitoring and analysis tool used with the 6500 series switches. It does not perform remote configuration changes.

# Answers to Review Questions

# Commands Used in This Book

This appendix provides all the different commands used in this book and their meanings. Use this as a study aid and as a desk reference.

The following list includes the commands used in this book for the IOS-based switches.

| Command | Meaning | Chapter |
|---|---|---|
| `auto qos voip` | Enables auto-qos on an interface | Chapter 9 |
| `class-map` | Matches traffic to a class | Chapter 9 |
| `custom-queue-list` *`list_number`* | Assigns the custom queue to an interface | Chapter 9 |
| Ctrl+Shift+6, then X | Used as an escape sequence | Chapter 2 |
| `duplex` | Sets the duplex of an interface, with half- or full-duplex | Chapter 2 |
| `enable secret` *`password`* | Sets the encrypted enable password of the switch | Chapter 2 |
| `hostname` | Assigns a name to the Catalyst switch | Chapter 2 |
| `interface` | Used to select an interface | Chapter 3 |
| `interface ethernet` *`module/port`* | Used to identify or set parameters on an interface on the switch | Chapter 2 |
| `interface fastethernet` *`module/port`* | Displays or changes parameters on the FastEthernet interfaces | Chapter 2 |
| `ip address` | Assigns an IP address to the switch | Chapter 2 |
| `ip cef` | Enables Cisco Express Forwarding | Chapter 7 |
| `mls qos trust` | Ensures that the CoS of the incoming frame is trusted | Chapter 9 |
| `no debug all(undebug all)` | Disables all debugging | Chapter 10 |
| `no spantree` | Turns off spanning tree for a VLAN | Chapter 4 |
| `policy-map` | Sets the policy for matched traffic | Chapter 9 |
| `port-channel mode` | Enables an EtherChannel bundle | Chapter 5 |
| `priority-group` *`list_number`* | Assigns the priority list to an interface | Chapter 9 |
| `priority-list` *`list_number`* | Creates the priority queue parameters | Chapter 9 |

| | | |
|---|---|---|
| `queue-list` *list_number* | Creates the custom queue parameters | Chapter 9 |
| `service-policy` | Applies the policy to an interface | Chapter 9 |
| `show buffers` | Displays the systems buffers | Chapter 10 |
| `show flash` | Displays the contents of flash memory | Chapter 10 |
| `show ip cef` | Displays the CEF interface conditions | Chapter 7 |
| `show mac-address-table` | Displays the contents of the CAM | Chapter 10 |
| `show processes` | Displays information about current system processes | Chapter 10 |
| `show run` | Displays the running-config of the switch | Chapter 2 |
| `show spanning-tree` | Used to view spanning tree information on a VLAN | Chapters 4 and 5 |
| `show spanning-tree uplink-fast` | Shows the UplinkFast parameters | Chapter 5 |
| `show tcam` | Displays data about the Tertiary CAM activity | Chapter 10 |
| `show version` | Displays the operating system version | Chapter 10 |
| `show vtp counters` | Shows the switches' VTP configuration | Chapter 3 |
| `shutdown` | Disables a particular interface | Chapter 2 |
| `spanning-tree` | Turns on spanning tree for a VLAN | Chapter 4 |
| `spanning-tree cost` | Configures a cost for an interface | Chapter 5 |
| `spanning-tree priority` | Configures the priority for an interface | Chapter 5 |
| `spanning-tree start-forwarding` | Enables PortFast on an interface | Chapter 5 |
| `standby ip` | Creates the HSRP address and enables HRP on an interface | Chapter 9 |
| `standby preempt` | Enables active preempting on an interface | Chapter 9 |
| `standby track` | Enables interface tracking related to an HSRP interface | Chapter 9 |
| `switchport` | Sets the characteristics of the interface, including VLAN membership and trunk configurations | Chapter 3 |
| `vlan` | Sets VLAN information | Chapter 3 |

| | | |
|---|---|---|
| vlan database | Enters VLAN configuration mode | Chapter 3 |
| vtp | Changes the VTP mode to server, transparent, or client; sets the domain name and password | Chapter 3 |
| wrr-queue bandwidth | Sets queue thresholds in weighted round robin queuing | Chapter 9 |
| wrr-queue cos-map | Establishes the class of service queues | Chapter 9 |

The following list includes commands used for configuring the 4000 series switch in this book.

| Command | Meaning | Chapter |
|---|---|---|
| clear mls entry destination *ip_addr_spec* *source ip_addr_spec flow protocol src_port dst_port [all]* | Allows all MLS entries to be cleared in addition to allowing specific entries to be terminated | Chapter 7 |
| clear trunk | Clears VLANs from a trunked port | Chapter 3 |
| Ctrl+C | Used as a break sequence | Chapter 2 |
| Ctrl+Shift+6, then X | Used as an escape sequence | Chapter 2 |
| show spantree uplinkfast | Shows the UplinkFast parameters and statistics | Chapter 5 |
| interface vlan # | Enables interface configuration mode for the specified VLAN interface | Chapter 6 |
| ip cgmp *proxy* | Enables CGMP on the specified interface on routers | Chapter 8 |
| ip igmp join-group *group_address* | Makes the router become an active member of the specified multicast group | Chapter 8 |
| ip igmp version (2\|1) | Applied to the interface and used to change the version of IGMP used on that interface | Chapter 8 |
| ip multicast ttl-threshold *ttl* | Applied to all border interfaces to enforce the scope or boundary of the IP multicast network | Chapter 8 |
| ip multicast-routing | Enables IP multicast forwarding on the router | Chapter 8 |
| ip pim dense-mode | Enables PIM dense mode operation on the interface | Chapter 8 |

| | | |
|---|---|---|
| `ip pim rp-address` *`ip_address group_access_list_number [override]`* | Manually configures an RP address on a multicast router | Chapter 8 |
| `ip pim send-rp-announce` *`type number`* `scope` *`ttl`* `group_list` *`access_list_number`* | Assigns specific multicast group addresses to an RP. The RP can then only announce that it knows multicast groups permitted by the access list specified | Chapter 8 |
| `ip pim send-rp-discovery scope` *`ttl`* | Configures RP Mapping Agent and allows the router to discover all RPs and group assignments | Chapter 8 |
| `ip pim sparse-dense-mode` | Enables PIM sparse-dense mode operation on the interface | Chapter 8 |
| `ip pim sparse-mode` | Enables PIM sparse mode operation on the interface | Chapter 8 |
| `mac-address` | Sets a specific MAC address on an interface | Chapter 6 |
| `mls rp ip` | Enables MLS on an external router, both global and interface specific | Chapter 7 |
| `mls rp management-interface` | Assigns the interface to the MLS-RP. This allows MLSP updates to use this interface | Chapter 7 |
| `mls rp vlan-id` *`vlan_id_number`* | Assigns the interface the proper VLAN number | Chapter 7 |
| `mls rp vtp-domain` *`domain_name`* | Assigns the interface to the VTP domain | Chapter 7 |
| `mtrace` | Displays the forwarding path based on group membership or the RPF | Chapter 8 |
| `ping` | Used for testing reachability | Chapter 8 |
| `session` | Connects the CLI to a session on a route processor module | Chapter 6 |
| `set cgmp enable` | Used on Catalyst switches to enable CGMP | Chapter 8 |
| `set enablepass` | Configures the enable password on a set-based device | Chapter 2 |
| `set interface sco` | Assigns an IP address to the management interface of the set-based switch | Chapter 2 |
| `set ip route` | Configures a default route on a set-based switch | Chapter 6 |

| | | |
|---|---|---|
| `set mls agingtime` *agingtime* | Sets the MLS aging time value to the specified value | Chapter 7 |
| `set mls agingtime fast` *fastagingtime pkt_threshold* | Allows the fast aging time and packet threshold to be set | Chapter 7 |
| `set mls enable` | Enables MLS on Catalyst switches. For most switches, this is set to on by default. | Chapter 7 |
| `set password` | Configures the usermode password on a set-based device | Chapter 2 |
| `set port channel` | Creates an EtherChannel bundle | Chapter 5 |
| `set port duplex` | Sets the duplex of a port | Chapter 2 |
| `set port speed` | Sets the speed of a port | Chapter 2 |
| `set qos map` | Sets the class of service mappings on a port | Chapter 9 |
| `set spantree` | Turns spanning tree off or on for a VLAN | Chapter 4 |
| `set spantree backbonefast` | Enables BackboneFast for a switch | Chapter 5 |
| `set spantree fwddelay` | Changes the forward delay time on a switch | Chapter 5 |
| `set spantree hello` | Changes the BPDU hello time on a switch | Chapter 5 |
| `set spantree maxage` | Sets how long a BPDU that is received will stay valid until another BPDU is received | Chapter 5 |
| `set spantree portcost` | Sets the STP port cost | Chapter 5 |
| `set spantree portfast` | Enables PortFast on a port | Chapter 5 |
| `set spantree portpri` | Sets the STP port priority | Chapter 5 |
| `set spantree portvlanpri` | Configures links to forward only certain VLANs | Chapter 5 |
| `set spantree root` | Makes a set-based switch a root bridge | Chapter 5 |
| `set spantree uplinkfast` | Enables UplinkFast on a port | Chapter 5 |
| `set system name` | Assigns a name to the Catalyst switch | Chapter 2 |
| `set trunk` | Configures trunking on a port | Chapter 3 |
| `set vlan` | Creates a VLAN and also assigns a port to a VLAN | Chapter 3 |

| | | |
|---|---|---|
| `set vtp domain` | Sets the VTP domain name | Chapter 3 |
| `set vtp mode` | Sets the VTP mode of the switch | Chapter 3 |
| `set vtp passwd` | Sets the optional VTP password | Chapter 3 |
| `show config` | Shows the configuration of the 5000 series switch | Chapters 2 and 6 |
| `show mls` | Shows MLS information on a switch | Chapter 7 |
| `show mls entry` | Provides MLS entry data on the MLS-SE | Chapter 7 |
| `show mls rp` | Provides global MLS information | Chapter 7 |
| `show mls rp interface` *interface* | Provides interface-specific MLS information | Chapter 7 |
| `show mls rp vtp-domain` *domain_name* | Provides MLS information for the VTP domain | Chapter 7 |
| `show module` | Shows the module and numbers of cards in the switch | Chapter 6 |
| `show port capabilities` *slot/port* | Shows the configuration of individual ports | Chapter 5 |
| `show port channel` | Shows the status of an EtherChannel bundle | Chapter 5 |
| `show spantree` | Shows the state of the STP per VLAN | Chapters 4 and 5 |
| `show vlan` | Shows the configured VLANs | Chapter 3 |
| `show vtp domain` | Shows the VTP domain configurations | Chapter 3 |
| `show vtp domain` | Provides VTP domain information on the switch | Chapter 7 |

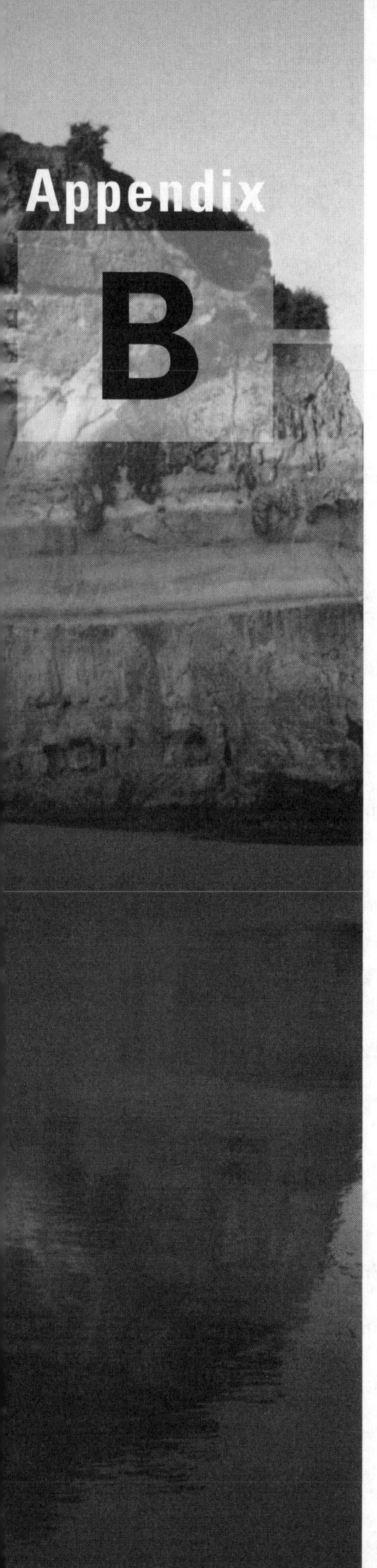


# Internet Multicast Addresses

Certain Class D IP networks in the range of 224.0.0.0 through 239.255.255.255 are used for host extensions for IP multicasting as specified in the Request for Comments (RFC) 1112 standard created by the Internet Engineering Task Force (IETF). The well-known addresses are assigned and maintained by the Internet Address Number Authority (IANA). RFC 1112 specifies the extensions required of a host implementation of the Internet Protocol (IP) to support multicasting.

A lot of abbreviations and acronyms are used in this appendix. The most important, found in the well-known addresses, are listed here:

**DHCP** Dynamic Host Configuration Protocol

**DVMRP** Distance Vector Multicast Routing Protocol

**OSPF** Open Shortest Path First

**PIM** Protocol Independent Multicast

**RIP** Routing Information Protocol

**RP** Route processor

This appendix describes the multicast addresses, the purpose of each address, and the RFC or contact acronym.

These addresses are subject to change. If you cannot find an address listed here that appears to be assigned, refer to the following location: `www.iana.org/assignments/multicast-addresses`.

**TABLE B.1** Multicast Addresses

| Address | Purpose | Reference/Contact Acronym |
|---|---|---|
| 224.0.0.0 | Base Address (Reserved) | RFC1112/JBP |
| 224.0.0.1 | All Systems on this Subnet | RFC1112/JBP |
| 224.0.0.2 | All Routers on this Subnet | JBP |
| 224.0.0.3 | Unassigned | JBP |
| 224.0.0.4 | DVMRP Routers | RFC1075/JBP |
| 224.0.0.5 | OSPFIGP All Routers | RFC2328/JXM1 |
| 224.0.0.6 | OSPFIGP Designated Routers | RFC2328/JXM1 |

**TABLE B.1** Multicast Addresses *(continued)*

| Address | Purpose | Reference/Contact Acronym |
|---|---|---|
| 224.0.0.7 | ST Routers | RFC1190/KS14 |
| 224.0.0.8 | ST Hosts | RFC1190/KS14 |
| 224.0.0.9 | RIP2 Routers | RFC1723/GSM11 |
| 224.0.0.10 | IGRP Routers | Farinacci |
| 224.0.0.11 | Mobile-Agents | Bill Simpson |
| 224.0.0.12 | DHCP Server/Relay Agent | RFC1884 |
| 224.0.0.13 | All PIM Routers | Farinacci |
| 224.0.0.14 | RSVP-ENCAPSULATION | Braden |
| 224.0.0.15 | All-cbt-routers | Ballardie |
| 224.0.0.16 | Designated-sbm | Baker |
| 224.0.0.17 | All-sbms | Baker |
| 224.0.0.18 | VRRP | Hinden |
| 224.0.0.19 | IP All L1Iss | Przygienda |
| 224.0.0.20 | IP All L2Iss | Przygienda |
| 224.0.0.21 | IP All IntermediateSystems | Przygienda |
| 224.0.0.22 | IGMP | Deering |
| 224.0.0.23 | GLOBECAST-ID | Scannell |
| 224.0.0.24 | Unassigned | JBP |
| 224.0.0.25 | Router-to-Switch | Wu |
| 224.0.0.26 | Unassigned | JBP |
| 224.0.0.27 | Al MPP Hello | Martinicky |

**TABLE B.1** Multicast Addresses *(continued)*

| Address | Purpose | Reference/Contact Acronym |
|---|---|---|
| 224.0.0.28 | ETC Control | Zmudzinski |
| 224.0.0.101 | Cisco-hnap | Bakke |
| 224.0.0.102 | HSRP | Wilson |
| 224.0.0.103 | MDAP | Deleu |
| 224.0.0.251 | mDNS | Cheshire |
| 224.0.1.0 | VMTP Managers Group | RFC1045/DRC3 |
| 224.0.1.1 | NTP Network TimeProtocol | RFC1119/DLM1 |
| 224.0.1.2 | SGI-Dogfight | AXC |
| 224.0.1.3 | Rwhod | SXD |
| 224.0.1.4 | VNP | DRC3 |
| 224.0.1.5 | Artificial Horizons-Aviator | BXF |
| 224.0.1.6 | NSS-Name Service Server | BXS2 |
| 224.0.1.7 | AUDIONEWS-Audio News Multi-cast | MXF2 |
| 224.0.1.8 | SUN NIS+ Information Service | CXM3 |
| 224.0.1.9 | MTP Multicast Transport Protocol | SXA |
| 224.0.1.10 | IETF-1-LOW-AUDIO | SC3 |
| 224.0.1.11 | IETF-1-AUDIO | SC3 |
| 224.0.1.12 | IETF-1-VIDEO | SC3 |
| 224.0.1.13 | IETF-2-LOW-AUDIO | SC3 |
| 224.0.1.14 | IETF-2-AUDIO | SC3 |
| 224.0.1.15 | IETF-2-VIDEO | SC3 |

**TABLE B.1** Multicast Addresses *(continued)*

| Address | Purpose | Reference/Contact Acronym |
|---|---|---|
| 224.0.1.16 | MUSIC-SERVICE | Guido Van Rossum |
| 224.0.1.17 | SEANET-TELEMETRY | Andrew Maffei |
| 224.0.1.18 | SEANET-IMAGE | Andrew Maffei |
| 224.0.1.19 | MLOADD | Braden |
| 224.0.1.20 | Any private experiment | JBP |
| 224.0.1.21 | DVMRP on MOSPF | John Moy |
| 224.0.1.22 | SVRLOC | Veizades |
| 224.0.1.23 | XINGTV | Gordon |
| 224.0.1.24 | Microsoft-DS | arnoldm@microsoft.com |
| 224.0.1.25 | NBC-PRO | bloomer@birch.crd.ge.com |
| 224.0.1.26 | NBC-PFN | bloomer@birch.crd.ge.com |
| 224.0.1.31 | Ampr-info | Janssen |
| 224.0.1.32 | Mtrace | Casner |
| 224.0.1.33 | RSVP-encap-1 | Braden |
| 224.0.1.34 | RSVP-encap-2 | Braden |
| 224.0.1.35 | SVRLOC-DA | Veizades |
| 224.0.1.36 | RLN-server | Kean |
| 224.0.1.37 | Proshare-mc | Lewis |
| 224.0.1.38 | Dantz | Yackle |
| 224.0.1.39 | Cisco-rp-announce | Farinacci |
| 224.0.1.40 | Cisco-rp-discovery | Farinacci |

**TABLE B.1** Multicast Addresses *(continued)*

| Address | Purpose | Reference/Contact Acronym |
|---|---|---|
| 224.0.1.41 | Gatekeeper | Toga |
| 224.0.1.42 | Iberiagames | Marocho |
| 224.0.1.43 | NWN-Discovery | Zwemmer |
| 224.0.1.44 | NWN-Adaptor | Zwemmer |
| 224.0.1.45 | ISMA-1 | Dunne |
| 224.0.1.46 | ISMA-2 | Dunne |
| 224.0.1.47 | Telerate | Peng |
| 224.0.1.48 | Ciena | Rodbell |
| 224.0.1.49 | DCAP-servers | RFC2114 |
| 224.0.1.50 | DCAP-clients | RFC2114 |
| 224.0.1.51 | MCNTP-directory | Rupp |
| 224.0.1.52 | MBONE-VCR-directory | Holfelder |
| 224.0.1.53 | Heartbeat | Mamakos |
| 224.0.1.54 | Sun-mc-grp | DeMoney |
| 224.0.1.55 | Extended-sys | Poole |
| 224.0.1.56 | Pdrncs | Wissenbach |
| 224.0.1.57 | TNS-adv-multi | Albin |
| 224.0.1.58 | Vcals-dmu | Shindoh |
| 224.0.1.59 | Zuba | Jackson |
| 224.0.1.60 | Hp-device-disc | Albright |
| 224.0.1.61 | TMS-production | Gilani |

**TABLE B.1** Multicast Addresses *(continued)*

| Address | Purpose | Reference/Contact Acronym |
|---|---|---|
| 224.0.1.62 | Sunscalar | Gibson |
| 224.0.1.63 | MMTP-poll | Costales |
| 224.0.1.64 | Compaq-peer | Volpe |
| 224.0.1.65 | IAPP | Meier |
| 224.0.1.66 | Multihasc-com | Brockbank |
| 224.0.1.67 | Serv-Discovery | Honton |
| 224.0.1.68 | Mdhcpdisover | RFC2730 |
| 224.0.1.69 | MMP-bundle-Discovery1 | Malkin |
| 224.0.1.70 | MMP-bundle-Discovery2 | Malkin |
| 224.0.1.71 | XYPOINT DGPS Data Feed | Green |
| 224.0.1.72 | GilatSkySurfer | Gal |
| 224.0.1.73 | SharesLive | Rowatt |
| 224.0.1.74 | NorthernData | Sheers |
| 224.0.1.75 | SIP | Schulzrinne |
| 224.0.1.76 | IAPP | Moelard |
| 224.0.1.77 | AGENTVIEW | Iyer |
| 224.0.1.78 | Tibco Multicast1 | Shum |
| 224.0.1.79 | Tibco Multicast2 | Shum |
| 224.0.1.80 | MSP | Caves |
| 224.0.1.81 | OTT (One-way Trip Time) | Schwartz |
| 224.0.1.82 | TRACKTICKER | Novick |

**TABLE B.1** Multicast Addresses *(continued)*

| Address | Purpose | Reference/Contact Acronym |
|---|---|---|
| 224.0.1.83 | DTN-mc | Gaddie |
| 224.0.1.84 | Jini-announcement | Scheifler |
| 224.0.1.85 | Jini-request | Scheifler |
| 224.0.1.86 | SDE-Discovery | Aronson |
| 224.0.1.87 | DirecPC-SI | Dillon |
| 224.0.1.88 | B1Rmonitor | Purkiss |
| 224.0.1.89 | 3Com-AMP3 dRMON | Banthia |
| 224.0.1.90 | ImFtmSvc | Bhatti |
| 224.0.1.91 | NQDS4 | Flynn |
| 224.0.1.92 | NQDS5 | Flynn |
| 224.0.1.93 | NQDS6 | Flynn |
| 224.0.1.94 | NLVL12 | Flynn |
| 224.0.1.95 | NTDS1 | Flynn |
| 224.0.1.96 | NTDS2 | Flynn |
| 224.0.1.97 | NODSA | Flynn |
| 224.0.1.98 | NODSB | Flynn |
| 224.0.1.99 | NODSC | Flynn |
| 224.0.1.100 | NODSD | Flynn |
| 224.0.1.101 | NQDS4R | Flynn |
| 224.0.1.102 | NQDS5R | Flynn |
| 224.0.1.103 | NQDS6R | Flynn |

**TABLE B.1** Multicast Addresses *(continued)*

| Address | Purpose | Reference/Contact Acronym |
|---|---|---|
| 224.0.1.104 | NLVL12R | Flynn |
| 224.0.1.105 | NTDS1R | Flynn |
| 224.0.1.106 | NTDS2R | Flynn |
| 224.0.1.107 | NODSAR | Flynn |
| 224.0.1.108 | NODSBR | Flynn |
| 224.0.1.109 | NODSCR | Flynn |
| 224.0.1.110 | NODSDR | Flynn |
| 224.0.1.111 | MRM | Wei |
| 224.0.1.112 | TVE-FILE | Blackketter |
| 224.0.1.113 | TVE-ANNOUNCE | Blackketter |
| 224.0.1.114 | Mac Srv Loc | Woodcock |
| 224.0.1.115 | Simple Multicast | Crowcroft |
| 224.0.1.116 | SpectraLinkGW | Hamilton |
| 224.0.1.117 | Dieboldmcast | Marsh |
| 224.0.1.118 | Tivoli Systems | Gabriel |
| 224.0.1.119 | PQ-Lic-mcast | Sledge |
| 224.0.1.120 | HYPERFEED | Kreutzjans |
| 224.0.1.121 | Pipesplatform | Dissett |
| 224.0.1.122 | LiebDevMgmg-DM | Velten |
| 224.0.1.123 | TRIBALVOICE | Thompson |
| 224.0.1.124 | UDLR-DTCP | Cipiere |

**TABLE B.1** Multicast Addresses *(continued)*

| Address | Purpose | Reference/Contact Acronym |
|---|---|---|
| 224.0.1.125 | PolyCom Relay1 | Coutiere |
| 224.0.1.126 | Infront Multi1 | Lindeman |
| 224.0.1.127 | XRX DEVICE DISC | Wang |
| 224.0.1.128 | CNN | Lynch |
| 224.0.1.129 | PTP-primary | Eidson |
| 224.0.1.130 | PTP-alternate1 | Eidson |
| 224.0.1.131 | PTP-alternate2 | Eidson |
| 224.0.1.132 | PTP-alternate3 | Eidson |
| 224.0.1.133 | ProCast | Revzen |
| 224.0.1.134 | 3Com Discp | White |
| 224.0.1.135 | CS-Multicasting | Stanev |
| 224.0.1.136 | TS-MC-1 | Sveistrup |
| 224.0.1.137 | Make Source | Daga |
| 224.0.1.138 | Teleborsa | Strazzera |
| 224.0.1.139 | SUMAConfig | Wallach |
| 224.0.1.140 | Unassigned | |
| 224.0.1.141 | DHCP-SERVERS | Hall |
| 224.0.1.142 | CN Router-LL | Armitage |
| 224.0.1.143 | EMWIN | Querubin |
| 224.0.1.144 | Alchemy Cluster | O'Rourke |
| 224.0.1.145 | Satcast One | Nevell |

**TABLE B.1** Multicast Addresses *(continued)*

| Address | Purpose | Reference/Contact Acronym |
|---|---|---|
| 224.0.1.146 | Satcast Two | Nevell |
| 224.0.1.147 | Satcast Three | Nevell |
| 224.0.1.148 | Intline | Sliwinski |
| 224.0.1.149 | 8x8 Multicast | Roper |
| 224.0.1.150 | Unassigned | JBP |
| 224.0.1.166 | Marratech-cc | Parnes |
| 224.0.1.167 | EMS-InterDev | Lyda |
| 224.0.1.168 | Itb301 | Rueskamp |
| 224.0.2.1 | "RWHO" Group (BSD) (unofficial) | JBP |
| 224.0.2.2 | SUN RPC PMAPPROC_CALLIT | BXE1 |
| 224.2.127.254 | SAPv1 Announcements | SC3 |
| 224.2.127.255 | SAPv0 Announcements | SC3 |

**TABLE B.2** Multicast Group Assignments for Class D IP Addresses

| Multicast Address | Group Assigned | Contact |
|---|---|---|
| 224.0.0.0–224.0.0.255 | Routing Protocols | |
| 224.0.1.27–224.0.1.30 | Lmsc-Calren-1 to 4 | Uang |
| 224.0.1.151–224.0.1.165 | Intline 1 to 15 | Sliwinski |
| 224.0.1.169–224.0.1.255 | Unassigned | JBP |
| 224.0.2.064–224.0.2.095 | SIAC MDD Service | Tse |
| 224.0.2.096–224.0.2.127 | CoolCast | Ballister |
| 224.0.2.128–224.0.2.191 | WOZ-Garage | Marquardt |

**TABLE B.2** Multicast Group Assignments for Class D IP Addresses *(continued)*

| Multicast Address | Group Assigned | Contact |
|---|---|---|
| 224.0.2.192–224.0.2.255 | SIAC MDD Market Service | Lamberg |
| 224.0.3.000–224.0.3.255 | RFE Generic Service | DXS3 |
| 224.0.4.000–224.0.4.255 | RFE IndividualConferences | DXS3 |
| 224.0.5.000–224.0.5.127 | CDPD Groups | BobBrenner |
| 224.0.5.128–224.0.5.191 | SIAC Market Service | Cho |
| 224.0.5.192–224.0.5.255 | Unassigned | IANA |
| 224.0.6.000–224.0.6.127 | Cornell ISIS Project | Tim Clark |
| 224.0.6.128–224.0.6.255 | Unassigned | IANA |
| 224.0.7.000–224.0.7.255 | Where-Are-You | Simpson |
| 224.0.8.000–224.0.8.255 | INTV | Tynan |
| 224.0.9.000–224.0.9.255 | Invisible Worlds | Malamud |
| 224.0.10.000–224.0.10.255 | DLSw Groups | Lee |
| 224.0.11.000–224.0.11.255 | NCC.NET Audio | Rubin |
| 224.0.12.000–224.0.12.063 | Microsoft and MSNBC | Blank |
| 224.0.13.000–224.0.13.255 | UUNET PIPEX Net News | Barber |
| 224.0.14.000–224.0.14.255 | NLANR | Wessels |
| 224.0.15.000–224.0.15.255 | Hewlett Packard | Van Der Meulen |
| 224.0.16.000–224.0.16.255 | XingNet | Uusitalo |
| 224.0.17.000–224.0.17.031 | Mercantile &Commodity Exchange | Gilani |
| 224.0.17.032–224.0.17.063 | NDQMD1 | Nelson |
| 224.0.17.064–224.0.17.127 | ODN-DTV | Hodges |

**TABLE B.2** Multicast Group Assignments for Class D IP Addresses *(continued)*

| Multicast Address | Group Assigned | Contact |
|---|---|---|
| 224.0.18.000–224.0.18.255 | Dow Jones | Peng |
| 224.0.19.000–224.0.19.063 | Walt Disney Company | Watson |
| 224.0.19.064–224.0.19.095 | Cal Multicast | Moran |
| 224.0.19.096–224.0.19.127 | SIAC Market Service | Roy |
| 224.0.19.128–224.0.19.191 | IIG Multicast | Carr |
| 224.0.19.192–224.0.19.207 | Metropol | Crawford |
| 224.0.19.208–224.0.19.239 | Xenoscience, Inc. | Timm |
| 224.0.19.240–224.0.19.255 | HYPERFEED | Felix |
| 224.0.20.000–224.0.20.063 | MS-IP/TV | Wong |
| 224.0.20.064–224.0.20.127 | Reliable Network Solutions | Vogels |
| 224.0.20.128–224.0.20.143 | TRACKTICKER Group | Novick |
| 224.0.20.144–224.0.20.207 | CNR Rebroadcast MCA | Sautter |
| 224.0.21.000–224.0.21.127 | Talarian MCAST | Mendal |
| 224.0.22.000–224.0.22.255 | WORLD MCAST | Stewart |
| 224.0.252.000–224.0.252.255 | Unassigned | Returned 29-Apr-03 |
| 224.0.253.000–224.0.253.255 | Unassigned | Returned 29-Apr-03 |
| 224.0.254.000–224.0.254.255 | Unassigned | Returned 29-Apr-03 |
| 224.0.255.000–224.0.255.255 | Unassigned | Returned 29-Apr-03 |
| 224.1.0.0–224.1.255.255 | ST Multicast Groups | RFC1190/KS14 |

**TABLE B.2** Multicast Group Assignments for Class D IP Addresses *(continued)*

| Multicast Address | Group Assigned | Contact |
|---|---|---|
| 224.2.0.0–224.2.127.253 | Multimedia Conference Calls | SC3 |
| 224.2.128.0–224.2.255.255 | SAP Dynamic Assignments | SC3 |
| 224.252.0.0–224.255.255.255 | DIS transient groups | IANA |
| 225.0.0.0–225.255.255.255 | Reserved | IANA |
| 232.0.0.0–232.255.255.255 | Source-Specific Multicast | DRC3 |
| 233.0.0.0–233.255.255.255 | GLOP Block | RFC3180 |
| 239.000.000.000–239.255.255.255 | Administratively Scoped | IANA/RFC2365 |
| 239.000.000.000–239.063.255.255 | Reserved | IANA |
| 239.064.000.000–239.127.255.255 | Reserved | IANA |
| 239.128.000.000–239.191.255.255 | Reserved | IANA |
| 239.192.000.000–239.251.255.255 | Organization-Local Scope | Meyer/RFC2365 |
| 239.252.000.000–239.252.255.255 | Site-Local Scope | Meyer/RFC2365 |
| 239.253.000.000–239.253.255.255 | Site-Local Scope | Meyer/RFC2365 |
| 239.254.000.000–239.254.255.255 | Site-Local Scope | Meyer/RFC2365 |
| 239.255.000.000–239.255.255.255 | Site-Local Scope | Meyer/RFC2365 |

**TABLE B.3** Multicast RFCs

| Reference RFC | RFC Title |
|---|---|
| RFC1045 | VMTP: Versatile Message Transaction ProtocolSpecification |
| RFC1075 | Distance Vector Multicast Routing Protocol |
| RFC1112 | Host Extensions for IP Multicasting |
| RFC1119 | Network Time Protocol (Version 1), Specification and Implementation |

**TABLE B.3** Multicast RFCs *(continued)*

| Reference RFC | RFC Title |
|---|---|
| RFC1190 | Experimental Internet Stream Protocol, Version 2 (ST-II) |
| RFC1723 | RIP Version 2: Carrying Additional Information |
| RFC1884 | IP Version 6 Addressing Architecture |
| RFC2114 | Data Link Switching Client Access Protocol |
| RFC2328 | OSPF Version 2 |
| RFC2365 | Administratively Scoped IP Multicast |
| RFC2730 | Multicast Address Dynamic Client Allocation Protocol (MADCAP) |

# The 2924 Switch Series Commands

The 2900 series switches are a range of low-cost access-layer switches. The entry-level models support standard layer 2 switching and up to 64 VLANs, while the 2948G-L3 provides layer 3 (CEF) switching. A Long Reach Ethernet (LRE) model is available to support metropolitan-area Ethernet connections.

If you would like a complete listing of the commands and the rationale behind the new and changed IOS commands, visit the Cisco website at `www.cisco.com`.

The (discontinued) 2926 series uses the CatOS operating system similar to the 4000 switches. Because these commands are largely limited to `set`, `show`, and `clear`, and are covered in detail in the main part of the book, you should refer to the relevant chapters for precise information about how to configure these switches.

The 2948, 2948G-L3, and 2980 switches all use standard IOS commands, and are not covered here. Please refer to the IOS commands throughout the book and in Appendix A to configure these models.

The 2912XL and 2924XL switches run a minimized version of IOS, with some slight variations in command format. These are the ones I propose to cover in this Appendix, because they appear nowhere else in the book.

This appendix is not designed to be the definitive list of commands for the 2900XL switches. It should, however, add to your general knowledge of the basic switch configuration where the 2900XL differs from the IOS.

# IOS Switch Commands

The standard Cisco IOS was used as the basis for the commands for the 2900XL switches. Some of those commands are still the same, and where I have not described a command you should assume that the regular IOS command does the job.

I have arranged the commands to resemble similar commands (on other switches) that appear in the main part of the book.

## Management and Administrative Commands

This first section deals with commands that can be grouped together as management and administration, such as setting global values for the switch.

`mac-address-table dynamic` This command adds a dynamic address entry to the address table.

`mac-address-table static` This command adds a static address entry to the address table.

## Interface Mode and Trunk Commands

The following commands are entered from the privileged interface configuration mode.

`duplex {`*`full`*` | `*`half`*` | `*`auto`*`}` and `no duplex` These commands set the interface duplex mode (the default mode is auto).

`port block` {*unicast* | *multicast*} and `no port block` {*unicast* | *multicast*} These commands block the flooding of unknown unicast or multicast packets to a port. (The default is to unknown unicast and multicast packets to all ports.)

`switchport access vlan` {*vlan-id* | *dynamic*} and `no switchport access vlan` {*vlan-id* | *dynamic*} These commands configure a port as a static-access or dynamic-access port. Access mode makes the port a member of the configured VLAN. Dynamic mode makes the port discover the VLAN assignment based on received incoming packets.

`switchport mode` {*access* | *multi* | *trunk*} and `no switchport mode` {*access* | *multi* | *trunk*} These commands set the port to become a trunk. (This operation is supported only in Enterprise Edition Software.)

`switchport trunk encapsulation` {*isl* | *dot1q*} and `no switchport trunk encapsulation` These commands set the encapsulation format on the trunk port. (This operation is supported only in Enterprise Edition Software.)

`switchport trunk allowed vlan` {*add vlan-list* | *all* | *except vlan-list* | *remove vlan-list*} and `no switchport trunk allowed vlan` These commands control which VLANs can receive and transmit traffic on the trunk. (This operation is supported only in Enterprise Edition Software.)

# VLAN and VTP Commands

As with some other switches, the VLAN information is contained inside a different database, so you have to enter the VLAN database configuration mode to alter VTP and VLAN information. This section shows some of the most useful commands.

## VLAN Database Mode

You must enter the VLAN database mode first. Once in this mode, the remainder of the commands in this section can be entered.

`vlan database` To enter the VLAN database, allowing advanced configuration of VLAN and VTP parameters, use the global command `vlan database`.

`vlan 1` This command configures a VLAN by its ID.

`vtp` This command configures the VTP mode.

`vtp domain` This command configures the VTP domain.

`reset` This command abandons the changes, but remains in VLAN database mode.

`apply` This command implements the changes, propagates them throughout the administrative domain, and remains in VLAN database mode.

`exit` This command implements the changes, propagates them throughout the administrative domain, and exits the VLAN database mode to return to the privileged mode.

## Spanning Tree Commands

The spanning tree commands are pretty unusual. In the first instance, only a single VLAN was supported on the switch (or if you like, no VLANs were supported), so all of the spanning tree commands applied to the whole switch. With the current support for up to 64 VLANs, new commands were created to allow spanning tree to be configured on a per-VLAN basis.

The negating of these commands is also pretty unusual, so I have added the commands for that as well.

### Global Commands

The following commands are entered from the privileged global command prompt.

`spanning-tree vlan 1` **and** `no spanning-tree vlan 1` This command enables spanning tree on the stated VLAN.

`vlan 1 {`*`ieee`*`|`*`dec`*`|`*`ibm`*`}` **and** `no vlan 1` **(reverts to default)** This command determines which version of spanning tree will be implemented.

`spanning-tree vlan 1 forward-time seconds` **and** `no spanning-tree vlan 1 forward-time` **(reverts to default)** This command determines the spanning tree forward timer.

`spanning-tree vlan 1 hello-time` *`seconds`* **and** `no spanning-tree vlan 1 hello-time` **(reverts to default)** This command determines the spanning tree hello timer settings.

`spanning-tree vlan 1 max-age` *`seconds`* **and** `no spanning-tree vlan 1 max-age` **(reverts to default)** This command determines the spanning tree aging timer settings.

`spanning-tree vlan 1 priority` *`bridge-priority`* **and** `no spanning-tree vlan 1 priority` **(reverts to default)** This command determines the spanning tree priority.

### Interface Commands

The following commands are entered from the privileged interface command prompt.

`vlan 1 cost` *`cost`* **and** `no vlan 1 cost` **(reverts to default)** This command determines the port spanning tree cost.

`vlan 1 port-priority port-priority` **and** `no vlan 1 priority` **(reverts to default)** This command determines the port spanning tree priority.

`vlan 1 portfast` *`interface`* **and** `no spanning-tree vlan 1 portfast` *`interface`* This command determines that the port will run in the spanning tree portfast mode.

## *show* Commands

This final section deals with a few of the more useful `show` commands. These commands are used to query the condition of general tables and specific ports on the switch.

`show mac-address-table` This command displays the MAC address table.

`show port block` This command displays the multicast and unicast filtering on the port.

`show port group` This command displays the assignation of ports to groups.

`show port monitor` This command displays the ports where monitoring is enabled.

`show port security` This command displays the ports where security is enabled.

# Glossary

**10BaseT** Part of the original IEEE 802.3 standard, 10BaseT is the Ethernet specification of 10Mbps baseband that uses two pairs of twisted-pair, Category 3, 4, or 5 cabling—using one pair to send data and the other to receive. 10BaseT has a distance limit of about 100 meters per segment. *See also: Ethernet* and *IEEE 802.3.*

**100BaseT** Based on the IEEE 802.3u standard, 100BaseT is the Fast Ethernet specification of 100Mbps baseband that uses UTP wiring. 100BaseT sends link pulses (containing more information than those used in 10BaseT) over the network when no traffic is present. *See also: 10BaseT, FastEthernet,* and *IEEE 802.3.*

**100BaseTX** Based on the IEEE 802.3u standard, 100BaseTX is the 100Mbps baseband FastEthernet specification that uses two pairs of UTP or STP wiring. To ensure correct signal timing, a 100BaseTX segment cannot be longer than 100 meters.

**20/80 rule** A rule indicating that 20 percent of what the user performs on the network is local, whereas up to 80 percent crosses the network segmentation points to get to network services.

**80/20 rule** A rule meaning that 80 percent of the users' traffic should remain on the local network segment and only 20 percent or less should cross the routers or bridges to the other network segments.

# A

**A&B bit signaling** Used in T1 transmission facilities and sometimes called "24th channel signaling." Each of the 24 T1 subchannels in this procedure uses one bit of every sixth frame to send supervisory signaling information.

**AAA** Authentication, Authorization, and Accounting: A Cisco description of the processes that are required to provide a remote access security solution. Each is implemented separately, but each can rely on the others for functionality. *See also: authentication, authorization,* and *accounting.*

**AAL** ATM Adaptation Layer: A service-dependent sublayer of the Data Link layer, which accepts data from other applications and brings it to the ATM layer in 48-byte ATM payload segments. CS and SAR are the two sublayers that form AALs. Currently, the four types of AAL recommended by the ITU-T are AAL1, AAL2, AAL3/4, and AAL5. AALs are differentiated by the source-destination timing they use, whether they are CBR or VBR, and whether they are used for connection-oriented or connectionless mode data transmission. *See also: AAL1, AAL2, AAL3/4, AAL5, ATM,* and *ATM layer.*

**AAL1** ATM Adaptation Layer 1: One of four AALs recommended by the ITU-T, it is used for connection-oriented, time-sensitive services that need constant bit rates, such as isochronous traffic and uncompressed video. *See also: AAL.*

**AAL2** ATM Adaptation Layer 2: One of four AALs recommended by the ITU-T, it is used for connection-oriented services that support a variable bit rate, such as voice traffic. *See also: AAL.*

**AAL3/4** ATM Adaptation Layer 3/4: One of four AALs (a product of two initially distinct layers) recommended by the ITU-T, supporting both connectionless and connection-oriented links. Its primary use is in sending SMDS packets over ATM networks. *See also: AAL.*

**AAL5** ATM Adaptation Layer 5: One of four AALs recommended by the ITU-T, it is used to support connection-oriented VBR services primarily to transfer classical IP over ATM and LANE traffic. *See also: AAL.*

**ABM** Asynchronous Balanced Mode: When two stations can initiate a transmission, ABM is an HDLC (or one of its derived protocols) communication technology that supports peer-oriented, point-to-point communications between both stations.

**ABR** Area Border Router: An OSPF router that is located on the border of one or more OSPF areas. ABRs are used to connect OSPF areas to the OSPF backbone area.

**access control lists** Used by Cisco routers to control packets as they pass through a router. Access lists are created and then applied to router interfaces to accomplish this.

**access layer** One of the layers in Cisco's three-layer hierarchical model. The access layer provides users with access to the internetwork.

**access link** A link used with switches that is only part of one Virtual LAN (VLAN). Trunk links carry information from multiple VLANs.

**access list** A set of test conditions kept by routers that determines "interesting traffic" to and from the router for various services on the network.

**access method** The manner in which network devices approach gaining access to the network itself.

**access rate** Defines the bandwidth rate of the circuit. For example, the access rate of a T1 circuit is 1.544Mbps. In Frame Relay and other technologies, there may be a fractional T1 connection—256Kbps, for example—however, the access rate and clock rate are still 1.544Mbps.

**access server** Also known as a "network access server," it is a communications process connecting asynchronous devices to a LAN or WAN through network and terminal emulation software, providing synchronous or asynchronous routing of supported protocols.

**accounting** One of the three components in AAA. Accounting provides auditing and logging functionalities to the security model.

**acknowledgment** Verification sent from one network device to another signifying that an event has occurred. May be abbreviated as ACK. *Contrast with: NAK.*

**ACR** Allowed Cell Rate: A designation defined by the ATM Forum for managing ATM traffic. Dynamically controlled by using congestion control measures, the ACR varies between the Minimum Cell Rate (MCR) and the Peak Cell Rate (PCR). *See also: MCR* and *PCR.*

**active monitor** The mechanism used to manage a token ring. The network node with the highest MAC address on the ring becomes the active monitor and is responsible for management tasks such as preventing loops and ensuring that tokens are not lost.

**address learning** Used with transparent bridges to learn the hardware addresses of all devices on an internetwork. The switch then filters the network with the known hardware (MAC) addresses.

**address mapping** A methodology that translates network addresses from one format to another so that different protocols can operate interchangeably.

**address mask** A bit combination descriptor identifying which portion of an address refers to the network or subnet and which part refers to the host. Sometimes simply called the "mask." *See also: subnet mask.*

**address resolution** The process used for resolving differences between computer addressing schemes. Address resolution typically defines a method for tracing Network layer (layer 3) addresses to Data Link layer (layer 2) addresses. *See also: address mapping.*

**adjacency** The relationship made between defined neighboring routers and end nodes, using a common media segment, to exchange routing information.

**administrative distance (AD)** A number between 0 and 255 that expresses the value of trustworthiness of a routing information source. The lower the number, the higher the integrity rating.

**administrative weight** A value designated by a network administrator to rate the preference given to a network link. It is one of four link metrics exchanged by PTSPs to test ATM network resource availability.

**ADSU** ATM data service unit: The terminal adapter used to connect to an ATM network through an HSSI-compatible mechanism. *See also: DSU.*

**advertising** The process whereby routing or service updates are transmitted at given intervals, enabling other routers on the network to maintain a record of viable routes.

**AFI** Authority and Format Identifier: The part of an NSAP ATM address that delineates the type and format of the IDI section of an ATM address.

**AIP** ATM Interface Processor: Supporting AAL3/4 and AAL5, this interface for Cisco 7000 series routers minimizes performance bottlenecks at the UNI. *See also: AAL3/4* and *AAL5.*

**algorithm** A set of rules or process used to solve a problem. In networking, algorithms are typically used for finding the best route for traffic from a source to its destination.

**alignment error** An error occurring in Ethernet networks, in which a received frame has extra bits—that is, a number not divisible by 8. Alignment errors are generally the result of frame damage caused by collisions.

**all-routes explorer packet** An explorer packet that can move across an entire SRB network, tracing all possible paths to a given destination. Also known as an "all-rings explorer packet." *See also: explorer packet, local explorer packet,* and *spanning explorer packet.*

**AM** Amplitude Modulation: A modulation method that represents information by varying the amplitude of the carrier signal. *See also: modulation.*

**AMI** Alternate Mark Inversion: A line-code type on T1 and E1 circuits that shows zeros as "01" during each bit cell, and ones as "11" or "00," alternately, during each bit cell. The sending device must maintain ones density in AMI but not independently of the data stream. Also known as "binary-coded, Alternate Mark Inversion." *Contrast with: B8ZS. See also: ones density.*

**amplitude** An analog or digital waveform's highest value.

**analog** Analog signaling is a technique to carry voice and data over copper and wireless media. When analog signals are transmitted over wires or through the air, the transmission conveys information through a variation of some type of signal amplitude, frequency, and phase.

**analog connection** Provides signaling via an infinitely variable waveform. This differs from a digital connection, in which a definite waveform is used to define values. Traditional phone service is an analog connection.

**analog transmission** Signal messaging whereby information is represented by various combinations of signal amplitude, frequency, and phase.

**ANSI** American National Standards Institute: The organization of corporate, government, and other volunteer members that coordinates standards-related activities, approves U.S. national standards, and develops U.S. positions in international standards organizations. ANSI assists in the creation of international and U.S. standards in disciplines such as communications, networking, and a variety of technical fields. It publishes over 13,000 standards for engineered products and technologies ranging from screw threads to networking protocols. ANSI is a member of the International Electrotechnical Commission (IEC) and the International Organization for Standardization (ISO).

**anycast** An ATM address that can be shared by more than one end system, enabling requests to be routed to a node that provides a particular service.

**AppleTalk** Currently in two versions, the group of communication protocols designed by Apple Computer for use in Macintosh environments. The earlier Phase 1 protocols support one physical network with only one network number that resides in one zone. The later Phase 2 protocols support more than one logical network on a single physical network, enabling networks to exist in more than one zone.

**Application layer** Layer 7 of the OSI reference network model, supplying services to application procedures (such as electronic mail or file transfer) that are outside the OSI model. This layer chooses and determines the availability of communicating partners along with the resources necessary to make the connection, coordinates partnering applications, and forms a consensus on procedures for controlling data integrity and error recovery.

**area** A logical, rather than physical, set of segments (based on either CLNS, DECnet, or OSPF) along with their attached devices. Areas are commonly connected to others by using routers to create a single autonomous system. *See also: autonomous system.*

**ARM** Asynchronous Response Mode: An HDLC communication mode using one primary station and at least one additional station, in which transmission can be initiated from either the primary or one of the secondary units.

**ARP** Address Resolution Protocol: Defined in RFC 826, the protocol that traces IP addresses to MAC addresses. *See also: RARP.*

**ASBR** Autonomous System Boundary Router: An area border router placed between an OSPF autonomous system and a non-OSPF network that operates both OSPF and an additional routing protocol, such as RIP. ASBRs must be located in a non-stub OSPF area. *See also: ABR, non-stub area,* and *OSPF.*

**ASCII** American Standard Code for Information Interchange: An 8-bit code for representing characters, consisting of 7 data bits plus 1 parity bit.

**ASICs** application-specific integrated circuits: Used in layer 2 switches to make filtering decisions. The ASIC looks in the filter table of MAC addresses and determines which port the destination hardware address of a received hardware address is destined for. The frame will be allowed to traverse only that one segment. If the hardware address is unknown, the frame is forwarded out all ports.

**ASN.1** Abstract Syntax Notation One: An OSI language used to describe types of data that are independent of computer structures and depicting methods. Described by ISO International Standard 8824.

**AST** Automatic Spanning Tree: A function that supplies one path for spanning explorer frames traveling from one node in the network to another, supporting the automatic resolution of spanning trees in SRB networks. AST is based on the IEEE 802.1 standard. *See also: IEEE 802.1* and *SRB.*

**asynchronous connection** Defines the start and stop of each octet. As a result, each byte in asynchronous connections requires 2 bytes of overhead. Synchronous connections use a synchronous clock to mark the start and stop of each character.

**asynchronous dial-up** Asynchronous dial-up is interchangeable with analog dial-up. Both terms refer to traditional modem-based connections.

**asynchronous transmission** Digital signals sent without precise timing, usually with different frequencies and phase relationships. Asynchronous transmissions generally enclose individual characters in control bits (called start and stop bits) that show the beginning and end of each character. *Contrast with: isochronous transmission* and *synchronous transmission.*

**ATDM** Asynchronous Time-Division Multiplexing: A technique for sending information, it differs from standard TDM in that the time slots are assigned when necessary rather than preassigned to certain transmitters. *Contrast with: FDM, statistical multiplexing,* and *TDM.*

**ATM** Asynchronous Transfer Mode: The international standard, identified by fixed-length 53-byte cells, for transmitting cells in multiple service systems, such as voice, video, or data. Transit delays are reduced because the fixed-length cells permit processing to occur in the hardware. ATM is designed to maximize the benefits of high-speed transmission media, such as SONET, E3, and T3.

**ATM ARP server** A device that supplies logical subnets running classical IP over ATM with address-resolution services.

**ATM endpoint** The initiating or terminating connection in an ATM network. ATM endpoints include servers, workstations, ATM-to-LAN switches, and ATM routers.

**ATM Forum** The international organization founded jointly by Northern Telecom, Sprint, Cisco Systems, and NET/ADAPTIVE in 1991 to develop and promote standards-based implementation agreements for ATM technology. The ATM Forum broadens official standards developed by ANSI and ITU-T and creates implementation agreements before official standards are published.

**ATM layer** A sublayer of the Data Link layer in an ATM network that is service independent. To create standard 53-byte ATM cells, the ATM layer receives 48-byte segments from the AAL and attaches a 5-byte header to each. These cells are then sent to the Physical layer for transmission across the physical medium. *See also: AAL.*

**ATMM** ATM Management: A procedure that runs on ATM switches, managing rate enforcement and VCI translation. *See also: ATM.*

**ATM user-user connection** A connection made by the ATM layer to supply communication between at least two ATM service users, such as ATMM processes. These communications can be uni- or bidirectional, using one or two VCCs, respectively. *See also: ATM layer* and *ATMM.*

**attenuation** In communication, weakening or loss of signal energy, typically caused by distance.

**authentication** The first component in the AAA model. Users are typically authenticated via a username and password, which are used to uniquely identify them.

**authority zone** A portion of the domain-name tree associated with DNS for which one name server is the authority. *See also: DNS.*

**authorization** The act of permitting access to a resource based on authentication information in the AAA model.

**auto duplex** A setting on layer 1 and layer 2 devices that sets the duplex of a switch port automatically.

**automatic call reconnect** A function that enables automatic call rerouting away from a failed trunk line.

**auto-negotiation** The process of two network devices communicating, trying to decide what duplex and speed will be used for data transport.

**autonomous confederation** A collection of self-governed systems that depend more on their own network accessibility and routing information than on information received from other systems or groups.

**autonomous switching** The ability of Cisco routers to process packets more quickly by using the ciscoBus to switch packets independently of the system processor.

**autonomous system (AS)** A group of networks under mutual administration that share the same routing methodology. Autonomous systems are subdivided by areas and must be assigned an individual 16-bit number by the IANA. *See also: area.*

**auto-QoS** A process whereby a router automatically determines if a port connection has special QoS requirement—for example, an IP phone—and allocates queue priority based on the needs without configuration.

**auto-reconfiguration** A procedure executed by nodes within the failure domain of a token ring, wherein nodes automatically perform diagnostics, trying to reconfigure the network around failed areas.

**Auto-RP** An IOS feature that allows multicast-enabled routers to detect RP and forward the summary information to other routers and hosts.

**auxiliary port** The console port on the back of Cisco routers that enables you to dial the router and make console configuration settings.

**AVF** Active Virtual Gateway: The term given to the router in a GLBP block that receives a virtual MAC address allocation from the active router. *See also: AVG* and *GLBP.*

**AVG** Active Virtual Gateway: The term given to the router in a GLBP block that allocates virtual MAC addresses. *See also: AVF* and *GLBP.*

**AVVID** Architecture for Voice, Video, and Integrated Data: This is a Cisco marketing term to group their convergence efforts. Convergence is the integration of historically distinct services into a single service.

# B

**B8ZS** Binary 8-Zero Substitution: A line-code type, interpreted at the remote end of the connection, that uses a special code substitution whenever eight consecutive zeros are transmitted over the link on T1 and E1 circuits. This technique assures ones density independent of the data stream. Also known as "Bipolar 8-Zero Substitution." *Contrast with: AMI. See also: ones density.*

**backbone** The basic portion of the network that provides the primary path for traffic sent to and initiated from other networks.

**BackboneFast** A method whereby, if the switch receives an inferior BPDU on a root port, the switch will begin figuring out who the new root bridge is in less time than normal spanning-tree convergence. This accelerates spanning-tree convergence after the failure of a non-directly connected network link.

**back end** A node or software program supplying services to a front end. *See also: server.*

**bandwidth** The gap between the highest and lowest frequencies employed by network signals. More commonly, it refers to the rated throughput capacity of a network protocol or medium.

**baseband** A feature of a network technology that uses only one carrier frequency—for example, Ethernet. Also named "narrowband." *Contrast with: broadband.*

**Basic Management Setup** Used with Cisco routers when in setup mode. Provides only enough management and configuration to get the router working so someone can telnet into the router and configure it.

**baud** Synonymous with bits per second (bps), if each signal element represents 1 bit. It is a unit of signaling speed equivalent to the number of separate signal elements transmitted per second.

**B channel** bearer channel: A full-duplex, 64Kbps channel in ISDN that transmits user data. *Compare to: D channel, E channel,* and *H channel.*

**beacon** An FDDI device or Token Ring frame that points to a serious problem with the ring, such as a broken cable. The beacon frame carries the address of the station thought to be down. *See also: failure domain.*

**bearer service** Used by service providers to provide DS0 service to ISDN customers. A DS0 is one 64KB channel. An ISDN bearer service provides either two DS0s, called two bearer channels, for a Basic Rate Interface (BRI), or 24 DS0s, called a Primary Rate Interface (PRI).

**BECN** Backward Explicit Congestion Notification: The bit set by a Frame Relay network in frames moving away from frames headed into a congested path. A DTE that receives frames with the BECN may ask higher-level protocols to take necessary flow control measures. *Contrast with: FECN.*

**best-efforts network** A network where traffic is forwarded with no QoS features and delivery is not guaranteed in any way.

**BGP** Border Gateway Protocol: This protocol has had four revisions. Version 4 of the interdomain routing protocol is most commonly used on the Internet. BGP4 supports CIDR and uses route-counting mechanisms to decrease the size of routing tables. *See also: CIDR.*

**bidirectional shared tree** A method of shared tree multicast forwarding. This method enables group members to receive data from the source or the RP, whichever is closer. *See also: RP (rendezvous point).*

**binary** A two-character numbering method that uses ones and zeros. The binary numbering system underlies all digital representation of information.

**BIP** Bit Interleaved Parity: A method used in ATM to monitor errors on a link, sending a check bit or word in the link overhead for the previous block or frame. This enables bit errors in transmissions to be found and delivered as maintenance information.

**BISDN** Broadband ISDN: ITU-T standards created to manage high-bandwidth technologies such as video. BISDN presently employs ATM technology along SONET/SDH-based transmission circuits, supplying data rates from 155Mbps through 622Mbps and beyond. *See also: BRI, ISDN,* and *PRI.*

**bit-oriented protocol** Regardless of frame content, the class of Data Link layer communication protocols that transmits frames. Bit-oriented protocols, as compared with byte-oriented, supply more efficient and trustworthy, full-duplex operation. *Compare to: byte-oriented protocol.*

**BoD** Bandwidth on Demand: This function enables an additional B channel to be used to increase the amount of bandwidth available for a particular connection.

**Boot ROM** Used in routers to put the router into bootstrap mode. Bootstrap mode then boots the device with an operating system. The ROM can also hold a small Cisco IOS.

**border gateway** A router that facilitates communication with routers in different autonomous systems.

**border router** Typically defined within Open Shortest Path First (OSPF) as a router that connected an area to the backbone area. However, a border router can be a router that connects a company to the Internet as well. *See also: OSPF.*

**BPDU** Bridge Protocol Data Unit: A Spanning Tree Protocol initializing packet that is sent at definable intervals for the purpose of exchanging information among bridges in networks.

**BRI** Basic Rate Interface: The ISDN interface that facilitates circuit-switched communication between video, data, and voice; it is made up of two B channels (64Kbps each) and one D channel (16Kbps). *Compare to: PRI. See also: BISDN.*

**bridge** A device for connecting two segments of a network and transmitting packets between them. Both segments must use identical protocols to communicate. Bridges function at the Data Link layer, layer 2 of the OSI reference model. The purpose of a bridge is to filter, send, or flood any incoming frame, based on the MAC address of that particular frame.

**bridge ID** Used to find and elect the root bridge in a layer 2 switched internetwork. The bridge ID is a combination of the bridge priority and base MAC address.

**bridging** A layer 2 process to block or forward frames based on MAC layer addresses. Bridges are lower speed, lower port density switches.

**broadband** A transmission methodology for multiplexing several independent signals onto one cable. In telecommunications, broadband is classified as any channel with bandwidth greater than 4kHz (typical voice grade). In LAN terminology, it is classified as a coaxial cable on which analog signaling is employed. Also known as "wideband." *Contrast with: baseband.*

**broadcast** A data frame or packet that is transmitted to every node on the local network segment (as defined by the broadcast domain). Broadcasts are known by their broadcast address, which is a destination network and host address with all the bits turned on. Also called "local broadcast." *Compare to: directed broadcast.*

**broadcast domain** A group of devices receiving broadcast frames initiating from any device within the group. Because they do not forward broadcast frames, broadcast domains are generally surrounded by routers.

**broadcast storm** An undesired event on the network caused by the simultaneous transmission of any number of broadcasts across the network segment. Such an occurrence can overwhelm network bandwidth, resulting in time-outs.

**brute force attack** A type of attack that bombards the resource with attempted connections until successful. In the most common brute force attack, different passwords are repeatedly tried until a match that is then used to compromise the network is found.

**buffer** A storage area dedicated to handling data while in transit. Buffers are used to receive/store sporadic deliveries of data bursts, usually received from faster devices, compensating for the variations in processing speed. Incoming information is stored until everything is received prior to sending data on. Also known as an "information buffer."

**buffer overflow** When a buffer has no room for additional frames or packets, it either drops new arrivals or clears out some additional space by dropping selective data already stored. The term for either of these processes is buffer overflow.

**bursting** Some technologies, including ATM and Frame Relay, are considered burstable. This means that user data can exceed the bandwidth normally reserved for the connection; however, this cannot exceed the port speed. An example of this is a 128Kbps Frame Relay CIR on a T1—depending on the vendor, it might be possible to send more than 128Kbps for a short time.

**bus** Any physical path, typically wires or copper, through which a digital signal can be used to send data from one part of a computer to another.

**BUS** broadcast and unknown servers: In LAN emulation, the hardware or software responsible for resolving all broadcasts and packets with unknown (unregistered) addresses into the point-to-point virtual circuits required by ATM. *See also: LANE, LEC, LECS,* and *LES.*

**bus fabric** A switch-fabric that uses an interrupt-driven internal bus.

**bus topology** A linear LAN architecture in which transmissions from various stations on the network are reproduced over the length of the medium and are accepted by all other stations. *Contrast with: ring topology* and *star topology.*

**BX.25** AT&T's use of X.25. *See also: X.25.*

**bypass mode** An FDDI and Token Ring network operation that deletes an interface.

**bypass relay** A device that enables a particular interface in the token ring to be closed down and effectively taken off the ring.

**byte-oriented protocol** Any type of Data Link communication protocol that, in order to mark the boundaries of frames, uses a specific character from the user character set. These protocols have generally been superseded by bit-oriented protocols. *Compare to: bit-oriented protocol.*

# C

**cable modem** A cable modem is not actually an analog device, like an asynchronous modem, but rather a customer access device for linking to a broadband cable network. These devices are typically bridges that have a coaxial cable connection to link to the cable network and a 10BaseT Ethernet connection to link to the user's PC.

**cable range** In an extended AppleTalk network, the range of numbers allotted for use by existing nodes on the network. The value of the cable range can be anywhere from a single number to a sequence of several touching network numbers. Node addresses are determined by their cable range value.

**CAC** Connection Admission Control: The sequence of actions executed by every ATM switch while connection setup is performed in order to determine whether a request for connection is violating the guarantees of QoS for established connections. Also, CAC is used to route a connection request through an ATM network.

**call admission control** A device for managing traffic in ATM networks, determining the possibility of a path containing adequate bandwidth for a requested VCC.

**call priority** In circuit-switched systems, the defining priority given to each originating port; it specifies in which order calls will be reconnected. Additionally, call priority identifies which calls are allowed during a bandwidth reservation.

**call setup time** The length of time necessary to effect a switched call between DTE devices.

**CAM** Content Addressable Memory: A storage system with unique data storage attributes used by some Catalyst switches. Unlike traditional memory banks, CAM data is stored so as to ensure that the actual location of the data holds some information.

**candidate packets** Packets identified by the MLS-SE as having the potential for establishing a flow cache. This determination is made based on the destination MAC (DMAC) address. The DMAC address must be a MAC addresses associated with a known MLS-RP. *See also: MLS-SE* and *MLS-RP*.

**CatOS** Abbreviation of Catalyst Operating System; the native operating system for certain Catalyst switches, such as the 4000, 5000, and 6500 series.

**CBR** Constant Bit Rate: An ATM Forum QoS class created for use in ATM networks. CBR is used for connections that rely on precision clocking to guarantee trustworthy delivery. *Compare to: ABR* and *VBR*.

**CD** Carrier Detect: A signal indicating that an interface is active or that a connection generated by a modem has been established.

**CDP** Cisco Discovery Protocol: Cisco's proprietary protocol that is used to tell a neighbor Cisco device about the type of hardware, software version, and active interfaces that the Cisco device is using. It uses a SNAP frame between devices and is not routable.

**CDVT** Cell Delay Variation Tolerance: A QoS parameter for traffic management in ATM networks specified when a connection is established. The allowable fluctuation levels for data samples taken by the PCR in CBR transmissions are determined by the CDVT. *See also: CBR* and *PCR*.

**CEF** Cisco Express Forwarding: A mechanism for forwarding packets using a replicated routing table and a forwarding database on the interface. Sometimes referred to by Cisco as one of their layer 3 switching mechanisms.

**cell** In ATM networking, the basic unit of data for switching and multiplexing. Cells have a defined length of 53 bytes, including a 5-byte header that identifies the cell's data stream and 48 bytes of payload. *See also: cell relay*.

**cell payload scrambling** The method by which an ATM switch maintains framing on some medium-speed edge and trunk interfaces (T3 or E3 circuits). Cell payload scrambling rearranges the data portion of a cell to maintain the line synchronization with certain common bit patterns.

**cell relay** A technology that uses small packets of fixed size, known as cells. Their fixed length enables cells to be processed and switched in hardware at high speeds, making this technology the foundation for ATM and other high-speed network protocols. *See also: cell*.

**Centrex** A local exchange carrier service, providing local switching that resembles that of an on-site PBX. Centrex has no on-site switching capability. Therefore, all customer connections return to the central office (CO). *See also: CO.*

**CER** Cell Error Ratio: In ATM, the ratio of the number of transmitted cells having errors to the total number of cells sent in a transmission within a certain span of time.

**CGMP** Cisco Group Management Protocol: A proprietary protocol developed by Cisco. The router uses CGMP to send multicast membership commands to Catalyst switches.

**Challenge** Used to provide authentication in Challenge Handshake Authentication Protocol (CHAP) as part of the handshake process. This numerically unique query is sent to authenticate the user without sending the password unencrypted across the wire. *See also: CHAP.*

**channelized E1** Operating at 2.048Mbps, an access link that is sectioned into 29 B channels and one D channel, supporting DDR, Frame Relay, and X.25. *Compare to: channelized T1.*

**channelized T1** Operating at 1.544Mbps, an access link that is sectioned into 23 B channels and 1 D channel of 64Kbps each, where individual channels or groups of channels connect to various destinations, supporting DDR, Frame Relay, and X.25. *Compare to: channelized E1.*

**CHAP** Challenge Handshake Authentication Protocol: Supported on lines using PPP encapsulation, it is a security feature that identifies the remote end, helping keep out unauthorized users. After CHAP is performed, the router or access server determines whether a given user is permitted access. It is a newer, more secure protocol than PAP. *Compare to: PAP.*

**character mode connections** Character mode connections are typically terminated at the access server and include Telnet and console connections.

**checksum** A test for ensuring the integrity of sent data. It is a number calculated from a series of values taken through a sequence of mathematical functions, typically placed at the end of the data from which it is calculated, and then recalculated at the receiving end for verification. *Compare to: CRC.*

**choke packet** When congestion exists, it is a packet sent to inform a transmitter that it should decrease its sending rate.

**CIDR** Classless Interdomain Routing: An IP addressing method designed to allow Class C addresses to be issued in blocks. Used by routing protocols such as BGP, OSPF and ISIS. *See also: BGP4.*

**CIP** Channel Interface Processor: A channel attachment interface for use in Cisco 7000 series routers that connects a host mainframe to a control unit. This device eliminates the need for a Front-End Processor (FEP) to attach channels.

**CIR** Committed Information Rate: Averaged over a minimum span of time and measured in bits per second (bps), a Frame Relay network's agreed-upon minimum rate of transferring information.

**circuit switching** Used with dial-up networks such as PPP and ISDN. Passes data, but needs to set up the connection first—just like making a phone call.

**Cisco Express Forwarding** *See: CEF.*

**Cisco FRAD** Cisco Frame-Relay Access Device: A Cisco product that supports Cisco IPS Frame Relay SNA services, connecting SDLC devices to Frame Relay without requiring an existing LAN. Can be upgraded to a fully functioning multiprotocol router. Can activate conversion from SDLC to Ethernet and Token Ring, but does not support attached LANs. *See also: FRAD.*

**Cisco hierarchical model** A Cisco model for building switched networks. The model consists of access layer devices, distribution layer devices, and core layer devices.

**Cisco IOS software** Cisco Internetworking Operating System software. The kernel of the Cisco line of routers and switches that supplies shared functionality, scalability, and security for all products under its CiscoFusion architecture. *See also: CiscoFusion.*

**CiscoFusion** Cisco's name for the internetworking architecture under which its Cisco IOS operates. It is designed to "fuse" together the capabilities of its disparate collection of acquired routers and switches.

**CiscoView** GUI-based management software for Cisco networking devices, enabling dynamic status, statistics, and comprehensive configuration information. Displays a physical view of the Cisco device chassis and provides device-monitoring functions and fundamental troubleshooting capabilities. Can be integrated with a number of SNMP-based network management platforms.

**Class A network** Part of the Internet Protocol hierarchical addressing scheme. Class A networks have only 8 bits for defining networks and 24 bits for defining hosts on each network. *Compare to: Class B network* and *Class C network.*

**Class B network** Part of the Internet Protocol hierarchical addressing scheme. Class B networks have 16 bits for defining networks and 16 bits for defining hosts on each network. *Compare to: Class A network* and *Class C network.*

**Class C network** Part of the Internet Protocol hierarchical addressing scheme. Class C networks have 24 bits for defining networks and only 8 bits for defining hosts on each network. *Compare to: Class A network* and *Class B network.*

**classical IP over ATM** Defined in RFC 1577, the specification for running IP over ATM that maximizes ATM features. Also known as "CIA."

**classification** Classification is the term applied to setting specific parameters inside the Type of Service and DiffServe fields in the IP header, thus requesting special handling by all routers in the traffic path. *See also: policing.*

**classless routing** Routing that allows use of Variable-Length Subnet Masks (VLSMs) and supernetting. Routing protocols that support classless routing are RIP version 2, EIGRP, and OSPF.

**CLI** command-line interface: Enables you to configure Cisco routers and switches with maximum flexibility.

**clocking** Used in synchronous connections to provide a marker for the start and end of data frames.

**CLP** Cell Loss Priority: The area in the ATM cell header that determines the likelihood of a cell being dropped during network congestion. Cells with CLP = 0 are considered insured traffic and are not apt to be dropped. Cells with CLP = 1 are considered best-effort traffic that might be dropped during congested episodes, delivering more resources to handle insured traffic.

**CLR** Cell Loss Ratio: The ratio of discarded cells to successfully delivered cells in ATM. CLR can be designated a QoS parameter when establishing a connection.

**CO** central office: The local telephone company office where all loops in a certain area connect and where circuit switching of subscriber lines occurs.

**collapsed backbone** A nondistributed backbone where all network segments are connected to each other through an internetworking device. A collapsed backbone can be a virtual network segment at work in a device such as a router, hub, or switch.

**collapsed core** One switch performing both core and distribution layer functions. Typically found in a small network, the functions of the core and distribution layer are still distinct.

**collision** The effect of two nodes sending transmissions simultaneously in Ethernet. When they meet on the physical media, the frames from each node collide and are damaged. *See also: collision domain.*

**collision domain** The network area in Ethernet over which frames that have collided will spread. Collisions are propagated by hubs and repeaters, but not by LAN switches, routers, or bridges. *See also: collision.*

**Common Spanning Tree (CST)** *See: CST.*

**composite metric** Used with routing protocols, such as IGRP and EIGRP, that use more than one metric to find the best path to a remote network. IGRP and EIGRP both use bandwidth and delay of the line by default. However, Maximum Transmission Unit (MTU), load, and reliability of a link can be used as well.

**compression** A technique to send more data across a link than would be normally permitted by representing repetitious strings of data with a single marker.

**configuration register** A 16-bit configurable value stored in hardware or software that determines how Cisco routers function during initialization. In hardware, the bit position is set by using a jumper. In software, it is set by specifying specific bit patterns used to set startup options, configured by using a hexadecimal value with configuration commands.

**congestion** Traffic that exceeds the network's capability to handle it.

**congestion avoidance** To minimize delays, the method an ATM network uses to control traffic entering the system. Lower-priority traffic is discarded at the edge of the network when indicators signal it cannot be delivered, thus using resources efficiently.

**congestion collapse** The situation that results from the retransmission of packets in ATM networks where little or no traffic successfully arrives at destination points. It usually happens in networks made of switches with ineffective or inadequate buffering capabilities combined with poor packet discard or ABR congestion feedback mechanisms.

**connection ID** Identifications given to each Telnet session into a router. The `show sessions` command will give you the connections a local router will have to a remote router. The `show users` command will show the connection IDs of users telnetted into your local router.

**connectionless** Data transfer that occurs without the creation of a virtual circuit. It has no overhead, uses best-effort delivery, is not reliable. *Contrast with: connection-oriented. See also: virtual circuit.*

**connection-oriented** Data transfer method that sets up a virtual circuit before any data is transferred. Uses acknowledgments and flow control for reliable data transfer. *Contrast with: connectionless. See also: virtual circuit.*

**console port** Typically an RJ-45 port on a Cisco router and switch that allows command-line interface capability.

**Content Addressable Memory** *See: CAM.*

**contention media** Media access method that is a baseband media—that is, first come, first served. Ethernet is an example of a contention media access.

**contiguous buffers** Contiguous buffers are formed from a single physical memory block.

**control direct VCC** One of three control connections defined by Phase I LAN emulation; a bi-directional virtual channel connection (VCC) established in ATM by an LEC to an LES. *See also: control distribute VCC* and *data direct VCC.*

**control distribute VCC** One of three control connections defined by Phase 1 LAN emulation; a unidirectional virtual channel connection (VCC) set up in ATM from an LES to an LEC. Usually, the VCC is a point-to-multipoint connection. *See also: control direct VCC* and *data direct VCC.*

**convergence** The process required for all routers in an internetwork to update their routing tables and create a consistent view of the network, using the best possible paths. No user data is passed during a convergence time.

**core block** If you have two or more switch blocks, the Cisco rule of thumb states that you need a core block. No routing is performed at the core, only transferring of data. It is a pass-through for the switch block, the server block, and the Internet. The core is responsible for transferring data to and from the switch blocks as quickly as possible. You can build a fast core with a frame, packet, or cell (ATM) network technology.

**core layer** Top layer in the Cisco three-layer hierarchical model, which helps you design, build, and maintain Cisco hierarchical networks. The core layer passes packets quickly to distribution-layer devices only. No packet filtering should take place at this layer.

**cost** An arbitrary value, based on hop count, bandwidth, or other calculation, that is typically assigned by a network administrator and used by the routing protocol to compare different routes through an internetwork. Routing protocols use cost values to select the best path to a certain destination: the lowest cost identifies the best path. Also known as "path cost." *See also: routing metric.*

**count to infinity** A problem occurring in routing algorithms that are slow to converge where routers keep increasing the hop count to particular networks. To avoid this problem, various solutions have been implemented into each of the different routing protocols. Some of those solutions include defining a maximum hop count (defining infinity), route poisoning, poison reverse, and split horizon.

**CPCS** Common Part Convergence Sublayer: One of two AAL sublayers that is service-dependent, it is further segmented into the CS and SAR sublayers. The CPCS prepares data for transmission across the ATM network; it creates the 48-byte payload cells that are sent to the ATM layer. *See also: AAL* and *ATM layer.*

**CPE** Customer Premises Equipment: Items such as telephones, modems, and terminals installed at customer locations and connected to the telephone company network.

**crankback** In ATM, a correction technique used when a node somewhere on a chosen path cannot accept a connection setup request, blocking the request. The path is rolled back to an intermediate node, which then uses GCAC to attempt to find an alternate path to the final destination.

**CRC** cyclic redundancy check: A methodology that detects errors, whereby the frame recipient makes a calculation by dividing frame contents with a prime binary divisor and compares the remainder to a value stored in the frame by the sending node. *Compare to: checksum.*

**crossbar** A switch-fabric comprising a matrix of totally connected cross-points. Sometimes referred to as a *matrix.*

**CSMA/CD** Carrier Sense Multiple Access with Collision Detection: A technology defined by the Ethernet IEEE 802.3 committee. Each device senses the cable for a digital signal before transmitting. Also, CSMA/CD allows all devices on the network to share the same cable, but one at a time. If two devices transmit at the same time, a frame collision will occur and a jamming pattern will be sent; the devices will stop transmitting, wait a predetermined amount of time, and then try to transmit again.

**CST** Common Spanning Tree: One spanning tree instance encompassing every VLAN in the switched network.

**CSU** channel service unit: A digital mechanism that connects end-user equipment to the local digital telephone loop. Frequently referred to along with the data service unit as "CSU/DSU." *See also: DSU.*

**CTD** Cell Transfer Delay: For a given connection in ATM, the time period between a cell exit event at the source user-network interface (UNI) and the corresponding cell entry event at the destination. The CTD between these points is the sum of the total inter-ATM transmission delay and the total ATM processing delay.

**custom queuing** Used by Cisco router IOS to provide a queuing method to slower serial links. Custom queuing enables an administrator to configure the type of traffic that will have priority over the link.

**cut-through** *See: cut-through frame switching.*

**cut-through frame switching** A frame-switching technique that flows data through a switch so that the leading edge exits the switch at the output port before the packet finishes entering the input port. Frames will be read, processed, and forwarded by devices that use cut-through switching as soon as the destination address of the frame is confirmed and the outgoing port is identified.

# D

**data compression** *See: compression.*

**data direct VCC** A bidirectional point-to-point virtual channel connection (VCC) set up between two LECs in ATM and one of three data connections defined by Phase 1 LAN emulation. Because data-direct VCCs do not guarantee QoS, they are generally reserved for UBR and ABR connections. *See also: control direct VCC* and *control distribute VCC.*

**data encapsulation** The process in which the information in a protocol is wrapped, or contained, in the data section of another protocol. In the OSI reference model, each layer encapsulates the layer immediately above it as the data flows down the protocol stack.

**data frame** Protocol Data Unit encapsulation at the Data Link layer of the OSI reference model. Encapsulates packets from the Network layer and prepares the data for transmission on a network medium.

**datagram** A logical collection of information transmitted as a Network layer unit over a medium without a previously established virtual circuit. IP datagrams have become the primary information unit of the Internet. At various layers of the OSI reference model, the terms *cell, frame, message, packet,* and *segment* also define these logical information groupings.

**Data Link Control layer** Layer 2 of the SNA architectural model, it is responsible for the transmission of data over a given physical link and compares somewhat to the Data Link layer of the OSI model.

**Data Link layer** Layer 2 of the OSI reference model, it ensures the trustworthy transmission of data across a physical link and is primarily concerned with physical addressing, line discipline, network topology, error notification, ordered delivery of frames, and flow control. The IEEE has further segmented this layer into the MAC sublayer and the LLC sublayer. Also known as the "Link layer." Can be compared somewhat to the Data Link Control layer of the SNA model. *See also: Application layer, LLC, MAC, Network layer, Physical layer, Presentation layer, Session layer,* and *Transport layer.*

**DCC** Data Country Code: Developed by the ATM Forum, one of two ATM address formats designed for use by private networks. *Compare to: ICD.*

**DCE** data communications equipment (as defined by the EIA) or data circuit-terminating equipment (as defined by the ITU-T): The mechanisms and links of a communications network that make up the network portion of the user-to-network interface, such as modems. The DCE supplies the physical connection to the network, forwards traffic, and provides a clocking signal to synchronize data transmission between DTE and DCE devices. *Compare to: DTE.*

**D channel** (1) data channel: A full-duplex, 16Kbps (BRI) or 64Kbps (PRI) ISDN channel. *Compare to: B channel, E channel,* and *H channel.* (2) In SNA, anything that provides a connection between the processor and main storage with any peripherals.

**DDP** Datagram Delivery Protocol: Used in the AppleTalk suite of protocols as a connectionless protocol that is responsible for sending datagrams through an internetwork.

**DDR** dial-on-demand routing: A technique that enables a router to automatically initiate and end a circuit-switched session per the requirements of the sending station. By mimicking keepalives, the router fools the end station into treating the session as active. DDR permits routing over ISDN or telephone lines via a modem or external ISDN terminal adapter.

**DE** Discard Eligibility: Used in Frame Relay networks to tell a switch that a frame can be discarded if the switch is too busy. The DE is a field in the frame that is turned on by transmitting routers if the Committed Information Rate (CIR) is oversubscribed or set to 0.

**DE bit** The DE bit marks a frame as discard eligible on a Frame Relay network. If a serial link is congested and the Frame Relay network has passed the Committed Information Rate (CIR), then the DE bit will always be on.

**default route** The static routing table entry used to direct frames whose next hop is not spelled out in the dynamic routing table.

**delay** The time elapsed between a sender's initiation of a transaction and the first response they receive. Also, the time needed to move a packet from its source to its destination over a path. *See also: latency.*

**demarc** The demarcation point between the customer premises equipment (CPE) and the telco's carrier equipment.

**demodulation** A series of steps that return a modulated signal to its original form. When receiving, a modem demodulates an analog signal to its original digital form (and, conversely, modulates the digital data it sends into an analog signal). *See also: modulation.*

**demultiplexing** The process of converting a single multiplex signal, comprising more than one input stream, back into separate output streams. *Contrast with: multiplexing.*

**denial-of-service attack** A denial-of-service attack, or DoS, blocks access to a network resource by saturating the device with attacking data. Typically, this is targeted against the link (particularly lower-bandwidth links) or the server. DDoS attacks, or distributed denial-of-service attacks, make use of multiple originating attacking resources to saturate a more capable resource.

**designated bridge** In the process of forwarding a frame from a segment to the route bridge, the bridge with the lowest path cost.

**designated ports** Used with the Spanning Tree Protocol (STP) to designate forwarding ports. If there are multiple links to the same network, STP will shut down a port to stop network loops.

**designated router** An OSPF router that creates LSAs for a multi-access network and is required to perform other special tasks in OSPF operations. Multi-access OSPF networks that maintain a minimum of two attached routers identify one router that is chosen by the OSPF Hello protocol, which makes possible a decrease in the number of adjacencies necessary on a multi-access network. This in turn reduces the quantity of routing protocol traffic and the physical size of the database.

**destination address** The address for the network devices that will receive a packet.

**dial backup** Dial backup connections are typically used to provide redundancy to Frame Relay connections. The backup link is activated over an analog modem.

**differentiated services** The name applied to the mechanism whereby routers in an internetwork forward data in queues configured to respond to specific bits—the Differentiated Services Code Points (DSCP)—in an IP header.

**DiffServe** *See: differentiated services.*

**digital** A digital waveform is one in which distinct ones and zeros provide the data representation. *See also: analog.*

**directed broadcast** A data frame or packet that is transmitted to a specific group of nodes on a remote network segment. Directed broadcasts are known by their broadcast address, which is a destination subnet address with all the bits turned on. *Compare to: broadcast.*

**discard eligible** In a Frame Relay network, frames which have the Discard Eligible flag set may be discarded at congested switches.

**discovery mode** Also known as "dynamic configuration," this technique is used by an AppleTalk interface to gain information from a working node about an attached network. The information is subsequently used by the interface for self-configuration.

**distance-vector routing algorithm** In order to find the shortest path, this group of routing algorithms repeats on the number of hops in a given route, requiring each router to send its complete routing table with each update, but only to its neighbors. Routing algorithms of this type tend to generate loops, but they are fundamentally simpler than their link-state counterparts. *See also: link-state routing algorithm* and *SPF.*

**distribution layer** Middle layer of the Cisco three-layer hierarchical model, which helps you design, install, and maintain Cisco hierarchical networks. The distribution layer is the point where Access layer devices connect. Routing is performed at this layer.

**distribution list** Access list used to filter incoming and outgoing route table entries on a router.

**DLCI** Data-Link Connection Identifier: Used to identify virtual circuits in a Frame Relay network.

**DNS** Domain Name System: Used to resolve host names to IP addresses.

**DSAP** Destination Service Access Point: The service access point of a network node, specified in the destination field of a packet. *See also: SSAP* and *SAP.*

**DSL** Digital Subscriber Line: DSL technologies are used to provide broadband services over a single copper pair, typically to residential customers. Most vendors are providing DSL services at up to 6Mbps downstream, but the technology can support 52Mbps service.

**DSR** Data Set Ready: When a DCE is powered up and ready to run, this EIA/TIA-232 interface circuit is also engaged.

**DSU** data service unit: This device is used to adapt the physical interface on a data terminal equipment (DTE) mechanism to a transmission facility such as T1 or E1 and is also responsible for signal timing. It is commonly grouped with the channel service unit and referred to as the "CSU/DSU." *See also: CSU.*

**DTE** data terminal equipment: Any device located at the user end of a user-network interface serving as a destination, a source, or both. DTE includes devices such as multiplexers, protocol translators, and computers. The connection to a data network is made through data channel equipment (DCE) such as a modem, using the clocking signals generated by that device. *Compare to: DCE.*

**DTR** data terminal ready: An activated EIA/TIA-232 circuit communicating to the DCE the state of preparedness of the DTE to transmit or receive data.

**DUAL** Diffusing Update Algorithm: Used in Enhanced IGRP, this convergence algorithm provides loop-free operation throughout an entire route's computation. DUAL grants routers involved in a topology revision the ability to synchronize simultaneously, while routers unaffected by this change are not involved. *See also: Enhanced IGRP.*

**DVMRP** Distance Vector Multicast Routing Protocol: Based primarily on the Routing Information Protocol (RIP), this Internet gateway protocol implements a common, condensed-mode IP multicast scheme, using IGMP to transfer routing datagrams between its neighbors. *See also: IGMP.*

**DXI** Data Exchange Interface: Described in RFC 1482, DXI defines the effectiveness of a network device such as a router, bridge, or hub to act as an FEP to an ATM network by using a special DSU that accomplishes packet encapsulation.

**dynamic entries** Used in layer 2 and layer 3 devices to dynamically create a table of either hardware addresses or logical addresses.

**dynamic routing** Also known as "adaptive routing," this technique automatically adapts to traffic or physical network revisions.

**dynamic VLAN** An administrator will create an entry with a server, which will be configured with the hardware addresses of all devices on the internetwork. The server then assigns dynamically used VLANs.

# E

**E1** Generally used in Europe, a wide-area digital transmission scheme carrying data at 2.048Mbps. E1 transmission lines are available for lease from common carriers for private use.

**E.164** (1) Evolved from the standard telephone numbering system, the standard recommended by ITU-T for international telecommunication numbering, particularly in ISDN, SMDS, and BISDN. (2) Label of a field in an ATM address containing numbers in E.164 format.

**E channel** echo channel: A 64Kbps ISDN control channel used for circuit switching. Specific description of this channel can be found in the 1984 ITU-T ISDN specification, but was dropped from the 1988 version. *Compare to: B channel, D channel,* and *H channel.*

**edge device** A device that enables packets to be forwarded between legacy interfaces (such as Ethernet and Token Ring) and ATM interfaces based on information in the Data Link and Network layers. An edge device does not take part in the running of any Network layer routing protocol; it merely uses the route description protocol in order to get the forwarding information required.

**EEPROM** electronically erasable programmable read-only memory: Programmed after their manufacture, these non-volatile memory chips can be erased if necessary by using electric power and reprogrammed. *Compare to: EPROM* and *PROM.*

**EFCI** Explicit Forward Congestion Indication: A congestion feedback mode permitted by ABR service in an ATM network. The EFCI can be set by any network element that is in a state of immediate or certain congestion. The destination end-system is able to carry out a protocol that adjusts and lowers the cell rate of the connection based on value of the EFCI. *See also: ABR.*

**EIGRP** *See: Enhanced IGRP.*

**EIP** Ethernet Interface Processor: A Cisco 7000 series router interface processor card, supplying 10Mbps AUI ports to support Ethernet Version 1 and Ethernet Version 2 or IEEE 802.3 interfaces with a high-speed data path to other interface processors.

**ELAN** Emulated LAN: An ATM network configured by using a client/server model in order to emulate either an Ethernet or Token Ring LAN. Multiple ELANs can exist at the same time on a single ATM network and are made up of a LAN Emulation Client (LEC), a LAN Emulation Server (LES), a broadcast and unknown server (BUS), and a LAN Emulation Configuration Server (LECS). ELANs are defined by the LANE specification. *See also: LANE, LEC, LECS,* and *LES.*

**ELAP** EtherTalk Link Access Protocol: In an EtherTalk network, the link-access protocol constructed above the standard Ethernet Data Link layer.

**enable packets** Packets that complete the flow cache. After the MLS-SE determines that the packet meets enable criteria, such as source MAC (SMAC) address and destination IP, the flow cache is established and subsequent packets are layer 3 switched. *See also: MLS-SE* and *MLS-RP.*

**encapsulation** The technique used by layered protocols in which a layer adds header information to the Protocol Data Unit (PDU) from the layer above. As an example, in Internet terminology, a packet would contain a header from the Physical layer, followed by a header from the Network layer (IP), followed by a header from the Transport layer (TCP), followed by the application protocol data.

**encryption** The conversion of information into a scrambled form that effectively disguises it to prevent unauthorized access. Every encryption scheme uses some well-defined algorithm, which is reversed at the receiving end by an opposite algorithm in a process known as decryption.

**end-to-end VLAN** VLAN that spans the switch-fabric from end to end; all switches in end-to-end VLANs understand about all configured VLANs. End-to-end VLANs are configured to allow membership based on function, project, department, and so on.

**Enhanced IGRP (EIGRP)** Enhanced Interior Gateway Routing Protocol: An advanced routing protocol created by Cisco, combining the advantages of link-state and distance-vector protocols. Enhanced IGRP has superior convergence attributes, including high operating efficiency. *See also: IGP, OSPF,* and *RIP.*

**Enhanced Image** An Enhanced Image runs on certain Catalyst 2950 switches and supports all features of the Standard Image, plus extra QoS, security, and traffic management. *See also: Standard Image.*

**enterprise network** A privately owned and operated network that connects most major locations in a large company or organization.

**enterprise services** Services provided to all users on the internetwork. Layer 3 switches or routers are required in this scenario because the services must be close to the core and would probably be based in their own subnet. Examples of these services include Internet access, e-mail, and possibly videoconferencing. If the servers that host these enterprise services were placed close to the backbone, all users would have the same distance to them, but this also means that all users' data would have to cross the backbone to get to these services.

**EPROM** erasable programmable read-only memory: Programmed after their manufacture, these non-volatile memory chips can be erased if necessary by using high-power light and reprogrammed. *Compare to: EEPROM* and *PROM.*

**error correction** A process that uses a checksum to detect bit errors in the data stream.

**ESF** Extended Superframe: Made up of 24 frames with 192 bits each, with the 193rd bit providing other functions including timing. This is an enhanced version of SF. *See also: SF.*

**Ethernet** A baseband LAN specification created by the Xerox Corporation and then improved through joint efforts of Xerox, Digital Equipment Corporation, and Intel. Ethernet is similar to the IEEE 802.3 series standard and, using CSMA/CD, operates over various types of cables at 10Mbps. Also called "DIX (Digital/Intel/Xerox) Ethernet." *Compare to: FastEthernet. See also: IEEE.*

**excess rate** In ATM networking, traffic exceeding a connection's insured rate. The excess rate is the maximum rate less the insured rate. Depending on the availability of network resources, excess traffic can be discarded during congestion episodes. *Compare to: maximum rate.*

**expansion** The procedure of directing compressed data through an algorithm, restoring information to its original size.

**expedited delivery** An option that can be specified by one protocol layer, communicating either with other layers or with the identical protocol layer in a different network device, requiring that identified data be processed faster.

**explorer packet** An SNA packet transmitted by a source Token Ring device to find the path through a source-route-bridged network.

**extended IP access list** IP access list that filters the network by logical address, protocol field in the Network layer header, and even the port field in the Transport layer header.

**extended IPX access list** IPX access list that filters the network by logical IPX address, protocol field in the Network layer header, or even socket number in the Transport layer header.

**Extended Setup** Used in setup mode to configure the router with more detail than Basic Setup mode. Allows multiple-protocol support and interface configuration.

**external route processor** A router that is external to the switch. An external layer 3 routing device can be used to provide routing between VLANs.

# F

**failure domain** The region in which a failure has occurred in a token ring. When a station gains information that a serious problem, such as a cable break, has occurred with the network, it sends a beacon frame that includes the station reporting the failure, its Next Addressable Upstream Neighbor (NAUN), and everything between. This defines the failure domain. Beaconing then initiates the procedure known as auto-reconfiguration. *See also: auto-reconfiguration* and *beacon.*

**fallback** In ATM networks, this mechanism is used for scouting a path if it isn't possible to locate one by using customary methods. The device relaxes requirements for certain characteristics, such as delay, in an attempt to find a path that meets a certain set of the most important requirements.

**Fast EtherChannel** Fast EtherChannel uses load distribution to share the links called a *bundle*, which is a group of links treated as a single link. Should one link in the bundle fail, the Ethernet Bundle Controller (EBC) informs the Enhanced Address Recognition Logic (EARL) ASIC of the failure, and the EARL in turn ages out all addresses learned on that link. The EBC and the EARL use hardware to recalculate the source and destination address pair on a different link.

**FastEthernet** Any Ethernet specification with a speed of 100Mbps. FastEthernet is 10 times faster than 10BaseT, while retaining qualities such as MAC mechanisms, MTU, and frame format. These similarities make it possible for existing 10BaseT applications and management tools to be used on FastEthernet networks. FastEthernet is based on an extension of IEEE 802.3 specification (IEEE 802.3u). *Compare to: Ethernet. See also: 100BaseT, 100BaseTX,* and *IEEE.*

**fast switching** A Cisco feature that uses a route cache to speed packet switching through a router. *Compare to: process switching.*

**FDDI** Fiber Distributed Data Interface: A LAN standard, defined by ANSI X3T9.5, that can run at speeds up to 200Mbps and uses token-passing media access on fiber-optic cable. For redundancy, FDDI can use a dual-ring architecture.

**FDM** Frequency-Division Multiplexing: A technique that permits information from several channels to be assigned bandwidth on one wire based on frequency. *Contrast with: ATDM, TDM,* and *statistical multiplexing.*

**FECN** Forward Explicit Congestion Notification: A bit set by a Frame Relay network that informs the DTE receptor that congestion was encountered along the path from source to destination. A device receiving frames with the FECN bit set can ask higher-priority protocols to take flow-control action as needed. *Contrast with: BECN.*

**FEIP** FastEthernet Interface Processor: An interface processor employed on Cisco 7000 series routers, supporting up to two 100Mbps 100BaseT ports.

**firewall** A barrier purposefully erected between any connected public networks and a private network, made up of a router or access server or several routers or access servers, that uses access lists and other methods to ensure the security of the private network.

**first in, first out** The default mechanism for servicing data in a queue is usually based on the first in, first out (FIFO) principle.

**Flash** electronically erasable programmable read-only memory (EEPROM). Used to hold the Cisco IOS in a router by default.

**flash memory** Developed by Intel and licensed to other semiconductor manufacturers, it is non-volatile storage that can be erased electronically and reprogrammed, physically located on an EEPROM chip. Flash memory permits software images to be stored, booted, and rewritten as needed. Cisco routers and switches use flash memory to hold the IOS by default. *See also: EPROM* and *EEPROM.*

**flat network** A network that is one large collision domain and one large broadcast domain.

**flooding** When traffic is received on an interface, it is then transmitted to every interface connected to that device except the interface from which the traffic originated. This technique can be used for traffic transfer by bridges and switches throughout the network.

**flow** A shortcut or MLS cache entry that is defined by the packet properties. Packets with identical properties belong to the same flow. *See also: MLS.*

**flow control** A methodology used to ensure that receiving units are not overwhelmed with data from sending devices. Pacing, as it is called in IBM networks, means that when buffers at a receiving unit are full, a message is transmitted to the sending unit to temporarily halt transmissions until all the data in the receiving buffer has been processed and the buffer is again ready for action.

**forwarding and filtering decision** The decision-making process that a switch goes through to determine which ports to forward a frame out of.

**FRAD** Frame Relay Access Device: Any device affording a connection between a LAN and a Frame Relay WAN. *See also: Cisco FRAD* and *FRAS*.

**fragment** Any portion of a larger packet that has been intentionally segmented into smaller pieces. A packet fragment does not necessarily indicate an error and can be intentional. *See also: fragmentation.*

**fragmentation** The process of intentionally segmenting a packet into smaller pieces when sending data over an intermediate network medium that cannot support the larger packet size.

**FragmentFree** LAN switch type that reads into the data section of a frame to make sure fragmentation did not occur. Sometimes called "modified cut-through."

**frame** A logical unit of information sent by the Data Link layer over a transmission medium. The term often refers to the header and trailer, employed for synchronization and error control, that surround the data contained in the unit.

**Frame Relay** A more efficient replacement of the X.25 protocol (an unrelated packet relay technology that guarantees data delivery). Frame Relay is an industry-standard, shared-access, best-effort, switched Data-Link layer encapsulation that services multiple virtual circuits and protocols between connected mechanisms.

**Frame Relay bridging** Defined in RFC 1490, this bridging method uses the identical spanning-tree algorithm as other bridging operations but permits packets to be encapsulated for transmission across a Frame Relay network.

**Frame Relay switching** A process that occurs when a router at a service provider provides packet switching for Frame Relay packets.

**frame tagging** VLANs can span multiple connected switches, which Cisco calls a switch-fabric. Switches within this switch-fabric must keep track of frames as they are received on the switch ports, and they must keep track of the VLAN they belong to as the frames traverse this switch-fabric. Frame tagging performs this function. Switches can then direct frames to the appropriate port.

**framing** Encapsulation at the Data Link layer of the OSI model. It is called framing because the packet is encapsulated with both a header and a trailer.

**FRAS** Frame Relay Access Support: A feature of Cisco IOS software that enables SDLC-, Ethernet-, Token Ring-, and Frame Relay–attached IBM devices to be linked with other IBM mechanisms on a Frame Relay network. *See also: FRAD.*

**frequency** The number of cycles of an alternating current signal per time unit, measured in hertz (cycles per second).

**FSIP** Fast Serial Interface Processor: The Cisco 7000 routers' default serial interface processor, it provides four or eight high-speed serial ports.

**FTP** File Transfer Protocol: The TCP/IP protocol used for transmitting files between network nodes, it supports a broad range of file types and is defined in RFC 959. *See also: TFTP.*

**full duplex** The capacity to transmit information between a sending station and a receiving unit at the same time. *See also: half duplex.*

**full mesh** A type of network topology in which every node has either a physical or a virtual circuit linking it to every other network node. A full mesh supplies a great deal of redundancy but is typically reserved for network backbones because of its expense. *See also: partial mesh.*

# G

**Gigabit EtherChannel** *See: Fast EtherChannel.*

**Gigabit Ethernet** 1000Mbps version of the IEEE 802.3. FastEthernet offers a speed increase of 10 times that of the 10BaseT Ethernet specification while preserving qualities such as frame format, MAC, mechanisms, and MTU.

**GLBP** Gateway Load Balancing Protocol: A protocol designed to provide redundancy of the client default gateway by using virtual addresses. In addition, the use of virtual MAC addresses allows all routers in a group to forward data. An alternative to HSRP. *See also: AVF, AVG,* and *HSRP.*

**GNS** Get Nearest Server: On an IPX network, a request packet sent by a customer for determining the location of the nearest active server of a given type. An IPX network client launches a GNS request to get either a direct answer from a connected server or a response from a router disclosing the location of the service on the internetwork to the GNS. GNS is part of IPX and SAP. *See also: IPX* and *SAP.*

**grafting** A process that activates an interface that has been deactivated by the pruning process. It is initiated by an IGMP membership report sent to the router.

**GRE** Generic Routing Encapsulation: A tunneling protocol created by Cisco with the capacity for encapsulating a wide variety of protocol packet types inside IP tunnels, thereby generating a virtual point-to-point connection to Cisco routers across an IP network at remote points. IP tunneling using GRE permits network expansion across a single-protocol backbone environment by linking multiprotocol subnetworks in a single-protocol backbone environment.

**guard band** The unused frequency area found between two communications channels, furnishing the space necessary to avoid interference between the two.

# H

**half duplex** The capacity to transfer data in only one direction at a time between a sending unit and a receiving unit. *See also: full duplex.*

**handshake** Any series of transmissions exchanged between two or more devices on a network to ensure synchronized operations.

**H channel** high-speed channel: A full-duplex, ISDN primary rate channel operating at a speed of 384Kbps. *Compare to: B channel, D channel,* and *E channel.*

**HDLC** High-Level Data Link Control: Using frame characters, including checksums, HDLC designates a method for data encapsulation on synchronous serial links and is the default encapsulation for Cisco routers. HDLC is a bit-oriented synchronous Data Link layer protocol created by ISO and derived from SDLC. However, most HDLC vendor implementations (including Cisco's) are proprietary. *See also: SDLC.*

**helper address** The unicast address specified, which instructs the Cisco router to change the client's local broadcast request for a service into a directed unicast to the server.

**hierarchical addressing** Any addressing plan employing a logical chain of commands to determine location. IP addresses are made up of a hierarchy of network numbers, subnet numbers, and host numbers to direct packets to the appropriate destination.

**hierarchical network** A multi-segment network configuration providing only one path through intermediate segments, between source segments and destination segments.

**hierarchy** *See: hierarchical network.*

**HIP** HSSI Interface Processor: An interface processor used on Cisco 7000 series routers, providing one HSSI port that supports connections to ATM, SMDS, Frame Relay, or private lines at speeds up to T3 or E3.

**holddown** The state a route is placed in so that routers can neither advertise the route nor accept advertisements about it for a defined time period. Holddown is used to allow time for bad information about a route to be propagated all routers in the network. A router generally places a route in holddown if a directly connected link fails.

**hop** The movement of a packet between any two network nodes. *See also: hop count.*

**hop count** A routing metric that calculates the distance between a source and a destination. RIP employs hop count as its sole metric. *See also: hop* and *RIP.*

**host address** Logical address configured by an administrator or server on a device. Logically identifies this device on an internetwork.

**HSCI** High-Speed Communication Interface: Developed by Cisco, a single-port interface that provides full-duplex synchronous serial communications capability at speeds up to 52Mbps.

**HSRP** Hot Standby Routing Protocol: A protocol that provides high network availability and provides nearly instantaneous hardware failover without administrator intervention. It generates a Hot Standby router group, including a lead router that lends its services to any packet being transferred to the Hot Standby address. If the lead router fails, it will be replaced by any of the other routers—the standby routers—that monitor it.

**HSSI** High-Speed Serial Interface: A network standard physical connector for high-speed serial linking over a WAN at speeds of up to 52Mbps.

**hub** Physical layer devices that are really just multiple port repeaters. When an electronic digital signal is received on a port, the signal is reamplified or regenerated and forwarded out all segments except the segment from which the signal was received.

# I

**ICD** International Code Designator: Adapted from the subnetwork model of addressing, this assigns the mapping of Network layer addresses to ATM addresses. HSSI is one of two ATM formats for addressing created by the ATM Forum to be utilized with private networks. *Compare to: DCC.*

**ICMP** Internet Control Message Protocol: Documented in RFC 792, it is a Network layer Internet protocol for the purpose of reporting errors and providing information pertinent to IP packet procedures.

**IEEE** Institute of Electrical and Electronics Engineers: A professional organization that, among other activities, defines standards in a number of fields within computing and electronics, including networking and communications. IEEE standards are the predominant LAN standards used today throughout the industry. Many protocols are commonly known by the reference number of the corresponding IEEE standard.

**IEEE 802.1** The IEEE committee specification that defines the bridging group. The specification for STP (Spanning Tree Protocol) is IEEE 802.1d. The STP uses SPA (spanning-tree algorithm) to find and prevent network loops in bridged networks.

**IEEE 802.1p** 802.1p specifies 3 bits in the 802.1Q header for allocation to Class of Service (CoS). This is analogous to quality of service in IP.

**IEEE 802.1Q** The specification for VLAN trunking is IEEE 802.1Q, which specifies additional fields inside any LAN frame.

**IEEE 802.3** The IEEE committee specification that defines the Ethernet group, specifically the original 10Mbps standard. Ethernet is a LAN protocol that specifies Physical layer and MAC sublayer media access. IEEE 802.3 uses CSMA/CD to provide access for many devices on the same network. FastEthernet is defined as 802.3u, and Gigabit Ethernet is defined as 802.3q. *See also: CSMA/CD.*

**IEEE 802.5** IEEE committee that defines Token Ring media access.

**IGMP** Internet Group Management Protocol: Employed by IP hosts, the protocol that reports their multicast group memberships to an adjacent multicast router. The first version, IGMPv1, enables hosts to subscribe to or join specified multicast groups. Enhancements were made to IGMPv2 to facilitate a host-initiated leave process, and IGMPv3 allows hosts to specify the list of hosts from whom they can receive traffic, blocking traffic from other hosts transmitting the same stream.

**IGMP Join process** The process by which hosts may join a multicast session outside of the Membership Query interval.

**IGMP Leave process** IGMPv1 does not have a formal leave process; a period of three query intervals must pass with no host confirmation before the interface is deactivated. IGMPv2 and IGMPv3 do allow the host to initiate the leave process immediately.

**IGMP Query process** The router uses IGMP to query hosts for Membership Reports, thus managing multicast on its interfaces.

**IGMP Snooping** An extension to CGMP, IGMP Snooping enables the switch to make multicast decisions directly, without the intervention of a router.

**IGP** Interior Gateway Protocol: Any protocol used by the Internet to exchange routing data within an independent system. Examples include RIP, IGRP, and OSPF.

**ILMI** Integrated (or Interim) Local Management Interface. A specification created by the ATM Forum, designated for the incorporation of network-management capability into the ATM UNI. Integrated Local Management Interface cells provide for automatic configuration between ATM systems. In LAN emulation, ILMI can provide sufficient information for the ATM end station to find an LECS. In addition, ILMI provides the ATM NSAP (Network Service Access Point) prefix information to the end station.

**in-band** *See: in-band management.*

**in-band management** The management of a network device "through" the network. Examples include using Simple Network Management Protocol (SNMP) or Telnet directly via the local LAN. *Compare to: out-of-band management.*

**in-band signaling** Configuration of a router from within the network. Examples are Telnet, Simple Network Management Protocol (SNMP), or a Network Management Station (NMS). *Compare to: out-of-band signaling.*

**insured burst** In an ATM network, it is the largest temporarily permitted data burst exceeding the insured rate on a PVC and not tagged by the traffic policing function for being dropped if network congestion occurs. This insured burst is designated in bytes or cells. *Compare to: maximum burst.*

**Integrated Services** Integrated Services networks use signaling protocols to establish an end-to-end path across an internetwork, with a predefined QoS applied to each traffic flow.

**interarea routing** Routing between two or more logical areas. *Compare to: intra-area routing. See also: area.*

**interface processor** Any of several processor modules used with Cisco 7000 series routers. *See also: AIP, CIP, EIP, FEIP, HIP, MIP,* and *TRIP.*

**internal route processor** Route Switch Modules (RSMs) and Route Switch Feature Cards (RSFCs) are called internal route processors because the processing of layer 3 packets is internal to a switch.

**Internet** The global "network of networks," whose popularity has exploded in the last few years. Originally a tool for collaborative academic research, it has become a medium for exchanging and distributing information of all kinds. The Internet's need to link disparate computer platforms and technologies has led to the development of uniform protocols and standards that have also found widespread use within corporate LANs. *See also: TCP/IP* and *MBONE.*

**internet** Before the rise in the use of the Internet, this lowercase form was shorthand for "internetwork" in the generic sense. Now rarely used. *See also: internetwork.*

**Internet protocol** Any protocol belonging to the TCP/IP protocol stack. *See also: TCP/IP.*

**internetwork** Any group of private networks interconnected by routers and other mechanisms, typically operating as a single entity.

**internetworking** Broadly, anything associated with the general task of linking networks to each other. The term encompasses technologies, procedures, and products. When you connect networks to a router, you are creating an internetwork.

**inter-VLAN routing** Cisco has created the proprietary protocol Inter-Switch Link (ISL) to allow routing between VLANs with only one Ethernet interface. To run ISL, you need to have two VLAN-capable FastEthernet or Gigabit Ethernet devices, such as a Cisco 5000 switch and a 7000 series router.

**intra-area routing** Routing that occurs within a logical area. *Compare to: interarea routing.*

**intruder detection** A system that operates by monitoring the data flow for characteristics consistent with security threats. In this manner, an intruder can be monitored or blocked from access. One trigger for an intruder detection system is multiple ping packets from a single resource in a brief period of time.

**Inverse ARP** Inverse Address Resolution Protocol: A technique by which dynamic mappings are constructed in a network, enabling a device such as a router to locate the logical network address and associate it with a permanent virtual circuit (PVC). Commonly used in Frame Relay to determine the far-end node's TCP/IP address by sending the Inverse ARP request to the local DLCI.

**IOS** Cisco's famous fully-inclusive Internetwork Operating System.

**IP** Internet Protocol: Defined in RFC 791, it is a Network layer protocol that is part of the TCP/IP stack and allows connectionless service. IP furnishes an array of features for addressing, type-of-service specification, fragmentation and reassembly, and security.

**IP address** Often called an "Internet address," this is an address uniquely identifying any device (host) on the Internet (or any TCP/IP network). Each address consists of four octets (32 bits), represented as decimal numbers separated by periods (a format known as "dotted-decimal"). Every address is made up of a network number, an optional subnetwork number, and a host number. The network and subnetwork numbers together are used for routing, while the host number addresses an individual host within the network or subnetwork. The network and subnetwork information is extracted from the IP address by using the subnet mask. There are five classes of IP addresses (A–E), which allocate different numbers of bits to the network, subnetwork, and host portions of the address. *See also: CIDR, IP,* and *subnet mask.*

**IPCP** IP Control Program: The protocol used to establish and configure IP over PPP. *See also: IP* and *PPP.*

**IP multicast** A technique for routing that enables IP traffic to be reproduced from one source to several endpoints or from multiple sources to many destinations. Instead of transmitting only one packet to each individual point of destination, one packet is sent to a multicast group specified by only one IP endpoint address for the group.

**IPX** Internetwork Packet Exchange: Network layer protocol (layer 3) used in Novell NetWare networks for transferring information from servers to workstations. Similar to IP and XNS.

**IPXCP** IPX Control Program: The protocol used to establish and configure IPX over PPP. *See also: IPX and PPP.*

**IPX spoofing** Provides IPX RIP/SAP traffic without requiring a connection to the opposing network. This allows a per-minute tariffed link, such as ISDN or analog phone, to support IPX without requiring the link to remain active.

**IPXWAN** Protocol used for new WAN links to provide and negotiate line options on the link by using IPX. After the link is up and the options have been agreed upon by the two end-to-end links, normal IPX transmission begins.

**IRDP** ICMP Router Discovery Protocol: Enables hosts to use the Internet Control Message Protocol (ICMP) to find a new path when the primary router becomes unavailable. IRDP is an extension to the ICMP protocol and not a dynamic routing protocol. This ICMP extension allows routers to advertise default routes to end stations.

**ISDN** Integrated Services Digital Network: Offered as a service by telephone companies, a communication protocol that allows telephone networks to carry data, voice, and other digital traffic. *See also: BISDN, BRI,* and *PRI.*

**ISL routing** Inter-Switch Link routing is a Cisco proprietary method of frame tagging in a switched internetwork. Frame tagging is a way to identify the VLAN membership of a frame as it traverses a switched internetwork.

**isochronous transmission** Asynchronous data transfer over a synchronous data link, requiring a constant bit rate for reliable transport. *Contrast with: asynchronous transmission* and *synchronous transmission.*

**ITU-T** International Telecommunication Union Telecommunication Standardization Sector: A group of engineers who develop worldwide standards for telecommunications technologies.

# L

**LAN** local area network: Broadly, any network linking two or more computers and related devices within a limited geographical area (up to a few kilometers). LANs are typically high-speed, low-error networks within a company. Cabling and signaling at the physical and Data Link layers of the OSI are dictated by LAN standards. Ethernet, FDDI, and Token Ring are among the most popular LAN technologies. *Compare to: MAN.*

**LANE** LAN emulation: The technology that enables an ATM network to operate as a LAN backbone. To do so, the ATM network is required to provide multicast and broadcast support, address mapping (MAC-to-ATM), and SVC management, in addition to an operable packet format. Additionally, LANE defines Ethernet and Token Ring ELANs. *See also: ELAN.*

**LAN switch** A high-speed, multiple-interface transparent bridging mechanism, transmitting packets between segments of data links, usually referred to specifically as an Ethernet switch. LAN switches transfer traffic based on MAC addresses. *See also: multi-layer switch* and *store-and-forward packet switching.*

**LAPB** Link Accessed Procedure, Balanced: A bit-oriented Data Link layer protocol that is part of the X.25 stack and has its origin in SDLC. *See also: SDLC* and *X.25.*

**LAPD** Link Access Procedure on the D channel. The ISDN Data Link layer protocol used specifically for the D channel and defined by ITU-T Recommendations Q.920 and Q.921. LAPD evolved from LAPB and is created to comply with the signaling requirements of ISDN basic access.

**latency** Broadly, the time it takes a data packet to get from one location to another. In specific networking contexts, it can mean either (1) the time elapsed (delay) between the execution of a request for access to a network by a device and the time the mechanism actually is permitted transmission, or (2) the time elapsed between when a mechanism receives a frame and the time that frame is forwarded out of the destination port.

**laws of physics delay** Delays that cannot be altered, such as the speed of electrical current traveling in a wire, or light in a fiber.

**layer 2 switching** Layer 2 switching is hardware based, which means it uses the MAC address from the hosts' NIC cards to filter the network. Switches use Application-Specific Integrated Circuits (ASICs) to build and maintain filter tables. It is OK to think of a layer 2 switch as a multiport bridge.

**layer 3 switch** *See: multi-layer switch.*

**layer 3 switching** A switching decision made with a layer 3 address as opposed to a MAC address.

**layer 3 switching module** A card or interface module performing layer 3 switching.

**layer 4 switching** A switching decision made with port and protocol or IPX socket information in addition to a layer 3 address.

**layered architecture** Industry standard way of creating applications to work on a network. Layered architecture allows the application developer to make changes in only one layer instead of the whole program.

**LCP** Link Control Protocol: The protocol designed to establish, configure, and test Data Link connections for use by PPP. *See also: PPP.*

**leaf router** The name given to a router occupying a specific topological location in a multicast network. A leaf router has no downstream PIM neighbors. Leaf routers always send PIM Dense Mode "prune" messages.

**leaky bucket** An analogy for the basic (generic) cell rate algorithm (GCRA) used in ATM networks for checking the conformance of cell flows from a user or network. The bucket's "hole" is understood to be the prolonged rate at which cells can be accommodated, and the "depth" is the tolerance for cell bursts over a certain time period.

**learning bridge** A bridge that transparently builds a dynamic database of MAC addresses and the interfaces associated with each address. Transparent bridges help to reduce traffic congestion on the network.

**LE ARP** LAN Emulation Address Resolution Protocol: The protocol providing the ATM address that corresponds to a MAC address.

**leased lines** Permanent connections between two points leased from the telephone companies.

**LEC** LAN Emulation Client: Software providing the emulation of the Link layer interface that allows the operation and communication of all higher-level protocols and applications to continue. The LEC client runs in all ATM devices, which include hosts, servers, bridges, and routers. The LANE client is responsible for address resolution, data transfer, address caching, interfacing to the emulated LAN, and driver support for higher-level services. *See also: ELAN* and *LES*.

**LECS** LAN Emulation Configuration Server: An important part of emulated LAN services, providing the configuration data that is furnished upon request from the LES. These services include address registration for Integrated Local Management Interface (ILMI) support, configuration support for the LES addresses and their corresponding emulated LAN identifiers, and an interface to the emulated LAN. *See also: LES* and *ELAN*.

**LES** LAN Emulation Server: The central LANE component that provides the initial configuration data for each connecting LEC. The LES typically is located on either an ATM-integrated router or a switch. Responsibilities of the LES include configuration and support for the LEC, address registration for the LEC, database storage and response concerning ATM addresses, and interfacing to the emulated LAN. *See also: ELAN, LEC,* and *LECS*.

**line loss** Losses associated with a cable. These could be because of poor quality installation or local interference.

**link compression** *See: compression.*

**link-state routing algorithm** A routing algorithm that enables each router to broadcast or multicast information regarding the cost of reaching all its neighbors to every node in the internetwork. Link-state algorithms provide a consistent view of the network and are therefore not vulnerable to routing loops. However, this is achieved at the cost of somewhat greater difficulty in computation and more widespread traffic (compared with distance-vector routing algorithms). *See also: distance-vector routing algorithm.*

**LLC** Logical Link Control: Defined by the IEEE, the higher of two Data Link layer sublayers. LLC is responsible for error detection (but not correction), flow control, framing, and software-sublayer addressing. The predominant LLC protocol, IEEE 802.2, defines both connectionless and connection-oriented operations. *See also: Data Link layer* and *MAC*.

**LMI** An enhancement to the original Frame Relay specification. Among the features it provides are a keep-alive mechanism, a multicast mechanism, global addressing, and a status mechanism.

**LNNI** LAN Emulation Network-to-Network Interface: In the Phase 2 LANE specification, an interface that supports communication between the server components within one ELAN.

**local explorer packet** In a Token Ring SRB network, a packet generated by an end system to find a host linked to the local ring. If no local host can be found, the end system will produce one of two solutions: a spanning explorer packet or an all-routes explorer packet.

**local loop** Connection from a demarcation point to the closest switching office.

**local services** Users trying to get to network services that are located on the same subnet or network are defined as local services. Users do not cross layer 3 devices, and the network services are in the same broadcast domain as the users. This type of traffic never crosses the backbone.

**local VLAN** A VLAN configured by geographic location; this location can be a building or just a closet in a building, depending on switch size. Geographically configured VLANs are designed around the fact that the business or corporation is using centralized resources, such as a server farm.

**loop avoidance** If multiple connections between switches are created for redundancy, network loops can occur. STP is used to stop network loops and allow redundancy.

**LSA** Link State Advertisement: Contained inside of link-state packets (LSPs), these advertisements are usually multicast packets, containing information about neighbors and path costs, that are employed by link-state protocols. Receiving routers use LSAs to maintain their link-state databases and, ultimately, routing tables.

**LUNI** LAN Emulation User-to-Network Interface: Defining the interface between the LAN Emulation Client (LEC) and the LAN Emulation Server, LUNI is the ATM Forum's standard for LAN emulation on ATM networks. *See also: LES* and *LECS.*

**LZW algorithm** A data compression process named for its inventors, Lempel, Ziv, and Welch. The algorithm works by finding longer and longer strings of data to compress with shorter representations.

# M

**MAC** Media Access Control: The lower sublayer in the Data Link layer, it is responsible for hardware addressing, media access, and error detection of frames. *See also: Data Link layer* and *LLC.*

**MAC address** A Data Link layer hardware address that every port or device needs in order to connect to a LAN segment. These addresses are used by various devices in the network for accurate location of logical addresses. MAC addresses are defined by the IEEE standard, and their length is six characters, typically using the burned-in address (BIA) of the local LAN interface. Variously called "hardware address," "physical address," "burned-in address," or "MAC layer address."

**MacIP** In AppleTalk, the Network layer protocol encapsulating IP packets in Datagram Delivery Protocol (DDP) packets. MacIP also supplies substitute ARP services.

**MAN** metropolitan area network: Any network that encompasses a metropolitan area; that is, an area typically larger than a LAN but smaller than a WAN. *Compare to: LAN.*

**Manchester encoding** A method for digital coding in which a mid-bit–time transition is employed for clocking, and a 1 (one) is denoted by a high voltage level during the first half of the bit time. This scheme is used by Ethernet and IEEE 802.3.

**matrix** A special type of switch-fabric. *See: crossbar.*

**maximum burst** Specified in bytes or cells, the largest burst of information exceeding the insured rate that will be permitted on an ATM permanent virtual connection for a short time and will not be dropped even if it goes over the specified maximum rate. *Compare to: insured burst. See also: maximum rate.*

**maximum rate** The maximum permitted data throughput on a particular virtual circuit, equal to the total of insured and uninsured traffic from the traffic source. Should traffic congestion occur, uninsured information might be deleted from the path. Measured in bits or cells per second, the maximum rate represents the highest throughput of data that the virtual circuit is ever able to deliver and cannot exceed the media rate. *Compare to: excess rate. See also: maximum burst.*

**MBONE** multicast backbone: The multicast backbone of the Internet, it is a virtual multicast network made up of multicast LANs, including point-to-point tunnels interconnecting them.

**MBS** maximum burst size: In an ATM signaling message, this metric, coded as a number of cells, is used to convey the burst tolerance.

**MCDV** maximum cell delay variation: The maximum two-point CDV objective across a link or node for the identified service category in an ATM network. The MCDV is one of four link metrics that are exchanged by using PTSPs to verify the available resources of an ATM network. Only one MCDV value is assigned to each traffic class.

**MCLR** maximum cell loss ratio: The maximum ratio of cells in an ATM network that fail to transit a link or node compared with the total number of cells that arrive at the link or node. MCLR is one of four link metrics that are exchanged using PTSPs to verify the available resources of an ATM network. The MCLR applies to cells in VBR and CBR traffic classes whose CLP bit is set to zero. *See also: CBR, CLP,* and *VBR.*

**MCR** minimum cell rate: A parameter determined by the ATM Forum for traffic management of the ATM networks. MCR is specifically defined for ABR transmissions and specifies the minimum value for the allowed cell rate (ACR). *See also: ACR* and *PCR.*

**MCTD** maximum cell transfer delay: In an ATM network, the total of the maximum cell delay variation and the fixed delay across the link or node. MCTD is one of four link metrics that are exchanged by using PNNI topology state packets to verify the available resources of an ATM network. There is one MCTD value assigned to each traffic class. *See also: MCDV.*

**Media Access Control** *See: MAC.*

**MIB** Management Information Base: Used with SNMP management software to gather information from remote devices. The management station can poll the remote device for information, or the MIB running on the remote station can be programmed to send information on a regular basis.

**MIP** Multichannel Interface Processor: The resident interface processor on Cisco 7000 series routers, providing up to two channelized T1 or E1 connections by serial cables connected to a CSU. The two controllers are capable of providing 24 T1 or 30 E1 channel groups, with each group being introduced to the system as a serial interface that can be configured individually.

**mips** Millions of instructions per second: A measure of processor speed.

**MLP** Multilink PPP: A technique used to split, recombine, and sequence datagrams across numerous logical data links.

**MLS** Multi-Layer Switching: Switching typically takes place at layer 2. When layer 3 information is allowed to be cached, layer 2 devices have the capability of rewriting and forwarding frames based on the layer 3 information.

**MLSP** Multi-Layer Switching Protocol: A protocol that runs on the router and enables it to communicate to the MLS-SE regarding topology or security changes.

**MLS-RP** Multi-Layer Switching Route Processor: An MLS-capable router or an RSM (Route Switch Module) installed in the switch. *See also: RSM* and *MLS.*

**MLS-SE** Multi-Layer Switching Switch Engine: An MLS-capable switch (a 5000 with an NFFC or a 6000 with an MSFC and PFC). *See also: MLS, NFFC, MSFC,* and *PFC.*

**MMP** Multichassis Multilink PPP: A protocol that supplies MLP support across multiple routers and access servers. MMP enables several routers and access servers to work as a single, large dial-up pool with one network address and ISDN access number. MMP successfully supports packet fragmenting and reassembly when the user connection is split between two physical access devices.

**modem** modulator-demodulator: A device that converts digital signals to analog and vice-versa so that digital information can be transmitted over analog communication facilities, such as voice-grade telephone lines. This is achieved by converting digital signals at the source to analog for transmission and reconverting the analog signals back into digital form at the destination. *See also: modulation* and *demodulation.*

**modemcap database** Stores modem initialization strings on the router for use in auto-detection and configuration.

**modem eliminator** A mechanism that makes possible a connection between two DTE devices without modems by simulating the commands and physical signaling required.

**modulation** The process of modifying some characteristic of an electrical signal, such as amplitude (AM) or frequency (FM), in order to represent digital or analog information. *See also: AM.*

**MOSPF** Multicast OSPF: An extension of the OSPF unicast protocol that enables IP multicast routing within the domain. *See also: OSPF.*

**MP bonding** MultiPoint bonding: A process of linking two or more physical connections into a single logical channel. This might use two or more analog lines and two or more modems, for example.

**MPOA** Multiprotocol over ATM: An effort by the ATM Forum to standardize how existing and future Network layer protocols such as IP, Ipv6, AppleTalk, and IPX run over an ATM network with directly attached hosts, routers, and multi-layer LAN switches.

**MSDP** Multicast Source Discovery Protocol: A support protocol used by multicast RP routers that allows them to use a TCP-based connection to share information with other RPs about active sources inside their own domains. *See also: RP.*

**MSFC** Multi-layer Switch Feature Card: A route processor (parallel to an RSM, or Route Switch Module) that is installed as a daughter card on Cisco Catalyst 6000 series switches. *See also: RSM.*

**mtrace (multicast traceroute)** Used to establish the SPT for a specified multicast group.

**MTU** maximum transmission unit: The largest packet size, measured in bytes, that an interface can handle.

**multicast** Broadly, any communication between a single sender and multiple receivers. Unlike broadcast messages, which are sent to all addresses on a network, multicast messages are sent to a defined subset of the network addresses; this subset has a group multicast address, which is specified in the packet's destination address field. *See also: broadcast* and *directed broadcast.*

**multicast address** A single address that points to more than one device on the network. Hosts joining a multicast group use this common address when receiving data sent to the group. Identical to group address. *See also: multicast.*

**multicast group** A group set up to receive messages from a source. These groups can be established based on Frame Relay or IP in the TCP/IP protocol suite, as well as other networks.

**multicast send VCC** A two-directional point-to-point virtual channel connection (VCC) arranged by an LEC to a BUS, it is one of the three types of informational link specified by phase 1 LANE. *See also: control distribute VCC* and *control direct VCC.*

**multi-layer switch** A highly specialized, high-speed, hardware-based type of LAN router, the device filters and forwards packets based on their layer 2 MAC addresses and layer 3 network addresses. It's possible that even layer 4 can be read. Sometimes called a "layer 3 switch." *See also: LAN switch.*

**Multi-Layer Switching** Multi-Layer Switching combines layer 2, 3, and 4 switching technology and provides very high-speed scalability with low latency. This is provided by huge filter tables based on the criteria designed by the network administrator. Carried out either in IOS or with an additional multi-layer switching module.

**Multi-Layer Switching Module** *See: Multi-Layer Switching.*

**multiplexing** The process of converting several logical signals into a single physical signal for transmission across one physical channel. *Contrast with: demultiplexing.*

**multistage queuing** Multistage queuing occurs when more than one queuing mechanism is applied, in an integrated fashion. An example might be Priority Queuing, where one queue uses Weighted Fair Queuing. *See also: Priority Queuing* and *Weighted Fair Queuing.*

# N

**NAK** negative acknowledgment: A response sent from a receiver, telling the sender that the information was not received or contained errors. *Contrast with: acknowledgment.*

**NAT** Network Address Translation: An algorithm instrumental in minimizing the requirement for globally unique IP addresses, permitting an organization whose addresses are not all globally unique to connect to the Internet, regardless, by translating those addresses into globally routable address space.

**NCP** Network Control Protocol: A protocol at the Logical Link Control sublayer of the Data Link layer used in the PPP stack. It is used to enable multiple Network layer protocols to run over a nonproprietary HDLC serial encapsulation.

**neighboring routers** Two routers in OSPF that have interfaces to a common network. On networks with multi-access, these neighboring routers are dynamically discovered by using the Hello protocol of OSPF.

**NetBEUI** NetBIOS Extended User Interface: An improved version of the NetBIOS protocol used in a number of network operating systems including LAN Manager, Windows NT, LAN Server, and Windows for Workgroups, implementing the OSI LLC2 protocol. NetBEUI formalizes the transport frame not standardized in NetBIOS and adds more functions. *See also: OSI.*

**NetBIOS** Network Basic Input/Output System: The API employed by applications residing on an IBM LAN to ask for services, such as session termination or information transfer, from lower-level network processes.

**NetWare** A widely used NOS created by Novell, providing a number of distributed network services and remote file access.

**network address** Used with the logical network addresses to identify the network segment in an internetwork. Logical addresses are hierarchical in nature and have at least two parts: network and host. An example of a hierarchical address is 172.16.10.5, where 172.16 is the network and 10.5 is the host address.

**Network layer** In the OSI reference model, it is layer 3—the layer in which routing is implemented, enabling connections and path selection between two end systems. *See also: Application layer, Data Link layer, Physical layer, Presentation layer, Session layer,* and *Transport layer.*

**NFFC** NetFlow Feature Card: A module installed on Cisco Catalyst 5000 series switches. It is capable of examining each frame's IP header as well as the Ethernet header. This in turn enables the NFFC to create flows.

**NFS** Network File System: One of the protocols in Sun Microsystems' widely used file system protocol suite, allowing remote file access across a network. The name is loosely used to refer to the entire Sun protocol suite, which also includes RPC, XDR (External Data Representation), and other protocols.

**NHRP** Next Hop Resolution Protocol: In a nonbroadcast multi-access (NBMA) network, the protocol employed by routers in order to dynamically locate MAC addresses of various hosts and routers. It enables systems to communicate directly without requiring an intermediate hop, thus facilitating increased performance in ATM, Frame Relay, X.25, and SMDS systems.

**NHS** Next Hop Server: Defined by the NHRP protocol, this server maintains the next-hop resolution cache tables, listing IP-to-ATM address maps of related nodes and nodes that can be reached through routers served by the NHS.

**NIC** network interface card: An electronic circuit board placed in a computer. The NIC provides network communication to a LAN.

**NLSP** NetWare Link Services Protocol: Novell's link-state routing protocol, based on the IS-IS model.

**NMP** Network Management Processor: A Catalyst 5000 switch processor module used to control and monitor the switch.

**node address** Used to identify a specific device in an internetwork. Can be a hardware address, which is burned into the network interface card, or a logical network address, which an administrator or server assigns to the node.

**non-blocking switch** A non-blocking switch introduces no delay to packets in the fabric.

**nondesignated ports** The Spanning Tree Protocol tells a port on a layer 2 switch to stop transmitting, stopping a network loop. Only designated ports can send frames.

**non-stub area** In OSPF, a resource-consuming area carrying a default route, intra-area routes, interarea routes, static routes, and external routes. Non-stub areas are the only areas that can have virtual links configured across them and exclusively contain an autonomous system boundary router (ASBR). *Compare to: stub area. See also: ASBR* and *OSPF*.

**NRZ** Nonreturn to Zero: One of several encoding schemes for transmitting digital data. NRZ signals sustain constant levels of voltage with no signal shifting (no return to zero-voltage level) during a bit interval. If there is a series of bits with the same value (1 or 0), there will be no state change. The signal is not self-clocking. *See also: NRZI.*

**NRZI** Nonreturn to Zero Inverted: One of several encoding schemes for transmitting digital data. A transition in voltage level (either from high to low or vice-versa) at the beginning of a bit interval is interpreted as a value of 1; the absence of a transition is interpreted as a 0. Thus, the voltage assigned to each value is continually inverted. NRZI signals are not self-clocking. *See also: NRZ.*

**NT1** network termination 1: An ISDN designation to devices that understand ISDN standards.

**NT2** network termination 2: An ISDN designation to devices that do not understand ISDN standards. To use an NT2, you must use a terminal adapter (TA).

**NVRAM** non-volatile RAM: Random-access memory that keeps its contents intact while power is turned off.

# O

**OC** Optical Carrier: A series of physical protocols, designated as OC-1, OC-2, OC-3, and so on, for SONET optical signal transmissions. OC signal levels place STS frames on a multi-mode fiber-optic line at various speeds, of which 51.84Mbps is the lowest (OC-1). Each subsequent protocol runs at a speed divisible by 51.84. *See also: SONET.*

**octet** Base-8 numbering system used to identify a section of a dotted decimal IP address. Also referred to as a byte.

**ones density** Also known as "pulse density," this is a method of signal clocking. The CSU/DSU retrieves the clocking information from data that passes through it. For this scheme to work, the data needs to be encoded to contain at least one binary 1 for each 8 bits transmitted. *See also: CSU* and *DSU.*

**one-time challenge tokens** Used to provide a single use password. This prevents replay attacks and snooping; however, it also requires the user to have a device that provides the token. This physical component of the security model works to prevent hackers from guessing or obtaining the user's password.

**OSI** Open Systems Interconnection: International standardization program designed by ISO and ITU-T for the development of data networking standards that make multivendor equipment interoperability a reality.

**OSI reference model** Open Systems Interconnection reference model: A conceptual model defined by the International Organization for Standardization (ISO), describing how any combination of devices can be connected for the purpose of communication. The OSI model divides the task into seven functional layers, forming a hierarchy with the applications at the top and the physical medium at the bottom, and it defines the functions each layer must provide. *See also: Application layer, Data Link layer, Network layer, Physical layer, Presentation layer, Session layer,* and *Transport layer.*

**OSPF** Open Shortest Path First: A link-state, hierarchical IGP routing algorithm derived from an earlier version of the IS-IS protocol, whose features include multipath routing, load balancing, and least-cost routing. OSPF is the suggested successor to RIP in the Internet environment. *See also: Enhanced IGRP, IGP,* and *IP.*

**OUI** Organizationally Unique Identifier: An identifier assigned by the IEEE to an organization that makes network interface cards. The organization then puts this OUI on each and every card they manufacture. The OUI is 3 bytes (24 bits) long. The manufacturer then adds a 3-byte identifier to uniquely identify the host on an internetwork. The total length of the address is 48 bits (6 bytes) and is called a hardware address or MAC address.

**out-of-band management** Management "outside" of the network's physical channels—for example, using a console connection not directly interfaced through the local LAN or WAN or a dial-in modem. *Compare to: in-band management.*

**out-of-band signaling** Within a network, any transmission that uses physical channels or frequencies separate from those ordinarily used for data transfer. For example, the initial configuration of a Cisco Catalyst switch requires an out-of-band connection via a console port. *Compare to: in-band signaling.*

**output buffer priorities** Refers to the use of queues applied to an interface buffer.

# P

**packet** In data communications, the basic logical unit of information transferred. A packet consists of a certain number of data bytes, wrapped or encapsulated in headers and/or trailers that contain information about where the packet came from, where it's going, and so on. The various protocols involved in sending a transmission add their own layers of header information, which the corresponding protocols in receiving devices then interpret.

**packet mode connections** Packet mode connections are typically passed through the router or remote access device. This includes Point-to-Point Protocol (PPP) sessions.

**packet switch** A physical device that makes it possible for a communication channel to share several connections; its functions include finding the most-efficient transmission path for packets.

**packet switching** A networking technology based on the transmission of data in packets. Dividing a continuous stream of data into small units—packets—enables data from multiple devices on a network to share the same communication channel simultaneously but also requires the use of precise routing information.

**PAD** packet assembler and disassembler: Used to buffer incoming data that is coming in faster than the receiving device can handle it. Typically, only used in X.25 networks.

**PAgP** Port Aggregation Protocol: The communication process that switches use to determine if and how they will form an EtherChannel connection.

**PAP** Password Authentication Protocol: In Point-to-Point Protocol (PPP) networks, a method of validating connection requests. The requesting (remote) device must send an authentication request, containing a password and ID, to the local router when attempting to connect. Unlike the more secure CHAP (Challenge Handshake Authentication Protocol), PAP sends the password unencrypted and does not attempt to verify whether the user is authorized to access the requested resource; it merely identifies the remote end. *Compare to: CHAP.*

**parity checking** A method of error-checking in data transmissions. An extra bit (the parity bit) is added to each character or data word so that the sum of the bits will be either an odd number (in odd parity) or an even number (even parity).

**partial mesh** A type of network topology in which some network nodes form a full mesh (where every node has either a physical or a virtual circuit linking it to every other network node), but others are attached to only one or two nodes in the network. A typical use of partial-mesh topology is in peripheral networks linked to a fully meshed backbone. *See also: full mesh.*

**particle buffers** Buffers created from physically separate but logically contiguous small blocks of memory.

**PAT** Port Address Translation: This process enables a single IP address to represent multiple resources by altering the source TCP or UDP port number. Sometimes referred to as *NAT overload.*

**payload compression** Reduces the number of bytes required to accurately represent the original data stream. Header compression is also possible. *See also: compression.*

**PCR** Peak Cell Rate: As defined by the ATM Forum, the parameter specifying, in cells per second, the maximum rate at which a source can transmit.

**PDN** Public Data Network: Generally for a fee, a PDN offers the public access to a computer communication network operated by private concerns or government agencies. Small organizations can take advantage of PDNs, aiding them in creating WANs without investing in long-distance equipment and circuitry.

**PDU** Protocol Data Unit: The name of the processes at each layer of the OSI model. PDUs at the Transport layer are called "segments," PDUs at the Network layer are called "packets" or "datagrams," and PDUs at the Data Link layer are called "frames." The Physical layer uses "bits."

**per-hop routing** Per-hop routing behavior refers to how packets are forwarded across an internetwork, with each router forwarding according to its own routing tables and priorities.

**PFC** Policy Feature Card: The PFC can be paralleled with the NFFC used in Catalyst 5000 switches. It is a device that is capable of examining IP and Ethernet headers in order to establish flow caches.

**PGP** Pretty Good Privacy: A popular public-key/private-key encryption application offering protected transfer of files and messages.

**Physical layer** The lowest layer—layer 1—in the OSI reference model, it is responsible for converting data packets from the Data Link layer (layer 2) into electrical signals. Physical layer protocols and standards define, for example, the type of cable and connectors to be used, including their pin assignments and the encoding scheme for signaling 0 and 1 values. *See also: Application layer, Data Link layer, Network layer, Presentation layer, Session layer,* and *Transport layer.*

**PIM** Protocol Independent Multicast: A multicast protocol that handles the IGMP requests as well as requests for multicast data forwarding.

**PIM DM** Protocol Independent Multicast dense mode: PIM DM utilizes the unicast route table and relies on the source root distribution architecture for multicast data forwarding.

**PIM SM** Protocol Independent Multicast sparse mode: PIM SM utilizes the unicast route table and relies on the shared root distribution architecture for multicast data forwarding.

**PIM sparse-dense mode** An interface configuration that enables the interface to choose the method of PIM operation.

**Ping** Packet Internet Groper: A Unix-based Internet diagnostic tool, consisting of a message sent to test the accessibility of a particular device on the IP network. The term's acronym (from which the "full name" was formed) reflects the underlying metaphor of submarine sonar. Just as the sonar operator sends out a signal and waits to hear it echo ("ping") back from a submerged object, the network user can ping another node on the network and wait to see whether it responds.

**plesiochronous** Nearly synchronous, except that clocking comes from an outside source instead of being embedded within the signal as in synchronous transmissions. The T1 and E1 hierarchies are plesiochronous.

**PLP** Packet Level Protocol: Occasionally called "X.25 Level 3" or "X.25 Protocol," a Network layer protocol that is part of the X.25 stack.

**PNNI** Private Network-Network Interface: An ATM Forum specification for offering topology data used for the calculation of paths through the network, among switches and groups of switches. It is based on well-known link-state routing procedures and allows for automatic configuration in networks whose addressing scheme is determined by the topology.

**point-to-multipoint connection** In ATM, a communication path going only one way, connecting a single system at the starting point, called the "root node," to systems at multiple points of destination, called "leaves." *See also: point-to-point connection.*

**point-to-point connection** In ATM, a channel of communication that can be directed either one way or two ways between two ATM end systems. *See also: point-to-multipoint connection.*

**poison reverse updates** These update messages are transmitted by a router back to the originator (thus ignoring the split-horizon rule) after route poisoning has occurred. Typically used with DV routing protocols in order to overcome large routing loops and offer explicit information when a subnet or network is not accessible (instead of merely suggesting that the network is unreachable by not including it in updates). *See also: route poisoning.*

**policing** When frames/packets arrive at an interface, they may be classified. In addition, queue sizes are configured to allow certain amounts of data through. Measuring whether data conforms to the permitted amount is called policing. *See also: classification.*

**polling** The procedure of orderly inquiry, used by a primary network mechanism, to determine whether secondary devices have data to transmit. A message is sent to each secondary, granting the secondary the right to transmit.

**POP** (1) Point of Presence: The physical location where an interexchange carrier has placed equipment to interconnect with a local exchange carrier. (2) Post Office Protocol (currently at version 3): A protocol used by client e-mail applications for recovery of mail from a mail server.

**port density** Port density reflects the capacity of the remote access device regarding the termination of interfaces. For example, the port density of an access server that serves four T1 circuits is 96 analog lines (non-ISDN PRI).

**PortFast** The configuration option that tells the switch to move directly from blocking mode to forwarding mode. Only to be used when a single PC is connected to the port.

**port security** Used with layer 2 switches to provide some security. Not typically used in production because it is difficult to manage. Allows only certain frames to traverse administrator-assigned segments.

**POTS** plain old telephone service: This refers to the traditional analog phone service that is found in most installations.

**PPP** Point-to-Point Protocol: The protocol most commonly used for dial-up Internet access, superseding the earlier SLIP. Its features include address notification, authentication via CHAP or PAP, support for multiple protocols, and link monitoring. PPP has two layers: the Link Control Protocol (LCP) establishes, configures, and tests a link; and then any of various Network Control Programs (NCPs) transport traffic for a specific protocol suite, such as IPX. *See also: CHAP, PAP,* and *SLIP.*

**PPP callback** The point-to-point protocol supports callback to a predetermined number to augment security.

**Predictor** A compression technique supported by Cisco. *See also: compression.*

**Presentation layer** Layer 6 of the OSI reference model, it defines how data is formatted, presented, encoded, and converted for use by software at the Application layer. *See also: Application layer, Data Link layer, Network layer, Physical layer, Session layer,* and *Transport layer.*

**PRI** Primary Rate Interface: A type of ISDN connection between a PBX and a long-distance carrier, which is made up of a single 64Kbps D channel in addition to 23 (T1) or 30 (E1) B channels. *Compare to: BRI. See also: ISDN.*

**priority queuing** A routing function in which frames temporarily placed in an interface output queue are assigned priorities based on traits such as packet size or type of interface.

**processing delay** The delay associated with packets being forwarded across a router fabric.

**process switching** As a packet arrives on a router to be forwarded, it's copied to the router's process buffer, and the router performs a lookup on the layer 3 address. Using the route table, an exit interface is associated with the destination address. The processor forwards the packet with the added new information to the exit interface, while the router initializes the fast-switching cache. Subsequent packets bound for the same destination address follow the same path as the first packet. *Compare to: fast switching.*

**PROM** programmable read-only memory: ROM that is programmable only once, using special equipment. *Compare to: EPROM and EEPROM.*

**propagation delay** The time it takes data to traverse a network from its source to its destination.

**protocol** In networking, the specification of a set of rules for a particular type of communication. The term is also used to refer to the software that implements a protocol.

**protocol stack** A collection of related protocols.

**Proxy ARP** Proxy Address Resolution Protocol: Used to allow redundancy in case of a failure with the configured default gateway on a host. Proxy ARP is a variation of the ARP protocol in which an intermediate device, such as a router, sends an ARP response on behalf of an end node to the requesting host.

**pruning** The act of trimming down the Shortest Path Tree. This deactivates interfaces that do not have group participants.

**PSE** Packet Switch Exchange: The X.25 term for a switch.

**PSN** packet-switched network: Any network that uses packet-switching technology. Also known as "packet-switched data network (PSDN)." *See also: packet switching.*

**PSTN** Public Switched Telephone Network: Colloquially referred to as "plain old telephone service" (POTS). A term that describes the assortment of telephone networks and services available globally.

**PTSP** PNNI Topology State Packet, used in ATM.

**PVC** permanent virtual circuit: In a Frame-Relay network, a logical connection, defined in software, that is maintained permanently. *Compare to: SVC. See also: virtual circuit.*

**PVP** permanent virtual path: A virtual path made up of PVCs. *See also: PVC.*

**PVP tunneling** permanent virtual path tunneling: A technique that links two private ATM networks across a public network by using a virtual path; the public network transparently trunks the complete collection of virtual channels in the virtual path between the two private networks.

**PVST** Per-VLAN Spanning Tree: A Cisco proprietary implementation of STP. PVST uses ISL and runs a separate instance of STP for each and every VLAN.

**PVST+** Per-VLAN Spanning Tree+: Allows CST information to be passed into PVST.

# Q

**QoS** quality of service: A set of metrics used to measure the quality of transmission and service availability of any given transmission system.

**queue** Broadly, any list of elements arranged in an orderly fashion and ready for processing, such as a line of people waiting to enter a movie theater. In routing, it refers to a backlog of information packets waiting in line to be transmitted over a router interface. Queuing disposition is the term applied to the order of packets in the queue.

**queuing** A quality of service process that enables packets to be forwarded from the router based on administratively defined parameters. This can be used for time-sensitive protocols, such as SNA.

# R

**R reference point** Used with ISDN networks to identify the connection between an NT1 and an S/T device. The S/T device converts the four-wire network to the two-wire ISDN standard network.

**RADIUS** Remote Authentication Dial-in User Service: A protocol that is used to communicate between the remote access device and an authentication server. Sometimes an authentication server running RADIUS will be called a RADIUS server.

**RAM** random access memory: Used by all computers to store information. Cisco routers use RAM to store packet buffers and routing tables, along with the hardware addresses cache.

**RARP** Reverse Address Resolution Protocol: The protocol within the TCP/IP stack that maps MAC addresses to IP addresses. *See also: ARP.*

**rate queue** A value, assigned to one or more virtual circuits, that specifies the speed at which an individual virtual circuit will transmit data to the remote end. Every rate queue identifies a segment of the total bandwidth available on an ATM link. The sum of all rate queues should not exceed the total available bandwidth.

**RCP** Remote Copy Protocol: A protocol for copying files to or from a file system that resides on a remote server on a network, using TCP to guarantee reliable data delivery.

**redistribution** A process used in Cisco routers to inject the paths found from one routing protocol into another routing protocol. For example, networks found by RIP can be inserted into an IGRP network.

**redundancy** In internetworking, the duplication of connections, devices, or services that can be used as a backup in the event that the primary connections, devices, or services fail.

**reference point** Used to define an area in an ISDN network. Providers used these reference points to find problems in the ISDN network.

**reliability** The measure of the quality of a connection. It is one of the metrics that can be used to make routing decisions.

**reload** An event or command that causes Cisco routers to reboot.

**remote access** A generic term that defines connectivity to distant resources using one of many technologies, as appropriate.

**remote services** Network services close to users but not on the same network or subnet as the users. The users would have to cross a layer 3 device to communicate with the network services, but they might not have to cross the backbone.

**rendezvous point** *See: RP.*

**reverse Telnet** Maps a Telnet port to a physical port on the router or access device. This enables the administrator to connect to a modem or other device attached to the port.

**RFC** Request for Comments: RFCs are used to present and define standards in the networking industry.

**RIF** Routing Information Field: In source-route bridging, a header field that defines the path direction of the frame or token. If the Route Information Indicator (RII) bit is not set, the RIF is read from source to destination (left to right). If the RII bit is set, the RIF is read from the destination back to the source, so the RIF is read from right to left. It is defined as part of the token ring frame header for source-routed frames, which contains path information.

**ring** Two or more stations connected in a logical circular topology. In this topology, which is the basis for Token Ring, FDDI, and CDDI, information is transferred from station to station in sequence.

**ring topology** A network logical topology comprising a series of repeaters that form one closed loop by connecting unidirectional transmission links. Individual stations on the network are connected to the network at a repeater. Physically, ring topologies are generally organized in a closed-loop star. *Contrast with: bus topology* and *star topology.*

**RIP** Routing Information Protocol: The most commonly used interior gateway protocol in the Internet. RIP employs hop count as a routing metric. *See also: Enhanced IGRP, IGP, OSPF,* and *hop count.*

**RIP version 2** Newer, updated version of Routing Information Protocol (RIP). Allows VLSM. *See also: VLSM.*

**RJ connector** registered jack connector: Used with twisted-pair wiring to connect the copper wire to network interface cards, switches, and hubs.

**robbed bit signaling** Also known as Channel Associated Signaling, robbed bit signaling operates on a per-channel basis rather than having a dedicated signaling channel.

**ROM** read-only memory: Chip used in computers to help boot the device. Cisco routers use a ROM chip to load the bootstrap, which runs a power-on self-test, and then find and load the IOS in flash memory by default.

**root bridge** Used with the Spanning Tree Protocol to stop network loops from occurring. The root bridge is elected by having the lowest bridge ID. The bridge ID is determined by the priority (32768 by default on all bridges and switches) and the main hardware address of the device. The root bridge determines which of the neighboring layer 2 devices' interfaces become the designated and nondesignated ports.

**round robin** A scheduling mechanism where queues are arranged as though in a logical ring around the output buffer. Packets are forwarded from queues as each rotates past the buffer.

**routed protocol** Routed protocols (such as IP and IPX) are used to transmit user data through an internetwork. By contrast, routing protocols (such as RIP, IGRP, and OSPF) are used to update routing tables between routers.

**route poisoning** Used by various DV routing protocols in order to overcome large routing loops and offer explicit information about when a subnet or network is not accessible (instead of merely suggesting that the network is unreachable by not including it in updates). Typically, this is accomplished by setting the hop count to one more than maximum. *See also: poison reverse updates.*

**route summarization** In various routing protocols, such as OSPF, EIGRP, and IS-IS, the consolidation of publicized subnetwork addresses so that a single summary route is advertised to other areas by an area border router.

**router** A Network layer mechanism, either software or hardware, using one or more metrics to decide on the best path to use for transmission of network traffic. Sending packets between networks by routers is based on the information provided on Network layers. Historically, this device has sometimes been called a "gateway."

**router on a stick** A term that identifies a single router interface connected to a single distribution layer switch port. The router is an external router that provides trunking protocol capabilities for routing between multiple VLANs. *See also: RSM* and *MSFC.*

**routing** The process of forwarding logically addressed packets from their local subnetwork toward their ultimate destination. In large networks, the numerous intermediary destinations that a packet might travel before reaching its destination can make routing very complex.

**routing domain** Any collection of end systems and intermediate systems that operate under an identical set of administrative rules. Every routing domain contains one or several areas, all individually given a certain area address.

**routing metric** Any value that is used by routing algorithms to determine whether one route is superior to another. Metrics include such information as bandwidth, delay, hop count, path cost, load, MTU, reliability, and communication cost. Only the best possible routes are stored in the routing table, while all other information may be stored in link-state or topological databases. *See also: cost.*

**routing protocol** Any protocol that defines algorithms to be used for updating routing tables between routers. Examples include IGRP, RIP, and OSPF.

**routing table** A table kept in a router or other internetworking mechanism that maintains a record of only the best possible routes to certain network destinations and the metrics associated with those routes.

**RP** (1) rendezvous point: A router that acts as the multicast source in a multicast network. Primarily in a shared tree distribution. (2) Route Processor: Also known as a "supervisory processor," a module on Cisco 7000 series routers that holds the CPU, system software, and most of the memory components used in the router.

**RSFC** Route Switch Feature Card: Used to provide routing between VLANs. The RSFC is a daughter card for the Supervisor engine II G and Supervisor III G cards. The RSFC is a fully functioning router running the Cisco IOS.

**RSM** Route Switch Module: A route processor that is inserted into the chassis of a Cisco Catalyst 5000 series switch. The RSM is configured exactly like an external router.

**RSP** Route/Switch Processor: A processor module combining the functions of RP and SP used in Cisco 7500 series routers. *See also: RP* and *SP*.

**RSTP** Rapid Spanning Tree Protocol: The IEEE 802.1w protocol that defines how spanning-tree convergence can be speeded up by reducing the number of spanning-tree modes and introducing a Hello protocol enhancement.

**RTS** Request to Send: An EIA/TIA-232 control signal requesting permission to transmit data on a communication line.

# S

**S reference point** ISDN reference point that works with a T reference point to convert a four-wire ISDN network to the two-wire ISDN network needed to communicate with the ISDN switches at the network provider.

**sampling rate** The rate at which samples of a specific waveform amplitude are collected within a specified period of time.

**SAP** (1) Service Access Point: A field specified by IEEE 802.2 that is part of an address specification. *See also: DSAP* and *SSAP*. (2) Service Advertising Protocol: The Novell NetWare protocol that supplies a way to inform network clients of resources and services availability on a network, using routers and servers. *See also: IPX*.

**SCR** Sustainable Cell Rate: An ATM Forum parameter used for traffic management, it is the long-term average cell rate for VBR connections that can be transmitted.

**scripts** A script predefines commands that should be issued in sequence, typically to complete a connection or accomplish a repetitive task.

**SDH** Synchronous Digital Hierarchy: The CCITT/ITU–TS standard for transport of data over fiber. Designed for worldwide use, SDH is partly compatible with SONET. The base rate for transmission is 155.52 Mbps. Widely used in Europe, although the standard is international.

**SDLC** Synchronous Data Link Control: A protocol used in SNA Data Link layer communications. SDLC is a bit-oriented, full-duplex serial protocol that is the basis for several similar protocols, including HDLC and LAPB. *See also: HDLC* and *LAPB*.

**security policy** Document that defines the business requirements and processes that are to be used to protect corporate data. A security policy might be as generic as "no file transfers allowed" to very specific, such as "FTP puts allowed only to server X."

**security server** A centralized device that authenticates access requests, typically via a protocol such as TACACS+ or RADIUS. *See also: TACACS+* and *RADIUS.*

**serialization delay** The delay associated with frames arriving at an interface. A function of the frame length and the arrival rate.

**server** Hardware and software that provide network services to clients.

**set-based** Set-based routers and switches use the `set` command to configure devices. Cisco is moving away from set-based commands and is using the command-line interface (CLI) on all new devices.

**Session layer** Layer 5 of the OSI reference model, responsible for creating, managing, and terminating sessions between applications and overseeing data exchange between Presentation layer entities. *See also: Application layer, Data Link layer, Network layer, Physical layer, Presentation layer,* and *Transport layer.*

**setup mode** Mode that a router will enter if no configuration is found in non-volatile RAM when the router boots. Enables the administrator to configure a router step-by-step. Not as robust or flexible as the command-line interface.

**SF** super frame: A super frame (also called a "D4 frame") consists of 12 frames with 192 bits each, and the 193rd bit providing other functions including error checking. SF is frequently used on T1 circuits. A newer version of the technology is Extended Super Frame (ESF), which uses 24 frames. *See also: ESF.*

**shared memory** A type of switch-fabric where the input and output queues are the same memory blocks but with separate pointers.

**shared trees** A method of multicast data forwarding. Shared trees use an architecture in which multiple sources share a common rendezvous point.

**signaling packet** An informational packet created by an ATM-connected mechanism that wants to establish a connection with another such mechanism. The packet contains the QoS parameters needed for connection and the ATM NSAP address of the endpoint. The endpoint responds with a message of acceptance if it is able to support the desired QoS, and the connection is established. *See also: QoS.*

**silicon switching** A type of high-speed switching used in Cisco 7000 series routers, based on the use of a separate processor (the Silicon Switch Processor, or SSP). *See also: SSE.*

**simplex** The mode with which data is transmitted. Simplex is a way of transmitting in only one direction. Half duplex transmits in two directions, but only one direction at a time. Full duplex transmits in both directions simultaneously.

**SLB** Server Load Balancing: A methodology for load balancing servers. A server farm is allocated a virtual address for clients to connect to and the router shares connections across the farm. *See also: HSRP.*

**sliding window** The method of flow control used by TCP, as well as several Data Link layer protocols. This method places a buffer between the receiving application and the network data flow. The "window" available for accepting data is the size of the buffer minus the amount of data already there. This window increases in size as the application reads data from it and decreases as new data is sent. The receiver sends the transmitter announcements of the current window size, and it may stop accepting data until the window increases above a certain threshold.

**SLIP** Serial Line Internet Protocol: An industry standard serial encapsulation for point-to-point connections that supports only a single routed protocol, TCP/IP. SLIP is the predecessor to PPP. *See also: PPP.*

**SMDS** Switched Multimegabit Data Service: A packet-switched, datagram-based WAN networking technology offered by telephone companies that provides high speed.

**SMTP** Simple Mail Transfer Protocol: A protocol used on the Internet to provide electronic mail services.

**SNA** System Network Architecture: A complex, feature-rich network architecture with several variations; created by IBM in the 1970s and composed of seven layers closely resembling the OSI reference model.

**SNAP** Subnetwork Access Protocol: SNAP is a frame used in Ethernet, Token Ring, and FDDI LANs. Data transfer, connection management, and QoS selection are three primary functions executed by the SNAP frame.

**snapshot routing** Snapshot routing takes a point-in-time capture of a dynamic routing table and maintains it even when the remote connection goes down. This allows the use of a dynamic routing protocol without requiring the link to remain active, which might incur per-minute usage charges.

**socket** (1) A software structure that operates within a network device as a destination point for communications. (2) In AppleTalk networks, an entity at a specific location within a node; AppleTalk sockets are conceptually similar to TCP/IP ports.

**SOHO** Small office, home office: A contemporary term for remote users.

**SONET** Synchronous Optical Network: The ANSI standard for synchronous transmission on fiber-optic media, developed at Bell Labs. It specifies a base signal rate of 51.84Mbps and a set of multiples of that rate, known as Optical Carrier levels, up to 2.5Gbps.

**source-route bridging** *See: SRB.*

**source trees** A method of multicast data forwarding. Source trees use the architecture of the source of the multicast traffic as the root of the tree.

**SP** Switch Processor: Also known as a "ciscoBus controller," it is a Cisco 7000 series processor module acting as governing agent for all CxBus activities.

**span** A full-duplex digital transmission line connecting two facilities.

**SPAN** Switch Port Analyzer: A feature of the Catalyst 5000 switch, offering freedom to manipulate within a switched Ethernet environment by extending the monitoring ability of the existing network analyzers into the environment. At one switched segment, the SPAN mirrors traffic onto a predetermined SPAN port, while a network analyzer connected to the SPAN port is able to monitor traffic from any other Catalyst switched port.

**spanning explorer packet** Sometimes called "limited-route explorer packet" or "single-route explorer packet," it pursues a statically configured spanning tree when searching for paths in a source-route bridging network. *See also: all-routes explorer packet, explorer packet,* and *local explorer packet.*

**spanning tree** A subset of a network topology, within which no loops exist. When bridges are interconnected into a loop, the bridge, or switch, cannot identify a frame that has been forwarded previously, so there is no mechanism for removing a frame as it passes the interface numerous times. Without a method of removing these frames, the bridges continuously forward them—consuming bandwidth and adding overhead to the network. Spanning trees prune the network to provide only one path for any packet. *See also: Spanning Tree Protocol* and *spanning-tree algorithm.*

**spanning-tree algorithm (STA)** An algorithm that creates a spanning tree using the Spanning Tree Protocol (STP). *See also: spanning tree* and *Spanning Tree Protocol.*

**Spanning Tree Protocol (STP)** The bridge protocol (IEEE 802.1D) that enables a learning bridge to dynamically avoid loops in the network topology by creating a spanning tree, using the spanning-tree algorithm. Spanning-tree frames called Bridge Protocol Data Units (BPDUs) are sent and received by all switches in the network at regular intervals. The switches participating in the spanning tree don't forward the frames; instead, they're processed to determine the spanning-tree topology itself. Cisco Catalyst series switches use STP 802.1D to perform this function. *See also: BPDU, learning bridge, MAC address, spanning tree,* and *spanning-tree algorithm.*

**SPF** Shortest Path First algorithm: A routing algorithm used to decide on the shortest-path spanning tree. Sometimes called "Dijkstra's algorithm" and frequently used in link-state routing algorithms. *See also: link-state routing algorithm.*

**SPID** Service Profile Identifier: A number assigned by service providers or local telephone companies and assigned by administrators to a BRI port. SPIDs are used to determine subscription services of a device connected via ISDN. ISDN devices use SPID when accessing the telephone company switch that initializes the link to a service provider.

**split horizon** Useful for preventing routing loops, a type of distance-vector routing rule where information about routes is prevented from leaving the router interface through which that information was received.

**spoofing** (1) In dial-on-demand routing (DDR), where a circuit-switched link is taken down to save toll charges when there is no traffic to be sent, spoofing is a scheme used by routers that causes a host to treat an interface as if it were functioning and supporting a session. The router pretends to send "spoof" replies to keep-alive messages from the host in an effort to convince the host that the session is up and running. *See also: DDR*. (2) The illegal act of sending a packet labeled with a false address, in order to deceive network security mechanisms such as filters and access lists.

**spooler** A management application that processes requests submitted to it for execution in a sequential fashion from a queue. A good example is a print spooler.

**SPX** Sequenced Packet Exchange: A Novell NetWare transport protocol that augments the datagram service provided by Network layer (layer 3) protocols, it was derived from the Switch-to-Switch Protocol of the XNS protocol suite.

**SQE** Signal Quality Error: In an Ethernet network, a message sent from a transceiver to an attached machine that the collision-detection circuitry is working.

**SRB** source-route bridging: Created by IBM, the bridging method used in Token Ring networks. The source determines the entire route to a destination before sending the data and includes that information in route information fields (RIF) within each packet. *Contrast with: transparent bridging.*

**SRT** source-route transparent bridging: A bridging scheme developed by IBM, merging source-route and transparent bridging. SRT takes advantage of both technologies in one device, fulfilling the needs of all end nodes. Translation between bridging protocols is not necessary. *Compare to: SR/TLB.*

**SR/TLB** source-route translational bridging: A bridging method that enables source-route stations to communicate with transparent bridge stations aided by an intermediate bridge that translates between the two bridge protocols. Used for bridging between Token Ring and Ethernet. *Compare to: SRT.*

**SS-7 signaling** Signaling System 7: The current standard for telecommunications switching control signaling. This is an out-of-band signaling that establishes circuits and provides billing information.

**SSAP** Source Service Access Point: The SAP of the network node identified in the Source field of the packet. *See also: DSAP* and *SAP*.

**SSE** Silicon Switching Engine: The software component of Cisco's silicon switching technology, hard-coded into the Silicon Switch Processor (SSP). Silicon switching is available only on the Cisco 7000 with an SSP. Silicon-switched packets are compared to the silicon-switching cache on the SSE. The SSP is a dedicated switch processor that offloads the switching process from the route processor, providing a fast-switching solution, but packets must still traverse the backplane of the router to get to the SSP and then back to the exit interface.

**SSM** Source Specific Multicast: An extension to the PIM protocol that removes the problem of finding the best server without having to resort to MSDP source discovery. SSM requires the network be running IGMPv3. *See also: PIM, MSDP,* and *IGMPv3.*

**Stac** A compression method developed by Stacker Corporation for use over serial links.

**Standard Image (SI)** The basic operating system used on some Catalyst 2950 switches. *See also: Enhanced Image.*

**standard IP access list** IP access list that uses only the source IP addresses to filter a network.

**standard IPX access list** IPX access list that uses only the source and destination IPX address to filter a network.

**star topology** A LAN physical topology with endpoints on the network converging at a common central switch (known as a hub) using point-to-point links. A logical ring topology can be configured as a physical star topology using a unidirectional closed-loop star rather than point-to-point links. That is, connections within the hub are arranged in an internal ring. *Contrast with: bus topology* and *ring topology.*

**state transitions** Digital signaling scheme that reads the "state" of the digital signal in the middle of the bit cell. If it is five volts, the cell is read as a one. If the state of the digital signal is zero volts, the bit cell is read as a zero.

**static route** A route whose information is purposefully entered into the routing table and takes priority over those chosen by dynamic routing protocols.

**static VLAN** VLAN that is manually configured port-by-port. This is the method typically used in production networks.

**statistical multiplexing** Multiplexing in general is a technique that enables data from multiple logical channels to be sent across a single physical channel. Statistical multiplexing dynamically assigns bandwidth only to input channels that are active, optimizing available bandwidth so that more devices can be connected than with other multiplexing techniques. Also known as "statistical time-division multiplexing" or "stat mux." *Contrast with ATDM, FDM,* and *TDM.*

**STM-1** Synchronous Transport Module Level 1. In the European SDH standard, one of many formats identifying the frame structure for the 155.52Mbps lines that are used to carry ATM cells.

**store-and-forward** *See: store-and-forward packet switching.*

**store-and-forward packet switching** A technique in which the switch first copies each packet into its buffer and performs a cyclic redundancy check (CRC). If the packet is error-free, the switch then looks up the destination address in its filter table, determines the appropriate exit port, and sends the packet.

**STP** (1) shielded twisted-pair: A two-pair wiring scheme, used in many network implementations, that has a layer of shielded insulation to reduce EMI. (2) Spanning Tree Protocol.

**stub area** An OSPF area carrying a default route, intra-area routes, and interarea routes, but no external routes. Configuration of virtual links cannot be achieved across a stub area, and stub areas are not allowed to contain an ASBR. *See also: non-stub area, ASBR,* and *OSPF.*

**stub network** A network having only one connection to a router.

**STUN** Serial Tunnel: A technology used to connect an HDLC link to an SDLC link over a serial link.

**subarea** A portion of an SNA network made up of a subarea node and its attached links and peripheral nodes.

**subarea node** An SNA communications host or controller that handles entire network addresses.

**subchannel** A frequency-based subdivision that creates a separate broadband communications channel.

**subinterface** One of many virtual interfaces available on a single physical interface.

**subnet** *See: subnetwork.*

**subnet address** The portion of an IP address that is specifically identified by the subnet mask as the subnetwork. *See also: IP address, subnetwork,* and *subnet mask.*

**subnet mask** Also simply known as "mask," a 32-bit address mask used in IP to identify the bits of an IP address that are used for the subnet address. Using a mask, the router does not need to examine all 32 bits, only those selected by the mask. *See also: address mask* and *IP address.*

**subnetwork** (1) Any network that is part of a larger IP network and is identified by a subnet address. A network administrator segments a network into subnetworks in order to provide a hierarchical, multilevel routing structure, and at the same time protect the subnetwork from the addressing complexity of networks that are attached. Also known as a "subnet." *See also: IP address, subnet mask,* and *subnet address.* (2) In OSI networks, the term specifically refers to a collection of computing devices controlled by only one administrative domain, using a solitary network connection protocol.

**subscribed** A host that has sent an IGMP join message is said to have subscribed to the group.

**SVC** switched virtual circuit: A dynamically established virtual circuit, created on demand and dissolved as soon as transmission is over and the circuit is no longer needed. In ATM terminology, it is referred to as a switched virtual connection. *Compare to: PVC.*

**switch** (1) In networking, a device responsible for multiple functions such as filtering, flooding, and sending frames. It works by using the destination address of individual frames. Switches operate at the Data Link layer of the OSI model. (2) Broadly, any electronic/mechanical device enabling connections to be established as needed and terminated if no longer necessary.

**switch block** An arrangement of layer 2 switches connecting users in the wiring closet into the access of the network.

**switch-fabric** The heart of the switch, where the actual switching process takes place. *See also: bus, shared memory,* and *crossbar.*

**switched Ethernet** A device that switches Ethernet frames between segments by filtering on hardware addresses.

**switched LAN** Any LAN implemented by using LAN switches. *See also: LAN switch.*

**switching fabric** The central functional block of any switch design; responsible for buffering and routing the incoming data to the appropriate output ports.

**Synchronous Digital Hierarchy** *See: SDH.*

**synchronous transmission** Signals transmitted digitally with precision clocking. These signals have identical frequencies and contain individual characters encapsulated in control bits (called start/stop bits) that designate the beginning and ending of each character. *Contrast with: asynchronous transmission* and *isochronous transmission.*

# T

**T reference point** Used with an S reference point to change a four-wire ISDN network to a two-wire ISDN network.

**T1** Digital WAN that uses 24 DS0s at 64KB each to create a bandwidth of 1.536Mbps, minus clocking overhead, providing 1.544Mbps of usable bandwidth.

**T3** Digital WAN that can provide bandwidth of 44.763Mbps.

**TACACS+** Terminal Access Control Access Control System: An enhanced version of TACACS, this protocol is similar to RADIUS. *See also: RADIUS.*

**tag switching** A high-performance technology used for forwarding packets. Based on the concept of label swapping, whereby packets or cells are designated to defined-length labels that control the manner in which data is to be sent. It incorporates Data Link layer (layer 2) switching and Network layer (layer 3) routing and supplies scalable, high-speed switching in the network core.

**tagged traffic** ATM cells with their cell loss priority (CLP) bit set to 1. Also referred to as "discard-eligible (DE) traffic." Tagged traffic can be eliminated in order to ensure trouble-free delivery of higher-priority traffic, if the network is congested. *See also: CLP.*

**TCAM** Ternary Content Addressable Memory: this uses a third binary option—the "don't care"—to make bridge table lookups faster. *See also: CAM.*

**TCP** Transmission Control Protocol: A connection-oriented protocol that is defined at the Transport layer of the OSI reference model. Provides reliable delivery of data.

**TCP header compression** A compression process that compresses only the TCP header information, which is typically repetitive. This would not compress the user data. *See also: compression.*

**TCP/IP** Transmission Control Protocol/Internet Protocol. The suite of protocols underlying the Internet. TCP and IP are the most widely known protocols in that suite. *See also: IP* and *TCP.*

**TDM** Time Division Multiplexing: A technique for assigning bandwidth on a single wire, based on preassigned time slots, to data from several channels. Bandwidth is allotted to each channel regardless of a station's ability to send data. *Contrast with: ATDM, FDM,* and *statistical multiplexing.*

**TE** terminal equipment: Any peripheral device that is ISDN-compatible and attached to a network, such as a telephone or computer. TE1s are devices that are ISDN-ready and understand ISDN signaling techniques. TE2s are devices that are not ISDN-ready and do not understand ISDN signaling techniques. A terminal adapter must be used with a TE2.

**TE1** A device with a four-wire, twisted-pair digital interface is referred to as terminal equipment type 1. Most modern ISDN devices are of this type.

**TE2** A TE2 device is a non-ISDN device which must be connected to an ISDN interface. This could be a non-ISDN phone or fax machine, or even a refrigerator. TE2 devices do not understand ISDN signaling techniques, and a terminal adapter must be used to convert the signaling.

**telco** A common abbreviation for the telephone company.

**Telnet** The standard terminal emulation protocol within the TCP/IP protocol stack. A method of remote terminal connection, enabling users to log in on remote networks and use those resources as if they were locally connected. Telnet is defined in RFC 854.

**terminal adapter** A hardware interface between a computer without a native ISDN interface and an ISDN line. In effect, a device to connect a standard async interface to a non-native ISDN device, emulating a modem.

**terminal emulation** The use of software, installed on a PC or LAN server, that enables the PC to function as if it were a "dumb" terminal directly attached to a particular type of mainframe.

**TFTP** Trivial File Transfer Protocol: Conceptually a stripped-down version of FTP, it's the protocol of choice if you know exactly what you want and where it's to be found. TFTP doesn't provide the abundance of functions that FTP does. In particular, it has no directory-browsing abilities; it can do nothing but send and receive files. *See also: FTP.*

**Thicknet** Also called "10Base5." Bus network that uses a thick cable and runs Ethernet up to 500 meters.

**Thinnet** Also called "10Base2." Bus network that uses a thin coax cable and runs Ethernet media access up to 185 meters.

**token** A frame containing only control information. Possessing this control information gives a network device permission to transmit data onto the network. *See also: token passing.*

**token bus** LAN architecture that is the basis for the IEEE 802.4 LAN specification and employs token passing access over a bus topology. *See also: IEEE.*

**token passing** A method used by network devices to access the physical medium in a systematic way based on possession of a small frame called a token. *See also: token.*

**Token Ring** IBM's token-passing LAN technology. It runs at 4Mbps or 16Mbps over a ring topology. Defined formally by IEEE 802.5. *See also: ring topology* and *token passing.*

**toll network** WAN network that uses the Public Switched Telephone Network (PSTN) to send packets.

**trace** IP command used to trace the path a packet takes through an internetwork.

**traffic shaping** Used on Frame Relay networks to provide priorities of data.

**transparent bridging** The bridging scheme used in Ethernet and IEEE 802.3 networks, it passes frames along one hop at a time, using bridging information stored in tables that associate end-node MAC addresses within bridge ports. This type of bridging is considered transparent because the source node does not know it has been bridged, because the destination frames are sent directly to the end node. *Contrast with: SRB.*

**transparent Ethernet** A variety of techniques used to make a customer's wide or metropolitan network look like an end-to-end Ethernet.

**Transport layer** Layer 4 of the OSI reference model, used for reliable communication between end nodes over the network. The Transport layer provides mechanisms used for establishing, maintaining, and terminating virtual circuits, transport fault detection and recovery, and controlling the flow of information. *See also: Application layer, Data Link layer, Network layer, Physical layer, Presentation layer,* and *Session layer.*

**trie** A pointer used with a data structure, where the data structure does not actually contain the data. This allows for data to be stored in the way that best suits the type of data being stored, and the lookup process to be decoupled from the data.

**TRIP** Token Ring Interface Processor: A high-speed interface processor used on Cisco 7000 series routers. The TRIP provides two or four ports for interconnection with IEEE 802.5 and IBM media. Ports may be set to speeds of either 4Mbps or 16Mbps independently of each other.

**trunk link** Link used between switches and from some servers to the switches. Trunk links carry information about many VLANs. Access links are used to connect host devices to a switch and carry only VLAN information that the device is a member of.

**TTL** Time to Live: A field in an IP header, indicating the length of time that a packet is valid.

**TUD** Trunk Up-Down: A protocol used in ATM networks for the monitoring of trunks. If a trunk misses a given number of test messages being sent by ATM switches to ensure trunk line quality, TUD declares the trunk down. When a trunk reverses direction and comes back up, TUD recognizes that the trunk is up and returns the trunk to service.

**tunneling** A method of avoiding protocol restrictions by wrapping packets from one protocol in another protocol's packet and transmitting this encapsulated packet over a network that supports the wrapper protocol. *See also: encapsulation.*

# U

**UART** The Universal Asynchronous Receiver/Transmitter: A chip that governs asynchronous communications. Its primary function is to buffer incoming data, but it also buffers outbound bits.

**UDP** User Datagram Protocol: A connectionless Transport layer protocol in the TCP/IP protocol stack that simply enables datagrams to be exchanged without acknowledgements or delivery guarantees, requiring other protocols to handle error processing and retransmission. UDP is defined in RFC 768.

**U reference point** Reference point between a TE1 and an ISDN network. The U reference point understands ISDN signaling techniques and uses a two-wire connection.

**unicast** Used for direct host-to-host communication. Communication is directed to only one destination and is originated from only one source.

**unidirectional shared tree** A method of shared tree multicast forwarding. This method allows only multicast data to be forwarded from the RP.

**uniquely** A host is uniquely identified by the MAC address, because this address is not repeated on any other host anywhere.

**unnumbered frames** HDLC frames used for control-management purposes, such as link startup and shutdown or mode specification.

**UplinkFast** Enables a switch to immediately begin forwarding frames on blocked ports when a failure is detected on the root port.

**upstream** Routers nearer to the transmitting multicast server are said to be upstream from the receiving client.

**UTP** unshielded twisted-pair: Copper wiring used in small-to-large networks to connect host devices to hubs and switches. Also used to connect switch to switch or hub to hub.

**VBR** Variable Bit Rate: A QoS class, as defined by the ATM Forum, for use in ATM networks that is subdivided into real time (RT) class and non-real time (NRT) class. RT is employed when connections have a fixed-time relationship between samples. Conversely, NRT is employed when connections do not have a fixed-time relationship between samples, but still need an assured QoS. *Compare to: ABR* and *CBR*.

**VCC** Virtual Channel Connection: A logical circuit that is created by VCLs (virtual channel links). VCCs carry data between two endpoints in an ATM network. Sometimes called a virtual circuit connection.

**VIP** (1) Versatile Interface Processor: An interface card for Cisco 7000 and 7500 series routers, providing multi-layer switching and running the Cisco IOS software. The most recent version of VIP is VIP2. (2) Virtual IP: A function making it possible for logically separated switched IP workgroups to run Virtual Networking Services across the switch ports of a Catalyst 5000.

**virtual circuit** Abbreviated VC, a logical circuit devised to ensure end-to-end communication between two devices on a network. A virtual circuit can be permanent (PVC) or switched (SVC). Virtual circuits are used in Frame Relay and X.25. Known as "virtual channels" in ATM. *See also: PVC* and *SVC*.

**virtual ring** In an SRB network, a logical connection between physical rings, either local or remote.

**VLAN** Virtual LAN: A group of devices on one or more logically segmented LANs (configured by use of management software), enabling devices to communicate as if attached to the same physical medium, when they are actually located on numerous different LAN segments. VLANs are based on logical instead of physical connections and thus are tremendously flexible.

**VLAN database** A special mode in 2900XL and 3500XL series switches where the administrator creates VLANs.

**VLSM** variable-length subnet mask: Helps optimize available address space and specify a different subnet mask for the same network number on various subnets. Also commonly referred to as "subnetting a subnet."

**VPN** virtual private network: A method of encrypting point-to-point logical connections across a public network, such as the Internet. This allows secure communications across a public network.

**VRRP** Virtual Router Redundancy Protocol: A standards-based alternative to Cisco's HSRP, providing a virtual router address for use as a host default gateway.

**VTP** VLAN Trunk Protocol: Used to update switches in a switch-fabric about VLANs configured on a VTP server. VTP devices can be a VTP server, client, or transparent device. Servers update clients. Transparent devices are only local devices and do not share information with VTP clients. VTPs send VLAN information down trunked links only.

**VTP modes** *See: VTP.*

**VTP pruning** VLAN Trunk Protocol is used to communicate VLAN information between switches in the same VTP domain. VTP pruning stops VLAN update information from being sent down trunked links if the updates are not needed.

# W

**WAN** wide area network: A designation used to connect LANs together across a DCE (data communications equipment) network. Typically, a WAN is a leased line or dial-up connection across a PSTN network. Examples of WAN protocols include Frame Relay, PPP, ISDN, and HDLC.

**weighted fair queuing** Default queuing method on serial links on all Cisco routers. An automated process for placing packets into a queue.

**weighted round robin** A fixed number of queues are serviced in round-robin fashion, each being configurable only as to the size of the queue. *See also: round robin.*

**wildcard** Used with access-list, supernetting, and OSPF configurations. Wildcards are designations used to identify a range of subnets.

**windowing** A flow-control method used with TCP at the Transport layer of the OSI model. Data is acknowledged by the receiver only at the end of a transmission window, which can vary in size according the network reliability.

**WinSock** Windows Socket Interface: A software interface that makes it possible for an assortment of applications to use and share an Internet connection. The WinSock software consists of a Dynamic Link Library (DLL) with supporting programs such as a dialer program that initiates the connection.

**wire speed** The term given to the process whereby data is forwarded through the switch with no appreciable delay. *See also: non-blocking.*

**workgroup switching** A switching method that supplies high-speed (100Mbps) transparent bridging between Ethernet networks as well as high-speed translational bridging between Ethernet and CDDI or FDDI.

# X

**X.25** An ITU-T packet-relay standard that defines communication between DTE and DCE network devices. X.25 uses a reliable Data Link layer protocol called LAPB. X.25 also uses PLP at the Network layer. X.25 has mostly been replaced by Frame Relay.

**X.25 protocol** First packet-switching network, but now mostly used in Europe. Replaced in U.S. by Frame Relay.

**XTAG** A locally significant numerical value assigned by the MLS-SE to each MLS-RP in the layer 2 network. *See also: MLS-SE* and *MLS-RP.*

# Z

**zone** A logical grouping of network devices in AppleTalk.

# Index

**Note to the Reader:** Throughout this index **boldfaced** page numbers indicate primary discussions of a topic. *Italicized* page numbers indicate illustrations.

## Numbers

# A

## B

## C

# D

## E

## F

# G

## H



## I

## J



## K



## L

## M

# N

# O

## Q

## R

## S

# T

## U



## V

## W



## X



## Z

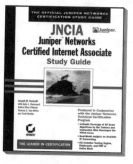

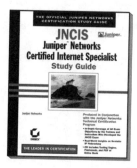

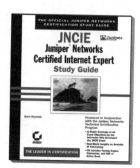

# The Complete Cisco Certification Solution

## CCNA: Cisco Certified Networking Associate

**For the CCNA Exam # 640-801**

**CCNA: Cisco Certified Network Associate Study Guide, 4th Ed.**
ISBN 0-7821-4311-3 · $49.99

**CCNA: Cisco Certified Network Associate Study Guide, Deluxe Edition, 3rd Ed.**
ISBN 0-7821-4314-8 · $89.99 

**CCNA Fast Pass**
ISBN 0-7821-4309-1 · $29.99 

**CCNA Certification Kit, 3rd Edition**
ISBN 0-7821-4315-6 · $169.98

**CCNA Virtual Lab, Platinum Edition**
ISBN 0-7821-3037-2 · $159.99

## CCNP: Cisco Certified Networking Professional*

***Prerequisite: Valid CCNA certification**

**CCNP: Building Scalable Cisco Internetworks Study Guide, 2nd Ed.**
ISBN 0-7821-4293-1 · $49.99 
*Building Scalable Cisco Internetworks Exam # 642-801*

**CCNP: Building Cisco Multilayer Switched Networks Study Guide**
ISBN 0-7821-4294-X · $49.99
*Building Cisco Multilayer Switched Networks Exam #642-811*

**CCNP: Building Cisco Remote Access Networks Study Guide**
ISBN 0-7821-4296-6 · $49.99 
*Building Cisco Remote Access Networks Study Guide Exam #624-821*

**CCNP: Cisco Internetwork Troubleshooting Study Guide**
ISBN 0-7821-4295-8 · $49.99 
*Cisco Internetwork Troubleshooting Study Guide Exam #642-831*

**Also Available:**

**CCNP Study Guide Kit, 3rd Edition.**
ISBN 0-7821-4297-4 · $159.96    covers all 4 exams

Visit **www.sybex.com** for all your Cisco certification needs.